Today's Public Relations

Today's Public Relations

An Introduction

ROBERT L. HEATH
University of Houston

W. TIMOTHY COOMBS
Eastern Illinois University

SAGE Publications
Thousand Oaks ▪ London ▪ New Delhi

For information:

 Sage Publications, Inc.
2455 Teller Road
Thousand Oaks, California 91320
E-mail: order@sagepub.com

Sage Publications Ltd.
1 Oliver's Yard
55 City Road
London EC1Y 1SP
United Kingdom

Sage Publications India Pvt. Ltd.
B-42, Panchsheel Enclave
Post Box 4109
New Delhi 110 017 India

Printed in the United States of America

Library of Congress Cataloging-in-Publication Data
Heath, Robert L. (Robert Lawrence), 1941–
Today's public relations: An introduction / by Robert L. Heath and W. Timothy Coombs.
  p. cm.
Includes bibliographical references and index.
ISBN 1-4129-2635-1 (pbk.)
  1. Public relations. I. Coombs, W. Timothy. II. Title.
HM1221.H43 2006
659.2—dc22

                                        2005013495

This book is printed on acid-free paper.

05 06 07 08 09 10 9 8 7 6 5 4 3 2 1

Acquisitions Editor:	Margaret H. Seawell
Associate Editor:	Margo Beth Crouppen
Editorial Assistant:	Sarah K. Quesenberry
Production Editor:	Laureen Shea
Copy Editor:	Carla Freeman
Typesetter:	C&M Digitals (P) Ltd.
Proofreader:	Scott Oney
Indexer:	Nara Wood

Brief Contents

Detailed Contents

Preface

*T*oday's Public Relations: An Introduction is a project that has been in the works for several years. It began as a challenge to create a text for the basic public relations course that maintained the best of other texts and built on recent research and theory. Public relations is a dynamic field, both in practice and because of the increasing research. Whereas little new thought existed in the early 1980s, since the middle of that decade, substantial achievement has occurred. This burgeoning literature has paralleled the growth in the numbers of students who study public relations. Today's public relations students stand on the shoulders of a century of practitioners who have honed this timeless discipline. They benefit from the richness of research and theory that emerges with each issue of major journals.

Now, students can have a text that explains public relations processes and functions as well as details how they can use messages to build mutually beneficial relations between organizations and key markets, audiences, and publics. Other texts tend to feature the processes of public relations, as part of the mass media. This text takes that foundation and builds on it in several ways. One of these ways is to draw on the heritage of rhetorical theory that has contributed much to the strategic design and use of messages as well as the critical evaluation of such messages. So, the text has historic origins but also seeks to encourage students to watch the Web for ways that technology will continue to reshape the practice of public relations. The Web not only gives another vehicle for organizations to communicate but also is loaded with the critical statements of activists. It is also a playground of misinformation and rumor that can damage the reputation and operation of good organizations.

Few professions are more important to society than is public relations. It is often more subtle and "silent" than other forms of professional communication. It tends to communicate through other communicators, such as getting stories out through reporters. Also, in comparison to other aspects of professional communication practice, public relations is less well understood and the victim of this misunderstanding. Recognizing this fact, the authors offer a text that builds on the heritage of public discourse that has been refined at least since the time of Aristotle and Plato. This book takes the view that public relations practitioners need to be strategic thinkers who know principles of message design, best public relations practices, and ethics. Add to this list an understanding of current research in public relations, and you have the makings of the next generation of public relations practitioners.

Chapter 1 is titled "Strategic Relationship Building: An Ethical Organization Communicating Effectively." This chapter draws on the timeless advice of leading rhetoricians that to communicate well, a person or an organization must first be good—ethical. This chapter sets the tone for the book by featuring the elements that lead to mutually beneficial relationships. Some years ago, academics and practitioners began to realize the potential in featuring relations as the foundation of relationship building. This book features that logic by advising that sound public relations practices cut two ways. One is to help the organization be a credible and ethical source of information and opinion. The second, then, is to know how to communicate effectively because the organization is good.

The wise practitioner learns how to think strategically and to listen to others, especially consumers and key publics who can influence whether the organization is successful. Markets, audiences, and publics can affect organizations' success by the choices they make and the actions they take. If they like the organization, they reward it by buying goods and services, contributing to it as a nonprofit, or supporting rather than opposing it during public policy battles. Along the way, practitioners have to understand their field; they have to know what public relations people do and how they think. To advance students' understanding of the practice, Chapter 1 distinguishes between public relations and marketing, advertising, and integrated communication.

Public relations may be as old as the human experience. Chapter 2 helps students to understand the profession by giving a solid historical discussion of key moments and pioneers of the profession. The record of public relations is mixed, but a continuing commitment to increase its professional standing can strengthen its positive role in society. Leading figures have not only practiced the profession in ways that help students understand the foundations of the profession, but these professionals have also worked to create professional associations that strengthen the practice.

Chapter 3 features principles and processes required to build mutually beneficial relationships. On this foundation, the next four chapters build a solid professional and academic basis for learning the profession by explaining how research is conducted (Chapter 4), how planning is central to the role public relations plays (Chapter 5), action plans (Chapter 6), and evaluation of results from public relations efforts (Chapter 7). The logic is that research helps practitioners to listen to their markets, audiences, and publics. What they hear can help identify whether relationships are strong and mutual—or fractured and contentious. Problems can be identified and understood to set the next step of planning and taking action. Planning and action steps are intended to create, maintain, and repair relationships as necessary to the success of the organization and the happiness of the people whose goodwill the organization needs. Evaluation allows practitioners and other managers the opportunity to assess how effective the public relations program is to help the organization manage these key relationships.

Chapter 8 explains theory in practice. Many academics and practitioners believe that theory strengthens the ability to practice public relations. Thus, they conduct research to unlock the mysteries of the profession and guide its development. This chapter explains how theory is created and how it can help practitioners to be more effective in building mutually beneficial relationships. This chapter offers theory that is basic to all public relations efforts and some that helps practitioners deal with crises and the risks that key publics experience. Theory can be used to manipulate, but it can also add value to relationships. To this end, Chapter 9 discusses ethics. It features the kinds of ethical challenges practitioners face each day.

The next four chapters build on these chapters to explain issues management (Chapter 10), strategic media choices (Chapter 11), strategies and principles of promotion and publicity (Chapter 12), and collaborative decision making (Chapter 13). Practitioners help their employers and clients discuss issues to assist society's efforts to create effective public policy. Controversy occurs. One strategic solution to controversy is to engage in collaborative decision making. *Today's Public Relations* is unique because of the attention it pays to topics such as crisis, risk, issues management, collaborative decision making, and promotion and publicity. It strives to be aware of what the successful practitioner needs to know and to explain that material in ways that can be applied successfully. Many public relations texts avoid substantial chapters on publicity and promotion despite the fact that much of what practitioners do supports this vital function.

Chapter 14 discusses the ways students can increase their ability to land that first job by preparing themselves during their college studies. Preparation requires many ingredients. These include knowing the principles and best practices of the profession, as well as having a solid sense of the ethics of effective public relations practice. Students need to build a strong portfolio to demonstrate their skills, have practical experience, including an internship, and participate in student organizations such as the Public Relations Student Society of America. As the last chapter (Chapter 15) points out, public relations is increasingly global and influenced by new media such as the Internet. The wise practitioner understands other people, other cultures, new media, and the challenges they present.

Along with the material in these chapters, the book features comments by working professionals to help students know "the business." Professional Reflections are placed near the ends of the chapters to help students follow in the footsteps of persons who have served the practice effectively and wisely. Each chapter challenges students to become increasingly aware of the role that the Web plays in the practice and the success of organizations. Ethical quandaries and case studies are used to keep students on their toes. Ethical pitfalls and challenges abound in the profession. Students need to become increasingly ethical to practice effectively and to advance the professional status of public relations. They will be challenged in life, and we constantly point to ethical pitfalls as well as successful cases. Each chapter starts with a vignette based on practical challenges, to set the course for the chapter. These vignettes frame and justify the discussion that follows in each chapter.

An Instructor's Resources CD provides teachers with assessment tools, as well as materials that will help students to further engage with the text. The disk includes Microsoft® PowerPoint® presentations for each chapter that may be used as lecture outlines. It also offers recommended resources, such as additional real-world cases, journal articles, and trade books that would nicely supplement the text. Web resources, which include the links in the book, are outlined as well. Furthermore, the CD outlines how to bring guest speakers into the classroom, set up field experiences for students, and more! Study guides that can be distributed to students as study aids or used to guide a review session can be found on the disk, as can a related test bank full of objective, short-answer, and essay test items. For instructors who do not assess their students using tests, the CD includes group and individual assignment ideas.

Acknowledgments

No book is the product of the efforts of the authors alone. This one is no exception. The authors acknowledge the imaginative and thoughtful help of several persons at Sage Publications: Margaret Seawell helped breathe life into this project when it seemed doomed. Margo Crouppen thoughtfully and systematically drew together the parts of the manuscript. Sarah Quesenberry was diligent and imaginative in finding visual material that would enrich the book. Laureen Shea helped keep the pieces from flying to the wind. Carla Freeman patiently and skillfully brought order and coherence to the final draft as it went to production. Along the way, in this book's development, many academics and professionals, including the following, read some or all of the working manuscript:

Mohan J. Dutta-Bergman, Purdue University

Tracy Senat, University of Central Oklahoma

Weiwu Zhang, Austin Peay State University

Diana Knott, Ohio University

Annnemarie Marek, University of Texas, Dallas

Beth Wood, Indiana University

Bonita Neff, Valparaiso University

To these people, the authors tip their hats and give thanks. We hope that we listened well to the advice and responded appropriately. Also to be thanked are legions of students who have contributed to this book by asking questions and seeking advice from the authors. They want to know how to practice ethically and effectively and how to use public relations to make their employers more ethical. We hope we have answered most of your questions in ways that truly give you solid grounding for a successful and enjoyable professional experience.

Strategic Relationship Building

An Ethical Organization Communicating Effectively

1

Vignette:
The Edison, New Jersey, Pipeline Explosion:
Texas Eastern Transmission in the Spotlight

On March 23, 1994, a natural gas pipeline owned by the Texas Eastern Transmission Corporation (TETCO), of Houston, Texas, exploded near the Durham Woods Apartments, in Edison, New Jersey. (TETCO was a subsidiary of Panhandle Eastern Transmission, now Duke Energy.) People for miles were shaken by the explosion, which occurred just before midnight. After the explosion, a fierce orange ball of fire could be seen all the way from network television offices in New York City. The chief engineer for the *New York Times* printing plant in Edison reported that the flames leapt 300 to 400 feet into the air and were so intense that headlights on nearby automobiles melted, giving the appearance that they were crying. Initial news reports indicated that at least 10 people were injured and that at least six apartment buildings were completely destroyed. People from the apartment complex milled about in the street, wearing only their nightclothes; many feared that all they owned had been destroyed. To make matters even worse, emergency personnel had no idea whether or not more explosions would occur. As the fire blazed, the dispatcher for the local fire department reported that the Mobil Chemical Company plant in Edison had also gone up in flames.

Explosion Creates Community Relations Crisis

SOURCE: Reprinted with permission from the *New Jersey Star-Ledger*.

Upon hearing the news, the mayor of Edison immediately blamed TETCO for the fire. The mayor took legal steps to force the pipeline company to cease its operations because they were unsafe. If you were the vice president for public affairs for TETCO, what would you do? How would you handle the mayor's action against your company? What facts would you want to know as you researched this crisis and prepared your response?

The executives who led the response to this need for public relations solutions had answers to these questions. Compare their response to what you might have done. See the vignette at the start of Chapter 5 to learn what they did.

Welcome to *Today's Public Relations:* Imagine that it's your first day on the job as a newly employed public relations professional. You are busy at your desk at 10:18 on a Monday morning. Your boss bustles in and tells you to have a media release ready by 4:00—your first important assignment in your new professional job. "Okay," you think to yourself, "no problem!" You have been trained to write a media release, but before you begin, you need to ask yourself why you are writing it. What do you want to accomplish with this media release? Even more important, consider what this media release means strategically for you, for your department, and for your organization. You must also consider how the media release will affect other organizations, groups of people inside and outside of your organization, and society itself. You must be strategic; you should make purposeful choices designed to achieve specific objectives.

In your preparation, you may consider rhetorical options that are SMART. The SMART approach to public relations thinks beyond tactics to consider all of the following options:

Societal value and meaning: The smart practitioner realizes that each statement and action can have consequences for the quality of society, the community where he or she works. Public relations and its clients do not operate in a vacuum. They are part of society.

Mutually beneficial relationships: Relationship building is required for public relations. A relationship is mutually beneficial when all of the involved parties gain from it and support it. Relationships are mutually beneficial when they are based on wise and sound ethical choices that foster the interests of all of the parties involved.

Advantages through objectives: Public relations is designed to achieve specific purposes, such as to raise awareness, increase understanding, align interests, share perspectives, compromise, reduce conflict, foster identification, and motivate action based on shared interests.

Rhetorical strategies: Rhetorical approaches to public relations require strategic planning based on research to decide on messages and tactics that can be used to achieve the objectives through specific message points. Rhetorical strategies include message development options: gaining awareness, informing, persuading, fostering identifications, and cocreating meaning to build bridges. Practitioners have an arsenal of strategies at their discretion to achieve their objectives: planning, research, collaborative decision making, and publicity coupled with promotion.

Tactics: Each specific public relations activity is a tactic. Writing and issuing a media release is a tactic, as is holding a media conference to respond to a crisis or creating and executing a publicity event to increase awareness for the grand opening of a shopping mall. Strategic responses force the practitioner to ask: What public relations tool should I use, what message content should we feature in our statements, and when should we implement our tactic?

If you have learned to think SMART, you ask questions and develop innovative solutions that make a difference, the heart of today's public relations. This text is designed to help you think tactically, strategically, and ethically about public relations and to teach you to ask questions and develop solutions that make a difference for your client by building mutually beneficial relationships with people who can positively or negatively affect the future of your client or employer. Public relations can help businesses, nonprofits, and governmental agencies to be successful.

Public relations is an integral part of national and global economies. Today's public relations practitioners contribute to all aspects of society, from passing laws to influencing consumer purchases to funding nonprofit agencies. Today's practitioners must face challenges that were often not addressed in the past. The professional practice of public relations requires more than merely being pleasant, meeting people, working with the media, and staging promotional events. Today, the profession is committed to creating, maintaining, and repairing strategic relationships in the face of conflicting interests and ethical choices. These relationships should equally benefit both your clients (or employer) and the people whose lives they affect. The need for creativity is constant. Strategic planning and critical thinking are vital for success. Ethical standards must guide every step of the process. Making a positive difference on behalf of clients or for your employer organization is the essence of professional public relations practice. To have a solid impact, you will need to be an ethical and strategic thinker as well as an effective communicator.

This book is actually designed for several audiences. A student may use it to prepare to become a professional practitioner, but practitioners who already work in public relations can also use it to increase their career knowledge and hone their strategic, ethical, and critical skills. Practitioners may find it invaluable in reviewing for their accreditation examinations.

Our first chapter poses an ethical quandary designed to develop your ethical and strategic reasoning so crucial in successfully practicing public relations. Included in this chapter, and throughout other chapters of this volume, autobiographical insights will offer a peek into what it's like to be a professional public relations practitioner. You will also find "Web Watchers," which challenge you to consider real-life examples of how public relations is practiced using the Internet; each Web Watcher encourages you to understand and appreciate the growing potential of cyberspace communication technology in the public relations process.

This chapter strives to help the reader to understand the complexity of public relations within the United States but also as part of a daunting global society composed of many voices, interests, and cultures. Practitioners must realize public relations is neither simplistic nor isolated from other organizations, organizational units, or groups. Public relations is complex. Many theories, much research, and decades of learning best practices help students to understand its role in society and identify when public relations is required. In broad strokes, theory is used to understand the processes of communication, its content, and the quality of relationships. Systems theory helps explain processes. Rhetorical heritage informs how people deal with meaning. Interpersonal communication, especially social exchange theory, gives insights into how relationships are created, maintained, and repaired.

Strategic Relationships:
Mutual Benefits

Today's public relations helps organizations build relationships. Relationships are strongest when they are mutually beneficial and characterized by "win-win" outcomes. Relationships are best when people share information that is accurate and relevant. Relationships require a commitment to open and trustworthy dialogue, a spirit of cooperation, a desire to align interests, a willingness to adopt compatible views/opinions, and a commitment to make a positive difference in the lives of everyone affected by your organization.

Before we continue to discuss this topic, let's look briefly at a relationship that has the potential for being mutually beneficial. In 2000, building-products giant Home Depot, Inc., created a relationship with the Forest Stewardship Council (FSC). The goal was to work together to select and market building materials that are harvested with environmentally responsible techniques. This accord ended a long and rancorous debate in which FSC charged Home Depot and other building-materials merchants with environmental destruction. This alliance could help Home Depot claim that its marketing techniques were environmentally responsible, thereby aligning its interests with environmental groups and with its customers who want quality but environmentally safe building materials. This relationship could also help Home Depot defend its marketing policies against the attacks of the more radical Rainforest Action Network. Other building materials companies (Wicke's, Lowe's, and Anderson Corporation, a window-building giant) joined in this coalition to meet FSC's environmental standards. These organizations engaged in two-way communication to collaboratively make decisions. This process could build trust, align interests, demonstrate environmental commitment, be cooperative, adopt compatible views/opinions, and commit to supporting the global market for building materials in an environmentally responsible manner. Once this agreement had been achieved, public relations could use media relations disseminate information about the agreement, attract and keep customers, and reduce activist criticism. This agreement strengthened Home Depot's reputation as being environmentally responsible. It added to FSC's image as an advocate for wise natural resource management.

A commitment to help build relationships calls for high ethical standards, strategic thinking, and effective communication. Quality relationships exist when people and organizations have compatible interests and share compatible views of the world. To assess the quality of a relationship, practitioners ask questions such as, "Is the donation to a school an investment in the community's future or merely a publicity stunt to attract favorable yet undeserved attention to an otherwise unethical company?"

Relationships can start, succeed, fail, and need repair. Similar interpretations of events and shared benefits are critical factors in any relationship. People can see and interpret the same event very differently—watch any "judge show" on television and you will appreciate how easy it is for people to interpret events differently. Organizations and their stakeholders need to share similar interpretations of events if the relationship is to run smoothly. *Stakeholders* have something of value (a stake). A stake might be customers' willingness to purchase goods and services. Home Depot and the other companies in the FSC alliance hope to be rewarded by the stakes (purchases and praise) of happy customers, reduced likelihood of regulatory constraints (stake), and praise rather than condemnation by environmental activists (stake).

Relationships are strongest when founded on shared interpretations that result from the cocreation of meaning. Environmentalists, such as FSC, communicate with building-materials companies to adopt shared views regarding ways to reduce environmental damage while marketing products to building-materials customers. Organizations and their stakeholders cocreate meaning by engaging in dialogue about message points basic to their relationships. People do not stay in relationships if they get nothing from them or if their views clash rather than align.

Today's public relations practitioners help their employers or clients to treat individuals and groups with honesty and respect. You might imagine yourself, for instance, working as a public relations practitioner for Home Depot (or one of the other building-materials companies) to meet and discuss these issues with FSC (or you could imagine working as a senior member of a public relations agency that was working that issue for its client, for example, Lowe's or Anderson). Viewed in these terms, the relationship between an organization and key stakeholders is the same as that between good friends who want the best for each other. Likewise, customers want good businesses to succeed, and citizens want good organizations—business, non-profit, and governmental—to continue their operations. Donors and members want nonprofit organizations to serve society. In your practice, you could work for such organizations, either as an employee in a public relations department or for an agency that has a contracted relationship with these clients.

BOX 1.1 CHARACTERISTICS OF A MUTUALLY BENEFICIAL RELATIONSHIP

- Openness: fosters two-way communication based on listening for and sharing valuable information, as well as being responsive, respectful, candid, and honest. One-way communication occurs when an organization "speaks" but does not listen to or acknowledge the merit in what other people and organizations "say."

- Trustworthiness: builds trust among publics and clients by being reliable, nonexploitative, and dependable.

- Cooperation: engages in collaborative decision making that ensures that the needs/wants of the organization and its stakeholders are met.

- Alignment: shares interests, rewards, and goals with those of its stakeholders.

- Compatibility of views/opinions: fosters mutual understanding and agreement, cocreates meaning.

- Commitment: supports the community by being involved in it, investing in it, and displaying commitment to it.

Relationship building is more than a buzzword. At its foundation, this concept is based on the principle of symbiosis, the foundation of biology—and even ecology. According to systems theory, all elements of nature prosper when they are in balance or experience harmony. This logic is applied to human society. Interpersonal relationship communication points out that people like relationships that reward them. When the relationship is not rewarding, they have no incentive to remain a part of it. The same can be said for the role of public relations. It seeks to foster harmony and balance between organizations and the people whose goodwill and support they need.

The Definition of Public Relations

The most effective way to begin to understand public relations is to define it. We have, in fact, repeatedly used the term *public relations* without pausing to define it! You may have your own definition, so let's not take for granted that your definition is the same as ours. Too often, people use a narrow and misleading definition of public relations. One such view considers public relations as little more than image building, a caricatured view that can reduce the practice to "flacks" who create a glossy or downright false image of an organization by "spinning" the truth. Those terms describe people who know how to lie and twist or spin issues during press conferences and other public forums to take the heat off of the organizations they represent. Another myopic view of public relations sees it as reputation management or impression management, whereby public relations mops up the mess left by unscrupulous business practices.

True, organizations want to be seen in the best possible light, but a good reputation is only part of their success. Let's avoid featuring a view of reputation management that leads some people to believe incorrectly that public relations distorts the truth to make a bad organization seem good. As we try to define public relations, we pay attention to the value that public relations adds to the organizations it serves as well as the people whose goodwill those organizations need. The essence of creating a good reputation or impression is to prove to stakeholders that the organization can create and maintain mutually beneficial relationships with them.

Our definition is lengthy but has to be in order to capture public relations' complexity. Public relations is the management function that entails planning, research, publicity, promotion, and collaborative decision making to help any organization's ability to listen to, appreciate, and respond appropriately to those persons and groups whose mutually beneficial relationships the organization needs to foster as it strives to achieve its mission and vision. This definition points to five key characteristics: (1) a management function, (2) the five major functions of public relations, (3) the practitioner's need to listen, appreciate, and respond, (4) the emphasis on mutually beneficial relationships, and (5) the achievement of a particular mission and vision. It is actually more important to appreciate these five characteristics than to memorize the definition verbatim.

The Public Relations Society of America (PRSA) officially defines public relations as a management function. As part of management, public relations managers should be intimately involved in selecting and implementing the organization's strategic goals by working alongside other managers who lead the organization. In this management function, public relations practitioners assist other managers to make sound strategic-planning and operating decisions. To do so, they anticipate, analyze, and respond to opinions of people and groups (stakeholders)—both inside and outside the organization—whose opinions and actions can affect the organization in positive or negative ways.

Because practitioners must work closely with other managers, they need to have a broad knowledge of the organization and all its operations, as well as an interest in the public policy and public opinion issues that are likely to affect the plans, activities, and outputs of the organization. Only then can practitioners anticipate and effectively help management respond to the needs of the organization and the interests of its stakeholders. You cannot have a meaningful discussion with other managers about operations or pending legislation if you have not bothered to analyze and understand them. The five functions of public relations—planning, research, publicity, promotion, and collaborative decision making—help to bring our definition to life.

Viewed in detail, these functions emphasize strong communication skills but entail a lot more than writing media releases or seeing that the balloons ordered for an event are the right color. Those tactics are important for successful public relations, but the definition asks practitioners to master strategic rhetorical processes of listening, appreciating what is heard, and responding to and even yielding to comments by stakeholder groups whose opinions and actions can make or break an organization. These public relations functions can achieve outcomes that are beneficial to the individual or the organization. Finally, the definition recognizes that an organization should be goal directed—pursue a mission and vision—and that public relations should help its employer or client organization to achieve those goals.

The Five Functions of Public Relations

The definition of public relations in this book spotlights five functions of public relations management: strategic planning, research, publicity, promotion, and collaborative decision making. In any organization, *functions* are the strategic actions that a person or an entire unit performs, including day-to-day operations as well as long-term planning. Let's look more closely at each of these functions to understand how each one helps to build mutual understanding needed to develop relationships among individuals, groups, and institutions.

The *strategic-planning* function positions the organization to respond to the needs, wants, and opinions of others. Planning involves counseling management's efforts to align their interests with those of their stakeholders. Public relations uses research to obtain data that can be used to refine planning decisions regarding which publicity activities and promotional campaigns can get the organization's message to its customers. Research helps define threats and opportunities that exist around the organization. Public relations activities are planned to support the plans and objectives of the organization. Public relations research and planning recognize the advantages of using collaborative decision making to build, maintain, or repair strategic relationships. For instance, building-materials companies seek positive relationships with environmental activists and customers. Thinking back to the vignette used to open this chapter, we can imagine that senior management at Texas Eastern Transmission (TETCO) wanted to repair its relationships with persons harmed and inconvenienced by the explosion and fire.

In recent years, public relations' role in strategic planning has become so influential that many organizations have created a new management position called the *chief communication officer* (CCO), the head of public relations, who works alongside others in top management. Capturing the essence of the CCO's job description, the *PRSA Blue Book* stated, "In helping to define and implement policy, the public relations practitioner uses a variety of professional communication skills and plays an integrative role both within the organization and between the organization and the external environment" (PRSA, 2003, p. B3). The CCO works alongside other key executives: chief executive officer (CEO), chief operating officer (COO), chief financial officer (CFO), and general counsel (the top lawyer for the organization). The CCO's duty is to ensure that the organization communicates effectively with its key markets, audiences, and publics, both internal and external.

The CCO is responsible for communicating with three kinds of people (stakeholders) with whom an organization wants to build mutually satisfying relationships: markets, audiences, and publics (we will refer to these as an organization's "MAPs"). A *market* is an identifiable group, current and potential customers, whom executives believe will want or need a product or service or will join and contribute to the community service activities of a nonprofit organization. An *audience* is some identifiable group of people an organization wants to reach with its message. A *public* is an identifiable group, either inside or outside of an organization, whose opinions on issues can affect the success of the organization. An *inside public* might be women or minority employees who feel they have not been treated fairly in terms of promotion and pay. An *external public* is an organization (such as FSC) or a group of individuals who share awareness of a problem, such as environmentalists. A public can pressure an organization to change its plans, policies, and priorities. MAPs need careful attention by any organization that seeks to foster effective and strategic relationships.

Public relations research is contextual and situational. Research seeks to understand *contexts,* such as markets (or customers), investors, employees, members of the public and business sectors, governmental officials, the media, and many other groups. Each group of people has its own opinions, concerns, and motivations. Your research can locate and examine the desires, beliefs, and attitudes of persons who can benefit or harm the organization. It is *situational* because opinions, tastes, wants, values, attitudes, and beliefs of these groups change. If a product is not selling well, that situation calls for research to discover whether it fits the tastes of targeted customers. If people are protesting a company's operations, that situation requires research to understand the merits of the activists' concerns.

PRSA advises practitioners to assist with the design, execution, and evaluation of research to understand the views of people outside of the organization. The *research function* can help managers know what to say in response to public policy issues and consumer concerns. Public relations management uses research to assess the impact of the organization's messages. It defines threats and opportunities. One specific objective of this research is to ascertain whether people believe the organization is socially responsible. Research can determine whether customers are aware of its products and services.

Publicity involves attracting attention and supplying information about a specific activity or attribute of the organization. Publicity employs media coverage to attract attention and inform targeted MAPs about an organization, product, service, need, or issue. Publicity could include a successful public relations effort to get local media to cover the grand opening of a new store or shopping center. Publicity, in this instance, is intended to attract shoppers' attention and give them information about the store or shopping center they can use when making purchases. To publicize the opening of a new shopping mall outside of Houston, Texas, a public relations firm encouraged reporters to feature the unique mix of businesses, the interesting architecture of the center, and its location. Publicity can alert battered women, for example, to the existence of a center where they can find shelter. Houston Area Women's Center uses periodic news reports as well as counseling through health and law enforcement professionals to help women know the array of services provided by the center. Publicity can attract donors' attention to the need for funding of this kind of shelter. Universities, for instance, routinely publicize their need for funding to support the library or special programs for students.

Promotion involves a series of publicity efforts that transpire for several days, weeks, or months to attract customers' attention and supply them with useful information. A promotional effort consists of a series of publicity events and news stories that are covered by the media so that MAPs become more aware of and informed about some organization, product, service, need, or issue. In contrast to a onetime publicity activity, promotion entails sustained efforts by public relations practitioners to attract continuing media attention. For instance, the shopping center might hold a publicity event each time a new store opens. To further the promotional effort, the shopping center can sponsor some activity to foster community support, such as an event for needy children to buy back-to-school clothes and supplies. Promotional activities can create or increase awareness for the shopping center and help to foster a community-minded reputation.

Collaborative decision making in public relations involves counseling leaders within the organization and fostering a decision-making style that respects the concerns of the publics affected by a decision. Consider the example of an organization looking to expand its manufacturing facility. The expansion option favored by the manufacturer would displace residents in one part of a tight-knit community. Collaborative decision making, however, would factor the citizens' concerns into the decision. Such counseling entails not only considering the interests of the organization but also the ramifications of policy, products, services, and operations as well as the organization's social and citizenship responsibilities. As a counselor, practitioners advise people at all levels of an organization about tactics, ethical actions, strategic solutions to problems, public policy decisions, and the best communication options to use in a given situation. Counseling involves taking stands and developing messages needed to participate in public dialogues, such as forums, town hall meetings, debates, and community or civic events to anticipate, understand, and represent the organization as having ideas that are valuable to the community in which it operates. The manufacturer, for instance, might run several open-door community forums to get a sense of citizen concerns and to better understand how to expand the facilities, which offer added local employment, though at the expense of some members of the community.

Public dialogues express differences of opinion and may result in conflict between the positions taken by the organization and concerned groups. For instance, environmentalists in the Pacific Northwest have opposed logging practices that they fear will destroy the habitat of spotted owls and damage water quality, due to erosion. In doing so, environmentalists threaten the jobs of the loggers, who worry that they may no longer be able to earn a living and care for their families. In this instance, practitioners could attend meetings to hear concerns expressed by loggers and environmentalists. Using this research, they can decide with their management the most constructive role for the organization. Based on the position taken by management, practitioners can inject opinions and data into the public dialogue, for instance, through media releases and public meetings. They can create and facilitate collaborative decision-making meetings, where the interested parties hammer out a mutually satisfying agreement.

Figure 1.1 depicts the five functions of public relations. The centerpiece in this model is strategic planning, the foundation of all activities. All public relations activities require planning for successful tactical implementation and goal achievement. The four outer circles capture the remaining functions of publicity, promotion, research, and collaborative decision making, all of which should be designed to build strategic relationships. The functions of public relations are interactive, helping the organization to attract and wisely use the resources it needs to accomplish its mission and vision.

Public Relations and Society

Public relations does not occur in a vacuum, but is the product of societies whose people and organizations interact to better themselves and shape their society. Through public discussion, people assert their points of view, criticize those of others, establish laws, and govern their behavior. This dialogue gives rise to each society—its arts and sciences, education, morality, and marketplace. Democratic society and free enterprise could simply not exist without this public examination of ideas.

To understand today's public relations, we need to discuss its social responsibility to serve the best interests of the marketplace and to wisely address ethical principles that define the public policies of society. A useful way to explore these points is to locate public relations within the rhetorical tradition. From there, we can appreciate why public relations must adhere to societal and marketplace responsibilities.

Figure 1.1: Five Functions of Public Relations as Relationship Building

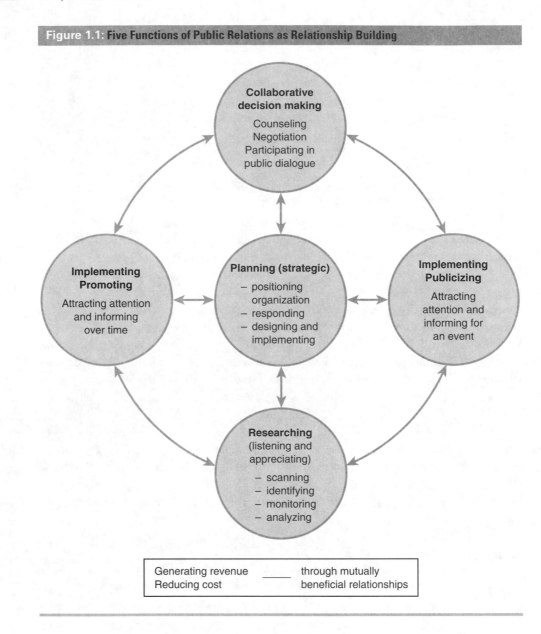

▶Public Relations and the Rhetorical Tradition

As a practice, rhetoric focuses on the skills needed to be effective in informing, persuading, making collaborative decisions, and cocreating meaning. Rhetoric ideally exists because people—MAPs—want information and evaluations they can use to make ethical and satisfying decisions. A rhetorical view of public relations assumes that factual evidence, reasoned argument, and ethical judgment are crucial to effective communication and solid relationships.

Why do we draw on rhetorical philosophy to support the practice of public relations? Writers on rhetoric examine the communication processes by which people influence the thoughts and actions of others by cocreating meaning. The very foundation of society is a body of law and constitutional principles that members of society contest and refine through discourse. Rhetoric assumes that people and groups publicly assert their views and demonstrate that their ideas are correct. They share in the formation of meaning that guides the choices people make in their daily lives. The cornerstone of rhetoric is strategic listening, appreciating, and responding to the concerns and opinions others hold.

We can trace the connection between rhetoric and public relations. In keeping with the tradition of rhetoric, public relations professionals can serve society to the degree that they meet or exceed societal expectations for ethical and effective public communication. Are they good listeners? Do they appreciate others' concerns? Are they committed to base judgment on sound fact and good evaluations? Do they prefer dialogue to monologue?

For centuries, rhetoric has been a critical part of the education of effective and responsible citizens. Today, the term *rhetoric* has fallen on hard times and is often used to refer to statements that are hollow, without substance. ("That is mere rhetoric!") The term can cause some people to feel discomfort because it is associated with a speaker or writer who cleverly manipulates an audience with empty statements. Students, however, encounter a more correct version of rhetoric in English, philosophy, classics, classical history, or speech communication classes, a definition that is far more positive and more accurate for understanding public relations. This debate over the best approach to rhetoric reaches back to the age of Plato, who criticized some of his contemporaries (for instance, Gorgias and Protagoras) who did manipulate audiences.

Rhetoric Is the Strategic Art of Effective Public Communication

That conclusion was formulated during a robust period in the history of Ancient Greece and Rome. In those societies, philosophers of rhetoric carefully developed principles for effective public communication and prescribed how people should manage their lives to be useful and ethically responsible citizens. The rhetorical heritage champions the principle that public communication is best when ethical people communicate effectively. As you shall see in Chapter 2, public relations practitioners have had identical concerns for centuries. Chapter 9 features the topic of public relations ethics.

The rhetorical heritage arose from dramatic changes in the government of Greece during the 5th century BC. Citizens needed to communicate effectively in court in order to reclaim property that had been unlawfully taken from them. Many of these people were not articulate. They wanted to know the principles and develop the skills of effective strategic communication so they could defend their property rights. In those days, there were no lawyers, so citizens had to be their own advocates.

Ancient Greeks respected the practical power of discourse and believed that individuals must use it ethically. Realizing that some statements were more effective than others, they sought answers to two basic questions: First, what are the best tactics and strategies of message development, design, and delivery for speaking and writing? Second, does good character help people to communicate with greater impact in society? These eternal questions are still being explored by today's public relations practitioners.

Not all ancient Greeks believed that skillful public communication was good for society. Plato thought, as many people do today, that rhetoric was a craft devoid of truth and devoted to trickery. His experience with courts in Greece led him to fear that tricky speakers could win their cases by using arguments that lacked substance and were not well reasoned, but rather appealed to people's prejudices and irrational impulses. Similar concerns persist about public relations practitioners who focus on image at the expense of substance. Remember how our definition of public relations sought to avoid the narrow definition of public relations as image?

BOX 1.2 IMAGE AND ADVERTISING

To help you think about image, we have included samples of communication tactics to demonstrate the interconnectedness of public relations and image-advertising campaigns. One of the most interesting public relations campaigns using advertising was sponsored by Mobil Oil Company, today part of ExxonMobil. Mobil's campaign was designed to convey the message that large companies are needed to solve large problems. Mobil's public affairs personnel believed that issue advertising could reach opinion leaders. To do so, they knew that ads had to be interesting and informative. One means for gaining interest was to tell a story—a fable. Does the use of a narrative in the "Peanuts" ad make its message more interesting and memorable? For more detail, see additional discussion of this campaign in Chapter 2.

Aristotle (1952), a Greek philosopher of rhetoric, believed that when people communicate in public, their arguments, evidence, and ideas naturally become better because they must withstand public scrutiny. Rhetoric is vital to society because it champions the open discussion of ideas and the careful examination of facts and information. People become persuaded by the quality of the evidence and reasoning that are provided to them by speakers or writers. They also are moved by emotional evaluations and the character of the communicator.

For Aristotle (1952), the essence of persuasion was factual evidence as well as careful and serious reasoning; he reasoned that rhetoric is "the faculty of observing in any given case the available means of persuasion" (p. 595). Either a statement is persuasive and credible because it is self-evidently truthful or because it can be proved so. Public communication gives other members of society the opportunity to democratically assess the quality of ideas that are advocated.

Of course, Aristotle also recognized that people can be fooled by false or flashy arguments. But he saw the positive rather than the negative side to this problem. Aristotle believed that people are not easily swayed from the opinions they hold. They resist influence and are thoughtful critics of what they hear and read. Aristotle concluded that even if people are misled for a while, eventually sound argument will

A Fable for Now:

Why Elephants Can't Live on Peanuts

The Elephant is a remarkable animal . . . huge, yet able to move quickly . . . stronger than any person, yet willing to work hard if properly treated.

One day, an Elephant was ambling through the forest. To her surprise, she found her path to the water hole blocked by a huge pile of sticks, vines, and brambles.

"Hello?" she called out over the barricade. "What gives?"

From behind the pile popped the Monkey. "Buzz off, snake-snoot," the Monkey shouted. "It's an outrage to little folk how much you take in, so the rest of us animals have seized the water hole and the food supply. You're gross, and we're revolting!"

"You certainly give that appearance," the Elephant noted quietly. "What's eating you?"

"It's *you* that's doing too much eating," the Monkey replied, "but we're going to change all that. Strict rations for you, fat friend. No more of your obscene profiteering at the feed trough." Overhead, a Parrot screamed: "From each according to your ability. To each according to our need. Gimme your crackers, gimme *all* your crackers!"

The Elephant was upset at this enormous misunderstanding. Yet, though her heart pounded, between the ears she was quite unflappable. "A moment, please," she said. "Though it may seem that I consume a great deal, it's no more than my share. Because I am large—not fat—it just takes more to keep me going. How can I work hard if you won't let me have the proper nourishment?"

The Monkey sneered. "Knock off that mumbo-jumbo, Dumbo," he said. "You already net more than a million Spiders. You take in more than a thousand Pack Rats. You profit more from the jungle's abundance than a hundred Monkeys!"

"But I also can haul tree trunks too heavy for any other creature," the Elephant said. "I can explore for new food supplies and water holes, and clear paths through the jungle with my strong legs. My feet can crush, my shoulders can pull, my trunk can lift. I am full of energy. I even give rides to the little ones. But I can't survive on peanuts."

Hours passed. The Elephant, denied access to her eating and drinking grounds, felt hungrier and hungrier, thirstier and thirstier. But soon, so did the other animals. For the sticks and vines that the animals had dragged together and woven into a barricade had become a solid dam, diverting the stream that fed the watering hole. "Help, help," the animals shouted, "crisis, crisis!"

The Elephant surveyed the scene. "Friends," she said, "see what a fix we're all in. Thank goodness I still have the energy to help. And, with your permission, I will." They quickly consented, and she set to work on the dam, pushing earth and pulling plants until the water hole again began to fill. "That's nice," the animals cried, greeting her undamming with faint praise.

"You see," the Elephant said, "you need a big beast for a big job, and a big beast has big needs. Not just to stay alive and growing, but to put a bit aside for tomorrow. And to have a bit extra for working especially hard, or for sharing with have-not animals."

She noticed that everybody had resumed drinking thirstily. Well, that tickled her old ivories, for all she really wanted was to be allowed to go on doing her customary work without any new wrinkles. No need for hurt feelings. After all, who ever heard of a thin-skinned Elephant?

Moral: Meeting America's energy needs is a big job and it takes big companies. If an energy company doesn't earn a profit proportionate to its size, it won't be able to seek and produce more energy. And that's no fable.

Mobil Oil's "Peanuts" Ad

© 1979 Mobil Corporation

This ad appeared in the *New York Times* of August 30, 1979.

prevail. Only through public discussion do people have the chance to hear many sides to each argument as they work to decide which is best.

You might agree that some people are not easily swayed yet concede that people of unethical character have the ability to manipulate others. Addressing this problem about 380 BC, Isocrates (1929b) argued that people who have good ethical character (ethos) are more likely than unethical people to gain acceptance for their ideas over time. Character, good or bad, cannot be hidden or suppressed. It is revealed, sooner or later, by what people say and do. The same is true for large organizations, whether for profit, nonprofit, or government. Their character, and that of their executives, is revealed in their language and actions, how they present their messages and conduct their business. The advantage in public discourse goes to people of sound ethical character. Realizing this fact, Isocrates challenged people to be honorable, because those whose reputations are tarnished have difficulty persuading people as others examine their character, motives, and ideas.

What features distinguish good ethics? Aristotle (1952) answered, "Good sense, good moral character, and goodwill" (p. 623). Goodwill is a crucial part of character, because, as Isocrates (1929a) realized, ethics keeps people from looking only at their own narrow interests. It challenges them to supply the ideas and arguments other members of society want in order to thoughtfully form their own opinions.

These traits are exhibited by excellent organizations and the persons who speak and write on their behalf. They are not the traits of the unscrupulous person or organization that would try to manipulate others' opinions and actions at all costs. Can a public relations practitioner go wrong by putting Aristotle's words on the wall of his or her office and living by them as simple, but sound, ethical principles?

The best advice from the rhetorical heritage is to be a good person—or a good organization—that communicates effectively. The 1st century AD Roman rhetorician Quintilian (1951) set forth a lofty challenge:

> My aim is to educate the true orator, who must be a good man (or woman) and must include philosophy in his studies in order to shape his character as a citizen and to equip himself to speak on ethical subjects, his special role. (p. 20)

What is the ideal orator—or anyone who engages in public discourse? On this point, Quintilian was firm: "My ideal orator, then, is the true philosopher, sound in morals and with full knowledge of speaking, always striving for the highest" (p. 20). He reasoned, "If a case is based on injustice, neither a good man nor rhetoric has any place in it" (p. 106).

Whether man or woman, today's practitioner cannot escape the challenge made by Quintilian two millennia ago. Public communication is inseparable from the character of the communicator. Table 1.1 summarizes the principles of the rhetorical heritage. These benchmarks still guide today's public relations practitioners' decisions about communication practices.

This brief insight into the rhetorical heritage is intended to cause you to think about challenges facing today's public relations practice; it may even give you a more positive view of rhetoric. This textbook presents public relations as a means for building

Table 1.1: Principles of the Rhetorical Heritage for Today's Public Relations Practice
The quality of public communication is inseparable from the character of the person and the accuracy of the ideas being advocated.
Public communication should be ethical, since no wise person will lie or distort the truth in public because critics can—and probably will—disclose those lies.
An individual's or organization's reputation can be harmed by not being ethical.
Ideas are improved when they are subjected to public scrutiny, where strong ideas inevitably prevail over weak ones.
Public statements should be built on well-selected evidence and sound reasoning that can withstand public scrutiny.
Public communicators should know and live an ethical life and achieve excellence in communication.
Public communicators of good ethical character are more likely than their unethical counterparts to gain acceptance for their ideas over time.
Public communication helps members of society listen to and read persuasive messages as a means by which important decisions are made.
People lose faith in society when they do not obtain information and advocated opinions that can be used to make individual and collective decisions.

strategic relationships through the ethical application of rhetorical principles. Thus, it is essential that these principles of rhetoric help you to examine the social responsibility, marketplace role, and ethical imperatives of public relations.

▶ Social Responsibility of Public Relations

Society is a marketplace of ideas, facts, values, and policies. Recall the flow and exchange of ideas you encounter when you pick up a magazine, read a book, listen to a commentator on radio, watch a television interview program, or listen to a public speech. Someone in public relations is a part of the public dialogue and must bear the social responsibility that goes with it.

Capturing these dynamics, Kenneth Burke (1969), a modern philosopher of rhetoric, called society "the Scramble, the Wrangle of the Marketplace, the flurries and flare-ups of the Human Barnyard, Give and Take, the wavering line of pressure and counter pressure" (p. 23). The "wrangle" transpires in public through various media and forums. The jargon of public relations features the concept of *publics*—groups of individuals who have a stake in the outcome of issues. Thus, the term *public* is a rich part of our language: public inquiry, public debate, publication, public record, public scrutiny, key publics, public opinion, public expectations, and public relations.

Public relations is conducted in view of society. As any savvy public relations person knows, every fact, action, choice, and preference has a way of suffering public scrutiny. The fabric of society is strengthened by public examination of solid facts, sound reasoning, and high ethical standards. Sham and deceit may occur in the substance and strategies some professionals choose to utilize. However, time and public scrutiny will reveal that they lack character and that their arguments lack credibility, as Isocrates taught. Reporters are keen to find and disclose sham, deceit, lies, and dishonesty.

Practitioners help alter the values of a society. Consider the activist group that works to create awareness that certain timber-harvesting methods will have undesirable long-term effects. The activist group may advocate legislation and regulation that alters how harvesting occurs, and society as a whole may benefit from such changes. Also think about the company that defends its practices by demonstrating how its conclusions are based on solid fact and sound reasoning. Such dialogue can mature to the point where collaborative agreements bring environmental practices into the marketing of home-building products.

Public relations professionals may assist in creating lifestyle or cultural changes. For instance, societal culture may change because what was unpopular becomes popular and fashionable. In these ways and thousands more, public relations can contribute to the society where it is practiced. Alcoholic beverage companies, for instance, have become sensitive to the potential for bad relationships with critics of their products. One countermeasure by this industry has been to preach responsible use of alcoholic beverages. One leader, Anheuser-Busch, has pressed its case on college campuses. These social responsibility campaigns have escalated in response to highly publicized cases of college students' deaths due to irresponsible alcohol consumption. Anheuser-Busch has contributed hundreds of thousands of dollars to campuses to promote safe and moderate consumption for students. The campaign has cautioned against underage consumption and binge drinking. These campaigns have used typical public relations tactics: posters, news stories in campus papers, T-shirts, coffee mugs, and screen savers that carry the message, "Drink responsibly if you drink." Beverage companies have even created management-level positions assigned the responsibility of promoting safe consumption practices.

Society expects professional public relations practitioners to meet high standards of truthfulness, candor, and openness. If public relations professionals do not rely on credible facts, they earn a bad reputation as "flacks." That term, along with "spin doctors," has become a part of the jargon in this society. Such derisive terms reflect a concern that mere words without substance can come to drive decisions.

The challenge of creating messages sensitive to society is dramatized by the difficulty companies have in becoming international and achieving harmony with different cultures around the globe. For instance, in the United States, companies are legally prohibited from engaging in fraud and graft. In many countries around the world, "consultants" receive pay to increase the chances a business will be allowed to operate or that the local newspaper will carry a practitioner's media release. This "consulting fee" may be nothing more than a payment—even a bribe—to be allowed to do business.

The social responsibility of public relations is to represent members of society in public discussions. Today's public relations is more likely to be based on decisions of what must be said to enhance the public dialogue. The outcome of this dialogue is a better society, building a strong community through the examination of sound reasons. Misusing public relations will only result in long-term damage to relationships and a reduced ability for the organization to function effectively.

▶Marketplace Responsibility of Public Relations

People and organizations use discourse to publicize, promote, and evaluate ideas and actions. Some ideas and actions relate to the purchase and use of products and services. Products would go unsold if sellers could not use a combination of publicity and paid advertisement to communicate with buyers. Services would go unnoticed if promotion and advertising did not tell consumers which organizations provide those services, where the services can be obtained, and how much they cost.

The marketplace requires the exchange of information. What do buyers want and need? What can sellers say that will help customers know what constitutes a good product or service? How can vendors build relationships if customers cannot trust the information and evaluations contained in public relations messages? A promotion for a Web site, for instance, might tout how it will save consumers time and money. The timing of such publicity might increase during the year-end holidays to encourage customers to choose between buying toys with a click of a mouse instead of fighting long lines at crowded toy stores.

Similar challenges face nonprofit organizations that must attract funds from members, donors, and supporters. How can nonprofit organizations convince persons to join and support the causes of the organization with their financial contributions? How can nonprofits convince persons who need their services that they are available and in a fashion that helps rather than harms persons whom the nonprofit should serve? A Web Watcher of sites such as iVillage's sponsored links to sites on breast cancer can help you appreciate how the Web allows for nonprofits to supply information to persons who are concerned about breast cancer and who want to engage in Internet conversation with others who have similar experiences (www.ivillage.com). By typing "breast cancer" into the iVillage "search" feature, for instance, an interested person can quickly gain access to M. D. Anderson Cancer Center and the National Breast Cancer Organization. These communication efforts serve the interests of victims of cancer and allow donors to conveniently contribute their finances to battle cancer.

Nonprofit organizations, such as the National Wildlife Federation, make statements that contain facts, values, and policy recommendations. These statements often conflict with what other organizations, particularly businesses and governmental agencies, say and do. Without rhetoric, how can nonprofits seek to convince others that their views are correct? Without such statements, how can they attract members—their markets—and form themselves into a potent public that organizations must negotiate with to solve the problems of society?

In these ways, organizations use rhetoric to respond to conditions in the marketplace. Such statements, however, are evaluated in light of standards of social responsibility. Every seller of goods or services must respect the social responsibilities of public communication. Nonprofits also compete in the marketplace for donations by addressing the concerns of key publics, such as environmental advocates who want building products without irresponsible destruction of nature.

▶An Ethical Organization Communicating Effectively

Public relations professionals must adhere to four principles in order to fulfill their social responsibility to society:

- Know what each key individual, group, or institution believes constitutes ethical behavior.
- Listen to what other members of society have to say.
- Ensure that public relations uses two-way communication.
- Build community through cocreated meaning.

First: *Know what each individual, group, or institution believes constitutes ethical behavior.* A public relations practitioner needs to appreciate which actions and policies please as well as offend members of the public. He or she should know which actions or policies foster community support, satisfied customers, or pleased donors. Once those standards are known, the organization should plan and manage its actions to meet them.

Public expectations are a standard that organizations must meet or exceed. Sometimes those expectations are unsound, but they cannot be ignored. Debates over environmental issues serve as excellent examples of potentially unsound expectations. Citizens often believe that they do not contribute to clean-air problems and therefore do not need to change their lifestyles. They are quick to blame air quality problems on industry. They may demand a quick and inexpensive solution when in fact a great deal of time and money is required to meet Environmental Protection Agency (EPA) clean-air standards. As a profession, public relations exists because it can help organizations to meet rather than fall short of public expectations. Such efforts begin with knowing the standards of social responsibility that must be met. The public relations person counsels his or her management regarding the standards others use to evaluate the organization—its policies, products, and services.

By professional training and engaging in best practices, the public relations practitioner serves as the eyes and ears of the organization. Through years of experience and a nearly compulsive consumption of news, practitioners know the ethics of what can be said and done in public and are wise to counsel executives about those standards. Such executives are often sheltered and are not routinely confronted with facing angry reporters and an unhappy public. In contrast, the public relations professional must meet the press and explain the actions of the organization in public. A wise practitioner learns to use news reports to know the concerns people voice about the organization.

The public relations professional needs to counsel the managers of organizations to listen to and heed criticisms. Executives of major and even minor organizations are often angered and insulted when they learn that key members of the public doubt the ethics of their operations, policies, products, or services. However, if organizations did not suffer criticism, public relations would be less needed. By the same token, if public relations practitioners can help organizations to act in ways that avoid criticism, the profession has served the organization and society quite well.

Second: *Listen to what other members of society have to say.* Public relations does not occur in a vacuum, but in situations where people interact to influence one another.

Their messages provide practitioners with valuable insights regarding the operating standards an organization must meet in its performance or address through public communication. An understanding of rhetoric helps practitioners recognize and analyze the strategic communication choices they have in light of the messages set forth by the organization's critics. The Fisher family, which founded Gap chain stores, learned this lesson. Gap stores market reasonably priced natural products for all ages. The controversy began when the Fisher family purchased 350 acres of timberland in Mendocino County, California, one of the hotbeds of environmental activism. The project began with high ideals, since the Fisher family is also a major donor to the Natural Resources Defense Council (NRDC). The timber controversy came to a boiling point when the family failed to realize the level of controversy that was being publicized by Julia Butterfly Hill, an outspoken Fisher foe who spent 738 days in an ancient redwood tree to save it from the lumber mill. Activists, including the NRDC, engaged in a boycott against Gap by publicizing the slogan "Save the Redwoods/Boycott the Gap."

Responding strategically requires knowing what others think and how strong their convictions are. By listening to the comments of others, people can become aware of what they must do to satisfy and not upset members of society. To know what must be said and done, a communicator learns to listen to and carefully consider the thoughts, concerns, needs, wants, and opinions of others.

Protesters Pressure Companies to Change Policies
SOURCE: Reprinted with permission from Shaun Walker, OtterMedia.com.

An organization can meet the needs and avoid collisions with stakeholder concerns only if it listens to them and is responsible and responsive. An organization can decide to change its performance to satisfy those worries or seek to persuade people that their concerns are unfounded. To meet this professional expectation, practitioners need a firm sense of communication strategies, ethical perspectives, and practical challenges. Through strategic listening, practitioners can determine what information others should know. They realize which arguments will and will not succeed. Careful listening helps practitioners realize that relationships depend on constructive actions as well as words. This analysis can lead them to recognize strengths and limits of what they are saying and doing to build mutually beneficial relationships.

Listening is an important public relations skill. Public relations practitioners should be able to appreciate what others say and write. Research is part of the public relations. Listening and carefully considering points others make can lead practitioners to appreciate the accuracy and persuasive power of those statements. No wise counselor ignores or dismisses reasonable positions. Conflicts should be resolved, not ignored, so that they do not boil over into controversy that attracts negative attention. After listening to the concerns of others, practitioners can devise communication plans—tactics and strategies—and counsel other managers to make decisions that lead to mutually beneficial relationships with MAPs.

Third: *Ensure that public relations is two-way communication.* Statements made in public invite response. Public statements are expected to withstand the challenges by other interested and articulate parties. For this reason, Lentz (1996) defended the principle that the public airwaves should foster dialogue rather than privilege some narrow interest; he concluded: "Truth should prevail in a market-like struggle where superior ideas vanquish their inferiors and achieve audience acceptance" (p. 1). In this manner, members of society contest ideas and weigh competing points of view to determine which ones should be adopted or rejected.

Public relations as two-way communication helps dispel the view of the public relations practice as a negative, manipulative approach to reputation management—to merely make the bad seem good. This view sees the public relations person as being able to put a "spin" or clever interpretation on what the organization has done or is doing that may be questionable. With such a spin, the individual is expected to restore the reputation and reduce public criticism even though the organization continues to act in ways that some think are offensive. The view that public relations is "spin-doctoring" weakens the credibility of the practice and damages its professional status. Let's consider an illustration of this technique. Imagine a large school district that has purchased some land for a new school. Some local residents sell their homes, but others refuse to do so. The school district obtains appraisals of the homes and offers to pay "market value." The problem is that the price of the homes is too low for the sellers to purchase comparable property. The school district threatens legal action against the home owners and begins proceedings to force them to sell at the offer price. Local reporters quote elderly citizens who say they will be on the streets if they sell. When asked about this deal, members of the school district say they have paid "fair market price" and believe the citizens have been treated fairly and that they are merely using the press to get higher prices for their property. Will the school district be believed, or rather tearful elderly poor citizens who are featured on camera at the top-of-the-hour television news? What is spin, and what is truth?

People who are interested in representing any organization, especially as public relations professionals, need to be two-way communicators. They must be committed to expressing views that support their client organization as well as community interests. They need to listen to people who criticize their organizations and recognize when such criticism has merit and when it deserves rebuttal. In fact, public relations practitioners should work to encourage comments even when they are negative. Properly examined ideas, evidence, values, and reasoning exchanges through dialogue can lead people and organizations to improve themselves and society (Wallace, 1963; Weaver, 1953, 1970). Two-way communication helps to reveal expectations of publics and to communicate to publics how those expectations are being met.

Fourth: *Build community through shared, cocreated meaning.* The savvy practitioner realizes that one voice, such as that of its employer, cannot dominate opinion. As parties engage in two-way communication in the effort to create, refine, and change opinions, meaning is cocreated. The attempt to build community through shared meaning is inherently rhetorical. Bryant (1953) defined rhetoric as "the function of adjusting ideas to people and people to ideas" (p. 413). Applying this principle, today's public relations seeks to cocreate meaning that adjusts organizations to individuals, groups, and institutions and adjusts individuals, groups, and institutions to organizations—"adjustment" is positive, not negative.

The imbalances of power in society are not etched in stone; they are subject to change. People who do not like the actions of organizations can oppose them. One of the most insightful commentaries on the cocreation of society was offered by George Herbert Mead (1934), who concluded that the mind, self, and society develop through dialogue. He observed,

> We tend to ignore the others and take into account only those which are immediate. The difficulty is to make ourselves recognize the other and wider interests, and then to bring them into some sort of rational relationship with the more immediate ones. There is room for mistakes, but mistakes are not sins. (pp. 388–389)

Shared identifications help forge lasting relationships. Nonprofit organizations, for instance, seek members of society who share their concerns and values. People for the Ethical Treatment of Animals (PETA) serves as a good example. The organization targets the use of furs taken from animals for the purpose of human vanity. Fur coats are not necessary to the quality of human life. Getting those identifications are easy. A more difficult identification results from PETA's criticism of the use of animals in research. They do not believe that animals need to be sacrificed for medial research. Segments of the population that oppose the sale of furs might not be so quick to identify with the criticism of using animals for medical research. (See PETA's Web site for examples of a variety of public relations tools.)

Today's public relations realizes that shared meaning allows people to identify with one another. Shared meaning lays the foundation for individuals to come to know and understand one another, as well as refine and shape each other's thoughts and preferences. Organizations and publics can come to agree on expectations as part of shared meanings—they operate from the same page. The only way to arrive at shared meaning is through two-way communication.

These four principles can serve as beacons to guide your practice of public relations. These principles seem very modern, but they result from controversies over the centuries. People have considered the role of language, messages, and meaning—rhetoric—in the building of societies and marketplaces that foster mutual interests. In future chapters, we will revisit the notion of shared or cocreating meaning to build community. For now, know that organizations are not entities with concrete boundaries. Organizations and the opinion environments in which they operate are cocreated through public discourse through tactics used to support rhetorical strategies.

Our trip through the rhetorical tradition may seem like a detour for understanding public relations. While students may question the current value of ideas taken from antiquity, the rhetorical tradition grounds public relations within a larger, older intellectual tradition. Public relations practitioners are public communicators, just like the rhetors of ancient Greece and Rome. Why is this important? Public communication carries a heavily ethical burden, a theme we will continue in Chapter 2 and feature in Chapter 9.

Even when selling goods or services, false information and weak arguments lead to inadequate conclusions. A community that is confronted with false information and weak arguments is likely to lose faith in collective decision making and the power of public relations. If customers cannot trust claims about products and services, they become cynical, angry, frustrated, and willing to punish the offending organization.

Social responsibility results when organizations respond to the power of public approval—the opinions, attitudes, or beliefs that define and justify an organization's operating principles and procedures. Opinions people hold about an organization—its positive reputation, services, policies, operations, or products—are vital to its ability to operate as it thinks best. By expressing approval or disapproval, opinion leaders set the boundaries on organizational action. They prescribe how the organization should conduct its activities. Favorable opinions are the basis of power. As long as organizations have the support of key segments of society, they have power to chart and realize their destinies. Favorable opinion is not given. It is earned by what organizations say and do. Even large companies (ExxonMobil comes to mind) realize that environmental spills, such as the *Exxon Valdez,* become part of its history. Those blotches on company image linger for years, even decades.

Drawing on principles of organizational citizenship, this text will emphasize ethics, effective communication, and best professional practices needed to build strategic mutually beneficial relationships. These principles should help you prepare for a successful career. The goal of this text is to help you think strategically about public relations and to learn to ask questions and develop solutions that make a difference and help your client organizations to be good citizens of society. We ask you to be SMART as you think and act as a professional practitioner. Learn the best tactics needed to achieve rhetorical strategies. See these as being the means by which you achieve advantages for employers and clients. Know that mutually beneficial relationships are crucial to your success. Recognize that you operate within societal constraints.

Marketing, Advertising, Public Relations, and Integrated Communication: Similarities and Differences

In today's public relations, it's not enough to know about your department or area of responsibility. To be effective within your organization, you must know the similarities and differences between your public relations responsibilities and those of other departments, especially advertising and marketing.

What distinguishes public relations from advertising or marketing? All three advance the goals of the organization through strategic planning and effective communication. One answer is to say that public relations positions the organization to enjoy long-term, mutually beneficial relationships. All three can foster an organization's reputation and increase its brand equity.

Advertising, marketing, and public relations are different, but they overlap. Let us consider the activities typical of marketing, advertising, public relations, and integrated communication. You should understand where each discipline is separate and where all of them overlap. This section examines marketing, advertising, public relations, and integrated communication to clarify and focus your understanding of professional public relations practice.

▶ Marketing: Creating and Positioning Products or Services

The primary responsibility of marketing is to create and position products or services. A *market* is a group of people who purchase or have the potential to purchase a product or service. A *product* is some object you can feel, touch, see, hear, smell, or taste, for example, a soft drink, an automobile, a telephone, or your favorite ice cream flavor. A *service* is a task or process performed for you, such as a haircut, an airplane trip, or an insurance plan; an insurance policy, however, would be a product. To create or position products or services, marketing departments must engage in the following activities.

Identifying and Developing Markets

Markets may be discovered by examining what people want or need. Some markets are carefully created by convincing people that they want or need something. For instance, soft drinks are wants rather than needs, while diapers are needs and not wants!

Positioning Products or Services, Including Creating Surrounds

The concept of market share suggests that any product or service fits into some complex of products or services. For instance, under the heading of movies, each movie, whether new or old, is a product line. Current-run movies compete against one another, television runs (new or old), and videos (new or old). *Surrounds* include items such as clothing, games, and toys that spin off from a movie, as well as popcorn, soft drinks, and candy. Movie theaters may also have video games. They may be located in malls, so some folks can go to the movie while others shop, or vice versa.

Pricing and Packaging

Within a product (or service) line, products can be positioned by price. People may prefer inexpensive products as bargains. Others may want the expensive ones because they believe you get more if you pay more. Price is a key consideration in marketing. Packaging can help to sell products and services. Packaging attracts attention to the product or service. For instance, the packaging for candy bars can be an important consideration. If "Hershey Kisses" were to change their foil packaging to waxed paper, would it attract or turn away consumers?

Advertising and Promoting Sales

Advertising is the paid placement of messages that attract attention to products or services, provide information, and recommend purchase. Marketing can advance sales by using advertising as well as gaining publicity and doing promotions through public relations. If you are doing public relations and your job is to attract publicity and pass out product coupons, you are in promotions.

Controlling Product Mix

By monitoring sales of products (or services) by types in markets and by regions, marketing people know how many to manufacture or order. They also know that they should not saturate a market, thereby killing the steady sale of products. Or they may want to flood a market that they believe will have a short half-life. Flooding damaged the "dot.com" segment of the new communication, e-commerce industry. Internet tools have been developed and sold to make fast profits rather than being used to build lasting business relationships.

Conducting Market Research

Companies and other organizations want to know whether they are reaching and satisfying people. They monitor sales and trends and work out complex models to track market trends and product/service preferences that can make or damage markets. Research begins with the assumption that the best predictor of future sales is the past satisfaction people have had with a product or service. Market research may use some version of *psychographics*, the study of personality traits and buying preferences. Such research might refine marketers' understanding of tastes in automobiles by age. Younger persons might favor small and responsive automobiles that are also economical to operate. Older persons prefer larger, safer, and more comfortable automobiles, for instance.

▶ Advertising: Creating and Paying to Place Informative and Persuasive Messages

The primary responsibility of advertising is to create informative and motivative messages and pay to place them in media designed to reach targeted audiences. Advertising is often a support department reporting to the marketing department. Some advertising departments stand alone. Advertising is a process and a tool. It helps marketing goals by informing and persuading customers, donors, and such. It also is a valuable tool for public relations. It assists efforts to create image, manage reputation, and address issues.

One key use of advertising is to help marketing create and respond to customer preferences and to interest consumers in a particular product or service. In addition to featuring products and services, advertising uses paid messages about the company, what some call "corporate" (institutional or image) advertising. To fulfill their responsibilities, advertising departments engage in certain activities.

Conducting Message Research

Research can be done as an ad campaign develops to reveal when customers are aware of the product/service and their intent to make a purchase. Messages can be pretested to determine whether they have flaws and if they are likely to have their intended impact on consumers. For instance, focus groups can be used to assess buyer satisfaction and whether reactions to products or services are positive or negative. They can determine the attention impact of messages as well as their appeal and believability. Such research can uncover questions audiences have about a product, service, or organization that advertising can address.

Creatively Developing Appeals and Messages

This traditional advertising function is art, not science, the ability to create an appealing message that catches and focuses attention and presses the activation buttons. Some advertising campaigns create cultural icons, from fictional characters such as Joe Camel, the Marlboro Man, and the Virginia Slims Woman to real-life personages such as Shaquille O'Neal or Michael Jordan. Kids want to "Be Like Mike!" Persuasive appeals and messages can be creatively established through visual images, fragrances, textures, and sounds.

Positioning advertising messages in relation to or as a response to competitors is everything in advertising and marketing. The goal is to feature products and services that do a better job of satisfying customers than competitors do. Automobiles are sold on the basis of the advantages they have in price, style, design, color, accessories, and durability.

Buying Time or Space

Advertising personnel are responsible for buying the media time or space desired to reach the targeted audiences. Buying time or space means that they purchase specific amounts of media time or print space. In addition to creatively using purchased time and space to feature products and services, advertising messages can be used in support of organizational positive reputation. They can address issues of importance to public policy debates. For instance, the Chemical Manufacturers Association (today called the American Chemistry Council) has used paid issue advertising to explain to target audiences and publics the operating changes that were reducing the environmental impact of chemical manufacturing facilities.

Creating Advertising Message Delivery Media Other Than Mass Media

Advertising specialists may select, design, or create means for reaching the targeted market with messages in ways other than the traditional mass media. This might include direct-mail advertising or impressive packaging, which creates an impression and increases the incentive for customers to buy a product while it is in their hands. Packaging can gain attention and use advertising messages related to the traits and advantages of the product to meet needs and satisfy wants. Advertising specialists create posters and other devices for attracting attention to products and services. These responsibilities may also involve the development of brochures, flyers, and direct-marketing devices such as product- or service-oriented key chains.

Assessing Message Reach and Impact

As a campaign is initiated and conducted, it may be monitored to determine whether key audiences and markets are receiving, noticing, reading, listening to, televiewing, believing, and acting on the messages.

▶ Public Relations: Creating Strategic Mutually Beneficial Relationships

Some marketing and advertising professionals might say that public relations' sole role includes putting out press releases and getting favorable "unpaid" media attention to aid in selling products, services, and the organization itself. But while these professionals might claim that public relations is merely image building, we will show you how public relations consists of much more than press releases and media events.

You have already read about the five functions of public relations: planning, research, publicity, promotion, and collaborative decision making. Below is a list of relationship-building activities that might be primarily the responsibility of public relations professionals. Note that we feature these as relationship-building responsibilities. Chapter 3 adds depth to the discussion of relationships that follows here.

BOX 1.3 PUBLIC RELATIONS, MORE OR LESS

"One of the unique characteristics of the public relations profession is how ill-defined the role is in most corporations" (Woodrum, 1995, p. 7). This observation should motivate practitioners to know what public relations is and to help other influential persons to adopt that view. Public relations is often more—as well as less—than what others expect it to be. It is more because it is a rich blend of five functions used ethically. It can be less, however, because practitioners cannot easily or ethically spin facts and solve problems merely by issuing a cleverly developed press release.

Marketing Relationships

By using publicity, promotion, articles, features, and similar techniques, public relations professionals assist their colleagues in marketing and advertising. Through marketing-communication efforts, public relations practitioners encourage people to learn about products or services (or fund-raising needs) and to see them as being of value. Public relations can use news stories, feature stories, events, and endorsements to increase the effectiveness of marketing efforts. Many people believe this is public relations' only function, which is unfortunate. Marketing relationships can also include relationships with donors, voters, or members.

Media Relationships

Building media relationships is one of the traditional tactics of public relations practitioners. In fact, some people mistakenly limit the practice of public relations to publicity through media relations. Advertising buys time and space in which to feature an organization's messages. In contrast, public relations practitioners prove to reporters that they have a newsworthy story the reporters need to tell to inform the public. Wise public relations persons know what reporters, editors, and program directors think are "newsworthy" details used to create and pitch stories. Each day, thousands of events and activities go unreported because of limited time and space in the news media. Mutually beneficial relationships with media reporters can increase the likelihood of an organization getting favorable commentary and exposure. During a crisis, positive relationships can reduce the damage caused by poorly chosen responses to the press, which lead to statements such as, "Spokespersons for the company refused to answer our efforts to contact them." Practitioners can be sources of choice if they build mutually beneficial relationships with the media. Commitment to be the first and best source of information regarding their organizations can create a trusting relationship with reporters.

Public Affairs/Governmental Relationships

Companies in particular, as well as activist groups, need highly educated personnel to monitor, create, modify, and kill legislation and regulations. Some people are offended by the notion that a company, for instance, should wield enough power to influence government policy. But if the interests of the company (or industry) and its key publics—the community—would be better off without a piece of legislation, then it should not exist. That message needs to be professionally communicated to build a relationship with other parties that have similar public policy agendas. Collaborations forge useful legislation and regulation in the public interest.

Community Relationships

Companies, governmental agencies, and activist groups seek to create, strengthen, and maintain mutually beneficial relationships with citizens. Such activities could be as limited as corporate sponsorship of a symphony or Little League teams. Even more vital goals center on doing what is necessary to improve and strengthen the community. Risk communication, for instance, is one aspect of community relationships. People who live and work in proximity to sources of danger, such as chemical companies or nuclear generation plants, want to know how safe they are and what to do in the event of an emergency. (To better understand this process, you may want to examine ChevronTexaco's home page as a Web Watcher.) Chevron (today ChevronTexaco) has been a leader in communicating with customers and neighbors about its environmental policies. The company became legendary for television and print ads that drew attention to its efforts and those of others to defend species and promote environmental quality.

Another example: Someone who lives near a nuclear power plant wants to know that it has three different types of sirens for specific types of emergencies and deserves to know what the various sirens mean and what emergency responses to follow when the sirens sound. Such persons also want to know—and deserve to know—about the safety features built into the plant. Closely examine the advertisement about the use of nuclear energy versus imported oil that was used by the U.S. Council for Energy Awareness (USCEA). The USCEA placed this ad in newspapers and magazines shortly after the Chernobyl disaster in the Ukraine, the world's worst nuclear accident. Do this ad and the public relations messages that would have accompanied it positively address community concerns? This ad was also part of the campaign to seek public support for nuclear generation by demonstrating that it can be safe if properly designed.

Activist Relationships

In the past three decades, companies and governmental agencies have learned that they often cannot ignore the concerns and complaints of activists, such as those involved with environmental issues. When people recognize problems and set out to correct them, they may band together and thus create or join an activist group to magnify their power. Companies and governmental agencies work proactively to understand, appreciate, and achieve mutually beneficial solutions to problems recognized by the activists. Companies and governmental agencies can use collaborative decision making to build strong relationships with activists. For example, you may recall the efforts of Home Depot to market environmentally safe building materials, mentioned earlier in this chapter.

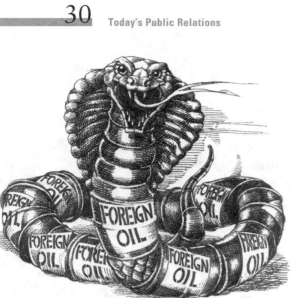

THE KISS OF DEATH?

We now import more than 40 percent of all the oil we use, and that percentage continues to grow. This excessive dependence on foreign oil could poison America's economy and our national security if our supply were ever disrupted.

But the more we use nuclear energy, instead of imported oil, to generate our electricity, the less we have to depend on uncertain foreign oil supplies.

America's 112 nuclear electric plants already have cut foreign oil dependence by 4 billion barrels since the oil embargo of 1973, saving us $115 billion in foreign oil payments.

But 112 nuclear plants will not be enough to meet our rapidly growing demand for electricity. We need more plants.

Importing so much oil is a danger America must avoid. We need to rely more on energy sources we can count on, like nuclear energy.

For a free booklet on nuclear energy, write to the U.S. Council for Energy Awareness, P.O. Box 66080, Dept. SK01, Washington, D.C. 20035.

U.S. COUNCIL FOR ENERGY AWARENESS

Nuclear energy means more energy independence.

© 1990 USCEA

As seen in May 1990 issues of The New York Times, The Washington Post, Natural History, The Leadership Network, The Economist, and Barron's; the May/June 1990 issue of State Legislatures; June 1990 issues of Reader's Digest, National Geographic, TIME, Sports Illustrated, Newsweek, U.S. News & World Report, Smithsonian, Business Week, Scientific American, Governing, and National Journal; July 1990 issues of Forbes and The Wall Street Journal; the July/August 1990 issue of American Heritage.

Foreign Oil Equals Loss of Freedom

SOURCE: Reprinted with permission from the Nuclear Energy Institute.

Customer Relationships

Someone in the organization needs to listen to the needs, concerns, and complaints of customers, donors, and others who purchase products or services. Public relations professionals should be intimately involved in customer relations. They can learn customers' preferences as well as their concerns and doubts about the quality of the product or service. With this knowledge, practitioners become advocates for customers to personnel in marketing and advertising so that the concerns can be addressed and problems can be solved. Practitioners can build mutually beneficial relationships so the products and services they promote are the first choice of customers, donors, and others.

Employee Relationships

While businesses, nonprofits, and governmental agencies communicate with external audiences, they also need to foster effective relationships with their employees. The goal of these relationships is to satisfy employees in order to increase productivity as well as motivate them to work toward increased product and service quality. Employees want to work for good organizations that communicate well. In turn, employees become ambassadors by speaking well of the organization.

Investor Relationships

Publicly traded companies (as well as other financial institutions) employ communication and relationship development specialists to ensure that companies are properly valued by financial analysts and fund managers. This public relations function requires a highly skilled and unusually highly paid practitioner to create, strengthen, and maintain long-term relationships with persons who invest in the company. In good times and stormy ones, a wise company seeks to demonstrate how investment—new and continued—is in the interest of the investor.

This list indicates that public relations professionals do more than merely support advertising and marketing, although savvy public relations people always realize that their immediate activity needs to be tied to some goal relevant to obtaining and wisely managing the revenue of the organization. In Chapter 3, we will elaborate further on the nature of strategic organizational relationships and public relations practice.

▶Integrated Communication: Creating Integrated Messages

As we near the end of this comparison of public relations, advertising, and marketing, we have one more topic to consider. In the past decade, a serious movement has occurred to create what is called *integrated marketing communication* or *integrated communication*. This trend has challenged marketing, advertising, and public relations to work together closely to support the organization's marketing effort. This movement, at least in part, was motivated by rising advertising costs and a realization that public relations messages may have more clout because people are more resistant to advertising messages than to publicity. The public questions the credibility of advertising but trusts the statements by reporters and other ostensibly objective third parties.

This integrated communication movement has resulted in battles regarding the relationships among marketing, advertising, and public relations. These battles have two dimensions: One is the struggle to control budgets, and the other is for "turf." Whether it is operating on a constrained or ample budget, each organization must think about how that budget needs to be divided. To make an effective decision, senior executives sometimes rely on what's called *return on investment* (ROI). That simply means that if senior management (or any other body with budget oversight) were to give you, the head of public relations, $500,000, they would want to know what you would do with that money. They would like an adequate return on investment. If they are a business, they want you to make more money for the organization than you cost. If they are a nonprofit, they want sufficient income to accomplish their charitable mission.

The second battle is for turf, managerial power. Managerial responsibility results in prestige, status, and visibility, as well as the budget authority to procure personnel, supplies, and office space. One sticking point in the discussion of integrated communication is the fear that marketing will control public relations. Such control can compromise the organization's ethics and limit the scope of its strategic activities. If public relations reports to marketing, many nonmarketing relationships will go unmanaged. And the ethics of public relations can be compromised. Public relations may be limited to speak well, even if inaccurately, about the organization's products and services. Integrated communication works best when public relations helps to get the marketing messages out, but public relations is not limited in the scope and ethics of this function.

This issue, a matter of budget and organizational turf, has become increasingly important and the contest more robust as managements have asked marketing departments to have a greater impact with less money. Over the past decade, advertising costs have increased dramatically. As a consequence, managers, including the head of marketing, look to public relations to help obtain "free" advertising: publicity and promotion. Public relations is expected to offset reduced budgets with free publicity.

This movement challenges public relations to engage in at least three activities with marketing and advertising. One is to share responsibility for reaching and satisfying customers. The second is to ensure that all organizational messages are integrated with and supportive of the advertising and marketing messages. In this sense, the organization is challenged to promote one theme even if it is tailored to its

Figure 1.2: The Relationships Between Marketing, Advertising, and Public Relations

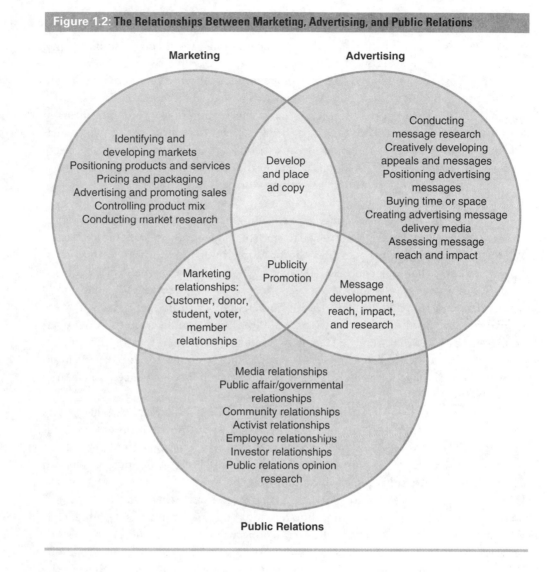

Figure 1.2: The Relationships Between Marketing, Advertising, and Public Relations

Marketing

Advertising

Identifying and
developing markets
Positioning products and services
Pricing and packaging
Advertising and promoting sales
Controlling product mix
Conducting market research

Develop
and place
ad copy

Conducting
message research
Creatively developing
appeals and messages
Positioning advertising
messages
Buying time or space
Creating advertising message
delivery media
Assessing message
reach and impact

Marketing
relationships:
Customer, donor,
student, voter,
member
relationships

Publicity
Promotion

Message
development,
reach, impact,
and research

Media relationships
Public affair/governmental
relationships
Community relationships
Activist relationships
Employee relationships
Investor relationships
Public relations opinion
research

Public Relations

different audiences' and markets' needs and wants. The third challenge is to promote and publicize goods and services in ways that reduce costs.

For some, integrated communication is a new theme. For many experienced public relations practitioners, it is standard practice. Public relations professionals realize that messages need to help inform, convince, and motivate audiences by reinforcing the same themes advanced by marketing and advertising. An organization will have problems if its product advertisements promote customer service while its financial messages and employee training stress reduced costs by spending less time with customers.

One major advantage to public relations, however, is its commitment to be the ethical conscience of the organization. It is expected to provide ethical balance to marketing and the interests of MAPs. And, as was demonstrated above, public relations needs to support marketing and advertising, but it has many additional relationship-building responsibilities.

One of our objectives in this discussion was to see where each of these three disciplines is unique and appreciate where they merge as one, at which point they constitute integrated communication. Figure 1.2 depicts the relationship between marketing, advertising, and public relations. Each circle contains the unique activities of marketing, advertising, and public relations. The intersection among circles indicates how the disciplines overlap. For example, the overlap between public relations and marketing centers on building relationships with customers; the overlap between public relations and advertising is message development, reach, impact, and research. Furthermore, all three intersect in the activities of publicity and promotion.

The "Magic Earth" Web site (Web Watcher) offers insights into the ways in which the advertising messages of a business mix with its public relations to position and promote its image. This company sells its products and services to other businesses. Public relations personnel issue media releases to announce business activities of interest to customers. We invite you to read the press releases, note the logos of the companies involved, and think about how they increase the value of the business, its brand equity.

Circumstances That Call for Public Relations

The study of public relations forces us to think about how organizations build effective relationships. Whether they are governmental agencies, businesses, or nonprofits, organizations wish to increase their monetary resources and achieve positive reputations. To earn these resources, organizations must create and maintain good relationships with key people or groups. Let us now consider the variety of organizations that require the strategic practice of today's public relations professionals.

Organizations That Need Public Relations

▶Business Organizations

Public relations can help companies increase their competitiveness by establishing mutually beneficial relationships with customers. Businesses use public relations to attract people to buy their products or services. Hospitals stay competitive by using public relations to demonstrate that they care about patients and provide excellent medical service. Automobile companies use special events to entice customers to buy the latest model. Customer relations programs look to reduce customer dissatisfaction and help customers to use products properly. Public relations can reduce conflict and friction between companies and their critics.

Reflections of an Account Executive

Lisa K. Merkl
Former Account Executive
Vollmer Public Relations
Houston, Texas

NOTE: This professional reflection was written by Lisa Merkl when she was in her second job. As is often the case, professionals move from one employer to the next as they advance. Today, Lisa is a Senior Science Writer/Editor in the Office of External Communication at the University of Houston. This reflection is offered to help students realize what they may be called on to know and to perform as they enter the profession. These challenges may be unique to a person in a large and diversified agency, but they are part of the skills and knowledge of the practice needed to participate in the profession.

V ariety and time—two of the most outstanding elements you'll experience working in an agency. You've got to be versatile and think quickly. In a single day, I am likely to cover the gamut from the petroleum to the entertainment industries. I've worked with clients in an array of industries, including popular music, real estate, education, retail, motor oil, telecommunications, industrial plant repairs, petroleum, aerospace, home services,

film distribution, health care, fine arts, and museums. No two days are alike.

Coming out of journalism and public relations degrees, I expected and looked forward to the wide variety of clients and industries I'd encounter, but the close eye kept on time has admittedly been the biggest adjustment. Living by a daily time log that's split up by 15-minute increments really gives you perspective on time as a commodity. The quarter hours that measure my day are critical—my salary and the agency's profit are a direct result of the hours I "bill" to each individual client.

I've dealt with both business-to-business and consumer media on local and national levels. I've pitched stories to print and broadcast outlets, including daily newspapers, business journals, oil and gas magazines, lifestyle magazines, aerospace journals, entertainment publications, AP reporters, local television news affiliates, and national network and cable television programs.

In a given day, I might perform any of a number of tasks:

- Write press releases, fact sheets, backgrounders, media alerts, and pitch letters.
- Build media lists.
- Brainstorm media angles.
- Create and personally deliver "media drops" that will draw extra attention to press materials.
- Make follow-up calls to the media regarding releases, press kits, or drops sent out.

▶Governmental Agencies

Governmental agencies must establish communication links with legislators as well as with the citizens they serve. They can use public relations to inform legislators and the

- Monitor the media and journalist message boards for leads on possible stories that might be appropriate for given clients' expertise or current offerings.
- Gauge analyst perceptions of publicly held clients.
- Set up and attend backgrounding sessions for clients with members of the media.
- Correspond and visit with reporters and assignment editors just as a "get to know you" for future reference.
- Attend live media remotes for TV or radio.
- Develop sponsorship packets for the launch of new projects, events, or products.
- Ghostwrite bylined articles on successful projects performed by the scientists, engineers, and technicians employed by clients.
- Write public relations plans and strategies for clients.
- Maintain client timelines.
- Review and edit clients' billing reports and compile status reports that explain the charges.
- Prepare meeting agendas and meet with clients.
- Maintain daily telephone and e-mail contact with clients.
- Monitor the media for trends relevant to clients' target industries.
- Review broadcast hits and print clips and calculate corresponding ad values for publicity recaps.
- Write speeches.
- Coordinate special event logistics.

- Attend special events surrounding new client products or services.
- Obtain collateral quotes for press kit folders, brochures, and direct mail pieces.
- Write brochure, Web site, and, occasionally, advertising copy.
- Liaise with advertising agencies and design firms for clients' non–public relations needs.

At times hectic, but more often exciting, I am on the cutting edge of setting public relations precedents. I mingle with media personalities and ultimately help shape the news and trends that billions of people follow each day. Opportunities abound. As a public relations professional, I create, innovate, and persuade, making my mark on the world. The power of PR to shape people's perceptions and make a difference in the way even one person goes about some facet of their life is a valuable gift.

Writing public relations plans, managing clients' public relations strategies, targeting media, writing press releases, and pitching stories creatively are rewarding tasks that I encounter every day, but when I get back evidence of measurable results, it takes it to a whole new level. One of my favorites is a "thank you" e-mail I received from one of my clients to tell me that the case study I wrote and placed for them in a publication brought them $1.5 million in new business. A testament to the power of public relations.

SOURCE: Reprinted with permission from Lisa K. Merkl.

public about services they provide and problems they solve. If agencies do not achieve and maintain public support, they can lose their funding and go out of operation. For instance, the mayor's office must attract attention to needed city services to justify increased taxes or to justify shifting funds from one budget priority to another. Federal agencies use media relations to report success stories. The Environmental Protection Agency reports success and failure in protecting endangered species.

▶Nonprofit Organizations

Nonprofit organizations use public relations to compete for membership and vie for political, volunteer, and monetary support for causes they represent. Hundreds of thousands of nonprofit groups operate in society, including the American Cancer Society, the National Wildlife Federation, agencies that serve battered women, and hundreds of colleges and universities. Although called "nonprofit," they have to compete for funds and communicate with donors and supporters. They must explain how they benefit society.

What types of organizations do not need public relations? Organizations that have no reason for strong and mutually beneficial relationships. Organizations that are indifferent to their reputations. Organizations that have little or no need to inform or persuade persons or groups. Can you identify any organizations that do not need public relations?

How Organizations Use Public Relations

Public relations enters the picture when an organization realizes that it needs to strategically build, maintain, or repair its relationships with persons, groups, and other organizations. Consider the following situations that challenge today's professional practitioners to make a difference for their organizations:

- Organizations want favorable attention and work to reduce criticism.
- Organizations need good working relationships, especially with reporters. Reporters can be powerful allies in disseminating information favorable to the organization. They can also discredit its reputation by revealing damaging details.
- Organizations work to survive crises.
- Organizations strive to inform people, as well as persuade them and shape their behavior.
- Organizations need revenue. Businesses want investors and customers. Governmental agencies want the support of legislators and citizens. Nonprofits work to attract supporters and donors.
- Organizations demonstrate how their interests align with those of citizens and customers.
- Organizations want to reduce costs that result from unproductive conflict.
- Organizations want to understand their MAPs.

This brief, but incomplete, list can help you imagine what public relations professionals do on a day-to-day basis, by serving the interests of clients, employers, and a wide array of individuals. Today's professional practitioners understand the dynamics of relationship building. They use their rhetorical and management skills to inform and persuade through the information that flows from an organization to people outside. They listen to opinions and concerns of people outside the organization and bring that information to the attention of management.

Conclusion

Chapter 1 should help you have a clearer picture of what public relations is and is not. The definition and five functions of public relations reveal its complexity. Public relations is not simply people skills or event planning; public relations requires the use of various management functions to build mutually beneficial relationships. A practitioner must learn a variety of skills and concepts that are central to the remainder of this book. The best practitioners are dedicated to truth, sound ethics, and policies that blend many interests.

Public relations is part of a larger rhetorical tradition. Public communication carries with it social responsibilities for maintaining the integrity of public discussions. We translated those responsibilities into four principles for organizations wishing to communicate ethically and effectively. We consider public relations' rhetorical roots as significant. These roots shape our views of what public relations is and how it should be practiced. We hope that you now have a better understanding and appreciation for how this book approaches public relations. We have asked you to think and act in ways that are SMART. The challenge is to learn tactics that can be used strategically to achieve outcomes that serve your clients and employers, as well as society.

Ethical Quandary: Unethical Organizations and Public Relations Practice

FURTHER
EXPLORATION

1

Classical thinkers knew, as we do today, that rhetoric could be used ethically or as a tool for achieving selfish ends. Consider the following questions: Can an unethical organization communicate effectively and sustain a positive reputation in public? Can unethical statements be effective over time? Should a public relations professional accept an assignment to work on a project that conflicts with his or her ethics?

Write a two-page position paper that answers these questions. Use comments from the chapter to justify your conclusion. Be sure to state the supporting reasons for your position. Come to class prepared to discuss your position.

Summary Questions

1. What kinds of organizations need public relations? What kinds of organizations do not need public relations? List five reasons why organizations need public relations. List five reasons why public relations helps those who want or need relationships with organizations.

2. What does "PRSA" stand for, and what does the organization that goes by those initials advocate regarding the practice of public relations?

3. Define *public relations.*

4. What are the five basic functions of public relations? Explain each function and tell what it does on behalf of the organization as well as its markets, audiences, and publics (MAPs).

5. Differentiate public relations, marketing, and advertising. How can they work together to achieve integrated communication?

6. What are the characteristics of a mutually beneficial relationship?

7. Define *rhetoric* and the *rhetorical heritage.*

8. What are the social and the market roles of public relations?

9. What four principles does rhetoric provide for the socially responsible practice of public relations?

10. What best practices are needed for an organization to achieve social responsibility?

Exercises

1. Study Table 1.1. Select one of the principles of the rhetorical heritage for today's public relations practice. Based on your reading in Chapter 1 and your experience, do you agree or disagree with the statement? Write an editorial in which you use three points that support or challenge the principle you have chosen.

2. Imagine that someone has just told you that public relations is nothing more than advertising and marketing. Based on your reading in Chapter 1, do you agree or disagree? Write a statement to be published by the PRSA that expresses your views.

3. Make contact with a public relations practitioner in your community. Show this person the Professional Reflection that is featured in Chapter 1. Ask the person to comment on how accurate that author's account is of publicity and promotion.

4. Do you agree with the definition of public relations in this chapter? If somebody made a derogatory comment about "public relations," what would you say in response? What three points would you make? Use the definition of public relations to justify your response.

5. Find a business, nonprofit organization, or governmental agency. See whether you can determine what it does to publicize and promote itself. How does it build relationships with its markets, audiences, or publics (MAPs)? Does it engage in collaborative decision making? If you can, contact the organization to help get answers to these questions. Also, ask whether it conducts research. How does it go about strategic planning?

6. Locate and study a nonprofit organization. What rhetorical positions does it take in its efforts to serve society when solving its problems?

Recommended Readings

Brown, C., & Waltzer, B. K. (2005). Every Thursday: Advertorials by Mobil Oil on the op-ed page of *The New York Times*. *Public Relations Review, 31*, 197–208.

Caywood, C. L. (Ed.). (1997). *The handbook of strategic public relations & integrated communications*. New York: McGraw-Hill.

Cropp, F., & Pincus, J. D. (2001). The mystery of public relations: Unraveling its past, unmasking its future. In R. L. Heath (Ed.), *Handbook of public relations* (pp. 189–204). Thousand Oaks, CA: Sage.

Dennis, L. B. (Ed.). (1996). *Practical public affairs in an era of change: A communications guide for business, government, and college*. Lanham, MD: University Press of America.

Elwood, W. N. (Ed.). (1995). *Public relations inquiry as rhetorical criticism: Case studies of corporate discourse and social influence* (pp. 13–23). Westport, CT: Praeger.

Grunig, J. E. (Ed.). (1992). *Excellence in public relations and communication management*. Hillsdale, NJ: Lawrence Erlbaum.

Harris, T. L., & Kotler, P. (1999). *Value-added public relations: The secret weapon of integrated marketing*. Lincolnwood, IL: NTC/Contemporary Publishing.

Heath, R. L. (1986). *Realism and relativism: A perspective on Kenneth Burke*. Macon, GA: Mercer University Press.

Heath, R. L. (2001). A rhetorical enactment rationale for public relations: The good organization communicating well. In R. L. Heath (Ed.), *Handbook of public relations* (pp. 31–50). Thousand Oaks, CA: Sage.

Heath, R. L. (2005). Rhetorical theory. In R. L. Heath (Ed.), *Encyclopedia of public relations* (pp. 749–752). Thousand Oaks, CA: Sage.

Hutton, J. G. (2001). Defining the relationship between public relations and marketing: Public relations' most important challenge. In R. L. Heath (Ed.), *Handbook of public relations* (pp. 205–214). Thousand Oaks, CA: Sage.

Kennedy, G. (1963). *The art of persuasion in Greece*. Princeton, NJ: Princeton University Press.

Kotler, P., & Armstrong, G. (2001). *Principles of marketing.* Upper Saddle River, NJ: Prentice Hall.

L'Etang, J., & Piecksa, M. (Eds.). (1996). *Critical perspectives in public relations.* London: International Thomson Business Press.

Stauber, J. C., & Rampton, S. (1995). *Toxic sludge is good for you: Lies, damn lies, and the public relations industry.* Monroe, ME: Common Courage.

Toth, E. L., & Heath, R. L. (Eds.). (1992). *Rhetorical and critical approaches to public relations.* Hillsdale, NJ: Lawrence Erlbaum.

Wells, W. (1997). *Advertising: Principles & practices* (4th ed.). Englewood Cliffs, NJ: Prentice Hall.

Woodrum, R. L. (1995). How to please the CEO and keep your job. *Public Relations Strategist, 1*(3), 7–12.

History of Public Relationships

2

Edward Bernays Promotes Lucky Strike Cigarettes

Edward Bernays called himself the "father of public relations." He wrote the first book on public relations, taught the first academic course in public relations, and was an expert at promotion—including self-promotion. In the late 1920s, he exploited principles of psychology and survey research to refine his practice. His interest in psychology may have come from the influence of his double-uncle, the famous Sigmund Freud, a pioneer in psychology.

Edward Bernays is famous for his strategic response to the image problems encountered by Lucky Strike cigarettes. Research by the American Tobacco Company revealed that women resisted smoking Lucky Strikes because the forest-green packaging clashed with their wardrobes. Management had two options: change the color, or change the market's perception of the color. The industry, under Bernays's tutelage, opted for the second decision and turned to public relations to implement the decision.

Bernays's campaign began with an invitation to a society matron to visit famous designers in Paris who would create forest-green gowns for a charity event. He then persuaded leading textile manufacturers to sponsor a Green Fashions Fall luncheon. Creating the Color Fashion Bureau, he invited fashion editors and art historians to discuss the significance of the color green. The Lucky Strike color was selected for the stationery that was used for correspondence about the event. Utilizing that stationery, he corresponded with interior decorators, art industry groups, department stores, and women's clubs.

Sales of Lucky Strikes slowly increased as the brand became more popular with women. Using the slogan "Torches of Freedom" during World War II, Lucky Strike demonstrated its

Edward Bernays, Father of Modern Public Relations

SOURCE: Copyright © Corbis.

patriotism and became the cigarette of choice by military service personnel, and the packaging changed to red, white, and blue. Also, the package featured a circle, which could be interpreted as being a bull's-eye in a target. Would you have thought changing women's perceptions of the color green was possible? Would this strategic use of public relations work in today's media-savvy society? Would changing the packaging make the brand more popular by appealing to patriotism? We should also note that in later years, as he learned of the potential health effects of tobacco smoke, Bernays voiced regret for having promoted Lucky Strike cigarettes.

This chapter can help you know the origins of your profession. As you are waiting for a class to begin, imagine that a friend of yours says that he or she cannot understand why anyone would study public relations, arguing that people go into public relations simply because they like to talk or socialize, and really do not have any otherwise useful skills. Besides, public relations is at best meaningless hype and at worst just a fancy way of lying. Your friend, of course, is simply repeating common misperceptions about public relations. First, public relations is not just "being good with people" or being able to talk flippantly and to socialize smoothly. Public relations is based on strong writing abilities and requires the mastery of various strategic management and tactical skills if a person is to have a successful career. A professional learns to apply an array of techniques, principles, and theories to public relations problems and opportunities— they are not just "people persons." Second, the mass media often misrepresent public relations by treating it as a way to hide the truth, reinforcing its reputation as substanceless hype.

Effective public relations is based on matching words and actions: There must be enough substance behind the words such that actions and words become one. This chapter continues your exploration into the true nature of the public relations profession, providing a historical context for the modern practice of public relations and its development toward becoming a profession. It uses the historical context of public relations to demonstrate the SMART approach to public relations: As you read about the persons who helped shape the field, consider how they have contributed Societal value and meaning as well as demonstrated the need to create Mutually beneficial relationships. Think about how they achieved Advantages through objectives as they employed a wide array of Rhetorical strategies and Tactics.

Historical Context

As we emphasize throughout this book, today's public relations practice is a complex of management and technical functions. Like many fields, public relations' earlier days were much less sophisticated and without standards. Understanding the history of public relations, its present state, and the dynamics shaping the future are important for a practitioner's personal growth and development. To appreciate today's professional practice and the potential of public relations, we must venture into our past to understand how we came to be the professionals that we are today. Using a simple chronological approach to public relations' history, this first section will focus on individuals and events that helped to shape the development of public relations. We will also show how emphases on promotion, publicity, planning, research, and relationship building have changed over time. By the end of the chapter, you will have a clearer picture of how the public relation profession works in today's society. Along with that picture should come an appreciation and pride in a field that employs many dedicated and honorable practitioners.

The *Encyclopedia of Public Relations,* edited by R. L. Heath (2005), is a valuable source for details on the history of public relations. It covers the origins of modern public relations, antecedents of public relations, biographical sketches, and historical events. Students, professionals, and the lay public find this work useful for understanding the people, events, times, and professional associations that have been particularly relevant in the evolution of public relations. Use the "List of Entries" in the beginning of the encyclopedia for quick access to topics that are relevant to this chapter.

▶Public Relations History: A Starting Reference Point

How people define the origins of public relations reflects what they believe it is. Many think of it as a paid, professional activity that occurred in the United States in the latter part of the 19th century. Large companies, such as railroads, engaged writers, including news reporters, to favorably describe land and opportunities in the midwestern and western United States. Those who think that public relations is media relations often feature this as a starting point. Others may point to the promotional skills of the great showman P. T. Barnum and his competitors. Again, this activity occurred in the middle years of the 19th century.

Because experts disagree over the exact origins of public relations, its history may not be entirely objective. However, we do know that society saw many changes around 1900, including the emerging use of mass media (newspapers), the continued rise of cities (urbanization), and the growth of manufacturing (industrialization). Because of these forces, we begin our time line of public relations' history near the dawn of the 20th century. It is in the start of modern society that organizations began to appreciate the value of public opinion—the collective opinions of many publics and markets. Corporations, nonprofits, and government agencies all realized that if people did not like or were opposed to them, it was much harder to operate effectively. Organizational leaders began to appreciate the usefulness of favorable opinions and would later understand the value of mutual relationships.

Public relations began to emerge as a way for organizations to cope with their environment, which included increased government regulation and sometimes sharply critical coverage in newspapers and popular magazines. Society and public relations became intertwined. Changes in each affected the other, and public relations was used to adapt to new societal values and to shape societal values. Public relations techniques have been used to promote significant societal changes, such as women's rights, civil rights, the cause of organized labor, and environmental responsibility. Changes in technology, such as the advent of radio, television, phones, faxes, and the Internet, each in its own time, also affected public relations by providing new tools for executing public relations activities. In fact, the various Web applications in this book are a testament to technology's continuing impact on public relations. Keep the links between society, public relations, and technology in mind as you read through the highlights from public relations' history that follow.

▶Antecedents of Public Relations

If we take an image-building and relationship management approach to public relations, we might argue that what we call "public relations" is virtually timeless. Kings and emperors used various forms of communication to assert their authority and to intimidate opponents. So did religious leaders. Is this public relations? We know that monarchs communicated with subjects. They gave instructions about when to plant and how to harvest crops. Such was the case in many ancient cultures, such as Persia and the Mayan culture of Mexico. These nobles built monuments. They created public displays of wealth and power. They made announcements to guide farmers through the planting and harvesting seasons.

Also masters of reputation building, Roman emperors had huge displays, or events, as they rode victoriously into Rome, with slaves and animals from conquered countries on display. Citizens might throw flowers into the path before these "heroes." These victors might ride in procession in spectacular chariots. Such publicity events might last for hours. At other times, these rulers might sit in the Roman Coliseum and watch animals and humans fight to the death. Was this public relations? When royalty died, massive tombs were often created. Was this image building part of their public relations? Were the liaisons and negotiations of these leaders with those of other countries contemporary public relations efforts called "government relations"?

History can hardly mark the first fairs where people gathered to show their produce and products. Today, we would probably think of fairs, especially world's fairs, as enormous publicity events. Jousts displayed the military ability of various kings and nobles. Such events were merely a variation of religious events. Pilgrimages may be treated as public relations. Masses of the faithful coming to worship can be viewed as public relations. Propagating the faith through preaching and the construction of churches—that too may be public relations. Songs and sermons conveyed messages of faith. Paintings and statues were crafted to inspire faith.

Can we imagine a time when royal marriages were used as part of relationship building? Ambassadors and other figures engaged in extensive government relations. Universities quickly enaged in promotion and alumni relations. They sought the finest scholars. Merchants sought investors—investor relations. Rulers sought painters and sculptors to create works or art and record grand events. Is that public relations? Painters, sculptors, architects, and composers sought patrons, as they do today. Is all of that public relations?

If we answer yes to all or at least most of the questions above, we are likely to see public relations as virtually as old as human civilization. But it was not known as a profession by that title until the 19th century. Before, it was likely to go by many names, but the goals, strategies, and tactics are timeless. And today, as in many of the past centuries, powerful individuals hire persons to communicate on their behalf to create image, develop reputation, and manage relationships. Even commisioned books and stories (by roving artists) are timeless antecedents of public relations.

Many texts on public relations describe turning points in government as evidence of antecedents of public relations. In 1215, Stephen Langton inspired several barons to confront King John of England. This moment of activist government relations led to the adoption of the Magna Carta. Also, the legends and facts of the American war of independence have been offered as evidence of how the tactics of public relations were used by the angry colonists to foment new government relations with England. By any standard, the Boston Tea Party was a "media event." It attracted media attention and portrayed the English tax system as being unjust. Symbols such as the Liberty Tree and slogans such as "Don't tread on me"—were these antecedents of modern public relations? Was the Declaration of Independence one of the greatest tactics of government relations of all time? It can be seen as a public relations backgrounder and fact sheet that listed grievances justifying resistance to the King of England.

Public Relations Time Line

By the 19th century, generations of individuals in all cultures, faiths, and countries had used tactics that could be honed even more to seek attention, provide information, influence attitudes, and motivate. These tactics were used strategically to build markets, form and topple governments, and attract the faithful. They were employed for conflict and confrontation as well as for collaborative decision making and negotiation. They called for people to identify with one another and, of course, to be dedicated against some other group of people.

Master publicist and promotor P. T. Barnum is among the first names to be typically linked to public relations. For much of the last part of the 19th century, he was a master promoter, widely recognized as perfecting the news value of hype and the art of the "pseudo-event." "Hyping" refers to the use of media news accounts to promote a topic through "puffery," or exaggerating its social relevance or entertainment value. A pseudo-event is a planned or staged event manufactured to create news and receive press coverage. A true showman, Barnum resorted to deception, hoax, and overexaggeration. He played to people's curiosity and touted the unusual: the world's smallest man and woman or the largest elephant, "Jumbo," or the strongest person.

During P. T. Barnum's era, public relations was a loose set of tactics to obtain newspaper coverage and secure public support. The objective was to promote and publicize anything that would draw paying crowds. There were no codes of ethics, sets of principles that maintained what was right or wrong. Still in its infancy, much of the public relations Barnum engaged in would be frowned on as manipulative and unethical by today's standards. Keep in mind that at the same time, medicine was a shady profession, and hospitals were viewed as places people went to die. Although today's practitioners often prefer to separate themselves from the likes of P. T. Barnum, he is an indelible part of history. Unfortunately, too many critics of the profession like to define public relations by its past limitations and not its ever-progressing contributions to society. Members of all professions, bankers, lawyers, and even police, have their growing pains and dark pasts. It is unfair to simply equate a current profession with its past actions in a knee-jerk fashion. As we move further through history, we will see indeed how far public relations has come from these early, reckless days.

WEB WATCHER: P. T. BARNUM

The reputation of Barnum ranges far beyond persons interested in the predecessors of our practice. An interesting Web site, http://home.nycap.rr.com/useless/barnum/index.html, which features "Useless Information," identifies words and phrases that Barnum popularized into the English language as part of his promotional strategies. These include "jumbo," "throwing your hat in the ring," "grandstanding," "The Greatest Show on Earth," "Siamese twins," and "Rain or Shine." This Web site makes an interesting point: "By the way, the only phrase that he is currently famous for is 'A sucker is born every minute.' Strangely enough, he never said this. It was actually stated by his competitor—a banker named David Hannum, owner of the Cardiff Giant (which later turned out to be a hoax)." This Web site reveals that Barnum was also a politician who served in the Connecticut State Legislature. In that capacity, "He is credited as casting the deciding factor in the senate vote for the abolition of slavery after the Civil War." This Web Watcher gives you additional insights into how important words are to practitioners and how they may influence the language of society.

Another Web site, "Celebrity Morgue.com", http://www.celebritymorgue.com/jumbo/, demonstrates Barnum's ability to exploit a photo-op. His famous "Jumbo" the elephant was killed by an unfortunate collision with a train in St. Thomas, Ontario, on September 15, 1885. This Web site affords an interesting glimpse of poor Jumbo, whose size was a news story even in his death. After a trip to the taxidermist, Jumbo continued to be part of Barnum's show.

As modern society began to take shape, public consent became increasingly important in policy making. Corporations used public relations in efforts to shape public opinion as a way to influence policy decisions. The "battle of the currents" is a stunning example of corporations using public relations to influence public opinion and policies, an early version of issues management, organized efforts to shape public policy decisions. The first public relations department was established in 1889 by George Westinghouse. He had organized a corporation to supply an alternating-current electricity, which competed with Thomas Edison's Edison Electric, which advocated the use of direct current. The battle between Edison and Westinghouse defined the electricity-generating industry, and both Edison and Westinghouse utilized public relations efforts to affect public opinion and policy decisions. Both were masters of the publicity and promotion tools needed to gain a competitive advantage and favorably present their companies.

Edison took his case to customers and public policy makers with a sponsored book titled *A Warning*. Details presented there, he hoped, would scare the public into favoring direct current. The polemic argued that alternating current is too lethal to be trusted into people's residences and neighborhoods; the book's appendix even ghoulishly listed persons who had been killed by electricity. Through his self-promotion, Edison may have been instrumental in the State of New York's decision to use alternating current to administer capital punishment (Cutlip, 1995). He demonstrated the potency of alternating current by having it used to kill horses and even an elephant. In 1889, Westinghouse countered Edison's attack with his own book, *Safety of the Alternating System of Electrical Distribution,* which extolled the virtues of his technology. Through public relations, Westinghouse won public support and ultimately government acceptance of his alternating current (AC). Today, we plug our computers into the wall and get AC current. Through promotion and publicity, corporations were using public relations—albeit one-way communication—to shape business and society.

Many battles of this time pitted large corporations against an increasingly critical mass media: the print media. At times, however, large corporations and the press worked together, even greasing each other's palms. The railroad industry serves as an excellent example. The Norfolk and Western Railroad, as did other lines, promoted itself and the cities it wanted to spawn by giving free passes to newspapermen. On their return from staged boosterism events along the railroad line, they wrote favorable stories, the cheapest "advertising" a railroad could get. Railroads needed customers. To create this customer base, railroads needed to attract settlers to obtain farmland and to support their local merchants (Olasky, 1987). When a train crashed, the reporters were even willing to stay away from the crash site to avoid negative publicity. Think about a recent train or airplane crash, and try to imagine reporters staying away from that sort of spectacle today.

Large corporations continued to grow, evolving into monopolies. Too often, powerful monopolies developed contemptuous attitudes toward their employees, the press, and segments of the public at large. Public support eroded as relationships could no longer be defended as mutually beneficial. Critics called for government reform of industry and to set limits on private sector activities. The railroads were among the most powerful economic and political forces at this time; even the elite saw reporters, their former promotional allies, turn to critics. A class of rich and powerful industrialists known as "robber barons" emerged from the monopolies. Famous robber barons included Cornelius Vanderbilt (railroads), J. P. Morgan (banking), Andrew Carnegie (steel), and John D. Rockefeller (oil). These men operated on the doctrine that the less the public knew of their operations, the more efficient and profitable business could be. Naturally, the robber barons were roundly criticized for underpaying their workers and the deplorable conditions under which their employees toiled.

Turn-of-the-century journalists known as "muckrakers" investigated and exposed the monopolistic robber barons' lack of product safety and general apathy about employees. The muckrakers were a reflection of a political movement known as the "Progressives," who wanted to use public relations in two prosocial ways. First, they wanted to create positive social change by molding the opinions of influential segments of the public. They sought to use public opinion to correct social ills, such as government corruption and the exploitation of workers. Second, they wanted to expose social ills and to build support for their cures. We can get a feel for public relations' role in the robber baron-muckraker battles by looking at two well-known muckrakers in detail, Upton Sinclair and Ida Tarbell. Sinclair and Tarbell make useful examples because they represent divergent types of progressive reformers.

Upton Sinclair was the "typical" muckraker, a crusader with a burning pen. Sinclair lived in the meatpacking neighborhoods of Chicago for 7 weeks to research the industry and used his experiences as the basis of the muckraking classic, *The Jungle*. Sinclair exposed the exploitation of the workers and the unsanitary preparation of meat, which included grinding rats, refuse—and the occasional employee—into the meat. His true goal was reform that would benefit the workers. Unfortunately, Sinclair fought for changes that never occurred, and he judged his effort a failure. The people focused on the scandalous meat preparation practices instead of on workers. Sinclair said he hit the public's stomach when he was aiming for its heart. The end result was only some superficial legislation, including the Pure Food Bill (1906), whose title was more impressive than its actual power. Moreover, lobbying and publicity by the meatpacking industry watered down the bite of the reform legislation. Just watch the news carefully, and you will see that many of the problems with the meat industry are still alive today.

BOX 2.1 ARMOUR PROMISES HIGH STANDARDS

On March 10, 1906, J. Ogden Armour published the second (and last) placed article in a series called "The Packers and the People" (*Saturday Evening Post*, p. 6). As head of Armour and Company, he concluded his discussion of the need for higher standards of sanitation in meatpacking. He pledged that "not one atom of any condemned animal or carcass finds its way, directly or indirectly, from any source, into any food product or food ingredient." See the concluding article on this topic to appreciate the character of placed stories, often in response to muckraker criticism.

Ida Tarbell was not your typical muckraker, but a well-known and respected biographer whose works included books on Abraham Lincoln and Napoleon. Surprisingly, Tarbell approached her subject with objectivity. When *McClure's* magazine hired her to write a history of the Standard Oil Company, she drew on public records, including court documents, and allowed Standard Oil to comment freely on her writings. The end result was a 19-part series in *McClure's*, titled "The History of Standard Oil." The opus detailed a variety of illegal practices by Standard Oil, including bribery, fraud, coercion, and violence. Standard Oil fought back with a promotion and publicity war. Standard Oil employed tactics such as having friendly journalists write negative reviews of the series and distributing millions of pamphlets presenting Standard Oil's side of the story to teachers, journalists, preachers, and community leaders. Ultimately, Standard Oil was deemed a trust, and the federal government ordered the monopoly to be split into a number of smaller companies. Both muckrakers and robber barons used public relations to shape how publics viewed their battles. Both sides wanted to shape policy decisions and attempted to do so by employing public relations in efforts to influence policymakers' opinions.

The Saturday Evening Post   March 10, 1906

Editor's Note—This is the second and concluding part of Mr. Armour's article, "The Packers and the People."

The Packers and the People

The Branch House and the Retailers

By J. Ogden Armour

There are two or three features in the packers' system of distributing dressed meats which demand at least passing attention. In the first paper of this series I showed, in detail, how the development of the modern refrigerator car completely revolutionized the meat business of the world. In accomplishing this wonderful transformation of food conditions, the refrigerator car had a powerful and indispensable ally in the form of the packers' "branch houses," or distributing agencies, containing a reserve of fresh meats in the best of refrigeration, awaiting the call of the local retailers.

Not only does the branch house relieve the local butcher of the burden of providing extensive refrigeration facilities of his own, but it also allows him to carry a smaller stock than he would otherwise be able to carry without danger of disappointment to his customers. Quite as important as either of these considerations is the fact that the local "branch" keeps at the demand of the retailers a supply of choice cuts ripened to just the right point. At call, the retailer is able to go out and get for his most select and discriminating customers the best cuts in the best of condition.

No feature of the packing and dress-meat business is more important than these branch house—none more important to the public as well as to the packer. Neither expense not attention to minutest detail is spared to make them models of what meat-houses should be, perfectly adapted to the purpose which they serve. They are built of the best materials that money can buy, and they are built on the best lines that ingenuity and experienced skill can contrive to secure perfect refrigeration and absolute cleanliness. In the up-to-date branch house building materials that are practically imperishable and impervious to outside influence are employed wherever possible. The floors are of cement. Storage and cooling rooms are lined with glazed tile, spotlessly white and smooth as glass. Not a cranny or crevice is left in which dust might gather or a germ hide from the frequent cleansings. All in all, they are as near dirt-proof, taint-proof and germ-proof as a building can be made.

These branch houses complete the packer's chain that takes the animal from farm or range, converts it into meat and sets it down at the retail meat merchant's door. We would hear less criticism of the packers if consumers could follow a steer from pen to slaughter-house; see it converted into "quarters" and "cuts" and hung in the cooler, transferred thence to a clean, cold car; transported under ice to the farthest part of the country, and finally deposited in the branch house. That would bring home to the consumer, as nothing else can, the fact that no part of the people's food supply receives more careful handling than does the meat that comes form the large packing-houses. In the absence of such a comprehensive inspection it would be a distinct benefit to the packers if the general public would take pains to visit and scrutinize the branch houses. They are always open to visitors. If there is a branch house of Armour & Co. in your vicinity, you are cordially invited to see for yourself just how the hated packer takes care of your meat supply.

The number of these branch houses maintained by the packers is very great. Armour & Co. have about three hundred of them in the United States alone. From the vast number of requests received from many sections of the country, asking for the installation of branch houses, it is very clear that these branches are looked upon by the people as being of great benefit to both the retailer and the consumer. Our aim is to protect the retailer and assist him in building up a secure and permanent trade.

A Help to the Small Butcher

In addition to the branch houses, we have, in many sections of the country, established smokehouses. Pickled hams, etc., are sent green to these points and are there smoked under our own supervision, after which they are sent to the branch house. This enables the dealer to get freshly-smoked meats.

One part of the system by which the packer distributes fresh meats to the people, through the local dealers, has been subjected to much criticism—and most unjustly, too. I refer to the "route car" by which meat is distributed to those towns not large enough to maintain a branch house or a distributing agency, or even to enable the retailer to order his meats in carload lots.

The accusation is that these cars are used to "peddle" meats and thus hurt the business of the local butchers. It is not true that this is a peddling proposition. These cars are certainly of great advantage and benefit to the local butchers as well as the consumers, and were brought into existence to meet the present requirements of the community at large, and are not fairly to be considered as an advantage to the packers so much as an advantage to the people. If the community were sufficiently large, carload lots could be shipped to these various points to much greater advantage to the packer and at a considerably less expense. But the demand in the small place is as urgent as it is limited; the retailers and the consumers there must have fresh meats, but they cannot take them in large shipments; therefore the route car is indispensable to the people of the small towns. It is far more expensive to ship in this way than to ship by the full carload. Every time one of these cars is cut out of a train and put on a siding the packer must pay from three to five dollars in addition to all the other transportation charges—and a car makes many such stops in the course of covering the route of small towns.

The Advantages of the Route Car

The question might be asked: Why not ship by local freight? Because meat would not arrive in good condition. Another reason for not shipping by local freight is that no dependence can be placed upon the arrival of meat thus shipped at a certain destination at any specific time. In short, this way is too slow and too unreliable for the transportation of fresh meats and meat products.

The car-route salesman visits all the towns along his route and takes orders for shipments to be made on a specific day, stipulating that the car shall arrive at each place at a certain day and hour—to be met by the wagons of the retailers of that town. This method of delivery is carried out regularly once or twice each week, as occasion demands, insuring the consumer the delivery of his meats in the very best condition. We do not sell to consumers, but reach them through the meat dealers in the various towns, and our method of putting the meats in their hands enables them to get a fresh supply at very short notice, which could not be done without the route car.

Showing the practical working of this method of distribution let me relate an instance: Mr. Boyd, formerly one of our branch-house managers at St. Louis, Missouri, is now extensively engaged in the retail meat business at Adrian, Michigan. From his wide experience in the branch-house meat business, he certainly knows whether it is now to his advantage, as a retail butcher, to secure his meats from these route cars. Mr. Boyd is now getting the bulk of his beef products from the route car running through his town, although he does, occasionally, go to the local butcher or slaughterer for some of his meats—but this only when he finds what he considers a "bargain."

Government inspection is another important feature of the packers' business. To the general public, the meat-eating public, it ought to appeal as one of the *most important* features of any and all business in the whole country. It is the wall that stands between the meat-eating public and the sale of diseased meat. This Government inspection alone, if there were no other business or economic reasons, would be an all-sufficient reason for the existence of the packing and dressed-meat business on a mammoth scale. It should, if understood, make the general public a partisan supporter of the larger packers.

Strangely enough, in view of its vital importance, the Government inspection has been the subject of almost endless misrepresentation—of *ignorantly or maliciously false statements.* The public has been told that meat animals and carcasses condemned as diseased are afterward secretly made use of by the packers and sold to the public for food in the form of both dressed meats and canned meats. Right here I desire to brand such statements as absolutely false as applied to the business of Armour & Co. I believe they are equally false as to all establishments in this country that are classed as packing-houses. I repeat: In Armour & Co.'s business *not one atom of any condemned animal or carcass finds its way, directly or indirectly, from any source, into any food product or food ingredient.*

Every meat animal and every carcass slaughtered in the Union Stock Yards, or in the stock yards at any of the markets of the United States, is carefully inspected by the United States Government. This inspection is supplemented, in practically all cases, by State or city inspection, or both. The live animals are inspected on the hoof and again when slaughtered.

The inspection by the United States Government is not compulsory on the packers in the strict legal sense of the term; it is more binding than if it were compulsory. *It is business.* Attempt to evade it would be, from the purely commercial viewpoint, suicidal. *No packer can do an interstate or export business without Government inspection.* Self-interest forces him to make use of it. Self-interest likewise demands that he shall not receive meats or by-products from any small packer, either for export, or other use, unless that small packer's plan is also "official"—that is, under United States Government inspection. This inspection is carried on under the direction of the Bureau of Animal Industry of the Department of Agriculture. The packer has nothing to say about the employment of the inspectors. They are assigned by the United States Government. The Government likewise is judge of their qualifications. It requires of them, first, that they shall have taken a full three-year course in veterinary science—as long a course as most States require for the admission of physicians and surgeons to practice. Then these educated veterinaries are selected by rigid civil-service examination.

Every meat animal that comes to the stock yards is first inspected on the hoof, as stated, by representatives of the Bureau of Animal Industry. All that show signs of disease are segregated and tagged as rejected by the United States Government inspectors. At regular intervals they are slaughtered (in Chicago under direction of the State officers) and consigned to other than food uses.

How the Consumer Is Insured

All carcasses—cattle, calves, sheep, hogs—are again rigidly inspected after slaughter. The internal organs affected by the various diseases to which meat animals are subject are examined. On the slightest sign of disease the carcass is rejected and so marked that it cannot escape observation. From the moment it is rejected, that carcass is in the custody of the United States Government agents and is by them personally followed to the rendering tank. It is hacked into small pieces, thrown into the tank and emerges only as grease or fertilizing material. This tankage product is in such form that it could not by any possibility be renovated to become a food product even if any packer were dishonest enough to attempt that. And if it were possible to evade inspection and use condemned carcasses or product from an "unofficial" packing-house, self-interest would again prevent it, because the packer would subject himself to speedy detection and exposure (if not endless blackmail) by the hundreds of employees who would be cognizant of his trickery.

This Government inspection thus becomes an important adjunct of the packer's business from two viewpoints. It puts the stamp of legitimacy and honesty upon the packer's product and so is to him a necessity. To the public it is an *insurance* against the sale of diseased meats.

Armour Challenged Competitors' Business Practices

Actually, robber barons were not keen to use public relations. Their first reactions were to seek the advice of their lawyers and business planners. Some business leaders sought to rebuke these attacks by threatening to withdraw advertising dollars from newspapers, but these efforts failed to influence the onslaught of negative publicity. Public relations eventually emerged as the wisest course of action.

▶ Hanging Out the Shingles

As pressure mounted on the industrial leaders, the demand for the first true public relations agencies began to form. Practitioners began to identify themselves as such. They made sure that corporate leaders knew their names and services. In this sense, they were "hanging out shingles" to attract clients.

The first public relations firm was established in Boston during the early 1900s. George Michaelis, Herbert Small, and Thomas Marvin founded the Publicity Bureau. They specialized in general press agent business, which meant they handled newspaper coverage. Press agents were hired to create or place favorable stories about corporations and the men who ran them.

The idea of public relations as a business for hire caught on quickly. Shingles were hung out in many cities. Several firms comprising ex–newspaper reporters sprang up to provide publicity and promotion services. For example, William Smith, a correspondent for the *New York Sun,* left his job to open his own publicity business. George Parker and Ivy Ledbetter Lee established the third New York firm in 1904. The Hamilton Wright Organization was formed in 1908 to promote international business such as trade between nations.

These needs by business led to the emergence of professional practitioners, many of whom have become icons. The typical professional practitioner was an ex–newspaper reporter. Some reporters were attracted to public relations because it offered them higher pay as company spokespersons. As each competent reporter decided to enter the profession, a business acquired a qualified practitioner and a critic was silenced. Many of these company spokespersons found their goals at odds with investigative journalists. This tension and mistrust continue to exist today.

These and other agencies successfully countered the negative publicity of the muckrakers. Many of these ex-reporters used journalistic methods for developing facts, obtaining publicity, and developing interpersonal contacts to represent their clients. They used the available means of public communication to publicize and promote the interests of their clients or employers. The focus was on tactics for publicity through press agentry, an attract-attention-at-all-costs mentality that has unsavory undertones.

One ex-reporter, Ivy Lee, distinguished himself from many practitioners of his era. Lee, noteworthy because he demonstrated both the promise and failings of public relations, was a Princeton graduate who went to work as a business reporter, specializing in politics. In 1903, he went to work for Seth Low's mayoral campaign, where he met George Parker, his future business partner. The publicity firm of Parker and Lee joined many public policy battles. They took utilities and railroads as clients. Lee was hired by the Pennsylvania Railroad in 1906. His primary assignment was to dispute the image that railroads were heartless. The campaign began with an article in a November 1907 *Moody's Magazine,* which proclaimed the virtues of railroads, arguing that they had expanded the West, carried goods to markets, made travel possible, and employed hundreds of workers (Lee, 1907). Based on the success of this campaign, a group of major railroads, in 1916, formed the Railway Executives' Advisory Committee to orchestrate press releases and publish articles on the industry.

Lee was hired in 1906 by George F. Baer, head of the powerful Coal Operators' Committee of Seven, to represent them in a coal strike. While working for Baer, Lee issued his "Declaration of Principles," a set of guidelines that opened the lines of communication between reporters and the business community. Lee advocated that the public should be informed of business and industry matters—the public was no longer a flock of sheep to be ignored. He realized that publicity unsupported by good works and ethical business practice was meaningless. He believed that organizational performance determines the amount, kind, and quality of publicity an organization will receive. Little did he know that his open approach to publicity would revolutionize press agentry and publicity into what many view as modern-day public relations.

Lee's open approach made coverage of the Baer coal strike easy for reporters and the public to follow, facilitating media coverage that enabled publics to follow the negotiations. Lee provided reports after each meeting and was available to answer questions. He generated favorable press coverage for Baer, which would lead him to be considered for other opportunities and eventually to be hired by people and organizations such as John D. Rockefeller and the American Tobacco Company.

The Rockefellers drew heavily on Lee to protect Standard Oil against Ida Tarbell's claims that John D. Rockefeller Sr.'s philanthropy was "tainted money" and from charges of violent strikebreaking in labor relations at their Colorado Fuel and Iron Company. Better known as the "Ludlow Massacre," the labor dispute resulted in 14 people being killed as a result of pro-management orders. Those killed included miners, their wives, and their children. Acting on orders from management, state troops opened fire on a tent city set up on the edge of town by striking miners; the miners had to leave their homes when on strike because the company owned their homes. Lee used pictures of Rockefeller dancing with miners' wives and a blitz of pro-management press and promotional materials to drown out the voice of the strikers. Lee was soundly criticized for presenting one-sided, factually inaccurate material in his bulletin, ironically titled "Facts in Colorado's Struggle for Industrial Freedom" (Raucher, 1968, p. 27). Most damaging was Lee's testimony before Congress. When Lee was asked, "What personal effort did you make to ascertain that the facts given you by the operators were correct?" he responded, "None whatever. I have no responsibility for the facts" (Ewen, 1996, p. 80). The answer was at odds with Lee's "Principles" and his motto of "Accuracy, Authenticity, Interest." Though technically more advanced than huckster P. T. Barnum, Ivy Lee's ideas of promotion and publicity often were no closer to the truth.

Around the time of his death, Lee came under further criticism for representing the German Dye Trust, an arm of Adolph Hitler's rising Third Reich. From 1933 to

1934, Lee worked for Interessen Gemeinschaft, Farben Industrie, better known as I. G. Farben or the German Dye Trust. Lee's role was as an expert on American public opinion. German businesses feared a worldwide boycott of German goods due to Nazi policies. Lee made recommendations for making German policies more palatable to Americans. While Lee was paid by I. G. Farben, he also consulted for the Hitler regime. He even advised Joseph Goebbels and met with numerous Nazi leaders, including Adolph Hitler. These connections led to the tag of "Nazi Advisor." The Congressional Special Committee on Un-American Activities was formed to examine the promotion of support for communism and fascism in the United States. The committee investigated Lee but did not find him guilty of any crimes—that was left to the press (Hiebert, 1966). The press painted Lee as a Nazi sympathizer. The committee's concerns over U.S. practitioners representing "reprehensible governments" led to the passage of the Federal Agents Registration Act (FARA) in 1938. FARA has the Justice Department monitor the actions of U.S. practitioners acting on behalf of foreign clients.

Despite the controversy at the time of his death in 1934, Lee should be remembered for several contributions to public relations. First, he advocated that business and industry should align themselves with the public interest, even though he himself may have fallen short of this mark. Second, he interacted with top executives and would implement programs only with the support of management. Third, Lee instituted open lines of communication with the media. Fourth, he emphasized the human elements of business, bringing public relations to the level of employees and the general public (Olasky, 1987). Lee exemplified how public relations often missed its mark to be truthful and to protect the public interest. Still, he articulated some important ideals for public relations to consider and opened the way for practitioners to work more directly with management. His firm, eventually named "Lee & Ross," because of his young partner Tommy Ross, lasted for more than 75 years.

Public relations personnel began working in-house during this time period as well. "Working in-house" meant that organizations were hiring public relations people full-time as employees and not just as consultants; people worked for the company directly and not through an agency. AT&T pioneered the in-house use of public relations practitioners. Arthur W. Page was selected to lead AT&T's public relations efforts. As a condition for accepting his public relations position with AT&T, Page made it clear that he wanted to provide input into policy formation. He knew that the company's performance would determine its reputation. Page's two principles are vital contributions to public relations. Page summed up his philosophy:

> All business in a democratic society begins with public permission and exists by public approval. If that be true, it follows that business should be cheerfully willing to tell the public what its policies are, what it is doing, and what it hopes to do. This seems practically a duty. (Griswold, 1967, p. 13)

Public relations practitioners serve best when top-ranking practitioners are part of each organization's management and strategic planning teams.

BOX 2.2 AT&T: A REGULATED MONOPOLY

Frederick P. Fish, who became president of the Bell Telephone System in 1900, recognized the need for his growing company to take its case to the public. If the public did not understand the advantage of a regulated monopoly, it would oppose that form of business arrangement. Raucher (1968) observed "that by 1906, the American Telephone and Telegraph Company had a general policy designed to placate public hostility and had methods for broadcasting the news about that policy" (p. 49). That policy was aggressively continued by Theodore Newton Vail when he became AT&T president in May 1907.

Vail was a master at publicity, promotion, and the cocreation of meaning. He sought to convince Americans that the phone company was operating in their interests. One of the first issue advertisements, put out by AT&T in 1908, emphasized the bond between the company and its customers: "The Bell System's ideal is the same as that of the public it serves—the most telephone service and the best, at the least cost to the user. It accepts its responsibility for a nation-wide telephone service as a public trust" (Garbett, 1981, p. 40). By 1910, Vail had converted these ideas into a consistent long-term campaign stressing the advantages of a privately run, publicly minded system (Schultze, 1981). A regulated monopoly allowed people in different parts of town and in different cities to talk to one another (Olasky, 1987).

One of the first major tests of this opinion formation strategy came in 1913, when the Justice Department initiated an antitrust suit charging that AT&T, through its control of Western Union, had created an impermissible monopoly. To defend itself, a newspaper series was started under the name of Vail (*New York Times,* September 4, 1913, p. 6). By May 1928, AT&T Publicity Director Arthur W. Page could announce their educational efforts had successfully convinced the public that the phone industry was best handled as a monopoly. But he also wisely cautioned company executives over still-lingering concerns (Raucher, 1968).

The early part of the century was alive with new strategies and tactics, as well as a burgeoning philosophy to guide the practice. In the years before World War I, other notable advances had occurred. Samuel Insull of the Chicago Edison Company established the first "bill stuffer" and external magazine, a publication sent to people other than employees, such as customers or investors. Theodore Roosevelt was the first president to use extensive news conferences and interviews to obtain support for his public works projects and policies. Nonprofit companies such as the American Red Cross and the National Tuberculosis Association opened press offices and utilized publicity programs, and the U.S. Marine Corps established a publicity bureau to promote the nation's military.

The next major advancement in public relations came with U.S. involvement in World War I. President Woodrow Wilson recognized the potential contribution of public relations. He named George Creel, a former newspaper reporter, to organize a comprehensive public relations campaign: the Creel Committee on Public Information. It was designed to advise Wilson, implement various war programs, and influence U.S. and world opinion. Creel assembled a talented group of journalists, scholars, press agents, artists, and members of other fields for the single purpose of mobilizing public opinion in favor of the war effort. The significance of the Creel Committee should not be overlooked by aspiring practitioners of public relations, for this is a rare instance in which a U.S. president appointed an official national committee to advise him on public relations matters. At that time, there was no campaign manual or precedents to guide or coordinate campaign efforts. The available means of communication, while well-known, had not been used in a single coordinated, national effort. Together, the Creel Committee members designed programs, obtained free media time and space, and counseled a nation on its wartime activities.

Much of the success of the U.S. war effort at home and abroad was attributed to the Creel Committee. It emphasized loyalty and patriotism as reasons for supporting the war. Liberty Loans were designed to help raise money; newspapers and magazines contributed countless amounts of free space and advertising; the committee convinced AT&T that the government needed control of the phone company for the war effort; and the Food Administration led activities to convince Americans to conserve food and other needed supplies. Thousands of businesses set up their own groups of publicity people to expand and build from the committee's effort.

The "Four-Minute Men" offer a good example of the planning that was becoming a part of public relations. Donald Ryerson created and ran the Four-Minute Men. These men were given 4 minutes during intermission at movie theaters to present a war message, a campaign in which over 75,000 men took part. Speakers were sent bulletins about the topic for their next speech. The information contained a list of points to cover, sample speeches, and warnings not to exceed the 4 minutes. Together, the Four-Minute Men presented 755,190 speeches and reached roughly 134,454,514 people (Lubbers, 1996). Each new speech required careful preparation and coordination; the bulletins had to be developed and monitored centrally from Ryerson's office. This was not simple promotion and publicity; public relations was now using planning as well.

Think of the Creel Committee as a conglomeration of people dedicated to obtaining public support through programmatic promotion and publicity. They were engaging in propaganda for the war, one-way communication designed to win acceptance of an idea. Propaganda pushes a target to accept an idea and is not interested in feedback or a dialogue. Propaganda is often associated with distortion, but its real focus is a one-sided presentation of an idea. Many members of the committee learned the public relations craft during the war effort. After the war, a large number went into private practice, serving other areas of society and the nation. Public relations quickly spread to organizations of all types. Public relations bureaus were active in churches, social work, business, colleges and universities, government, labor and social movements, and politics. Public relations firms grew in number all across the country.

No one better exemplifies the trend toward the institutionalization of public relations than Edward Bernays, who perfected his "science" in the Creel Committee. Bernays delighted in self-aggrandizement, calling himself the "father of public relations."

He started as a press agent for the Creel Committee, where he dreamed of making a life's work at what he called the "engineering of consent." In 1923, Bernays coined the term "public relations counsel" in his first book, *Crystallizing Public Opinion*. He also taught the first course on public relations at New York University. He married Doris Fleischman in 1922; she also practiced public relations and began a lifelong career as a public relations counselor, offering advice to corporations, government agencies, and a host of U.S. presidents, including Calvin Coolidge and Herbert Hoover.

Doris Fleischman had an important public relations career too. She did much of the behind-the-scenes work for Bernays, as well as her own, more visible work. While an early feminist, Doris Fleischman was also "the woman behind the man" as an often silent partner in Bernays's public relations practice. Doris did much of the writing, including work for the U.S. War Department and the American Tobacco Company. She was even a ghostwriter for many speeches and strategy papers that bore the name Edward Bernays. Her most visible effort was working on the 1920 NAACP (National Association for the Advancement of Colored People) Convention in Atlanta, Georgia. She met with state and local officials in order to secure a successful event (Tye, 1998).

To promote Ivory Soap and make bathing more popular with stubborn children, Bernays organized national soap-carving contests in public schools. Contests were judged by a soap council, who made sure that only Ivory Soap was used. Undoubtedly, many of these sculptures ended up in the family bath. To promote bacon, Bernays arranged for a group of doctors to comment favorably on the virtues of eating a hearty breakfast. Venida, an industry leader in the manufacture and sale of hairnets, was dismayed by a change in women's fashions after World War I: Women adopted the bobbed hairstyle. They didn't need expensive hairnets—a market was lost but could be regained. Bernays urged artists to praise the "Greek coiffure" appearance that could be achieved with hairnets and convinced labor commissioners to recognize the safety advantages of women wearing hairnets in the workplace.

Another giant in the institutionalization of public relations was Carl Byoir, who refined the use of special events. One of his greatest achievements came as the result of his participation in the effort to defeat polio, a crippling disease rampant across the country during the late 1940s and early 1950s. He advised the President's Committee for the Infantile Paralysis campaign to enlist and empower mothers to work on behalf of children. The theme was the "March of Dimes," and contributions came in one dime at a time. That continues to be a major way of gaining funds to cure childhood diseases. After Byoir retired, George Hammond took over this agency's leadership for many of his 50 years with the firm. The continuity of these agencies became one of the hallmarks of American public relations.

Perhaps no firm was more successful than the creation of John W. Hill and Don Knowlton. This firm began in Cleveland in 1927. It became "Hill & Knowlton" when they became partners in 1933.

John W. Hill

SOURCE: Reprinted with permission from Hill & Knowlton.

At the encouragement of major clients, its headquarters moved to New York City in 1938, during the Great Depression. It opened an office for governmental relations in Washington, D.C., in 1944. Branches were opened in other cities, then countries, leading to Hill & Knowton, International. As did many other pioneers, it built a client list of major industries and trade associations. It represented steel and iron, tobacco, alcohol, chemicals, retail, household and cosmetic products, heavy manufacturing, banking, the aircraft industry, and oil. It counseled nonprofits and foreign governments. It helped American companies expand into global markets. Its growth parallels that of its clients and perhaps led some of them to success. Hill built a talent pool and fostered a philosophy that stressed the need for businesses to work hard to convince communities they deserved to operate there. If communities would not accept the industry, then the industry had to change to adapt to the community. To Hill, people were the lords of the land. Public opinion, public interest, integrity, and public approval were the cornerstones of his career and agency philosophy. No matter how humble, people had every right to expect the best from industry. Industry had to meet the standards of public interest. Long after Hill left the firm bearing his name, it was associated with some scandalous activities. Without doubt, that would not have happened under his direction and would have perplexed him deeply. He never got over his small-town, Indiana values, no matter how rich and powerful he became.

As is the case with any person, field, or profession, rapid growth necessitates time to mature. Building on successes from previous decades, public relations matured as a practice during the middle years of the 20th century. Generations of practitioners honed a loose set of press agentry and special events tactics into an integrated, sophisticated practice requiring specialized knowledge, experience, and skills—technical and strategic. Now practitioners worked to stabilize their position in the organization and to develop additional expertise. Advancements took the form of strategic planning and research, working smarter and more cost-effectively. As a field, public relations grew by meeting the challenges brought on by World War II. Television was emerging as a major mass medium, and persuasion research conducted by the U.S. government during World War II provided new ideas for shaping the opinions of targeted audiences, especially as the major powers fought the cold war. Activist social movements also worked to dramatically change the cultural values and issue priorities of the nation. Business and industry began a slow trend away from occasional and defensive public relations options to more positive, proactive, and continual programs.

Social science research tools such as surveys, focus groups, and computerized data analysis were becoming more widely utilized to examine opinions of key markets, audiences, and publics. Practitioners such as Earl Newsom pioneered the use of social scientific research to counsel managements and design as well as evaluate campaigns. The first minority-owned public relations firms were forming and being hired to communicate with minority communities. The first agency specializing in political public relations was formed by Clem Whitaker and Leone Baxter in San Francisco. Growth in communication technologies offered opportunities and challenges to practitioners as fax machines and the Internet appeared. Proactive public relations, ethnic relations, social science research, and political public relations would diversify and shape future practice.

In addition to Leone Baxter, many other women contributed to the profession of public relations. (See Box 2.3, which gives brief biographical sketches of some leading women and minority practitioners.) Minority practitioners have long served the profession as well. They have joined and supported the primary professional associations but have also developed their own associations, such as the National Black Public Relations Association. See the *Encyclopedia of Public Relations* for descriptions of male and female practitioners, some of whom are also people of color.

BOX 2.3 PROMINENT WOMEN AND MINORITIES IN PUBLIC RELATIONS

As they have in other professions, women and minorities have made steady progress to develop and apply their skills in public relations. Some are mentioned in the body of this chapter. Here is a list of others who deserve recognition.

Joseph Varney Baker (1908–1995) was the first African American to gain national prominence. He owned his own firm, which he started in 1934. He was the first African American to become APR (Accredited in Public Relations). He specialized in communicating with the Black consumer market for clients such as DuPont, Procter & Gamble, and major Black entertainers.

Ann H. Barkelew (1935–) retired from Fleischman-Hillard in 2001. She specialized in retail public relations working for Dayton-Hudson and was the first female member of its management committee.

Phyllis Berlowe (1922–2000) began her career by studying journalism. She established the Berlowe Group and specialized in working with the food industry.

Alice L. Beeman (1919–2003) was the first woman president of the Council for the Advancement and Support of Education (1974). She worked in higher-education public relations.

Judith Bogart (1936–) was the second woman to preside over the Public Relations Society of America (PRSA) (1983). She specialized in nonprofits, such as hospitals and the Girl Scouts.

Dorothy Gregg (1920–1997) earned her PhD on the way to becoming the first woman appointed as a corporate officer of Celanese Corporation. She was vice president of communication there from 1975 to 1983. She started her career with U.S. Steel and ended it with Ruder, Finn, and Rotman, from 1983 to 1987.

Denny Griswold (1908–2001) was cofounder and editor of *PR News*. She gained her experience working for some of the male pioneers of the profession and brought experience to help convince senior management of the need for high standards of corporate responsibility.

Caroline Hood (1909–1981) became synonymous with the Rockefeller Center in New York City, where she became the senior practitioner. She was the first woman appointed to the PRSA Board of Directors (1951).

E. Roxie Howlett (????–) was a West Coast practitioner who operated in Portland and San Francisco. She was a leader in those communities and a volunteer in nonprofit public relations.

Barbara Hunter (1927–) was the head of a New York firm that specialized in the food and beverage industry. She was a president of the PRSA and stressed the need for practitioners to stay abreast of social trends.

Lee Jaffe (1899–2001) worked for the New York Port Authority, where she was a leader in rebuilding and revitalizing New York City. One of her major projects was the creation of the World Trade Center, which was destroyed by a terrorist attack on September 11, 2001.

Inez Y. Kaiser (1918–) was a teacher who turned to a career in public relatons. Her specialities centered on home economics and fashion. She was the first African American woman to cover fashion shows, in which she led in working with Black models, and helped to established Black fashion and beauty.

Ruth Kassewitz (1928–) had a varied career in public relations and advertising. In 1969, she became the director of communications for the Metro-Dade County Department of Housing and Urban Development (Florida). She specialized in public information campaigns and citizens' advisory boards.

Moss Kendrix (1917–1989) moved from being a journalist in the Black media to public relations. He specialized in marketing, especially Coca-Cola. He was a leader in the National Public Relations Roundtable and in community relations.

Marilyn Laurie (1939–) was the first woman to hold a senior position at AT&T. She was one of the originators of Earth Day. She owned her own firm and worked for many nonprofits.

Amelia Lobsenz (1922–1992) was the first woman president of the International Public Relations Association. She owned an agency that developed a major client list in home care products, beauty products, and automobiles.

Rosalee A. Roberts (1943–) was PRSA president in 1992. In that capacity, she worked to create a new vision for the organization and worked to revitalize it. She practiced in Omaha, Nebraska, where she worked for health care, food, and beverage clients.

Jean Schoonover (1920–) became president of Dudley-Anderson-Yutzy (D-A-Y) in New York City, the first major agency there to be owned and operated by women.

Rea Smith (1918–1981) provided organizational leadership for the development of the PRSA, where she worked. She not only developed the professional staff there but also led in the development of the Foundation for Public Relations Research and Education and the PRSA Code of Ethics.

Whereas men had launched the profession in the late 1800s and formed the first firms in the early 1900s, 100 years later, women had come to play a leadership role and began to form the majority of practitioners. Enrollments in classes in public relations by 2000 were predominantly women. Such trends even fostered concerns that the profession would lose status, as had been the case in teaching and nursing, for instance, when the majority of professionals became women. But women and minorities made steady progress.

In part, they advanced because of the leadership of women and men who were supportive of them. One such woman was Betsy Ann Plank. You will find her Professional Reflection at the end of this chapter. She worked in large agencies and in the telephone industry. The latter was notoriously male dominated. Plank was educated at the University of Alabama and worked in Chicago. She started her career there in 1947 and matured to be a major figure in the Daniel J. Edelman firm, which she joined in 1960. Based on those credentials, she became the director of public relations planning for AT&T before moving to Illinois Bell, which today is SBC Communications. She is the first lady of PRSA and was the first woman president and the chair of the committee that created PRSSA, the student wing of this national professional organization. She won a Golden Anvil award in 1977, and the Paul M. Lund Service Award and Patrick Jackson Service Award in 2001. She was the first woman elected professional of the year (1979) by readers of *Public Relations News*. Of all her accomplishments, however, she is most proud of her work on behalf of students through PRSSA. She wanted other students to walk in her footsteps and wanted those footsteps to be true and straight—especially for young women entering the profession.

Although women made progress, they did so in a male-dominated profession. During World War II, government and business began again to work hand in hand to support and win mutually beneficial outcomes. Before the bombing of Pearl Harbor in 1941, the government's information effort was largely unorganized. After much consideration, President Roosevelt issued an executive order to create the Office of War Information (OWI). Elmer Davis, a former news and radio reporter, was named to direct the effort. OWI was unable to achieve the same level of prominence as the Creel Committee did; nonetheless, OWI contributed to the field. It is credited with helping the public relations practice expand in the military and business. OWI developed more techniques and trained more practitioners—about 75,000 total—than its predecessor, the Creel Committee.

Technological advances brought new media to the forefront of practice. Advertisements were broadcast on the radio, on billboards, on streetcars, in magazines, and through direct mail. Radio was beginning to become the dominant mass medium during the 1940s. Public relations people were very active in creating the public service announcements (PSAs) that began appearing during World War II. PSAs, which run free of charge, about governmental or nonprofit events, programs, or services, are still found on radio today. Advertising would emerge as a billion-dollar industry by the early 1930s, with print media in the form of newspapers and magazines dominating mass dissemination of information. By the 1970s and 1980s, the communication tide shifted to electronics. Television and then the Internet each revolutionized communications and altered public relations practices. The speed and variety of communications kept changing with each new innovation. Public relations practitioners had to understand how best to utilize the various media to achieve their objectives.

The American Medical Association's (AMA) public relations campaign to defeat President Truman's national health insurance plan embodies the research and planning emphasis on public relations. In January of 1948, President Truman announced a plan for compulsory national health insurance. Under his plan, the federal government would ensure that all Americans had health insurance. The AMA saw national health insurance as a threat to a physician's autonomy and quickly hired the public relations firm of Whitaker & Baxter to help them defeat the national threat. During a 1-year period, the AMA would spend over a million dollars on the campaign, making it the most expensive public relations campaign to date. Research showed people were afraid of socialism during this time period. Socialism was linked to communism, and both were seen as very bad. The AMA's campaign labeled national health insurance as "socialized medicine." A coordinated mix of pamphlets, publicity, public speaking, and endorsements from respected figures and organizations were used to spread the word about socialized medicine.

The AMA's public relations effort successfully achieved its objectives. Before the campaign, 58% of the American people favored national health insurance, and Congressional mail ran 2.5 to 1 in favor of it. A year after the campaign, only 39% of the American people favored national health insurance, and Congressional mail ran 4 to 1 against it. Was it really the campaign? Since a 1949 survey found that 75% of Americans referred to national health insurance as "socialized medicine," it seems the message did reach the publics as intended (Starr, 1969). Research and planning were the cornerstone of the AMA's successful use of public relations to defeat national health insurance.

Bernays led the way toward a theory-based practice. Many can applaud the theory he articulated, even it they disagree with its principles and conclusions. Typical of his views was this statement, made in 1928:

> The conscious and intelligent manipulation of the organized habits and opinions of the masses is an important element in democratic society. Those who manipulate this unseen mechanism of society constitute an invisible government which is the true ruling power of our country. (Bernays, 1928, p. 9)

This one-way view of public relations using theory to conduct behind-the-scenes manipulation was extended into his book *The Engineering of Consent,* published in 1950 (Olasky, 1987).

The role of the public relations counselor continued to evolve as practitioners became advisors to management. However, they were not hired because they were able to craft and send out press releases or hold press conferences or design brochures—they advised. For example, Earl Newsom was hired by Henry Ford II to advise on a United Automotive Workers (UAW) strike. Newsom drafted a strongly worded, four-page letter to the UAW for Ford. The letter signaled a tough negotiation ahead, as Ford complained about the 773 work stoppages since 1941 and the 38.8% drop in worker efficiency. The letter indicated both points would be a part of the negotiation. Later, Newsom drafted a speech for Ford about labor relations. After 12 drafts, Ford presented the speech on January 9, 1946. The press hailed Ford as an "industrial statesman" for his recognition of unions as an enduring part of the business landscape and calling for labor and management to cooperate with one another (Cutlip, 1994). Attracted to large corporations, large public relations firms stabilized in metropolitan areas such as Chicago, New York, Philadelphia, Washington, and Los Angeles.

In the middle decades of the 20th century, investor relations became an increasingly refined part of public relations practice, aimed at the objective of providing facts and opinions to investors. Investor relations started when, in 1858, for instance, the Borden Company issued a financial report to stockholders. In 1877, railroad tycoon Jay Gould opened a press bureau for his Union Pacific Railroad to disseminate positive information about the company. Around 1888, the Mutual Life Insurance Company hired a press agent, Charles J. Smith, to write press releases and enhance the company's public standing.

The stock market crash in 1929 created a crisis of confidence for all large institutions, especially free enterprise industries and regulatory agencies. Prior to the Depression, which prompted creation of a strong Securities and Exchange Commission (SEC), few ethical standards guided the practice of representing the market value of a publicly traded company. For instance, George Gunton was a popular economist who championed the free enterprise system in his capacity as editor of *Gunton's Magazine;* while in that position, he received a $15,000 annual retainer from Standard Oil.

Part of the reason for the stock market crash was the practice of using puffery to feature stocks. Reporters and public relations persons often claimed that companies— their share values—were worth well beyond their actual value. Newspaper reporters sometimes wrote stories that falsely lauded the investment value of companies: Richard Edmondson of the *Wall Street Journal,* William Gomber of *Financial America,* Charles Murphy of the *New York Evening Mail,* J. F. Lowther of the *New York Herald Tribune,* William White of the *New York Evening Post,* and W. F. Walmsley of the *New York Times.* Several of these reporters were in fact paid guns of publicist Newton Plummer. Such practices led to the formation of the SEC, which enforced standards of investor relations practice, including fines and imprisonment, to ensure that stock market information is accurate and easily available to all interested investors. As was true for other aspects of the profession, investor relations had added to the practice, but many improvements were needed for the advancement of professionalism.

▶ The Practice Becomes Professional

Professionals tend to start as individuals applying their skills for fees and salaries. Once these professionals realize that they have a unique set of talents and skills, they move to create professional organizations. They even innovate the development of curricula in colleges and universities, where professors prepare students to become members of the profession. During the late 1930s and through the post–World War II era, educational institutions began to offer public relations courses, such as principles of public relations. Books and journals on public relations tactics were published.

Professional organizations began to strengthen the practice. The National Association of Accredited Publicity Directors, founded in 1936, consisted primarily of East Coast practitioners. This organization was renamed the National Association of Public Relations Counsel in 1944. Meanwhile, the American Council on Public Relations was founded by Rex Harlow in 1939. The American Council was primarily composed of members from the West Coast.

What was needed was an association that embraced practitioners from across the nation. To fulfill that end, the Public Relations Society of America (PRSA) was founded in 1948, from the merger of the National Association of Public Relations Counsel and the American Council on Public Relations. The American Council had been formed in 1961, largely consisting of members from the Washington, D.C., PRSA; it then merged with the American Public Relations Association in 1961. The mergers were a natural outgrowth of professional development. It makes better sense to have one national organization than a number of smaller, regional ones; the organization will be stronger financially and politically. Through these mergers, national and international associations of public relations began. Now chapters of such organizations exist in major cities, states, regions, nations, and continents.

PRSA and the International Association of Business Communicators (IABC) have emerged as the leading professional trade associations for public relations practitioners. PRSA listed the following as its purpose:

> The purpose of the Public Relations Society of America Foundation, Inc., is to function in accordance with its charter under section 403 of the New York State Corporation Law as a not-for-profit organization and under Section 501(c)3 of the U.S. Internal Revenue Code of 1954, for the purpose to foster, sponsor and conduct research, education and continuing education in public relations, and to perform any acts, including the raising of funds, necessary or incidental to carrying out public relations research and education programs that advances the value of public relations in helping to serve the public good. (PRSA, 2005)

IABC stated at its Web site the following purpose:

> IABC, the International Association of Business Communicators, is the leading resource for effective communication. We provide products, services, activities and networking opportunities to help people and organizations achieve excellence in public relations, employee communication, marketing communication, public affairs and other forms of communication. People around the world, in every industry as well as the public and nonprofit sectors, have taken advantage of our resources to advance their careers and meet organizational objectives. IABC specializes in helping people and organizations: Think strategically about communication, Measure and clarify the value of communication, Build better relationships with stakeholders. (IABC, 2005)

IABC reports at its Web site this impressive bit of history:

> IABC began in 1970 as a merger between the American Association of Industrial Editors and the International Council of Industrial Editors. Corporate Communicators Canada joined IABC in 1974. In its first year of operation, IABC had 2,280 members and a budget of approximately U.S. $100,000. Twenty-five years later, IABC's membership has grown to more than 12,500 worldwide with an annual operating budget of U.S. $3.6 million. (IABC, 2005)

▶Return of Activism

At the same time public relations was making substantial advances, another force occurred that would dramatically challenge the practice. The 1960s, 1970s, and early 1980s witnessed the rise of many public activist movements. As in the years of the robber barons, key segments of the public became dissatisfied with business practices and demanded more social accountability on issues such as civil rights and consumer protection. "Environmental protection" became an anthem around the world. People were bothered by poor quality, unsafe products, failure to live up to claims in advertising, service after the sale, and the failure of companies to demonstrate actual concern for the buying public. Consumer organizations such as the Consumer Federation of America and Ralph Nader's the Nader Organization sprang up to fight for the rights of consumers. Ralph Nader rose from obscurity to a leadership role in consumer rights through a battle with General Motors (GM). In 1965, Nader wrote *Unsafe at Any Speed,* a critique of automobile safety that centered on the Chevrolet Corvair, a rear-engine GM product. In 1966, the *New York Times* revealed that GM had hired private investigators and harassed Nader because of the book. GM's attack on Nader made him even more famous in the press: GM inadvertently had acted as Nader's press agent to promote his cause.

The government began to respond to public pressure with more regulation. Of the 35 major health, safety, and environmental laws that had been passed by 1982, starting with the Dangerous Cargo Act in 1877, 26 came into being in the 1960s and 1970s (Renfro, 1982; for more discussion of laws and regulation, see Heath, 1997). These cover tobacco and alcohol abuse, flammable fabrics, poison prevention packaging, mine and railroad protection, water pollution, clean air, noise control, lead-based paint restrictions, food quality, and myriad other issues. More regulation and legislation affecting corporate performance was written into law in the United States in the past 30 years than in all of U.S. history before that time.

By the end of the 1960s, the civil rights movement, women's rights, gay rights, environmentalism, the labor movement, the farm movement, the peace movement, and space exploration were all issues garnering grassroots public support for action. Many of these movements utilized public relations techniques for publicity and promotion to advocate their cause. These social movements acted to diversify the mass public into publics geared toward specific social issues and concerns. Through public relations, the activism also served to shape public values. By the early 1990s, concern for the environment became a stable value in U.S. society. Organizations were trying to find ways to include "green" messages in their public relations efforts. McDonald's exemplifies this change in direction. In the 1980s, McDonald's was at the center of environmentalists' anger; their use of polystyrene packaging made them a prime target. By working with the Environmental Defense Fund on a waste reduction program, McDonald's became recognized as the most environmentally friendly corporation by the mid-1990s. Part of the turnaround was to use public relations to explain and to promote the company's new environmentally friendly initiatives and actions.

WEB WATCHER: MCDONALD'S

Look at http://www.mcdonalds.com to see whether the company has a press release announcing the environmental record McDonald's has achieved, and more recently its position on healtly lifestyles that include fast food. One media release issued in February 2000 read in part as follows:

> McDonald's Honored by U.S. Environmental Protection Agency: CONSERVATION AND RECYCLING EFFORTS EARN "WASTEWISE" AWARD
>
> WASHINGTON, D.C.—The U.S. Environmental Protection Agency on Thursday presented McDonald's USA with its WasteWise Partner of the Year award, in recognition of its ongoing commitment to significant solid waste reduction.
>
> The EPA cited McDonald's industry-leading recycling track record and its continual review and evaluation of packaging materials, with an eye on always trying to find the most efficient materials available.

Whereas McDonald's worked on the issue of conservation in the late 1990s and early 2000s, by 2004, it was devoting strategic planning and communication to the issue of obesity and fast food. Another visit to its home page revealed, for instance, a press release from 2004 on its "balanced lifestyles platform." It proclaimed its commitment to the public's healthy food choices, physical activity, and education. As do many other companies, McDonald's uses the Web in its public relations efforts to attract customers, to invite audiences to learn about the company and a healthy lifestyle, and to address key publics' concerns about fast food's role in public health issues.

A bit of investigation at this site will lead to the company's statement of corporate responsibility.

Public relations practitioners responded to increasing public concerns, but with some difficulty. They had become sophisticated in management, communication, and use of the media to reach the people. But the battle of corporate America against increasingly sophisticated and dedicated grassroots activism strained their professional training—almost to a breaking point.

By understanding the organization and its stakeholders, public relations practitioners have the necessary information to respond effectively on behalf of their organizations or clients. Public relations practices now have an established role with business, activism, nonprofits, and government. Social scientific research had increased sophistication to analyze the opinions of markets and publics. Technology added new means for public communication. Schools of journalism and mass communication and speech communication were producing academically trained practitioners. Professional associations developed thoughtful publications and continuing education to strengthen their members' technical and strategic skills. Society had delivered a new set of challenges to public relations practitioners, and they had responded with the maturity that comes from experience. But activism still concentrated its efforts to change the fundamental principles and values of society.

As a response to the growing power of activists, leading public relations practitioners as well as scholars in business administration and ethics created and advanced what came to be called "issue management." Activism exploded in the 1960s and 1970s, as these were times of social upheaval, with civil rights and the antiwar movement as examples. The tumultuous activism of the 1960s and 1970s attacked the standards of business ethics and created the great era of reform. According to tradition, in 1977, W. Howard Chase coined the term "issue management," which he designated as a new science of corporate communication response to critics of business activities. Chase drew on his experience at American Can Company and other leaders, such as advertising expert John E. O'Toole and public relations legend John W. Hill. O'Toole may have coined the term "advocacy advertising," advertisements that sell ideas, not products or services. This sort of discussion spurs companies such as Mobil Oil Company (today part of ExxonMobil) to engage in thought-provoking op-ed advertising.

BOX 2.4 MOBIL OIL'S "PEANUTS" OP-ED

Mobil Oil Company believed that the voices of activism in the 1970s could eventually lead to the destruction of the large corporation as a business entity. In defense, it launched a series of advertisements. One appeared in the *New York Times* of August 30, 1979, titled "Why Elephants Can't Live on Peanuts." This campaign is an important part of public relations history because it blended advertising and public affairs communication. It also took corporate messages to the editorial pages of newspapers and magazines. (See "Mobil Oil's 'Peanuts' Ad" in Chapter 1.)

Speaking as chairperson of the Issue Management Association, W. Howard Chase (1982) offered a widely quoted definition:

Issues management is the capacity to understand, mobilize, coordinate, and direct all strategic and policy planning functions, and all public affairs/public relations skills, toward achievement of one objective: meaningful partici- pation in creation of public policy that affects personal and institutional destiny. (p. 1)

Chase stressed the proactive aspect of issues management that "rejects the hypothesis that any institution must be the pawn of the public policy determined solely by others" (p. 2). Based on his experience with Allstate Insurance Company, Raymond Ewing (1987), a leader in the development of issues management, defined it as "simply public policy research, foresight, and planning for an organization in the private sector impacted by decisions made by others in the public sector" (p. 18).

Public relations had finally come of age. Organizations with established programs, while continuing a concern for publicity and promotion, were moving beyond publicity to encompass strategic planning and research in their programs. Practitioners were recognizing their contributions to society and to the organizations they served. Public relations counseling became a recognized discipline. Academic education, in addition to seat-of-the-pants experience, was necessary for entry into the field. What was there left to do but to establish the parameters for the next stage of public relations development, a professional field of study and practice?

In summary, we end this section by noting the many ways in which the practice of public relations has come a long way since the primitive publicity of showman P. T. Barnum. Over the years, public relations has become more sophisticated, emphasizing planning and research to improve the effectiveness of its efforts to inform publics, alter attitudes, change behaviors, and build mutually beneficial relationships. Progressive practitioners have embraced the importance of relationship building, even featuring that concept in the mission and vision statements of professional associations. Yet in other ways, public relations remains a prisoner of its inescapable past. The news media—rightly or wrongly—too often equate public relations with publicity, and exploitive practitioners still use manipulative promotion and publicity to reinforce this view. Public relations is a noble profession when practiced correctly. Janus-faced Bernays himself embodies the evil and good of public relations. He helped to popularize smoking for women before the full health effects of smoking were known, opening the floodgates for a new cigarette market and future health problems. By the 1960s, when the health effects were made public, Bernays became a public opponent of smoking and used his public relations skills to develop many anti-tobacco campaigns. Public relations has become a sophisticated social science tool, with the potential to be used for both good and evil purposes. As you read the next section, you will see how many professional associations are working to get future practitioners such as yourself to use public relations responsibly.

Creating the Future

Many dynamics have the potential to shape the professional practice of public relations. For example, technology continues to change and grow at a very fast pace, and global economies, markets, and activism create a need for culturally sensitive practitioners. Markets are also diversifying partly due to technology and because public relations is scientifically targeting audiences around the globe.

Scott M. Cutlip, often called the "dean of public relations faculty," and the leading historian of our field, concluded in *The Unseen Power* some revealing observations:

> The public relations specialist contributes to the Miltonian principle of the self-righting process in a democracy, a principle embedded in historic decisions of the U.S. Supreme Court. The advocate's role is essential in a democracy that must be responsive to the public will and dependent on the conciliation of public and private interests in a mutually rewarding manner. (Cutlip, 1994, p. xii)

Table 2.1: Five Stages of Public Relations Growth in the United States	
Stage	*Key Events in U.S. History*
Foundations Use of existing public forms of communication.	Colonization of America American Revolution Western Expansion
Expansion Publicity and promotion used throughout society.	Industrial Revolution Creation of corporations
Institutionalization Increased sophistication of PR tactics in society.	Muckrakers World War I Depression
Maturation Use of strategic planning and research.	World War II Cold war Activist movements
Professionalization Focus on building strategic relationships with key stakeholders and seekers.	Stakeholder management Issues management Investor relations

This mandate requires students to mature into practitioners who can help organizations to become ethically responsible in their activities and effective in their communication—the essence of the rhetorical tradition.

Practitioners cannot take themselves for granted and rest on past accomplishments. They will be required to constantly raise the level of performance. Two recent books call for practitioners to recommit to ethical practice. Stauber and Rampton (1995) charged the industry with denying the public access to information vital to their health and well-being, and the very title of their book characterizes their indictment: *Toxic Sludge Is Good for You: Lies, Damn Lies, and the Public Relations Industry*. A more balanced but nevertheless critical review of the practice was written by Ewen (1996): *PR! A Social History of Spin*. Ewen indicted the profession for believing that "truth is something that can be merchandised to the public" (p. 80). For Ewen, public relations' ability to convince publics into believing that harmful corporations have their best interests at heart can dwarf the ethical traditions we have discussed.

As a profession moves to create its future, it must have a balanced, objective, and candid assessment of itself. It must recognize its weaknesses and improve upon them, as well as continue to develop its strengths. This chapter has attempted a balanced portrayal of public relations' growth. It has undoubtedly featured the positive, while downplaying the negative. Still, while every profession has its positive icons, it must also be willing to learn from persons who have discredited the profession with their unethical choices. As outlined in Table 2.1, public relations has evolved as a dynamic profession that has met and will continue to meet many challenges.

Conclusion

What can be made of the history of public relations? It features dates, characters, and events. But all of that can be subsumed under the essence of history. What have we

A Full Calendar

**Betsy Plank
Principal
Betsy Plank Public
    Relations
Chicago, Illinois**

NOTE: In this reflection, Betsy Plank reflects on one part of her 50-year career. By many, she is considered to be the most influential woman practitioner. She contributed to the development of the practice, earned many awards, and served as an officer of the Public Relations Society of America. She is most pleased by the fact that she helped establish the PRSSA as a way of building the practitioners of the future. The *Encyclopedia of Public Relations* presents a biographical sketch of Ms. Plank.

There is no such thing as a less-than-10-hour day—and I've loved every one of them, even those laced with frustrations or beginning with 7 a.m. meetings. (When I graduated from corporate life and resurrected my counselor shingle, one "never-again" for this congenital night person was any meeting before mid-morning. So far, I've kept that promise to me.)

Meetings. They populated the corporate culture—more than I ever encountered in prior agency life. Some for information exchange. Others for presentations. Too few for outright decision making. Most for debate, negotiation and persuasion. All lifeblood to the corporate anatomy of a telephone company whose customer base was Everyone Out There.

On any typical day, there were two meetings before noon—usually one with division managers to assess work in progress. Over the years, my department's responsibilities in the statewide enterprise included economic development; issues management; community and educational relations; executive programs, memberships and speech-writing; consumer and urban affairs; research; directory covers and Customer Guide Pages; the corporate contributions and art programs; exhibits; graphic and video production; and—early on—employee relations in all its guises: print, TV, hotline, face-to-face discussion programs, and communications counsel to Human Resources/Labor Relations.

Note that nothing in all that had anything to do with press conferences or releases for public media—a radical departure from those earlier agency days which teethed on the tools of marketing communications.

In its halcyon years, the departmental staff reached 114. When I left in the early nineties, it was 70-plus and—like everything else in the company—still downsizing. Nevertheless, our responsibilities remained the same, and most involved building respected relationships with key leaders and other external audiences—all of whom have vested interests in a public utility. All were our clients. So were the other departments in that highly technological service company.

One Thursday on the desk calendar noted a 9 a.m. staff meeting and a 10:30 a.m. meeting with Operations about the proposal for Chicago's first area code split. There was no lunch date, which left room to return phone calls, to check with Cynthia, who kept me and our office on track, and to make inroads on correspondence.

In the interoffice stack this day there was a letter to the president from an irate V.I.P. who had also complained to the Illinois Commerce Commission about being omitted from the latest Chicago phone directory. He fumed, "I've undoubtedly lost business and am considering legal action." The president's handwritten note to me was terse. "Investigate and prepare response." (Turned out that the management of the writer's downtown high-rise had leased a block of service from another telecommunications company but then overlooked reporting tenants' names and numbers to our directory people. Ah, the labor pains of new competition!)

A scheduled afternoon preview of a video rough-cut at the studio has a line through it— postponed for an emergency meeting with the Law Department to discuss threatened intervention by a minority action group against an upcoming rate case.

After that lengthy and heated session, I left to connect with the Chicago Community Relations Manager, asking him to connect with the group leaders, gather intelligence, try to defuse the problem, and to report back—by Tuesday at the latest.

Following that call, I began to wrestle reluctantly with the latest edict from Finance about company-wide budget cuts. (Be careful what you wish for. Climbing the ladder to the corner office often tilts one's agenda from the joys of the practice to managing budgets, politics, and people, who usually have more fun than you.)

Early evening—after the phone subsided—was "think time" with a handful of colleagues to revisit the subject of the new area code. How to get it accepted—despite the growing and noisy protests of communities, chambers of commerce,

and businesses which perceived the change as costly, inconvenient, and—most curious—a "put down." Even residence customers were expressing sudden deep affection for their familiar area code and resisting the prospect of change.

To company engineers and computers, the "case" was obvious and immutable: the numbers available to the established area code were running out. But human nature doesn't always yield to numbers. There was real possibility of a public relations nightmare.

After considering the customer attitudes, our conclusion that night was to lubricate the inevitable by presenting the painful arithmetic in a more persuasive way: Running out of numbers meant that the metropolitan economy was thriving and growing. That spelled new business, new jobs, new services—trade-offs everyone could cheer about. (Ultimately that persuasion worked: The change was accepted and became prelude to a decade of continuing roll-out of new area codes, ignited not only by the economy but also by portable and car phones.)

That night, however, was the genesis of the strategy—reached after analysis, discussion and debate, plus a few war stories about the difficulties of dealing with human behavior. It was problem solving at its best, and I was proud of us.

We left the tableful of empty coffee cups and paper scraps, turned off the lights and headed home to sainted spouses, the microwave and the late news.

However, not before a quick calendar check. Tomorrow, it reminded me, would begin with one of those 7 a.m. meetings.

SOURCE: Reprinted with permission from Betsy Plank.

learned from those dates, characters, and events? Previous practitioners such as Ivy Lee, Arthur Page, Leone Baxter, Edward Bernays, and Doris Fleischman were deeply interested in finding the available means of public communication and combining them with the most ethical and effective interaction. They were committed to fostering the interests of their client organizations and society. Continuing a concern for strategic relationships based on ethical interaction and organizational performance will be a challenge for future generations. We encourage you to follow in their footsteps.

History often focuses on leaders who made a field. We believe that the equation is the opposite: A field makes leaders. While dynamics such as those previously mentioned will shape the available means of public communication and how that communication takes place, they are not the key to the future of the practice. You are the key. Your education, your dedication, your willingness to think and act strategically combined with your ability to plan and implement creative programs will make the difference. Your concern for ethics and representing your client or organization will make the difference. Your view of yourself as a professional or a career craft person will make the difference.

Based on what we have covered in this chapter, are you prepared now to answer the questions we asked in the chapter opening? Can you defend your discipline by pointing to its history? What does your knowledge of that history contribute to how you will practice public relations?

WEB WATCHER: PROFESSIONAL ORGANIZATIONS IN PUBLIC RELATIONS

Throughout this chapter, you may have noticed the Web sites of several professional organizations for public relations practitioners. Can you find the Public Relations Society of America (PRSA), the International Association of Business Communicators (IABC), and the Association for Educators and Journalists in Mass Communication (AEJMC) Web sites on the Internet? Visit their Web sites to answer the following questions. What are the unique characteristics of each? How are they similar and different? What are the membership requirements and dues? Which organization would be a better fit for your interests?

FURTHER EXPLORATION

Ethical Quandary: Thanks for the Referral

Your nonprofit organization asks you to design a publicity program around a special event. After careful consideration of your workload and the importance of the event to the organization, you suggest that the particular project requires the expertise of an outside firm. With the approval of the nonprofit, you refer the project to a competent friend who has recently opened her own public relations firm. After several meetings, your friend is selected by the organization to publicize the event. As a token of appreciation, she sends you a $100 coupon to a nice local restaurant to thank you for the business. Is it ethical to accept the coupon? Why? Why not? What do you say to your friend? What have your learned about the history of public relations that would guide your decision?

Summary Questions

1. What role did publicity and promotion with newspaper reporters play in the western expansion of the United States?

2. How did P. T. Barnum contribute to our society's language and to the use of promotion and publicity by the entertainment industry?

3. Identify some historical examples of events, publicity, promotion, sports information, political communication, media relations, governmental relations, and issues management.

4. Has public relations been used by the "establishment" as well as those groups that criticize the "establishment"?

5. What are "muckrakers"? What role did they play in the institutionalization of public relations?

6. Who were some of the early practitioners, and where did they work before becoming paid practitioners?

7. Name five of the early practitioners of the 20th century. Which one was most influential, and why was the person so influential?

8. What do you believe was Ivy Lee's major contribution to the practice of public relations? What was Edward Bernays's chief contribution? What was John W. Hill's chief contribution?

9. What role did the Creel Committee play in the evolution of the practice?

10. When did investor relations start? What led to its growth in the 20th century?

11. What were the key trends during the periods of professionalization?

12. In what years did the Public Relations Society of America (PRSA) and the International Association of Business Communicators (IABC) start?

13. Name some of the books and journals that have helped to shape the practice in the past 20 years.

14. What are two global challenges that face practitioners over the coming decades?

Exercises

1. Select a practitioner, and write an obituary or a tribute to this person. You may select a person of historical importance or a person who is practicing today. In the piece you write, give basic details, including the person's academic study and professional training. Assess the person's contribution to the practice. You might consider contacting a person who has held a leadership position in the Public

Relations Society of America (PRSA), the International Association of Business Communicators (IABC), or the Public Affairs Council. You might select a prominent academician whose works you are beginning to explore. Many resources offer biographical materials, especially the *Encyclopedia of Public Relations.*

2. Interview some of the current leadership in a local (or national) chapter of the Public Relations Society of America (PRSA) or the International Association of Business Communicators (IABC). Write a short history of the chapter.

3. Select an industry, company, nonprofit, or governmental agency and search through library archives for details about their public relations efforts. Write a short critical examination of the organization's public relations efforts.

4. Interview the public relations officer for your college or university. Write a short critical examination of its public relations efforts.

5. In each chapter, we present a professional reflection of a practitioner. You should have read one for this chapter and for Chapter 1. Select a practitioner or academician. Contact this person. Interview the person. (You can conduct the interview by e-mail.) Write a professional reflection for this person.

Recommended Readings

Brown, C., & Waltzer, B. K. (2005). Every Thursday: Advertorials by Mobil Oil on the op-ed page of *The New York Times. Public Relations Review, 31,* 197–208.

Davidson, P. (1941). *Propaganda and the American Revolution, 1763–1783.* Chapel Hill: University of North Carolina Press.

Heath, R. L. (1997). *Strategic issues management: Organizations and public policy challenges* (see especially chap. 2). Thousand Oaks, CA: Sage.

Heath, R. L. (2005). *Encyclopedia of public relations.* Thousand Oaks, CA: Sage.

Henry, S. (1998). Dissonant notes of a retiring feminist: Doris Fleishman's later years. *Journal of Public Relations Research, 10,* 1–35.

Miller, K. S. (1999). *The voice of business: Hill & Knowlton and postwar public relations.* Chapel Hill: University of North Carolina Press.

Parenti, M. (1986). *Inventing reality: The politics of the mass media.* New York: St. Martin's Press.

Pearson, R. (1992). Perspectives on public relations history. In E. L. Toth & R. L. Heath (Eds.), *Rhetorical and critical approaches to public relations* (pp. 111–130). Hillsdale, NJ: Lawrence Erlbaum.

Ross, I. (1959). *The image merchants.* Garden City, NY: Doubleday Press.

Schmertz, H. (1986). *Good-bye to the low profile: The art of creative confrontation.* Boston: Little, Brown.

Stewart, M. (1992). Alfred Fleishman. *International Public Relations Review, 15,* 19–20.

Tedlow, R. S. (1979). *Keeping the corporate image: Public relations and business: 1900–1950.* Greenwich, CT: JAI Press.

Managing Mutually Beneficial Relationships

3

Making a Difference: World Wildlife Fund

With over 1.3 million members in the United States alone, the World Wildlife Fund (WWF) is one of the largest and most powerful nonprofit environmentalist groups in the world. Fulfilling its ambitious goal of "saving life on earth," the WWF protects and saves endangered species and has battled global threats to the environment that other groups won't touch. The WWF has rescued nature reserves in Nepal, fought deforestation in the Amazon, defended the rain forests of Cameroon, and ensured that America's sustainable fishing industries remain ecologically sound. But the WWF does not endorse political candidates, nor does it engage in reactionary politics that simply seek to punish those who fail to live up to its environmental standards. Instead, the WWF's remarkable success lies in an approach to activism that cultivates two-way relationships and maintains clear objectives that leave no question as to what WWF members must accomplish. This relationship-building approach rejects the antagonistic tactics of protest and confrontation favored by activists of earlier generations in favor of engaging corporations, communities, governments, and other groups in partnerships that recognize that meaningful change is best effected through proactive cooperation and not reactive contention. The end result of the WWF's forward-looking agenda is over 2,000 successful projects since the organization's inception in 1961.

Although the WWF cooperates with four key groups—corporations, governments, communities, and other environmental groups—it is the often environmentally unfriendly corporations that become the primary targets of the organization's actions. The WWF's efforts to revamp the sustainable fishing industry perfectly demonstrate just how successful mutually beneficial relationships can be.

With the United Nations reporting that 60% of the world's fisheries are dangerously overfished or fished to the point of exhaustion, the WWF has cooperated with Unilever, the world's largest producer of frozen fish, to form the Marine Stewardship Council (MSC), a group that consults with fisheries and environmentalists to recommend standards for sustaining both corporate profits and ecological balance. This strategy has proved a boon for the Alaskan salmon. Major seafood buyers are given incentives to buy salmon

Be a
FORCE
FOR
NATURE

WE MUST JOIN TOGETHER TO PROTECT OUR WORLD OR WE COULD LOSE ALL IT GIVES US. TO LEARN HOW YOU CAN HELP, ORDER YOUR FREE WORLD WILDLIFE FUND ACTION KIT.

TOGETHER, WE CAN BE A FORCE FOR NATURE
800-CALL-WWF | worldwildlife.org

Saving Life on Earth

SOURCE: Photo by Tim Davis/Getty Images. Reprinted with permission from Plowshare Group.

stamped with the MSC's approval, local governments are pleased that indigenous fishing industries rich in culture and history are being protected, and environmentalists are assured that salmon fishing is responsibly regulated.

In another example, the WWF has succeeded in preserving the rain forests of Cameroon, which are continually plagued by the threat of local logging industries. Recognizing that the destitute Cameroonian government, one of the poorest in the world, is ill-equipped to deal with logging and poachers, the WWF has joined forces with the Forest Stewardship Council, another environmental group, and corporations in Cameroon, the United Kingdom, and Belgium to promote sustainable forestry guidelines. Under the WWF's guidance, British and Belgian home-building corporations have pledged to buy Cameroonian timber rather than the cheaper woods of rogue Far East companies who fail to meet the Forest Stewardship Council's sustainability guidelines. Moreover,

consumer groups in the United Kingdom and Belgium, whose environmental awareness has been raised by the WWF's efforts, have promised to use only certified lumber.

Again, the WWF's trustworthy reputation as a relationship builder becomes the catalyst for environmental practices that do not shortchange the fiscal needs of industry. The WWF received *Wall Street Journal's SmartMoney* magazine's "Top Environmental Charity" award for 1998, proof positive that unlike many reactive environmentalist groups, its success lies in its appreciation of the need to foster—and not hinder—business relationships. Since then, the WWF has consistently been rated by the Council of Better Business Bureaus and *SmartMoney* as a top charity because of its environmental effectiveness and wise stewardship of its contributors' dollars. That is a sound foundation for mutually beneficial relationships. Nature is the benefactor of this organization's sound public relations.

O rganizations look to public relations to fulfill a variety of goals and objectives. Traditionally, these have ranged from handling publicity and promotion campaigns to highly sensitive counseling of upper management on delicate issues. Increasingly, managements have learned to look to public relations to help their organizations build mutually beneficial relationships (MBRs) with key stakeholders, which come in many variations. Part of that challenge is to refine the organization's ethical standards and corporate responsibility.

Relationship theory in recent years has made gains in refining the practice, but that approach to public relations is not new. As any thoughtful person will understand, the antecedents of public relations were always sensitive to relationship building—even though many relationships have ended up being lopsided or asymmetrical. For many years, practitioners and theorists have considered the role of relationship building in the practice of public relations. One of the earliest and most powerful statements on this topic was written by John W. Hill (1958), principal founder of Hill & Knowlton. He said,

> When we look at the work of corporate enterprise, we may properly say that every corporation *has* public relations. It has them whether management is interested in the ways of public opinion or not. It has them because the corporation deals with employees, stockholders, customers, neighbors, government functionaries, and many others—with all of whom it has many relationships.
>
> The corporation thus is constantly involved in public relations, even if management gives them no special thought or concern or guidance. . . .
>
> But when a management decides to guard, improve, or develop this asset, "public relations" becomes the label for *a function*. Here the term that took a plural verb becomes singular, so that now we say: "Public relations is a function of top management in every well-managed corporation." (p. 4)

Many other writers on public relations have taken a view that relates to relationship building. Heath (1994) reasoned that executives are called on to meet the challenge of successfully managing their organizations by meeting or exceeding the expectations of their stakeholders. Managements can't long be successful if they violate the conditions of a relationship. When they meet those conditions, the quality of the relationship can help them during a crisis (Betz, 1996). Along similar lines, Broom, Casey, and Ritchey (1997) featured the need for organizations to understand the conditions needed for solid relationships. Ledingham and Bruning (1998, 2000; Ledingham, 2005) have featured these strategic options in their relationship management theory of public relations.

Relationship management is a fundamental rubric of public relations. It calls on an understanding of the systems that can affect the future of an organization, as well as the meaning and quality of relationships. Thus, public relations theory draws on systems, rhetorical heritage, and social exchange theory to explain and improve the practice. These theoretical options also justify the role of public relations as helping to make society function better so that harmony displaces division and symmetry is championed over asymmetry.

As explored in Chapter 2, rulers and religious figures over the past centuries have been interested in image, reputation, issue positions, and relationships. These often are not separable. In fact, they are the stuff of public relations. As in interpersonal relationships between two people, relationships in the public arena are strongest when they are mutually beneficial and characterized by a "win-win" situation in which all parties achieve the results they desire. By this definition, the strength of a relationship is tested by the desire of each party to sustain it in its current form.

This chapter explores three lines of analysis relevant to relationship building and management. One is the rationale for MBRs. The second investigates the role of message development objectives as vital to relationship development. The chapter ends with more attention to the conditions and venues whereby relationships are needed for an organization to be successful.

Mutually Beneficial Relationships

Building MBRs calls for high ethical standards, strategic thinking, responsible planning, and effective communication. Quality relationships exist when people and organizations have compatible interests and share compatible views of the world. To assess the quality of a relationship, the public relations professional asks questions such as, "Is the donation to a school an investment in the community's future or merely a publicity stunt to attract favorable yet undeserved attention to an otherwise unethical company?"

Many people in society think of public relations as merely "spin-doctoring" and image management—deployed to hide the truth and to cover unethical or dangerous actions committed by an organization. This perception is made stronger by mass media, which usually support it. An MBR approach to public relations counteracts this view, because win-win situations benefit both an organization and the people of society as a whole.

As the efforts of the WWF illustrate, serious relationship building requires time, effort, and the outlay of social, political, and economic resources. These same concerns inform any person's interpersonal relations with friends and family, and the sensitivities people use in gauging their personal relationships can serve as a model for global business relations. Just as you must be sensitive and empathetic enough to repair a personal relationship when you have been selfish or uncaring, so must organizations take into account the excitable, fragile, and even fickle feelings of stakeholders in order to build, maintain, and repair professional relationships.

Stakeholders are persons or groups that have something of value in relation to an organization. Furthermore, the wise public relations practitioner must not merely respond to stakeholders' needs but also, like a knowing friend, be able to shrewdly and empathetically anticipate those needs before they go unfulfilled. If people or organizations have stakes others want or need, then the persons who want or need those stakes are *stakeseekers*. The exchange of stakes can include selling and buying goods. It can negotiate the interests of a community to have a freeway system that does not harm property values.

A long-term relationship flourishes when it provides mutual benefit; if it is not mutually beneficial, then there is no rational incentive for the "losing" party to continue the relationship. For this reason, consumers do business with competitors, and activists fight to build a better quality of life.

The diplomatic premises of *exchange, empathy,* and *maintenance* that characterize personal relationships also hold true for relationships between organizations and stakeholders. Remember that organizations are stakeseekers who want the stakes held by others. The role of public relations, then, is to analyze these relationships, to identify what offends, appeases, and pleases stakeholders, and to know how to strengthen, weaken, and exploit the emotional and practical qualities of these relations to achieve the desired effects. But the mutual benefits of public relations do not merely respond to needs and wants—they can shape them too. For example, in the late 1980s and early 1990s, the Regional Bell Operating Companies (RBOCs) used public relations to change blasé public attitudes toward a telecommunications industry that had come under fire for monopolistic business practices. The RBOCs brought to public attention the stranglehold long-distance carriers held over the public and lobbied to be released from their government regulations in order to compete openly with long-distance giants such as Sprint and MCI. In 1996, Congress responded by passing the revolutionary Telecommunications Act, which, by ending the restrictions that forced the RBOCs to remain noncompetitive, has created a competitive environment that offers RBOCs more freedom and consumers more choice. In this way, public relations can mold public opinion by publicizing unfair practices and enlightening the public about the reciprocal benefits their organization can, under the right circumstances, potentially provide.

▶ Defining Mutually Beneficial Relationships

Mutually beneficial relationships (MBRs) are defined as relationships that substantially and symbiotically benefit all parties subject to the policy of a group or organization. As mentioned earlier, these relationships are strongest when they are mutually beneficial and characterized by a win-win situation in which all parties achieve the results they desire. From an organizational standpoint, the public relations practitioner should cooperate with stakeholders, meet and shape their expectations, and align their interests with those of the corporation the public relations practitioner represents. While the organization will attempt to live up to stakeholders' expectations and reflect their interests, it is also the organization's duty to adjust and correct what it perceives to be any unrealistic or misinformed notions that stakeholders might hold. We can't be doctrinaire—two-way good, one-way bad. Information can be persuasive, too. MBRs, then, are a way to be most effective and persuasive as well as being the most ethical. To facilitate this goal, organizations must practice *two-way symmetrical communication,* in which interaction causes changes on both sides of the organization-stakeholder relationship, as a way to promote mutual understanding between an organization and important stakeholders. Such interaction is best when it is dialogue rather than monologue.

The public relations crisis that befell the garment industry well illustrates how such adjustments come into play. Activist groups have long criticized the brutal, slavish working conditions of the sweatshops in developing nations that supply garment makers such as the Gap, Eddie Bauer, and Nike. In the 1990s, when activists threatened to boycott these corporations until they ceased operations in countries lacking progressive labor laws, public relations divisions proposed and advanced a common solution in response. Explaining why they could not afford to leave these countries, many garment makers instead voluntarily adopted codes of conduct for their suppliers. In turn, the garment makers asked activist groups to accept the codes as a viable compromise.

WEB WATCHER: APPAREL INDUSTRY

The apparel industry has worked to develop and enforce its own codes of conduct. This is important given the continuing interest in child labor, corporal punishment, and other labor issues. Visit the "Apparel Industry and Codes of Conduct" Web site, at http://www.dol.gov/ilab/media/reports/iclp/apparel/main.htm, to see the efforts to address labor issues. Pay particular attention to how child labor is defined and limited.

Importantly, this compromise between the two factions did not mean that the sweatshop controversies were magically dispelled with a convenient dash of public relations. Concerns over sweatshop exploitation are as intense as they ever were, and even a balanced compromise will not always fully satisfy either side. But instead of Nike and other manufacturers responding to activists with a defensive, knee-jerk position of counterproductive denial and avoidance, the intervention of public relations has resulted in a concrete, progressive achievement: the codes of conduct. Controversies, clashes, and injustices will always exist as long as there are conflicting interests—how progressively and how peacefully those conflicts are resolved is ultimately the real measure of public relations success. This is the test of fostering a mutually beneficial exchange of stakes between stakeholders and stakeseekers. These cases also illustrate how the buying dollars of customers are stakes they hold and how businesses compete, seeking those dollars. In exchange, customers want to give stakes to companies that, in turn, give the stakes of being responsible employers.

MBRs help build positive operating environments for organizations. Let's consider the hypothetical example of two gravel-mining companies vying to open two pits in the same town at the same time but embarking on different strategies to secure their much-needed mining permits. Cross Industries rendezvoused with local politicians and negotiated for their permits secretly, while Ethical Mining, Inc., met openly with local officials and community groups, even throwing a barbecue bash as part of their demonstration on the effects and benefits of their proposed pit. By the year's end, it came time to review each rival company's proposal, and public hearings allowed community members to publicly support or oppose each candidate. Community members were outraged to learn of the clandestine meetings between Cross Industries and local bigwigs, and the local sheriff's department needed to shield Cross's executives from both hurled epithets and hurled bottles. Its invalid operating permits were revoked, and all hopes of opening their pit were dashed. Surprisingly, when it came time to vote for Ethical Mining, they too lost, effectively defeated by the prevailingly negative sentiments toward the gravel industry created by Cross's unethical, backdoor practices. Though disappointed, Ethical Mining returned the following year with more plans, more meetings, and more barbecues. This time, they sent out surveys and held focus groups to find out the specific concerns of the townspeople and alter their plans to assuage those fears.

Through persistence, enough votes were generated honestly for the gravel pit to open the following year. Because Ethical Mining took time to cultivate a relationship with stakeholders rather than hastily lunging for the falsely perceived roots of power, they created an MBR that saw their bottom line and community interests as symbiotic partners instead of stealthy opponents.

▶ Mutually Beneficial Relationships and Return on Investment

The incentive to foster MBRs operates on an intrinsically rational model of rewards and punishments that sees self-interest and an interest in stakeholders' well-being as mutually inclusive. Stakeholders grant their *stakes*—goods, services, and other elements of value—to organizations that please them, and they punish organizations that misbehave by granting their stakes to the offending organization's competitors. Therefore, the premise of mutual benefits and inclusion is also a basic law of the marketplace.

As a public relations practitioner, you should thus learn to think in terms of *return on investment* (ROI). ROI is the "return" or results for a given use of money or resources in an enterprise, usually calculated as profit or cost savings. To effectively counsel managements, practitioners need to have high ethical standards, know ROI thinking, and understand the law of MBRs. All organizations seek positive ROI, in other words, to generate more revenue than they spend. This is usually achieved through wise planning and resource management. One of the greatest wasters of resources is failed public relations, as, for example, disgruntled activist groups may muster a costly boycott, leak embarrassing media reports, and file enough lawsuits to stymie daily corporate operations. All of these tactics are designed to financially cripple the organization, not only making it less competitive but also weakening its public image to the point where it must cave in on demands.

As someone embarking on a professional career, you will need to think seriously about ROI. Even nonprofits such as the WWF must be cost-effective, and so too must your efforts generate more than they cost; at the very least, you must be prepared to outline how the money spent on your public relations projects can recoup itself. Another way of thinking about MBRs is to imagine diminishing the gap between what an organization actually does and what stakeholders expect it to do: The smaller the gap, the more authentic the MBR. When firms' operations fail to meet stakeholder expectations, *legitimacy gaps* widen, fostering the desire by stakeholders to correct—or punish—those operations through selling stock, activism, or boycotts. But ROI thinking also encapsulates our MBR philosophy: Executives obviously want the greatest return for the least cost, and if public relations functions properly, it can help their organizations anticipate dire community needs before those unfulfilled needs can balloon into anger and discontent. By offering speedy, economic, and culturally sensitive solutions to potentially costly legitimacy gaps, public relations justifies its budget, earns its keep, and inarguably provides ROI.

The efforts of McDonald's to become environmentally friendly and responsible to customers' interest in health provide another excellent illustration of aligning corporate and public interests. In the early 1990s, McDonald's was still serving its sandwiches in environmentally unfriendly polystyrene clamshell packages, even though environmentalism was quickly becoming a concern of mainstream, middle-class America. Because public opinion demanded change, McDonald's decided to appease the public by mounting a campaign that encouraged recycling polystyrene. Early tests showed, however, that consumers thought the campaign was insufficient and merely addressed the effects of the problem rather than striking at the root cause. Responding to public needs, McDonald's joined forces with the Environmental Defense Fund in 1993, setting in motion a series of initiatives designed to put McDonald's at the environmental forefront of all fast-food chains. The first step was rejecting polystyrene altogether in favor of biodegradable paper containers. In addition, McDonald's now builds new restaurants entirely from recycled materials and refuses to purchase beef from deforested rain forest land. In November of 2000, McDonald's even received an award from the Environmental Protection Agency (EPA) for its outstanding achievements. The corporation's alignment of its values and practices with the proenvironmental values of its consumers and stakeholders operates on two levels: First, it voices a concern for the environment, as expressed through public relations; and second, it moves that concern into the realm of concrete action through philanthropy and corporate responsibility.

In similar fashion, merely proclaiming its food to be healthy and blaming consumers for eating too much would sound self-serving and defensive. It would strain the relationship with its customers, who have been encouraged to trust McDonald's to provide healthy food in appropriate portions. The menu has to change, as does the entire marketing plan. This is the public relations solution to its customer relations, as well as its relationships with other fast-food businesses, legislators, regulators, litigators, and activists.

Establishing Mutually Beneficial Relationships

So far, this chapter has explained why it is strategically important to implement MBRs, but how exactly does one go about it? In reality, there are no particular public relations tools whose use lets you know when an MBR exists. In a sense, using public relations is like using a language: Anybody can use the linguistic tools that are words, sentences, and punctuation, but not everybody can use them correctly or effectively. Just as people who do not understand the rules of grammar can use the same common vocabulary words that are used by people who speak correctly, so are press releases, statistics, and other public relations tools equally available to all practitioners, regardless of how well or how ethically they practice. Some practitioners may ignore information about stakeholders, and others may try to force changes in stakeholders' views, but those seeking a healthy, reciprocal relationship will use the principle of *adjustment* outlined above.

MBRs are reflected not in the use of certain tools, but in the ways they are used: how well the practical "vocabulary" of public relations tools is placed within the ethical "grammar" of MBRs. The commitment to building MBRs must become a philosophical, ethical, and strategic approach that allows the public relations practitioner and the organization to view stakeholders as partners, not enemies. Building and maintaining relationships will also be a rhetorical challenge, whereby the responsibility you take for the words you use determines how healthy your relationships will be. Relationship building often poses rhetorical problems. They are situational demands for statements that inform, persuade, negotiate, resolve conflict, and collaborate in decision making.

It is not enough to know that positive relations and two-way communication are important—one must know how to actually create and facilitate them. We can identify five critical factors necessary for creating an MBR:

- Aligning with stakeholders by maintaining a consistent *voice*
- Making sure messages are true and trustworthy
- Providing open, two-way communication
- Being proactive
- Identifying and creating opportunity

▶Keeping a Consistent Voice

A relationship-building approach to public relations realizes that all of what the organization does and says communicates information about an organization. People experience and make sense of an organization, its management, its reputation, and its products and services by what it does just as much as by what it says. Markets, audiences, and publics (MAPs) interpret the reputation of the organization by what it says and does—and by how well what it says corresponds to what it does. The public identity created by the combination of what an organization does and says is called its *voice,* and the public relations professional must make it a priority to ensure that the organization's voice is always clear, coherent, and consistent.

Producing a *consistent voice* means that an organization's statements and actions should reinforce one another. The organization cannot pick and choose which of its public statements it will honor and which it will ignore or betray; ideally, it should always honor all of these statements. Likewise, the organization's advertising, marketing, and public relations departments should be adapting the same overriding information, evaluations, and conclusions to meet the needs and concerns of their individual audiences. All public communications should be integrated such that the organization speaks with a single, coherent voice and the information shared with one stakeholder reflects the same theme and content that is used in dialogues with other stakeholders, even if the interests of those other stakeholders differ. Consider the advertising campaigns of Ben & Jerry's Ice Cream, a company that has made its charitable actions into a major selling point and a key part of its voice. Ideally, Ben & Jerry's internal communications and employee training should be thematically consistent with both their *image advertising* (targeted to potential investors) and their *product advertising* (targeted to potential consumers). The product advertisements might include placing claims of Ben & Jerry's commitment to environmentalism on individual ice cream cartons to encourage consumers to buy the product, while the image advertisement would explain to investors how this sales technique boosts revenue by addressing the "green" sympathies of consumers. Simply, the same message can be fashioned around the needs of different audiences without altering the message's central theme.

Closely aligned with the role of voice is the idea that public relations is a form of *symbolic action,* whereby publics respond to an organization based not so much on what the organization is, but on what they think it represents. A perspective of symbolic action recognizes that basically everything, from language to physical actions, is understood in terms of symbolic meaning. Thus, when people or organizations interpret an action, they attribute motives to it in order to draw their conclusions. The importance of this symbolism becomes more obvious when we take into account *relativism,* or the idea that an event has no single, universal meaning and can be interpreted differently by people depending on their varying locations, nationalities, customs, traditions, languages, and personal prejudices.

Symbolic action is not a "code word" for abstract meanings without concrete action, but an admission that we must take responsibility for what our actions—good or bad, noble or selfish—could potentially symbolize to others. Unfortunately, the news media regularly and simplistically use the phrase "public relations" to mean empty words without responsible action, implying that public relations is just spin. We, however, would in fact argue the opposite: Words not supported by actions cannot be called authentic public relations in the first place.

While many people continue to demonize public relations, it may actually offer more opportunities for two-way communication than traditional one-way communication of the news media because it takes an intermediary position between organizations and stakeholders. Because the marketplace is inherently a two-way arena where stakeholder and stakeseeker meet, the idea of symbolic action indicates that inconsistent voice—a breakdown between what an organization says and what it does—can have disastrous effects for that organization. Stakeholders will, for example, expect Ben & Jerry's to fulfill their promise of environmental charity; if it were ever found out that Ben & Jerry's was falsifying its claims, the company could very well be finished. Remember that it is your obligation as a public relations professional to protect your organization and to not reinforce the negative stereotype of the profession as mere spin.

You can better appreciate the importance of a consistent voice when you consider the disastrously inconsistent voice adopted by Mitsubishi Motors. In the mid-1990s, the Equal Employment Opportunity Commission (EEOC) charged Mitsubishi with sexual harassment, reportedly widespread throughout its manufacturing plant in Normal, Illinois. Mitsubishi's initial reaction was to totally deny the charges, attack the EEOC for even making such claims, and orchestrate a worker protest at the EEOC's Chicago offices. However, Mitsubishi's abrasive, uncooperative response led many to criticize the company, and Mitsubishi's encouraging its own workers to stand up for the company was seen not only as a cheap tactic, but possibly coercive. Eventually, the company changed its tactics—switched its voice—and hired former Labor Secretary Lynn Martin as a consultant as part of their efforts to build a harassment-free workplace. But Mitsubishi had underestimated the degree to which the public would negatively interpret the symbolism of their initial denial, and stakeholders remained unconvinced of the company's sincerity, even though Martin gave Mitsubishi a positive report. The public found Mitsubishi's quick turnaround from firm denial to admission and reconciliation difficult to believe. As a result, its corporate credibility suffered as many female buyers rejected Mitsubishi as a choice.

▶Making Sure Messages Reflect the Truth

As the spokesperson for an organization, the public relations practitioner must often develop or deliver messages prepared by others in the organization. Sources can be varied and include senior management, such as the chief executive officer (CEO) and chief operating officer (COO). Regardless of the source, spokespersons often find themselves in the unenviable position of relying on unfamiliar information prepared by strangers. Nevertheless, professionals have the ethical and practical responsibility of knowing the truth and telling it—one cannot repeat lies or half-truths and then later blame an erroneous source once the truth is exposed. Because lies are almost always discovered at some point, practitioners must make every reasonable attempt to verify the information they must deliver to stakeholders. Untruths not only damage the client's and practitioner's reputations but also hurt the reputation of the entire profession and reinforce the worst stereotypes about spin and public manipulation. Assume that the public will be as critical as you are of the information you receive, and approach your sources and their information critically so that your presentations will withstand the scrutiny of MAPs.

Imagine the feelings of a vice president of public relations who suffered the following incident. She worked for a publicly traded, multinational company. She was called by a business writer, who inquired about rumors that her CEO was in conversation with the CEO of another company about a merger. She asked her CEO about this matter. He said, "I have not had any conversations with the CEO of that company about a merger." She reported that information to the reporter and was shocked to see a news story the next day include statements from e-mails between the two CEOs. Had they been in "conversation"? Was she made to look like a fool? Was she betrayed? Was her relationship with her CEO and this reporter damaged?

Three basic pieces of advice should guide public relations practitioners when searching for accurate facts:

- Rely on *primary resources,* such as interviews with key players and consultants' reports when trying to select accurate information. Barring forgery or falsification, it is nearly impossible to dispute the accuracy of primary resources. Then, consider the *secondary resources*—others' commentaries on the primary resources—and don't hesitate to diplomatically correct their errors or misconceptions.
- Refer to archives, commissioned research, focus groups, interviews, surveys, and other primary resources to make your opinions as credible and well informed as possible. In terms of public relations, credibility should encompass equality, fairness, trustworthiness, corporate responsibility, and, with respect to products and operations, safety.
- Carefully craft your message to best capture and convey the facts and your intended symbolic meaning. These *message choices,* based on your primary and secondary resources along with fact-based research, should position you on the behalf of your clients while satisfying the needs of the community.

No matter how much research and fact-checking you do, you will always face an element of uncertainty when you present your message. Even the best research will unlikely be exhaustive, and because ideas are relative and even statistics are open to symbolic interpretation, contentious audiences and publics may debate the validity of facts you take for granted. But if you anticipate possible counterarguments and prepare for the symbolism your message choices might *potentially* have, the natural conflict of ideas between an organization and stakeholders can be healthy and productive and prompt mutual growth and enlightenment.

In most cases, information and opinion survive because of the prevailing—and relativistic—preferences of a community. Simply, what is considered "true" is largely a function of what stakeholders believe to be true. Again, problems arise when the relative positions of organizations and stakeholders produce conflicting claims on "the truth." Consider the 1997 example of Philip Morris attempting to revitalize its sagging line of Virginia Slims, a cigarette targeted at women. Trying to make smoking an appealing practice for young women in a strongly antismoking public environment, Philip Morris toured the United States to recruit up-and-coming female musicians, signing them to lucrative record contracts on its "Woman Thing Music" label. The CDs, however, could be purchased only in special promotional packages of Virginia Slims cigarettes. Anti-smoking critics accused Philip Morris of exploiting female musicians and implicating them in a crass marketing scheme. Defenders of the company argued that Philip Morris, whose Virginia Slims tennis tour was in 1970 the first professional women's tennis tournament in the world, was benefiting underappreciated, underpaid female artists and that the company had always had women's interests at heart. While it is possible that each side's claims are valid, controversy surrounding the campaign was sufficiently negative to work against its promotional value.

This case stresses the reality that companies have multiple stakeholders, whose values and interests can be in conflict. Problems and differences cannot always be resolved through communication. For that reason, changes in policy are important statements about a company's commitment to building and maintaining MBRs.

▶ Ensuring Two-Way Symmetrical Communication

At the core of most current public relations practices is the idea of two-way communication, which ensures that organizations and stakeholders are engaged in dialogue rather than monologue. Today's public relations assumes that messages are part of a discourse of statement and counterstatement, of give-and-take. This type of communication helps organizations listen to stakeholders, understand and appreciate what is being said, adjust to a changing business environment, and make necessary adjustments.

But even sustained two-way communication cannot always prevent misunderstandings and misperceptions. For example, even under the guidance of open communication, stakeholders often harbor unrealistic views of the profits made by manufacturers, presuming CEOs always rake in astronomical profits when the economy runs smoothly. In truth, this is hardly the case—just ask any "dot-com" executive who has filed for bankruptcy—and organizations need public relations to remedy faulty beliefs that create public discontent from fallacious reasoning. Stakeholders must be told—and convinced—that the organization might not be able to aid a community because the astronomical profits the community imagines do not exist. On the other hand, when it is obvious an organization can afford to make a difference, the public will expect it to do so. Environmental stakeholders demanded a radical environmental consciousness of McDonald's. Its budgeting and marketing had to become tailored to these environmental expectations, otherwise the company would suffer negative publicity and controversy. It would suffer image damage if it were to be known to make multi-billion-dollar profits by exploiting the environment. Likewise, today, it must work to be in harmony with the growing concern over the public health implications for consumers of its products.

Being Proactive

Unfortunately, the term *proactive* has become a cliché in both the business world and the media, often because people misuse the word. But the proactivity of two-way communication, as opposed to the reactivity of one-way communication, is a crucial element of modern public relations. Adopting a *proactive approach* means being able to anticipate important events and stakeholder concerns and addressing them in the early stages, before they can turn into public relations problems. This goal is achieved by constantly analyzing and responding to environmental factors—those internal and external to the organization that can affect its success. In a *reactive approach,* on the other hand, organizations wait for events and stakeholder reactions to unfold before taking action. Dealing with environmental protesters only when they are picketing outside of corporate headquarters or with the aftereffects of an oil spill or chemical leak are examples of the reactive approach at work.

Yet being proactive does not simply mean beating the critics to the punch or "winning" a debatable issue, because such actions are still one-sided and self-interested. They do nothing to build the trust required for successful long-term relationships. Eventually, angry, tenacious stakeholders will also act in their own self-interests, pressing the issue and discovering that you've merely covered up a questionable or offensive word or deed instead of addressing it straightforwardly. The goal of proactivity should never be to quickly remove or hide offensive policies or statements, but to actively engage in dialogic relationships that place the organization's voice and stakeholder voices on the same level, and realize that reactivity is a short-term answer and that MBRs are a long-term solution.

The value of proactivity can be seen by looking at the controversy surrounding air bags. It has been convincingly demonstrated that front-passenger air bags reduce traffic deaths for most passengers, and new cars come standard with front air bags. However, warnings accompany these air bags. Small adults and even older children can be harmed and even killed by the bags as they operate. Small children are safer in the backseat, especially in properly designed and tailored car seats. Side-impact air bags have proven more controversial, however, and car manufacturers have been more reluctant to add them, despite pressure from U.S. safety officials.

In this example, a proactive automobile manufacturer could view the situation as an opportunity. By working with the government, the manufacturer could potentially save money by basing its research and development with evolving government regulations and might even be able to positively influence the legislative process, all the while creating goodwill with both government agencies and consumers. A reactive manufacturer would shortsightedly only wait for regulations to be passed and then try to catch up with more innovative competitors, thus getting to the market later, losing the chance to influence policy-making decisions, and running the risk of needless cash outlays if the new regulations made old research obsolete. For these reasons, responsible companies realize that proactivity requires being engaged with issues from the start rather than denying the potential worth of critics' comments and waiting to see how a public policy battle unfolds.

Too often, risk communication and crisis management are reactive and short-term in nature. The *crisis management plan* (CMP) is basically a kind of damage control, spelling out what plans should be implemented when crises strike. Proactive crisis management, on the other hand, consists of long-term sustained effort and oversight: It searches for weaknesses that could later become crises and looks to eliminate or at least reduce any foreseen risks. For instance, if safety standards had been reviewed, revised, and reinforced, the nuclear disaster at the Chernobyl nuclear plant might have been averted by understanding a design flaw that led to the partial nuclear meltdown that forced thousands from their homes. Proactivity is also in the financial best interests of private corporations, for it seeks to solve problems before they become costly. In the 1970s, insurance companies pressured auto manufacturers to design safer cars not only to save more lives but also because the bottom lines of insurance companies would benefit if cars could withstand more damage. In this case, the economic concerns of the insurance industry worked hand in hand with consumer safety. These topics will be expanded in later chapters. Here, the key point is that from the outset, today's public relations calls for engagement to build MBRs.

It is certain that reactivity will always be a reality in public relations practice; after all, it is impossible to anticipate all eventualities and events. A reactive stance is required when an organization is caught off-guard by an issue or when stakeholders realize a problem the organization was unaware of. At these times, organizations must exhibit

Shell in Action

SOURCE: Reprinted with permission from Shell Oil Company.

a delicate balance of responsibility and sensitivity in such situations, and message choice becomes particularly crucial. Yet as a best practice, the sage practitioner is proactive and stands in front of a rhetorical problem or emerging issue, rather than defensively hiding behind it.

▶ Finding and Creating Opportunities

In the process of being proactive, practitioners seek to build relationships and to create new ways to strengthen relationships with stakeholders, as well as to identify potential trouble spots. As part of this process, practitioners seek to find and create new opportunities. An *opportunity* is any circumstance by which an organization can serve the community to the mutual advantage of both. The difference between finding and creating is in the timing: A *found opportunity* has already been stated publicly, whereas a *created opportunity* is created from a latent need or desire that you have perceived but that has yet to be publicized. For example, if a local neighborhood association petitions a city for a new park, that would constitute a found opportunity for the construction company hired to do the job. But if the construction company were to actively search for a community in need of its services and could convince that local neighborhood association that a safe place for children to play would be in its best interests, that would be a created opportunity. But whether found or created, the organization must take the general initiative to strengthen its ties with local stakeholder groups.

What if a substantial market existed that your organization had not yet tapped? In his article "Strategically Reaching the Gay Market," Public Relations Society of America (PRSA) strategist Eric Ewell (1996) outlined the kind of strategic initiatives involved in creating new opportunities for previously invisible markets. Ewell's statistical analysis revealed that the U.S. gay and lesbian market is largely well educated and affluent, and, with multiple income households averaging $51,624 for gay men and $45,927 for lesbians, it could be as large as $514 billion annually. Strategic public relations campaigns can identify messages and channels that have historically appealed to the community, such as arts, entertainment, and fashion. The gay and lesbian market, which may have a greater interest in social activism than other communities, can also become linked with fund-raising and governmental services. For example, gays and lesbians might be more inclined to buy a certain product if a percentage of the proceeds went to fund AIDS research or antidiscrimination public service ads. Therefore, it is the job of the public relations professional not to merely perfect relationships with preexisting markets but also to be aggressive and perceptive enough to find entirely new markets.

To be effective, a search for opportunities must be systematic. The kind of situational analysis that opportunity-searching calls for can be summarized by these questions:

- What improvements can be made in how the organization operates?
- Can the market arena be improved?
- Can a product or fund-raising activity be presented more favorably?
- Can the public policy arena be improved?
- Would a change in public policy help the community?

- What can be done to create and strengthen community relationships?
- Who can the organization serve that it is not serving?
- Who has not heard of the organization that can benefit from a relationship with it?

These questions suggest that relationship building requires strategic thinking, making sound ethical choices, and focusing on the balance of needs and interests between the organization and each of its stakeholders. This public relations effort is most likely to achieve the organization's goals and objectives when it is proactive. It needs cocreated meaning.

Message Development Objectives

Although public relations is not limited to communication, communication is the lifeblood of MBRs. Through communication, organizations and stakeholders are able to align their interests and to benefit from the relationship. But actions are a vital part of the strategic options organizations can use to build relationships. The astute observer will realize that actions communicate a great deal about the quality of relationships and help define the organization's reputation.

It is too broad to simply say communication creates MBRs. The term *communication* is very ambiguous, and such a statement provides little guidance for a public relations practitioner. Five specific message development objectives (MDOs) are central to public relations practice: gain attention, inform, persuade, engage in collaborative decision making, and cocreate meaning. The MDOs are the specific communication objectives practitioners can use in their efforts to construct MBRs. The MDOs convert the five factors for establishing MBRs outlined in the previous section into the specific objectives necessary to build MBRs. This section defines the five MDOs and explains how they can be applied using a variety of stakeholder examples.

▶ Types of Message Development Objectives

Developing an MBR is not simple or easy. It requires careful thought, effective planning, and ethical decisions. Any complex process is more easily understood by dividing it into easier-to-understand parts. In a way, the MDOs are parts of the MBR development process. They help practitioners to understand the challenge, including the rhetorical problems, that must be addressed in serving clients, employers, and the people whose goodwill is needed for the organization to succeed.

Attention

No relationship can exist if the two parties do not know each other exist and what is on each other's mind. Organizations must attend to stakeholders and vice versa if there is to be any relationship. Potential customers, for instance, do not appear until they know a product or service exists. Similarly, candidates rely on name recognition to win elections. Organizations and stakeholders must pay attention to one another if an MBR has any chance to form.

BOX 3.1 GAINING ATTENTION AND REPORTING

Public relations efforts related to public policy can attract attention to problems that need solution and to their potential solutions. Although the details used in the formation of public policy may be difficult for laypeople to understand and interpret, public relations practitioners are challenged to keep messages simple so that interested parties have a chance to understand the issues and know why some policies are favored and others are opposed. Gaining attention for information relevant to a company's (stock's) values is not merely a strategy of investor relations; it is a requirement of the Securities and Exchange Commission (SEC). The SEC requires companies to report all information in a timely manner (as soon as possible) that can have an effect on the value of stock. That means that if buyers or sellers would use the information in making a buy, sell, or hold decision, it must be reported so that all interested parties have an opportunity to obtain it at the same time. Investor relations often makes reports to attract attention to a company's share value, especially when it is positive.

Information

For a relationship to progress, each side needs to learn more about the other: They need information. Relationships develop as a function of the two parties sharing information. Investors, for example, thrive on information about an organization. They want as much financial data as possible when investing money. Conversely, the more information an organization knows about potential investors, the more effectively it can target messages to them. We need information in order to understand whether interests are aligned and whether the relationship has the potential to be mutually beneficial. Information is the name of the game in investor relations. Also, practitioners realize that having information about something may achieve understanding but does not constitute agreement. Often companies and activists, for instance, are aware of the same facts but may differ in how they are to best be interpreted.

Tons of accounting data are generated and summarized for analysts (buy- and sell-sides), stockbrokers, investment bankers, fund managers, stockholders, and officials of the SEC. Information demonstrates the current financial value of the company and is used to project its future worth. Sell-side analysts interpret financial information and recommend that investors buy, hold, or sell shares in specific companies. Buy-side analysts receive information from many sources and help the organizations they represent (such as mutual funds) to decide to buy, sell, or hold certain stocks. Stockbrokers advise individual investors. They often work for major companies that advise individual investors. Investment bankers supply expertise and funding to help a company launch the sale of many shares of its stock, such as occurs during an initial public offering, the act of going public by beginning to trade a specific stock on one of the exchanges. Fund managers are in charge of deciding which stocks should be bought, sold, or held by a mutual fund. A mutual fund allows investors to share in the ownership of many companies' stocks at one time.

Schools engage in communication and strategic-planning efforts to keep students and other members of the community informed on programs, needs, and accomplishments of students. Students can be channels of communication to other MAPs and are themselves MAPs. Through them, communities can be reached to better understand the constraints and accomplishments of educational institutions. Information is important in political campaigns and public policy actions. Public relations can help to ascertain what publics want to know to make an intelligent decision about candidates for an office or a public policy position. Once this is known, the objective is to tell what the candidate can and will do to serve the voters' and publics' interests.

Persuasion

Sometimes organizations and stakeholders need to change one another's attitudes or behavior through persuasion. Some theorists who study public relations frown on persuasion. They may not realize that activists are trying to persuade management on some issue. Persuasion theory has developed for more than a century to understand the processes people go through as they make decisions. Psychologists and communication theorists have developed theories and tested hypotheses to better understand this process. Such work sheds light on the ways people form and use beliefs and attitudes in making decisions. This literature is vast but can be summarized simply as resulting from attempts to explain the ways individuals influence one another. Thus, *persuasion* can be discussed and described as the process of human influence. Its rich body of research shows that people can be influenced by others but they are also capable of influencing themselves. They seek messages to form beliefs and attitudes on the way to making what they hope to be rewarding decisions.

Persuasion is not inherently unethical. Universities will try to persuade alumni to donate money. Animal rights activists will try to persuade companies to end product testing on animals. Persuasion is a natural part of the alignment process and is often used to ensure that both sides are receiving benefits from the relationship. The American Lung Association may try to persuade smokers to change in order to improve smokers' health. The local public television station may try to persuade noncontributing viewers to contribute to the station's upkeep. Children's advocates call for improved public policies to protect children's interests. They work to persuade donors to contribute money to foster children's welfare.

Thus, the question of how persuasion and ethics connect focuses on both the process and the ends. If the persuasion process distorts and shapes the decision to the advantage of the source against the interest of the receiver, it is unethical. But if the influence, such as motivating people to drive safely or contribute to a charity, is not manipulative and used for a bad end, then it is ethical. If both parties benefit, then persuasion is mutually beneficial and ethical.

Marketing communication can recommend that customer needs and wants can be satisfied by using a product or service. Public relations attempts to persuade customers to adopt a particular persona about the organization and view the organizational products and services favorably compared with those of its competitors. Nonprofit organizations struggle for legitimacy, as they must prove that they deserve contributor and donor support. Nonprofits do so by demonstrating the needs that they serve through their efforts. For instance, colleges and universities demonstrate that they contribute intellectual and social benefits to society. Although nonprofits rarely compete openly with other groups, each struggles to attract its share of limited resources. Because they are cause oriented, nonprofits demonstrate the seriousness of the problems that need remedy, often engaging in telemarketing to raise funds or motivating people to attend fund-raisers and make donations to help to achieve the group's strategic missions.

Organizations seek to persuade activists to adopt their point of view. The opposite is also true. This rhetorical exchange is constructive—if the participants see it as dialogue, not monologue. Persuasion can have positive community outcomes; if it allows citizens to understand and compare issue positions, it can even lead to collaborative decision making.

Collaborative Decision Making

MBRs suggest participation by both parties in the relationship. Participation should include decision making. Important decisions should be made in a collaborative fashion; both parties contribute to and have a voice in the decision. Unilateral decisions, those made by only one party in the relationship, violate the spirit of MBRs. Consider how many schools now involve students, parents, and alumni in decisions about dress codes, drug abuse, campus safety, and school performance on standardized tests. Both parties should contribute to decisions if both are to benefit from the decision. Unilateral decisions will either favor the decision makers or make the non–decision makers feel powerless and patronized—as if they are unable to look after their own best interests.

Businesses and other organizations have been prone to adopt an employee relationship approach that is called "command and control." This means that management designs work and tells employees what to do. An alternative approach is based on collaborative decision making. In keeping with that approach, public relations can help employees to be involved in organizational decisions by opening channels of communication and reporting the success stories that arise from employees participating in decision making. One chemical company in the Houston area has a 35-employee editorial board that decides the content of the employee newsletter, and management honors employees' requests for information by providing it for the newsletter.

Instead of taking activist battles to the street, the front page of the newspaper, or top-of-the-hour television or radio news, organizations have learned that creating problem-solving mechanisms can be useful. Collaborative decision-making efforts solve the problems that activists raise. In such efforts, activists have to be reasonable or lose their appeal to the community. For instance, rather than opposing the environmental groups trying to save the dolphins, tuna processors such as Starkist and Bumble Bee switched to buying tuna from fishermen who did not use nets that needlessly ensnared and killed dolphins. Collaborative efforts can make products more appealing and strengthen marketing advantage while satisfying homemaker requirements.

Cocreation of Meaning

Parties in an MBR need to be on the same page; they need to see and interpret the world in a similar fashion. Cocreation of meaning suggests that the organization and stakeholder share meanings—they have similar values, attitudes, and beliefs—which permit them to see events in the same way. Shared meaning promotes alignment.

Let us consider an example of an industrial accident that injures a number of workers. The organization will want to cocreate the meaning of the industrial accident with stakeholders. Ideally, the crisis is seen as an accident, something that is unavoidable and a necessary cost or risk of doing business. If employees create a different meaning, such as organizational negligence, there is a problem with these competing meanings. Cocreation of meaning is essential to the alignment function of MBRs. Narratives and identification both aid in the cocreation of meaning.

Narratives

Walter Fisher (1987), a leading communication theorist, has posed the tantalizing theory that narrative is the most basic form of communication. People tell stories to communicate facts and to shape values and attitudes. Narratives are so basic to human nature that news reports typically feature the elements of who, what, when, where, why, and how. If Fisher is correct, then people organize their lives as stories and their culture suggests appropriate and inappropriate ways to think and act. As you look at advertisements, do you think they tell a story? In such cases, they suggest that if we live a narrative involving the featured service or product, then we will live happily ever after. Sometimes they begin, "Once upon a time a person had a problem. . . ." But when she or he used a specific product the person lived happily ever after.

People are naturally drawn to narratives: dramas involving competing and conflicting characters. Even as children hearing bedtime stories, we enjoy a compelling plot in which good and evil do battle. The entire sports-entertainment industry is built on the human need for narratives: We cheer heroes and boo villains. People come together when they share narratives. Employees learn about and become a part of the organization when they learn and use the organization's stories. Narratives are another way to share meanings. People share meanings when they have similar views of the heroes, villains, and plots of stories. Through narratives, organizations and stakeholders can learn about one another and share meanings, both of which contribute to the formation of MBRs.

Public relations marketing messages often stress endorsements and testimonials. By featuring ordinary people or celebrities who use a product or a service, narratives are created to help customers think of themselves using the products or services as well. America's Dairy Farmers and Milk Processors have used a variety of celebrities in their "Got Milk?" campaign. Basketball player Kevin Garnett and tennis stars Venus and Serena Williams are among the celebrities to wear the signature milk moustache of the campaign. Each nonprofit has a story to tell. It features what it is doing, what it has done, and its commitment to the future. Stories are a substance of its fund-raising. Human interest stories abound that can attract donor and membership attention and prove that the organization contributes to the public interest.

Got Milk?

SOURCE: Reprinted with permission from Lowe Worldwide.

Stories are often the lifeblood of nonprofits. Many use the "poster child" theme to demonstrate the stark reality of a specific disease and its cure or rehabilitation. Stories help nonprofits to personalize their causes, from "once upon a time" to "happily ever after." Actress Roma Downey, speaking for Save the Children, tells the story of a specific child in a developing country. Potential donors see the child, and Save the Children's mission becomes personalized through the story. A vital part of the strategic mission of nonprofits is to think in terms of problems and project their solutions. Organizations are wise to enact a narrative of cooperation rather than combat. If the competing interests are thought of as characters in the drama, activists can often portray business leaders, other activists, or governmental officials as the bad guys. People for the Ethical Treatment of Animals (PETA) launched the successful "Murder King" Web campaign as a parody and protest against Burger King. Burger King is clearly the villain in PETA's tale of animal abuse. For that reason, a narrative of cooperation is preferred to confrontation by enlightened organizations working with activists. Journalism entails storytelling. Stories—news stories—are the stock-in-trade of those in the media. They think of the world in terms of story. They respond to press releases and other pitches by public relations persons in terms of whether what the public relations person says, or wants to have said, is indeed a story worthy of publication or broadcast.

Identification

People often share similarities or see part of themselves in another person or organization. Shared similarities can be called "identification." People, especially students, identify with their schools. People say "we won" or "we lost," not "the team" won or lost. The people are not members of the team, but through identification feel they are a part of the team. The school mascot becomes their identity: We are the fighting "Tornadoes," and "I am a Tornado." Identification can be a powerful motivator for changing attitudes and behaviors. We modify attitudes and behaviors to become more similar to those people or organizations with which we identify. Consider how people try to emulate their role models. It follows that identification can be a useful force in MBRs. Mutual identification should facilitate alignment as parties will want to become even more alike, including the meanings they attribute to events. Identification can promote alignment.

Identification is a key concept in Kenneth Burke's (1969) theory of rhetoric. As Quesinberry (2005) pointed out, achieving identification is a continuing challenge to public relations practitioners. They call for stakeholders to share common ground of interests, facts, and values. These can promote a sense of similarity, needed for a successful relationship, so that people want to support an organization rather than oppose it. This logic has implications for marketing, as well as the management of issues. It is vital to building MBRs.

Membership is a source of personal identification. People like to be attached to that which succeeds and benefits society. Nonprofit organizations create logos to identify themselves and differentiate themselves from similar groups. One of the best examples is the symbolism associated with colleges and universities, such as school colors, campus style, school pride, and mascots. Pins, buttons, and bumper stickers are important paraphernalia of identification. People come to see their self-concept and self-interest as part of their commitment to nonprofit organizations.

People in communities identify with organizations and industries in their community. The objective of sound public relations is to generate positive identification between the organization and the community in which it operates. People's identification can be called "community pride." Pride is a positive sense of community and a belief that the organization operates in the public interest. The opposite feeling, division, can occur when antagonism exists between organization and the community. Any sense of identification results from the relationship people believe exists between them and the organizations in their community.

BOX 3.2 IDENTIFICATION IN ACTION

People belong to nonprofits because they identify with the objectives. Through their memberships, they create new identifications. Some people identify with the victims that require the help of the organization. For instance, people identify with greyhounds that are bred to race. Once they no longer have that value, the dogs may be destroyed. That once was routine practice. Now the solution is to "adopt a greyhound." Nonprofits have used identifications, such as Mothers Against Drunk Driving (MADD) or mothers for March of Dimes. Mothers, as part of their hearth and home values, often see participation in nonprofits as a vital part of their identification.

Relationship Types and Tools

Later chapters discuss many of the types of relationships needed for an organization's success as well as the tools that can be used by practitioners to build, maintain, and repair those relationships. This final section of this chapter briefly reviews the factors relevant to relationships and points to the many kinds of stakeholder relationships and tools needed to be successful.

▶Conditions of Relationship Development

Chapter 1 introduced a list of factors that are relevant to solid relationships. No single list of factors is definitive. Based on research and practical observation, these seem quite important: openness, trustworthiness, cooperation, alignment of interests, compatibility of views and opinions, and commitment.

Standard lore advises organizations to be *open*. One of the tests of openness is their ability to be the first and best source of information relevant to all of their activities. It is obvious that organizations are privileged to keep trade secrets, information that gives them a competitive advantage. We may expect an organization to provide information about its operations, policies, products, and services, which publics legitimately want and need to make decisions. But a company, for instance, need not divulge trade secrets as long as they have proprietary value and don't compromise the genuine interest of some publics. Likewise, companies can implement antiterrorism measures. They can and should explain these measures in part. However, a full and open explanation could very well be used against the company and its stakeholders by terrorists.

Organizations need to think in terms of *building trust*. They must act and communicate in ways that foster trust. They start down this road by recognizing how vulnerable various interests may be to the organization's decisions and actions. Trust is built when organizations serve as stewards for the interest of their stakeholders and stakeseekers. Trust is built by understanding and meeting the expectations their MAPs hold for the organization. For instance, if the organization is expected to operate with high levels of employee and neighbor health and safety, then that must be the case. People deserve to trust the organization to do and say the "right thing."

Organizations should be *cooperative*. They must be willing to work with their constituents. They need to be proactive in spotting and solving problems. If they are called to hearings, they should come forward and be willing to defend their operations and executive choices. They need to communicate with their critics in ways that demonstrate a commitment to fostering relationships that are mutual.

If they are cooperative, organizations can demonstrate that their interests are aligned with their stakeholders'. A company wants customers to trust its product safety claims. Quite frankly, then, its products must meet or exceed safety standards. The organization demonstrates that its interests align with its stakeholders' when the interests of both are aligned. Customers want a safe product that performs as promoted, for instance. In this regard, the company must demonstrate aligned interests. A nonprofit wants to achieve a social good, such as protecting battered women. It demonstrates its ability to do that and appeals to donors to contribute because of these aligned interests.

Compatible views are crucial to a relationship. If a company claims to be committed to environmental responsibility as part of its relationship-building effort, its definition of environmental responsibility needs to be compatible with that of its publics. If the organization wants to attract the best and brightest employees, it needs to demonstrate that it has views that are compatible with that kind of employee.

Commitment is an essential ingredient in relationships. Is the company committed to product safety? Does the company hide behind legal interpretations when some higher ethical standard is more appropriate? Is the governmental agency truly committed to building better roads, improving public school education, or fostering public health? Commitment is a combination of action and statement: the good organization communicating well.

▶Venues and Tools

Because public relations deals with relationships with multiple publics, it operates in many venues and has several tools at its discretion. Brief attention to these relationship options suggests the variety and strategic challenge of public relations.

Customer relations is vital to businesses. Promotion and publicity are functions of public relations used to attract the interest of customers and motivate them to make purchases. However, businesses need to be open to customers' questions and complaints. Through tools such as home pages and FYIs, they can help customers to get value from their purchase. Customer relations can also listen to complaints and collaborate to solve problems.

Media relations is one of the traditional venues of public relations. Reporters want the organization to be open and committed to being the first and best source of information. They want to obtain relevant information. Media releases are issued to inform reporters. Practitioners create backgrounders, conduct press conferences, and provide material at their home pages to satisfy reporters' needs for information to develop stories on schedules.

Alumni relations help colleges and universities to accomplish their missions and visions. Alumni serve as a source of support, including financial contributions, needed for a successful educational institution. How can the relationship be mutual? What do alumni want in exchange for their financial support? They want information of educational accomplishment. They want to have and know about events such as homecoming, plays, musical performances, and student accomplishments. They want to know of the achievements of faculty. They want successful athletic programs.

Follower relations sustain nonprofits, such as activist groups. Activist organizations seek people who have aligned interests. They must demonstrate their commitment to achieve outcomes relevant to the cause. They ask for financial support from followers and must deliver successful outcomes, such as species protection, in exchange. This relationship, as is the case for all relationships, depends on social exchange—mutual benefit.

Investor relationships depend on information that is openly provided. This information must be relevant to investors' desires to buy, sell, and hold stock. The information must be timed so that all investors have an equal chance to get it and use it to make decisions. Investors must be able to trust the quality of the information. They want a business that has interests aligned with theirs.

This very brief list suggests some of the many kinds of relationships that are relevant to public relations efforts to broker the exchange between MAPs and organizations. Building, repairing, and maintaining relationships are essential to public relations. As John Hill wrote, organizations have public relations whether they are constructive and mutual or not. These relationships must be founded on solid ethical choices and a demonstrated commitment to corporate responsibility. The goal of effective public relations is to help the organization to be good and communicate effectively.

Conclusion

This chapter has detailed the idea of mutually beneficial relationships (MBRs), what we feel is the defining quality of today's public relations. We began by defining MBRs, moved to discussing how to establish MBRs, and ended with some of the objectives used in constructing MBRs. MBRs require an organization to meet stakeholder expectations, cooperate with stakeholders, and align organizational interests with those of its stakeholders. With multiple and often conflicting stakeholders, managing MBRs is not always easy. Five factors are essential to establishing MBRs: keeping a consistent voice, making sure your messages reflect the truth, ensuring two-way communication,

Engaging in Community Relations

Graham Painter, APR
Senior Vice
   President—Corporate
   Communications
Sterling Bank
Houston, Texas

Note: This professional reflection was written by Mr. Painter when he was the vice president of Public Relations for CenterPoint Energy of Houston, Texas, successor to Houston Lighting & Power Co. (HL&P). His comments demonstrate how positive commitment to community relations is essential, although not without challenges. He recognizes the need for mutually beneficial relationships with customers.

It was turning out to be another South Texas scorcher. As the sun began to light up the sky, you could already see there wasn't a cloud in sight. It was barely 6 a.m., and the temperature stood at 89, heading up to the triple digits again. I started the day by scanning the local paper to see the new count: over 120 dead in Texas from this summer's furnace-like heat. Thank God for air-conditioning.

Trouble is, not everyone in Texas has air-conditioning, and many of those who do can't afford to run it. Air-conditioning can really drive an electric meter, and if you're on a fixed income trying to make ends meet, air-conditioning may be an unaffordable luxury. Except that in a summer of unprecedented and relentless heat, air-conditioning and the electricity to run it both take on very different roles.

Over the previous weeks, we'd issued a number of news releases warning customers of the unusual heat and offering to make extended payment arrangements for anyone who needed them. Our president was quoted as saying customers should not refrain from using air-conditioning for fear of defaulting on their electric bills and having the power cut off. HL&P will work out a payment plan with anyone who needs one, he said.

Others were helping, too. The federal government had allocated $1 million to the Houston area for heat relief. The money was being administered by a local charity, and we had offered space at one of our Houston offices to help them screen applicants. The building was conveniently located on a number of city bus routes and had lots of small offices to give the applicants some privacy while they were interviewed.

At 9:30 my phone rang. The executive in charge of the building where customers were being screened was having a problem. Hundreds of people were in line to apply, she said, far more than expected, and the line wrapped around the block. The heat was really climbing, there was little shade, and the crowd was getting restless. Now a television news crew was setting up. I asked our media relations manager to drive over and help out.

In the meantime, I was scheduled to meet with the company president on a plan he had to move funds from power plant payments to public aid. It had never been done before and would require the approval of the state Public Utility Commission. We needed to determine how much to recommend be moved and to anticipate what questions the regulators would have. What would consumer groups say? Do we need to explain the complex accounting issues to the news media? Is there a better way to help?

At about 10:30, the media relations manager called. "It's a disaster," she said in staccato bursts, clearly agitated. "Hundreds in line, withering heat, and rumors that the interviewers won't be able to see everybody today. A fight broke out over positions in line, and one lady fainted. Police, concerned about more heat strokes in the crowd, recommended that the fire department spray a cooling mist over those in line—all filmed by local TV. Moments ago, pandemonium, but order is now being restored."

"Is the lady getting medical help?" I asked.

"Yes, fire department paramedics are here."

"Have you had a chance to talk with reporters?"

"Not all of them," she said. "Some left before I could get to them. I'm calling them now; but be sure to watch the news at noon."

All the local television stations covered the event. The coverage was up-close and breathless, and an incorrect message came through on every broadcast: Customers lining up to beg for extra time to pay their light bills got hosed down by police.

That afternoon we communicated with every television and radio station and the city's major newspaper explaining what had really happened. Customers weren't begging for extra time to pay their bills, they were seeking federal funding, and HL&P had loaned its offices to help agencies administer the money. The company also had numerous assistance plans in place to help low income customers.

The local evening news set the story straight. But the incorrect earlier stories had now moved to the networks. That's right, that same exciting footage of fainting and spraying was now on all networks plus CNN, and the story was the original "wrong" version: People seeking help from their power company get hosed by police!

There was a real temptation to drop everything and fight the incorrect coverage, but my experience with network news is not good. Trying to get a correction to yesterday's news is normally a monumental waste of time. The media manager and I caucused on the phone that night. We decided to avoid being defensive and instead focus entirely on positive actions. We discussed holding a news conference and rolling out the president's funding plan with him as the speaker. We also committed to focusing on all the other positive things we were doing to help customers cope with the heat. My day was over after midnight, but I needed to be at work early the next day to get internal buy-in to our plan.

The aftermath of the event was positive. Regulators quickly approved our president's innovative plan to move an unprecedented $5 million into an account for public aid to be administered by a local United Way agency. It was the largest such amount we knew of ever being donated by a power company. The news conference got significant positive local coverage and, more importantly, the money provided a real shot in the arm for people trying to make it through Texas' hottest summer on record. Most importantly, there was no loss of life in our area from lack of electric power. A month later, hardly anyone remembered that we'd been blamed for the misinterpreted event. Staying cool when the news got hot was the right choice.

SOURCE: Reprinted with permission from Graham Painter.

being proactive, and identifying and creating opportunity. Message development objectives help practitioners to use the five factors; they are the specific communication objectives practitioners can use to construct MBRs. Each of the eight message development objectives was defined and multiple examples of each were given featuring relevant stakeholders. As public relations evolves as a field, it becomes more complex. As practitioners, your understanding of public relations must be as complex as the field itself if you are to be an effective practitioner. We believe it is important that practitioners understand MBRs and understand how to pursue them on the job.

Strategic decisions of the kinds discussed in this section, and throughout this chapter, should highlight the challenges of the profession. As you think back on what this chapter has meant to you, reflect on the objectives at the beginning of the chapter. Do you believe the chapter helped you to accomplish those objectives? Do you have a better appreciation for relationships as the building blocks of public relations? Are you more aware of guidelines that can help you know how to enhance relationships as part of your professional practice? Do you better understand the types of relationships that are valuable to an organization's success? Do you know the message development objectives that can be used to an create, sustain, and repair relationships?

The management of relationships requires strategic stewardship. Companies and other types of organizations learn the hard way that they cannot act only in their interests. They must serve larger interests. In the most general sense, this is called the "public interest," even though each public has its unique interest. In fact, its unique interest defines its nature as a public. The organization can use message development objectives to achieve its stewardship of these interests.

FURTHER EXPLORATION

3

Ethical Quandary: The Quality of Relationships as the Basis of Ethics

In 1990, Hill & Knowlton, a prestigious U.S. public relations firm, had a $10.7 million contract with the Citizens for a Free Kuwait. Essentially, the organization was paying Hill & Knowlton to make people aware of Kuwait and how it was suffering from an invasion by Iraq. Others claim it was a thinly veiled attempt by the Kuwaiti government to build support for U.S. and international intervention on its behalf. In addition to the usual press conferences, "Free Kuwait" rallies and T-shirts, video news releases, and advertisements, Hill & Knowlton did extensive preparatory work for witnesses testifying before the Congressional Human Rights Caucus. The testimony has been considered a pivotal step in getting the United States to support military intervention. The most compelling testimony was given by Nayirah, a 15-year-old Kuwaiti who testified to Iraqi soldiers taking babies from incubators in Kuwait and leaving them to die on the floor. This is an example of the "atrocity story," which historically has been a popular tool for winning support for wars. President George H. W. Bush used this image numerous times in his pro-intervention speeches.

The story became a rallying point for factions in the United States that wanted to send troops to fight the Iraqis. Unknown to most hearing the testimony, Nayirah was the daughter of the Kuwaiti ambassador to the U.S. Moreover, two independent aid agencies and interviews with doctors at the Kuwaiti hospital could not confirm the story.

Hill & Knowlton came under intense fire after two network broadcasts and two books broke the story after the Gulf War. While no one believes Hill & Knowlton created the Gulf War, people do wonder if it is right for public relations firms to use their persuasive skills to encourage participation in a war in order to promote military intervention. Did the campaign use fictional emotional images to blunt a legitimate dialogue over military intervention in the Gulf? What responsibility does Hill & Knowlton have to reveal its true client? The U.S. government requires detailed paperwork for foreign clients of public relations practitioners. The records show that over 90% of the money came from the Kuwaiti government. Hill & Knowlton should have known the identity of the real client. Did the audiences consuming their messages have the right to know? These two issues raise relational issues for Hill & Knowlton and for the Kuwaiti government. Did the desire to make money override moral and ethical concerns at Hill & Knowlton? How will this episode affect the reactions of audiences to future efforts from Hill & Knowlton? How will these revelations affect how publics in the U.S. react to future foreign policy issues relating to Kuwait? Both the nature of the ethical dilemma and its possible effects on future relationships must be considered.

Consider the criteria of effective relationships. Which of the guidelines can help you to consider the connection between the quality of a relationship and its need for ethical standards? Write a short essay in which you critique the ethical choices in the Kuwait case. Use each of the five guidelines as a part of your essay.

Summary Questions

1. What are the characteristics of a mutually beneficial relationship (MBR)?

2. Why is the objective to build, repair, and maintain MBRs a sound philosophical approach to public relations?

3. What five guidelines can be applied to build MBRs?

4. What is the common misconception related to being proactive?

5. Why is two-way communication essential to building MBRs?

6. What does it mean for an organization to have a consistent voice?

7. Give an example of an organization creating an opportunity.

8. How are always being proactive and identifying and creating opportunities related?

9. Select a typical relationship identified in the chapter. Think of a specific organization that fits that kind of relationship. Explain why it fits that relationship and how it can use message development objectives (MDOs) to succeed in building that relationship.

10. What is an MDO?

11. What does it mean for an organization to pursue cocreation of meaning?

12. How are narrative, identification, and symbolic convergence related to the cocreation of meaning?

13. Why is attention an MDO?

Exercises

1. Find a copy of an annual report for a publicly traded company, for a nonprofit organization, or for a governmental organization. (Note: You may be able to find these reports at organizations' home pages on their Web sites.) Analyze this report for efforts to cocreate meaning. What meaning was the organization trying to cocreate with its stakeholders? Did the author of the document use narratives, symbolic convergence, and/or identification to cocreate meaning? What narratives were used, and how did they attempt to cocreate meaning? What symbolic perspectives were used in the documents, and how did they attempt to cocreate meaning? What efforts were used to establish identification, and how did they attempt to cocreate meaning?

2. Research a local nonprofit organization. Find out its mission and what special challenges it faces trying to achieve that mission. Also, identify which MDOs are used. Then, evaluate how well or poorly it uses these MDOs. What else could the organization do to build MBRs?

3. Follow the campaign of a politician in the newspaper, on television, and on the radio. In your research, differentiate between the candidate's use of paid advertisement and the accounts of the candidate's activities, image, and policy positions that appear in news stories. Were any events used to attract attention to the candidate and create identifications between the candidate and key constituent groups? Identify which MDOs were used in the campaign. Then, evaluate how well or poorly these MDOs were used. What else could the campaign do to build MBRs?

4. Do research to locate a problem that exists within your community. Explain what organizations might have a stake in this problem. How could these organizations use the problem as an opportunity? What actions would be necessary to use these opportunities to achieve the mission of the organization?

Recommended Readings

Beach, L. R. (1996). *Decision making in the workplace.* Mahwah, NJ: Lawrence Erlbaum.

Bowman, C. (1990). *The essence of strategic management.* New York: Prentice Hall.

Dilenschneider, R. L. (1996). Leadership in the 21st century. *Public Relations Tactics, 3*(8), 27.

Dozier, D. M., Grunig, L. A., & Grunig, J. A. (1995). *Manager's guide to excellence in public relations and communication management.* Mahwah, NJ: Lawrence Erlbaum.

Fishbein, M., & Ajzen, I. (1975). *Belief, attitude, intention, and behavior.* Reading, MA: Addison-Wesley.

Heath, R. L. (1997). *Strategic issues management: Organizations and public policy challenges* (see especially chap. 1). Thousand Oaks, CA: Sage.

Hunger, J. D., & Wheelen, T. L. (1993). *Strategic management* (4th ed.). Reading, MA: Addison-Wesley.

Hunt, T., & Grunig, J. E. (1994). *Public relations techniques.* Fort Worth, TX: Harcourt Brace.

Kelly, K. S. (1991). *Fund-raising and public relations: A critical analysis.* Hillsdale, NJ: Lawrence Erlbaum.

Kelly, K. S. (1998). *Effective fund-raising management* (see especially chap. 10). Mahwah, NJ: Lawrence Erlbaum.

Ledingham, J. A., & Bruning, S. D. (2001). Management community relationships to maximize mutual benefit: Doing well by doing good. In R. L. Heath (Ed.), *Handbook of public relations* (pp. 527–534). Thousand Oaks, CA: Sage.

Spicer, C. (1997). *Organizational public relations: A political perspective.* Mahwah, NJ: Lawrence Erlbaum.

Trujillo, N., & Toth, E. L. (1987). Organizational paradigms for public relations research and practice. *Management Communication Quarterly, 1,* 199–281.

Wilson, L. J. (2001). Relationships within communities: Public relations for the new century. In R. L. Heath (Ed.), *Handbook of public relations* (pp. 521–526). Thousand Oaks, CA: Sage.

4

The Value of Research

arberton Citizens Hospital (BCH) was founded in 1915 to serve the residents of Barberton, Ohio (population 27,000+), a blue-collar suburb of Akron. In 1996, BCH became part of a for-profit hospital chain. The current owner is Triad Hospitals, Inc., of Plano, Texas. A 2001 survey found that people in the area perceived BCH as "low-tech" and that patients were sent to other area hospitals for specialty services. This is not a very desirable position of a hospital among its markets, audiences, and publics. BCH realized some changes needed to be made.

In 2002, BCH decided to expand its facilities. The expansion would provide new services, improve existing facilities, and provide much-needed parking. Their old parking deck was outdated and in an inconvenient location for its new emergency room. The only space to expand was into an adjacent city park. BCH would require eight acres from the park. The city charter stipulated that a two-thirds vote of the citizens, a supermajority, was

Making a Difference in Barberton

SOURCE: Reprinted with permission from Barberton Citizens Hospital.

required to transfer park land. The issue would be placed on a special May 2003 ballot. The challenge facing BCH was to win two thirds of the vote. Before taking any action, managers at BCH needed to understand the situation. The best way to understand a situation is to conduct research, a systematic collection of information/data.

BCH conducted a survey of potential voters in January of 2003. If BCH already had enough support, everything would be fine. The survey found that 51% approved of the sale, 44% opposed, and 6% were undecided. BCH was well short of the 67%. In fact, 29% of those opposed were strongly opposed, meaning it would be difficult to change their views. Focus groups were conducted to get a deeper understanding of how the supporters, opponents, and mixed publics viewed the issue. The focus group results suggested that people needed to understand why the park was the best option for expansion and who was endorsing the sale. BCH now had a better understanding of the situation. BCH knew it faced a rhetorical problem; they needed to build support to win the vote. Research gave insights into the types of information they should include in their messages.

The vignette used to open this chapter illustrates a strategic approach to public relations. Research, more precisely preliminary research, sheds light on the problem. The information collected in the research is used to guide the planning and execution of the campaign. Then, research skills are used to evaluate the public relations efforts to determine success or failure. This is the basic four-step public relations action: research, planning, execution, and evaluation. We view the need for public relations actions to be rooted in rhetorical problems. This chapter provides an overview of what research is, the two basic types of research, the primary research methods used in public relations, research to understand rhetorical problems, and research to understand markets, audiences, and publics (MAPs).

Research

Research is the systematic collection and interpretation of information. Another name for information is *data*. *Systematic* means there is a focus or point to the information collection. When you go to the library to research a paper, you have a focus. You are looking for information relevant to your paper topic. Similarly, public relations practitioners collect information related to their concerns. In the BCH example described in the opening vignette, they needed information about how people would vote on the park land sale issue. Research that helps to explain the current situation is called *preliminary research,* and it is used to plan the public relations effort. In contrast, *evaluative research* is used to determine the success or failure of a public relations effort. Both forms of research use the same basic methods and tools; the difference is the focus. This chapter concentrates on preliminary research that is used to inform the planning (Chapter 5) and execution (Chapter 6). Evaluative research is covered in Chapter 7.

Research can be categorized a number of different ways. Common categories for research include (a) theoretical and applied, (b) primary and secondary, and (c) informal/qualitative and formal/quantitative. Exploring these categories will give you a better sense of the richness that is research.

▶Applied and Theoretical Research

Theoretical and applied research concentrate on the different goals of research. *Theoretical research* seeks to test theories or parts of theories. In Chapter 8, five public relations theories are discussed. Each had been the subject of multiple research studies designed to "test" whether the theory holds true. The goal is to develop and to advance theory. *Applied research* seeks solutions to everyday problems. A public relations researcher may be interested in improving the retention of information from a public health message. The goal is to solve practical problems. At times, research can be both theoretical and applied. An applied study might help to advance theory, and a theoretical study might find practical solutions to problems (Stewart, 2002). Public relations research by its nature is "practical," meaning that even theoretical research will be applied. There may be theoretical physics, but not theoretical public relations. All five theories in Chapter 8 have produced research that provides solutions to problems encountered by practitioners, as well as advancing theory.

▶Primary and Secondary Research

Primary and *secondary* differentiate research based on whether or not the information collected is original or was collected by some other person or organization. When you, someone else in your organization, or a paid consultant collects information to address a specific concern, that is *primary research. Secondary research* involves examining studies that are already published or data that were collected for some other project but could prove useful to you. Gallup and Harris public opinion polls, U.S. Census data, *Fortune* magazine's "Most Admired Companies," and Environmental Protection Agency (EPA) data on hazardous chemical release responses are all secondary research. You can find secondary data at government Web sites, some corporate Web sites, libraries, and online databases. Primary and secondary research share the same methods; the difference is whether or not the data are original or preexisting. In secondary research, you might reanalyze the data yourself or use summaries of the data provided by the original researcher. The advantage is that someone else spends the time and money to collect the data. The disadvantages are that it may not be the exact information you need, and you may not know how accurate the information is (Stacks, 2002).

▶ Informal and Formal Research

The informal/qualitative and formal/quantitative is the most frequently used categorization of research. That is why we are using it to organize the discussion of research methods. Research methods, tools for collecting information, can be divided into informal and formal. *Informal research* is very subjective; the people collecting the data can interpret the information in different ways. For instance, the case study is an informal method. The data are observations, and researchers then interpret the information—decide what the data mean to them. Five different people can look at the same case study information and come to different conclusions about what management did right or wrong in the situation. However, information methods can provide details of what people think or feel. In the BCH example, an informal method (focus group research) was used to understand how voters felt about the land sale issue. Informal research methods are often referred to as *qualitative research*.

Formal research is objective. The data are collected in the form of numbers and analyzed using statistical programs. The statistical analysis is objective because there are set rules for interpreting the results of various statistical analyses. Five researchers looking at the results of the same statistical test will reach the same conclusion. Because of the reliance on numbers, formal research is often called *quantitative research* (Stacks, 2002). Both formal and informal research have their strengths and weaknesses. A full discussion of research methods is beyond the scope of this book. We want to familiarize you with some of the basic research methods you will utilize in public relations. We have selected the three most common research methods used in public relations: in-depth interviews and focus groups, content analysis, and surveys.

In-Depth Interviews and Focus Groups

An in-depth interview is a semistructured interview. Job and marketing interviews are structured interviews, in which the interviewer asks a set series of questions. The in-depth interview allows the interviewee (person being asked the questions) to control the interview. The interviewer has a set of general questions designed to get the interviewee talking. The questions are open-ended, which means the interviewee can say whatever he or she likes. Closed-ended questions give interviewees a set list of options from which to choose, such as "agree, neutral, or disagree." The interviewer listens to the interviewee and asks follow-up questions to get additional information about the topic. Where the interview goes after the initial question depends on the response of the interviewee, because the interviewer is developing follow-up questions based on those responses. A series of in-depth interviews may be on the same topics and use the same basic questions but can go in very different directions. Accenture, an international management consulting firm, used a series of in-depth interviews to collect information from past and prospective clients. The interviews were designed to discover how this target group was defining high-performance business. The in-depth interviews were based on open-ended questions, such as "How do you define high-performance business?" Respondents did not give the exact same answers.

Focus groups are like in-depth interviews in which 3 to 20 people are interviewed at the same time. A moderator leads the group through the interview by asking open-ended questions and probing people's responses. The quality of an in-depth interview or a focus group is dependent on the skill of interviewer/moderator. The skilled interviewer/moderator asks relevant follow-up questions and digs deeper into the answers. In-depth interviews and focus groups are excellent for finding out why people feel or think a certain way or what information they would like to know. BCH used focus groups to find out what people wanted to know about the park land sale. Accenture used focus groups to determine that Tiger Woods was a perfect reflection of high-performance business. That is why he became a fixture worldwide in Accenture's corporate image advertising.

Both in-depth and focus groups are audio-recorded and then transcribed. Transcription involves writing down exactly what each person said in the interview or focus groups. Sometimes focus groups are videotaped, and people's nonverbal reactions are examined by researchers. The researchers might look at facial expressions or gestures used when giving a response. The transcripts are then analyzed for themes. *Themes* are when people give similar responses. For BCH, people wanting to know why the park was the best expansion option is an example of a theme. Themes suggest how people think or feel. Finding themes is a matter of interpretation: There is a subjective element to informal methods. Three researchers might look at the same transcripts and select different themes. Still, in-depth interviews and focus groups are cost-effective ways for understanding MAPs.

Content Analysis

Content analysis is "a systematic, objective, and quantitative method for research messages" (Stacks, 2002, p. 107). Any written material can be content analyzed, even transcripts from in-depth interviews and focus groups. Content analysis is a bridge between informal and formal research. Effective content analysis is objective, and the messages are translated into numbers that can be statistically analyzed. Many audits are content analysis. If you were to audit your Web site to determine the different types of information presented on the Web site or online discussions of your organization to determine positive and negative statements, you would be using content analysis. Cingular Wireless audited other wireless companies' teen programs before developing one of its own. The audit involved identifying the content of each teen program.

The key to content analysis is developing a reliable category system and training coders. Content analysis begins by determining your unit of analysis, the things you are actually going to count. A unit of analysis can be words, themes, or stories. You then create a category system. The category system provides the boxes in which you place the units. For instance, media coverage of an organization is often coded as favorable, neutral, or unfavorable. Cingular developed a system for coding the advice wireless companies gave teens for using wireless phones while driving. The categories need to be mutually exclusive and exhaustive. *Mutually exclusive* means a unit cannot fit in more than one box. *Exhaustive* means most of the data fit into a specific category. You want over 90% of the units to fit into a category. Any time you code, you create an "other" box for units that do not fit. If over 10% of your data go into the "other" box, it is time to rethink the categories, because they are not exhaustive.

People trained to use the category system are called *coders*. Coders then code: They place units into the categories. Content analysis involves two or more coders. A key to being objective and systematic is that the coders agree on how a unit should be coded.

Agreement is called *intercoder reliability*. There are specific statistical analyses you can use to compute intercoder reliability. You want agreement on at least 90% of all codes; the coders disagree less than 1 out of 10 times. Only precise categories will lead to high levels or agreement/reliability. Content analysis moves away from one person's subjective interpretation of a message to two or more people agreeing on the interpretation of a message.

Surveys

Surveys are the most common research method used in public relations. A survey is "a method of gathering relatively in-depth information about respondent attitudes and beliefs" (Stacks, 2002, p. 175). A survey is composed of a series of questions or items. These items are typically closed-ended questions; the respondent is given a limited set of response options from which to choose. Box 4.1 provides some sample survey items and scales. BCH used surveys to determine how many people opposed, supported, or were neutral on the park land sale. The answers to the survey items are then converted to numbers and examined using statistical programs. Box 4.1 has some notes on converting survey items into data.

BOX 4.1 SAMPLE SURVEY ITEMS AND SCORING

Below are the directions and items for the Organizational Reputation Scale (Coombs & Holladay, 2002). This scale uses the Likert Scale.

INSTRUCTIONS: Think about the case you have just read. The items below concern your impression of the organization and the crisis. Circle one number for each of the questions. The responses range from 1 = STRONGLY DISAGREE to 5 = STRONGLY AGREE.

1. The organization is concerned with the well-being of its publics.	1 STRONGLY DISAGREE	2	3	4	5 STRONGLY AGREE

1. The organization is concerned with the well-being of its publics.   1 STRONGLY DISAGREE   2   3   4   5 STRONGLY AGREE

2. The organization is basically DISHONEST.   1 STRONGLY DISAGREE   2   3   4   5 STRONGLY AGREE

3. I do NOT trust the organization to tell the truth about the incident.   1 STRONGLY DISAGREE   2   3   4   5 STRONGLY AGREE

4. Under most circumstances, I would be likely to believe what the organization says.   1 STRONGLY DISAGREE   2   3   4   5 STRONGLY AGREE

5. The organization is NOT concerned with the well-being of its publics.   1 STRONGLY DISAGREE   2   3   4   5 STRONGLY AGREE

Each item is given a numerical value or score based on the response of the participant. For items 1 and 4, a "1" is given "1," a "2" is given a "2," and so on. Items 2, 3, and 5 must be reverse scored because the item is worded negatively. A "1" is given a "5," a "2" is given a "4," and so on. A score for Organizational Reputation is calculated by adding up the scores from the five items; the higher the score, the stronger the perceptions of the organization's reputation. An organization can score as high as 25 or as low as 5.

A semantic differential scale could be used to measure organizational reputation as well. Sample items might include the following:

1. Dishonorable   ____ ____ ____ ____ ____   Honorable
2. Trustworthy   ____ ____ ____ ____ ____   Untrustworthy
3. Harmful   ____ ____ ____ ____ ____   Helpful

You can give the responses to the semantic differential scales numerical scores 1 to 5, just like the Likert scale responses. Item 2 would be reverse coded, because the favorable descriptor is on the left.

Respondents can be given a survey in a number of ways, including in person, over the phone, by land mail, by e-mail, or by visiting a Web site. Each method has its advantages and disadvantages. Table 4.1 reviews those advantages and disadvantages. Earlier, we noted that this is not a book on research methods. There are a number

Table 4.1: Comparing Administration Techniques for Surveys

	Advantages	Disadvantages
Postal Mail	Covers large geographic area Reasonable cost Selective sampling Anonymity for respondents Leisurely response for participants	Low response rate Slow return time Cannot clarify items Respondents are unknown
Telephone	Covers large geographic area Random-digit dialing sampling Can clarify items Moderate response rate	High staffing costs Research may influence responses Feels like marketing No visual items possible Only get who is at home
Face-to-face	Can collect observable data Can develop rapport High response rate	High staffing costs Research may influence responses Liability if interviewers are injured while collecting data
Online	Data are entered directly into the computer Somewhat novel	Technology cost Technology competence

SOURCE: Stewart (2002).

of excellent books on that subject. However, we do need to cover a number of concepts to provide an accurate picture of public relations research. Box 4.2 provides tips on how to write surveys, which are sometimes called *questionnaires*. When we talk about surveys, we need to address sampling.

BOX 4.2 SURVEY/QUESTIONNAIRE DESIGN

Surveys, especially printed ones, are also known as questionnaires. Writing a good questionnaire is not as easy as picking a scale and jotting down a few questions/items. Good questionnaires have properly written questions and effective design. This box reviews key points for writing questions/items and overall questionnaire design.

Writing Effective Questions/Items

1. Make the questions clear, including the words. Do not use jargon. Also avoid vague questions, such as "Do you like water?" Does this mean to drink, to swim in, or to view?

2. Keep questions short. Long questions can become confusing.

3. Provide complete instructions for how people should answer the questions. Should they circle their responses? Should they select only one response?

4. Be realistic in what people can recall about your organization and/or message. Asking people to recall trivial material or asking for very detailed recall will yield bad results because human memory does have limits.

5. Avoid "double-barrel" questions—questions that ask two things at once. "How do you feel about our new delivery options, and is the speed of delivery what you desire?" The respondent faces a dilemma—which question should be answered? How will you know which one he or she answered when you are evaluating the data?

6. Avoid biased words or terms. "Do you like the despicable marketing tactics used by McDonald's?" The words shape the respondents' reactions.

7. Avoid leading questions, questions that suggest the answer/response in their wording. "Do you believe that Congress should prohibit insurance companies from raising rates?" "You wouldn't want to go to Rudolpho's Restaurant for the company's annual party, would you?"

Questionnaire Design

- Stay focused on the purpose. Make sure the questions address the information you need to collect.

- Do not make it too long. Respondents will get fatigued and either stop answering questions or provide you "quick" answers.

- Vary the questions to avoid respondents falling into a pattern. Do not make all the questions either positively or negatively worded. Respondents may begin to skim the questions and follow a pattern rather than reading them carefully. Say you have three questions about the community relations of your organization. "1. The organization treats the community well." "2. The organization is a *positive* influence in the community." "3. The organization works to solve community problems." It would be best to alter the second question to read "2. The organization is a *negative* influence in the community." This breaks the pattern of positively worded questions and helps you to determine whether respondents are actually reading each item.

You use surveys to find information about MAPs—to listen to them. Odds are that you will not be able to survey every possible MAP; that is too expensive and time-consuming. Instead, you select a group of people from a MAP to complete the survey. This selection of people is known as a *sample*. How you select the sample has important implications for the information you collect. The more the sample reflects the characteristics of your target group, the more certain you are that the results reflect how that target group feels. The technical term for a sample that reflects your target group is a *representative sample*.

A representative sample is created through scientific selection of the sample. Sampling techniques can be scientific or unscientific. Table 4.2 reviews the primary sampling methods. Unscientific samples are *convenience samples*. You use people who are easy to get, rather than carefully selecting the sample. A *representative sample* means you are very confident that the information provided by your sample reflects how the larger target public feels. In the BCH example, the use of a scientific sample allows management to understand where voters stood on the park land sale issue. A nonscientific sample is not considered representative: It may or may not reflect how the larger target audience feels or thinks. Time and financial constraints may limit your ability to generate a scientific sample (Stacks, 2002).

Audits: Combining Research Methods

It would be a mistake to think that public relations practitioners use only one research method to collect information. In reality, a number of methods might be used to collect the information necessary to build an effective public relations effort. The communication audit is an excellent illustration of using multiple methods. An audit can be used to identify MAP perceptions of an organization, perceptions of messages, or perceptions of the organization's communication vehicles (Kinnick, 2005). Audits are receiver oriented because they ask receivers how they feel about an organization, its communication channels, and/or its messages.

Table 4.2: Sampling Methods

A. Probability Samples: These use random selection of the people in the sample. Every person in the targeted MAP (what is called a "sampling frame") has an equal chance of being included in the sample.

  1. Simple Random Sampling: Names are selected at random from a complete list of names. A computer typically does the random selection.
  2. Systematic Sampling: A list of possible people is compiled, a starting point is selected at random, and then every "nth" (7th or 31st, for example) name is selected from the list.
  3. Stratified Random Sample: People are first categorized by some characteristic (stratified). Then a simple random or systematic sample technique is used to draw a sample from each group/strata.

B. Nonprobability Samples: These do not involve random selection and may be biased in some way. There are times when a researcher cannot determine a complete sampling frame, so a nonprobability sample is used.

  1. Convenience Sample: Researchers simply take whoever is available: for example, students in a class or diners in a restaurant.
  2. Purposive Sample: Researchers select participants based on certain characteristics, such as lifestyle or driving habits. Research attempts to recruit people with these characteristics.
  3. Snowball Sample: This is also known as a networking sample. People who participate in the study are asked to recruit others to participate or to provide the names of people they know who might participate (Holladay, 2005).

Lerbinger (1997) divided audits into three categories: public relations audits, communication audits, and social audits. Public relations audits examine how well the messages and channels are at building positive relations with MAPs. A practitioner might use the public relations audit to evaluate the organization's reputation and determine how well it matches its identity (how management thinks the organization should be perceived) or to check on whether certain communication channels are reaching the desired MAPs. Communication audits are used to evaluate communication vehicles and to determine whether messages reached the desired MAPs. Social audits evaluate an organization's social responsibility actions, such as whether people are aware of the actions and MAPs' perceptions of the organization as socially responsible.

The communication audit can serve to illustrate how audits mix methods. Our objective is to improve the number of times and length of time customers visit MacCorp's Web site. We begin with a focus group and in-depth interviews with customers to find out why they visit the Web site and what content would make the Web site more attractive to them. This qualitative/subjective information would be used to construct a survey that we send a randomly selected sample of customers. The focus would be on determining what information people want at the Web site. Next, we would perform a content analysis of the Web site. The content analysis would indicate whether or not the Web site has the information desired by the customers. The content of the Web site would be adjusted to better suit the needs of the customers. We have used all the research methods discussed so far to make MacCorp's Web site more appealing.

WEB WATCHER: SILVER ANVIL AWARDS

The Public Relations Society of America (PRSA) presents the Silver Anvil awards annually to recognize excellence in public relations. PRSA has an archive of summaries of past winners at its Web site (http://prcdemo.prsa.org/silveranvil.htm). Visit the site and find a summary. The address takes you to the search engine for the Silver Anvils. Answer these two questions using your summary: "What type of information was collected for formative research?" and "How did this information shape the objectives of the public relations action?"

BOX 4.3 JOHN HILL

John Hill, one of the cofounders of the Hill & Knowlton Agency, offered the following advice to practitioners and corporate managers: "A corporation or an industry may find itself faced by unfavorable public opinion because people are unaware of the facts. The way is then open for the corporation to attempt to change the public attitude and to win people to its point of view. On the other hand it may be wise to change an unpopular policy, making a frank acknowledgement of need for change. Such declaration of honest intent will usually meet with public approval" (Hill, 1958, p. 39).

Using Research to Solve Rhetorical Problems

In this section of the chapter, we shift from explaining research methods and concepts to applying them. As noted earlier, public relations research is *applied:* It tries to solve problems or utilize opportunities. This section examines how research is used to understand the situation and MAPs, two vital concerns when either solving a problem or using an opportunity. Researching these topics provides the information practitioners need to be strategic. Strategic public relations efforts are developed to achieve specific goals. Before developing strategy, the practitioner must understand the situation he or she is facing. We think of the situation as a rhetorical problem. Each public relations effort may be designed to solve one or more rhetorical problems. A *rhetorical problem* is the perceived or actual gap between what a market, audience, or public believes and does and what it should believe and do. In terms of public relations, a rhetorical problem is a gap in agreement, alignment of interests, cocreated meaning, shared understanding, shared facts and their interpretation, motivation, interests, evaluations, behavior, or conclusions. A difference of opinion is a rhetorical problem. A difference in motivation is a rhetorical problem.

A rhetorical problem exists when managers are challenged in knowing what to do or say to create, maintain, or restore mutually beneficial relationships. If customers knew about a company's products or services, they would not need to be informed through publicity and promotion. If donors were willing to give money to support an organization's charitable mission, they would not need to be motivated. If activists approved of the company's operations, practitioners would not need to deal with conflict through negotiation and collaborative decision making. If executives knew what was on the minds of customers or activists, they would not need to listen to them—to conduct research. In short, if all went well, executives would not need the functions performed by public relations. Because rhetorical problems arise, strategic-planning responses are needed.

A threat is a problem. A missed opportunity would be a problem. Seeing an opportunity and not responding to it: That is a problem. Not making the proper response to a threat or an opportunity—each would be a problem. Allowing an emergency to become a crisis that turns into an issue: That is a problem. Having potential customers or donors (audiences) unaware of the charity and those that need it: That is a problem. If these people were not properly informed of the organization's products, services, and charitable activities, that would be a problem. If they were not motivated to buy products or contribute money to the organization, that would be a problem. If the organization is not open to its customers or donors and does not demonstrate its commitment to them, that is a problem. Having deteriorating relationships with key stakeholders: That is a problem. Having deteriorating relationships turn into an issue leading to laws and regulations: Those are problems. Not looking for and responding to opportunities—those would be problems.

A rhetorical statement—public relations response—is strategic communication selected from an array of options. Strategic selection of the statement or action is calculated to maximize the outcomes for all interested parties.

As a threat, a rhetorical problem is a concern or an issue position that one or more entities (such as an activist group) has developed to which an organization must respond. A crisis would be one example, as would the rhetorical appeals of an activist group that is challenging—criticizing—assumptions basic to the organization's operations. A rhetorical problem can result from market shift, drop-off in donations or alumni support, need for additional donations or alumni support, and changes in consumer behavior. The list is endless but helps us to imagine the array of key places public relations is expected to assist client organizations.

As an opportunity, a rhetorical problem is an issue, concern, or question that the organization raises in an effort to get key MAPs to see and acknowledge the importance of the position, learn about it, become comfortable with it, and adopt a mutually beneficial position on it.

Strategy is vital to management. Plans are developed to achieve goals through the use of public relations strategies and tactics. Public relations is a means, not an end. It serves organizations by helping them to achieve their strategic business plan. A strategic business plan guides the best way to accomplish a mission or vision; it explains how an organization gets where it wants to go. Strategy requires knowing what needs to be done. Research, systematically collecting information, is the means practitioners use to gain the knowledge required to develop strategies. Research helps the practitioners to understand the situations and MAPs they must address. Rhetorical problems demand action. To be effective, practitioners must understand the situation surrounding the rhetorical problem and MAPs that are involved. Research is what allows us to understand the situation and MAPs.

▶Situational Assessment

Conducting a situational assessment to isolate problems is the first step in strategic action. If your car has a flat tire, that is a problem. If you are hungry, that is a problem. If a pan of food begins to smoke on the stove, that is a problem. If you eat too much, that is a problem. If you find yourself engaged in an unresolved conflict, that is a problem. If you have opinions different from those of someone whose cooperation you need, that is a problem. If you offend someone important to you, that is a problem. If you want someone to do something he or she doesn't want to do, that is a problem. If you and that person need to cooperate but want to do something different, that is a problem.

This logic suggests that if we have a problem, then we want to discover a solution. If you have a flat tire, what would you do? Would you replace the flat tire with a properly inflated spare tire? Would you call an emergency road service? Would you flag down another motorist to get help? Would you ask a passenger in your car to change the tire? Would you call your folks, husband, wife, boyfriend, or girlfriend? If you have a problem, what is the solution? That reminds us of the sage observation of a professional colleague, a vice president of public affairs, and a PRSA Fellow. He told a public relations management class one evening that his job description could be reduced to three words: expert problem solver.

"Situational" problems are "rhetorical" problems. This is a way of thinking about a public relations problem and its strategic response. This reasoning reinforces the assumption that public relations professionals are problem solvers. A public relations—rhetorical—problem requires either a communication response or a strategic change in how the organization operates. The problem may wisely and ethically be solved by both.

Senior public relations practitioners offer the sage advice that you should never present a problem to management without having one or more solutions in mind. The formulation of a solution begins with research and situational assessment. When management poses a problem to you, you should not think of what can be done to deny the problem or blame it on some entity. The constructive, proactive response is to work to solve the problem in the most ethical and mutually beneficial manner.

BOX 4.4 ANALYZE AND RESPOND TO RHETORICAL PROBLEMS

- Conduct situational analysis
  - Listen to and understand stakeseekers—MAPs
  - Listen to and understand stakeholders—MAPs

- Identify rhetorical problems
  - Action, threats, or opportunities
  - Communication, threats, or opportunities
  - Market: message, communication processes, and actions
  - Audience: message, communication processes, and actions
  - Public: message, communication processes, and actions
  - Lack of awareness on the part of a market or audience
  - Lack of motivation on the part of a market or audience
  - Lack of information on the part of a MAP
  - Disagreement or difference of opinion between the organization and its MAPs
  - Lack of a positive relationship between the organization and its MAPs
  - Different zones of meaning: lack of cocreated meaning between the organization and its MAPs

- Identify mutually beneficial outcomes

- Identify message development objectives
  - Attract attention: Publicize and promote
  - Inform: Publicize and promote
  - Cocreate meaning
  - Engage in collaborative decision making
  - Build or repair relationships

- Identify communication style and relationship development options
  - Openness
  - Trust
  - Dialogue
  - Responsiveness: commitment
  - Alignment of interests

- Consider and reconcile ethical and corporate responsibility quandaries

To illustrate this line of analysis, we offer many potential sources of rhetorical problems. For each of the following, several rhetorical responses are possible. We suggest some below. You may think of others as you continue to learn to think strategically. As always, we ask, *What would you do?* Which message development objectives would you select? Which public relations tools would you employ to work to resolve the rhetorical problem? To answer that question, we discuss issues management in Chapter 10, strategic use of media in Chapter 11, publicity and promotion message design in Chapter 12, and negotiation/collaborative decision making in Chapter 13.

- Lack of awareness (attention and/or knowledge) on the part of a market, audience, or public to a product, service, image, aspect of the organization's reputation, or preferred action.
- Lack of motivation to act in a manner that is in the best interests of both parties.
- Difference in attitude (the way in which something is evaluated): Attitudes held by the key market, audience, or public differ in critical ways from those of the organization.
- Difference in belief (the way an attribute is associated with something): Beliefs held by the key market, audience, or public differ in critical ways from those of the organization.
- Misunderstanding/disagreement (co-orientation): Extent to which the opinions and issue positions of the organization and one or more stakeholders differ.
- Inaccuracy (co-orientation): Extent to which the market, audience, or public does not know the opinion of the organization on a crucial matter.
- Dissatisfaction (co-orientation): Extent to which the values or attitudes of the market, audience, or public differ from those of the organization on some critical matter.
- Attack (priorities of values, differences of belief and attitude; differences in platform of fact, evaluative premises, or conclusion): Extent to which a public criticizes the actions, policies, statements, issues position, service, or product of the organization. Attack can come from activists, other organizations (intra- or interindustry), or government.
- Drop in business (revenue generated—charitable donations, follower support): Trends are a natural part of the life of an organization. Increases constitute opportunities. Drops are threats. The key problem is the reason for the drop.
- Drop in community support: Relationships can deteriorate. Whereas once the community thought positively of an organization, that opinion may shift to neutral or negative. One of the most dramatic shifts in the past 30 years has been the loss of confidence on the part of the general public in the United States in regard to their perception of the trustworthiness and honesty of corporate leaders. Three decades ago, in 1966, 55% of the public had "a great deal of confidence" in the capability and moral qualities of corporate leaders. By 1976, the confidence level had fallen to 16% (Kelly, 1982). 1983 Gallup research placed the figure at 18% for those who gave business executives "very high" and "high" ratings for honesty and ethics. In the battle of trustworthiness during the 1980s, corporate leaders trailed TV commentators (33%), journalists (28%), and newspaper reporters (26%) ("Honesty and Ethical Standards," 1983). A decade later, some figures remained relatively the same, but others showed dramatic change: Business executives (20%), newspaper reporters (22%), television commentators/reporters (28%), U.S. senators (18%), and members of Congress (14%) ("Honesty and Ethical Standards," 1993). In 2000,

nurses were found to be the most honest and ethical (79%). Other medical personnel and teachers at all levels were in the 60% range. Business executives continued to be about 20%, and that was before the Enron scandal (and others). Elected government officials, professional communicators, lawyers, and some business types (especially insurance and real estate) were at the bottom ("Nurses Remain at Top of Honesty and Ethics Poll," 2000).

- Drop in reputation: Attributes are used to define an organization. They can be positive or negative. A drop in reputation can occur because positives become less positive and negatives become more negative. A drop can also result when fewer positives are associated with the organization and more negatives are associated with it.
- High cognitive involvement: This is an increase in the extent to which a key public believes its self-interest is positively or negatively affected in ways that lead it to focus attention on organization as a cause or a solution for that increase.
- Conflicting interests and zones of meaning: Conflicts result from strongly held differences of opinion on crucial matters.
- Nonaligned interests and zones of meaning: Zones of meaning are compatible when they lead to similar conclusions and support the same themes and actions. Conflict results when they are not aligned, when interests are seen to be at odds rather than compatible.
- Lack of identification/mixed identifications and identities: Identification results when people think that their identities (the terms they use when they think about themselves) are similar to (aligned with) those the organization uses to present itself.
- Disagreement over definitions, facts, evaluations, problems (definition and importance): Facts are basic to reasoning. A rhetorical problem can result when the facts known or believed by an organization are different from those known or believed by key stakeholders.
- Disagreements of ranked priorities: The organization may hold the same facts as do one or more stakeholders but reason from them differently.
- Polarization: Division occurs instead of merging. This happens when opinions, evaluations, goals, and interests are incompatible and key markets, audiences, or publics think of themselves as being different rather than identified with the organization.
- Distrust: Extent to which the market, public, or audiences lacks faith in what the organization does or says.
- Relationship deterioration: Extent to which elements that define a relationship suggest a negative rather than a positive trajectory toward the entities, thinking that their interests, opinions, and actions are mutually beneficial.

Today's public relations practitioner is a problem solver. Each practitioner is expected to spot problems and develop strategic and tactical plans to solve those problems. Goal-oriented thinking suggests that practitioners need to set goals and select the tactics required to achieve them. To assess rhetorical problems and develop strategic responses, practitioners analyze their MAPS.

MAPs: A Picture of the Territory

The ethical approach to rhetorical public relations features the need to know what customers like and dislike about the organization, especially its policies, activities, products, and services. Savvy organizations want to know what their MAPs know, don't know, and want to know. Public relations requires the ability to understand and communicate with people based on the current or potential relationship between them and organizations. Effective communication requires that messages be tailored to the needs and interests of people. This communication is a dialogue and the basis for cultivating relationships. Relationships require listening and understanding. They work best when the participants hold each other in positive regard. They depend on shared information and cocreated meanings. They need constant nourishment to maintain support and prevent opposition. Efforts are needed to ensure that the relationship is open as well as based on trust, cooperation, compatible views, aligned interests, and commitment. In this way, it becomes mutually beneficial.

Organizations may have to communicate with a few, hundreds, thousands, or millions of people. It simply is impractical to treat each person as an individual and communicate with people on a one-to-one level. By necessity, a public relations practitioner must cluster people into useful groups. By useful, we mean that the people in the groups have certain traits, attitudes, values, or behaviors; they are similar in some meaningful way. Knowing their similarity helps in the design of messages and the selection of channels to communicate with them. Identifying and dividing people into groups is called *segmentation,* a topic that will be further developed in this chapter.

Chapter 1 defined a *market* as an identifiable group whom executives believe will want a product or service from a business or will join and contribute to the activities of a nonprofit organization. An *audience* is a group who may be interested and could become sufficiently cognitively involved to prefer one product in competition with another or to become attentive to a public policy issue. What is a *public?* Is it an individual who has the authority or capacity to make decisions that affect an organization? Is it a group of people who organize to confront an organization to challenge its business practices? Is it the media? A successful public relations practitioner must be able to effectively identify MAPs. Creating a MAP assumes a practitioner has a clear understanding of what constitutes a market, an audience, or a public. Moreover, people shift from audience to market or public. Figure 4.1 is a visual representation of how the three are connected. They cease being a market and become a public. Because they are a public, they are also a market. A rhetorical approach to public relations considers how fluid these changes are, because people can shift from one category to another.

Practitioners must be able to understand these categories of people well enough to know how to align their interests with the organization, how to solve mutually perplexing problems through collaborative decision making, and how to cocreate meaning. *MAP analysis* is a view of the ways people connect with the organization. They can be a market that supports the organization financially (donate money or buy its products, for instance). They can be a public for that organization because they are cognitively involved in a public policy issue that might affect the interests of the organization and the relationship they have with it. They can be an audience for additional

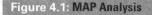

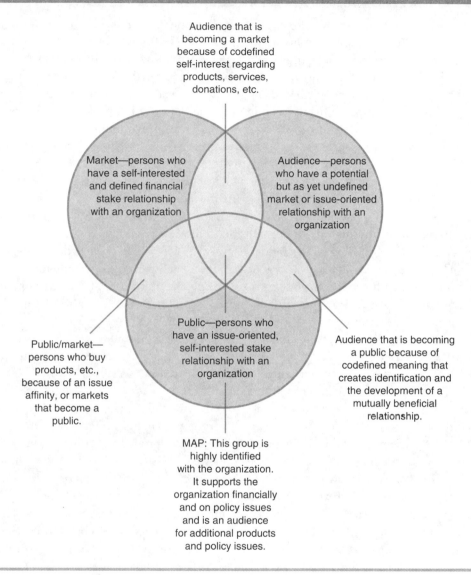

Figure 4.1: MAP Analysis

products or opportunities to donate money, and they are an audience for additional issues that arise.

A second consideration is the ways in which scholars and practitioners come to gain insights into MAPs. Practitioners and scholars conduct research and understand the opinions and actions of how people act in a collective manner. Research attempts to understand how people develop market preferences, what attracts their attention as audiences, and why they become attached to issues and even progress to being activists. All three topics have implications for the practice of public relations as practitioners seek to communicate, gain attention, inform, persuade, engage in collaborative decision making, and cocreate meaning.

Publics can be markets when they buy products because of their identification and relationship with an organization. For instance, environmental activists often buy products from activist groups, such as the National Wildlife Federation. This organization markets T-shirts and sweatshirts as well as other personal items that are part of the organization's efforts to brand its identity with environmental issues. In this way, the organization can identify with its followers, who constitute a public that can be marshaled against organizations targeted by the National Wildlife Federation as harming the global environment.

A market can become a public if it is aware of a problem and is cognitively involved in the solution of the problem based on the quality of product (bacterial contamination of meat, for instance) or the way the product is manufactured (through the use of child labor, for example). Consumers may become outraged by the actions and policies of a business or industry. These publics can vote with their purchase dollars. They can also appeal for governmental pressures to force the business or industry to operate in a more responsible manner. For example, because of its use of sweatshops, Nike faced consumer boycotts and legislation for regulating overseas garment operations.

▶Traditional Segmentation

The segmentation of MAPs is one of the most fundamental, day-to-day strategic functions in the world of professional public relations practice. Your colleagues in advertising and marketing and others in organizational management will use the concept of segmentation to refer to key constituents, and thus, you will need to know them in order to be an equal participant in discussions and decisions. The concepts are commonly used, and public relations practitioners must be able to understand the terms and be able to design strategic communication to effectively contribute to organizational achievement.

To think about segmentation means to think strategically—rhetorically—about what motivates a person's needs and wants. The idea behind segmentation is rather simple: Divide a market, audience, or public into subgroups such that the members are more like each other than like nonmembers of the segment. In general, segments must be definable, mutually exclusive, measurable, accessible, reachable with affordable communications, and large enough for organizational products or services to make a reasonable profit.

The terminology used in this section can become very confusing. Stakes and the MAP approach are forms of segmentation, ways to divide people into useful groups. Stakes are the first layer. While people share similar stakes, there is room for wide variation among the stake segments. For instance, investors are viewed as a specific stakeholder group, people looking to make a profit. However, people invest for different reasons. Some are looking for short-term profit, others are saving for retirement, and some consider only socially responsible organizations for investment.

MAP analysis adds a second layer to the segmentation and makes the segments more precise. MAP analysis should lead you to note that some persons are aware of your product, service, or policy issue but might not have a well-formed opinion (attitude) about it. Thus, they would not likely take action for or against the product, service, or issue without additional information and opinion. They may need to see a self-interesting motive to take action. In contrast, another MAP segment might currently use a product or service, or they might support or oppose a specific issue position. For that reason, they would need to be approached in different ways—with different messages—than the persons who are just becoming aware and forming opinions. The MAP analysis segments people into specific MAPs, giving practitioners useful insights into how the people relate to the organization.

Traditional segmentation, involving procedures commonly used in marketing and public relations, is the final layer in the MAP process. We gain even finer, more refined insights into a segment when we add in traditional segmentation methods. Traditional segmentation provides insights into values, beliefs, behaviors, communication preferences, and communication channel usage.

Segmentation has become one of the more influential concepts in marketing that has permeated the thinking of managers and researchers. Segmentation involves dividing MAPs into smaller groups that are similar to one another in some way. They may share similar interests, values, or education levels (Lenskold, 2003; McDonald & Dunbar, 2004). The goal was to identify financially lucrative segments of a market and to develop products specifically to fit the needs and wants of that segment.

In today's professional environment, segmentation involves "differential response." General differences in customers', donors', followers', or students' behavioral responses can be identified through variables or characteristics that predict such a response (e.g., attitudes, demographics, or geographic location). For example, why does a consumer choose Diet Pepsi over Diet Coke? What aspects of the product or what characteristics of the customer motivate this choice? Answers to these questions would result from differential responses. The answers to those questions allow a public relations professional to design a communication program that encourages the purchase of Diet Pepsi over Diet Coke by members of the market segment. Such segmentation not only helps the practitioner to know what to say to feature appropriate characteristics of the product, for example, but also to select the best channels to reach this targeted market or audience.

Two types of variables are traditionally used in segmentation: objective and inferred variables. *Objective variables* involve the use of secondary sources to identify and segment. This kind of variable includes demographics, the media-specific groups of individuals used to obtain information and form opinions, and geographic location. By using data based on those variables, a profile can be used to identify MAPs based on the opinions they hold. Such variables, however, are not very effective in making predictions of behaviors. Demographic categories, for instance, do not necessarily predict the opinions people hold or the actions they are likely to take.

Inferred variables are developed through direct interaction with a targeted group of people. Variables such as perceptions, cognitions, and attitudes provide for the prediction of desired behaviors and other effects. These variables are researched by using surveys, focus groups, and interviews, to name only a few of the typical research methodologies.

Most researchers and practitioners in the fields of marketing, advertising, and public relations utilize social-psychological situational variables to identify and segment. The term *social-psychological situational variable* refers to inferred or objective variables that reflect social or psychological characteristics that are generally situational in nature. For example, social characteristics could be economic or ethnic background, gender, or the region of the country or the generational era in which an individual was born. Psychological characteristics could be attitudes about a product, perceptions of an organization, or cognitive decision-making processes.

Can you think of other social or psychological variables? As you wander through a grocery store or a shopping mall, try to imagine the different sorts of individuals most likely to prefer various kinds of products. For instance, expectant parents may focus on certain types of items. Their shopping lists may change once the child has arrived. Those purchases are likely to be different from those of youngsters or persons who have retired. Go to a large book and magazine store and browse the shelves, imagining the different categories of readers.

BOX 4.5 SEGMENTATION TOOLS

Various social scientific research tools are used to learn more about what is on the minds of MAPs. For example, researchers have used personal values to identify and predict consumer behavior in marketing campaigns. One such approach, called VALS (Values and Lifestyles), features a combination of hierarchical needs and the extent to which people are inner or outer directed. VALS is premised on people expressing their personalities through their behaviors. Personality traits are used to understand consumer behavior so it is not applicable to other types of stakeholders. VALS was developed and is licensed through SRI International. VALS divides consumers into eight categories: Innovators, Thinkers, Achievers, Experiencers, Believers, Strivers, Makers, and Survivors.

This system attempts to profile markets based on the value hierarchy unique to each group. For instance, one group of consumers could be faced with frugal survival, whereas another spends money to achieve self-actualization. Is the purchase of an expensive sports car an expression of frugal survival or self-actualization? Which value is at play when a person buys an economical automobile that is reliable and does not have many "add-ons"?

Psychographic research is quantitative and originates with the activities, interests, and opinions (AIO) of consumers. Today, psychographics goes beyond AIO to include attitudes, values, demographics, and media patterns. Psychographics is more than simply lifestyles. It represents personality traits. In addition to psychographics, geodemographics (geographic localities of individuals as defined by variables such as age, education, or income) can be used to understand the wants and needs of key constituents. One such instrument, called PRIZM (Potential Rating Index for Zip Markets), assumes that similar kinds of people group together or that as people group together, they become similar in their opinions and marketing tastes. The logic of this approach fits many of the themes we have addressed in our discussion of message development objectives. As people in a community (geographic location) discuss and deal with shared problems and have similar experiences, they cocreate meaning. Thus, they come to have similar attitudes based on their life experiences and lifestyles.

Research and Ethics

Research is not just a one-way street that is used to develop effective messages. Research also should be used to understand MAPs so that the organization can adapt to them and communicate with them rather than "communicate at" or manipulate them. MAPs can have different and even conflicting ethical standards. A bank may try to use prudent practices when granting loans. If this bank is not careful, some publics may criticize it for discriminatory practices. The bank needs to understand what its stakeholders believe to be discriminatory practices. A bookstore chain may consider what standards customers and potential customers use to decide what counts as pornographic. The chain would avoid stocking magazines and books its markets and audiences might consider offensive.

Research can help an organization know the ethical standards that are prized by its MAPs. It can monitor the opinions of the MAPs to determine whether it is violating any of the expectations its stakeholders have about its policies and operations. Automobile companies stopped using live animals in crash tests because people thought the process was cruel to the animals and not particularly helpful in determining crash effects on humans.

Society's ethical standards change over time. Organizations are wise to use research to observe and monitor changes in ethics. Research should monitor these changes to honestly understand them rather than to merely seek to exploit them. Smith & Wesson, a major gun maker, was the first company to accept governmental concessions on firearms safety and sales practices. The move mirrors the growing view in the United States that such practices are good and right.

Research and Relationship Building

Today's public relations requires strategic efforts to build mutually beneficial relationships. Thus, research is productively used to assess and monitor the quality of relationships between the organization and its stakeholders and stakeseekers. In relationships, the goal is to align the client organization's interests with those of its stakeholders and stakeseekers. A vital part of creating such alignments is to communicate in ways that foster rather than harm the creation and maintenance of relationships. Several communication styles lead to mutually beneficial relationships:

- Openness: Listens to and appreciate others' points of view; engages in two-way communication; is open and responsive to ideas, concerns, needs, and wants.
- Trustworthiness: Builds trust by being reliable, nonexploitative, and dependable.
- Respectfulness: Shows regard for the ideas and opinions of others.
- Commitment: Builds trust through shared control and empowerment; supports the community by being involved in it, investing in it, and displaying commitment to it.
- Alignment of interests (attitudes and beliefs): Works to build relationships through mutually beneficial attitudes and beliefs.

- Cooperation: Negotiates and engages in collaborative decision making.
- Achievement of dynamic change needed for a growing relationship: Adapts to others as well as acknowledges how others adapt to the organization.
- Compatibility of views/opinions: Fosters mutual understanding and agreement; cocreates meaning.

Each of these factors is important to the development of mutually beneficial relationships. Each offers a focal point for your research. As you design research, think of how each factor can be measured to see whether it is helping or harming relationships with the MAPs.

Let's ask some questions to integrate the communication styles into effective research required for today's public relations. Do MAPs think the client organization listens to and appreciates their attitudes, wants, desires, or concerns? Does the organization demonstrate respect for the opinions and concerns of others? In the opinion of MAPs, is the client organization open and responsive to their ideas, concerns, needs, and wants? Do they think the organization works to build trust through shared control and empowerment? Do they think that their interests align with those of the client organization? Based on their experience with the client organization, do they think it is willing to negotiate and engage in collaborative decision making? Is the client organization perceived to be willing to achieve dynamic change needed for a growing relationship? Answers to any one or combination of these questions are useful to a public relations practitioner. Each question seeks insight into the quality of the organization's relationships with each MAP.

Research should be conducted prior to initiating changes in what the organization does and says. It should be used to monitor change. It can evaluate the effectiveness of the strategic business and communication plan. It estimates the consequences of what is being done and said.

Conclusion

In this chapter, we have introduced you to research, a vital public relations skill set. The modern practitioner cannot hope to succeed without some understanding of the types and basics of research. Research allows a practitioner to see and to understand MAPs. It permits timely and strategic actions; the practitioner knows when to act and what should be accomplished. The wise practitioner will utilize research to inform ethical choices, to facilitate relationship building, and to develop strategic responses. Research is used throughout the public relations process. This chapter emphasized formative research, understanding the MAPs and the situation. Chapter 5 will illustrate how research is used in the second phase of a public relations action, planning. Chapter 6 shows how research translates into practice. Chapter 7 will elaborate on the evaluative function of research. Research is a process of collecting and interpreting information that can be used to create strategy and to assess its success or failure.

Research in Public Relations

**Tom Watson
Head of the School
of Communication
Charles Sturt University
Bathurst, Australia**

NOTE: Dr. Tom Watson was chairman (2000–2002) of the Public Relations Consultants Association (U.K.) and formerly managing director of Hallmark Public Relations, Winchester, England.

For years I have illustrated the role of research in planning public relations programs with a joke along the lines of:

A gentleman walking along a road sees a yokel sitting by the roadside. *"I say, my good man, is this the way to Woop Woop?"*

"Well, sorr," the yokel replies in his broad country accent, *"I wouldn't start from here."*

And how many PR programs "wouldn't start from here" but, worse, launch into an abyss of hope and hype? Too many sally forth like headless chicken in circles of rapidly diminishing energy and end up with the client or employer losing faith in the practitioners and in public relations methodology.

Like many other practitioners, I have found it difficult to convince clients of the need for research to set the planning benchmarks. Faced with upfront expenditure on research before any "real work" begins, they appeal to the practitioner's "creativity" and "experience" and promise to spend more on the program itself.

However, many of us have had to find ways around the client's indifference to research through media analysis, "dipstick" research among reporters and stakeholders, use of existing published data, and scanning the Internet. All these inputs can be used to form views that can establish benchmarks. Their validity may not be strong as specially commissioned research, but no practitioner should ever rely on dubious "creativity" to plan a program.

FURTHER EXPLORATION

4

Ethical Quandary: Using Research to Build Relationships

Using research and segmentation tools to define and understand MAPs can rely on stereotypes. Is it unethical to think in terms of stereotypes? Is it strategically and rhetorically unsound? Is it unethical to ask which stakeholders think the operations and policies of the organization are legitimate, appropriate, and ethical? This assessment can consider whether the reputation of the organization is positive or negative in the judgment of each MAP. Reputation is a group's attitude toward an organization

When research is used, it does make a major difference to strategic planning. In the early 1990s my (then) consultancy was advising the proponents of a new town in southern England. By using focus group discussions, we identified two important factors that had not arisen before in the debate over land-use and the provision of housing.

These were that the less vociferous members of the community (the so-called silent majority) were unhappy with the type of housing that had been built in the past 20 years and they wanted their voices heard. From this research, we turned the campaign's potential strategy away from reliance on political lobbying to a much broader community involvement. This information would not have arisen had my client not believed in fundamental research and the testing of all assumptions.

The new town is high on the agenda for future development, with many of its features and facilities proposed by "silent majority" discussion groups that were formed as a result of the research. In the UK, it was once said that "the British like going into the future by looking backwards" and research is needed to unlock the real attitudes of people and not just those whose voices are loudest.

So how do we convince budget holders that research pays dividends? Two quite separate imperatives are now driving an expansion of research methodology and its application to all aspects of program development and monitoring. The first is the increasing use of procurement executives to negotiate public relations programs which have Key Performance Indicators (KPIs). The KPIs and program objectives need research in order to be established with accuracy. The second is the increasing demand for measurement of program outcomes. Together, these two imperatives will foster an expansion of expenditure on research and planning. It is up to practitioners themselves to improve their knowledge of research methods and thus put a more convincing case to budget holders. The methodology is readily available and does not cost a fortune to apply.

SOURCE: Reprinted with permission from Tom Watson.

(its officials, personnel, policies, operations, products, and services). Such evaluations help executives to predict whether stakeholders will act favorably toward or against the organization. Reputation is an assessment of how well an organization meets stakeholders' expectations. Another consideration of reputation is the extent to which it favorably differentiates the organization from others, especially those in competition for the same resources.

Write an essay to justify three ethical principles that you believe practitioners should follow as they work to segment and understand MAPs so that they can increase the quality of communication with them and build strong relationships with them.

Summary Questions

1. What is research?
2. How do preliminary and evaluative research differ from one another?
3. How do formal and informal research differ from one another?
4. What are the basics of conducting a focus group or an in-depth interview?
5. What is the importance of intercoder reliability and mutually exclusive categories in content analysis?
6. What is a survey?
7. What does it mean to have a representative sample?
8. Is there a difference between Likert and semantic differential scales?
9. When does a rhetorical problem occur?
10. What is involved in a situational assessment, and how does it help to form strategy?
11. What does it mean to say that MAPs are fluid?
12. What are the two types of variables used in segmentation?
13. What are VALS, and how do they help public relations practitioners?

Exercises

1. Find a Web site that is designed to appeal to a market, an audience, and a public. Describe what you believe is the basis for the positive or negative relationship between the organization and the market, audience, and public. Identify the stakes that are sought by the organization and by the market, audience, and public.
2. Select an organization and conduct its stakeholder/stakeseeker analysis. List as many stakeholders and stakeseekers as you can and identify the stakes and the conditions needed for their positive exchange. Find at least two stakeholders who are likely to be in at least partial conflict.
3. As a small group, analyze various publics regarding a student issue on your campus. Think of an issue that affects students. Identify the kinds of students who constitute a specific public-identification group, a specific public-attentive group, a mass public-attentive group, and a mass public-general public. What events would you plan and implement to attract mass and media attention in the discussion and determination stage? Be prepared to share your example with your classmates.
4. Select a for-profit or nonprofit organization, and conduct market segmentation. What factors do you believe best account for your understanding of the market? What meaning does the market share that could be useful in a communication campaign? Can you perform a nested segmentation analysis so that you see how different persons might want or need the product or support the nonprofit but for different reasons?

5. Select one of the MAP relationships that is featured in the chapter. Imagine that you are a practitioner who is advising management on the strength of your relationship with the MAP, the messages that form a common ground with the MAP, where differences might exist between you and the MAP, and how you might strengthen or build a relationship with the MAP. Imagine the differences between communicating with a market or public versus communicating with an audience on this topic.

Recommended Readings

Heath, R. L. (Ed.). (2005). *Encyclopedia of public relations*. Thousand Oaks, CA: Sage.

Matera, F. R., & Artique, R. J. (2000). *Public relations campaigns and techniques: Building bridges into the 21st century*. Boston: Allyn & Bacon.

SRI Consulting Business Intelligence. (2004). *About VALS*. Retrieved July 10, 2004, from http://www.sric-bi.com/VALS/

Stacks, D. W. (2002). *Primer of public relations research*. New York: Guilford Press.

Stewart, T. D. (2002). *Principles of research in communication*. Boston: Allyn & Bacon.

5

Elements of Planning

The Edison, New Jersey, Pipeline Explosion Revisited

Let's return to the vignette we introduced at the beginning of Chapter 1. That vignette gives us the opportunity to apply much of what we have learned since Chapter 1.

The vignette in Chapter 1 focused on a pipeline explosion in Edison, New Jersey. We promised that we would return to that case and tell you how the crisis was managed. Promise kept! The vignette sets up the discussion of strategic public relations planning to build relationships, the theme of this chapter.

Soon after the explosion occurred, the mayor of Edison blamed the pipeline company Texas Eastern Transmission (TETCO), a subsidiary of Duke Energy (formerly Panhandle Eastern Transmission). A public recognized a problem and sought someone to blame for the problem. Publics were cognitively involved with the problem; they saw it as related to their self-interests. The mayor saw the explosion in his political self-interest. He wanted to protect the interests of his constituents.

The crisis was detected by the apartment dwellers, who heard and felt the explosion. (Luckily, no one was seriously injured.) The crisis attracted network news attention in New York City. Company pipeline crews noted a problem and began immediate crisis mode actions. TETCO management in Houston was alerted. It marshaled its forces and flew to Edison.

The crisis response team consisted of crisis response experts and senior management, including the vice president of public affairs. When

Successful Response to Community Relations Crisis

SOURCE: Reprinted with permission by the Public Relations Society of America (http://www.prsa.org).

the crisis response team arrived in Edison, they were confronted with angry citizens, angry officials—the start of a public that was looking to form and take action against the company. To them and others, the explosion scene resembled a battlefield with damaged buildings, burned-out automobiles with melted headlights that had a comical "teary" look, and a crater 120 feet wide and 60 feet deep. The explosion displaced 2,000 people. Many were without more clothing than they had grabbed as they fled their apartments.

By the time the crisis response team arrived in Edison, it had formulated its specific crisis response, which focused on three priorities. Each priority was designed to demonstrate that TETCO was a good company that wanted a mutually beneficial relationship with members of the community where it operates, a key to building community relationships:

Priority 1: Care for victims. A fund of $7 to $10 million was allocated to assist the victims. $5,000 was given to families whose apartments were burned, and $1,000 was given to other families as needed. In addition, $350 per person, per week was paid to cover living expenses, and the company covered temporary housing costs for 2 months. Teams were assigned to assist victims and work with local officials.

Priority 2: Assist and cooperate with the National Transportation Safety Board (NTSB), the federal agency that oversees pipeline safety. Investigation revealed that third parties had damaged the pipeline when they buried parts of a pickup. The NTSB quickly concluded that TETCO was not liable for the fire.

Priority 3: Restore the pipeline into service. It is a major transportation line for providing natural gas to users in the Northeast.

To accomplish these three priorities, TETCO knew that it had to build (rebuild) a relationship with the mayor, community members, and other elected officials (including those at the federal level) to solve this problem, restore people's lives as well as could be done, and put the pipeline back into service. The company wanted to use public relations to achieve a mutually beneficial relationship (collaborative decision making).

It began to implement its plan within 12 hours of the explosion and half a continent away from corporate headquarters. One of the first steps was to begin to contact local community groups. One of these was the local branch of United Way. Since the company had no reputation with this particular group, its leaders were encouraged to contact the head of United Way in Houston. She spoke highly of the corporate good citizenship of the company. That report laid a foundation of trust with key groups in Edison. In this way, TETCO used one mutually beneficial relationship to create, maintain, or repair the relationship with the citizens of Edison.

In the days that followed, the team fielded hundreds of media inquiries. The media swarmed to the site because the fire was visible from New York City, it was close to major media centers, and it was a dramatic human interest event. As everything seemed to be moving toward normal and the pipeline neared going into operation, the local mayor called on a county judge to impose a restraining order that prevented the company from putting the pipeline into operation. The company knew it would win a court battle. The NTSB ruled that it was not responsible for the explosion and the county judge could not impose such a rule in a federal matter. But if a big company crushes a small-town mayor, the company loses as it seeks to win.

Thus, the company opted for a communication win instead of a legal win. It went to the media with facts about how it had assisted victims, even though the company was not liable. It applied principles of narrative theory and told a story of a good company being opposed by a bad mayor—one motivated by political gain. This story shifted (redefined) the anger of the community from the company to the mayor, who was playing politics. This evaluation led the mayor to negotiate a series of steps that led to a media event. At that event, the mayor and a senior TETCO official cooperated in giving the order and taking the actions to put the restored pipeline back into service. A good company had communicated effectively to achieve a mutually beneficial relationship with its key markets, audiences, and publics.

Today's public relations requires planning and strategic thinking. The public relations plan of an organization must fit with and support its strategic business plan. This is true regardless of whether the organization building public relations is a business, a nonprofit, or a governmental agency.

Public relations planning is no different from other kinds of planning. It requires research, planning, taking action, and evaluation. Chapter 4 discussed research. This chapter focuses attention on how research is incorporated into planning to formulate the actions that need to be taken. Chapter 6 will describe how to take action. Chapter 7 will explain how to evaluate the success of the plan and its implementation.

Planning and Strategic Thinking

Practitioners learn to think in terms of a formula of steps. Research. Plan. Implement the plan. Evaluate the plan. Refine the plan. Implement the plan, and so forth. These steps capture the essence of the strategic thinking public relations managers use to make their organization or unit more effective. Public relations practitioners increase their effectiveness by helping to develop the organizational plan and by using public relations planning to enhance the total organization.

137

Effective management along with effective public relations requires two levels of planning. First, the organization must have a plan to accomplish its mission and vision. Each department, as well, must have a plan to accomplish the objectives needed to assist the total organization in its efforts to be effective. Thus, a public relations department has a master plan. To foster appropriate relationships with each of its markets, audiences, and publics (MAPs), it should also have a plan.

TETCO had a community relations plan, one needed to create and maintain (even repair) relationships between the organization and the citizens in communities where it operates. Once the explosion occurred, that community relations plan and even its overall crisis response plan became the framework for developing, implementing, and evaluating the specific plan that would be used to restore its relationship with the citizens of Edison, New Jersey. It used that plan to accomplish the corporate plan of restoring the operation of its pipeline.

In most cases, an organization does not succeed by accident. Leaders of successful organizations think strategically; they act purposefully. Strategic organizations formulate plans to guide their actions in a specific direction; they know where they are going and how to get there. Successful public relations practitioners must have a strategic focus as well.

Imagine you want to drive from Chicago, Illinois, to Columbus, Ohio. You could get in a car and begin driving southeast, taking any road that sent you in the desired direction. That is not a strategic approach, although it might be fun and might eventually lead you to your destination. To be strategic, you could conduct research. For your research, you might buy detailed maps or use an Internet map, plot the quickest route, and locate places to stop to eat and to buy gas. You might use the Web to check on road construction. That would be a strategic approach.

Public relations entails building relationships with MAPs. To help set the tone for discussing strategic planning, you need to consider the planning challenges that are central to the following cases. One case asks you to consider what plan you would develop to achieve the objective of creating market interest through publicity for a new toy called "Tickle Me Elmo." Another raises the question of how to attract an audience to information relevant to breast cancer. The last focuses on a public that can affect how an industry, shrimpers, operates. Mature public relations practitioners think in terms of MAPs.

▶ Attracting a Market for Tickle Me Elmo

Imagine for a moment that you work in the public relations department for a national toy company. A new toy is being introduced for the holiday. The marketing plan is to sell at least 400,000 units. It is a *Sesame Street* "muppet." The public relations plan calls for publicity efforts to increase awareness of the toy. Your boss asks you to handle the campaign and wants a plan in 2 days. What do you do?

Here is an actual answer to that question. A toy company sought to attract attention of its key market—persons who purchase toys for children. Publicity campaigns are often used to attract the attention of a market to a product designed to appeal to that market. This particular publicity campaign launched a new toy so effectively that demand outstripped supply. The most sought-after toy during that holiday season was "Tickle Me Elmo," produced by Tyco Toys, Inc. This *Sesame Street* muppet was predicted to sell

400,000 units. Freeman Public Relations, Inc., wanted to give the product a boost, with the objective of achieving or exceeding this sales objective. Using a strategy similar to that employed to promote the "Cabbage Patch" dolls several years before, Freeman sent a Tickle Me Elmo to TV talk show host Rosie O'Donnell for her 1-year-old son. Then, the company sent 200 more Elmos to her. She used them on air as rewards for members of the audience who said the word "wall." Her guests that day were actor Tom Hanks, comedian Dom DeLuise, singer Willie Nelson, and Cliffy Clinkscales, an 11-year-old basketball whiz. The guests were charming and played with the dolls. This publicity effort increased sales. Store clerks were inundated with requests for Elmo. Parents worked hard to buy one so as not to disappoint their children. This most sought-after toy surpassed the 400,000 initial business plan projection and sold over 1,000,000 units. The rhetorical objective was to attract favorable attention and to provide the market with information about a new toy. The toy company wanted to sustain its relationship with its key market, leading both to be mutually satisfied. Toy buyers are a market. They do not need to be convinced to buy toys. They are targets to be motivated to buy specific toys. Thus, the rhetorical challenge is to attract their attention to a specific toy and demonstrate how it appeals to the wants of the market.

Publicity: Got to Have an Elmo

SOURCE: Copyright © Getty Images.

▶ Attracting an Audience of Potential Breast Cancer Victims

Each person is a potential victim of various diseases and illnesses. For this reason, people are the targets of messages created by many members of the medical community. They are an audience waiting to be intercepted by one of these messages. For various reasons, people look for health-related information. They might ask their physicians or contact a society, such as the American Cancer Society, to obtain information. They might read magazine articles, hear television programs, and talk with friends and relatives. They search the Web for information. Each person is a potential market who needs or wants medical services. They are a potential public; they might become issue oriented on some topic, seeking to influence public policy. They may need medical services.

Your boss walks into your office and asks you to consider the publicity plan to increase women's awareness of breast cancer information. Your organization also wants to be seen as a continuing source of information, and you want to partner with a corporation that sees breast cancer as part of its customer relations program. Your job assignment is to create a publicity plan to be launched on the Web to attract an audience of women.

Here is an actual response to that public relations plan. The "iVillage" Web site is devoted to many women's topics, such as birth control, depression, potty training, work, and recipes. At one time, this site featured a list of facts:

- An estimated 178,700 new cases of invasive breast cancer will be diagnosed in 1998.
- Approximately 43,500 deaths will occur in women from breast cancer in 1998.
- One in eight women will get breast cancer in their lifetime.
- Breast cancer risk increases with age, and every woman is at risk.
- Every 11 minutes, a woman dies of breast cancer.
- Seventy-eight percent of women with breast cancer are over 50 years of age.
- Approximately 1,600 cases of breast cancer will be diagnosed in men in 1998, and 400 of those men will die.
- More than 1.6 million women who have had breast cancer are still alive in the United States.
- Breast cancer is the leading cause of cancer death in women between the ages of 15 and 54 and the second cause of cancer death in women 55 to 74.
- Sixty-two percent of Black women diagnosed with breast cancer experience a 5-year survival rate, while 79% of White women experience 5-year survival.
- The first sign of breast cancer usually shows up on a woman's mammogram before it can be felt or any other symptoms are present.
- Risks for breast cancer include a family history, atypical hyperplasia, delaying pregnancy until after age 30 or never becoming pregnant, early menstruation (before age 12), late menopause (after age 55), current use or use in the last 10 years of oral contraceptives, and daily consumption of alcohol.
- Early detection of breast cancer, through monthly breast self-exam and particularly yearly mammography after age 40, offers the best chance for survival.
- Ninety percent of women who find and treat breast cancer early will be cancer free after 5 years.
- Over 80% of breast lumps are not cancerous, but benign, such as fibrocystic breast disease.
- Estrogen replacement therapy (ERT) helps reduce the risk of breast cancer for the first 10 years of treatment; after 10 years of ERT, a woman's risk of breast cancer increases 43%.
- You are never too young to develop breast cancer. Breast self-exam should begin by the age of 20.

Web sites such as this may be sponsored by women's groups or by companies that sell women's products, such as Avon and Gillette. They may be created as a service by cancer research and treatment facilities, such as M. D. Anderson Cancer Center in Houston, Texas, or national associations, such as the American Cancer Society. Information provided can help women to make informed decisions.

It can alert them to the problem and various solutions (gain attention). It can cocreate meaning. It can lead them to collaborative decisions. One additional feature is the links that such sites provide to facilitate a person's efforts to acquire information. These companies, societies, associations, help groups, and institutes seek mutually beneficial relationships with audiences whom they work to reach.

Avon uses the tagline "The Company for Women" in its corporate reputation branding effort. At its home Web page, it features the breast cancer crusade as part of its strategic philanthropy. To build a mutually beneficial relationship with its primary market, women, it demonstrates its

Relationship Building Through Aligned Interests

SOURCE: Copyright © Rod Rolle/Getty Images.

commitment to women and women's health. Avon created the Avon Worldwide Fund for Women's Health and has raised millions of dollars for the cause of international women's health. Under its section on corporate responsibility, Gillette features women's cancer programs.

The Web site of the American Cancer Society (ACS) provides information to answer the following questions:

- Who gets breast cancer?
- How has the occurrence of breast cancer changed over time?
- Who survives breast cancer?
- Who is at risk of developing breast cancer?
- What are the signs and symptoms of breast cancer?
- How is breast cancer treated?
- Can breast cancer be prevented?
- What are the current disease control strategies for breast cancer?
- What research is currently being done on breast cancer?
- What resources are available in your community?
- What is the ACS doing about breast cancer?

The ACS home page features medical updates and news you can use. A key objective of this effort is to attract an audience to the information that women can use to save their lives. Accomplishing this objective is a first step toward the objective of reducing the death toll of women (and men) to breast cancer. All of these organizations are worthy of a Web Watcher.

▶ **Responding to a Public
Concerned About Ridley Turtles**

You work for a government agency in Texas. Its mission is to protect wildlife while also supporting commercial activities that entail the wise management of natural resources. Your boss has reminded you of this public relations plan, one that calls for your agency to build relationships between activists seeking to protect animals and commercial activities, such as shrimp harvesting. The Texas Gulf Coast region prides itself on its seafood. Shrimpers and turtle advocates are on a collision course. What is your public relations plan to deal with these publics?

Over the past two decades, a running battle has occurred between persons who engage in the shrimp-harvesting business and activists who are concerned that traditional harvesting methods lead to unnecessary drowning of Ridley turtles. (As a Web Watcher, search for "Ridley turtles," and look for the home page of an organization called HEART.) Shrimp are harvested in open waters using large boats that drag nets behind them. These nets skim just above the seabed (mud, sand, or coral). Shrimp are scooped into the nets. Those nets also catch turtles. Turtles, unlike fish or shrimp, need to breathe air from above the water surface periodically. If they get caught in the nets, they are likely not to get to the surface and breathe before they suffocate. To prevent this ecological tragedy, activists have pressured the government to require shrimpers to use turtle-excluder devices (TEDs) in the nets. TEDs are openings in the nets that allow turtles to leave the nets as they rise toward the surface. TEDs also allow some shrimp to escape. If shrimp escape, shrimpers have to use more time and fuel to fill their nets. It costs them more to operate when they use the TEDs. This increased operating cost lowers their profit. Thus, they oppose these devices. The groups who have pressured the shrimpers have moved to seek boycotts of produce that is not harvested in an ecologically responsible manner. One such group, called HEART, has used billboard ads and encouraged restaurants to use only shrimp that are harvested in an environmentally responsible manner; it supplies information and opinions at its home page. Collaborative decision making has been difficult to achieve between the shrimpers— the industry—and this public. The concern of the industry is that the sympathy for the cause of the public can lead to even greater restrictions on their harvesting methods and may result in boycotts that reduce the size of their market. If you were a public relations counselor for the shrimp-harvesting industry, what would you do? What would you do if you represented the seafood restaurant industry? How would you map this public, along with its corresponding markets and audiences? Note that persons who oppose the traditional harvesting methods differ from a market. They are a public because they are concerned about an issue. They take action on that issue, which could affect the market or public policy that influences the operations of the seafood industry.

These three cases were intended to heighten your appreciation of strategy. Moreover, the cases illustrate the links between formative research and planning. The information collected through research is used to plan the public relations action.

Understanding the situation and MAPs allows a practitioner to decide what must be done to address the problem or utilize the opportunity.

Planning: The Basics

Planning requires situational assessment, setting objectives, deciding on how to achieve those objectives, implementing the plan, and seeing whether it works. There are three basic elements to planning: objectives, project management documents, and budgets. This section explains the value of each to overall public relations efforts.

▶ Types of Objectives

There are a variety of ways of categorizing objectives. (Box 5.1 presents the 12-category objective system proposed by McGuire, 1989.)

- Being exposed to a message
- Attending to a message
- Liking or becoming interested in a message
- Comprehending the message
- Acquiring the skills to use the information and evaluation contained in the message
- Yielding to the message
- Storing the message content in memory
- Recalling the message content from memory
- Deciding on the basis of the information retrieved
- Behaving in a manner that is based on the information
- Reinforcing behavior that leads to positive outcomes
- Consolidating behaviors that are positive so that they become routine and repeated

These 12 stages explain how individuals make decisions. Knowledge of these stages helps practitioners make strategic decisions as they supply the information people need and want. This model demonstrates why MAPs consist of people who are at various stages in their decision processes.

McGuire's work helps practitioners to divide objectives into three basic categories: knowledge, attitude, and behavior. Knowledge focuses on MAPs learning new information. Knowledge ranges from simple awareness to understanding a message (comprehension) to remembering specific information in a message (Coombs, 2005). McGuire's exposure, attention, liking, comprehending, and acquiring skills all relate to knowledge. Acquiring a skill reflects learning information. You are unlikely to learn information if you cannot understand it, do not like it, pay it no attention, or are never exposed to it.

(Text continues on page 148)

BOX 5.1 MCGUIRE'S 12 STEPS OF OPINION FORMATION AND BEHAVIOR

McGuire (1989) identified 12 possible objectives. You would match the type of objective to the needs of the situation and MAPs. McGuire's work helps to avoid the mistake of assuming that all MAPs are of one mind. That approach to public relations may be too general to strategically support our efforts—especially those to be more focused in the target we select to reach and the message we design to accomplish our goals. Consider McGuire's developmental stages of the thought and action persons go through as they are influenced, or influence themselves, through the acquisition of information and opinion.

Knowing this sequence can help public relations practitioners analyze the place in the sequence where they find various members of MAPs at any moment in time. Using the stages of this sequence, practitioners can estimate the kinds of information and opinion that can be used to influence the targets of their campaigns. This model also makes practitioners realize that they must listen to and appreciate their target because they must understand what it wants in the way of information and influence.

1. *Exposure to communication.* One of the realities of message impact is that people must be exposed to a message several times before they become aware of it and think about it. Each individual is subjected to hundreds or thousands of messages each day. People pick and chose between these messages. They pay attention to some. Most they ignore. One of the challenges facing the practitioner is to increase the likelihood that key MAPs will become aware of the messages. One of the strategies of public relations is to provide information in strategic ways so that their MAPs can obtain it. The first stage is to gain people's attention.

2. *Attending to the message.* To attend to a message means that the person pauses from doing something else and gives partial or full attention to it. One classic assumption is that messages have greater likelihood of gaining attention if they relate to the self-interest of the person or to some altruistic interest the person has. Markets and publics may already have a self-interest that motivates them to attend to the message.

Practitioners may need to design each message to appeal to the self-interest of audiences to stimulate them to attend to it. Self-interest increases the likelihood people will pay attention to a message. Let's review some key points on this topic. The example of people agreeing to volunteer illustrates many of the points.

- A public relations practitioner can predict that people will find something attention gaining simply because it is novel or otherwise visually, aurally, or conceptually attractive or markedly unattractive or interesting. A message or action may gain attention because it is distinct, appeals to emotions, is repeated, or is thought to be useful.

You decide to volunteer for the Special Olympics. Their brochures contained stories about participants. The emotions in the stories about how the program changed participants' lives caught your attention.

• Attention is likely to result when people become involved with some topic or action. Involvement may occur because of an individual's *personality traits*. People who have different personalities find that events, messages, issues, choices, products, or services appeal to them with different degrees of interest.

• Involvement can occur when an individual finds *connections* or *relevance* between an event, choice, product, service, or issue and experiences he or she has had. Attention is greater if the person sees the topic as being relevant to his or her self-interest. You have a strong interest in sports, so the Special Olympics were consistent with your self-interests.

• Involvement may result because a situation, event, or message *threatens or confirms the self-concept* of the individual. You see yourself as a helping person, and coaching in the Special Olympics will confirm that self-concept.

• Some issue, product, choice, service, or event can create involvement because it has *consequences* for the person's future. You plan on coaching in the future, so working with the Special Olympics will build toward that goal.

• A message or other stimulus gains attention because people think the information it contains is useful. Petty and Cacioppo (1986) argued that people want information that helps them form useful opinions—attitudes and beliefs. An opinion is useful it if leads to decisions and actions that are rewarding and avoids those that are not rewarding. For this reason, people who are involved with an issue, product choice, choice among services, and some social need are more likely to have well-formed opinions relevant to the choices they need to make. Involvement increases people's ability to remember or recall relevant facts. They seek and share information with other people during conversations on those topics that are related to their self-interest. They are more likely to talk about, listen to messages about, read about, or teleview topics related to their self-interests.

3. *Liking, becoming interested in some topic, issue, event, product, service, or opinion choice.* Liking is created when something seems rewarding. People are attracted to some topic, product, service, person, or organization because its benefits outweigh its costs. It is pleasing. It satisfies needs or wants—or at least seems to be satisfying. Some people who learned about the proposed location of Disney's "America" theme park, which was to be located in Haymarket, Virginia, part of historic Prince William County, were offended by the idea. They were interested in the issue because they disliked the harm it would do to their community.

4. *Comprehending the message.* Over time, people obtain information and opinions that help them to believe they understand an issue or topic. To that extent, they feel that they comprehend the information and the choices that it helps them to make. They become more comfortable with a product or service as they think they understand it. They seek and retain information that helps them understand a product, service, or issue.

5. *Skill acquisition.* As people acquire skills, they learn how to do something. They even learn how to think about something. One of humans' life skills is to make decisions. Parents let children decide which flavor of ice cream they want. Later in life, they are more prepared, for instance, to decide which make of automobile they want to purchase.

6. *Yielding to the message or other stimuli.* As people become more informed, they may change an existing attitude or create a new one. Yielding is the stage in this process, McGuire concluded, at which people create or change their attitudes.

7. *Memory storage of content or agreement.* If people find information and opinions important to them, they will likely store those items in their memory so they can recall them when they need them. For instance, persons might hear an entertainment news item about their favorite music group coming to town for a concert. That information is stored to be retrieved. If individuals learn information that persuades them that a product seems to have favorable traits, they store that information to use during their shopping.

What increases the likelihood that people will remember messages? Familiarity is one factor. Novelty is a second. A third factor is the importance of the information. A fourth factor is the degree to which the information is associated with markedly positive or negative stimuli. People recall information by categories, such as things to eat/not eat and automobiles to like/dislike. If people rehearse their thoughts, they are more likely to remember them. For this reason, if you think to yourself, "I need to remember this cold remedy or tell someone the name of the remedy," you are more likely to remember it. Retention is increased if people take actions that are relevant to the idea to be recalled. If people try a product, such as taste a soft drink, they might be more likely to recall that experience when they have the chance to choose that product later. The same could be predicted for a service that they have the opportunity to try during a trade show. For instance, at a trade show, potential customers might play with a computer program. That experience could lock into their memory and affect a subsequent purchase.

8. *Information search and retrieval.* Once the information is stored, people have to be able to *recall* it as they need it. As we stand in front of a rack holding several products, such as cold remedies, can we remember which

one has the trait that we learned through advertising or public relations messages? Which rock band is coming to town? When is it coming? Where can fans get tickets?

9. *Deciding on the basis of the information retrieved.* A decision can result either because persons recall the information they stored to make a specific decision or because of the information they recall that is relevant to the decision. We know that recall can be imprecise. We also know that after making a decision, we may recall something that would have affected our decision if we had remembered it before we made the decision.

10. *Behaving in accord with the decision.* Based on what they learn and recall, people can proceed to make their choice. They buy one product or service in preference to its competitors. They vote for one candidate and not for others. They decide to seek the treatment of a physician or a dentist, instead of not obtaining medical or dental treatment.

The theory of reasoned action can help practitioners understand how people chose one behavior as opposed to alternative ones (Ajzen & Fishbein, 1980). It builds on the theory of information integration, which reasons that people's actions or behaviors are based on their attitudes toward the behaviors *and* their opinions of what persons important to them would want them to do.

This last factor is a subjective norm: people's sense of what they think others want them to think or do. If they have a positive attitude toward a behavior, they want to take that action. But if people whom they respect don't want them to take the action, they have a quandary. As a matter of behavioral intention, people's actions result from a balanced choice between what they want to do and what they think others want them to do. If both parts of the equation agree, then the choice is easy. If the parts conflict, then people can experience a little and even substantial dissonance. Practitioners are wise to recognize these two parts of people's preferences and behavior. Communication and relationship building should recognize the potential conflict.

11. *Reinforcing desired acts.* If people find that a choice (of a product, for instance) satisfies their needs or wants, they prefer it again. Public relations practitioners are wise to predict that people will do or believe that which has satisfied them in the past. If people try something and like it, they are likely to try it again. If they have disliked something, they are likely to not prefer it in the future.

12. *Postbehavior consolidating.* McGuire recognized that people become predictable because they find increased reason—consolidate their behavior—to continue to prefer and to do that which they have found repeatedly rewarding.

An attitude is an evaluation, an expression of preferences—a like or dislike. That means it has positive, neutral, or negative valence. It can be held in different degrees of strength. Attitudes express preferences. When people yield, they are changing their attitudes. The Walt Disney Company once tried to build a theme park on part of a historic Civil War battlefield in Virginia. In opposition to the plan, protesters voiced their outrage and boycotted against Disney. Some persons were indifferent (neutral) to the plan, Disney, or both. Those who liked Disney probably did not take part in the boycott over the Civil War battlefield. The protesters held negative attitudes that motivated them to act. To guide behavior, an attitude needs to be stored in our memories, be recalled when relevant, and be used when making a decision.

Knowledge, what people believe, shapes their attitudes, which, in turn, influence behavior. Of course, people are not always that orderly or predictable. Sometimes they form attitudes without much knowledge and engage in behaviors counter to their attitudes. This set of circumstances warns us about the difficulty of setting and accomplishing objectives. Behavior change is the most difficult objective, followed by attitude change, and then knowledge gain. It is relatively easy to get people to learn new information. However, people will resist changing their attitudes and behaviors.

Research helps a practitioner to understand where MAPs are in the progression of objectives. Practitioners, for instance, might need to get information to audiences to create awareness and motivate them to be aware of some matter. Practitioners can supply information that helps customers to comprehend some issue, to be motivated to act, or to consolidate their decisions. For people who are considering traveling to a theme park, practitioners might help them to comprehend the fun they can have. Practitioners might motivate those who are about to make the choice. Practitioners might supply information to help people consolidate their decisions. A practitioner might, for instance, as a customer relations gesture, give them a souvenir and a brochure to remind them of the fun they had.

Similarly, practitioners should recognize that people who are only becoming aware of an issue are different from those who have taken public stands on that issue. One audience is beginning to learn about an issue, while the other public is looking for reinforcement to justify continuing to oppose a company's activities. For these reasons, practitioners think in terms of MAPs. They realize that people are different in their attitudes, beliefs, and behaviors. Research can help to put people into categories based on similarities, but there are always categories.

CHALLENGE BOX

Consider a product, a service, and a policy issue. Using McGuire's model, identify which stage you have achieved with each. Think of messages that you might use as a practitioner to attract an audience to become a market and then move that market to repeated behavior. Why do some people become aware of an issue—thus becoming an audience and a potential public for that issue? Why do some people become deeply involved in that issue, whereas others do not? If a parent had a child killed in a DWI (driving while intoxicated) car accident, use this model to explain his or her commitment to Mothers Against Drunk Driving (MADD), a national campaign to reduce such accidents.

Writing Objectives

Public relations actions look to create some sort of change in the rhetorical situation. Your motivation for engaging in public relations is to facilitate a change that will in some way benefit the organization and its stakeholders. Objectives are central to any public relations effort because they establish the measure of success or failure. To be more precise, we mean *outcome objectives*. The outcome objective establishes the conditions that must be met for the public relations action to be considered a success— to determine whether the desired changes were achieved. A proper outcome objective is measurable and specific (Coombs, 2005). You cannot have an objective if you cannot measure it, because there would be no means to evaluate it. Chapter 7 will expand on the topic of evaluation.

To be specific, an objective must include the desired amount of change and the target MAP for the change. Without having a target amount of change, you have no measure of success or failure. Let us consider a few examples. Objectives that simply say "to increase awareness of the organization" or to "collect blood" are too vague. One could argue that any awareness or any blood collected would constitute success. A proper objective would indicate the precise amount of change, such as "To increase awareness of the organization by 15%" or "To collect 20 pints of blood."

Even our revised objectives remain vague because they do not specify the target MAP for the change. We have researched the MAPs, so we know whom we should target. This should be placed in the objective because it will influence the message design, the topic of Chapter 6. By specifying the target, we know who should be receiving the messages and who should be experiencing the change (whom we will target during evaluation). The earlier objectives could be revised as follows: "To increase awareness of the organization by 15% among potential customers" and "To collect 20 pints of blood from new donors in the community." This discussion of objectives reflects a larger concept in management known as *management by objective* (MBO). MBO will be explained later in this chapter. MBO is based on the organization trying to attain specific objectives (Hallahan, 2005). These public relations plans need to fit and help to achieve the larger organizational goals.

We must keep one additional point in mind when we use objectives that seek an increase or decrease. To know whether something increased or decreased, you must measure it before and after your public relations effort. Assessing the knowledge, attitude, or behavior before the public relations action provides what is called a *benchmark*. A benchmark is a starting point against which you compare later results (Stacks, 2005). It is much like the way parents track the height of their children as they grow. Your measure after the public relations action can then be compared to the benchmark to see whether the desired increase or decrease was achieved. In the case from Chapter 4, Barberton Citizens Hospital created a benchmark when its survey found that only 51% of the citizens favored selling the park land to the hospital.

▶ Program Management Documents

Public relations planning needs to consider the planning terminology used in many organizations. A public relations action can be a program; a long-term effort; or a project, a temporary, organized effort that creates a unique product or service (Hallahan, 2005; Martin & Tate, 1997). A project has a specific time frame for completion, is composed of a series of related tasks or events that must be coordinated, and seeks to accomplish a specific objective (Davidson, 2000). Whether a program or a project, to be an effective project, a public relations action requires documents that outline the planning process, what are called *program management documents*. Many professions use project management ideas, including public relations, advertising, marketing, construction, and architecture. The planning documents detail the tasks to be completed, who is assigned to complete the tasks (staffing), and the time it will take to complete the tasks (the calendar).

The first step in developing a planning document is to identify all the tasks necessary to complete your public relations action—achieve your objective(s). A list of all the tasks necessary to complete the public relations action is known as the *work breakdown structure*. The second step is to identify how much time each task with take. The third step is to identify the chronological order of the tasks and which tasks are dependent on other tasks. Once you have the tasks, time, and sequence, you are ready to determine how much time the project/public relations action will take to complete (Davidson, 2000). One mistake novices make is to simply add up all the time of the tasks. Box 5.2 illustrates a project time calculation. The seasoned planner knows some tasks can be completed simultaneously (done at the same time), while others are sequential (you must complete one before starting another). Once you determine which tasks are simultaneous and which are sequential, you can calculate the time the project will take. Box 5.2 shows the difference between careful calculation and simply adding up all the tasks. One other piece of advice: Build in time for external contingencies, factors beyond your control that might slow you down. Weather problems, equipment breakdowns, or missed delivery times can create delays. Over time, you will learn how to see potential delays and work them into your program planning.

BOX 5.2 TASKS FOR THE NEWSLETTER

Terry is the editor for his organization's quarterly newsletter. Each edition contains 8 to 10 stories. Key tasks are collecting information for the stories, writing the stories, getting approval of the stories, deciding the layout for news stories, printing the newsletter, and distributing the newsletter. Terry has two other people in the department who help to research and write the stories. Below are the main tasks and time:

Task	Time
Research and writing a story	5 days ($\times$ 10 stories)
Approval of stories	6 days
Layout	2 days
Printing the newsletter	3 days (includes shipping)
Distributing the newsletter	1 day

> If we simply added up all the days, it would be 62 days. However, 3 stories can be researched and written simultaneously. With 10 stories, the time for researching and writing would be 20 days. The remaining tasks must be done in sequence. This would take 12 days. Terry can plan on the newsletter project taking as little as 32 days.

Public relations departments vary in how they construct planning documents. One option is a simple matrix. A matrix or grid lists the central issues along the top of the document and the components of the plan (i.e., strategies, situation, etc.) down the left-hand side of the page. This will create a series of squares or quadrants. Each quadrant is filled in with the objectives, messages, strategies, and tactics relevant to the issues. Your list of central issues will vary from project to project. The matrix is useful as a checklist. It helps you understand whether key points have been covered and to see what tactics have been developed for each quadrant. On a recent project, one coauthor helped to develop a planning matrix for a public hearing. The matrix listed the key issues in the policy discussion across the top, and the left-hand side listed the key message themes needed to for the hearing. The quadrants were filled with the names of people delivering testimony on the theme and the general content of their messages.

A variation of the grid is to use the matrix as a list of questions that need to be answered. Your plan involved answering each of these key questions. Turney (2004) has provided a list of 10 questions for a strategic public relations plan: (1) Who are the organization's key target audiences? (2) Why is this audience important to the organization? (3) What view does the organization want this audience to have of it? (4) What is the audience's current view of the organization? (5) What issues and appeals are important to this audience? (6) Which media does this audience use and trust the most? (7) How does this audience's current view of the organization differ from the desired one? (8) What message themes will have the greatest impact on this audience? (9) What are the best ways of reaching this audience? (10) Who will serve as the organization's primary contact for working with this audience?

Common tools for creating planning documents are Gantt Charts and PERT Charts. While old standards, both are still widely used because they allow for tracking of tasks, time, and staffing all in one (Davidson, 2000). Both are visual representations of the tasks and times. The charts will have the tasks listed on the left side and the time running on the bottom. Computer software, such as "Microsoft Project" or "Primavera Project Planner," can be used to develop either type of chart. Organizations may have preferences, so learn which planning tool your organization uses. The charts are modified as the project progresses to show what has been accomplished and when. Both allow people to easily see where a project is, how long it has taken, what needs to be done, and how much time is left. The weakness of the Gantt and PERT Charts is that they do not display specific tactics and messages for the key tasks.

▶ Budgets

The planning documents will help you calculate the budget. The tasks will help you to identify costs such as personnel (e.g., hiring a graphic designer), commodities (e.g., paper, envelopes, etc.), and services (e.g., having a brochure professionally printed). Organizations differ in how budgets are developed and monies allocated. The key skill is being able to identify all potential costs accurately. Forgetting about a costly item or underestimating costs will cause you to go over budget. You must learn the costs associated with various tasks if you are to create effective budgets.

Public Relations and Strategic Planning

Public relations is a means, not an end. It serves organizations by helping them to achieve their strategic plans. A strategic plan is a means by which they accomplish their missions or visions. Organizations are more likely to realize their missions and visions if they are good and can communicate effectively to build mutually beneficial relationships (see Box 5.3 on "Mission and Vision Statements"). Public relations can help an organization achieve its mission and vision. To do so, each public relations department or agency should state its own mission and vision statement. How public relations serves an organization reflects the mission to which it is dedicated.

BOX 5.3 MISSION AND VISION STATEMENTS

An organization needs to know where it is going. In this boxed feature, we present the mission statements of three organizations: ChevronTexaco Corporation (business), Greenpeace (nonprofit), and the Natural Resources Conservation Service (government agency), which is a division of the U.S. Department of Agriculture. Consider these mission and vision statements, and think of how they influence what is said and done by employees, members, supporters, and other stakeholders and stakeseekers.

Three Mission and Vision Statements

Mission and vision statements express how the executives want to position their organization in regard to its environment: its competitors, marketplace, public policy arena, stakeholders, stakeseekers, and community standards of corporate responsibility. Executives ask, "What is the mission of our organization that makes it unique, differentiates it from other organizations, and gives us a clear idea of where the organization is going?" Hunger and Wheelen (1993), academic experts on strategic planning, observed, "The corporate *mission* is the purpose or reason for the corporation's existence" (p. 14). Compare the following statements for a business, a nonprofit, and a government agency.

1. *ChevronTexaco Corporation:* Chevron/Texaco Corporation, one of the world's largest integrated petroleum companies, takes pride not only in its products and services but also in the way it conducts its worldwide operations. The company's principles and values are embodied in "The ChevronTexaco Way," which provides an integrated framework for its strategies and goals. The company's mission and vision statements are part of "The ChevronTexaco Way."

"Developing vital energy resources around the globe"

"A global enterprise highly competitive across all energy sectors, the newly formed company brings together a wealth of talents, shared values and a strong commitment to developing vital energy resources around the globe."

"ChevronTexaco aims to set the standard not only for goals achieved but for how we achieve them. As important as our financial and operating performance is—our goal is to be No. 1 among our competitors in total stockholder return—our underlying values, more than anything, define who we are."

"The ChevronTexaco Way: Our vision is to be the global energy company most admired for its people, partnership and performance."

2. *Greenpeace:*

"Greenpeace is an independent, campaigning organisation that uses non-violent, creative confrontation to expose global environmental problems, and force solutions for a green and peaceful future. Greenpeace's goal is to ensure the ability of the Earth to nurture life in all its diversity."

3. *Natural Resources Conservation Service* (a division of the U.S. Department of Agriculture):

MISSION—To provide leadership in a partnership effort to help people conserve, improve, and sustain our natural resources and environment.

VISION—Harmony between people and the land

Note: You might compare the Greenpeace mission statement with that stated by the World Wildlife Fund, which is featured in Chapter 3. WWF thinks of itself as a research and collaborative decision-making organization. The mission of Greenpeace commits it to confrontation and highly visible challenges to protect the environment and human health.

A properly stated mission defines the unique purpose that sets a business or other organization apart from others of its type. The mission identifies the scope of the organization's operations by which it obtains and uses revenue and builds mutually beneficial relationships. The mission is the theme that runs throughout the planning and operations of the organization.

Mission statements should translate into objectives. Objectives are standards by which the organization's activities can be empirically assessed. The statement is most serviceable when members of the organization can measure how well strategies serve to accomplish the mission. The mission statement captures key attitudes of the organization, such as those regarding growth, innovation, and quality.

Public relations efforts grow out of two kinds of strategic planning. One is the strategic planning, often called *strategic business planning,* that is created by the executives of the organization. This plan is formulated and implemented so that the entire organization can achieve its mission. In support of the strategic business plan, each department in the organization needs to develop its unique plan, which it implements to help the entire organization to be successful.

This second kind of strategic-planning process occurs at the department or unit level. For this reason, public relations plans—in general and for each specific project—are created, budgeted, and implemented by the public relations department (perhaps in conjunction with an external agency).

As do the organizations that it serves, public relations operates in two broad contexts: the marketplace and the public policy arena. In the marketplace, each organization competes for dollars from customers, followers, or donors. The public policy arena consists of legislative, regulatory, and judicial decision makers. In the public policy arena, legislative bodies create laws that are implemented by regulators in the executive branch of government and enforced by the courts.

In market competition, each organization must obtain in an ethical manner the income it needs to accomplish its mission. An organization's ability to conduct its market activities may be affected by public policy. For this reason, organizations may strategically seek to change public policy in order to accomplish their missions. In these ways, executives of each organization work to protect and promote the interest of the organization and the persons who are affected by it.

Does the quality of relationships the organization creates and maintains affect its ability to survive and thrive? Today's public relations is founded on the principles of building and maintaining mutually beneficial relationships. It requires a strong commitment to fostering the interactive relationship between organizations and their MAPs. Relationship building is inherently a two-way process. It consists of giving and getting stakes in exchange. It is committed to communicating with stakeholders based on what they believe, what they want to know, and what they expect from the relationship. It promotes wise and ethical actions based on openness that builds trust. Public relations can help the organization to be good—to meet standards of corporate responsibility—and to communicate effectively.

This rhetorical approach to public relations is committed to the principle that all of what the organization does and says has communicative impact. People experience and make sense of an organization and its management, reputation, products, services, and ethics by what it does and says. What the organization does and says is its "voice" (Heath, 1994). Public relations professionals can help the organization to speak in a clear, coherent, and consistent voice in all that it does and says.

Voice means that all of the statements—advertising, marketing, public relations—tailor information, evaluations, and conclusions to meet the needs, interests, concerns, and opinions of each MAP. Communication needs to be integrated. For instance, messages shared with investor analysts need to express the same theme and content that is used in dialogue with employees, regulators, activists, other members of an industry, and consumers.

A rhetorical approach to public relations demonstrates that statements are true through all actions by the organization—all of the experiences people have with it. Wise and ethical organizations demonstrate their commitment to quality relationships by all that they do and say. For instance, through product advertising, publicity, and promotion, they say, "Trust us when we tell you about the quality and price of our products; they will satisfy you."

That approach to strategic planning is good business. Quality relationships increase the willingness of key MAPs to reward rather than punish organizations. Stakeholders want to grant their stakes to organizations that please them. If displeased, they will withhold them or give them to another organization. Thus, quality relationships can have market advantage. The logic of organizational strategic planning—and public relations—is simple: Stakeholders prefer to give their stakes to those stakeseekers that do most to achieve a balance of mutual interests. Organizations must compete against one another for resources. They seek favors. They work to increase and manage their markets or please their donors or other constituents. They work to attract investors, contributors, and donors. They want to avoid unproductive and dysfunctional media, governmental, and activist relations.

For these reasons, as a public relations practitioner, you should learn to think in terms of *return on investment* (ROI). To achieve ROI, you need to add value to the efforts of your client—to help the organization to accomplish its mission by generating and wisely managing its resources. ROI means that an organization's efforts should generate more revenue than they cost. This logic also applies to public relations.

If public relations functions properly, it helps the organization listen in order to learn what needs to be known to create beneficial relationships. Then, it offers solutions—strategic responses to the needs, interests, and concerns of MAPs. In that way, public relations justifies its budget and earns its keep. Practitioners do so by knowing and becoming expert in implementing strategic responses to rhetorical problems facing their client organizations. Today's public relations practitioners learn to make a difference in bottom-line performance. To do so, they recognize and solve rhetorical problems that work against the creation and maintenance of mutually beneficial relationships.

WEB WATCHER: STRATEGISTS, INC.

We have presented a discussion of planning in this chapter. Now it is time to go and see how public relations practitioners talk about and conduct planning. Strategists, Inc., is a public relations consulting firm that prides itself on planning. Visit the following section of their Web site: http://www.strategistsinc.com/services-strategic-planning.htm. Look under the headings "strategic planning" and "plan writing." See how they define these concepts and look at examples that summarize their work in strategic planning and plan writing. You will get a feel for how organizations bring to life the planning concepts in this chapter.

▶ Management by Objective: Planning by Setting Goals

Management by objective (MBO) continues to be a popular method for creating and implementing organizational strategies. The logic of MBO is this: In light of what others are doing and thinking, what factors are at play that can help or harm your organization's efforts to achieve its mission? Achieving that goal requires situational analysis. What needs to be done and said to make or keep the organization (your department, campaign, or job) effective? That question grows out of objective setting and strategic implementation of the means to accomplish that objective. What do you need to do or say to accomplish your (and the organization's) objectives to satisfactorily take advantage of opportunities and avoid or minimize threats? That is the essence of MBO: thinking strategically. That logic asks that you develop your plans—within ethical guidelines—to accomplish (or help others accomplish) what needs to be done to move the organization in the desired direction.

MBO is a nice logic that applies feedback—evaluation/assessment—to determine how well the strategies, as implemented, achieve their objectives. It is consistent with our earlier discussion of objectives in the public relations action. Evaluation measures whether the plan as implemented has achieved the objectives needed to help the organization to accomplish what it must and desires to do. Feedback is implemented through evaluative research. It requires knowing what the organization wants to achieve and setting measures to determine whether it was successful.

This process builds in stages. Each stage is likely to exist and impinge on the organization's success whether it is planned or more accidental, or coincidental:

- *Rhetorical situation:* circumstances surrounding the organization that will affect its ability to achieve what it desires. It must know, consider, and adapt to its situation if it is to achieve its mission.
- *Objectives* (mission and vision): the goals the organization seeks to accomplish in its efforts to achieve its mission.
- *Plan:* the means by which the organization strategically intends to accomplish its objectives. The plan includes message development options and actions.
- *Implementation:* strategic options that are chosen and budgeted to be used as the means for putting the plan into operation.
- *Feedback/evaluation:* hard and soft evidence used to determine the extent to which the strategic options as implemented are accomplishing what they must and should for the organization to achieve its mission, in light of the situation.

Now, the effort of the organization might end with evaluation—especially if it is favorable. That could be shortsighted, even disastrous, for at least two reasons. One, the situation around the organization constantly changes, including the strategic planning, implementation, and assessment of other organizations, as well as dynamic change on the part of MAPs. The success and failure of other organizations in their strategic efforts can be a factor in what your client organization needs to plan, implement, and accomplish.

Second, plans succeed to various degrees. Sometimes they accomplish more than expected. Sometimes they achieve success with less effort than anticipated. Sometimes they fall short of expectations. The logic of MBO is that feedback evaluation is a stage in an ongoing effort. The organization should seek constant change by building on its success.

Based on how well the plan accomplished its objective, in light of the situation, the plan can be refined, objectives reshaped, and implementation continued or modified. In this manner, MBO is a dynamic mode of thinking and acting.

- *Feedback/evaluation* (as situational analysis): continual listening to the market and sociopolitical arenas, as well as stakeholders or stakeseekers who impinge on the organization.
- *Objectives redefined/revised:* refining objectives in light of continual situational assessment and the organization's ability to design and implement a feasible strategic plan.
- *Plan redefined/revised:* refining the means for achieving objectives, in light of situational changes and success in implementing key plans.
- *Implementation redefined/revised:* refining means for putting the plan into play.
- *Feedback/evaluation:* continued listening to the situational factors to which the organization needs to respond.

This analysis forms a spiral of ongoing, adaptive strategic planning, implementation, and assessment.

Conclusion

Strategic thinking grows out of the analysis of the kinds of relationships that are necessary for the organization to achieve its mission. Savvy public relations experts learn to use relationships to define goals and strategies. Planning activities for a successful team effort are derived from discovering an opportunity or threat: formative research. That logic is basic to the discovery and analysis of the rhetorical problem facing the organization. In the vignette at the beginning of this chapter, TETCO did not just react, even in a crisis. Management carefully considered the situation, MAPs, and relationships before responding. The response was strategic and designed to restore mutually beneficial relationships in the community in which it operated.

Your formative research informs your planning process. In planning, you are developing measurable objectives, creating a plan, and developing a budget. An effective objective demands that you quantify your results and specify your target MAPs. Your plan requires you to identify all tasks that need to be completed and the sequencing of the tasks. Your budget needs to list all possible costs you might encounter. Proper planning is the most effective way to prepare a public relations action. Planning creates focus and seeks to eliminate surprises such as last-minute tasks that need to be completed or budget items that were overlooked. Your planning documents tell you what needs to be done and how much it will cost.

Making a Difference

Helen I. Ostrowski
Global CEO
Porter Novelli
New York City,
New York

I'm sure just about everyone in our profession has encountered the vexing question (usually accompanied by a quizzical look): "So . . . public relations is more than press releases?" This is when I contemplate going into teaching—but then remember experience is the best teacher of all.

Of course much of our time as public relations professionals is spent parsing our words, making sure the nuance is just so, and ensuring every fact is absolutely correct. Just as much time is spent with journalists, advocates, community leaders, employees, analysts and a host of other constituents to ensure we are truly listening and creating the kind of dialogues in which we can successfully tell our stories. Our craft is one of well-articulated persuasion.

But what I've loved most about what we do is the power to make a difference. And that difference doesn't come just through words or deeds alone, but truly understanding our audiences and the world they live in to gain the insights necessary to drive creative ideas that truly have an impact. Ideas that create awareness of a problem or issue. Ideas that shift attitudes. Ideas that alter behavior. Ideas that change minds.

Making a difference isn't about altruistic platitudes or idealistic programs. It's about creating a more favorable environment in which an organization's idea, service or issue can take seed and flourish and where we can see measurable progress. Creating that environment depends on solid strategic planning—based in research—with results you can measure.

What has been particularly rewarding is to see how well organizations are employing public relations—and how sophisticated it's become since I started in the profession. Gillette, for example, now uses public relations in advance of all other disciplines before major new product launches, because the company has found it can create the receptivity it needs for its marketing and sales. As a result, public relations often leads the way in finding new insights that inform not only the public relations program, but the marketing program as well. For example, when the company was getting ready to launch a new shaving product for women, Sensor, it planned to use the same

In addition, you can track tasks and costs as the public relations project progresses. You will know whether you are on schedule and on budget or if corrections are necessary. In the third season of NBC's *The Apprentice*, a team leader simply started high-tech, high-performance approach that worked so well in launching the men's product. However, research for the public relations program into women's attitudes toward shaving discovered that women blame themselves when they fumble the job, whereas men blame the product—creating an entirely new strategy and messaging for the women's program. By the way, I never fail to get knowing nods from women whenever I talk about this case history.

Some of the most fervent believers in public relations are marketers—and small wonder, when you consider that public relations is every bit as rigorous a discipline as marketing. In many ways, marketers are the new converts to public relations, as they've seen its power in shaping markets, increasing user acceptance and building loyalty (to name just a few virtues). Public relations has always been part and parcel of the corporate firmament in helping with financial markets or managing issues. But businesses and governments alike have also become just as savvy as their marketing counterparts, and today public relations programs carried out by these groups look an awful lot like marketing programs: intensive research to understand audiences, testing of messages and ideas, and then measuring impact after the campaign has been launched. It wasn't until the National Institutes of Health found out in testing that consumers couldn't make sense of this medical problem called "cholesterol" unless they could quantify it somehow: hence, the "know your number" campaign that galvanized public attention to this life-threatening condition and led the way to better testing and treatment. Likewise, when the State of Florida decided to spend its tobacco settlement monies on educating teens about the dangers of smoking, it took extensive research into kids' psyches to realize the way to reach them *wasn't* through telling them how bad smoking was for them— it would be by appealing to kids' sense of being manipulated by the tobacco industry. Thus was born the Truth campaign, recognized globally for its success in lowering teenage smoking.

Obviously, the biggest difference we make is as individuals in the lives of those we touch—professionally and personally. But because our profession is built on understanding what makes people tick—how they think, what they believe and what they *could* think or believe in the future—we have tremendous power in shaping how our society accepts change, the true dynamic of public relations.

Did someone say we're more than press releases? Happily, all it takes is one experience with a successful public relations campaign, and that vexing question turns to: "Tell me how we can measure what we're doing." But that's a reflection for another day!

SOURCE: Reprinted with permission from Helen I. Ostrowski.

a project without planning. It turns out that he bought items he did not need and did not have the money to buy items the team did need. He did not consider the tasks or budget until it was too late. He admitted his mistake and was "fired" by

Donald Trump. There is reality to this reality show. Failure to plan can result in practitioners losing accounts and/or jobs. Planning sets the stage for action (Chapter 6) and is critical to evaluation (Chapter 7). Planning is the glue that binds together the elements of the public relations process.

Ethical Quandary: Building Ethics Into Planning

Explain at least three ethical reasons that you would use when advising a client or an organization's executive management who wants to exploit or correct a damaged relationship. Let's imagine that the client knows that a competitor is not meeting customers' or donors' expectations (a damaged relationship opportunity). Or you might imagine that a client's product or service is not as good "as advertised" but the client wants a promotional campaign to deny or divert attention from that fact (a damaged relationship threat). Or you might imagine that a consumer reporter has made allegations about a product or service (even a fund-raising tactic or the use of charitable contributions) that you believe to be untrue (a crisis based on a threat to a relationship). Ethical decisions can be based on high moral principle—doing what is right—and on pragmatics—what works is good. Would you build your case on either of these principles? What three points would you make to guide the selection of public relations responses to the rhetorical problem? How are these three points connected to the strategic responses you would advise making to solve the rhetorical problem?

Summary Questions

1. Define *mission* and *vision*. Explain why these statements are best when they contain outcomes that can be measured.

2. How is return on investment (ROI) a part of strategic business planning and of strategic public relations planning?

3. How is planning related to strategy?

4. What are the characteristics of an effective objective?

5. What are the three basic types of objectives?

6. How do objectives relate to benchmarking?

7. What are program management documents?

8. What are the steps in creating a planning document?

9. What are the two kinds of strategic planning?

10. What is management by objective (MBO)?

Exercises

1. Find a Web site for a business, governmental agency, or nonprofit organization. Look to see whether the organization states its mission statement. If you were the public relations officer for the organization, what plan would you recommend to increase awareness, to inform, to persuade, to listen, and to engage in collaborative decision making so that the organization could achieve its mission and vision?

2. Develop a public relations plan to help increase the visibility of your Public Relations Student Society of America (PRSSA) chapter. If you are on a campus that has no chapter, develop a plan to convince faculty members and administrators that a chapter should be established on the campus. To achieve your plan, do you need to research the Web site of the Public Relations Society of America (PRSA) and PRSSA to determine what requirements need to be met to create or promote your chapter? To whom should you listen to learn more about the challenges to creating or increasing awareness for your chapter?

Recommended Readings

Allen, R. W. (1995). Rebuilding trust in a world of disbelief. *Public Relations Strategist, 1*(4), 13–16.

Carroll, A. B. (1998). Stakeholder strategy for public relations. *Public Relations Strategist, 3*(4), 38–40.

Dozier, D. M., Grunig, L. A., & Grunig, J. A. (1995). *Manager's guide to excellence in public relations and communication management.* Mahwah, NJ: Lawrence Erlbaum.

Ferguson, S. D. (1999). *Communication planning: An integrated approach.* Thousand Oaks, CA: Sage.

Gaschen, D. J. (1998). Managing the growth of your business (and getting a good night's sleep). *Public Relations Tactics, 5*(7), 12–13.

Heath, R. L. (1997). *Strategic issues management: Organizations and public policy challenges* (see especially chap. 1). Thousand Oaks, CA: Sage.

Hon, L. C. (1997). What have you done for me lately? Exploring effectiveness in public relations. *Journal of Public Relations Research, 9*, 1–30.

Hon, L. C. (1998). Demonstrating effectiveness in public relations: Goals, objectives, and evaluation. *Journal of Public Relations Research, 10*, 103–135.

Hunger, J. D., & Wheelen, T. L. (1993). *Strategic management* (4th ed.). Reading, MA: Addison-Wesley.

Kazoleas, D. (2005). Program/action plans. In R. L. Heath (Ed.), *Encyclopedia of public relations* (pp. 648–650). Thousand Oaks, CA: Sage.

Kelly, K. S. (1991). *Fund raising and public relations: A critical analysis.* Hillsdale, NJ: Lawrence Erlbaum.

Stern, S. (1998). Building long-term relationships. *Public Relations Tactics, 5*(7), 11–12.

Suggs, S. (1998). Goodwill hunting: How community service can recharge your career. *Public Relations Tactics, 5*(12), 24–25.

Turner, L. J. (2005). Elmo's story: A ticklish media creation. *Public Relations Review, 31,* 297–299.

Weintraub, A., & Pinkleton, B. E. (2000). *Strategic public relations management.* Mahwah, NJ: Lawrence Erlbaum.

Wilson, L. J. (2001). Extending strategic planning to communication tactics. In R. L. Heath (Ed.), *Handbook of public relations* (pp. 215–222). Thousand Oaks, CA: Sage.

Taking Action
Strategic Messaging

6

How Many Chips?

Teachers look for innovative ways to teach children. One teacher liked to use real-life problems to help children learn to count. She wanted to make counting important to the students. This teaching technique created a rhetorical problem for Nabisco, which advertises that each 18-ounce bag of Chips Ahoy! contains at least 1,000 chocolate chips. The teacher challenged the children to count the chips in several bags. They did. The totals they counted ranged from 340 to 680—far below the advertised claim. The children were shocked. Is there truth in advertising? Nearly 100 angry letters prepared by children in these classes were sent to Nabisco. That is the rhetorical problem. What is the solution? A company spokesperson visited the school in assembly. Through her research, she had learned that the children counted only the chips they could see in each cookie. Using a public relations tool called an "event," she placed a bag of cookies in a colander and soaked them until only the chips remained. The students counted again. The total number was 1,181 (Blackburn, 1997). This is an excellent example of customer relationship building. It rests on the creation of a platform of fact the children could use in understanding the quality of the product—as well as the reputation of the company. Strategically solving this public relations problem required developing a strategy and implementing it. The company could have conducted the experiment and reported the results in a letter. Instead, it wanted to engage the students in a scientific experiment to test the accuracy of the company's advertising message claims. To do that, it needed to implement the

Proving the Accuracy of Advertising Claims

SOURCE: Reprinted with permission from *Chance*. Copyright 1999 by the American Statistical Association. All rights reserved.

demonstration. The company wanted to be correct—a good company—and wanted to communicate that point effectively. That required strategic thinking coupled with successful implementation.

The SMART approach to public relations (Societal value and meaning, Mutually beneficial relationships, Advantages through objectives, Rhetorical strategies, and Tactics) requires that practitioners understand how to take action by knowing the array of tools that are available to achieve strategic outcomes. Each of these can be used in the proper time and place. To think and act SMART, practitioners master an array of public relations tools. Each is like a tool in a toolbox. It has its specific application. Strategic and ethical practitioners ask whether each tool has social value and contributes to shared meaning that advances the public interest. Can any tool help or harm relationships? Tactics are employed to accomplish definable objectives. They are rhetorical since they can be used to influence or achieve outcomes.

The SMART approach is rhetorical. That means that tools and tactics are selected and employed because of what they can accomplish in regard to the stated objectives. Tactics are employed to make the strategies work and achieve the objectives. This SMART approach to public relations begins with research, entails strategic planning, requires tactical implementation, and ends with evaluation. In this way, the public relations practitioner keeps the activities alive and vital to accomplish specific outcomes.

Thinking Strategically and Tactically

To take action, public relations practitioners need certain personal traits and professional skills. In Box 6.1, you will find lists of the qualities that are critical to a public relations practitioner. These lists represent the skills, knowledge, and personal traits that employers find most desirable. The qualities featured reflect the preferences of PRSA (Public Relations Society of America), PRSSA (Public Relations Student Society of America), and the Commission on Public Relations Education Study. Because these skills are expected of practitioners, they should be central to each student's professional development. They make the practitioner more tactical.

BOX 6.1 QUALITIES OF A PUBLIC RELATIONS PRACTITIONER

Public Relations Society of America

- Analytic/critical thinking
- Ability to work well under pressure
- Imagination and creativity
- Communication skills/writing
- Self-confidence
- Diplomacy
- Organization and planning skills
- Internet research skills

Public Relations Student Society of America

- Effective written communication
- Persuasive speaking/presentational skills
- Problem solving/critical thinking
- Decision making
- Active listening
- Editing
- Research/information gathering
- Production skills (desktop publishing, layout, graphics)
- Computer skills (basic plus desktop publishing and Internet)

1999 Commission on Public Relations Education Study

- Self-starter
- Writing news release
- Organized
- Interpersonal skills
- Critical thinking/problem solving
- Flexible
- Word processing/e-mail
- Knowledge/interest in current events
- Constructively accepts criticism

The Public Relations Society of America (PRSA) is the largest professional organization of public relations practitioners. It works hard to be a leader in education for the field. PRSA wants to ensure that quality job candidates enter the job market, because its members are the future employers. The Public Relations Student Society of America (PRSSA) is the student version of PRSA and part of its effort to improve public relations education. In 1999, the Commission on Public Relations Education, a collection of leading public relations educators and practitioners, released a report updating curriculum requirements for undergraduate and graduate education in the United States. To help the commission, a survey of practitioners and educators was completed, asking them to evaluate what students should be able to do on the job, qualities of a good hire. The list you see is the one compiled from the practitioners who responded to the survey.

Writing regularly is at the top of all the lists about public relations qualifications. But if you look closer at Box 6.1, you will see the value of strategy and tactic. Practitioners value the ability to engage in analysis/critical thinking. As a public relations practitioner, you need to be *analytical*, capable of identifying and dissecting issues. Part of the challenge of being a successful practitioner is to recognize problems before the happen and once they happen. Recognizing a problem is the first step. Being able to think strategically and tactically is the second.

One of the differences that distinguishes the strategic thinker is knowing that public relations tactics are not an end in and of themselves. Tools and strategies are used to achieve objectives and accomplish goals. Public relations is valuable because it helps organizations to be more effective. To make organizations more effective, public relations can strategically and tactically help them to build, repair, and maintain mutually beneficial relations. See the conclusion stressed in Box 6.2.

BOX 6.2 MEANS, NOT AN END

Public relations is a means, not an end. It serves an organization by helping it to achieve its strategic business plan. The strategic business plan is the means by which an organization's management seeks to achieve its mission or vision. The strategic public relations plan is the means by which public relations practitioners work to help management achieve the organization's business plan. Having a good plan based on sound research lays the foundation for implementation. At some point, the practitioner must take action.

The strategic process begins by knowing which relationships practitioners must build, maintain, or repair. Once this challenge is firmly in mind, they need to select public relations tactics to accomplish those objectives. This line of thinking has three components: (a) Understand the dynamics of the relationship, (b) think in terms of message development objectives, and (c) select and use appropriate public relations tools. Message development objectives include

- Gaining attention
- Providing useful information (informing) desired by the market, audience, or public (MAP)
- Persuading and being persuaded through dialogue, within ethical limits
- Engaging in collaborative decision making
- Cocreating meaning through narratives and identification

Strategic planning addresses message development objectives. It begins by listening—conducting research or being attentive to MAPs. It entails observing the messages and deciding which stakeholders agree and disagree with the message positions that are relevant to the organization's interests. It determines which markets or publics are aware of (or not aware of) certain facts and hold various opinions. When the organization and the stakeholder agree on the issue, the relationship is positive, and when they disagree, it can be negative. Positive relationships lead to stake giving; negative relationships result in stake withholding. In the largest sense, public relations tactics allow practitioners to take actions to solve problems of awareness, knowledge, agreement, and motivation. Practitioners consider what needs to be said, how it should be said, and what communication tools are needed to engage in successful and ethical communication.

Formulating Messages

To respond to a rhetorical challenge, practitioners decide what must be said. They want to present a message in its most appealing way. They also know that what they say must address what the MAPs want to know. Practitioners understand that they must listen to others to be able to respond appropriately. As practitioners and the persons they communicate with work together, the end product is cocreated meaning. The objective is to create meaning that fosters mutually beneficial relationships. This challenge raises two lines of questions.

▶ Message Points

One way of thinking about messages considers the *message points* that need to be put before each MAP for their consideration. A message point is some fact or opinion about a product or a service that a practitioner wants a customer to remember.

Message points are also used to present a desirable persona of the organization, one that advances its reputation. Thus, for instance, in the case of a furniture store, one message point would be the products that it sells. Another would be its location. If it is having a seasonal sale or publicizing the grand opening of a new location, that is a message point. If an event, such as an appearance by a celebrity or music group, is going to be part of the grand opening, that information becomes a message point. Perhaps the opening is going to be associated with a charitable fund-raiser. That information becomes a message point. In this way, the practitioner has in mind the rhetorical problem (notifying people of the opening and motivating them to visit the store) and the substance of the message that needs to be set into play to solve the rhetorical problem. This would be the message of publicity and promotion. Thus, message points are the most basic but essential elements of the response to the rhetorical problem. They help cocreate meaning.

What about the messages in a controversy? That too can be resolved into message points. Message points surface during honest disagreements between an organization and a public. Each side of a controversy may be convinced it is correct. It asserts its views—key facts and opinions. For instance, communities around the nation find citizens pitted against one another over the "wild" deer issue (Sledzik, 1997).

The "wild" deer issue arises and becomes a problem as people move from cities to suburbs; they have invaded the territories of wild animals. One species, deer, can flourish where people live. Some people protect the deer because they are beautiful. Under protection, the deer become pets. For other members of a community, they are nuisances because they cause car accidents and destroy landscaping. To research the impact of "wild" deer on the local environment, including residents' property,

Deer Population Divides Communities and Strains Relationships

SOURCE: Copyright 2005 Houston Chronicle Publishing Company.

requires knowing something about the total financial impact, the number and kinds of deer involved, and the most humane means for deer population management. In this kind of controversy, message points come from many directions and voices—in a dialogue—which members of local government are challenged to address.

To address this issue through dialogue, message points of fact and evaluation are weighed, leading to the formation of a policy. Collaborative decision making helps determine what the key message points are, which facts and evaluations are best because they withstand public scrutiny, and which policy solves the collectively experienced problem. In this case, collaborative decision making may be needed to explore which competing message is correct. Again, this communication effort can result in cocreated meaning through dialogue.

This line of thinking, a *concurrence model,* uses a series of questions to determine the agreement or disagreement between an organization and each relevant stakeholder/stakeseeker in the specific rhetorical problem. The assumption is that high agreement, understanding, and satisfaction is good—a co-orientation assumption. When conflict is high, we have competing and unaligned zones of meaning. Thus, a practitioner may begin to take action by addressing the elements of the message needed to respond to the rhetorical problem:

- What do you want the group to know?
- What do they know?
- What do you want them to believe?
- What do they believe?
- How do you want them to evaluate the circumstances of the situation?
- How do they evaluate the circumstances of the situation?
- What criteria do they use?
- What criteria do you want them to use?
- What conclusions do you want them to draw?
- What conclusions do they want to draw?
- Where is there difference?
- Where is there agreement?
- How significant is the agreement?
- How substantial is the disagreement?
- Which differences can be reduced or eliminated?
- Is the relationship strengthening or deteriorating because of differences?

Concurrence can be looked at from the point of view of each MAP as well. For instance, what do you believe, and what do they want you to believe? If we put this analysis into the context of a rhetorical problem, we can think of it this way: Differences that are strongly held are likely to be threats; they can lead to conflict. Opportunities arise out of agreement and unmet challenges.

Based on that analysis, let's combine message development objectives with considerations of the relevant message points. To do so, let's remind ourselves that we are interested in facts: what is empirically known, evaluations (preferences), and conclusions/solutions. Attitudes are evaluations based on beliefs. Preferences are expressions of value.

Informative and persuasive message points can be used to achieve the information, attitude, and/or behavioral objectives discussed in Chapter 5.

Informative Message Points

Situational analysis asks key questions: What facts need to be put into play? What facts are being put into play by key stakeholders? The message development objective features this prescription: Incorporate into message points the information that can create mutual understanding, satisfaction, and agreement. By returning to the Nabisco "Chips Ahoy!" case, we can consider the informative message points the company wants to demonstrate to the children, teacher, and parents:

- Each bag of Chips Ahoy! contains at least 1,000 chocolate chips.
- Nabisco is willing to prove its advertising claims under public scrutiny.
- Nabisco responds to customer inquiries.

Persuasive Message Points

Situational analysis asks key questions: What attitudes are at play? Are they ones that are likely to lead to the wisest, most mutually satisfying outcomes? What can be changed? What can be reinforced? What changes need to be made by the client organization in light of prevailing opinions? The message development objectives are a strategic persuasion response to the rhetorical problem:

- Nabisco is an honest company.
- Nabisco is an open company.
- Nabisco respects children as customers.
- Nabisco supports public education practices.
- Nabisco tells the truth.
- Nabisco makes a good product.
- Buy Nabisco products.

You can use this logic to think about an organization's reputation. Its reputation is a composite of what people know about it and the attitude they have toward it.

Messages consist of facts, opinions, and action statements. Behind each of these are sets of premises that people use to guide their reasoning. As practitioners take action, they select the premises or address premises that are fundamental to the decision confronting each MAP. Messages do some or all of the following:

- *Use widely accepted premises:* These messages accept the premises that are widely held by key MAPs and use them to cocreate meaning. For instance, safety is a widely accepted premise that can be used in public health and safety messages, such as "Don't drive drunk" or "Friends don't let friends drive drunk."
- *Defend premises:* Over time, premises and assumptions of society change. Key groups work to change premises as part of their rhetorical role in society. Messages may be used to stop or slow the change. For instance, as lawsuits have become more frequent and settlements larger, tort reform groups have

defended the premise of limited liability ("Stop lawsuit abuse!") and fostered individual responsibility. (Product design costs everyone money when they have to be overdesigned to prevent product design abuse in lawsuits.)

- *Advocate new premises:* As well as defending the status quo, messages can be designed to change it. Although being healthy is a standard premise shared (cocreated as a zone of meaning) throughout society, the standards of health change. One standard that has changed in the past two decades is the "healthy glow of tanned skin," which may be a first step toward skin cancer, a growing medical problem.

- *Champion or challenge public policies:* Messages may champion public policies or challenge them. The insurance industry lobbied aggressively, and successfully, for legislation that would force automobile manufacturers to make safer cars. This was a smart business effort, as well as one that was socially responsible, on the part of the insurance industry. It believed that lives and suffering could be saved if people had safer automobiles. And insurance rates could be lower and profits higher.

- *Enlist supporters to act on specific policies and recommendations:* Activist groups, for instance, enlist followers to act on policies or recommendations. This can entail giving money for specific environmental projects or writing Congress to pressure action on environmental legislation. In a similar fashion, messages of this sort are targeted at markets. If you believe our product is as good as we say it is, then buy it! That marketing logic underpins a lot of publicity and promotion.

▶ Formulating Message Points

Message points involve the careful crafting of words. We have selected three resources we feel are important to constructing messages that will build mutually beneficial relationships: narratives, identification, and persona. Each of these resources can be used to build your message points.

Narratives

Messages are based on and apply common narratives. People live and think in terms of stories. They report the events that occur in their lives as stories. They make and execute plans as stories. For these reasons, narrative theory is vital to the formulation of messages used by public relations practitioners. After having seen the demonstration on how to count cookies, will the schoolchildren report to their parents, siblings, friends, and grandparents that each bag of Chips Ahoy! contains at least 1,000 chips? Will they tell the story of the assembly, meeting the company representative, counting the chips, and drawing conclusions? Will they and the person who buys cookies purchase that brand, based on this cocreated meaning?

Identification

Identification is vital to relationships. In a sense, identification can be simplified by the following axiom: Birds of a feather flock together. For this reason, public relations practitioners work to identify with MAPs. In turn, they ask that this identification be reciprocated. Identification is a vital part of marketing publicity and promotion. Companies try to position themselves so they demonstrate how they identify with the needs and wants of customers. They create a persona that links to that of their customers. Nabisco wants children, parents, and teachers to identify with it as a good and honest company. How would identification work in the "wild" deer scenario? First, community government needs to work to help residents identify with the community to see the deer population as a community problem, not a problem of "them"— the opposition. The community is less likely to achieve a satisfactory solution if it is divided along more narrow identifications of "deer lovers" and "deer killers." By seeing this as a joint deer population management problem, the community has the spirit to work together toward a mutually beneficial solution.

Persona

Organizations' personae are revealed by what they say and do, and how they say and do it. An organization's persona is shaped by what is said and written about it. A persona is the residue of the encounters MAPs have with the organization. Personae can be inferred from ad message content, communication tactics, kinds of issues addressed, and the relationship the source states, implies, assumes, or seeks with key publics.

A persona can affect how key publics react to the organization's public policy stance, and its public policy stance helps establish its persona. A persona can also affect and be affected by its products, services, fund-raising activities, and impact on the community. A persona influences how well the organization is received in the marketplace and public policy arena. MAPs react to an organization's persona based on their identification with it.

Public relations helps tell the narrative the organization is attempting to create and enact. Its persona is like a character in a play, novel, or film. It needs to be clearly defined and presented in a manner that is convincing and fosters a mutually beneficial relationship with stakeholders and stakeseekers. The persona or character enacted by an organization results from the residue of what key MAPs know of its actions and statements.

Personae are the roles the organization takes on or is expected or perceived to take on. Roles are archetypal, such as "objective advocate," "policy innovator," "informed source," and "friendly advisor." Consider these personae: freedom fighter, informed source, savior through technology, policy innovator, business advisor, environmental protectionist, policy corrector, and protector of children.

CHALLENGE

Think of organizations that you believe exhibit or achieve each of these personae, and consider the personae you believe are presented by organizations with which you are familiar.

Advocates of public policy issue positions exhibit personae that are vital to the campaign they are waging. The same can be said for the marketing and fund-raising efforts of organizations. Governmental agencies work to define and portray personae aligned with their missions and interests of key MAPs. For instance, the FBI and the Justice Department seek different personae than do welfare agency departments such as the Department of Education and the Department of Housing and Urban Development (HUD). The Department of Commerce differs from the Department of Defense.

Similar tailoring exists for activist group personae. Some activist groups position themselves—portray a persona—as being extreme, active, and radical demanders of policy change: Greenpeace, for example. In contrast, the Audubon Society is more staid, and the World Wildlife Fund positions itself to support research and fund species preservation.

Universities strive for unique personae, reflected in their academic programs, admission and graduation standards, athletic programs, campus mascots, students, alumni, and faculty. Fund-raising organizations tailor their missions and demonstrate their personae as a vital part of their efforts to generate and apply funds in ways that foster and sustain long-term relationships between donors and benefactors of those funds.

Personae can be interpreted by applying four concepts that are vital to the rhetorical positioning of organizations through their public relations: differentiation, association, identity, and goodwill. Let's think about each one and its implications for public relations.

Activists Appeal to Followers by Aligning Interests

SOURCE: Reprinted with permission from the National Audubon Society.

- *Differentiation* results when products, services, issue discussions, operations, policy positions, mission, and marketing strategies (including fund-raising) make an organization unique—different from other organizations.
- *Associations* result from the traits or attributes that result from the actions, values, and traits that typify the company or group—such as being proenvironmental.
- *Identity* is the archetype that characterizes the organization—bold advocate, technical expert, wise advisor, defender of the environment, or protector of abused women.
- *Goodwill* results when policies and actions taken by the organization benefit others and advance community interests—those of stakeseekers and stakeholders.

Persona and Identification

People identify with organizations that align with their interests and shared meaning. Through dialogue between employees and management, a persona can arise that

A Technical Communication Professional Flexes With Changing Times

Marty Moore, MS
Senior Practitioner
Specializing in
Communication
Technology
Washington, D.C.

E-commerce was going to change the way the world did business. Venture money flowed as fast as business plans utilizing the power of the Internet could be submitted. Companies were hiring as quickly as candidates could come in the door. Companies rushed to put "dot-com" behind their name. If you did not, you were seen as behind the times. Suddenly, it all changed. The market was suddenly demanding e-commerce companies show revenue and a profitability plan. Companies without a salient business model were being financially punished. Instead of "dot-com," pure Internet companies were being called "dot-bombs."

The company I worked for utilized the Internet as a complementary sales channel for thousands of software publisher clients. Founded in 1994, the company is a leading global e-commerce outsource provider, offering clients complete e-commerce systems and services. Its commerce services grow businesses quickly and profitably. Our services include e-commerce strategy, site development and hosting, order and transaction management, system integration, product fulfillment and returns, e-marketing and customer service.

As the economy began to falter, the key for us was to create a consistent message. While other e-commerce companies chose to frequently "reinvent" themselves, we were determined that creating a simple, concise set of messages was the best methodology. We positioned ourselves as a "leading global e-commerce outsource provider."

is mutually satisfying and aligns interests. Employees identify with the organization where they work. Managements identify with employees. Products are featured as means by which customers can identify with the organization. We often call this "brand loyalty," which translates into "brand equity." They may disidentify with a product or organization when they see the purchase of the product or the support of the organization as conflicting with their identity. Students identify with their schools or universities. They identify with other students from their schools or universities. Persons with commitment to environmental protection identify with environmental groups and disidentify with organizations that they believe harm the

Our contention was that outsourcing saves time and money and yields a faster return on investment.

For the most part, we opted not to rely on advertising to build its brand. Instead, we utilized public relations techniques. Senior management decided advertising was a method to purchase a reputation; however, public relations was a better method to building a world-class reputation through third-party, expert endorsements. Without the combination of advertising and public relations, we have to work harder at getting the idea of e-commerce outsourcing as part of the media's and potential clients' agendas. Our plan was to develop our concept of being a "leading global e-commerce outsourcer"; we developed our message and used it faithfully without alteration.

Public relations is a powerful tactic in the high-tech arena. Our public relations efforts crossed all departments. However, we had a heavy focus on industry analyst relations, investor relations and media relations. These three key efforts needed to be congruent. Our public relations focused on the efforts of reaching all stakeholders, evangelizing the idea of e-commerce outsourcing.

Our media relations efforts continued to focus on four areas. First is the technology media. We worked with the most established technology brands. Our goal was to leverage the power of these brands to continue to build awareness. The second focus area was the financial media. The company achieved consistent, double-digit growth since the company was founded. Third, our focus was the trade media. At the height of the "new economy," there were many "trade rags." Finally, what we have deemed the tier-one publications were our target. These publications include the weekly business media that tend to focus on business trends rather than specific companies. With four focus areas, each demanding different variations of the same message—a technology, financial, trade and business message—we remained committed to the concept of outsourcing.

SOURCE: Reprinted with permission from Marty Moore.

environment. Identification is shared meaning (even campus rivalries) and aligned interests.

Identification can predict product purchase. It may be a vital part of the reason why students choose one college over another. It seems to be key to alumni association membership and sustained contributions to alma maters. If people identify with animals and other parts of the environment, are they likely to join and support environmental movements? If they identify with the targeted group of a nonprofit, such as cancer victims, are they likely to support its efforts? For that reason, we can understand why people support the American Cancer Society. The list of identifications is endless.

WEB WATCHER: THE AD COUNCIL

In 1942, the Ad Council began creating messages designed to help the American people. Their mission is "to identify a select number of significant public issues and stimulate action on those issues through communications programs that make a measurable difference in our society" (Ad Council, 2004). People from advertising and public relations volunteer their time to create the public service announcements (PSAs) the Ad Council uses to tackle public issues, such as their famous "Smokey the Bear" campaign. The Ad Council maintains a section of their Web site that has messages from their current campaigns. The address is http://www.adcouncil.org/campaigns/. Visit the Web site, and select a specific campaign that has a sample newspaper PSA to print. Based on the message in the PSA, answer these questions: (1) What do you think the objective is, and (2) Who do believe the target is for the PSA? Finally, what clues in the message helped you to answer these questions?

Conclusion

Research and planning set the stage for a practitioner to take action. Taking action involves creating messages and then sending them to your targeted MAPs. This chapter focused on creating messages. Chapters 11 and 12 will explore selecting tactics and channels for delivering your messages. We have discussed the idea behind message strategies and how these relate to message development objectives. There is still a great deal you will need to learn about creating public relations messages. That is why a public relations major will be required to take a course in public relations writing. We can only introduce the subject in the introductory textbook. Once practitioners have begun to take action by formulating messages, they need to decide which tools of the trade are most useful to achieve the message development objectives. Chapter 12 provides recommendations for the selection and use of various public relations tools.

FURTHER
EXPLORATION

6

Ethical Quandary: Sustaining Mutually Beneficial Relationships

Consider whether a relationship can be sustained if it is not mutually beneficial. What role does ethics play in the creation and maintenance of a relationship? Is a relationship ethical when one entity benefits more than the other one does?

Summary Questions

1. What is the SMART approach to public relations?
2. What does it mean to say public relations is a means, not an end?
3. What do message development objectives include?
4. What are message points?
5. What are some of the different types of message points?
6. How is a concurrent model used to determine agreement or disagreement between an organization and stakeholder/stakeseeker?
7. Why are narratives valuable in messages?
8. How does an organization use messages to create identification with MAPs?
9. What is the connection between messages and an organization's persona?
10. What are the four rhetorical concepts used to build a persona?

Exercises

1. Find a public relations message from an organization and locate the following:
   a. The organization's persona
   b. The message point
   c. The rhetorical concept used to build the persona

2. Find a different message that develops a narrative. What is the organization's role narrative? What values or beliefs does the narrative use to build identification between the organization and MAPs?

Recommended Readings

Adams, W. C. (1995). Marrying the functions: The importance of media relations in public affairs planning. *Public Relations Quarterly, 40*(3), 7–11.

Broom, G. M. (1982). A comparison of sex roles in public relations. *Public Relations Review, 8*(3), 17–22.

Broom, G. M., & Dozier, D. M. (1986). Advancement for public relations role models. *Public Relations Review, 12*(1), 37–56.

Cameron, G. T., Sallot, L. M., & Curtin, P. A. (1997). Public relations and the production of news: A critical review and theoretical framework. In B. R. Burleson (Ed.), *Communication yearbook 20* (pp. 111–155). Thousand Oaks, CA: Sage.

Coombs, W. T. (1995). Choosing the right words: The development of guidelines for the selection of the "appropriate" crisis-response strategies. *Management Communication Quarterly, 8*, 447–476.

Douglas, D. F., Westley, B. N., & Chaffee, S. H. (1970). An information campaign that changed community attitudes. *Journalism Quarterly, 47,* 479–487, 492.

Gibson, D. (2002). Recalls of body parts: Problems and solutions. *Public Relations Quarterly, 47*(3), 36–43.

Mendelsohn, H. (1973). Some reasons why information campaigns can succeed. *Public Opinion Quarterly, 37,* 50–61.

Metzler, M. S. (2001). The centrality of organizational legitimacy to public relations practice. In R. L. Heath (Ed.), *Handbook of public relations* (pp. 321–334). Thousand Oaks, CA: Sage.

Moffitt, M. A. (1999). *Campaign strategies and message design.* Westport, CT: Praeger.

Moffitt, M. A. (2001). Using the collapse model of corporate image for campaign message design. In R. L. Heath (Ed.), *Handbook of public relations* (pp. 347–356). Thousand Oaks, CA: Sage.

Teller, H. R. (2002). Building a winning corporate personality. *Public Relations Strategist, 8*(1), 18–23.

Temple, K. R. (2002). Setting clear goals: The key ingredient to effective communications planning. *Public Relations Quarterly, 47*(2), 32–35.

Evaluation of Public Relations Efforts

7

"Moving the Needle" and Making a Difference

The late 1990s witnessed an increased concern over cholesterol. Although it was a major factor in heart disease, Americans did not understand what high cholesterol really meant or how to control the "bad" cholesterol in their diets. Parke-Davis and Pfizer, the pharmaceutical leaders in cholesterol lowering, joined forces with the American Heart Association to change this situation. The end result was a program called "The Cholesterol Low Down Rewards Program." The program combined national and local events in major cities such as Seattle, St. Louis, New Orleans, New York, San Francisco, Cleveland, and Phoenix. To drive media coverage, three celebrity spokespersons were used: Regis Philbin, Debbie Allen, and Dick Clark. Each celebrity has a personal connection to high cholesterol. Regis Philbin and Dick Clark both have high cholesterol, and Regis is a heart disease survivor as well. Debbie Allen had lost four relatives to heart disease related to high cholesterol, including her father.

The program was targeted toward men and women over the age of 40; this is the group that needs to be aware of high cholesterol and be tested for it. The program had multiple elements. The first element was to raise awareness through national and local media events. One or more of the celebrity spokespersons were part of each event. The second element was a cholesterol screening at each of the local Cholesterol Low Down events. Participants who had cholesterol scores over 200 mg/dL were identified as "screeners" and were advised to

Making a Difference Through Public Relations

SOURCE: Reproduced with permission © 2005, American Heart Association.

confer with a physician and enroll in The Cholesterol Low Down Rewards Program. The Cholesterol Low Down Rewards Program was the third element. This was a behavior modification program designed to reduce cholesterol in a person's diet. When a screener enrolled, he or she received a Hallmark Card from Debbie Allen and Dick Clark, which included a cholesterol checklist and a follow-up prerecorded phone message from Dick Clark urging the person to see his or her physician. Those who mailed in proof of a physician's visit received a gift package that included a fanny pack, a Cholesterol Low Down T-shirt, and copies of the books *Practical Tips & Recipes* and *Fitting in Fitness*. There were two main objectives. The first was to increase awareness of cholesterol as a health issue by 20% for people over the age of 40. The second was to motivate 50% of the high screeners to enroll in The Cholesterol Low Down Rewards Program.

The awareness objective was evaluated using a pre- and posttest assessment of cholesterol awareness. From a survey of 400 adults over age 40, there was a 23% increase in awareness of cholesterol as a health issue—Objective 1 was achieved. The behavioral objective was assessed using the number of "screeners" who enrolled in The Cholesterol Low Down Rewards Program. Of those "screeners" found to have high cholesterol, 77% joined The Cholesterol Low Down Rewards Program—Objective 2 was achieved. In the end, Parke-Davis, Pfizer, and the American Heart Association had solid evidence that their public relations effort was a success.

As many meetings did, this one focused on new business development. New business development is the lifeblood of an agency. Clients issue a request for proposal to let prospective agencies tell them what they can do "to make a difference" for the client. So, as the conversation addressed the current request for proposal, it began to focus on what the team always called "moving the needle." That was a planning term for thinking about the rhetorical problem and formulating a measurable solution.

Team members knew that they had to assess the situation, understand the relevant goals and objectives, understand the rhetorical problem, think in terms of action, and know how to evaluate the service to the client.

Today's conversation addressed a client's request for service that could increase customers' understanding of the unique qualities of a high-tech innovation. The client was engaged in business-to-business marketing. That means the client sold products to companies that used those products to reach an end user, a retail customer. Research had indicated that many of the customers did not understand the innovation—what it was, how it worked, and why it was better than those designed and manufactured by competitors. That was the job. The client wanted an agency that could "move the needle." The team thought strategically and built into the proposal measures that could be used to evaluate the success of the campaign. Thus, the proposal was crafted and submitted to the prospective client.

In Chapter 5, we talked about the need to know the territory if you were going to take a trip. Research is much like a road map. It lets you know where you are. Evaluation lets you know whether or not you reached your destination. If you planned on going to Seattle, did you arrive in the Emerald City, or did you find yourself in Portland? Portland is a nice place to be, but not if you meant to be in Seattle. Evaluation is the research that is done at the end of a public relations action; it tells you whether or not you were successful. In fact, evaluation is a culmination of the previous three steps: Everything you have done has led to this point. Your initial research helped you understand the situation, your planning set the objectives you pursued, and the execution put your plan into action. All that is left is to determine whether your efforts were a success or failure, and why. Do not forget the "why." If we made it to Seattle, we would want to know why we made it so we could do it again if need be. If we arrived in Portland, we should learn why so that we do not make that mistake again. Learning is a critical feature of evaluation; it helps us to repeat successes and avoid failures.

Reaching the Final Destination: Evaluation

By necessity, this chapter will review some of the information from Chapter 5. Since evaluation is research, we need to mention the ways to collect data. You may also reread the Professional Reflection from that chapter. Moreover, evaluation is based on objectives, so we need to revisit some of the types of objectives. The review nature of this section highlights the fact that the four steps in the public relations action are closely connected and dependent on one another.

▶ Relevance of Evaluation

Public relations academic James Grunig (1983) made the following observation about evaluation in public relations: "Just as everyone is against sin, so most public relations people I talk to are for evaluation. People keep on sinning, however, and PR people continue not to do evaluation" (p. 28). Grunig is one in a long line of public relations insiders who lament the failure of public relations people to engage in evaluation. You might be tempted to conclude that if public relations people generally avoid it, maybe we shouldn't bother. That is a reasonable but dangerous conclusion. Evaluation is central to establishing public relations' value in the organizational world.

The SMART (Societal value and meaning, Mutually beneficial relationships, Advantages through relationships, Rhetorical strategies, Tactics) approach to public relations requires that every effort be made to evaluate the success of the total public relations program as well as specific public relations initiatives. In the largest sense, strategic practitioners ask whether their practice has social value and contributes to shared meaning that advances the public interest. One focal point of that analysis is the quality of the relationships between the organization and its markets, audiences, and publics (MAPs). Strategic approaches seek advantages to the organization and MAPs by working to accomplish specific and well-defined objectives. The SMART approach is rhetorical. That means that strategies are selected and employed because of what they can accomplish in regard to the stated objectives. Tactics are employed to make the strategies work and achieve the objectives. This SMART approach to public relations begins with research, entails strategic planning, requires tactical implementation, and ends with evaluation. In this way, the public relations practitioner keeps the activities alive and vital to accomplish specific outcomes.

Evaluation is proof that public relations is making a difference for an organization. Of course, this assumes your evaluation shows that your actions are successful. If you claim that your public relations efforts lead to an improvement in how the community perceives your organization, you'd better have data to prove that. Evaluation provides those data. Shortly, we will discuss how to establish changes in perceptions. Evaluation provides justification for the public relations department's existence: It shows it is contributing to organizational goals and objectives.

Evaluation is one of the management functions practitioners need to master. Encroachment, nonpublic relations people running public relations departments, is a real concern in the profession. Public relations personnel cannot expect to become managers and run a department if they do not understand and use evaluation. You might think it is no big deal if an outsider runs a public relations department, but look more closely. Nonmanagers in public relations make less money than managers. Encroachment helps to suppress pay scales across the field. A public relations practitioner must know and employ evaluation to be part of management.

For the reasons noted above, the Public Relations Society of America (PRSA) has been crusading to make evaluation commonplace in public relations efforts. We have talked before about the Silver Anvil Awards PRSA uses to recognize outstanding public relations works. One of the four points used to judge Silver Anvil nominees is their evaluation efforts. Judges note this is still the weakest part of most entries, but at least there is an effort being made to promote the use of evaluation in public relations. This chapter explains the evaluation process, the value it provides practitioners, and why evaluation is often left undone.

BOX 7.1 "MOVING THE NEEDLE" OR "SHOWING THE BROCHURE"

How practitioners think about evaluation says a lot about whether they approach their work strategically as a manager or functionally as a technician. For instance, as you mature in your profession, will you think in terms of return on investment or as a person who "does public relations"? Do you seek funding for public relations projects by arguing that you can work to return some specific advantage by spending the funds? Do you merely "do public relations" with the funding you receive? The first way of thinking is managerial and strategic. The second is more typical of public relations technicians. The first approach requires that you measure the results of your strategies of public relations. The second might lead you to merely display your publications and clippings to demonstrate what you have been doing. Managers move the needle, working to advance from where their organization is to a more favorable status. Technicians produce "brochures," which they use to show what they do.

Process Versus Outcome Evaluation

When is evaluation not evaluation? When you use only process evaluation. These two lines are not meant to be a bad joke; they are meant to highlight a serious flaw in evaluation efforts. Many practitioners mistake process for outcome evaluation. By discussing each, we shall see why this is a serious error.

▶Process

Process evaluation monitors what you do during a public relations effort. It is basically a checklist of everything you said you were going to do when you developed your plan. A failure to do what you planned to do can be the reason your public relations action failed; process evaluation can offer some learning insights. Examples of process evaluation would be sending out news releases, assessing the readability level of the public relations message, and deciding between two different forms of a message. Now, all three of these factors are important to your public relations action. If your news releases were not sent, you will not generate any publicity. If your message is written at too high a readability level, your target may not understand it. If you do not pretest your message options, you will not know which one your target might prefer. It is easy to determine whether or not you mailed your news releases, and most process evaluation is fairly easy to do. Readability is part of the "Spellcheck" program on Word, while focus groups can be used to determine which of two message options your target might prefer. If we return to our travel metaphor, process evaluation involves checking the route we planned to take. Did we stay on that route, or did we take a wrong turn?

The PRSA has noted that a problem still exists with Silver Anvil entries that confuse process with outcome evaluation. Historically, public relations practitioners have relied on press clips, now including Internet clips, as proof of success or failure of some specific public relations campaign. *Clips* are copies of stories that mention your organization's name and some special message point, for instance, Web sites that mention your organization or posts of information about your organization to discussion forums or Weblogs. Practitioners use clips, or clippings, to try to quantify the amount of publicity generated by a public relations department. Clippings have two limitations. First, they reduce public relations to simply publicity, and by now you should know there is much more to public relations than that. If all public relations does is generate clippings, it is not a management function at all. The old standby was to convert the publicity into advertising dollars: How much would it have cost to buy X column inches in a newspaper or Y minutes on a television show? While it is still helpful to calculate coverage in terms of dollars, it is not an effective evaluation tool—it is a process.

Second, using clippings as a primary research tool assumes that all publicity is equal and that all publicity is good. Strategic public relations practitioners know both of those assumptions are untrue. Publicity needs to be examined for its quality. The quality of clippings is assessed through content analysis—a coding system. An organization develops coding categories to assess the content of the clippings.

The coding typically involves a set of topics such as customer service, product quality, treatment of employees, and so on. For each topic, the clippings are assessed to determine whether the comments about the topic are positive, negative, or neutral. For instance, Burrelle's Information Services charts favorable and unfavorable stories. They can even customize their evaluations to fit a content analysis system developed by its customer. You can create the categories, and Burrelle's will automatically place the clips into your categories and generate reports for you.

Imagine your organization is about to start a new program for providing college scholarship money to local students. Your objectives might center on awareness of the scholarship program (to have 60% of the community aware of the new scholarship program) and improving perceptions of the organization's commitment to the community (to have the organization's community commitment score increase from 5 to 7 among community leaders). You would want to know more than simply how much media coverage was generated. You would want to know whether the program was mentioned and, if so, whether the coverage was favorable or unfavorable. Moreover, did the coverage discuss the organization's larger commitment to the community? If so, were the discussions favorable or unfavorable? By examining specific content factors, you will get a better picture of whether or not the publicity was supporting your objectives. Obviously, stories that discuss the scholarship program but complain it is a sad attempt to buy goodwill would not support your community commitment objective.

Today, clipping services cover the Internet as well as print and broadcast media. Discussion groups, Weblogs, and Web sites are examined along with the online news outlets. An organization can receive daily updates on what is being said about them (the topics) and how it is being said (assessment of content).

In its advice about Silver Anvil entries, PRSA states that clips are a measure or process, not an outcome. Publicity is a means, not an end. What do you hope to achieve with the clips? Increased brand awareness? A more favorable reputation? Clients want to see specific results, what you have accomplished, not simply what you have done.

A recent Silver Anvil winner included a process objective among its outcome objectives. The objective was to increase awareness of the relationship between insulin resistance, diabetes, and cardiovascular disease among the at-risk population. Notice the objective is less effective because it does not specify an amount of change for awareness. Awareness was evaluated using media impressions, the number of people potentially exposed to the topic from the publicity that was generated. Just because people might have been exposed to a message does not mean they saw or heard the message. The process of getting attention (publicity) was evaluated, not the outcome of actual awareness of the topic.

▶Outcome

An outcome objective is a true assessment of a public relations effort's success or failure. Success or failure is determined by whether or not we achieved the objective(s) set for the public relations action. Objectives can be classified as knowledge (learning new information), attitude (changing evaluations of an attitude object), or behavior (altering how people act). Remember a good objective is measurable and indicates the amount of desired change. If we cannot measure an objective, we cannot engage in evaluation; that is why measurability it vital to an objective. We also need to know what we are shooting for: how much change we hope to achieve or the amount of something we hope to reach. Let us consider a few objectives and how we can use various social scientific research methods to assess them:

1. "To collect 275 pints of blood during the September blood drive."

2. "To have 50% of potential consumers be aware of 'Furbies' the day after the product launch."

3. "To have community perceptions of the organization's community commitment improve from a rating of 3.5 to 4."

4. "To have 15% of local residents begin using the new home recycling tubs on trash day."

5. "To increase awareness of Accenture's consulting services by 20% among potential customers."

6. "To increase by 7% those at risk for high blood pressure modifying their salt intake."

Objectives 1, 4, and 6 are *behavioral objectives;* they try to modify how people act. The assessment for both 1 and 4 is very simple: counting. For Objective 1, we could simply count the pints of blood collected. For Objective 4, we count the number of people using the new home recycling tubs on trash day and divide by the total number of people putting out trash. When it is easy to see, you can use simple observation to evaluate behavioral objectives. Objective 6 is more complicated to assess—we cannot go around and check the salt intake of everyone in our target group. We do not have the time and resources, and people do not like to be watched all the time. An alternative to observation is to use surveys or structured interviews that ask questions about diet and salt usage. To assess the objective, we must collect information before (benchmarking) and after (posttest) the public relations action. We cannot determine whether there is an increase from our public relations action unless we know our starting point, the benchmark of the behavior. If we just measured behavior after the campaign and we found 8% were modifying their salt intake, we would not know whether that change was a result of our actions. It could be that 6% were modifying their diets before the public relations action; thus, our efforts had a 2% increase. Precision in evaluation is critical, and knowledge of social scientific research will improve precision.

Objectives 2 and 3 are *attitudinal;* they try to change how people feel toward something. Surveys and structured interviews are best to assess attitudes. Again, pre- and postmeasures are critical to evaluating success when you desire change. The process involves collecting data before your public relations effort, executing the effort, and collecting data after the public relations effort is completed. The only way to show change is to compare pre– and post–public relations effort data. The data need to be collected in the same fashion. If you used a survey, the same items need to be on the survey you used to collect pre- and postevent data. In most cases, you will not be able to collect preevent data until you have decided your objective. Sometimes you are fortunate and your formative data are appropriate for the preevent data.

We cannot assess change if we do not have a benchmark for comparison. The same is true for *knowledge objectives*. We must assess what people know before a public relations action if we are to determine whether our action changes what they know. Recall in the opening vignette that Parke-Davis, Pfizer, and the American Heart Association collected pre- and posttest assessments of awareness of cholesterol as a health risk to determine whether their awareness objective was a success or not. Last, Objective 5 is a type of knowledge objective, because it helps to determine what percentage of potential customers are aware of Accenture's consulting services.

You may have noticed that in discussing the evaluation research, focus groups and in-depth interviews were not mentioned. These qualitative measures are best suited for exploratory research, understanding the situation, rather than for evaluation. Evaluation relies on quantitative measures because we must quantify, or give numbers to, our results because our objectives are quantities, that is, percentages and amounts. Qualitative measures are a poor match for the demands of evaluation.

Appropriate Evaluative Data

In this section, we have used the term *data*. As noted in Chapter 4, *data* simply means "information." As a practitioner, you need to know what types of data (information) are appropriate for evaluative research. Awareness is assessed through surveys that measure awareness, familiarity, and knowledge of specifics about a product, organization, or issue. Surveys can be used to assess attitudes and behavior. People can be asked about their degree of community support, how much they trust an organization, their perceptions of an organization (reputation) or a product (brand), the job satisfaction of employees, their intent to purchase a product, or any behavioral changes they have made.

An example will help to illustrate selecting the right data. Ledingham and Brunig have developed relationship management theory. The theory is incorporated into Chapter 3 and outlined in Chapter 8. The key aspect of the theory is determining the quality of a relationship between an organization and its stakeholders. A survey has been developed that evaluates the key dimensions of the relationship: trust, openness, credibility, intimacy, similarity, immediacy, agreement, accuracy, common interest, and relational history (Ledingham, 2005). Studies using relationship management theory create a benchmark using the survey instrument, then use the same instrument to collect data about the relationship after the public relations action.

As noted earlier, surveys are used when a behavior cannot be observed easily. We cannot watch people eat and assess whether they are following a low-fat or low-carbohydrate diet. Some behavior can be observed and counted. Common observable behavior includes voting, donations (money, goods, or blood), attendance at an event, information requests, Web visits, participation in an event, number of people volunteering, number of people e-mailing or writing letters, market share, sales figures, and stock prices. In Chapter 4, we used the example of Barberton Citizens Hospital

(BCH) trying to win a local vote to allow the city to sell it some park land for an expansion. In the end, 77% voted yes on the sale of the park land—BCH exceeded its target of 67% voting for the park land sale. The key to evaluation is determining the best way to measure, or collect data about, the objective. This will not be difficult if you crafted a proper objective. As noted in Chapter 5, an effective objective must be measurable. Failure to create a proper objective dooms an evaluation effort.

WEB WATCHER: THE AD COUNCIL

In the Chapter 6 Web Watcher you were introduced to the Ad Council. It creates public service announcements (PSAs) designed to improve society. The Ad Council hopes to achieve attitude and behavioral changes. The Ad Council reflects the value of evaluation by devoting a section of its Web site to the topic. The address is http://www.adcouncil.org/research/impact_of_psas/. Visit the Web site and select a specific campaign whose impact is discussed at the site, then answer these two questions: What type of objective was the campaign pursuing? How was the objective measured?

Value of Learning

Whenever you complete a public relations effort, you have expended a great deal of time, effort, and often money. To maximize the return on your investment, you should learn as much as possible from the public relations action. Part of evaluation is understanding why the effort was a success or failure. By understanding "why," we learn and grow as public relations practitioners and develop resources to be used in future public relations efforts. Learning creates an institutional memory.

▶ Reasons for Success or Failure

There are no guarantees of success in public relations, because we are dealing with people and people are hard to predict. In fact, the 1982 PRSA Code of Conduct told practitioners that they could not ethically promise specific outcomes. Managers know that any action taken by an organization should have a postmortem, an assessment of what went right and what went wrong. The idea is to keep what worked while improving or eliminating what went wrong. An organization wants to repeat success and avoid future failure. Let us consider an example. A state Special Olympics program was not successful in placing stories about athletes in local papers. Their placement rate was around 5%. A new member of the public relations staff wanted to improve that rate, so she reviewed the past failures. She found a possible problem in the way the news releases were written; they did not follow the standard format the media likes, and the media list had not been updated in years. Two problems were identified and corrected for the next year. Placement rates shot up to over 50% once the changes were made. Public relations people should learn from their mistakes, as painful as that might be. In contrast, The Cholesterol Low Down Rewards Program was very successful, and the plan served as a blueprint for future actions: The organizations decided they would repeat the program for a number of years.

▶Institution Memory

Learning requires people to remember. The same holds true for an organization. People change jobs in organizations and sometimes leave the organization. The danger is losing what a person knows when he or she leaves a public relations department; hence the need for an institutional memory. An institutional memory for a public relations department is a record of exactly what they have done, the evaluation of the efforts, and lessons learned from the postmortem. An institutional memory requires thorough documentation and systematic storage of information.

Contributing to Community Building

SOURCE: Reprinted with permission from Special Olympics and ShopKo.

It is important to keep complete records of what is done during a public relations effort. This would include background information collected, the records for planning and reasons for key decisions, sample materials and reasons for selecting specific media and tactics, and data collected for the evaluation. Of course, the records are informed by the postmortem. You should indicate in your records any piece of the public relations action you thought was especially good or bad—document the lessons learned for future use. Documentation goes back to public relations being based on facts rather than gut instincts. Go back and find out exactly what you did or what worked in the past; do not rely on someone's memory of events. Memories are selective and subject to error; get the hard facts from the documentation. There is one other benefit to documentation: legal issues. If an organization is ever taken to court over a public relations action, you will be able to document exactly what was done. If you operate in a legal and ethical fashion, that documentation will serve as your defense. If you operate like Enron or Tyco, those documents will help the prosecution.

Documentation is only as good as its storage system. I can store and recall gigabytes of documentation, but if I or another person cannot make sense of the storage system, it is hard to use. Think about when you use online databases. The information is organized in a systematic fashion, so anyone with some knowledge of the system can retrieve what he or she needs. Millions of people use LexisNexis to find background information because it is thorough and easy to use. Store your information in a consistent manner, and divide the information into meaning units. For instance, information about public relations actions can have four broad categories: formative research, planning, execution, and evaluation. Each broad category will have subcategories. For instance, planning might include targets, objectives, messages, tactics, budget, and PERT charts. The key is consistency: Organize every public relations effort using the same system of categories and subcategories. Consistency allows for easier retrieval and comparison between public relations efforts.

The Failure to Evaluate

So, if so many people in public relations believe in the value of evaluation, why is it still done infrequently? There are three common reasons for not evaluating: People lack the proper training, budgets often lack funds for evaluation, and there is not enough time. In discussing research, we have mentioned the need to understand the basics of social science research. Many of those currently in the public relations field have had no formal training in social science research, so they do not know the best ways to engage in evaluation. The 1999 Commission Public Relations Education Report recognized this flaw and recommended that a class in research methods be required for public relations majors. If evaluation is research, future practitioners must be equipped with the proper knowledge and skills. As time goes by, lack of proper training is becoming less of an excuse.

Lack of money is a cold reality in the public relations world. We have never heard a practitioner say that he or she had too much money to spend on a department's activities. When budgets run short, evaluation is often trimmed, because it is the last task to be completed. Or a budget is too small even to include evaluation. When Xavier University in Cincinnati conducted a Sesquicentennial celebration that was nominated for a Silver Anvil Award, they were given a grant to fund their preevent survey research. However, there was no money for a postevent survey. Their Silver Anvil materials acknowledged the value of evaluative research but noted they could not afford a postevent survey because no one had donated money for such research. The Xavier officials lacked the funds to conduct the desired evaluative research. Given the need to prove what public relations can contribute to an organization, evaluation needs to become a higher budget priority for public relations managers.

One of the authors was working on a project with a not-for-profit hospital. Part of the public relations effort involved winning community support for the hospital's position on an upcoming vote on whether or not a specialized surgical center should be built in the area. The vast majority of the budget was dedicated to newspaper advertising about the issue. The hospital wanted to make sure the community knew its position and why the hospital was taking a stand on the controversial issue. There was not enough money to conduct pre- and postevent attitude surveys, nor was there enough time. The vote was tied to when the group proposing the surgical center filed its paperwork. The public relations effort was condensed into a 6-week time frame for action. It was not possible to collect preevent data and execute the necessary actions in 6 weeks. With no benchmark data, there could be no evaluation. We did not have the money or the time to conduct proper evaluative research.

At times, public relations research can be extremely expensive. A major survey or extensive content analysis could cost thousands of dollars. Major companies, large nonprofits, or big governmental agencies might be able to afford such costs. Even then, the smart organization wants to know what it can know. At times, cost-effective measures are available, even though they might not meet all of the standards for solid research.

For instance, chemical manufacturers need to know how well their messages on safety preparedness and community health are getting across to key publics. A few years ago, such companies were required to communicate the worst-case-scenario risks in their communities. That means they were required by the Environmental Protection Agency (EPA) to determine the most extensive potential damage to area residents that could occur if the most dangerous chemical were to be suddenly released in massive amounts under the worst prevailing wind. These companies were required to show the map of the people who would be affected.

Companies complied with this requirement, but they took this opportunity to communicate their safety and health preparedness emergency response programs. They held public meetings where community residents could come to listen to presentations by all members of the dialogue, including community leaders and environmental activists. Tables were arranged so that the community members could meet and visit with members of area companies responsible for public safety. They could talk to elected officials and to members of the fire and police departments who would participate in emergency response.

As they left, members of the community were asked to complete a response card with only a few questions. One question asked whether they believed they had learned valuable emergency response and community preparedness information. They could indicate whether their concerns were taken seriously. They were invited to indicate whether they thought their relationship with the industry was helped or harmed by such meetings. Responses were favorable, in the 95% range. Such studies can be criticized for not being solidly scientific, but even these responses could alert industry, government, and activists to potential trouble spots. The study was conducted by students from a local university so that the citizens could believe the study was as objective as possible. They were given an opportunity to provide comments as well as to mark responses numerically. One benefit of the study was a recurring comment: "Thanks for giving us the chance to fill out these forms. That indicates that someone truly cares about what we think."

Simplifying Evaluation

Evaluation can be tied to objectives and goals—to processes and outcomes. The art and science of evaluation is knowing where to look and knowing what to look for.

▶ Column Inches

The easiest form of evaluation simply is whether the information in a media release (or press conference) was reported, and reported accurately. Much attention has been paid over the years to ad equivalency: getting publicity without using advertising. The assumption is that publicity counts as much or more than advertising. Whether such is the case is debatable, but at the most basic level of evaluation, a practitioner can know that his or her release had news value.

▶ Attitude and Knowledge Measures

In previous chapters, we have emphasized attitude and knowledge as important public relations outcomes. Did a campaign increase the targets' (MAPs') knowledge—what they know and believe before and after the communication? Did it change or at least reinforce their attitudes? These questions can be measured, using standard social science techniques such as surveys, interviews, and focus groups.

▶ Behavior

As strange as it might seem, behavior is often the easiest of the several ingredients in this model to measure. If a publicity effort is intended to create a lot of interest in the opening of a theatrical or music production, one measure is box office. How many tickets were sold? If the campaign was designed to motivate more people to give blood, the easy measure is a comparison of this year's and last year's total pints contributed.

Conclusion

Evaluative research can be used to address all elements of the public relations process. For instance, it can measure message impact on awareness, opinion, and motive or action. It can be used to assess the quality of the relationship between people and the organization. This measurement can be done periodically, such as every year or every 5 years, to determine whether the relationship is improving or deteriorating. Surveys can determine whether the organization and its MAPs share meaning, whether they identify with one another, and whether they operate from compatible or competing narratives.

Thus, today's public relations is increasingly theory and research driven. What academics and practitioners learn about successful approaches to public relations can be used as the foundation for evaluation. It is a rhetorical process that employs strategies and tactics to achieve specific outcomes. Research is a vital part of the process because it is a way of listening to MAPs. Listening is vital to successful strategic public relations. Evaluation is more than an indicator of success or failure. It provides insights into the quality of your relationships with MAPs and the quality of your public relations work.

This section concludes the overview of the four-step process of public relations effort. We have led you from understanding the situation to planning the effort, executing it, and evaluating your results. As you progress through a sequence of public relations courses, you will encounter courses that build on this knowledge and reinforce this four-step process. These four chapters include ideas you will deal with regularly throughout your public relations education and career.

Ethical Quandary: Choices About Evaluation

You are in charge of public relations for a proposed "surgicenter." Surgicenters are for-profit clinics, typically established by physicians who invest in the project. A surgicenter provides specialized care, such as cardiology or a limited range of inpatient surgeries; these are the "profitable" procedures for most hospitals. A surgicenter targets profitable medical procedures to generate earnings for the center. The local general hospital is opposed to the planned surgicenter. The hospital views the surgicenter as predatory and as having a negative effect on the community. A surgicenter reduces the profit margin of nearby hospitals, making it more difficult to provide the medical services that lose money, such as trauma, emergency rooms, and psychiatric care.

The surgicenter and hospital have been debating the issue in the local newspaper. A state licensing agency will make the final decision on approval for building the surgicenter. The state licensing agency does factor how the community feels about the project into their final decision. The people planning the surgicenter decide to commission a public opinion poll about the issue. You will be collecting the data for the poll. You know that by framing questions in a biased manner, you can change the results of the poll. You design the questions so that they favor the surgicenter. Do you claim success in your public relations effort (winning public support) when your data show support for the surgicenter? Do you report the results to the local newspaper? Provide a rationale for your decisions.

Summary Questions

1. Why is evaluation important to a public relations practitioner?
2. How do process and outcome evaluation differ? Why is it misleading to confuse the two?
3. What are the three basic types of outcome objectives commonly used in public relations? Give an example of how you might collect evaluative data for each one.
4. What is the relationship between evaluation and learning?
5. What is institutional memory and its relationship to evaluation?
6. Why do some public relations practitioners choose not to use evaluation?

Exercises

1. Go to the PRSA Web site and navigate to the collection of Silver Anvil Award winners. The site provides summaries of the winners, arranged by year and topic. Select and review the summaries and identify the evaluative technique(s) used and the type of outcomes objectives that were used.
2. You are part of a team that wants to increase student awareness and use of recycling containers on campus. How would you go about evaluating your effort? Include in your discussion the type of data (information) you would collect, how you would collect data, and when you would collect data in relation to the execution of your campaign.

Recommended Readings

Boje, D. M. (2001). *Narrative methods for organizational and communication research.* Thousand Oaks, CA: Sage.

Broom, G. M., & Dozier, D. (1990). *Using research in public relations: Applications to program management.* Englewood Cliffs, NJ: Prentice Hall.

Coombs, W. T. (2005). Public relations research. In R. L. Heath (Ed.), *Encyclopedia of public relations* (pp. 693–696). Thousand Oaks, CA: Sage.

Hallahan, K. (2001). The dynamics of issue activation and response: An issue process model. *Journal of Public Relations Research, 13,* 27–69.

Handwerk, P. S. (1998). Winning support for the function, ensuring relevancy to corporate strategy and measuring results. In W. Pedersen (Ed.), *Making community relations pay off: Tools & strategies* (pp. 35–37). Washington, DC: Public Affairs Council.

Stacks, D. W. (2003). *Primer of public relations research.* New York: Guilford.

Stacks, D. W. (2005). Benchmarking. In R. L. Heath (Ed.), *Encyclopedia of public relations* (pp. 74–76). Thousand Oaks, CA: Sage.

Yungwook, K. (2001). Measuring the economic value of public relations. *Journal of Public Relations Research, 13,* 3–25.

Public Relations Theory in Practice

8

Theory to the Rescue

I t is 10:31am. A loud boom is heard, and the floor of the public relations office at West Pharmaceuticals rocks, along with all the other buildings at the North Carolina facility. You look out the window and see a large black cloud rising from the production facility. Employees are running from the facility. Your phone rings, and you know that call is activation for West Pharmaceuticals's crisis management plan. As part of the crisis management team, you will help orchestrate the company's response. Time is in short supply. Immediately, the team must determine whether an evacuation is necessary and how to send the appropriate warning to people living near the facility (community stakeholders). You must account for all of the employees and determine the number of injured or dead (employee stakeholders). You must assess the damage to determine whether production can be resumed and how long that might take (employee, customer, and investor stakeholders). You will also need to document all actions related to the crisis for government investigators (government stakeholders).

Everyone knew the risk of the company's operations. Chemical-manufacturing processes can be dangerous. People can be burned, even killed, if an explosion occurs. Property can be damaged. A risk is a calculated chance that something good or bad happens. An explosion, however remote, signals a crisis, because a company simply cannot operate without some risk.

Facing the Media During a Crisis

SOURCE: Copyright © REUTERS/Ellen Ozier/Landov.

Within an hour of the explosion, you will need to make a statement for the news media and have spokespeople ready and available if needed (media stakeholders). You are facing the communication problems common to any crisis. The crisis team will need to select a crisis response strategy: what the organization chooses to say and do in response to the crisis. These choices will affect your organization's reputation and financial performance (Coombs & Holladay, 2001). Your advice needs to be informed and supported by research. You will be exercising your critical thinking skills by applying principles and theory from public relations to help solve this problem.

Public relations is a professional practice that is guided by best practices tested through experience as well as theory and research. Much of what practitioners do on a daily basis reflects what are called *best practices*. These best practices are honed strategies and tactics that result from experience—and trial and error. Simply wanting to rely exclusively on best practices, many practitioners and students like to discount theory and research based on principles of practice. This is a mistake.

All employers value critical thinking skills, the ability to analyze and solve problems. Research is conducted and theory developed to focus and refine the analysis needed to solve problems. In fact, even trial and error results in "street-level" theory and research. That way of knowing what to do and how to do it is similar to research. Trial and error often "tests hypotheses."

The best practitioners and academics are trained to be researchers who also love theory. Legends of public relations such as Earl Newsom, John W. Hill, and Edward L. Bernays read extensively and drew on social scientific research current at the time of their work. Newsom sought insights from social science to help him understand the opinions of markets, audiences, and publics (MAPs). He was a keen student of the developing social science techniques of using survey data to gain insights into the fabric of thought that is woven into what we call "public opinion." Hill too studied leading thinkers who were crafting an understanding of public opinion and was also fascinated with understanding opinion leaders. Bernays was the double-nephew of Sigmund Freud and read extensively about the mysteries of the human mind.

Theory and principles (abbreviated theories) guide analysis and problem solving. They provide guides for understanding the problem (analysis) and suggest potential solutions (problem solving).

This chapter discusses the concept of theory and how it is used in public relations to solve problems. In the first section of this chapter, we explain what theory is and how it is created. The remaining sections illustrate the development and application of public relations theory to crisis management and risk communication.

The Movement Toward Theory

A significant advancement in public relations education and practice has been the movement from accepted wisdom and "seat-of-the-pants" thinking to reasoned action: decisions guided by principles and theory. Even when practitioners apply best practices learned from experience, they are applying theory, whether they know it or not. Students are taught principles, grounded in theory, which recommend certain courses of action when confronted with a public relations problem such as the need to develop or to maintain mutually beneficial relationships. Critical strategic thinking is utilized as students apply these principles to public relations problems. Students apply these principles when they become practitioners. In this way, public relations moves from mere hunches to reasoned action.

Defining Theory

People use the term *theory* in very different ways. This is problematic, because we may use the term and assume everyone agrees on what it means. As a result, theory must be clearly defined to prevent misunderstandings. A theory is a systematic interpretation of a phenomenon that specifies the relationship between variables; it explains how things work by establishing relationships between concepts/variables (Neuliep, 1996). Theories move beyond simple description in an attempt to explain *why* things happen. Objects fall to the ground; observing that fact, Sir Isaac Newton developed a theory of gravity to explain the phenomena he saw. By identifying the functions of theory, we move beyond a vague definition and gain greater insight into the term.

Three objectives are the outcome of using theory: (1) organization/explanation, (2) prediction, and (3) control. A theory begins by observing phenomena and then organizing concepts/variables to explain what is observed. A theory organizes by isolating a set of relevant concepts/variables and specifying how they are related to one another. Organizing is an explanation of a phenomenon; it tells us why things occur regularly. Models, or visual depictions of relationships, are often used to illustrate the organization/explanation function of theories. A theory allows for prediction; we anticipate what outcomes and effects will occur. Gravity predicts that if we throw a ball into the air, it will hit the ground and that the higher we throw the ball, the harder it will hit the ground.

Public relations and communication are social sciences. In social science, predictions deal in degrees of certainty, not absolutes as in the world of the physical sciences. Social science prediction indicates that we generally know what will happen but we cannot be 100% sure it will happen. Control stems from prediction. A theory offers control by indicating which actions will be most effective or appropriate. By altering our actions, we can direct or regulate a phenomenon. Through control, a theory suggests guidelines for behavior. In public relations, theories provide guidelines for handling stakeholders and developing mutually beneficial relationships.

Language of Theory

The use of the term *theory* is clarified further by examining its vocabulary. The theory vocabulary includes phenomenon, concepts/variables, and propositions. A *phenomenon* is the event or thing you are trying to explain. Newton wanted to explain why things always fall down and not up. *Concepts* or *variables* are the terms we use to denote processes that would be hard to discuss or describe if we did not give them a name. A variable is a form of shorthand. Instead of saying "a force that draws things down," we can say "gravity." Concepts/variables are the building blocks of theory.

Propositions establish the relationships between variables and establish the assumptions the theorist holds to be true. Propositions are also known as *postulates* or *axioms*. When we are testing propositions, we call them hypotheses. *Hypotheses* are conjectural or speculative relationships between two or more variables that can be tested empirically.

Theory Building

Theory building can be divided into four stages: (1) asking, (2) observing, (3) theorizing, and (4) checking. Asking is the starting point. The theorist decides he or she wants to explain some phenomenon. Observing involves descriptive research designed to understand the phenomenon. The theorist looks for patterns and identifies the relevant variables. Some people take observing to be the same as theorizing. Thus, they might look to see how practitioners respond during press conferences. Based on this observation, they might generate a list of what to do or not do when holding a press conference. Think of principles as abbreviated theories because they lack the theorizing and checking elements of theory building. Theorizing involves developing reasons *why* the phenomenon occurs. The theorist needs to articulate the relationship between the variables and to develop his or her propositions. Checking involves research designed to test the hypotheses generated by the theory. Typically, propositions are translated into hypotheses, which can be accepted or rejected. The theorist uses the results to refine his or her theory or to modify the theory. Checking is an ongoing process; theorists continually test and refine their ideas (Anderson & Ross, 2002).

Exemplar Public Relations Theories

Over the years, public relations has drawn theories from other disciplines, such as mass communication and psychology. In this chapter, we would like to focus on five theories developed specifically for public relations: excellence theory, contingency theory, relationship management theory, situational crisis communication theory (SCCT), and risk communication theory. These theories can be applied to the rhetorical problems that practitioners face. The first three represent general approaches to understanding the practices of public relations, while the last two focus on specific applications of public relations. We shall review the main features of the theories while developing in greater detail the applied nature of SCCT and risk communication.

▶Excellence Theory

Excellence theory evolved from the work of James E. Grunig at the University of Maryland. Grunig was a pioneer in public relations research and used a grant from the International Association of Business Communicators (IABC) to fund the excellence research. Excellence theory has a broad focus, as it tries to explain how the public relations practitioner can serve as a communication manager in the dominant coalition (executive cadres). By serving in this communication management function, the practitioner can contribute to the overall effectiveness of an organization (Grunig, 1992). In other words, public relations can be a part of planning and decision making (a management function) and help the organization to realize its strategic plan. The core of excellence theory is the same as the one promoted in this book, "to build good long-term relationships with strategic publics" (Grunig, Grunig, & Dozier, 2002, p. 57).

Excellence theory derives its name from the search for factors that make public relations "excellent," which, in turn, helps organizations to be effective. The researchers studied 327 organizations and refined a list of principles or factors of excellence. The principles represent a series of propositions that prescribe how public relations and organizations should be structured to maximize mutually beneficial relationships between the organization and its MAPs. The 10 principles of excellence have been condensed into eight broad variables (Bowen, 2005). Organizations that embrace these principles will be more effective:

1. *Value of communication:* Chief executive officers (CEOs) and top management must understand the value of public relations and communication.

2. *Contribute to strategic organizational functions:* Public relations is a part of the organization's strategic planning. Public relations is part of the decision-making group in the organization and acts to represent the views of the stakeholders to the other members of management.

3. *Perform the management role:* There are two roles in public relations, technician and management. The technician simply creates materials such as news releases. The manager is involved in planning and decision making. Organizations are more effective when their top public relations people act as managers.

4. *Use the two-way symmetrical model of public relations:* There are four models of public relations: press agentry (seeks publicity), public information (disseminates accurate information), two-way asymmetrical (scientific persuasion), and two-way symmetrical (mutual understanding). The one-way model simply sends information, while the two-way uses research to understand stakeholders. The two-way symmetrical approach is a dialogue between the organization and its stakeholders. The two sides influence one another and try to understand each other's perspectives.

5. *Potential to practice the ideal model:* For a public relations department to utilize the two-way symmetrical model and the managerial role, people in the public relations department must have the skills necessary to accomplish both. Practitioners must understand research, such as the principles outlined in Chapter 4, to use the two-way symmetrical model. Practitioners must understand management concepts, such as the planning discussed in Chapter 5, to serve in the managerial role. The excellent public relations department has practitioners with research and strategic management skills and knowledge.

6. *Activism as positive energy:* Activism is when stakeholders seek/communicate to the organization the need for change. Excellent public relations departments have a high level of activism. Activism is part of the dialogue between the organization and the stakeholders. Knowing what stakeholders want allows practitioners to better represent their needs and concerns in the planning process, thereby building a stronger foundation for mutually beneficial relationships.

7. *Organizational culture and structure:* The organizational culture must be participative and empower employees to make decisions. Rigid, hierarchical structures discourage communication, so more organic structures are found in excellent organizations.

8. *Diversity as a strength:* Public relations departments are stronger when they are diverse in terms of gender and race. Organizations have diverse stakeholders. A public relations department that reflects the diversity of the stakeholders can better understand and represent the interests of the stakeholders.

Excellence theory is normative: It prescribes how a public relations department should be structured and function. The research identified a variety of factors that serve to create excellence in public relations (Bowen, 2005). The excellence research found that public relations can improve the operation of the organization building mutually beneficial relationships with MAPs. The theory also provides guidelines for creating an excellent public relations practice.

▶ Contingency Theory

The focus of contingency theory is on managing the conflict between an organization and its MAPs. No matter how good the public relations, there will be conflicts that arise between various MAPs and the organization. Conflict is recognized as a natural and positive force in the MAP-organization relationship. Organizations and MAPs will have different goals, values, and so on. The key is how those differences are bridged—meaning cocreated.

Contingency theory places the conflictual and strategic relationships between MAPs and the organization on a continuum anchored by "pure advocacy" and "pure accommodation." *Advocacy* means each group pursues its own self-interest, while *accommodation* means each party considers the other party's interests. Contingency reflects the fact that how the two sides interact varies over time and by the situation (Shin, 2005). How an organization treats a market, audience, or public in one situation may be very different from how it treats it at another time.

The organization-MAP relationship is dynamic, meaning it is always shifting and changing. Organizations and MAPs both pursue their self-interests in a relationship and measure the success of the relationship against those self-interests. The response to the conflict is some mix of advocacy and accommodation. That mix is a function of how well each response helps achieve desired outcomes—reach strategic purposes. Research has demonstrated that as contingencies change, the strategies organizations and MAPs use to manage conflict will change.

A variety of contingencies contribute to the selection of strategies, including trust, the issue creating the conflict, and top management support. Glen T. Cameron, the primary researcher involved with this theory, along with his colleagues (Cameron, Cropp, & Reber, 2001), has identified 86 factors and 11 categories (threats, relationship characteristics, issue under consideration, individual characteristics, industry environment, internal threats, political/social/cultural environment, organization's characteristics, external publics, management characteristics, and public relations department characteristics). The factors are grouped along external and internal dimensions. These factors limit the degree of accommodation a public relations practitioner can adopt when dealing with a MAP conflict. Contingency theory explains the factors that affect how public relations practitioners can strategically manage conflicts (Shin, 2005).

▶ Relationship Management Theory

Relationship management theory reflects the growing concern in public relations for managing the relationships between an organization and its MAPs, a key element of this book as well. John Ledingham and Steven Bruning have been the primary researchers advancing relationship management theory. *Relationship* becomes the core of public relations and is defined as "the state which exists between an organization and its key publics in which the actions of either can impact the economic, social, cultural or political well-being of the other" (Ledingham, 2003, p. 184). The relationship is managed through the communication between the organization and the MAPs. Public relations becomes a strategic resource for managing the relationship. The success or failure of public relations is then measured by the quality of the organization-MAP relationship (Ledingham, 2005).

Relationships are an *exchange* relationship. Consistent with the focus of this book, the interaction must be mutually beneficial if it is to continue. Both sides must be getting something from the relationship. Public relations uses communication to make sure there is mutual benefit to the relationship. Relationship management theory emerges from four developments in public relations:

1. Realization that relationships are central to public relations

2. View of public relations as a management function, not just a technical one

3. The identification of key dimensions to the organization-MAP relationship

4. Construction of models of the organization-MAP relationship

Focusing on relationships and the management of relationships sets the foundation for this theory. If you do not see relationships as central to public relations or following a management function, relationship management theory makes little sense. The dimensions and models allow practitioners to evaluate the organization-MAP relationship and to track its development and progress. We can determine the quality of the relationship and whether the relationship is progressing as it should. The key dimensions are trust, openness, credibility, intimacy, similarity, immediacy, agreement, accuracy, common interest, and relational history.

There are three types of relationships in relationship management theory: interpersonal, professional, and community. The *interpersonal relationship* is "personal interactions between the organizational representatives and the public members" (Ledingham, 2005, p. 741). The *professional relationship* is the how the organization delivers professional services to the MAPs. The *community relationship* is how well the organization is perceived to support community concerns. The objective of public relations is to use communication and actions (behaviors) from the organization to build mutually beneficial relationships (Ledingham, 2005).

Relationship management theory articulates 10 principles that should be used to build the organization-MAP relationship:

1. The core of public relations is relationships.

2. A successful relationship benefits the organization and MAPs.

3. The organization-MAP relationship is dynamic.

4. Relationships are driven by the wants and needs of the organization and MAPs.

5. Effective management of relationships will increase the understanding between organizations and MAPs.

6. The success of organization-MAP management is measured by relationship quality.

7. Communication is the strategic tool for managing relationships.

8. Relational history, nature of interactions, frequency of exchange, and reciprocity influence the organization-MAP relationship.

9. Organization-MAP relationships can be categorized by type.

10. Relationship building can be applied to all aspects of public relations (Ledingham, 2005).

▶ Situational Crisis Communication Theory

Situational crisis communication theory (SCCT) was developed for the narrow aspect of public relations known as *crisis communication*. SCCT centers on the use of crisis response strategies to protect the organization's reputation. SCCT evolves from converging lines of communication research (Benoit, 1995; Benson, 1988; Coombs, 1995; Hearit, 1994) that state that the effectiveness of communication strategies is dependent on characteristics of the situation. The argument is that the situation helps to determine an appropriate response. The rhetorical problem for SCCT is the need for organizations to respond to a crisis. By understanding the crisis situation, a crisis manager can choose the most appropriate response.

Crisis managers use crisis response strategies to protect the organization's reputation. The organizational reputation is a valuable resource that can affect recruitment, stock prices, and even sales (Davies, Chun, da Silva, & Roper, 2003; Fombrun & Van Riel, 2003). SCCT argues that the best way to protect the reputational resource is by selecting the crisis response strategies that best fit the *reputational threat* presented by the crisis. The reputational threat is assessed by a two-step process. The first step is to identify the crisis type. A crisis type is the frame used to interpret the crisis (e.g., Lerbinger, 1997). Table 8.1 lists and defines the primary crisis types used in SCCT. Research in SCCT has found that crisis types vary by the level of crisis responsibility, the amount of responsibility MAPs believe the organization has for the crisis. Perception of crisis responsibility is a reputational threat because it is negatively related to organizational reputation (Coombs & Holladay, 1996, 2001, 2002). The crisis types form three crisis clusters and are based on the reputational threat/attributions of crisis responsibility: mild, moderate, and severe reputational threats. Table 8.1 indicates which crisis types belong to each of the three clusters.

The second step is to determine whether there is a crisis history, whether or not an organization has experienced similar crises. SCCT research has shown that a history of similar crises intensifies the reputational damage of a crisis (Coombs & Holladay, 2001). Crisis types and crisis history are combined to determine the reputational threat of a crisis situation. Determining the crisis type provides an initial assessment of the reputational threat by indicating the level of crisis responsibility associated with the crisis. This initial assessment is then adjusted if there is a history of similar crises. For example, a crisis with a mild reputational threat and a history of crises will become

Table 8.1: SCCT Crisis Types by Crisis Clusters

Victim Cluster: In these crisis types, the organization is also a victim of the crisis. (Mild Reputational Threat)

Natural disaster: Acts of nature, such as an earthquake, damage an organization.

Rumors: False and damaging information about an organization is being circulated.

Workplace violence: Current or former employee attacks current employees on site.

Product tampering/Malevolence: External agent causes damage to an organization.

Accidental Cluster: In these crisis types, the organizational actions leading to the crisis were unintentional. (Moderate Reputational Threat)

Challenges: Stakeholders claim an organization is operating in an inappropriate manner.

Megadamage: A technical accident occurs in which the focus is on the environmental damage from the accident.

Technical breakdown accidents: A technology or equipment failure causes an industrial accident.

Technical breakdown recalls: A technology or equipment failure causes a product to be recalled.

Preventable Cluster: In these crisis types, the organization knowingly placed people at risk, took inappropriate actions, or violated a law or regulation. (Severe Reputational Threat)

Human breakdown accidents: Human error causes an industrial accident.

Human breakdown recalls: Human error causes a product to be recalled.

Organizational misdeed with no injuries: Stakeholders are deceived without injury.

Organizational misdeed management misconduct: Laws or regulations are violated by management.

Organizational misdeed with injuries: Stakeholders are placed at risk by management, and injuries occur.

a moderate reputational threat. The level of threat is important because it drives the selection of crisis response strategies.

Crisis response strategies are what the organization says and does after a crisis hits—the response to the rhetorical problem. These rhetorical resources vary in the degree to which each accepts responsibility for the crisis and addresses the concerns of victims. *Deny strategies* claim there is no crisis (denial) or try to prove the organization has no responsibility for the crisis (scapegoating). *Diminish strategies* attempt to minimize the organization's responsibility (excuse) and/or the seriousness of the crisis (justification). *Rebuild strategies* provide compensation and/or apologize for the crisis. *Reinforcing strategies* include telling stakeholders about past good works (bolstering) and praising stakeholders (ingratiation). Reinforcing strategies are only supplemental and must be used with one of the other three. Table 8.2 lists and defines the crisis response strategies used in SCCT. Crisis managers can use a combination of

---

Table 8.2: SCCT Crisis Response Strategies

Deny Strategies

Attack the accuser: Crisis manager confronts the person or group, claiming something is wrong with the organization:
"The organization threatened to sue the people who claim a crisis occurred."

Denial: Crisis manager asserts that there is no crisis:
"The organization said that no crisis event occurred."

Scapegoat: Crisis manager blames some person or group outside of the organization for the crisis:
"The organization blamed the supplier for the crisis."

Diminish Strategies

Excuse: Crisis manager minimizes organizational responsibility by denying intent to do harm and/or claiming inability to control the events that triggered the crisis:
"The organization said it did not intend for the crisis to occur and that accidents happen as part of the operation of any organization."

Justification: Crisis manager minimizes the perceived damage caused by the crisis:
"The organization said the damage and injuries from the crisis were very minor."

Rebuild Strategies

Compensation: Crisis manager offers money or other gifts to victims:
"The organization offered money and products as compensation."

Apology: Crisis manager indicates the organization takes full responsibility for the crisis and asks stakeholders for forgiveness:
"The organization publicly accepted full responsibility for the crisis and asked stakeholders to forgive the mistake."

Reinforcing Strategies

Bolstering: Tell stakeholders about the past good works of the organization:
"The organization restated its recent work to improve K–12 education."

Ingratiation: Crisis manager praises stakeholders:
"The organization thanked stakeholders for their help."

crisis response strategies as long as they are free of contradictions (Ihlen, 2002). For example, it is a contradiction/problem if crisis managers use deny strategies with any strategies that acknowledge a crisis has occurred.

SCCT maintains that crisis managers must provide instructing and adjusting information before taking any action designed to address reputational concerns. *Instructing information* helps MAPs cope physically with a crisis. Examples include telling people to evacuate an area or to return a defective chain saw. *Adjusting information* helps MAPs to cope psychologically with the crisis. Examples include expressions of sympathy and telling MAPs what is being done to avoid a repeat of the crisis (Sturges, 1994). Crisis managers should never utilize crisis response strategies designed to protect the organization's reputation until adjusting and instructing information has been delivered.

In SCCT, crisis managers select crisis response strategies based on the reputational threat of the crisis. Mild reputational threats require only instructing and adjusting information. Moderate reputational threats require diminish strategies. Severe reputational threats demand reinforcing strategies. Deny strategies can be used for rumors or challenges, such as charges that your organization is acting in an immoral manner. Reinforcing strategies can be used with any crisis. Table 8.3 provides a summary of the SCCT guidelines for the use of crisis response strategies.

Table 8.3: SCCT Guidelines for Crisis Response Strategy Selection

1. Provide Instruction Strategies for All Crises With Victims
    A. When needed, provide warnings to stakeholders.
    B. Provide directions for how stakeholders should alter behaviors/expectations because of the crisis.

2. Provide Adjustment Strategies for All Crises With Victims
    A. Express concern for victims.
    B. Provide information about the cause of the crisis, when available.
    C. Provide information about corrective action–what is being done to prevent a repeat of the crisis—when relevant.

3. Select the Appropriate Crisis Response Strategy(ies) to Protect the Reputation
    A. For crises with minimal attributions of crisis responsibility (victim crises) and a history of similar crises, use the diminish crisis response strategies.
    B. For crises with low attributions of crisis responsibility (accident crises) and no history of similar crises, use diminish crisis response strategies.
    C. For crises with low attributions of crisis responsibility (accident crises) and a history of similar crises, use rebuild crisis response strategies.
    D. For crises with strong attributions of crisis responsibility (preventable crises) use the rebuild crisis response strategies regardless of crisis history.
    E. For rumor and challenge crises, use deny crisis response strategies when possible.
    F. Use reinforcing crisis response strategies as supplements to the other crisis response strategies.
    G. Try to maintain consistency in crisis response strategies by not mixing deny posture strategies with either the diminish or rebuild posture strategies.
    H. For crises with minimal attributions of crisis responsibility (victim crises) and no history of similar crises, informational and adjustment strategies alone are enough.
    I. Be prepared to change crisis response strategies if the crisis situation mutates and demands a different response to effectively protect the organization's reputation.

Some people make the mistake of assuming an organization should simply use highly accommodative crisis response strategies, especially apology, for any crisis. The evaluation of the crisis situation must consider the legal and financial limitations as well. The apology strategy does incur legal liability (Fuchs-Burnett, 2002). Hence, an organization may avoid more victim-protecting or responsibility-accepting response strategies because they cannot afford them and/or do not wish to assume the legal liability. These are real constraints that affect the operation of a crisis team. At times, reinforcing strategies are overly expensive and overkill. Crisis response strategies have costs for organizations. The more accommodative strategies have higher financial costs for an organization (Coombs, 2004). Compensation has obvious costs, whatever was paid to the MAPs. Apologies open an organization to financial costs from lawsuits. An apology admits responsibility. That admission of responsibility is used by victims of the crisis to win financial settlements in civil lawsuits (Fuchs-Burnett, 2002). Moreover, research has shown that using highly accommodative strategies offers no greater reputation protection in moderate reputational threat than the prescribed diminish strategies. The same holds true for just using instructing and adjusting information for mild crises (Coombs & Holladay, 1996; Coombs & Schmidt, 2000). The point is that an organization should use highly accommodative strategies only when necessary. It saves wasting financial resources.

SCCT attempts to understand, to explain, and to provide prescriptive actions for crisis communication. SCCT uses an understanding of the reputational threat of the crisis to select crisis response strategies that should maximize reputational protection.

▶Risk Communication Theory

Society exists for the collective management of risk. Police and fire personnel are trained and equipped to respond to specific emergencies. Medical researchers work to unlock the mysteries of diseases. Each person is at some risk to suffer various diseases. The common cold is one disease. So are cancer and heart attack. Physicians study and train to treat disease. Diet experts recommend that certain foods be eaten and others be avoided. Engineering students learn principles needed for safe design, construction, and operation. They design and build roads that reduce the risks of collisions. They design cars that are safer. The scandals of corporate cheating have demonstrated the risks of financial investment and employment. Greedy executives can ruin a company, leading to hundreds of employees being laid off and investors ruined. Note that once that sort of risk occurs, crisis communication is needed. Because of this role in society, public relations practitioners serving all types of organizations are at the forefront of risk communication.

Some experts are trained to identify and reduce risks. Others communicate about risks. Risk communication is vital to public relations. For instance, "environmental public relations" has become one of the best-paying jobs of the profession. Industries have learned that fear of risk can strain their relationships with customers and neighbors. So they have developed specific protocols of community relationships that allow them to engage in dialogue with people who live near dangerous facilities.

Risk results from products, services, or processes that can harm health, safety, or environmental quality. Organizations that are believed to create these risks are expected to manage them in ways that satisfy the expectations of the MAPs. Those organizations may need to change how they operate as well as how they communicate. In both cases, rhetorical problems emerge that require strategic solutions. They are central to companies' relationships with employees and communities. In this way, as well, risk and crisis communication are first cousins.

Let's think about risks in our lives. Automobile and traffic safety. Medical treatment. Financial investments. Pesticides, herbicides, and food additives. Electromagnetic fields. Drunk driving. Safe sex. Releases of toxic chemicals. Crime. Airline safety. Recreational accidents by children in playgrounds. Certain kinds of fat in foods. Natural hazards such as earthquakes, fires, hurricanes, floods, and tornadoes. Occupational safety. Safety in the home. Biotechnology. Radiation. Terrorism. What risks have we left off of this list?

A risk is a matter of uncertainty. Will some event or outcome happen? If a gambler bets on the spin of a roulette wheel, which number will win? If a person buys a stock, will it go up or down or be static? If a couple marries, will they divorce? If a person drives drunk, will someone be injured—or arrested? The chemical-manufacturing industry defines risk as (a) a hazard (for instance, toxic or flammable materials), (b) the possibility something will go wrong, and (c) the consequence when something does go wrong. Many other industries, nonprofits, and governmental agencies think this way.

Risks result in two kinds of outcomes: negative and positive. A gambler can win or lose. A student can pass or fail. Risks have magnitude: large or small. Although people know risks occur, no one wants to be the one to suffer the negative consequences.

There are three basic kinds of risk. The first is *natural risks,* such as violent weather, which result from the physics of nature. The second kind of risk occurs because of what others do. For instance, biotechnology researchers can create risks by the plants they create through genetic alteration. The third kind of risk people encounter results from their lifestyle choices: for example, drunk driving, abuse of alcohol, drug abuse, or overconsumption of fat, salt, and sugar.

Risk communicators may enter the picture to make people aware of risks and to advise them how to avoid risks and what to do if a risk manifests itself. For instance, public relations practitioners may work for chemical-manufacturing companies. They may help get the word to employees regarding their risk of exposure to chemicals or the potential of explosion and fire. These practitioners offer instructions on how to work safely and how to "shelter in place" (get into safe cover) if an incident occurs. Professional communicators work on public safety campaigns (drive safely) and public health campaigns (know the signs of cancer and be vigilant). They tell people to "see a doctor." They advise people to use sunscreen, to exercise regularly, and to take other measures to increase good health.

IN CASE OF CHEMICAL EMERGENCY

Wally says:

Wally

1. Go inside
2. Listen to AM 530
3. Stay off the phone

Provided by your local Deer Park
Emergency Planning Committee 713-478-7298

Sheltering in Place

SOURCE: Reprinted with permission from Deer Park, TX LEPC.

The theory of risk communication has continued to refine the principles that guide effective strategies. One traditional approach to risk communication was for technically trained experts to determine the degree to which people are at risk and recommend changes in business practices, or lifestyles, and assume that a rational decision model prevailed. If technical experts determined that a risk did not occur, they reported that conclusion to concerned publics, saying, "Trust us!"

Today's public relations doubts the value of the word of the *expert*. Current theory realizes that collaborative decision making is a vital part of risk communication. People may receive and consider messages provided about risks, but they like to feel control over those risks. One way to increase control is to empower collaborative decision making. For this reason, patients like to discuss various treatments of their diseases, and community members like to be able to discuss risks that companies create. Activism results from the desire to discuss risks. Industries, for this reason, have various kinds of community advisory committees in which they meet, share information, and listen to people who live and work near these facilities.

If a practitioner works for groups such as the American Heart Association, he or she is likely to engage in risk communication. Nonprofits look for opportunities to communicate with key audiences regarding how they could, for instance, change their diets or increase their exercise to reduce the chances (risks) they would suffer heart disease. They use a Web site to present message points. They may create interactive dialogue by which interested persons could raise questions and voice concerns.

Researchers from many disciplines study risks. Some calculate the likelihood that various risks will occur. By these calculations, people come to know for an entire population how many people might, for instance, be hit by a meteor, be struck by lightening, die from a bee sting, or be seriously injured in a car accident.

Other researchers study risk perception. They note how variables affect perception of risk: catastrophic potential, familiarity, understanding, uncertainty, controllability, voluntariness of exposure, effects on children, effects manifestation, effects on future generations, victim identity, dread, trust in institutions, media attention, accident history, equity, benefits, reversibility, personal stake, and origin. Some risks are frightening because of a catastrophic potential, such as attacks by terrorists. People may not worry about risks that are familiar, such as those related to driving an automobile. People don't like to have risks forced on them (voluntariness). They dread some risks, such as disfiguring surgeries. Risks that affect children and subsequent generations are scary. No one wants to be the victim of a negative risk, no matter how unlikely.

Several variables influence how people communicate about risks. These include support, harms and benefits, risk tolerance, uncertainty, trust, self-interest and altruistic values, cognitive involvement, control, and knowledge.

Support is the outcome objective of managing the organization's response to the concerns of key publics. Either a risk exists or it does not. It is controllable in various ways and degrees—or it is not. Public relations seeks to displace opposition with support by (a) making appropriate strategic business plans, (b) engaging in effective issues monitoring and analysis, (c) using public policy planning in the mutual interest of stakeholders, (d) seeking to meet key publics' expectations of corporate responsibility, and (e) communicating in ways that maximize the control people feel is reasonable to achieve harmony and foster multiple stakeholders' mutual interests. People support that which benefits them and oppose that which harms them. Note that these elements are featured in Chapter 10, which discusses issues management.

Harms and benefits are important aspects of the risk assessment equation. Krimsky and Golding (1992) observed, "Expected utility theory comprises a set of decision rules that define rational behavior. It is generally assumed that people would follow these rules if they had sufficient information and time to dwell on the consequences of alternative decision paths" (p. 356). People may infer that they receive benefits (or suffer harms) and then decide whether they suffer risks that are intolerable. Those who think they are harmed do not support the source of risk.

Risk tolerance is an important concept. Just as everyone is not equally aware of the risks in a community or the emergency response measures they should take to increase their safety, all members of a community have a different sense of the degree to which a risk exists and whether it is harmful. They differ in their risk tolerance—a measure of how knowledgeable they are of a risk and accommodating to it. Women, for instance, tend to be less tolerant of technical risks than are men.

Uncertainty is a concept that defines risk. Risk is the likelihood (probability) that an event will occur and that it will be tolerable or severe. Albrecht (1988) concluded that uncertainty is "the lack of attributional confidence about cause-effect patterns" (p. 387). Driskill and Goldstein (1986) reasoned that individuals suffering turbulent or unstable conditions become more attentive to information that will help them cope with their environment; they found people are not always able to reduce their uncertainty with information alone. Uncertainty may not result merely from the lack of information but may also occur when people lack appropriate premises to use to draw conclusions from information they do have.

Trust is a complex variable. Those who create or interpret risks would like for publics to "trust" them. Trust is not granted, but earned by what is said and done. Trust results from the amount of control an audience believes it can exert over sources of risk information and assessment. As Kasperson concluded, "There is not a single risk communication problem; there is not a single social trust problem. There are many problems, and they are different" (cited in Davies, Covello, & Allen, 1987, p. 45). Trust is affected by vulnerability, predictability, and reward dependability. As noted above in discussing crisis, the history of the organization is a major factor in publics' willingness to trust. If the organization gives reason to be trusted, then it will enjoy publics' trust. It earns trust by properly working with people to mitigate the likelihood and consequences of various risks.

Self-interest or altruistic values predict whether publics and audiences will be cognitively involved with public policy issues leading them to recognize which arguments are relevant, to have more knowledge on a topic, and to communicate about it (Heath & Douglas, 1991; Heath, Liao, & Douglas, 1995; Nathan, Heath, & Douglas, 1992). Persons who believe they are at risk become more thoughtful in their analysis of message content and work harder to obtain information and opinion through conversation, reading, listening to news, and televiewing.

Cognitively involved persons can be reached with information and argument even though they may resist them, whereas less involved persons are likely to ignore informational presentations and discussions of the risk. Involved persons are more critical of information and arguments than are their less cognitively involved counterparts (Petty & Cacioppo, 1986). Perception that risk exists and is unacceptable—or at least deserving of concern—correlates with cognitive involvement.

Control has particular relevance for the analysis of and strategic response to crises and risks. Persons who indicate that they do not support what they fear are high-risk chemical facilities exhibit a greater need for control in comparison to supporters of such facilities. People tend to believe that they benefit more from sources of risk if they think the managements of such facilities, perhaps in conjunction with government regulators, properly control their operations. Chemical workers, persons employed by a source of risk, believe that the managements of such facilities exert more self-control over their operations than do persons who do not work in the industry. An increased sense of shared control over the risk and its potentially harmful outcomes is likely to lead to greater harmony between the organization and its stakeholders and stakeseekers.

Knowledge is one of the most problematic variables in this analysis. One view of risks is that people use knowledge to make rational risk assessments. As alluring as that proposition is, we know that people distort risk decisions because of emotion. One underpinning assumption in risk assessment is that experts can obtain scientific knowledge about the degree to which a risk exists, use that knowledge to properly abate the risk, and supply concerned publics with the details of the risk and means for its abatement. The assumption is that once key publics receive technical information, they make informed decisions and their concern will lessen.

Risk communication is most strategic and ethical when it is used to increase a sense of control by the publics, the stakeholders, who believe the risks can affect them or someone or something toward which they hold altruistic values. In the simplest sense, people acknowledge the risks of life but want to know who causes them and whether those sources of risks are responsible: Are they willing and able to exert the appropriate levels to control to prevent or respond to crises?

In this way, crisis and risk are connected. They are also tied to issues. An issue may become a crisis. A crisis can mature into an issue. If a risk is appropriately managed, it is less likely to become an issue and a crisis is less likely to occur.

Risk communication theory postulates that support is more likely to be granted when people believe that benefits outweigh the negative aspects of a risk. Persons who are more risk tolerant tend to believe such is the case. The more uncertain people are about a risk, the more likely they are to be less tolerant and to seek more control of the risk. If one or more organizations can demonstrate the willingness and ability to properly manage risk, they are more likely to be supported rather than opposed in their efforts.

As people believe a risk relates to their self-interest or the object of their altruism, they are more likely to be cognitively involved. This leads to their willingness to seek and receive information. If they are more cognitively involved, they tend to like more informative messages and stronger arguments to help them understand and formulate opinions and behavioral intentions. They want control. That can come through knowledge. All of this functions best when it occurs in an infrastructure that allows dialogue rather than monologue.

A linear, expert source approach to risk communication may not be as successful as other approaches. An alternative is to see all of the concerned persons engaged in dialogue. Ethically and pragmatically, people want to engage in risk discussion, and they deserve to be included. Whose life is this anyway? Dialogue includes all of the people who want to be involved. This view is referred to as a *communication infrastructure*, which brings together company spokespersons, government officials, activists, and concerned citizens. Each states its case but needs to listen to and give regard for the comments and concerns of other voices in this dialogue.

People who are less risk tolerant have more negative views of the health-and-safety impact of an industry. They are less likely than risk-tolerant individuals to believe that the costs of living and working in proximity to risks generates personal or community benefits that outweigh potential harms. Knowledge of the source of risk and its potential harms may not differentiate these two groups of individuals. What people know or understand may not be as important as what they believe based on their interpretation of the facts. Thus, when practitioners and academics suggest that both sides of a controversy must understand one another, that is only halfway to agreement. Low-risk-tolerant individuals believe that the source of risk is less willing and able to exert appropriate control over their activities. Low-risk-tolerant persons tend to be less certain they know the consequences of living and working in proximity to these companies (Heath, Seshadri, & Lee, 1998; Nathan et al., 1992).

This theory features the role of cognitive involvement. As predicted, when persons believe that an industry will harm their economic interest, they experience more involvement. Involvement increases because they worry that their self-interests will be harmed. Of interest, however, is that some people may see positive benefits from living near a chemical-manufacturing facility, while their neighbors fear negative consequences. Either high degrees of positive or negative involvement may occur. Simply stated, people respond to risks based on whether they believe they will gain or lose because of the risk (Heath et al., 1995). People with high positive or negative involvement are most likely to support or oppose an issue and more likely to take action for or against the company. Thus, we have the dynamics of public dialogue: differences of opinion and interest on the part of key publics. Individuals who are more highly involved seek and interpret information about the risk and take action.

One of the problems regarding risk communication is the inability or unwillingness of people to know as much about a risk as they might—or even think they do. Risk issues are often complex, requiring expertise in gathering and interpreting information. However, people don't easily believe and often don't understand what experts say. Experts can engage in what people think of as "technobabble," or scientific terms. Very few people in a community know what is going on in the community, what chemicals are produced, how the companies operate, and how safe living and conditions are. Nevertheless, people can hold strong opinions in the absence of knowledge. Even though people are not well informed, those who are better informed seem to be more supportive of the companies that generate risks (Heath & Abel, 1996b).

Rather than types of knowledge about chemicals and processes, the most important form of knowledge to increase a feeling of risk tolerance answers the following questions: Is the industry working hard to operate safely? Are they prepared to warn citizens if something happens that might harm them? Will they use sirens and telephone emergency response systems to alert citizens to dangers? Does the industry work hard to let people know about these emergency response systems? People who believe the industry scores high on these questions are more risk tolerant and more supportive of industry. Nevertheless, people are concerned about the industry; they are not complacent. Communities in which industry and government cooperate to create and implement emergency warning communication and response systems generate the most support among residents (Heath & Abel, 1996a). Empowerment gained from working together cooperatively—collaboratively—strengthens relationships between industry, government, and citizens (Heath & Palenchar, 2000).

These effects can be demonstrated in another way. People who live closest to such companies may benefit most but also be at greater risk. Is proximity to a source of risk a factor? Those farthest from the source of risk (more than 20 miles) may have the most fear. Openness in communication and efforts to build trust lead to support rather than opposition. Trust correlates negatively with cognitive involvement (concern), uncertainty, and dread. Support is positively correlated with openness, knowledge, and trust (Heath et al., 1998).

Experts are a vital part of risk communication infrastructures. One category of these is the industrial hygienist. Hygienists who are employed in the industry show significant differences from nonemployees, especially in terms of level of cognitive involvement, uncertainty, use of business as sources of information, perceived knowledge of risks, and confidence in the industry's willingness to exert self-control to abate risks. Those employed in the industry rely heavily on technical information from technical journals. Those not employed in the industry get most of their information from local news media; they rely on the kinds of accounts and interpretations reported here to understand the degree of risk in the community. Employees use the local media simply to monitor issues, not as sources of how well the industry is doing to operate safely (Heath & Gay, 1995, 1997).

Symmetry has long been a topic important to the practice of public relations. Risk communication theory reveals that even concerned citizens are more supportive if they believe they are in dialogue with the industry and government. Even those who consider themselves to be activists are more supportive than are those who believe themselves to be outside of the communication and decision-making loop. Activists believe they can influence the trajectory of risks toward a safer community in which to live and work. They not only believe the industry is willing and able to control its processes but are also confident that community pressures increase industry's safe performance (Palenchar & Heath, 2002).

The extent to which people support rather than oppose an organization that creates risks depends on their social awareness and their sense that "rightness" is occurring.

Persons who are merely pragmatic in their views of industry are less supportive. Thus, industry or government (or both) need to demonstrate that they are concerned about the public's welfare and are doing what is right to produce value for the community. Such analysis can find publics that may be segmented as "concerned," "willing to accept industry and move on," and "don't want to know." Sharing values and demonstrating concern helps the community to appreciate, understand, and tolerate these sources of risk (Palenchar & Heath, 2002).

People in any community where industry or government creates risks to health and safety may have a supportive or unsupportive relationship with these entities. To reduce opposition and gain support, these organizations must demonstrate commitment to the well-being of local citizens. Such commitment is demonstrated through actions and statements. It demonstrates that the industry and the local residents have aligned interests and share common values. As is argued throughout this book, organizations must build public relations—relations with their key publics. This is not a fleeting or momentary activity. It is not something that can be accomplished easily. Trust requires demonstrated commitment rather than narrow self-interest. In this way, risk communication truly demonstrates all that is good and useful about the practice of public relations.

Risk communication offers many professional challenges. People don't like to change their lifestyles to be healthier. People worry that their health and safety are being harmed by industrial processes. Rhetorical responses to the needs of MAPs can be a vital part of professional practice. They can build relationships in which people enjoy healthier and safer lives. They foster community—one of the central goals of today's public relations.

We end this section with some observations that can help you think strategically and ethically as you are called on to respond to risk concerns by MAPs:

- Accept the desire on the part of key publics to exert control over factors they worry affect them and other entities for which they have concern.
- Collaborate with them to engage in information gathering, risk assessment, and risk control. This effort is likely to require effective communication and decision-making infrastructures.
- Empower community members by demonstrating to them that through their participation in decision making they are a constructive part of the risk assessment and control process.
- Build trust over time through community outreach, collaborative decision making, and demonstrations that community expectations are met or exceeded by product design, manufacturing procedures, and emergency response.
- Participate in the risk assessment and communication process; don't attempt to dominate it.
- Have as your goal the outcome of the members of the community believing that through the risk assessment and decision-making process, they have achieved better conclusions or have been unable to honestly and candidly find fault with the decisions of others.

WEB WATCHER: RESEARCH AND THEORY

We have provided just a glimpse into the array of theories available in public relations. Professor Kirk Hallahan at Colorado State University has a section of his Web site about public relations devoted to research in public relations. The Web site address for public relations research is http://lamar.colostate.edu/~hallahan/articles.htm. Visit the Web site and look through his categorization of public relations research. See whether you can find sample research from each of the five theories presented in this chapter. Also, develop a list of theories we did not cover. This Web site will be a useful resource in future classes if you are a public relations major. The *Encyclopedia of Public Relations* (Heath, 2005) is another excellent source of brief descriptions of key theories.

Conclusion

Elaine was hired by EVP Electronics to develop a community relations program. EVP has largely neglected the local community where its facilities are located. Elaine uses relationship management theory to guide the creation of EVP's community relations program. Her basic premise is that there must be mutually beneficial relationships established between EVP management and community leaders. Communication is the way to develop and manage those relationships. Her first action is to assess the current quality of the relationship between EVP and community leaders. She uses the scales developed for relationship management theory to assess the relationship quality. The results suggest the two weakest dimensions are trust and credibility. Community leaders have little trust in EVP and do not view it as very credible. Elaine realizes she must address these two concerns as she builds and communicates the new community relations program. Elaine has used theory to address a challenge she faced on her new job.

Some practitioners reject the role of theory in their practice. They want a simple formula to follow that will always allow them to be effective. That is not what theory and research provide. It helps practitioners to be better critical and analytical thinkers. To that end, this chapter has explained what a theory is and justified the relevance of theories in public relations practice. In public relations, theories are meant to be applied: They are designed to help understand and to solve problems public relations practitioners will face. We have used risk and crisis communication to illustrate how theory is used to solve problems and guide public relations actions. Critical thinking is an essential job skill.

Practitioners cannot be effective at critical thinking unless they have a variety of theories and principles that can be applied to their problems. Our discussions of mutually beneficial relationships throughout this book include a variety of theories and principles that can be applied toward building, maintaining, or repairing organization-stakeholder relationships. Part of being an effective practitioner is staying current with the latest developments in theory. By learning new tools, you can hone your practice.

Connecting Theory and Planning

**John Beardsley, APR
Counselor in Public
    Relations
1995 President,
    Public Relations
    Society of America**

"The threat of a loss has a greater impact on a decision than the possibility of an equivalent gain." In the lingo of economists, losses loom larger than gains.

A midsized midwestern manufacturing company decided it needed to shut down one of its plants and lay off 25% of its workforce. The 96-year-old company had never done anything like this before and, quite frankly, had no idea what to expect. How would the employees who were being let go react? What about those who were staying? And would the surrounding community, in which the company had been a neighborly but low-profile resident for so many years, be supportive or resentful? Public relations planning had to deal with these several uncertainties.

The foundation for the resulting plan came from a paper published in the early 1980s by two psychologists, Nobel laureate Daniel Kahneman and the late Amos Tversky. Kahneman and Tversky wondered why people make risk-seeking decisions in situations where risk-averse behavior would seem to be expected.

Risk aversion has been a topic of study by economists since the 1730s. Here's an example: Suppose you're given a choice between a sure gain of $80 and an 85% chance of winning $100 but a 15% chance of winning nothing. You're more likely to choose the sure gain of $80, even though the gamble has an "expected value" that's $5 higher. On the surface, that's not rational behavior; in fact, it's risk-averse.

Kahneman and Tversky conducted extensive research on this kind of behavior, and they noticed something unusual. Let's say you're forced to choose between a sure loss of $80 and a risk that involves an 85% chance of losing $100 and a 15% chance

FURTHER
EXPLORATION

8

Ethical Quandary: Ethics in Relationships

Imagine that you are a fairly successful public relations consultant. The core of your business is built around your "fusion theory" of stakeholder relationship development. Your theory helps to identify and to resolve problems with MAPs. Along of losing nothing. The same numbers as above, but applied to a loss instead of a gain. And in this case, you'll usually take the gamble. Now that's not rational, either, because the value of the gamble is $5 more than the value of the sure loss. So it's risk-seeking.

What makes people behave so differently in these situations? Kahneman and Tversky wanted to know. Their research provided the answer. The "investigations of the psychology of preferences demonstrated several intriguing discrepancies between subjective and objective conceptions of decisions," they said. Their conclusion: "The threat of a loss has a greater impact on a decision than the possibility of an equivalent gain." In short, "preferences between gains are risk-averse and preferences between losses are risk-seeking."

Using the "psychology of preferences" as a guideline, the company's public relations plan for the plant closing was designed to recognize that laid-off employees, the ones facing a loss, were definite prospects for risk-seeking behavior, perhaps even going so far as breaking windows, damaging equipment, and slashing tires, while the employees who kept their jobs were likely to want to keep a low profile and therefore shouldn't be expected to stand up as gung-ho cheerleaders for management's new view of the company's future. Doing so would be too risky. And the neighboring community—well, they would probably just wait and see how things went.

The objectives of the public relations plan were (a) to humanize the company's regret for having to take such an action, even though it was necessary to ensure the continuing success of the enterprise; (b) to describe the supportive programs being offered to laid-off workers; (c) to minimize employee/customer/supplier anxiety; and (d) to reduce so-called "survivor sickness" among remaining employees. The objectives were accomplished.

The lesson from Kahneman and Tversky: People will take greater chances when it comes to avoiding losses than they will when going after gains. That's pretty useful behavioral knowledge for public relations practitioners.

REFERENCE: Kahneman, D., & Tversky, A. (1982, January). The psychology of preferences. *Scientific American*, 160–173.

SOURCE: Reprinted with permission from John Beardsley.

the way, you have defined your variables, developed instruments for assessing each variable, and specified the relationships between the variables. However, you have never fully tested the theory for fear it may be wrong and people will no longer use it. Should you continue to sell this theory to clients as a solution to their relationship problems? Write a rationale for your answer. How would the answer change if a preliminary test found no support for the key relationships used to build the fusion theory?

Summary Questions

1. What are the three functions of theory?

2. What is a theory?

3. Why does it matter that public relations can be considered a social science?

4. What are the four stages of theory building, and what are the key actions taken during each stage?

5. What are the key variables in risk communication theory?

6. What is the major focus of excellence theory?

7. What makes situational crisis communication theory (SCCT) prescriptive?

8. What is the central concern in contingency theory?

9. How are relationships evaluated in relationship management theory?

Exercises

1. Look through the news reports to find an example of a crisis and the organization's response to the crisis. Use situational crisis communication theory (SCCT) to assess whether or not the response fits the crisis situation.

2. Look through articles in either the *Journal of Public Relations Research* or *Public Relations Review,* and find an article that claims to be using a theory. How well does the theory in the article meet the three functions of theory presented in this chapter?

Recommended Readings

Cameron, G. T., Cropp, F., & Reber, B. H. (2001). Getting past platitudes: Factors limiting accommodation in public relations. *Journal of Communication Management, 5*(3), 242–261.

Cancel, A. E., Cameron, G. T., Sallot, L. M., & Mitrock, M. A. (1997). It depends: A contingency theory of accommodation in public relations. *Journal of Public Relations Research, 9,* 31–36.

Coombs, W. T. (2005). Crisis and crisis management. In R. L. Heath (Ed.), *Encyclopedia of public relations* (pp. 217–221). Thousand Oaks, CA: Sage.

Coombs, W. T. (2005). Crisis communication. In R. L. Heath (Ed.), *Encyclopedia of public relations* (pp. 221–224). Thousand Oaks, CA: Sage.

Grunig, J. E. (2001). Two-way symmetrical public relations: Past, present, and future. In R. L. Heath (Ed.), *Handbook of public relations* (pp. 31–50). Thousand Oaks, CA: Sage.

Heath, R. L. (2001). A rhetorical enactment rationale for public relations: The good organization communicating well. In R. L. Heath (Ed.), *Handbook of public relations* (pp. 11–30). Thousand Oaks, CA: Sage.

Heath, R. L. (2005). Mutually beneficial relationships. In R. L. Heath (Ed.), *Encyclopedia of public relations* (pp. 552–556). Thousand Oaks, CA: Sage.

Lyon, L., & Cameron, G. T. (2004). A relational approach examining the interplay of prior reputation and immediate response to a crisis. *Journal of Public Relations Research, 16,* 213–242.

Palenchar, M. J. (2005). Risk communication. In R. L. Heath (Ed.), *Encyclopedia of public relations* (pp. 752–755). Thousand Oaks, CA: Sage.

Wan, H. H., & Pfau, M. (2004). The relative effectiveness of inoculation, bolstering, and combined approaches to crisis communication. *Journal of Public Relations Research, 16,* 301–328.

9

Ethical and Legal Restraints on Public Relations Practice

Nike Corporation is a leader in sports apparel marketing. In recent years, its corporate policies and marketing strategies have been criticized. Critics have claimed that Nike, like many other companies, has bought products that are produced in sweatshop conditions. Key arguments in that criticism have merged in a case called *Kasky v. Nike,* which has implications for how and when public relations practitioners communicate. Increasingly, public relations messages have come to be treated like those of their advertising cohorts. When the message is commercial speech, the messages cannot be misleading. For public relations practitioners, then, the distinction between commercial and noncommercial speech is important. Traditionally, under the protection of the First Amendment of the U.S. Constitution, companies and others in society have been able to engage in noncommercial speech, sometimes called "political" or "issues speech," without the worry that legal restraints or injunctions would be used to constrain these messages. In sum, commercial speech needs to be scrupulously accurate, but noncommercial speech is freer to voice opinion based on fact. The reason for the high standard for commercial speech is the need for customers to be able to take at face value the statements made in ads, publicity, and promotion as they decide whether to purchase various goods and services.

The elements of this case reach back into the mid- to late 1990s. At that time, Nike, like its

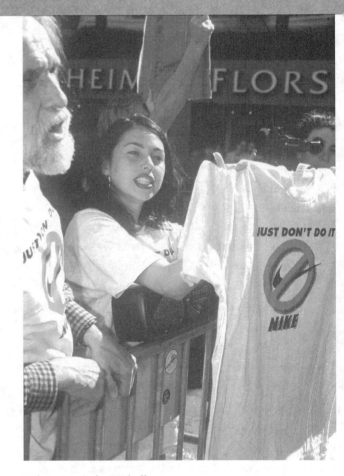

Nike's Sweatshop Challenge

SOURCE: Copyright © Getty Images.

competitors and other kinds of companies, routinely contracted with companies owned and located in countries such as Korea, Vietnam, Taiwan, China, Thailand, and Indonesia. With few exceptions, the employees in these manufacturing facilities were young women under the age of 24. All contractors for these goods are required to sign a Memorandum of Understanding. This agreement commits the purchasing company to work to ensure compliance on the part of the manufacturing companies. The standards of work relate to minimum wage, overtime, child labor, holiday, vacations, insurance benefits, and working conditions, including comfort and safety. One of the safety issues is sexual abuse. Under attack by critics, Nike began to survey compliance and used accounting firms to conduct spot checks of labor and environmental conditions. The consulting firm they hired was cochaired by Andrew Young, a former ambassador to the United Nations. Young, in this capacity, issued a statement that no violations were found by his firm. Activist critics, on the basis of key countries, such as Vietnam, issued statements that contradicted that conclusion. Thus, we have by definition an issue of fact. What is the truth in this matter? As a company, Nike became known as a purveyor of sports apparel made on human misery.

Not surprisingly, Nike countered with a public relations campaign, aimed in part to repair and manage its reputation. To address its side of the issue, the company issued press releases and used other tactics to respond to the mounting allegations that it had become the iconic exploiter of sweatshop labor. Having access to the text of these responses, Marc Kasky identified what he believed to be six misrepresentations of fact. With these claims, he filed a complaint under California's Business and Professions Code sections 17200 and 17500. In response to this action, Nike and other respondents argued that the filing is contrary to the First Amendment of the U.S. Constitution. The controversy surrounding this action centers squarely on what elements distinguish commercial (not protected by the U.S. Constitution) and noncommercial speech, which is protected. Protection means that it cannot be regulated. Regulation assumes that buyers need to be protected from claims in commercial speech. The law assumes that noncommercial speech is corrected because of the dialogue—debate—that surrounds an issue discussed in the various kinds of communication.

Summarizing a complex legal argument is difficult, and impossible in the detail of this opening vignette. The Supreme Court has not ruled on this case. Thus, the boundaries of commercial and noncommercial speech are not clarified in this case. Those arguments challenging Kasky reason that large companies should be constrained from making statements about their policies and actions that have commercial and reputational value, even when those statements do not specifically address the quality of a product or service. Opponents of this position believe that statements about a product or service need regulation, but those relevant to corporate policies, especially in terms also of government policies in other countries, need open debate where opinions may conflict over interpretation. Thus, they would argue that the public interest is served by such "issue" communication. Time will tell—and guide your practice—on these matters.

A central theme of today's public relations is that to be an effective communicator requires being an ethical communicator. This theme reinforces the basic principle of the rhetorical heritage discussed in Chapter 1: the challenge of being a good organization communicating well. It assumes that if a communicator is not ethical, that fact will be revealed and the communication efforts of the person or organization will fail.

To better understand the legal and ethical implications of the practice, this chapter investigates ethical principles, codes of ethics, and legal principles. These affect how practitioners conduct themselves on behalf of their clients. What practitioners want to say and do on behalf of clients is limited by legal and ethical principles. These principles are derived from an insightful understanding of the role communication plays in society. The ethical and legal principles of the practice are derived from a simple premise. Communication is allowed—even encouraged—when it serves the interests of society.

A Good Organization Communicating Well

A profound misconception is that the First Amendment of the U.S. Constitution gives unlimited protection to the person or organization that wants to express—speak, write, depict, or portray in graphics or pictures—some idea. In their interpretation of the First Amendment, courts are far more interested in protecting people's right to hear, read, see, or teleview than the right to proclaim, persuade, or inform. If you are a communication major, you may have had—or perhaps will have—a course in communication law and ethics. Those are standard courses in departments and colleges where public relations is taught. You may already have a sense of the legal and moral guidelines that will shape your practice from such a course.

In either case, you will be expected to learn that freedom of communication, the right to free expression, is governed not by what is good for the individual wanting to communicate, but what is good for society. Typically, such discussions are based on a few profound principles. Information is power. Opinion is power. Discussions of First Amendment rights and responsibilities consider whether society is stronger if its citizens have the freedom to receive information they want and the opportunity to learn others' opinions. In this way, they and society are empowered with the information and opinion they need to make wise decisions. How should organizations, as well as people, be constrained in their rights to speak on issues? Consider, for instance, the implications of the case in Box 9.1.

BOX 9.1 RACKETEERING AND THE ETHICAL
AND LEGAL PRACTICE OF PUBLIC RELATIONS

In 1997, a Florida state judge was asked to review civil-racketeering allegations against Hill & Knowlton, one of the nation's largest public relations firms—a unit of WPP Group. The charge against the firm was that its communication efforts to play down the risks of smoking during the 1950s and 1960s constituted industry conspiracy under Florida's racketeering law. The charge was that members of the firm conspired with members of the tobacco industry to perpetrate a crime onto persons who smoked and persons who had to pay for the health costs of persons who smoked. The Florida state judge dismissed these charges because the alleged conspiracy happened too long ago. In addition, Hill & Knowlton had stopped working for the tobacco industry in 1968. This case poses a legal problem: Can practitioners "racketeer"? Racketeering legislation was created to prosecute criminals who conspired to commit criminal acts, such as those typically associated with Mafia leaders who do not kill or extort, but who conspire to see that such criminal acts occur. This discussion also raises an ethical problem: Should the public relations industry represent clients that they believe harm society? This case study's legal problem may be far-fetched, but it suggests how prosecuting attorneys believe that communication actions can violate criminal statutes. So much for unlimited freedom of speech.

As a public relations practitioner, can you imagine the power of sharing information and expressing opinions that can affect other people's interests? Public relations is about power. It must be used wisely and ethically. It can empower an organization. It can empower stakeholders and stakeseekers of that organization. Power is exerted through buying—going down the street with credit cards and cash in hand—selecting products or services purveyed by competing vendors. Power is the ability to give money and volunteer time and services to various nonprofit organizations. Power exists when we can use governmental agencies to solve the collective problems of society. Deciding to protest as an active public is a commitment to take a role in the formation and implementation of public policy aimed at improving society. All of these actions assume that power results from the acquisition and use of information and the opinions of others to shape crucial decisions.

To feature power as a central aspect of public relations is unique. It can unnerve some persons who think that public relations is too powerful, having the "power" to manipulate by sneaking through people's mental defenses. For this reason, legal and regulatory restrictions are placed on persons—businesses and nonprofits—to prevent them from lying in the content of advertising or distorting the truth through public relations communication.

Power in a society should be shared. It can be the basis of conflict, a fight for advantage. The choice we hope you make in your practice is central to our definition of public

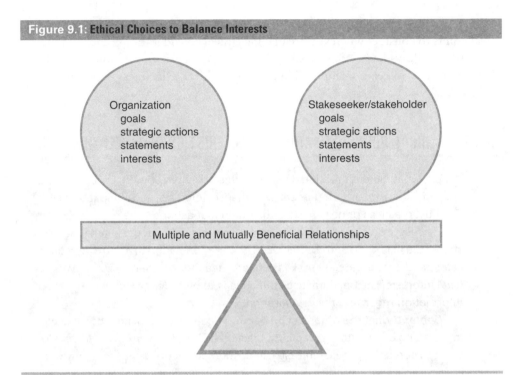

Figure 9.1: Ethical Choices to Balance Interests

Organization
goals
strategic actions
statements
interests

Stakeseeker/stakeholder
goals
strategic actions
statements
interests

Multiple and Mutually Beneficial Relationships

relations as the managerial and technical communication strategies required for building and maintaining mutually beneficial relationships between client organizations and their stakeholders and stakeseekers. This means achieving a balance of interests, by devising goals and strategies that lead to mutually beneficial ends. This balance is captured in Figure 9.1.

Power is fundamental to ethics. If we do not acknowledge power and discuss it thoughtfully and thoroughly, we cannot appreciate many ethical quandaries. Consider the following, for instance: power to lie. Power to withhold information. Power to manipulate. Power to empower. Power to make good, wise, and informed decisions. This last point is clearly and resoundingly captured by Robert Jackall (1995): "Successful public relations depends on its practitioners' abilities to provide audiences with convincing reasons for justified belief in some product, client, or cause" (p. 14). This view assumes that the public interest is the foundation for the ethical choices made by professional public relations practitioners.

To frame our discussion of the ethical, legal, and regulatory constraints on public relations practice, consider this line of analysis. What happens to persons and organizations that act and speak in ways that affect others but do not act ethically—are they meeting prevailing community standards? Those persons and organizations are likely to be forced to act more ethically through lawsuits and regulatory restrictions. Those two options frame the discussion that follows. Ethical principles and codes of professional ethics, as well as legal and regulatory constraints, shape the way people practice and employ public relations.

Today's rhetorical approach to public relations suggests that you have at least four focal points to consider when you are making ethical considerations. Each of the focal points that follows has a counterpart principle that is basic to relationship building: The philosophy of relationship building stresses ethical principles, as is summarized in Box 9.2.

BOX 9.2 ETHICAL PRINCIPLES AND CHARACTERISTICS OF A RELATIONSHIP

Action: what the organization does. It is ethical when it demonstrates cooperation, openness, trust, commitment, alignment of interests, and compatible views. The best practices principle is to understand that actions have meaning.

Process: how the organization communicates. It is ethical when it demonstrates that it is open and committed in its communication to inform, persuade, listen, and collaboratively make decisions needed to achieve mutually beneficial interests. The best practices principle is to be the first and best source of information regarding the organization.

Content: what the organization communicates. It is ethical when it is willing to stand behind its messages, subject them to public scrutiny, and develop them to serve the public interest. The best practices principle is to communicate content that supports the mutual interests and needs of all parties.

Product: what the organization helps to accomplish. It is ethical when it is willing to work toward cocreated, negotiated, and aligned interests and compatible views. The best practices principle is to work toward mutually beneficial outcomes.

- What the organization *does*—its actions, policies, practices, and procedures—can be examined to determine whether they conform to public standards of ethical behavior.
- How an organization communicates can draw attention to its ethical choices. Think of this as communication *process*. Elements of the communication process include when, where, how, and with whom the organization communicates—or does not communicate. Process features trust and openness.
- What the organization communicates—the *content* of its messages—is subject to ethical scrutiny. This focal point can include not only the words used (and other symbols) but also the facts, evaluations, opinions, and conclusions that are contained in its messages. Ethical considerations that people might have include wondering whether the organization is telling the truth, spinning the truth, or fabricating what it hopes will be believed to be the truth.
- The outcome—*product*—of the message and communication process can also be a focal point. If messages lead people to believe one conclusion when another is more correct, critics will conclude that the organization violated an ethical principle.

This chapter takes a relationship-building approach to the legal and ethical constraints on the practice of public relations. The chapter will examine codes and principles of ethics related to the practice of public relations. To frame this discussion, consider whether that which builds, maintains, and strengthens relationships in mutually beneficial ways is ethical. Codes of professional practice are means by which professionals challenge and police one another to know and adhere to those standards. Laws and regulations coerce compliance with community standards because some practitioners and other members of the organization are insensitive to community standards or flaunt those standards for selfish interests—or both.

Ethical Issues:
A Relationship Approach

One of the running observations that is often made in the study of journalism or public relations is that persons with ethics enter journalism and those without ethics practice public relations.

We do not ask you to agree or disagree with that observation, but we encourage your self-examination. Ask yourself this question: Am I willing to undertake the professional responsibility to ensure that I will be the best available supplier of information and opinion through my practice of public relations because I realize that any lower standard can harm the profession and the society it serves?

That challenge asks you to think about your profession *and* the society it serves. It does not ask you to think only about the interests of your client. If you serve your profession and society, you will do justice to your client. If you do not serve society and your profession, you will damage your client. If you place your client's interests above those of your profession and society, you will do substantial damage to all three. Those are daunting challenges. Consider the implications of those challenges throughout this chapter. Can you ethically serve one interest above others and build mutually beneficial relationships?

Journalists who are asked whether they trust public relations practitioners as credible sources of information often say they do not. So, they don't trust practitioners in general, but they do have specific practitioners whom they trust. A huge amount of "news" that appears in newspapers and newsmagazines—as well as on radio and television—results from reporters, editors, and news directors using information gained from press releases and questions posed to practitioners. So, the information supplied by public relations practitioners can't be that bad—if it is that usable. Without doubt, however, reporters trust some practitioners much more than others. That observation suggests the value of effective media relationship building. To help build bridges, the Public Relations Society of America (PRSA) chapters sponsor Media Days to bring together practitioners and reporters. A synergistic relationship—love/hate—exists between them. Dialogue can help to bridge gaps of trust.

This chapter examines ethical constraints on public relations, the codes of professional conduct that practitioners need to support and use to guide their practices and the legal guidelines that need to be followed. The order of those topics has a compelling logic to it. If people knew and adhered to ethical constraints in their practice, no codes or legal restraints would be needed. Codes and laws or regulations are set into place and enforced because some small number of individuals is prone to act in ways that violate professional and societal expectations. How we define our practice, including its code, is a statement of our ethics.

As Kenneth Burke (1966) reasoned, "By the ethical dimension (of our language), we express our characters, whether or not we intend to do so" (p. 28). All of what public relations practitioners do and communicate reveals their ethical principles.

A profession achieves its status if it is able to accomplish four goals:

- Serve society in a useful, constructive manner.
- Develop a set of practical skills that is unique to the profession.
- Create a body of literature and theory that is unique to the profession.
- Formulate and apply ethical standards that are unique to the profession.

For this reason, we challenge students of the practice to prescribe and uphold a code of ethics, a code of professional performance that can guide their actions and strategic choices as practitioners.

Stressing that point, Seib and Fitzpatrick (1995) directed attention to that principle by defining the role of public relations: "Every profession has a moral purpose. Medicine has health. Law has justice. Public relations has harmony—social harmony" (p. 1).

Public relations practitioners should have unimpeachable ethical standards, and they need to know the legal and regulatory constraints that affect what they and their clients can say and when they can say it. Proper ethical choices foster community by creating and maintaining mutually beneficial relationships. As Kruckeberg (1997) wrote, "Professional ethics are shaped by two distinct forces: the wider moral principles of society; and the aims of the profession" (pp. 34–35).

That is a daunting challenge. *Gallup Poll Monthly* reports the results from its "Honesty and Ethics" trend. We have included a graphic of those data over many decades for you to examine (see Table 9.1). One startling discovery is that most professions have suffered substantial reduction in public regard—a matter of declining deference. From a high of about 50% at the end of the 1950s, public perception of the honesty and ethics of corporate leadership has slipped dramatically. Cynicism characterizes the nation's mood. Advertising practitioners are rated extremely low. Public relations practitioners are not included in the survey, but we can imagine they also would be rated quite low—as might also be the case for marketing personnel. Recall that we discussed this trend in Chapter 4, where we emphasized how data can be used in research to track trends that can affect the quality of relationships between organizations and their stakeholders/stakeseekers.

Some major influence leaders and opinion makers in society receive shockingly low ethics scores in the opinion of the public. A list of those who in 2003 were below 30% approval rating includes TV reporters/commentators, bankers, journalists, business executives, building contractors, local officeholders, U.S. senators, lawyers, TV talk show hosts, real estate agents, labor union leaders, congresspersons, state

Table 9.1: Honesty and Ethics Trend (percentages for "very high" and "high" combined)

	1976	1981	1985	1988	1990	1993	2000	2003
Nurses	NA	NA	NA	NA	NA	NA	79	83
Druggists/pharmacists	NA	59	65	66	62	65	67	67
Clergy	NA	63	67	60	55	53	59	56
College teachers	49	45	53	54	51	52	59	59
Medical doctors	56	50	58	53	52	51	63	68
Policemen	NA	44	47	47	49	50	55	59
Dentists	NA	52	56	51	52	50	58	61
Engineers	49	48	53	48	50	49	56	59
Funeral directors	NA	30	32	24	35	34	35	NA
TV reporters/commentators	NA	36	33	22	32	28	22	NA
Bankers	NA	39	38	26	32	28	37	35
Journalists	33	32	31	23	30	26	21	25
Newspaper reporters	NA	30	29	22	24	22	17	NA
Business executives	20	19	23	16	25	20	22	18
Building contractors	23	19	21	22	20	20	23	NA
Local officeholders	NA	14	18	14	21	19	26	NA
U.S. senators	19	20	23	19	24	18	24	20
Lawyers	25	25	27	18	22	16	17	16
TV talk show hosts	NA	NA	NA	NA	NA	16	NA	NA
Real estate agents	NA	14	15	13	16	15	19	NA
Labor union leaders	12	14	13	14	15	14	17	NA
Congresspersons	14	15	20	16	20	14	22	17
State officeholders	NA	12	15	11	17	14	21	NA
Stockbrokers	NA	21	20	13	14	13	20	15
Insurance salespersons	NA	11	10	10	13	10	16	12
Advertising practitioners	11	9	12	7	12	8	11	12
Car salespersons	NA	6	5	6	6	6	10	7

SOURCE: Data provided based on the Gallup Poll.

officeholders, stockbrokers, insurance salespersons, advertising practitioners, and car salespersons. This profile continues today, suggesting that the era of deference to authority has come to an end. People just don't trust many kinds of leaders to be honest and ethical.

How can a community be strong if influence leaders in markets (business leaders, advertising persons, and salespeople) are so distrusted? On the public policy side, local, state, and federal legislators are not respected. The same is true of reporters and other media opinion makers.

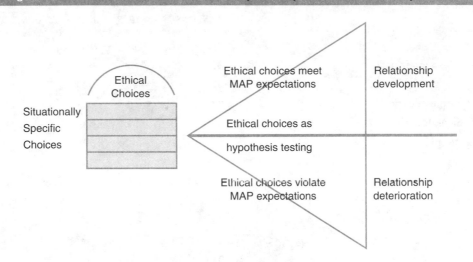

Figure 9.2: Ethical Choices That Build or Destroy Mutually Beneficial Relationships

What interpretations can we make of these data? One is to consider that however low the reputation of public relations might otherwise be, it is also affected by the reputation of the organizations it counsels and communicates on behalf of. Seib and Fitzpatrick (1995) thought that "much of the distrust of public relations professionals derives from the lack of public trust in the institutions they represent" (p. 7).

To help you understand the concept of relationship-based ethics needed for community building, we encourage you to adopt a perspective-taking view of ethics. Learning to think and act ethically should not be limited to thoughts of "what can I get away with doing." Practitioners need to approach ethics from the point of view of the persons who are watching, reading, and listening to what they and their clients do and say. The goal is to meet or exceed community standards. Figure 9.2 graphically presents this choice and its outcomes. Perspective taking means learning to think of the ethical standards others expect of us—as professionals.

Balancing Absolute Versus Relative Ethics

Critics of public relations point to the ethics of the practice. They complain that practitioners lack ethics, which means they fail to meet the ethical standards preferred by the critics. Critics expect practitioners to know and abide by their absolute standards of ethics. Therein lies one of the problems of the practice: knowing what those absolute standards might be. The second problem is following standards as though they were absolute. Some have even called for "super norms," universal principles of ethics that can guide actions across all situations and for all time.

The search for absolutes is the responsibility of philosophers. The search for ethical practice is the responsibility of those persons who are dedicated to the profession.

One approach to ethics is to feature the negative. In this sense, individuals or society says what should *not* be done. People are told what *not* to do. In contrast is the positive ethics of doing what is right, as opposed to not doing what is wrong. Where do we look for those standards? You should be restrained by ethics—the good of society—in terms of what you say and do. In similar fashion, you should be offended by some things others say and do—or refuse to say and do—and through your professional practice oppose such ethical choices.

Our perspective-taking point of view asks us to consider when we should yield to absolute standards or relative standards—depending on what is the interest of society. First, think of society as a collective of individuals who want the best for each other, an ideal view. Next, think of ethics as knowing and doing what is best for the mutual benefit of society—or the societies—in which our clients operate. For this reason, knowing ethical expectations of a society not only consists of understanding universal principles but also suggests the value of conducting research to monitor the relativistic subtleties of each era in each society.

Jackall (1995) added perspective to the battle between absolute and relative standards of ethics. He observed that "absolute moral claims usually convince only the claimants, even though such sentiments often silence opponents through their appealing, high-minded simplicity or effective slogans that obliterate important distinctions" (p. 15). Such difficulties result from the fact that the diversity of thought in our society undercuts moral absolutes.

Let's dwell for a moment on two principles that might offer absolute standards for the practice of public relations. One is the Golden Rule: Do to others as you would have them do to you. How can we apply this to public relations ethics? Let's rephrase the Golden Rule in several ways to focus on its implications for the practice.

Listen to others as you would have them listen to you. Appreciate the points of view and concerns held by others as you would wish them to appreciate your viewpoints and concerns. Give the information and opinion you would want others to give you if you were in their circumstances and they were in yours, for example, as a counselor or spokesperson for a company, nonprofit organization, or governmental agency. We can check information for its accuracy and statements for their truthfulness as we would want others to similarly verify the accuracy of information. We can challenge ourselves to communicate in a timely and open fashion as we would expect others to communicate with us if we were buying a product or services, listening to key messages, or making public policy decisions.

We can offer a second absolute principle that might guide your practice of public relations. Act in a professional manner and counsel your clients in such a manner that you never have to be concerned by what would be written about them or about your professional judgment on the front page of the newspaper or presented at the top-of-the-hour radio or television news story. This simply means that you use ethical judgment that leads to praise rather than criticism by your peers and by the markets, audiences, and publics (MAPs) of the organizations you counsel.

ETHICS PROBE

Identify three absolute principles by which you believe you can conduct professional public relations practice. Write your principles on a sheet of paper, and exchange papers with someone who has done the same. Think, if you can, of exceptions to the absolutes the other person has proposed.

Meeting Public Expectations

One of the best standards of values is termed "front-page" or "top-of-the-hour" thinking. Simply stated: Don't do or say anything—don't allow your client to do or say anything—that you would not want to appear on the front page of newspapers or at the top of the hour on radio or television news. If you don't want it to appear in public because it will "look bad," then don't do it. That is a perspective you can take as you define public expectations. News reports typically focus on what ethical judgments have been made that violate community standards.

Knowing and meeting community standards, for this reason, becomes central to the effort to create, implement, and police professional codes of ethics. As Kruckeberg (1997) reasoned,

> A code of ethics specifically codifies the group's relationship to society. Ethics codes must be consonant with the expectations of society; however, within those parameters, society allows professional groups the freedom to determine specifically what they ethically may do within their relationships to society. (p. 35)

The challenge to meet high ethical standards results from considering the consequences of failing to do so. Expectations do not exist in a vacuum. They result from the goals that join MAPs to the interests of the organization. Organizations are obligated to consider the interests and expectations of multiple stakeholders and stakeseekers. Taking a systems approach to such matters, Bivins (1992) reasoned that all of the parties affected by an instance deserving public relations have goals. Those goals can be seen as mutually exclusive or complementary. Rather than asking what's best for the client or for me, the practitioner must ask what's is best for all of the interests. That's what the stakeholders and stakeseekers expect.

ETHICS PROBE

Look at the practice of public relations and the management of organizations from the point of view of a member of a MAP. What three expectations do you have of the way that the organization, through its public relations, listens, responds, and appreciates—strives to achieve and maintain mutually beneficial relationships?

Achieving Openness as the Basis of Mutually Beneficial Relationships

Tell the truth. Be transparent. Those prescriptions are basic to the practice and serve as mandates that cross the lips of critics of public relations. Sometimes it is difficult to know the truth. Telling the truth can be hurtful. In addition, "truth" often is a matter of contention and debate. What some persons believe to be the truth may not satisfy others as being the truth.

Be open and candid. Even the government will not allow companies to disclose some facts. Companies and other organizations, such as the federal government, are privileged to hold information as secret. Information relating to criminal charges can be withheld until an appropriate time. Information regarding issues of national security are privileged to be known to a select few individuals—for the good of the country. Under some circumstances, personnel data may not be disclosed to the public. Companies may keep proprietary information secret, such as formulas they have developed for product design, or data, such as that held by oil companies regarding the location of oil and gas reserves.

Engage in dialogue responsibly. Can an organization ethically advocate that one issue position is superior to another? Can an organization remain silent when it believes that one issue position is superior to another? These questions frame points made by Hanson (1996), who stated that in public dialogue,

> all participants must serve as guarantors of the free exchange of ideas, even by those with limited resources and access. This view, held by the majority of public affairs professionals today, means that the practitioner must continually balance advocacy for his or her own organization with the commitment to the airing of all important voices on any public concern. (p. 424)

Don't spin, although you must frame your points. Organizational managers have an instinct to hide, obscure, or spin "bad" information, and that information can lead to negative opinions. Savvy practitioners know the value of getting such information out—being open—in ways that give reporters and critics less reason to hound management for the true and full disclosure of details. A cover-up and false denial typically lead to or occur during crisis circumstances. Hanson (1996) observed, "The client's instinct may be to bury the information. The practitioner may know or believe it must be revealed, to satisfy the law or to protect the organization from greater long-term damage" (p. 426). Spinning means that you give an interpretation to information and a story that privileges only the organization's interest. Framing entails giving a perspective to information and a story that helps MAPs understand in terms of their perspectives.

ETHICS PROBE

Think of three kinds of information that an organization must always be willing to provide in its efforts to demonstrate that it is committed to open communication. Think of three kinds of information that an organization is privileged to keep to itself and still be considered to be willing and able to demonstrate its ethically strategic efforts to achieve and maintain mutually beneficial relationships. Note: Some kinds of personnel information may be privileged. What kinds of personnel information can be kept from the public without violating the trust the public has in the organization? Would members of a community deserve to have information about personnel who work for a school district as opposed to information about employees of a company? What if that company provides health services, such as a hospital?

Making Strategic Responses Based on Privileged and Proprietary Information

An organization is not required to tell everything about itself. Companies are allowed to protect trade secrets, such as manufacturing processes, from public scrutiny. If they have formulas, such as the ingredients in a soft drink, they can keep them secret. If a military equipment contractor designs special devices that increase the fighting capability of a tank or ship, for instance, those can be kept secret. Companies may know the medical condition of certain employees that they may not make public.

So, on one hand, organizations can keep secrets. How does that square with the discussion of being open and creating trust? Again, we ask that you take the community perspective. The community wants information if it is in the interest of the community to know that information. Would making the information public help the members of the community to make decisions they are unable to make without the information? Would making the information public harm the public—the public interest?

ETHICS PROBE

If an oil company has information about oil reserves, can it keep that information from its key publics, even investors? Why would the company want to keep that information secret? What about the financial status of the organization? Can it keep that information secret? Can it keep information as secret if the company is publicly traded as if it were closely held? What information can the government keep secret? If coaches had been violating recruiting guidelines in ways that could lead to NCAA sanctions, should the public relations officer of the college or university help keep that information secret?

Achieving Taste and Good Judgment in the Practice of Public Relations

Publicity and promotion are valuable tools in strategic public relations plans. Good news can be bad news. Publicity and promotion can go too far. They can attract too much attention—and attention for the wrong reason. They can attract the wrong kind of attention. The restraint on such efforts is *taste*. From the perspective of the community, how can a campaign attract favorable attention and stay within the bounds of good taste?

That is not merely an ethical quandary or moral brain twister. Imagine for a moment that you have been assigned the account of handling the publicity for the *Sports Illustrated* bathing suit issue. That is a major part of the marketing effort of the magazine. Large circulation attracts higher advertising space revenue. So, you have the incentive to sensationalize the publicity that surrounds the models and the issue. After all, isn't it easy to attract attention to beautiful women in swimsuits? Aren't

swimsuits an integral part of the sports industry? Doesn't *Sports Illustrated* report on the sports industry? Aren't males the primary readers of *Sports Illustrated?* So, what's the issue? Who cares who is offended, as long as the issue attracts attention and readership grows?

Stateman (1997) focused on the balance between publicity and publicity with good taste. The *Sports Illustrated* bathing suit issue is a dominant media event for 2 to 3 days in this country. So, attracting attention is relatively easy, although reporters want a new angle each year, so their story of this story does not get stale or narrowly focus on "just another issue with beautiful women in swimsuits." The magazine wants

AIDS Awareness Campaign

SOURCE: Reprinted with permission from the City of Los Angeles AIDS Coordinator's Office.

the issue to be "wholesome." That is a code word for tasteful, within the bounds of community standards. The publishers do not want readers to be ashamed to have the magazine on their reading tables and coffee tables—if the children or moms happen by, for instance. So the standards of the issue—standards of taste—are implied. The issue and its publicity must not strain family values. Art Berke, director of communications for *Sports Illustrated*, made the following point:

> The swimsuit issue is a wholesome edition. It's something we feel we handle very tastefully and we want to project that in the publicity we do. Frankly, the best part of my job is that we don't have to get publicity for publicity sake. If we feel that it is not going to be absolutely positive, we don't have to do it. (quoted by Stateman, 1997, p. 4)

From the community perspective, the issue of taste is not always easy to establish. But that is the nature of ethical judgments. "Wholesome" may be one of those public relations "spins" that give the profession a bad name. But it can also be a community standard, a blend of physical attractiveness enhanced with clothing. The standard of taste is this: If it would shock the sensibilities of the community, then it is not wholesome. It violates standards of taste.

ETHICS PROBE

What response would you make to the city or county health director if he or she approached you as a public relations professional and made the following request: "We want to conduct an AIDS awareness campaign by using one line of text on a billboard campaign. The line of text is 'Sex can kill. Prevent AIDS.' And we want a graphic of a condom on the billboard." Is that in keeping with standards of good taste?

Making Actions Speak for Values

Actions speak louder than words. That point should be emblazoned on each practitioner's "ethics manual." Each public relations counselor makes that point clear to managements that are working to create and implement organizational plans and operations. Organizations can subscribe to a code of ethics. But if their actions do not enact the ethics preferred by their MAPs, those managers have failed to make the statement they need to build mutually beneficial relationships—and thereby earn the stakes held by their stakeholders.

Recall the definition of public relations proposed in Chapter 1: Public relations is the management function that entails planning, research, negotiation, promotion, and publicity to foster an organization's ability to strategically listen to, appreciate, and *respond* to those persons and groups whose mutually beneficial relationships the organization needs to achieve its mission and vision. When we selected the key word *respond*, we did so to stress the importance of the statements *and* the actions.

Actions are statements. If a company, for instance, says that it cares about its customers, it must act to prove that it means what it says. For the organization to speak well, it must be good. It needs to blend into actions and statements all of what it adheres to in regard to ethical principles it uses in its planning and operations. People use the actions of the organization to interpret the meaning of the statements the organization makes. Actions need to fit with statements.

ETHICS PROBE

Find examples in your community in which companies or other organizations say one thing and do the opposite.

Building and Protecting Trust

Rather than relying on codes and prescriptive statements, you might find it useful to search for key concepts to use to define the ethical limits of your practice. One concept might be trust. If you asked a reporter to trust you about details you are giving during a crisis surrounding financial problems of your client's organization, what would you expect the reporter to do? What is trust? How do you create it? Is it a vital part of the mutually beneficial relationship we have advocated for effective media relations? "Trust is the expectation that arises within a community of regular, honest, and cooperative behavior, based on commonly shared norms, on the part of other members of that community" (Fukuyama, 1995, p. 26). Trust is acting in ways that take the actions and statements of one another at face value, in a positive effort to achieve mutually beneficial relationships.

Trust is earned, it is not granted. It is earned by what individuals and organizations do and say. Recognizing this challenge, Fukuyama (1995) reasoned that "people who do not trust one another will end up cooperating only under a system of formal rules and regulations, which have to be negotiated, agreed to, litigated, and enforced, sometimes by coercive means" (p. 27). This ethic of trust challenges practitioners to seek high standards in their professional practice and through their counsel to their clients. The goal is to act in ways that create trust without formal rules, regulations, and the coercive force of government, including lawsuits.

ETHICS PROBE

Give three ethical guidelines that could be followed to increase the likelihood that key MAPs would trust an organization.

Recognizing and Aligning Interests

Who does the practitioner represent? Where does his or her loyalty lie? Your first answer might be to say that the loyalty rests with the client. A strong case can be made that the first loyalty must be to the community if the requirement of being loyal to the client is going to be meaningful. The community interest becomes the basis for the counseling that senior practitioners are expected to achieve as they aid, guide, and communicate with and on behalf of clients.

Loyalty is owed both to the client and to organizations that compete against a client. A conflict of interest occurs when a practitioner seeks, tries, or is expected to serve the interest of two or more organizations whose missions lead them to compete against one another. The obligation of the practitioner rests with the person who pays the invoices or signs the paychecks. However, the practitioner must also know, appreciate, and never compromise working relationships—especially competitive ones—with other organizations.

ETHICS PROBE

Let's say that you have the opportunity to counsel and conduct public relations efforts on behalf of two competitors — at the same time. Must you choose one competitor in preference to the other? Can you think of ethical ways in which you could serve both at the same time? What three guidelines would you use to make your decision, and how would you state those guidelines to the satisfaction of the clients?

Codes of Professional Conduct

Codes of conduct are guidelines for appropriate behavior. Organizations and professional associations often have codes of conduct. These codes of conduct are sources of guidance for public relations practitioners. To be professional requires the creation and enforcement of "agreed-upon standards."

> Professionals have the burden of policing their own ranks to assure that public relations is practiced by all of its professional members in a manner conforming to such agreed-upon 'professional' ethics. (Kruckeberg, 1997, p. 34)

What do codes of professional standards accomplish? As Kruckeberg (1997) answered, they define and clarify the relationship between the profession and society. Practitioners can look to organizational and professional codes for insight into ethical public relations practices. But more important, practitioners are actively involved in shaping the codes of conduct for the profession and the organization.

▶Organizational Codes

Public relations personnel should play a role in shaping their organizations' codes of conduct as well as following them. Public relations is often thought to be a profession of liars and spinners: persons who twist the truth, stonewall, sandbag, and distort facts and opinions. That is hardly the kind of person who could or should set the ethical standards of an organization. By the same token, public relations persons are most familiar with community standards, at least insofar as those expectations are expressed by the reporters. Practitioners know what offends the press. They also know who has to face reporters when the organization's activities offend them: the practitioners themselves. Nevertheless, practitioners are often not involved in the creation and implementation of codes of operating ethics (Heath & Ryan, 1989). As an example of a company code of conduct, see Box 9.3, "Matrikon Code of Conduct."

BOX 9.3 MATRIKON CODE OF CONDUCT

Laws and Regulations

All company associates are expected to comply with the laws and regulations of all jurisdictions where Matrikon conducts its business. No individual shall encourage another individual to circumvent applicable laws or regulations, nor the rules of honest business conduct, nor shall they condone any such violation.

We adhere to the principles of the "Canadian Corruption of Foreign Public Officials Act" and the "United States Foreign Corrupt Practices Act." This legislation prohibits offering or giving anything of value to foreign government officials, or making unlawful political contributions in order to obtain or retain business or to influence an official decision. Liability under this legislation cannot be avoided through the use of agents or third-party intermediaries, and the penalties for contravention of this legislation are severe.

Fair Treatment of Individuals

All individuals employed or associated with Matrikon will be treated with respect, dignity, and equality. We are committed to equal opportunity for all employees, without bias based on differences in culture, ethnicity, color, religion, gender, sexual orientation, age, marital status, national origin, or handicap. We will provide a workplace free from all forms of discrimination, including sexual and other forms of harassment. (Refer to Matrikon's Harassment policy.)

Conflicts of Interest

Our general rule is that company associates should avoid any activity, investment or interest that is, or appears to be, in conflict with the business or their employment with Matrikon. Potential conflicts of interest must be disclosed and resolved including where a company associate:

- Acts as an officer, director, employee, partner, agent, consultant or client for any of Matrikon's competitors, suppliers or contractors.
- Engages in other outside employment where there is a potential for conflict. Management should be informed of such external employment to ensure that no conflict exists and that your job performance with Matrikon is not adversely affected.
- Directly or beneficially holds a substantial (greater than 10%) financial or other interest in any business or organization with which Matrikon has business dealings, and the employee or their family could receive a benefit from transactions with Matrikon.
- Participates in a venture where Matrikon has expressed a business interest.

Where appropriate, Matrikon may request written disclosure of outside business interests to determine compliance with the Code. As well, an individual may wish to provide Matrikon with such disclosure in advance. Matrikon will review the circumstances and issue a letter indicating the awareness of the individual's actions or involvement, and that (in the outlined situation) there is no conflict of interest; or, alternatively, Matrikon may specify appropriate action required to ensure compliance with the Code.

Confidential Information

You will not disclose information about Matrikon, its business decisions, its shareholders, partners, clients, or other associates unless it is part of your job duties or you have written consent from Matrikon. This includes both internally-generated information and confidential information received from external sources.

Unless there is a "need to know," this information should be kept out of sight, and not disclosed whether it is at work, home, in public, or elsewhere.

Insider Information/Investment Activity

From time to time, company associates will have inside information that may not be known to the general public. This may be information about new products, plans or processes, mergers, acquisitions, negotiations relevant to significant business deals, contracts, sales, lawsuits, or special relationships with others.

Under securities legislation, the company associate of Matrikon may be considered to be in a "special relationship" with certain shareholders, and partners of Matrikon. It is not permitted to use undisclosed material information (including material facts and material changes) concerning Matrikon, its shareholders or partners to your personal advantage, or the corresponding disadvantage of others in the securities market. It is also prohibited for a person with such information to give it to others, or "tipping," so that the other person may improperly make use of the information.

For more detailed guidelines regarding the use, disclosure and restrictions of this information, you may refer to Matrikon's Blackout standards and Disclosure (Information Dissemination) standards.

Gifts and Other Benefits

Company associates will not give or offer, directly or indirectly, anything of significant value to a business associate or government official to influence or reward an action. Conversely, we will not accept a gift, favor, loan, special service, payment, or special treatment of any kind where such items could be viewed as creating an obligation or influencing a business decision. Where usually-accepted business practices permit or require, and where appropriate to the business role and responsibilities of the individuals, provision of meals, entertainment, or promotional gifts of a reasonable value is acceptable. If you are uncertain about the appropriateness of a proposed business gift, you are encouraged to speak to your manager.

The payment or receipt of bribes or "kickbacks" is strictly prohibited.

Agents, Consultants, and Representatives of Matrikon

This Code applies equally to agents, consultants, subcontractors, or representatives acting on Matrikon's behalf. We will not retain such parties in an effort to circumvent our standards or business values.

Company Resources (Assets)

All company associates are required to protect and use company resources (assets) for the advancement of Matrikon's business. Tangible company resources (assets) include, but are not limited to, equipment, supplies and vehicles. Other resources (assets) may include intellectual property, and can be inventions, discoveries, ideas, trademarks, trade secrets, and patents.

For further information regarding company resources (assets), refer to our Employee Secrecy and Inventions Agreement. You are reminded to follow your obligation in your agreement.

Copyrights and Licenses

All company associates will respect all copyrights and other intellectual property protections, including those relating to software or hardware, trademarks, and trade secrets used by Matrikon. More details are provided in the Acceptable Computer Usage and Information Security Standards.

Political or Public Activities and Contributions

All company associates will not use or contribute company time, funds, or assets for the benefit of any political party, candidate, or official, except as permitted by law and authorized in advance by the Chief Executive Officer (CEO). Attendance at political functions, or at functions widely attended by industry counterparts, is acceptable and does not require approval. These standards do not intend to restrict your personal involvement, use of your personal (individual) resources for political or public activities.

Records and Reporting

All activities conducted by or on behalf of Matrikon are subject to audit. Such audits may include a review of any related hard copy or electronic record. Full, prompt, and accurate recording of operating and financial information, in accordance with Canadian Generally Accepted Accounting Principles, is required. No secret or unrecorded funds or assets shall be established or maintained. Provision of intentionally erroneous or misleading documents or invoices to accommodate other parties is also prohibited. We will maintain documentation supporting corporate transactions and all other accounting entries. All company associates will co-operate with Matrikon's auditors at all times.

SOURCE: Reprinted from http://www.matrikon.com/corporate/about/conduct.asp

Ethics officers for companies often rely more on legal counsel and human resource specialists than do public relations practitioners (Fitzpatrick, 1996b). As you undertake the challenge of becoming a public relations professional, what will you come to know, and what will you do to make public relations more central in these matters? After all, public relations is committed to helping organizations manage themselves in ways that are mutually beneficial to all stakeholders and stakeseekers. Isn't that a first step toward having public relations professionals help to institutionalize ethics?

►Professional Organizations

The Public Relations Society of America (PRSA), the Public Affairs Council, the International Association of Business Communicators (IABC), and the public relations associations in various countries all have codes that specify ethical behavior. PRSA's code is an example of how these documents evolve and change over time. The last major revision was in 2002. Box 9.4 presents the main elements of the PRSA Code and an extended example illustrating the conflict of interest provision.

BOX 9.4 PRSA CODE OF ETHICS

The PRSA Code has six provisions:

1. Free flow of information
2. Competition
3. Disclosure of information
4. Safeguarding confidences
5. Conflicts of interest
6. Enhancing the profession

Conflicts of Interest

Core Principle

Avoiding real, potential, or perceived conflicts of interest builds the trust of clients, employers, and the publics.

Intent

- To earn trust and mutual respect with clients or employers.
- To build trust with the public by avoiding or ending situations that put one's personal or professional interests in conflict with society's interests.

Guidelines

A member shall:

- Act in the best interests of the client or employer, even subordinating the member's personal interests.

- Avoid actions and circumstances that may appear to compromise good business judgment or create a conflict between personal and professional interests.
- Disclose promptly any existing or potential conflict of interest to affected clients or organizations.
- Encourage clients and customers to determine whether a conflict exists after notifying all affected parties.

Examples of Improper Conduct Under This Provision

- The member fails to disclose that he or she has a strong financial interest in a client's chief competitor.
- The member represents a "competitor company" or a "conflicting interest" without informing a prospective client.

SOURCE: PRSA Code of Ethics. Reprinted from http://www.prsa.org/_About/ethics/conflicts.asp?ident=eth5

The PRSA Code offers guidelines to persons who practice public relations. However, only members of PRSA are obligated to follow their code and are subject to punishment for violating it. Anyone can claim to practice public relations. Many so-called practitioners draw intense media coverage with their often unethical tactics. The profession has no mechanism for preventing the abuse of public relations. Over the years, the idea of licensing public relations has been discussed. This would require practitioners to be licensed like lawyers and medical doctors. There are many problems with licensing, such as who would create the tests and monitor compliance. The idea has never progressed very far.

BOX 9.5 SBC AND FLEISHMAN: HILLARD ETHICAL ISSUES

Fleishman-Hillard is one of the largest public relations companies in the world. It has a global network of offices as well as offices in 22 locations in the United States. It started in St. Louis, Missouri, in 1946, with Al Fleishman and Bob Hillard, growing to more than 80 offices on five continents.

Fleishman-Hillard became embroiled in a controversy in its work with SBC, a telecommunication company. David Lazarus, a reporter for the *San Francisco Chronicle,* was collecting information on a story about a possible strike by SBC employees. One of his sources was Marc Bien, who was identified as a vice president of corporate communications for the telecommunications giant SBC Communications. The story was written quoting Bien as an SBC employee. The contention is that Bien is employed by Fleishman-Hillard, not SBC. SBC's own internal documents list Bien as a "nonemployee," who is payed by Fleishman-Hillard. His business card indicates he works for SBC, and he works in the firm's San Francisco office. Internal SBC documents show that about a half-dozen SBC vice presidents are in reality Fleishman employees. However, these people present themselves as SBC executives.

Lazarus wrote a follow-up story about the "misrepresentation." Ed Presper, a Fleishman-Hillard spokesman, said that Bien was under no obligation to identify himself as an outside contractor while speaking to the reporter about SBC's use of outside contractors. Kathy Cripps, president of the Council of Public Relations Firms, a leading industry organization (of which Fleishman is a member), said, "Our code of ethics makes it very clear that member firms must be truthful with the media and the public. The code does not seem to be being followed here" (Lazarus, 2004).

The question is, does the case really constitute an ethical violation? One way to make ethical evaluations is through the use of the Potter Box, created by Harvard University philosopher Ralph Potter. The Potter Box examines four elements of the ethical case: situation, values, loyalty, and principles. The situation details the ethical dilemma by providing the facts in the case and includes multiple points of view. In public relations, you would consider the point of view of the organization and key MAPs involved in the case. Values would be the values involved in the case, such as legal or professional values. Values are the standards various groups use as standards of choice. Loyalties ask, "To whom are you loyal?" You identify with those with whom your primary loyalties would be in the case. Principles are the ethical principles used to guide your decision. The Potter Box uses five central ethical principles: (1) Aristotle's Golden Mean—you balance the claims of two sides by seeking the middle ground; (2) Judeo-Christian Person of Ends—you are to be unselfish and to help others; (3) Mill's Principle of Utility—you seek the greatest good for the largest number of people; (4) Rawls's Veil of Ignorance—you remove all self-interests and consider the decision without these biases; and (5) Kant's Categorical Imperative—you treat everyone and every situation the same; what is right for one is right for all.

Use the Potter Box to determine whether Fleishman-Hillard acted ethically. Consider the situation from the perspective of Fleishman-Hillard and then from that of a customer reading the news stories. Does your answer change as your loyalties shift? Should that be the case given that public relations should balance the needs of the client and society? You may need to collect additional information about the case to complete this exercise.

WEB WATCHER: ETHICS AND PROFESSIONAL PRACTICE

You have read about the ethical concerns of public relations. Now it is time to see how serious practitioners in the profession take ethics. Visit the ethics section of the Public Relations Society of America (PRSA) Web site (http://www.prsa.org/_About/ethics/). At the site you should (1) review the matrix of ethical dilemmas to get a deeper understanding of the types of ethical issues faced by practitioners and (2) complete one of the six ethical case studies to see how PRSA recommends approaching ethics. Look for the PRSA Member Code of Ethics. You can also find it in *The Blue Book,* a PRSA publication that is sent to every member. You can also find material on ethics at the home page of the International Association of Business Communicators.

Legal Constraints: Limits on the Professional Practice of Public Relations

The environment in which the profession of public relations is practiced is becoming more litigious, and the laws are increasingly complex. Practitioners may not be prepared to meet these challenges. "Many public relations professionals may be placing themselves and client organizations at risk of legal liability because they have little or no familiarity with important legal issues that affect public relations activities," concluded Fitzpatrick (1996a, p. 1). This conclusion was based on a survey of 1,000 PRSA members' familiarity with commercial speech, contracts, financial public relations, copyright, privacy, libel, access to information, SEC regulations, and professional malpractice.

Based on survey results, Fitzpatrick concluded that most practitioners are only "somewhat" or "not at all familiar" with these legal issues. That finding is troubling. But the picture becomes worse when she also reports that most of the work of practitioners is not reviewed by legal counsel. The bottom-line conclusion of these findings: Practitioners' ignorance of the law coupled with their failure to use legal counsel put themselves and their clients at risk.

To assist your efforts to understand the law, you may want to have legal counsel periodically review your practice. Or you may wish to ask your clients to seek legal counsel prior to and after the design of a campaign. You need to continue your education. Read professional journals. Keep up-to-date on communication law, perhaps by visiting a college campus every 3 to 5 years to purchase the current text being used for the course on communication law and ethics. You might purchase a text, such as Ralph Holsinger and Jon Paul Dilts's (1997) *Media Law.*

In the sections that follow, we do not pretend to provide all of the information you will need on legal matters to ensure that your practice will avoid legal pitfalls. By knowing something about the law, you should become encouraged to ask questions, continue your study, and seek counsel when you see warning flags. We cannot make you legal experts, but we will alert you to the primary legal concerns faced in public relations.

▶Copyright Law

Copyright protection extends to the creative work of individuals and organizations. It protects the proprietary interest the creators of the work enjoy as the benefit of their talent. Copyright protection is extended to anything that is in a fixed and tangible form. This would include written documents, songs, Web pages, photographs, films, and even an original dance move. Copyright can cover anything that you can hear, see, or touch. Once material is created, it has copyright protection. You, as the creator, are the only one who can legally use the materials. You can place the copyright symbol © on any original material you create. You need to register for a copyright with the U.S. Copyright Office in order to sue for financial damages. Material is typically covered for the life of the creator plus 50 years. Photographs, however, are for life plus only 25 years. You need to check specific laws, such as the Berne Convention, to determine international copyright protection (see "What Is Copyright Protection?" 2004).

If you quote other people's work, you must get permission. At least, you may be obligated to indicate the source of the work. If you are benefiting financially or in reputation from your work, which includes their work, you are obligated to take appropriate efforts to share your reward with the original creator. This means that you may have to pay the creator to use some or all of his or her work. An example would be using a "Dilbert" comic strip on a company's publication. Scott Adams, the creator of Dilbert, would need to give permission for its use and receive a fee for its use. Failure to do so would violate copyright law. One mistake people make is thinking that just because a work is on the Internet, it is free to be used. That is not the case at all. Any material presented on or created for the Internet has full copyright protection unless the author specifies he or she has abandoned the copyright, that is, releases the material to the public domain. Whenever a copyright expires or is abandoned, the material enters the public domain and is free for anyone to use.

Public relations departments and agencies get into some sticky situations if they do not think about and properly prepare for the acquisition and use of others' creative work. For instance, if you create something, say a graphic, as a part of your work assignment on a project, you cannot claim it and use it as though it were your property. If you used company time, equipment, materials, or other employees, the work was done for the company and is not your private work.

What if you create something at home, in the evening after work, not for a specific project, and on your own computer? What if you ask in an agency meeting, "Would this graphic help?" If the agency and client use the graphic, they are likely to be obligated to pay for it. You may retain subsequent use of it. That means that you could sell it to someone else.

One exception to other copyright provisions is captured in the concept of fair use. Fair use does not require permission from the creator of the material. However, there are limits to fair use. This provision or interpretation of copyright laws allows persons or organizations to have limited use of others' work. The key to fair use is the amount of another person's work that is used and the context or way in which it is used. Using a line of a song or poem could be allowed as fair use. Using a portion of a larger graphic or painting could be fair use. Limited use of quoted passages from a book or report could be fair use. If you write a criticism of a book (or of other kinds of artistic works), you are likely to be able to quote or otherwise use limited amounts of the subject of your discussion without having to gain permission. Generally, fair use is reserved for works that involve news reporting, parody, research, or education (Leeper, 2005).

The savvy practitioner is wise to notify the person or organization that owns a copyright and indicate the use prior to actually using it in a public relations presentation. It is wise to give attribution, such as a list of credits, so that all of the world will know who the actual creator was.

▶ Trademark Law

A trademark is a distinctive word, symbol, phrase, product shape, picture, or logo associated with an organization. An organization does not want other people or organizations to use their trademarks. When someone else uses your trademark, this can be infringement and you have legal rights to stop other people using your trademark. For maximum legal protection, an organization needs to register trademarks with the Patent and Trademark Office. A trademark with the ® mark is registered. However, a variety of state statutes provide common-law protection for trademarks. *Common law* means that if an organization uses a trademark for a period of time, it is given some legal rights to that trademark, even without filing with the federal government.

To prevent someone else from using its trademark, an organization has to prove "likelihood of confusion." This means the use of the trademark leads to confusion among consumers. The consumers think they are buying a product or service from one company when they are really buying from another company. For instance, you buy a shirt with a "swoosh" on it because you believe it was made by Nike, but it was not. To win a likelihood-of-confusions case, an organization must have a defendable trademark (registration is useful), there must be similarity between the two trademarks, and the two companies must sell similar goods and services. In total, there are eight factors for likelihood-of-confusion listed in Table 9.2.

Table 9.2: Likelihood-of-Confusion Criteria

1. Similar impressions created by the two marks (look and/or sound alike).
2. Use of the marks for similar goods or services.
3. The strength of the original trademark.
4. Evidence proving that consumers are confused.
5. Intent to create confusion with the new mark.
6. How close the goods are in stores.
7. How careful consumers are when examining the goods.
8. Likelihood that a product line will expand.

More recently, the Federal Trademark Dilution Act (1995) has been used to protect trademarks. "Famous" trademarks are protected against dilution, meaning no one else can use the trademark, even if they sell very different products or services. Courts are still trying to work out what constitutes a "famous" trademark. One clear violation is when the famous trademark is used by a company in an "unsavory or unwholesome" way. Such abuse of a trademark would hurt the company owning that trademark. The use of Coca-Cola to sell cheap picnic supplies is an abuse of a famous trademark. Even though Coca-Cola does not sell picnic supplies, its famous trademark is diluted by being associated with inferior products.

The Internet has brought domain names into the trademark dispute. The domain name is the address name for a Web site. What can a company do if its name or a name of one of its products is legally purchased as a domain name? Obviously, the company would want that domain name, but some other party beat them to securing it. MTV and McDonald's are two of many large organizations meeting this fate. The Anticybersquatting Consumer Protection Act provides some relief. An organization can legally be awarded the domain name using its trademark if the owner of the domain tries to sell the domain to the company for a profit, is using the domain name to sell goods or services, or is using the domain name to tarnish the trademark. An example is the domain "candyland.com." "Candlyland" is a famous children's game sold by Hasbro. However, an adult entertainment company was first to secure the domain name. Hasbro sued and won. The adult entertainment firm was using the trademark for commerce and was tarnishing the trademark. The Internet is a blessing and curse for trademarks. It is easier to find people misusing a trademark online but also easier to abuse a trademark online. Companies must be vigilant in their efforts to protect their trademarks. A failure to actively protect a trademark permits anyone to use it in the future (Trademark Law, 2004).

▶ Privacy

Federal and state statutes protect the privacy of individuals under specific circumstances. This means that an organization or public relations practitioner could violate a law or regulation if certain kinds of information are made public. In general, protected information is that which would motivate and allow others, public and private, to intrude into the lives of individuals. One kind of protected information relates to an employee's work performance; another is a patient's (or employee's) medical condition.

Privacy laws, laws that protect privacy, extend protection to trade secrets and other proprietary information. This issue is often a two-edged sword. On one hand, a company could protect the details about a product innovation from public scrutiny. That protection would keep competitors from learning valuable proprietary information that they could use, without the cost of research and development, to compete against the company that spent money to create the innovation. That protection is appropriate, although in the case of pharmaceutical development, for instance, proprietary data must be made available to the Food and Drug Administration (FDA).

The bad news related to privacy and property rights results from the requirement by the Securities and Exchange Commission (SEC) that publicly traded companies must make public all information that has material value for the strength of the company's financial performance. Innovation, such as product development, for instance, is important to a company, since a better or unique product has market advantage. Likewise, if an oil company discovers a crude oil or natural gas reserve, that information could be valuable to competitors. Investors and investment analysts want such details to help them evaluate the strength, current and potential, of a company's financial performance.

In recent years, you have probably heard details about internal memoranda and research documents that were prepared by a company. Considerable reporting has centered on that matter in regard to practices of the tobacco industry. Did executives' communications with one another indicate they knew the health hazards of tobacco? If a company created information about components of a cigarette or its manufacturing process, must that company make the information public—or is it protected as proprietary? If the company finds that a product harms people's health, must it publish that information?

Privacy is also an issue relevant to activities of governmental agencies and the practice of public information officers. The Freedom of Information Act (1966) opens most governmental files to public scrutiny. This provision can strain relationships between the agencies and their key stakeholders. The stakeholders may be offended by the information they find. They may fight to gain access to information. Of related interest is the fact that once private sector information is given to a government agency, that information may no longer be protected as it might have been if the company had not been forced to report it to the agency. Secrets can become public, thereby resulting in relationship problems between organizations and their MAPs.

If you are a public information officer for a governmental agency, do you have to help the organizations you counsel to not violate open-meeting laws? As well as being interested in the requirements for ensuring privacy, you may have professional obligations for seeing that your clients are appropriately open to their stakeholders and stakeseekers. Typical open-meetings laws specify that the date, time, place, and agenda of public meetings be posted. This notice becomes a contract with the public to meet as specified.

All matters of public interest must be conducted in public. A city council, for instance, might use a closed executive session to discuss a personnel matter, for instance, the review of the city manager. After private discussions, the council typically is obligated to publicly take appointment, reappointment, or termination actions—moving and passing an agenda item—regarding the specific individual. The same can be true of budget items.

▶Defamation: Libelous and Slanderous Attacks

Can you imagine working in public relations for an activist group, such as an environmental organization, and being asked to put out a press release in which you make claims about the character of the CEO of a company who wants to cut old-growth timber? If you make statements about this person's character, motives, and approaches to business practices, can you and your organization violate his or her rights? Can this person win a lawsuit that alleges that you and your organization defamed his or her character?

Defamation assumes that people's character is worth money to them. If a person makes a false and malicious statement that harms another's character, a successful lawsuit can be mounted against that person. *Libel* is that sort of statement made in a tangible form, for instance, written in print or presented in graphics, such as a cartoon. *Slander* is a spoken attack.

Libel requires proof of three types. The offending statement(s) must be published. It must identify the person who claims he or she was defamed. It must defame, that is, lower the reputation or estimate others would have of the person's character. The target of such statements may be offended, but not be defamed. Defamation charges require factual presentation that material damage did or might have resulted because the statement harmed the person's reputation.

What do you need to be sure you can do or say in the event that your statements go to trial? *Truth* is one aspect of your defense. Can you prove that the person is as "bad" as you allege? Have you violated your *privilege* to comment on matters that occur that concern you? If you are a party to some agreement and you characterize the agreement as being bogged down or violated by a person because of the person's bad character, you may be privileged to hold and express that opinion because you are a party to the events. The final defense is your ability to make *fair comment* about something that you believe, or have every reason to believe, to be true. But you might be wrong because you did not have all of the facts or misinterpreted them in a manner that others would understand as being a legitimate, but incorrect interpretation.

►Environmental Law

Companies and other organizations whose processes affect the environment can be required to gather and report data about their organization's impact on the environment. In chemical manufacturing companies, for instance, environmental experts play a pivotal role in gathering data about their emissions. They are required to keep records regarding the manufacture, storage, and transportation of chemicals that the Environmental Protection Agency (EPA) believes cause health and environmental damage.

Typical environmental laws include the Emergency Planning and Community Right-to-Know Act of 1986, Section 3 of the Superfund Amendments and Reauthorization Act of 1986 (SARA Title III). This federal legislation mandated that the public has the right to know what chemicals and other potentially hazardous materials are manufactured, stored, and transported in their communities. The law was intended to increase the flow of technical information from experts to lay publics and to open channels of commentary between them. Responding to this initiative, the chemical industry proactively undertook what it called its "Responsible Care" program.

►Employee Law

The Occupational Safety and Health Administration (OSHA) requires that employees be notified of specific working conditions. For instance, if their work leads them to make contact with chemicals that appear on the EPA list mentioned in the previous section, they must be notified.

Employees deserve to know their rights, for instance, those under the Americans with Disabilities Act (1990). If they have specific disabilities, they qualify for certain kinds of assistance. They deserve a working environment that is as friendly to their disability as possible. Employees deserve to know their rights to decide whether they have been or are being discriminated against because of their particular demographic category. They deserve to know their rights and the appropriate actions if they have been or are being subjected to sexual harassment.

Employees deserve to know this information. Likewise, management needs to know its obligations to meet workplace requirements. They need to know and understand the law and regulations. They need to know how their employing organization expects them to act in regard to such laws to ensure compliance with them. For these reasons, practitioners who are working to build employee relationships will find that their practice is shaped by OSHA guidelines.

BOX 9.6 OTHER RELATED LEGAL POINTS

The Securities Exchange Acts of 1933 and 1934 gave the Securities and Exchange Commission (SEC) authority to oversee statements made by publicly traded companies. All persons who might trade (buy or sell) a stock deserve to receive relevant material information in a timely manner. Material information is facts about the company's financial performance that would lead the prudent investor to decide to buy, sell, or hold shares in a specific company. Know whether your message might affect stock prices and the SEC regulations you must follow.

The Food and Drug Administration (FDA) has the power to regulate what can and must be said about food and drug products. The FDA can regulate statements about food and drug products that could lead persons to use them incorrectly. If your messages involve food or drug products, know the FDA rules.

The Internal Revenue Service (IRS) can affect how and when you communicate. The power of the IRS to shape a company's communication campaign results from its ability to determine which expenditures are legitimate business expenses. If corporate dollars are not deductible, executives are reluctant to participate in communication campaigns.

Perjury assumes that the wise practitioner does not make or allow those he or she counsels to make statements in a court of law or a governmental hearing that are not true. Perjury is making statements under oath that are known to be false.

Fund-raising activities receive special tax code status because they are performed by nonprofit organizations. These 501(c)(3) organizations operate in a nonprofit status and therefore do not pay taxes. Federal, state, and local regulations exist, and public relations practitioners must be aware of and honor them.

Managing Global Expectations in Internet Time

David P. Stangis
Director, Corporate
   Responsibility
Intel Corporation

At Intel, and I presume many other global companies, the definition and practice of managing expectations has evolved greatly over just the last few years. Just yesterday it seems we were a company owned by institutional investors and concerned about being good neighbors in the communities in which we operated and our employees lived. Managing expectations meant communicating with shareholders en masse and supporting a limited number of community programs.

A few things happened to change all that. A certain 5-tone musical identity campaign, coupled with a doubling in revenues, employees, manufacturing sites and share price (a few times) brought a whole new level of attention and expectations. Concurrent with these changes was the buildout of the Internet economy enabling real-time shared information across the globe and a shift in the Intel stockholder base. Not only had the mix of shareholders shifted from primarily institutions to a mix including almost half individual investors, the growing universe of socially responsible investors looked to Intel as a potential investment.

At Intel, Corporate Responsibility grew not out of an executive edict, but from within existing external relationships. Corporate Responsibility as a function at Intel didn't come about until the end of 2000. Prior to that, I managed expectations one-on-one and face-to-face in a role we called Environmental, Health, and Safety External Affairs. Frankly, communities', investors' and even employees' initial interests centered around whether the company was performing as expected in terms of preventing pollution and providing a safe workplace for employees and the community.

Conclusion

Most public relations practitioners are ethical and honorable people: They know the proper way to practice public relations. As a new practitioner, you can draw guidance from existing professional codes of conduct and from your organization's own

For 3 years, I met with investors, members of our site communities, and even homeowners and businesspeople near sites we were considering growing in. Over time, the questions expanded from the environment to ethical performance, supply chain management, diversity, and privacy generally. Was Intel the kind of company "I could be happy living next to, working for or owning"? The other phenomenon that occurred at the same time was that many groups with a "cause" saw Intel as either a source of needed funds or a sexy "high-tech" name to have on their list.

Internet time also meant that I had to manage Intel's relationship with one stakeholder as though I were managing the relationship simultaneously with every interested stakeholder. My words or presentations to one group could, within days, be in the hands of similarly interested stakeholders around the globe. One misspoken statement personally, or by anyone at Intel, now has immediate repercussions, not only in the local community as before, but everywhere.

I implore, and have worked to instill, a more operational and tactical approach to Corporate Responsibility. If I'm the one who needs to represent the responsible behaviors of Intel to external stakeholders, I want to be sure I not only have the facts and data to back up my words but also have insight and intelligence into what might be tomorrow's, next month's or next year's burning issue.

Corporate Responsibility today means digging into and understanding the operations and practices around environmental performance, human resource policies, technology advancement, marketing and corporate governance. It also means using (or developing) a management system capable of identifying emerging issues specific to your industry and the marketplace. Professionals need to move far beyond understanding communications and learn to be lifelong students of psychology, technology, global business and local economics in order to manage expectations in today's environment. Tomorrow's leaders will need to surpass reaction and model anticipation, predication and engagement to be truly successful.

SOURCE: Reprinted with permission from David P. Stangis.

code of conduct, if it has one. In addition to these ethical boundaries, you need to learn the legal constraints of public relations. In most of your work, there will be no ethical or legal dilemmas. However, by knowing the legal limits, you are less likely to violate them, and by appreciating the ethical concerns, you can make appropriate choices if the situation arises. The effective public relations practitioner is prepared—that includes ethically and legally.

Ethical Quandary: Practicing for a Multinational and Keeping Your Ethics

A leading practitioner posed the following question to a graduate class in public relations management: If you are advising a client from a country where bribery is the custom, including bribing reporters to write a positive story, how do you advise that client when it wants to offer money for a positive story in the United States? Then, the practitioner turned the story around. If you were representing a U.S. company that was operating in a country where bribery was part of journalism, what would you say? If the client said, "We want you to help us get a story in the key newspapers," what would you say, especially if your client were Accredited in Public Relations (APR)? What code of ethics is a person who is APR sworn to uphold? What does it say about bribing reporters? What does the code of ethics of the Society of Professional Journalists say to reporters who wish to receive something of value from any person or company? The answers to these questions are important to anyone who wants to practice public relations in an ethical manner, especially a manner that supports the principles of the Code of the Public Relations Society of America. Kruckeberg (1997) has an important opinion regarding the performance of companies in many countries with differing standards of ethics; he claimed that "corporations are morally obligated to maintain a level of behavior consonant with their publicly identified ethical standards but they may need occasionally to compromise their ethical standards to respect the values of others" (p. 35). What is the limit to such compromise if a U.S. company is operating abroad? What about a transnational company headquartered in a country that encourages bribes? Whose values need to be compromised? Such questions are not easy to answer. In his book titled *Trust*, Francis Fukuyama (1995) made this wise and relevant observation: "One can easily know the right thing to do intellectually, but only people with 'character' are able to do them under difficult or challenging circumstances" (pp. 35–36).

Summary Questions

1. What is protected speech? What are the differences between commercial and political speech?

2. Why are ethics vital to the quality of relationships? What are the advantages of thinking about ethics in terms of a balance of interests in society?

3. How are action, process, content, and product key elements of how we think about the ethics of the public relations process?

4. In addition to creating standards of ethics to guide the profession, what other factors are necessary for the practice of public relations to achieve true professional status?

5. What is the difference between absolute and relative standards of ethics?

6. How are ethics of public relations connected to the expectations of markets, audiences, and publics (MAPs)?

7. Why is openness a key aspect of public relations ethics?

8. If practitioners get paid for achieving publicity, why is community taste part of the ethics of public relations?

9. How are trust and aligned interests part of public relations ethics?

10. Differentiate *libel* and *slander*. What are the points that can be made to defend against charges of libel?

11. What is copyright? How does it affect the way in which people deserve to be paid for their creative efforts. Include in your discussion the principles of fair use.

12. If you are supposed to openly provide information, how can you do that and adhere to legal provisions that certain information is proprietary and some information is not to be made public?

Exercises

1. Find a case of an organization that violated an ethical standard and one that violated a legal standard. Write a two-page essay on each case to indicate what could have been done to achieve the strategic outcome without violating any ethical or legal standards.

2. Based on the principles of the PRSA Code and/or the IABC Code, indicate which five ethical principles you will include in the personal code by which you conduct your practice. In a group with other students, discuss those principles and select and frame those principles into a list that each of you would be pleased to have printed on a plaque and placed in your office. One way to raise ethical principles in a profession is to continually discuss them. Let's consider the advice of Jackall (1995):

    > Discussing concrete issues that have moral significance with colleagues in a regular, disciplined way can be invaluable in this regard. Indeed, only sustained, focused discussions can help clarify what rules actually apply in a given situation and how these rules compare with rules in use in analogous professional situations. Such discussions also cultivate the habits of mind that enable businessmen and -women to discern such rules accurately, evaluate them carefully from many different perspectives, and make reasonable and defensible decisions (p. 18).

3. As you begin to draw conclusions on this line of inquiry, write down the slogan about selecting which clients to represent that you want to place on your desk as you practice public relations. What would the slogan say? Will you put that slogan on your business cards and present them to prospective clients? Will you make clear to your boss the standard of ethical persuasion that you have written down?

4. Do you agree with one of the slogans often quoted by public relations practitioners: Never say or do something that you do not want on the front page of the newspaper or at the top-of-the-hour news segment? Why is this a good ethical standard?

5. In the chapter, we stressed the ethical principle of a company, nonprofit, or governmental organization committing to be the first and best source of information. In terms of the nature of community and the rhetorical tradition, why is this a good ethical statement?

6. Examine the dimensions of relationships that we have discussed throughout this text. Select one of them and write a two-page essay on one of the legal principles discussed in the chapter. Show how the legal principle and the dimension of a relationship are compatible or incompatible.

Recommended Readings

Bowen, S. A. (2005). Ethics of public relations. In R. L. Heath (Ed.), *Encyclopedia of public relations* (pp. 294–297). Thousand Oaks, CA: Sage.

Daugherty, E. L. (2001). Public relations and social responsibility. In R. L. Heath (Ed.), *Handbook of public relations* (pp. 389–402). Thousand Oaks, CA: Sage.

Day, K. D., Dong, Q., & Robins, C. (2001). Ethics in public relations: Theory and practice. In R. L. Heath (Ed.), *Handbook of public relations* (pp. 411–422). Thousand Oaks, CA: Sage.

"The Dream" in danger. (1995). *Public Relations Strategist, 1*(1), 44–45.

Frederick, W. C., & Weber, J. (1990). In W. C. Frederick & L. E. Preston (Eds.), *Business ethics: Research issues and empirical studies* (pp. 123–144). Greenwich, CT: JAI Press.

Holsigner, R., & Dilts, J. P. (1997). *Media law* (4th ed.). New York: McGraw-Hill.

Kelly, K. S. (2001). Stewardship: The fifth step in the public relations process. In R. L. Heath (Ed.), *Handbook of public relations* (pp. 279–289). Thousand Oaks, CA: Sage.

Leeper, K. A. (2001). The measurement of ethics: Instruments applicable to public relations. In R. L. Heath (Ed.), *Handbook of public relations* (pp. 435–440). Thousand Oaks, CA: Sage.

Seeger, M. W., Sellnow, T. L., & Ulmer, R. R. (2005). Codes of ethics. In R. L. Heath (Ed.), *Encyclopedia of public relations* (pp. 138–140). Thousand Oaks, CA: Sage.

Sellnow, T. L., Seeger, M. W., & Ulmer, R. R. (2005). In R. L. Heath (Ed.), *Encyclopedia of public relations* (pp. 140–142). Thousand Oaks, CA: Sage.

Stauber, J. C., & Rampton, S. (1995). *Toxic sludge is good for you: Lies, damn lies, and the public relations industry*. Monroe, ME: Common Courage.

Strenski, J. B. (1995). The ethics of manipulated communication. *Public Relations Quarterly, 40*(3), 33–35.

Tedlow, R. S. (1979). *Keeping the corporate image: Public relations and business: 1900–1950*. Greenwich, CT: JAI Press.

10

Monitoring and Managing Issues

General Motors Sets the Record Straight With *Dateline NBC*: The Issue of Safety

General Motors (GM) designed and manufactured Chevrolet and GM pickup trucks with two 20-gallon gasoline tanks installed in each vehicle. The tanks were located on the sides of the pickups. Several consumer safety groups claimed that this design was unsafe. The tanks were alleged to be unsafe because they were located outside of the heavy steel frame of the pickup. If a vehicle with this design were struck from the side, the collision could cause a fire. Between 1973 and 1992, 250 people had died from side-impact collisions in which one or more tanks ruptured and caught fire. The Insurance Institute for Highway Safety, an insurance industry group, urged the National Highway Traffic Safety Administration to recall the pickups because they were unsafe. GM responded that the pickups were safe because they met federal safety standards, but internal GM memos indicated that company officials were aware of the safety design problems. The company eventually changed the design.

To any manager of public relations for GM, the events up to this point would be challenging enough, but this issue took an interesting twist. On November 17, 1992, *Dateline NBC* featured the safety issue as part of its consumer-reporting mission. The episode titled "Waiting to Explode?" included video footage of GM pickups exploding during tests involving collisions on their sides. The episode included details suggesting that top safety experts concluded that the side-mounted tanks had led to more than 200 deaths. Also featured in the episode was a mother of a young man who lost his life in his 1985 model pickup. Those vivid images would likely lead consumers to fear purchasing the vehicles. Investors could worry that

Fair Testing

SOURCE: Copyright © Landov.

lawsuits would hurt GM as an investment opportunity. Public policy officials, such as federal regulators, might take action against GM. Consumer activist groups were likely to obtain and use copies of the footage in their campaign for automobile safety. What would you do? How do you propose that GM manage this issue and rebuild its reputation? What is the mission of GM? What damage would an environmental and situational analysis reveal about the marketability of this vehicle if the news report were accurate? Is the call for increased vehicle safety design a public policy issue if the record is not corrected? Did GM use high standards of corporate responsibility in the design and marketing of its vehicle? What is the rhetorical problem?

This vignette was chosen to challenge your analytical ability. What strategies would you recommend, and what tactics would you use to solve this issue? The case involves GM's integrity and its reputation and brand equity. The issue is product safety. What facts are central to this issue? In your analysis of this case, did you take a multiple stakeholder/ stakeseeker approach? Did you consider the relevant media relationships, customer relationships, investor relationships, public policy relationships, consumer group, or activist relationships, to name a few? Identify the stakes and stakeholders. What message development objectives and public relations tools would you use?

Actual case outcome: An investigation revealed that employees of NBC had rigged incendiary devices in the pickup bodies to make them explode dramatically to obtain maximum news impact. Based on that fact, GM decided to sue NBC. GM set out to rebuild its reputation for manufacturing safe, reliable, and economical vehicles. GM took the offensive and contested NBC's right to accuse GM of misjudgment in the design and manufacture of its pickups (Hearit, 1996). On February 9, 1993, Jane Pauley and Stone Phillips, program anchors, read an apology. GM dropped the suit. Is the GM design unsafe? Did this story prove that fact? In any case, it might be a dangerous automobile, but this news story concocted information to "spin" the version of the story they wanted to put on the air.

Today's public relations practitioner finds many challenges and opportunities. These challenges need careful response because they are relevant to the client organization's mission and vision. Strategic public relations can help an organization achieve its strategic business plan. To do so requires wise and ethical choices to meet the challenges and exploit the opportunities needed to create, repair, and sustain mutually beneficial relationships between the organization and its key stakeholders and stakeseekers. Differences over issues can harm the relationship between the organization and its key publics. Agreement is a fundamental ingredient to building identifications needed for relationships.

Chapter 1 laid the foundation for the discussion of issues management as a public relations responsibility. It emphasized the role of rhetorical dialogue that members of society can use to forge public policy. To serve the interest of community building, public relations has a social responsibility to help society formulate and implement public policy that solves problems and makes society better.

In this dialogue, businesses may be criticized because some people and organizations are offended by what they do and say. They might, for instance, make unsafe products. Outcry and protest can lead to legislation that forces companies to achieve higher standards. Nonprofit groups seek to influence public policy. For instance, anti-gun advocates oppose the sale of some or all types of firearms and promote the use of special locks to protect children. The National Rifle Association (NRA), a nonprofit group, opposes those public policies. Government agencies play a central role in the formation and implementation of public policy. The Environmental Protection Agency (EPA), for instance, works to achieve a cleaner society by imposing regulations on business operations, government operations, and the lifestyles of citizens.

Some challenges and opportunities require publicity and promotion. Those public relations functions are used primarily to increase awareness, inform, persuade, and cocreate meaning. The typical outcome of these functions is to generate more income for the organization. Businesses engage in publicity and promotion to attract customers. Nonprofits use publicity and promotion to attract donors, followers, members, and contributors. Universities, for instance, use these public relations functions to attract students, who pay fees and tuition. They want to encourage donors—especially alumni—to contribute money to the academic and athletic programs. Government agencies use publicity and promotion to feature their usefulness to citizens so that legislators and executive officers of government give a reasonable share of tax and fee revenues to the agencies, so they can do their business. Politicians use publicity and promotion (including featuring what the agencies do that is good for society) to run for office and promote their candidacies.

If we think along these lines, we realize that public relations conducts situational analysis to determine what needs to be done to create, maintain, and repair relationships with markets and audiences. Those are vital aspects of today's public relations, but it entails much more than that.

To expand your horizon regarding the role public relations plays in the success of organizations, this chapter looks at how and why practitioners conduct situational analysis. This situational analysis and strategic response allows them to know who opposes and supports the actions of the organization and how conflict can be avoided or resolved. Issues management monitors issues, sets high standards of corporate responsibility, and communicates a tough defense and smart offense to steward the ideas that guide society.

Giving Voice to the Organization Through Issues Management

Issues management engages in power politics. Activists seek to control businesses and governmental agencies by creating issues agendas and pressuring specific kinds of action (Davis & Thompson, 1994).

If publics in the situation in which the organization operates are offended by how it acts, they will pressure it to change. This pressure can be brought to bear directly on the organization through appeals for change. The pressure may be exerted through efforts to generate negative news coverage for its actions and policies. If these tactics fail, activists can work to hammer the organization into a shape they prefer by using governmental power: legislative, legal, or executive policy. This is the realm of issues management, to help organizations to inform, persuade, collaboratively make decisions, and cocreate meaning with publics.

Based on years of issues management experience with Allstate Insurance, Raymond Ewing (1987) came to believe that issues management "developed within the business community as an educational task aimed at preserving the proper balance between the legitimate goals and rights of the free enterprise system and those of society" (p. 5). Issues management is a foresight discipline that can serve the needs of nonprofits, advocacy groups, and governmental agencies, all groups of people who assert their interests through public policy formation, mitigation, and adaptation. Thus, Ewing reasoned, "A corporation exists for the *optimization* of the satisfactions of its stakeholders" (p. 32).

This chapter focuses attention on publics and audiences rather than markets and audiences. It examines the nature of issues, the way in which issues can constitute threats and opportunities, and the ways in which organizations monitor and respond to issues. Responses can include changing the organization so that it is not offensive and legitimate. We call this "improving its corporate responsibility." Responses can entail the use of issue communication. Communication occurs in many forms and through a rich array of tools. Beyond media relations, the tools include using the Web, preparing executives to appear on talk shows, participating in government hearings, and using issue advertising.

To begin our analysis, revisit the discussion in Chapter 4 about publics and audiences, and about stakeholders and stakeseekers. This analysis will be expanded below with discussion of the problem of the legitimacy gap and the need for organizations to listen to customers and publics.

What is an issue? It is *a contestable difference of opinion, a matter of fact, evaluation, or policy that is important to the parties concerned.* An issue can be framed as a question—as a rhetorical problem. In the case of the GM pickups, the issue was safety: Is the design safe? The rhetorical response suggests an answer to the question. What businesses provide the best of each product or service? When is a new store opening? Is a specific product safe? Is it selling at a fair price? How available or reliable is a product or service? Does an organization engage in unethical behavior? Does an organization pollute the environment? Does an organization harm persons' health, safety, or quality of life? Does an organization engage in discriminatory business practices? Is the organization committed to building relationships with its key communities?

What is an issues management view of public relations? It is *the management of organizational and community resources through the public policy process to advance organizational interests and rights by striking a mutual balance with those of stakeholders and stakeseekers.* It supports strategic business planning; champions high standards of corporate responsibility; identifies, monitors, and analyzes issues; and communicates to foster understanding and minimize conflict between the organization and the people whose support it needs.

Based on this foundation, the next section looks at issues management as a strategic function.

▶Issues Management as a Strategic Function

Managements want their organizations to succeed. For that reason, managements must solve two challenges as they create and implement an effective strategic plan. One is to maximize their income, the money they take in to accomplish their mission. The other, and it is crucial to issues management, is to reduce costs. Bottom-line observation: Conflict costs money. If you reduce conflict, you reduce cost. If you reduce cost, your revenue goes further.

Publics want to use conflict to cost organizations money. This is a power resource effort to force organizations to change policies, procedures, and practices that offend publics.

To make this point, let's recall the definition of publics in Chapter 4. A public is a group of people that share a view, pro or con, and have an interest in some problematic public policy issue. This definition means that some people, such as environmentalists, believe, or share a view, that an industrial plant is polluting. The members of this group, the public, form an organization, protest the plant management, and lobby government to take action against the plant. This is a public policy rather than a market issue. In its protest, the public might boycott products, but sometimes they cannot. So, they may have limited marketplace influence, whereas they may be able to exert influence through government. Thus, the issue is one of public policy. It is public policy because it is policy changed or imposed through government—the public sector.

This controversy between the public and the manufacturing plant is an issue. An issue is a contestable matter of fact, value, or policy. That means that people and organizations can debate an issue; they take sides on that issue. The debate constitutes a conflict between two competing points of view. Both points of view cannot be "true" or "best" at the same time.

Issues of fact result from differences of opinion about specific facts or their interpretation. For instance, in 1999, Houston, Texas, for a short time earned the distinction of the city with the worst air quality, a distinction that has much more often been held by Los Angeles, California. Houston needed to reduce its pollution so that it could meet federal guidelines. Such analysis is objective, a matter of fact, as well as subjective, a matter of opinion. The county tax assessor contested the estimate the EPA had used to determine the magnitude of the problem in Harris country, where Houston is located. He discovered that the EPA had overestimated the number of cars, their ages, and sizes. Therefore, the magnitude of air pollution was lower than what the EPA believed. This is a contestable fact.

An issue of value is one that is highly subjective. Two parties may contest an issue whereby each party simply *evaluates* it differently. For instance, People for the Ethical Treatment of Animals (PETA) objects to the abuse and slaughtering of animals for food and fur. Both sides of this controversy agree that animals are slaughtered—a matter of fact. PETA views the abuse and killing of animals as unethical; industries that are scrutinized by PETA do not see the killing of animals as unethical. As a means for heightening awareness of the ethical evaluation of the fast-food industry, PETA offered 10,000 "Unhappy Meals." This was an obvious play on the brand equity of the "Happy Meal." The unhappy meal kit featured a picture of Ronald McDonald carrying a bloody ax. The company name was changed to "McCruelty's." The box featured the picture of a cow breaking out of the box. Each kit contained pictures of bloody animals, straw dabbed with red paint, a stuffed Ronald covered in blood and holding a butcher knife, anti-meat stickers, and toy animals with paint depicting their slashed throats.

An issue of policy results from a difference of opinion regarding what should be done; for example, recommending that actions either be taken voluntarily or by the force of government policy, the EPA might require—as a matter of public policy—residents of the city of Houston to reduce their speed limit to 55 miles per hour, to restrict the hours that construction vehicles could be operated, and to reduce industrial plant emissions. Each of these is a policy. A policy refers to preferred actions. In the case of the remedy

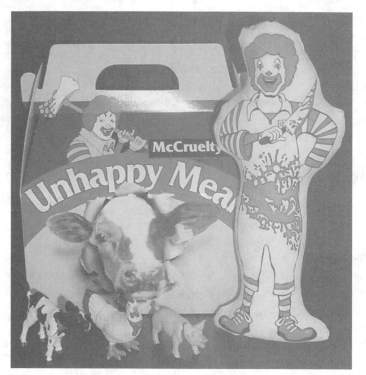

Eating Meat Is Murder!

SOURCE: Reprinted with permission from PETA.

for Houston's air quality, many policies are proposed and debated. Interests push against interests in this public policy debate.

These issues, differences of opinions, are the basis of why one entity opposes another, leading to an issue. Why do organizations offend publics? Publics have expectations, such as product safety. When a company or industry offends those expectations, publics want to force the company or industry to be less offensive. If a company manufacturers tires that are unsafe, people can exert influence in the marketplace by not buying the tires. They may also petition government to regulate the industry more closely. They may sue the industry as a class action.

The objective of such power resource plays is to force the company or industry, for instance, to act in ways that come closer to the expectations of the industry. Sethi (1977; see also Heath, 1997) has provided an excellent model of this deteriorating relationship as he described what he called the legitimacy gap (see Figure 10.1).

Issues management as a strategic function seeks to reduce the legitimacy gap. If it is successful, it can reduce costs and even increase the willingness of markets, audiences, and publics (MAPs) to do business with it—to be followers, customers, and supporters, such as legislators who fund government agencies.

Part of the success of issues management is to help society create narratives that cocreate meaning and lead to collaborative decision making. This topic is explored in the next section.

Figure 10.1: Gap Between Organization's Performance and Publics' Expectations

Organization
Performance
Activities   ⟷   Gap   ⟷   Publics'
Policies   Expectations

    BASES OF GAP
       Differences of fact
       Differences of policy
       Differences of value

▶Issues Management as Strategic Narratives

Protest takes a narrative form. Critics of an industry work to create a narrative that blames it for some predictable damage. In Chapter 5, we described the battle between HEART, an organization committed to save the Ridley turtles, and the shrimp-harvesting industry. HEART works to create the narrative that shrimpers drown turtles in their nets. This needless killing endangers the species. An endangered species can be doomed to extinction. Thus, HEART wants strictly imposed and enforced restrictions on the shrimping industry. The goal is to change the narrative from one where turtles become extinct to one where they thrive.

In such efforts, activists paint their opponents in the most negative terms. They vilify opponents' characters, condemning them for having low moral standards. For instance, PETA claims that persons who kill animals or consume products made from dead animals are murderers. They say the same about medical researchers who use animals in medical research and training. They want children to realize that animals are killed so they can have hamburgers and hot dogs, along with other similar foods. PETA volunteers splatter red paint on fur coats to demonstrate the narrative that animals are murdered so that their furs can be used for the vanity of humans.

Activists attack technologies and substances that are sold to consumers. Anti-tobacco activists point to the personal and social narratives of suffering, death, and high medical costs as the narrative attached to that industry. Persons who protest environmental damage from industrial processes claim that children and other members of society suffer health problems. Critics of genetic engineering argue that mutations will occur. These mutations can lead to dire consequences. Persons who eat foods that have been genetically altered may eventually produce mutant offspring. Or animals, including insects, that eat those plants may mutate and become uncontrollable monsters.

Such narratives focus on the elements of a news story: Who, when, where, why, how, and what? They paint the character of their attacks in negative terms, while presenting themselves positively. They foster plot lines and themes that pose choices. These choices lead either to dire consequences or much better alternatives. They call for voluntary changes. If those changes are not forthcoming, they seek public policy changes to force the offenders to change or even cease to operate. Issues management, then, tends to be a contest of good and evil, especially in the messages presented by activists. Activists use protests and publish newsletters that dramatize their versions of these narratives.

More moderate players in the issues management ballpark use more muted narratives to pose choices. The automobile safety activists, such as Ralph Nader, worked in loose coalition with the automobile insurance companies to create design standards that would make automobiles safer. Activists believed cars were unsafe, or at least could be safer. Insurance companies wanted to reduce the cost of insuring motorists against injury. Together, these forces of change created a car safety narrative that led to increased governmental standards. Automobile manufacturers have had to make safer automobiles.

Issues manifest themselves as narratives. Issues management provides a set of strategic responses that organizations, including activists, can use in these public policy battles. Consumer activists challenge manufacturers to create safer products, thereby hurting the market for irresponsible companies. Nonprofits create issues by dramatizing specific conditions, such as environmental damage, homelessness, or family violence. Government agencies create issues by advocating higher or lower standards, such as air quality standards. Companies create issues by advocating higher or lower standards, such as policies related to privacy on the Internet.

These narratives create controversy and conflict. As is demonstrated in the next section, they pose choices that become important to strategic public relations.

▶Issues Management as Strategies for Influencing Choices

Issues management requires that the organization reduce the legitimacy gap. To do so, it can increase each organization's ability to meet or exceed the expectations of its MAPs. Or it can communicate with them. Either action or communication, or both, can help solve a controversy.

Based on this analysis, a public relations view of issues management centers on the options organizations have as they work to create, maintain, and repair relationships with publics and audiences. Several strategic responses are possible, each of which can reduce the legitimacy gap:

- The organization can create and implement a strategic business plan that results in operations that are supported rather than opposed by its publics.
- The organization can argue (inform and persuade) publics and audiences that its actions are not as bad as believed.
- The organization can argue that the expectations of the publics and audiences are unjustified.
- The organization can inform the publics and audiences about what it is doing to end or reduce the offense.
- The organization can collaboratively make decisions with the publics and audiences that lead to interpretations of fact, value, or policies that are mutually satisfying.
- The organization can collaboratively make decisions with the publics and audiences that solve the problem that creates the gap.
- The organization can cocreate a meaning with the publics and audiences that bring harmony rather than disharmony.

This brief review of the public relations responses to issues suggests that message development objectives offer practitioners many options in their efforts to resolve differences. Such efforts also entail one of the key public relations functions: It requires that organizations listen to their publics and audiences. An organization needs to understand the publics' or audiences' perspectives on issues if they are going to be resolved. The organization cannot operate from only its one perspective but must also take its critics' perspectives into account in terms of what it does and says—how it communicates and what it communicates.

Audiences are important in this analysis of the quality of relationships between the organization and its MAPs. Activists, for instance, seek to enlarge the number of people who hold their views, that is, share their perspectives on some issue, such as consumer product safety. Activists appeal to audiences, persons who do not see themselves attached to the issue, but who might make that connection. Audiences can be targeted by organizations employing issues management. Effective public relations may inform, persuade, collaboratively make decisions, and cocreate meaning with audiences, which reduces their incentive to become publics.

The choices people make can affect the success of organizations. Some choices have public policy implications. If stakeholders like an organization, what it does and says, they are willing to see that it operates with minimal constraints from legislation, regulation, and legal guidelines. Legislation is passed to reward or punish organizations and individuals for what they do and say. For instance, legislative bodies can pass laws that raise taxes or impose restrictions on the quality of products a company (and industry) produces. If legislators are convinced that cars are unsafe as designed and manufactured, they can set higher standards that the manufacturers must meet. Legislators can set clean-air and clean-water standards.

Regulators are in the administrative or executive branches of government. The president, governor, or mayor, for instance, is the head of an administrative branch of government. Regulators implement the laws and ordinances passed by the legislative bodies. Sometimes regulators have enormous power for this reason.

The courts are a vital part of the public policy arena. The organization may seek to influence public policy by engaging in lawsuits. This is a standard tactic of activists. For instance, when the EPA seemed unwilling to impose air quality standards on cities, various environmental groups threatened to sue the EPA to force it to take action. The anti-tobacco interests have sued the tobacco industry. Some suits were filed by families and some by the attorneys general of various states. Industries may sue to prevent the imposition of public policy standards.

Viewed in this way, public relations plays a vital role in organizations' management of issues. Public relations persons may work with members of legislatures (government relations). They may create coalitions with other parties to influence issues, take corrective actions, and shape public policies. Public relations can help to find and build the harmony, the shared perspectives and mutually beneficial relationships needed to resolve the conflict between the organization and its publics and audiences.

As we discuss in the next section, public relations practitioners can manage issues by aligning their organizations' interests with those of the stakeholding and stakeseeking markets, audiences, and, especially, the publics.

▶Issues Management as Strategies for Aligning Interests

The legitimacy gap is a powerful way of examining the extent to which an organization's interests align with the interests of its MAPs. Relationships are influenced by the alignment of interests. For instance, many problems arose when a waste management company (garbage company) bought a parcel of land and then tried to persuade members of the community, including nearby residents, that a garbage dump (landfill) should be located there. Citizens—publics—protested the sites of these dumps.

Faced with these time-consuming and revenue-draining difficulties, waste management companies changed their tactics. Instead of engaging in conflict and confrontation, they went to the cities and said, "We are consultants in the waste management business.

We would like to work with you to solve your solid waste (garbage) problems." So, rather than having interests in conflict, they learned the virtue of aligning interests and collaboratively making decisions. They used government relationship and community relationship building as ways to create and maintain positive relationships by aligning the interests of the company with the community.

Organizations come to issues from different points of view and sets of dynamics. Nonprofits raise issues because it is in the interest of the causes they serve to do so. Nonprofits may raise issues on both sides of the abortion issue. Thus, pro-life and pro-choice advocates oppose one another. They seek to influence legislation, regulation, and legal interpretations. They do so by aligning interests with a cause and identifying with the persons who support that cause.

Companies raise issues. They may seek to align interests with advocates of automobile safety, for instance. The firearm industry, in defense of its market, aligns its interest with advocacy groups such as the National Rifle Association (NRA) and persons, including lawmakers, who favor gun ownership.

Companies may raise issues that oppose other industries. The automobile insurance industry aligns interests with car safety advocates and with car owners. By aligning interests of this kind, the insurance industry gains political support and allied voices in the public policy arena.

Medical researchers, physicians, and other members of the medical profession aligned their interest against the tobacco interest, primarily starting in the early 1950s and reaching a major plateau in 1964 with the Surgeon General's Report. The tobacco interest aligned its interests with legislators from states where tobacco is grown and processed, and with industries, such as vendors and advertisers, that reap the benefits of tobacco sales. Through various appeals to smokers, the industry sought to align interest against regulators who sought—and succeeded—in limiting the places where people could smoke. Thus, for instance, in the workplace, airplanes, restaurants, and public buildings, areas where smoking could occur were often banned or limited.

The alignment of interests results from finding persons and groups that share a set of facts, an interpretation of those facts, evaluations, and policy positions. Publics are likely to have well-formed opinions that either align with or collide against those of other advocates. Audiences can become the target of appeals to attract them to (identify with) one side or another of an issue because of some other aligned interest.

In one sense, such alignments lead to a fracturing of society as individuals, organizations, and groups favor competing sides of issues. This fracturing can polarize opposing interests. By the opposite dynamic, organizations seeking to manage interests can work to find and build on the aligned interests that resolve conflict rather than create and magnify it. Identifications can be fostered. Public relations practitioners can serve society by adding to the quality of that society, by fostering harmony and seeking policies that make society better.

Such is likely to be the case when organizations take positions on issues that look to align the interests of the members of society, rather than pit interests against one another. For these ways, issues management is strategic. Public relations practitioners, along with other executives, make decisions based on fact, evaluation, and policy preferences that can advance the good of society.

This first section has explained how public relations gives voice to organizations as they participate in dialogue that can create, maintain, and change relationships needed to form public policy that serves society. Issues management is the public policy side of the practice of public relations. It calls on community relationships, media relationships, activist relationships, follower/supporter relationships, and government relationships. The goal is to align strategic interests to solve society's problems. The next section explains how public relations practitioners engage in issues management, as we examine issues management in action.

Issues Management in Action

Some academics and practitioners believe that public relations has long been a part of issues management or that issues management has long been a subfunction of public relations practitioners. In the 1970s, the term *issues management* was popularized by senior practitioners who worried that public relations professionals were not exerting sufficient influence at executive levels in their organizations. These practitioners believed that traditional public relations functions, especially publicity and promotion, were not responding to corporate critics whose angry public protest pointed to the likelihood that how businesses and government operated was about to change. People had become offended by many aspects of business and government.

Recognizing that issues management is vital to the future of an organization's well-being, Ewing (1987) observed that "issues management is about power" (p. 1). If organizations want to influence the public policy agenda, they must have power based on the soundness of the issue position they take. They can change society's policies because they offer sound reasons to justify the positions they advocate. These positions need to align the interests of key players, build effective and mutually beneficial relationships, and advance the interests of the community.

In the face of such public outcry, some critics of public relations as it was practiced in the 1970s thought that it was reactive rather than proactive: It was oriented to publicity and promotion, mere "feel good" and "smiley-faced activities" designed to get favorable press attention. Critics feared that senior public relations counselors were brought into the strategic-planning loop too late to be useful. Public relations practitioners who fostered interest in issues management thought they could "expand the role of public relations beyond media relations and product publicity to a senior management problem-solving function critical to the survival of an organization" (Tucker, Broom, & Caywood, 1993, p. 38).

Practitioners and academics wanted to make public relations more central to the situational analysis needed to avoid collisions with stakeholder publics. For this reason, if public relations was merely a communication discipline, it lacked the confidence of management and intellectual foundations to help organizations reduce the friction between themselves and actual or potential critics. This change in direction required development of strategies of issues identification, monitoring, analysis, and response.

Out of a robust discussion of the relationship between issues management and public relations, some people concluded that it is a public relations function. Others think it embraces public relations. Let's not quibble at the moment. Let's challenge today's public relations to take an issues management perspective.

We launch our views on issues management by noting loudly that we do not think that organizations can manage issues. Some critics of issues management suggest that it sounds like people who support the concept believe organizations—especially large corporations—can (and should or should not) manipulate issues. Persons who take this view tend to believe that "manage" is synonymous with "manipulate."

The opposite end of the continuum has people reasoning that "you cannot manage issues," so you don't need to think about issues management. What happens, happens. Put a pretty face on dire circumstances. If life hands you lemons, make lemonade. Perhaps people who hold this view believe that organizations cannot take actions, including communication, to defend themselves or change themselves to reduce conflict with their publics.

Today's public relations is performed through managerial and technical functions. These functions are selected and implemented to help the client organization achieve its mission. Using the steps of strategic planning, issues management engages in the following sequence of steps:

- *Mission and vision statements:* What the organization wants to accomplish will be supported by some and opposed by others. Issues management can help the organization position itself so that it reduces friction and maximizes support. Part of this positioning requires effective communication.
- *Situational assessment:* The opinions of key publics affect the environment in which the organization operates. Issues management requires that public relations practitioners carefully monitor the environment of opinions and rising or falling issues that can affect the destiny of the organization. The assessment looks for opportunities and threats.
- *Strategy formulation:* Strategies of issues management can be divided into two broad categories. From the first chapter, we have stressed the importance of the good organization communicating well. The first strategy is to be a good organization, one that performs in ways that do not offend the expectations of its audiences and publics. The second strategy is to work in dialogue with other interested parties to examine ideas, information, and issues looking for best solutions to problems.
- *Strategic adjustment and relationship development:* As issues change, strategies need to be adapted to them to reflect these changes. The issue might require certain facts that must be introduced into the dialogue. The issue might center on certain evaluations. It might examine which policies are best to solve the problem. Things happen. Things change. Public relations practitioners need to adapt to the dynamics of issues so that they work to align interests and resolve the issue.
- *Evaluating the strategic plan:* As always, practitioners need to be able to assess the extent to which their strategic choices and the implementation of their communication efforts have been successful. If harmony increases, the issue has been wisely managed. If conflict and friction continue and even increase, then new strategic options are needed.

▶Positioning the Organization: Setting Objectives

As we have reasoned from the first chapter, this view of organizational performance assumes that the organization must be "good" before it communicates effectively. This view of issues management does not limit the function to media relations, customer relations, or government relations. It engages in planning to establish mutual interests and achieve harmony.

Many approaches have been advocated for managing issues. For instance, Renfro (1993) highlighted four intelligence activities: "(1) scanning for emerging issues, (2) researching, analyzing, and forecasting the issues, (3) prioritizing the many issues identified by the scanning and research stages, and (4) developing strategic and issue operation (or action) plans" (p. 64). A lot has been made of the matter of observing and predicting emerging issues. A widely adopted model, presented by Chase (1984), features issue identification, analysis, change options, and action program. Acknowledging the influence of Chase, J. Johnson (1983) offered a model that Hainsworth and Meng (1988) used to feature scanning/monitoring, identification/prioritization, analysis, decision (strategy), implementation, and evaluation.

Today's public relations requires that practitioners identify and solve issues—rhetorical problems. That means that they learn to bring to bear on those problems strategies selected to get the job done. They have an array of strategic responses. They know that message content is vital. It must be understood and managed in coordination with the parties with whom the organization seeks to build and maintain mutually beneficial relationships. Issues management assumes that an organization must understand its MAPs—what they know and believe, as well as their evaluations of the world around them. An issues management approach to public relations knows that the organization must be adjusted to fit into its community and that the community can be adjusted to support the organization's goals. This dialogue is the essence of today's public relations.

Issues management requires that objectives be stated to guide the process. Practitioners ask, "What do we need to accomplish to help the organization achieve its mission and vision?" Activists may set the objective of raising and aggressively pressing issues to seek change, such as to reduce cruelty to animals or reduce the threat of family violence. Companies may set the objective of helping to create environmental policy that allows for them to operate, but in ways that do not have negative impact on the environment. Government agencies may set the objective of creating and implementing effective public policy. For instance, the Federal Trade Commission wants communication policy that protects consumers against false and misleading product advertising claims. The Natural Resources Conservation Service wants to reduce soil erosion by the wise management of farmland and large construction sites.

Tied to these organizational objectives, we can find specific objectives that are relevant to the practice of public relations:

- To understand the issue, the motives of the persons who press for the issue, and the relationships that affect how the issue will be decided.
- To monitor the situation—to listen to critics and others who take issue positions—to understand what they say and their motives and interests.
- To inform, to be sure the key facts relevant to the issue are available for the persons to consider as they think about the issue.

- To persuade (convince) audiences and publics of some positions and to be persuaded in turn, so that the best conclusions are made. To motivate people to help press for the issue to be resolved. To motivate people to reduce their protest once the problem is solved.
- To engage in collaborative decision making and negotiation to align interests, reduce conflict, and solve problems that propel the issue.
- To cocreate meaning that aligns interests, reduces conflict, and solves problems that propel the issue.

The ultimate objective of the issues management program is to reduce friction between the organization and voices in society. To accomplish this goal requires three kinds of plans:

- *Business plan:* The strategic business plan allows the organization to position itself so that it reduces—or creates—friction to force needed changes in society.
- *Public policy plan:* The strategic public policy plan articulates approaches to aligning interests and effecting public policy change.
- *Issue communication plan:* This plan articulates the communication options that are needed to voice the opinions the organization believes are best on the issue.

As the organization sets its objectives, it needs to ask whether an issue poses a threat or offers an opportunity. If the organization thinks of issues as threats, it is likely to respond reactively and oppose the issue and debate aggressively with its proponents. This may be a good tactic, but it might also blind the organization to the need to change itself or the advantages that can be gained by changing itself.

Issues may offer opportunities. Proactive organizations look to see whether change can improve the relationship between themselves and the MAPs. This proactive response helps organizations to see debate and change as a positive rather than threatening option.

▶Achieving Corporate Responsibility: Getting the House in Order

Public relations is confronted with the reality that an organization must be good if it intends to be an effective communicator. If an industry creates a product that it knows is addictive and kills its customers, it has to manufacture the issue positions it takes, in part by shading the truth, twisting the truth, and ignoring the truth. Effective public relations assumes that the organization can set forth message points that withstand the challenge by opponents.

Of related importance, issues management can help reduce the legitimacy gap. This means that organizations know what their MAPs expect of them and try not to offend or violate those expectations.

Imagine, therefore, that you were expecting company. You want them to be pleased by what they find as they visit where you live. Thus, you clean house. The same is true for organizations that want to be effective issues managers. They need to clean house. They need to reduce friction by meeting the expectations of their stakeseekers and stakeholders.

Savvy practitioners and managers know the standards of corporate responsibility. They meet or exceed those standards. To the extent to which they are able to do this, they increase the chances that they can build, maintain, and repair mutually beneficial relationships.

Let's say, for instance, that a logging company has been using forestry methods that offend environmentalists. These methods reduce the natural habitat and increase erosion. One option of issues management would be for the company to claim through advertising and public relations that these methods do not do serious damage. The campaign might charge that the environmentalists expect unreasonably high standards. The campaign might allege that meeting high standards is likely to force the company to go out of business, hurting the local economy and causing layoffs. These message points may sound typical. They also might not solve the conflict. They can motivate activists to work harder to stop what they see as damage.

In contrast, the company might invite the activists to help meet the challenge of staying profitable while not harming the economy. The company might begin to implement better forestry techniques that do less damage to the environment.

The first step in corporate responsibility is to listen to critics to know the standards they expect and to aspire to high standards of performance. This means that issues managers need to be able to recognize the motivators for issues and, with them, the violations of standards of corporate responsibility.

Four key factors seem to be associated with issues that lead to concern, outrage, conflict, protest, and even calls for increased legislation, regulation, and legal action. You may want to think about these factors to see whether they signal the potential for controversy.

- *Fairness:* People want to be treated fairly. If they believe that businesses charge too much for products or services and if they can't challenge those costs through competition, people are prone to ask legislators or regulators to reduce these costs.
- *Equality:* People do not want to feel that they have been treated unequally. In recent years, Americans with disabilities have fought to ensure that they have equal access to businesses and public buildings. Individuals do not want to discover that they receive less equal treatment because of age, race, or other condition when they seek a job, a raise, a promotion, or other benefits from their work.
- *Environmental aesthetics:* Since the 1960s, concern for the quality of the environment has risen steadily. Many environmental groups are committed to fighting to protect species, such as Ridley turtles, as part of their commitment to environmental quality.
- *Safety:* Consumer safety has become a huge issue. People believe they should be properly warned and protected so they cannot be hurt when they use products.

Motivators such as these are vital indicators of the sorts of issues that can lead to controversies over standards of corporate responsibility. Managers, including public relations professionals, are wise to know these standards and recognize the need to meet them.

Knowing what to do is part of the equation. Achieving the standards of corporate responsibility is the other part. Organizations are wise to impose new and better standards of responsibility to avoid the cost of controversy and overregulation. Savvy senior practitioners frequently counsel senior managements to change proactively and then communicate that change to demonstrate commitment to the interests of their MAPs.

Be a good organizational citizen. Let the world know what you have accomplished. Be willing to use those standards as ways of attracting business and reducing the cost of controversy.

▶ Scouting the Terrain: Listening for Threats and Opportunities

Public relations practitioners, whether engaged in marketing or public policy battles, should be the ears and eyes of the organization. They should be excellent listeners who can spot threats and opportunities. They need to know how to conduct research.

Early in the emergence of interest in issues management, many scholars and practitioners wanted to know how to spot issues as soon as possible, while they were emerging. Now, many of those practitioners have recognized that early response is not the advantage and that many issues simply seem never to go away.

To be a good researcher or listener, practitioners who are engaged in issues management need to accomplish several stages of issues monitoring. Like the scouts in the old Western movies, they need to know the terrain. They need to be experts at conducting situation analysis. To so do, they need to engage in issue scanning, identification, analysis, monitoring/tracking, and prioritization. We examine each of these in order.

BOX 10.1 SCOUT THE TERRAIN: LISTEN FOR THREATS AND OPPORTUNITIES

Issue scanning: Requires constant efforts to watch for issues. This process is similar to actions of persons who look for warnings on a radar screen.

Issue identification: A crucial step. Issues managers know that some issues are more important—pose threats or offer opportunities—than others. This step requires identifying the issues that are most likely to have a positive or negative impact on the client organization.

Issue analysis: Issue managers need to be experts on issues. They also need to be part of teams of experts who can help to understand the nature of issues and their likely impact on the organization. Analysis is a way of "thinking smart" about an issue. It looks for opportunities as well as threats. Analysis can help the organization prepare its responses to the issue. This can include changing corporate responsibility or communicating to be sure that the best information, evaluation, and policy positions are featured in the discussion of the issue.

Issue monitoring/tracking: Issues don't last forever, nor do they usually die suddenly. Sometimes issues that seem to have died resurface. Issue monitoring is the strategy of watching to see the life cycle of the issue. Does it progress to the point that it becomes legislation, regulation, or litigation?

> *Issue prioritization:* Organizations make a mistake if they try to manage too many issues. For this reason, they have to decide which issues deserve the most attention at a given time and which allow for the most influence. Some may require response because they are based on false information or assumptions/evaluations and constitute grave threats to the organization.

Issue Scanning

Imagine the following conversation. You are a senior practitioner in a nice office, at work on the company newsletter. You have several staff members working on it and are striving to get it to the printer soon to meet deadlines. Your phone rings. It is the chief executive officer (CEO). He says, "Do you know that we have about 40 people outside of the Big X manufacturing facility? I just saw it on CNN. They are protesting the vapors that come out of our cooling tower and offensive odors. What do you know about this?" Do you reply:

1. "I am busy with the employee newsletter and will deal with those protesters when I have finished."

2. "I don't know anything about protesters, and besides, public relations deals with marketing, not protesters."

3. "I'll get on this right now."

4. "I have talked with our plant manager, who has been meeting with those people. He has me scheduled to meet with them tomorrow. I am going to include our environmental experts and staff members of the city and county. I know that they worry about the emissions they see, but those emissions are harmless clouds of water vapor from the cooling towers. I have a report from a local college professor to support that conclusion. The odor problem began when we changed our operating procedures and introduced a new chemical. It stinks, it really does! We did not prepare for that in our operations. The plant manager is committed to changing processes, but that will take about 6 months. We have invited the leader of the protest, a member of city staff, a member of the county staff, and the college professor to monitor the progress in making the change. We have two reports that indicate that the chemical poses no health problems, but it does stink. We can't deny that. The plant manager had asked the protesters not to protest. I had asked them not to protest. They decided to protest. That is their First Amendment right. I respect their choice, even though I don't agree with it. Our plan is to end this issue by giving information, allowing them to monitor the project, and having them discuss the issue. Let's see if that does the trick. If so, we will also report those changes to employees in a forthcoming issue of the employee newsletter. We will do a feature story on the success of the project in our community relations and environmental report. Do you think that we have covered all of the bases to date?"

Grade the various responses with a letter grade of A, B, C, D, or F.

Your grade probably reflects the practitioner's ability not only to scan for issues but also to respond quickly and appropriately. One of the key points to scanning is that sometimes an issue emerges only when it hits CNN, but organizations have more response time if they are aware earlier.

Issue scanning depends on spotting issues, as early as possible. You can grasp the concept of scanning best by thinking about a radar screen. We are familiar with the scenario of the person sitting before a screen looking for "blips," something that appears on the screen. The screen maintains continuous surveillance of the environment, looking for something.

That is what issue scanning entails. Practitioners are expected to be constantly on the lookout for issues. They need to see them as soon as possible to give the maximum chance for early response.

One place that practitioners can scan is the standard media; however, most issues are well established by the time they become the bases for standard media news stories.

To get an earlier warning, scanning should focus on research reports in technical, medical, or social scientific journals. Such papers may also be posted on the Internet, so that is a good place to scan. Early warning can increase if the scanning includes reading activist and government literature. Activists give speeches, make news statements, publish newsletters, and post statements on their Web sites.

Practitioners should have a network of scanners. Persons with technical expertise, such as engineers and environmental quality experts, should be encouraged to look for studies, reports, and claims made about technical risks and issues. They should be encouraged to make reports on their findings. Battles over environmental quality, for instance, start in the scientific community and may migrate to the standard popular press.

CHALLENGE BOX

Select an organization. Scan the popular press, the Web (Web Watcher), and some other relevant sources for issues that can help or harm this organization.

Some companies and activists groups, even governmental agencies, create Q&As or chat rooms/bulletin boards on the Internet. They encourage critics to raise issues and ask questions. In this way, they can "scan" for issues by having the issues come to them.

Rumors abound on the Internet. For instance, have you ever heard of a chemical called "sodium laureth sulfate" or "sodium lauryl sulfate" (SLS)? If you learned about these in the past several years, it might have occurred because a friend forwarded an e-mail warning to you from the Internet. The standard statement began with a personal greeting and warning from your friend. Then, you might have been encouraged to "check the ingredients listed on your shampoo bottle, and see if they have a substance by the name of sodium laureth sulfate, or simply SLS." The warning stated that this is used in powerful cleansers to produce foam. It is "strong." "It is also proven that it can cause cancer in the long run, and this is no joke." So the note continued. The e-mail included product names that contained the substance. It said that a researcher at the University of Pennsylvania conducted the study. Some e-mails even said that Health Canada had concluded the chemical is harmful and banned it.

Scanning means rummaging for warning signs. This e-mail was one. A quick Web search could also reveal that Web sites were set up that included this chemical as one of the "most wanted," meaning a bad actor.

That search could also reveal a site, established on February 12, 1999, that claimed this to be an "Internet Hoax." It said the e-mail note your friend forwarded was a hoax. First, "Health Canada has investigated the chemical and found no scientific evidence to suggest that SLS causes cancer. It has a history of safe use in Canada." Second, "Health Canada contacted the University of Pennsylvania Health System and found that it is not the author of the sodium laureth sulfate warning and does not endorse any link between SLS and cancer." A Web search could disclose a debate over this and other chemicals. Sites abound to raise concerns and to address them (Web Watcher).

The point of this study is that issues pop up all over the place. They may be well founded, or hoaxes. Both need to be addressed. Scanning helps to spot them as early as possible. Since many issues are related to studies and claims that require technical knowledge, the practitioner is wise to have well- and diversely educated scanners on the team.

Issue Identification

Issue identification follows issue scanning. At first, you might think that scanning and identification are the same, but they are not. Scanning requires constant vigilance to spot something that might be an issue; identification involves determining whether a problem or concern exists that poses a threat or opportunity for the organization.

If the issue seems sufficiently threatening or promising, it is logged into the issue analysis system. An issue becomes more identifiable once it begins to receive more attention by the media and other organizations and publics. Usually, issues take on importance once they are promoted as part of the issue agenda by legitimate reporters, activists and other nonprofits, businesses, and governmental agencies. They receive more attention and become more defined as a part of the larger dialogue on that topic.

CHALLENGE BOX

Watch the evening local and national news, including CNN, for one week. Also read one national or large local newspaper and one news magazine for one week. Identify at least three issues that are reported in more than one outlet. Identify who is keeping the issues alive and for what motives. Are these issues part of a larger agenda, especially those that are motivated by equality, fairness, environmental quality, and safety? Think of one reason why this is an issue that an organization needs to analyze and monitor.

Issue Analysis

Issue analysis is required once issues have been identified as deserving more detailed scrutiny. Analysis focuses on several aspects of an issue. The first is the merits of the issue. Is the issue based on fact? Persons who are concerned about the Ridley turtles monitor their numbers and watch for what they call "strandings," turtles that have been killed or drowned as part of the shrimp harvesting. For the activists, these facts substantiate their position. Shrimp harvesters and governmental agents monitor the issue by observing the numbers of turtles and strandings.

Issue analysts investigate the evaluations and motivators that are likely to serve as incentives for advocates to attract media and other stakeholders' attention to the issue. Such analysis centers on the nature of the problem that is being discussed to ask why its advocates believe it is a problem. Odors are a problem for people who live near manufacturing facilities. Odors may signal toxic materials. They are offensive to the quality of life. They can hurt property values.

This sort of analysis plumbs the depths of problem recognition and centers on the degree to which stakeholders see the problem as relating to their interests, such as personal health, or altruistic interests, such as environmental quality, including Ridley turtle survival. Analysis asks whether there is a problem, whether stakeholders think there is a problem, and whether they see it as affecting them.

Issue analysis investigates the nature of the groups, their power in the public policy arena, and the flashpoint potential of an issue. Powerful groups can easily keep issues alive. Less powerful groups struggle and fail to keep them alive. One of the ways an issue stays alive is to be associated with a flashpoint where people are outraged to learn about the issue and realize its impact. In recent years, "tender tissue" issues have plagued government and industry. The concern is that various technologies, such as vinyl, chloride, and electromagnetic fields, damage children's tender tissue, increasing their health risks. Whereas we might not be overly concerned about health consequences on adults, we may be prone to see the flashpoint of issues related to children. Media reporters like human interest stories, and they love those regarding children.

Issue analysis looks at large opinion trends, such as the increasing or decreasing sensitivity of society to be concerned about environmental or economic issues. Such analysis also looks more specifically at the implications of the issue for the organization. It may look at the implications for industry, groups of similar-cause nonprofits, or governmental agencies that address specific types of issues.

Issue analysis examines the potential impact on the organization. Some issues offer opportunities. For instance, businesses that operate at high standards can see their competition harmed by calls for safer products. Some competitors sacrifice safety for design or manufacturing costs. They could be harmed or forced out of business, leaving more of the market for their competition. Nonprofits can benefit from increased interest in a particular disease. For instance, if a celebrity becomes victim to a medical problem, such as breast cancer, that offers an opportunity to conduct fund-raising because insufficient federal or state funding is available to help specific classes of women.

Issue analysis can also consider whether the issue will harm their operations or chances of conducting nonprofit fund-raising. If a state government wants to raise taxes on business operations, it can make companies that do business in that state less competitive than businesses that operate in other states. If a company is taxed in Illinois whereas its competition in Indiana is not, competition for sales in other states harms the one that is taxed. A call for higher environmental pollution reduction may damage a company's ability to invest money in new product development, because it has to spend money to reduce air emissions. In this way, analysis looks for the consequences of the issue on the operations of the company, nonprofit, or governmental agency.

To strengthen issues analysis, Renfro (1993) advised the use of issue briefs that define and explain the issue; explore its various positions, sides, and options as well as the parties that have an interest in it; determine the nature, timing, and mechanics of the potential impact of the issue; and guide attention to additional sources of analysis regarding the issue. These briefs are "thinking documents" that precede the formulation of issue position papers, which, based on the data captured by the briefs, assert the position and tactics executives are going to take on the issue.

CHALLENGE BOX

Analyze an issue. Identify the motivators and the points of difference that are likely to keep it alive. Consider whether the issue is one of fact, value, or policy—or more than one of these. What incentive and power do its advocates have for keeping it alive? Explain why you believe it will stay alive or fade in importance. What impact will this issue have on companies, nonprofits, or governmental agencies? Who are these companies, nonprofits, or governmental agencies?

Analysis examines the organizations and persons who attach themselves to an issue. *Issue legitimators* are key persons or organizations that have so much credibility that they can make an issue legitimate by taking a side on it. For instance, an issue regarding the carcinogenic effects of a substance might be debated. If the American Cancer Society or the EPA indicates that it has reason to be concerned about the health effects of the substance, that gives the issue more legitimacy. If either places the substance on its list of known carcinogens, that changes the legitimacy of the issue once more.

Issue Monitoring/Tracking

Issue monitoring/tracking watches the trajectory of issues. It asks whether an issue is becoming more potent or is losing steam. Tracking can entail many kinds of research that were discussed in Chapter 4. See Box 10.2 for the uses of research in issues management.

BOX 10.2 ISSUE MONITORING AS PUBLIC RELATIONS RESEARCH

Finding facts: Archival research issues managers must know the facts. They need to use archival research to scan and monitor issues in the media. These media can be the general media or specialized media. The general media are a good source to spot issues that have become strong enough for media reporters to be interested in them. Most issues begin in scholarly or activist literature. The Web is a good source of archival data. Commissioned studies can give valuable insights into the substance of an issue. Trade associations often conduct commissioned studies for industry, as do research institutions and college professors.

Interviews: Interviews are an excellent means for getting information and opinions of key persons. If you have reason to think that an issue might have merit, you could interview experts who have researched and written about the issue or issues that are related to it. You can also interview persons who have responsibility for monitoring the issue, such as leading activists or experts in government agencies. You might call these persons to determine the status and substance of an issue.

You might interview persons who have been affected by the issue. For instance, if you are responsible for monitoring an issue, such as discrimination in the workplace, you are wise to have interviewed people on both sides of that issue. Talk to persons who believe they have experienced discrimination. Learn their views. Also talk to persons who have investigated their allegations.

Focus groups: One of the best uses of focus groups is to determine whether issues have flashpoints. You might pose key questions to a targeted group of individuals. For instance, if a governmental agency is seeking to change tax policy so that it would hurt the older segment of the population, focus groups could be used to determine whether they would respond to this issue and demand certain actions of their legislators. Focus groups are an excellent means for deciding whether specific issue positions or organizational policies offend the attitudes and evaluations of key MAPs. Focus groups can also be used to test messages to determine how they need to be framed so they relate to the interests of the key publics and audiences. Focus groups can be used to determine the best way to explain an issue, especially if it is highly technical. How can it be explained clearly and credibly?

Surveys: Surveys are a good way to ascertain the opinions of larger segments of the population. Archival research can reveal studies, such as those by national or regional polling groups. Organizations commission surveys to determine what strategic audiences and publics know, believe, and are willing to do—the actions they are willing to take. They might, for instance, be willing to write letters to their local, state, or federal representatives expressing their views on the issue.

Content analysis: Content analysis is an excellent means for determining the trajectory of an issue. This research technique entails reading and comparing media reports. Media reports can be monitored, for instance, by determining whether the issue received top-of-the-hour or front-page attention or has slipped. Content analysis can reveal whether an issue is growing or waning as a news story topic. It can indicate whether specific facts, evaluations, or policy positions are being reported. It can reveal whether the facts being reported are accurate and whether they are interpreted appropriately.

Renfro (1993) contended that an issue matures through six stages: *birth* (the result of key changes), *definition* (some persons or groups characterize the issue), *name* (attach it to a few terms that give it identity), *champion* (key players become identified with and advocate the issue), *group* (interested parties become definable as a demographic or interest group), and *media recognition* (editors, reporters, and news or program directors believe the issue is worth reporting because it has or deserves the status of news). A crucial stage is naming ("Those who define the issue win the debate"), which can lead to complementary advice ("Redefine the issue to win a new debate") (Renfro, 1993, p. 40).

The birth of an issue begins when an individual or a group experiences strain. *Strain* occurs when someone believes that a problem exists. A problem is a discrepancy between what is and what ought to be. For instance, environmentalists experience strain when species inventories reveal a decline in the population of some animal or plant. Once strain occurs, mobilization can begin. At this stage, several individuals or groups become active. They communicate with themselves, the offending organizations, and the media to raise awareness of their concern. They create or use an existing organization to bring pressure to change some policy.

Confrontation occurs when the pressure is brought to bear. This pressure can exist in meetings with executives of the offending organization. It can result in increased stories placed in the media to draw general attention to the issue and increase or broaden awareness of the issue. At this stage, advocates also try to broaden and deepen the concern audiences and publics feel for the issue. Confrontation can lead to battles in hearings, in the drafting of legislation, and on the legislative floors. Battles can be waged in regulatory hearings and even in court.

At some point, the sides engage in negotiation. Smart public relations issues managers try to get to this stage as quickly as possible. Chapter 13 discusses collaborative decision making. During this phase of issues management, the sides of the issue work to find a mutually acceptable solution to the problem. They find a way to align interests and achieve an outcome that restores or builds a mutually beneficial relationship.

During the final stage of an issue, the sides work to build support for the agreement that was achieved through collaborative decision making. Industry leaders communicate to build consensus within an industry for some newly adopted policy. Activists and other nonprofit organizations work to convince followers that a wise decision was achieved. Government leaders work to convince constituents that a solid outcome was achieved. The result of these communication efforts is to cocreate meaning that leads to harmony in place of conflict.

BOX 10.3 STAGES OF AN ISSUE FROM EMERGENCE TO RESOLUTION

Strain

Mobilization: Emerging issue

Confrontation

    Informal clash

    Media clash

    Potential legislative action

    Prelegislative action

    Legislative action

    Legal/administrative/litigation

Negotiation

Resolution

Issue monitoring and tracking requires that practitioners watch the growth, evolution, death, stagnation, or culmination of an issue. The lives and fates of issues, like people, take many turns and twists. Some have happy outcomes. Others are painful and problematic. An issues management program is able to chart these directions and understand why the issue progresses as it does.

CHALLENGE BOX

Select an issue that has matured into legislation. This legislation is likely to have had some regulatory impact. It may have been litigated, even reviewed by the U.S. Supreme Court. Select an issue that has at least resulted in legislation. Identify when it was first discussed in the general media. Determine the various groups and individuals who took sides on the issue. Find out whether it continues to be controversial.

Issue Prioritization

Issue prioritization goes beyond issue analysis. Issue analysis is used to determine which issues deserve the most attention because of threats and opportunities they pose for an organization. This step goes beyond analysis to determining the response options that seem best. One response is to give in to the issue's advocates. Another is to oppose them, on the grounds that their facts and analysis are incorrect or potentially harmful to the organization and to society.

Issue prioritization can entail changing the strategic business plan of the organization to reduce threats or take advantage of the opportunities. It can require that the organization implement higher standards of corporate responsibility.

Issue prioritization may lead to government relations activities, including lobbying and the creation of legislative initiatives. It can require the expenditure of money for an issue communication campaign. The next section addresses the strategies and challenges of issue communication.

CHALLENGE BOX

Identify an issue that took one direction for several years, such as resistance to critics. See how that issue changed the priorities of the company, or even an entire industry. The tobacco industry is an interesting case to study. By 2000, several lawsuits had been settled with states over the medical costs that were created by tobacco products. Further litigation was pending. States required that the industry improve its record regarding sales of products to persons who were underage. States required that the industry fund anti-smoking campaigns. By July of 2000, companies such as Philip Morris were conducting national advertising campaigns to tell key MAPs about their improved operations. They claimed to have learned their lesson and to have adopted higher operating standards.

Recall the grading exercise we used to introduce this section. Based on what you have learned about issue monitoring, would you change the grade you gave for the various responses that could have been given by the practitioner who was facing a protest at his or her manufacturing facility? Let's ask three more questions. Should the practitioner have notified senior management that a protest was going to occur so they would not have to learn about it from watching network news? Should the person have identified the message points that were being used to communicate with the upset community residents? Should the practitioner have told the executive how collaborative decision making could solve this problem?

BOX 10.4 STRATEGIC APPROACHES TO ISSUES MANAGEMENT: MONITORING, TRACKING, ANALYZING, AND RESPONDING

- Monitor issues
  - Scan to identify issues—radar screens
  - Analyze issues to understand the advocates' positions as well as the rationale for their positions
  - Track the trajectory of issues given the advocates and the prevailing opinion environment
- Enlist issue identifiers, monitors, and analysts among other disciplines in the organization
- Form issue analysis teams: matrixing internal and external expertise
- Develop issues matrices that compare the company position to those of the stakeholders
- Implement appropriate standards of good citizenship
- Know the communication options that can be used to engage in issue discussions
  - Know what should be said—situational analysis and corporate issue positions
  - Know what must be said—situational analysis and corporate issue positions
  - Develop and implement issue positions that conform with corporate issue positions

▶Communicating About Issues: Issue Response

Communication is one option in issues management. The first option is to change the organization so that it meets or exceeds the expectations of its stakeholders. If those expectations are incorrect or if the organization is raising rather than combating the issue, communication is a vital option.

BOX 10.5 TECHNIQUES FOR DEVELOPING ISSUE COMMUNICATION

- Recognize whether the issue at hand is one of fact, evaluation, or policy.
- Develop issue papers and backgrounders to support your organization's point of view on each issue.
- In an executive summary or opening statement, feature the key point that is central to the issue paper or backgrounder.
- Build the issue paper or backgrounder around three to five message points that support the issue position that is championed.

- Establish the context of the issue in terms of positives and negatives; frame alternative positions in terms of positive or negative outcomes for the organization and its stakeholders.

- Refute opposing positions by showing where they lack fact, make incorrect interpretations of fact, are based on the wrong values, or lead to unwise policy.

- Keep the language of the document simple; avoid or define technical terms and concepts so they can be understood by lay audiences.

- Have executives and internal experts become spokespersons for issue positions; supply talking points for spokespersons to use as they work to feature facts, evaluations, and policy positions.

- List third parties that can be contacted to confirm the points you are working to support.

- Communicate as part of a larger set of voices; create third-party (including trade associations) alliances on issues.

Issue communication is a response to a rhetorical problem. A rhetorical problem results when some problem has the potential of working against the creation and maintenance of mutually beneficial relationships. A rhetorical problem can result from disagreement or misunderstanding. It may occur when parties operate out of different values, attitudes, needs, or wants. If two parties have conflicting facts or interpret them differently, a rhetorical problem can result. If a group (public) or set of individuals (audience or market) thinks and acts differently than what the organization desires, prefers, or thinks advisable, a rhetorical problem exists.

The challenge facing the practitioner is to isolate the issue at the heart of the problem and recommend corrective actions and communication strategies that can create, repair, maintain, restore, or strengthen the relationship. For instance, in the case of Disney's "America" theme park, the publics that opposed the location of the park, on part of a Civil War battlefield in Virginia, believed that it would harm the countryside and spoil the legacy of persons whose lives were given for a sociopolitical cause. The issue confronting Disney was where it could locate the park to generate the highest revenues. Disney had not properly identified and analyzed the issues at hand. Its strategic response put the company on a collision course with several key publics. That case, mentioned in Chapter 5, demonstrates the principle that when differences occur, they center on an issue.

An issue is addressable through the use of facts (information) and evaluative premises (attitudes). The issue is capable of being resolved through communication or actions. People may come to think an issue is more of a problem than it is. Or they may believe that an issue is less serious than facts and sound judgment would suggest. In this way, an issue is contestable.

An issue has at least two sides. It arises from a difference—a choice. How the issue is resolved can have important consequences for the relationship between the various interested parties. Relationships depend on alignment of interests, seeing mutually beneficial reasons for holding one opinion as opposed to another or taking one action versus some other action.

Part of the rhetorical challenge to public relations practitioners is listening to others to determine when an issue exists. Once issues are identified, they need to be analyzed to determine how important their resolution is to the parties concerned. Practitioners are expected to look at the issue from other parties' points of view. Practitioners can increase their appreciation of others' points of view by understanding their reasoning and determining why the issue is important for them.

People cocreate meaning that allows them to coordinate their activities. They learn which opinions and actions are rewarding or produce harmful outcomes. They realize that the actions of others can have consequences for their well-being. They attempt to create informed opinions that lead to desirable outcomes.

The rhetorical tradition challenges and informs public relations practitioners on how to help people to achieve relationships, hold opinions, and take actions that are mutually beneficial. This strategy is called *perspective taking*—thinking as others think—listening to them and appreciating their points of view. Perspective taking is inherent in rhetoric. Each strategic response is based on the concerns, opinions, needs, and wants of others. It recognizes what it must say and which points cannot be sustained given the critical judgment of MAPs.

We sharpen our definition of MAPs by thinking of each of these categories of persons as stakeseekers or stakeholders. Stakeseekers seek something of value from stakeholders. Stakeholders can give or withhold something as part of the exchange with stakeseekers.

Several communication functions are vital to the practice of public relations: to attract attention (gain awareness), inform, persuade, negotiate, and cocreate meaning. Public relations practitioners use communication tactics on behalf of their clients in the public interest. They counsel the clients regarding the available, best, and required communication responses as each situation dictates.

Framing the Issue

Issue communication begins with strategic efforts to frame the issue. Disney "America" framed the issue as a commercial effort to provide visitors with an interesting opportunity to learn more about the history of the Civil War. Opponents framed the issue as commercial clutter and damage to the countryside, which was made more damaging because it commercialized the valor and sacrifice of the soldiers and noncombatants who were affected by the war. As mentioned in the opening vignette of this chapter, *Dateline NBC* framed the story about the gas tanks on GM pickups as an issue of safety, which was the accurate issue, but went too far in creating information that would support the issue. Shell UK framed the issue of the disposal of the Brent Spar as the best environmentally responsible business decision—to sink the disused oil collection buoy in the North Sea.

Greenpeace focused only on the environmental impact of the proposal to scuttle the Brent Spar.

An issue does not just occur, nor does it occur in a vacuum. It is framed by those who discuss it. Organizations seek to frame an issue so that it privileges their side. If they go too far in this strategic option, they are likely to alienate their oppositions.

Wise practitioners know that they should frame issues so that they lay a foundation for aligning the interests of the persons who are involved with and affected by the issue. They are wise to avoid framing the issue in a way that threatens the interest of their opponents and forces them to make an undesirable choice. For instance, companies have made serious mistakes when they frame manufacturing-plant-facility environmental damage by pitting jobs and taxes against the threat of closing the plant. They mistakenly believe they can badger opponents by saying that "if we are forced to change, we will have to close the plant." That sort of framing privileges the organization and disempowers the opponents. It is bound to fail.

Informing

Issues need a foundation in fact. The objective of issue communicators is to see that the best information is available for interested persons to make a decision. They also work with the issue discussants to see what is the best way of framing and interpreting the information to understand the problem and its solution.

Shell UK brought together scientists and policymakers to generate research and decide what the best business decision would be to dispose of the Brent Spar in an environmentally responsible way. It commissioned studies and made the findings of those studies available to the parties that were interested in the disposal of the structure. GM brought information to bear that would allow viewers to know that NBC had "manufactured information" in its attempt to create a more damaging news story about the gas tanks in pickups.

Putting information into play is not easy. Sometimes the facts are hard to know, if they can be known. For instance, one of the widely debated issues is whether facts support the conclusion that we are experiencing global warming. Related to that is the information that would indicate what causes contribute to global warming, if it is occurring.

Despite the difficulty of knowing the facts, they should help ground interpretations of problems and the development of solutions. One of the obligations of effective public relations is to share the facts, to inform MAPs, to the extent that facts are available. Issue communication should be informed discussion.

Persuading

Persuading entails convincing and motivating. Activists seek to shape attitudes and motivate people to act on issues. The same can be true for the private sector organizations as well as government.

Evaluations are often a key part of issue communication. For instance, if people believe that toys are unsafe, they will not buy them. Toy manufacturers, first of all, have to be sure that toys are safe and then be in a position to persuade people that they are safe. Safety is an evaluation that can be supported. On environmental quality issues, judgment may prevail over information. For instance, clear-cutting may be seen as an environmentally offensive means for harvesting trees: cutting down acres of trees that take hundreds of years to grow and only minutes to fell.

Issue communication needs to be based on a platform of evaluation as to whether the opinions and evaluations of the various sides can be voiced and considered, and some compromise achieved. Sometimes compromise cannot be achieved. Those are the types of issues that trouble people and organizations for years.

Part of the persuasion that exists with issues is the formulation of public policies that reflect the information and opinions of the issue disputants. Public policy is the written or unwritten guidelines that guide personal and organizational behaviors. Issue discussion focuses on which policies are best for society and the interested parties.

Community activists focused attention on the potential damage that Disney "America" could have on the Virginia countryside. Civil War enthusiasts had different opinions—evaluations—of the way in which the heritage of the veterans and former slaves should be honored. They did not believe that this heritage should be commercialized.

BOX 10.6 WRITING EFFECTIVE ISSUE COMMUNICATION

- Frame the issue discussion in terms of the target stakeholders' self-interests.

- Use fact sheets to provide information.

- State propositions along with their supporting reasons.

- Cast issue statements in terms of narratives that the targeted stakeholders can appreciate.

- Feature the target stakeholders' self-interests as a way to gain interest and frame the issue discussion.

- Consider using Q&A formats.

- Build common ground and use it to frame the discussion of the issues.

- Make sure that your communication features a few relevant message points.

Building Relationships

The quality of relationships affects the ways in which issue discussants resolve differences and engage in collaborative decision making. Today's public relations requires effective relationships, which help parties to solve differences and reduce conflict based on issues. The way in which issues are managed is likely to help or harm relationships.

For this reason, we stress that the elements of an effective relationship need to guide the operations, communication style, and content, as well as the approach to resolving differences about issues:

- *Openness:* Fosters two-way communication that involves listening/sharing valuable information. Issue discussion is best when the participants are open, responsive, respectful, candid, and honest.
- *Trustworthiness:* Builds trust by being reliable, nonexploitative, and dependable. The more diverse the issue is, the more important trust becomes a factor in the quality of communication. Spokespersons should demonstrate that they deserve to be trusted because they are committed to being valued and credible sources of information, evaluation, and policy position statements. They demonstrate trust by acting beyond their self-interests.
- *Cooperation:* Cooperates to make decisions by engaging in collaborative decision making that ensures that the needs/wants of the organization and its stakeholders are met. Issue communication is likely to fail if it does not demonstrate a commitment to work with the interested parties to frame the issue, obtain the proper information, evaluate the information, consider and reconcile value differences, and achieve a wise and widely accepted policy. The parties demonstrate their commitment to these ends by being cooperative in their discussion of issues.
- *Alignment:* Aligns interests, rewards, and goals with those of its stakeholders. One reason for an issue is that interests are not aligned or seem to not be aligned. Issue discussants increase the quality of issue communication by seeking positions that align the interests of the discussants.
- *Compatibility of views/opinions:* Fosters mutual understanding and agreement, cocreates meaning. Issues by definition arise because views and opinions are not or seem not to be compatible. They seem to be at odds with one another. Issue discussants are wise to find the common ground they share with their stakeholders and use that to resolve differences.
- *Commitment:* Supports the community by being involved in it, investing in it, and displaying commitment to it. Issues arise because one entity believes that another entity is committed to different goals or means to achieve goals. Issue discussants should demonstrate that they are committed to discovering solutions to problems and resolving differences.

By applying these characteristics of a relationship, issue discussants can increase the quality of communication and reduce the friction that forces them apart. The objective is to find a common ground and be committed to using it to formulate and implement the best policies, those that satisfy the interests of the organization and its stakeholders.

The communication, in this way, needs to be strategic. All of the efforts of the issues management plan need to be focused on solving the rhetorical problem that the organization creates or that is brought up by other issue discussants. The sequence of strategic decisions is featured in Box 10.7.

BOX 10.7 STRATEGIC APPROACHES TO ISSUE RESPONSE

- *Rhetorical situation/rhetorical problem:* Circumstances surrounding the organization that will affect its ability to achieve what it desires. It must know, consider, and adapt to its situation if it is to achieve its mission. Among the key factors that affect the mission of the organization are issues that it raises, as does its stakeholder publics. The organization either creates a rhetorical problem or wisely responds to a rhetorical problem.

- *Objectives* (mission and vision): The goals the organization seeks to accomplish in its effort to achieve its mission. The organization needs to solve the problem so that it can seize opportunities or reduce the conflict associated with to the threats posed by stakeholders who press issues.

- *Plan:* The means by which the organization strategically intends to accomplish its objectives. The plan includes message development options and actions. The plan is a means by which the organization raises and promotes issues or responds to them to reduce the likelihood that others will impose undue standards on the organization.

- *Implementation:* Strategic options that are chosen and budgeted to be used as the means for putting the plan into operation. One of the liabilities of a hypervigilant organization is that lots of issues analysis can be done and position papers can be prepared. The organization needs to do something, the right something, to see that the issue resolves to the mutual benefit of it and its stakeholder publics.

- *Feedback/evaluation:* Hard and soft evidence used to determine the extent to which the strategic options as implemented are accomplishing what they must and should for the organization to achieve its mission, in light of the situation. One of the key kinds of research is evaluative. This can include, for instance, survey research that determines whether key audiences and publics believe an issue and feel that it should be sustained. Feedback can also be obtained by monitoring the trajectory of an issue in the legislative process.

Issue communication requires the development of message points that capture and express positions that are defensible. Several guidelines can be employed as practitioners strategically develop message points to be fostered during issue communication. The following guidelines can serve as best practices that can increase the effectiveness of issue communication:

- Assert and defend facts relevant to the issue.
- Simplify issues and relate them to stakeholder interests and values.
- Demonstrate a commitment to issue stewardship.

- Acknowledge and address genuine differences of opinion and policy.
- Avoid character assaults on critics; acknowledge disagreements, and rise above the fray.
- Present issue positions so that they correspond to or improve the prevailing societal narratives.
- Cast public policy issue positions so that they build mutually beneficial relationships.
- Work to keep your side of the issue alive in media reports and with opinion leaders.
- Avoid addressing issues that will die because proponents are unable to sustain them because they lack a foundation of fact or emotional appeal.
- Encourage credible third parties to support and comment favorably on your issue positions.
- Create issue dialogues that demonstrate commitment to the community interest.
- Build message content and use communication vehicles that foster the best interests of the community.
- Open the dialogue to many participants rather than ignoring or trying to stifle legitimate and concerned voices.
- Frame your issue positions in terms of the mutual interests of key stakeholders and the organization you are representing.

Collaborative Decision Making

The traditional version of issue communication, as well as public relations, called for organizations to debate issues in public. Today's public relations acknowledges that the strategic option may have merit, but collaborative decision making is a vital part of issue communication. It brings interested parties together and gives them a voice in solving the rhetorical problems for forming the best policies.

Chapter 13 delves deeply into collaborative decision making, but the following best practices can help you to address strategic issue communication:

- Know the mutual benefits to be achieved through issues management.
- Look for points of consensus and "win-win" outcomes.
- Avoid adopting a "win-loss" approach when discussing issues and resolving conflict.
- Frame issue positions in terms of the mutual best interests of stakeholders and the community.
- Recognize that most issues entail multiple stakeholding advocates, each of whom has a unique interest in the issue and its resolution.
- Demonstrate community interest and issue stewardship by sharing the floor rather than by dominating it.
- Frame issue positions in terms of your technical expertise, community goodwill, and commitment to solve problems.
- Recognize that activists like to moralize issues. Adapt your issue position to the values of your key stakeholders.

If issues are managed successfully, they can result in compromise and mutually beneficial decisions. If they are managed badly, they can result in crisis. Also, crisis can become an issue. Several guidelines may help to prevent an issue from becoming a crisis:

- Prevent media reporters, nongovernmental organizations (NGOs), and government officials from framing issues without your comments. If you are silent, your position cannot influence the way in which issues are framed. This can result in a discussion that forces you to take a reactive rather than a proactive stance on the issues.
- Be proactive; become engaged in the dialogue as early as possible.
- Avoid being characterized as unresponsive and irresponsible in regard to the issue.
- Inject a calm and rational tone into issue discussions to counterbalance any moralizing and hyperbolic tone that is introduced by activists, media, and government officials.
- Admit when you are wrong—have taken an indefensible issue position—and demonstrate stewardship by taking the proper corrective actions.
- Avoid personalizing the issues by attacking the character or integrity of opponents.
- Work to frame issues that favor your interest and the interests of your key stakeholders.

Cocreate Meaning

Communication and other issue response options can be used to reduce conflict and foster agreement. Such options assume that both sides in a controversy are likely to give ground in the effort to discover the most satisfying policy option.

Shared narrative can be one means by which issue discussants cocreate meaning that reduces the friction. Issues often arise as one party sets forward a narrative that paints an unfavorable picture of some company, industry, nonprofit (including activists), or governmental agency. This narrative unfolds as news stories. It features the persona of the good players and of the bad players at odds with one another. It focuses on the scripts of opposition, as well as on plots and themes that feature moral options. Such narratives often pit good against evil. Activists are particularly adept and rhetorically privileged to make such dramatic statements.

To resolve issues, discussants need to cocreate and gain acceptance for narratives that feature the cooperation and harmony of issues management, which leads to positive outcomes for the parties concerned.

Identification is a powerful rhetorical force in issue communication. It pits persons who identify with good causes against people who are characterized as supporting bad causes. In environmental battles, identifications may be seen as being based on (a) environmentalists who want to protect the environment against (b) corporate or governmental interests who would destroy nature. Issue motivators are a primary source of the basis for identification. Persons who oppose certain chemicals position themselves as calling for others to identify with them for good health, by opposing the forces that would destroy health.

To resolve issues, discussants need to cocreate identifications that feature the common ground and common interests that resolve differences and foster mutually beneficial outcomes.

People can feel outrage when they receive evidence and are asked to evaluate specific actions that offend their value systems. They have seen a forest that has been clear-cut, for instance, even if it is only in the publications of environmental activists. They share the concern of parents everywhere who strive to prevent harm to their children that results from unsafe toys. They have experienced unfair actions and therefore can empathize with others who are experiencing unfair treatment. In this way, issue communication can foster symbolic convergence by having people think about, experience, and recall experiences that they share that create concern for the policies and actions of the offending organizations.

To resolve issues, discussants need to focus on facts, evaluations, and policy options by addressing the common experiences of publics and audiences to help them think of positive resolution of problems and the constructive end to conflict.

This section ends with a discussion of issue communication tactics. That is the final step in a series of issues management efforts to creatively respond to threats and opportunities as ways of advancing the mission and vision of the organization. Issue discussants create rhetorical problems that can require new and improved standards of corporate responsibility to reduce the legitimacy gaps. Issue monitoring is required to help the organization listen to its critics, understand its situation, and adapt to that situation. Part of that adaptation is to be a constructive issue communicator who is dedicated to helping to solve problems with the best information, persuasion, relationship building, collaborative decision making, and cocreated meaning. The next section reviews communication tools that can be used in issue communication.

▶ Selecting Issue Response Tools

Sophisticated campaigns strategically utilize every communication channel available to reach key publics and build or adapt to zones of meaning that are mutually beneficial. In this effort, many modes of communication are worth consideration. The options in issue communication range from paid advertisements, to placed information through traditional public relations strategies, to responses to media inquiries and statements made by various issue discussants.

In addition to developing content and working to present it in ways that are useful to issue discussants, practitioners need to strategically select the communication vehicles that foster issues management.

Many vehicles are available for the presentation of the issue positions favored by an organization. Some of these may need to be placed in the media, either through advertising or placed news stories or responses to reporters' inquiries. Whatever form the statements take, they should be based on issue papers. Organizations are wise to prepare issue papers that they can use to advance their position on issues. These position papers can be used to respond to critics and media inquiries. Several considerations are worth keeping in mind as you develop issue papers. A position paper can be developed for each issue by following these guidelines:

- Discuss issues by using words that stakeholders can understand. Some issues are complex because they involve technical jargon. This jargon needs to be used in discussing or debating issues with experts but must be translated for lay audiences and publics.
- Feature the component parts of the issue discussion, whether fact, value, or policy.
- Present opposing views and more than one side of an issue; demonstrate how your side is the best point of view given the analysis.
- Avoid using threats and other strategies that seem to privilege your position and interest while disempowering your opposition.
- State both sides of the issue, your client organization's and the opposing view.
- Present information in "layers," starting with summaries or capstone statements, and then providing in-depth discussions. The extra layers offer supporting materials to enrich your organization's position on the issue.
- State conclusions in ways that are memorable and easily incorporated into conversation. Frame these conclusions so they can be used as talking points by persons who speak on the issue. Speeches can be based on these talking points, but so can media conferences and backgrounders.
- Integrate the organization's expertise and reputation into issue statements.
- Demonstrate a tone of fairness and regard for the issue discussants.

Issue communication is challenging because it often requires the ability to discuss complex technical issues in terms that can be understood by the lay public. Informative persuasive messages need to be developed that can be understood and used in news stories by reporters. These messages may also need to be targeted to well-educated and technically savvy listeners and readers.

The challenge in issue communication is to develop carefully tailored messages and then to make them available to publics and audiences through a wide array of communication vehicles. Here is a list of such vehicles. This list is not intended to be exhaustive, but suggests the wide range of possible means for reaching key stakeholders.

- Issue advertising
- Sponsored books/editorials
- Negotiation
- Executive comments
- Public affairs programming
- Press releases/media relations
- Personal contact with opinion leaders by key staff and management personnel
- Video and satellite presentations to internal and external audiences
- Congressional testimony/public hearings

- Mailings to constituencies
- Bill stuffers
- Conference papers presentations
- Trials
- Open houses/issue workshops
- Educational information relevant to activist, government, or industry issues that can be distributed through schools
- Joint research efforts
- Citizens advisory panels/committees
- Placed and commissioned articles
- Employee communication
- Internal and external newsletters
- Speakers bureaus
- Annual financial or special topic reports
- Videos mailed to key audiences and on request
- Op-eds placed on editorial pages
- Talk show appearances
- E-mail and bulletin boards
- Billboards
- Special issue documents
- Scholarly papers (commissioned)
- Citizens advisory committees
- Lobbying
- Web sites
- Legislative position papers
- Collaborative decision making

Several guidelines are useful to keep in mind when selecting and using communication vehicles. You should look for and develop vehicles that give you third-party endorsement. For instance, you may ask experts to comment on the issue position you take. You can tell reporters that such experts look forward to being interviewed for news stories and editorial comment. Such third-party experts can be invited to participate in panels, hearings, talk shows, and citizens advisory panels/committees.

Citizens advisory panels/committees (CAPs/CACs) are a widely used tool of community relations. Companies that operate near residential communities and pose a health or safety threat to those communities find CAPs/CACs to be a useful vehicle for on-the-record discussions that help to bridge gaps of understanding, agreement, and satisfaction. Influential community leaders, concerned citizens, and company representatives come together on a periodic basis, such as monthly, to work through agendas of policy issues, performance concerns, and technical information. CAPs/CACs have been operated by the chemical-manufacturing industry, the nuclear waste management organizations, and water quality organizations. They have been fostered by companies, industries, and governmental agencies as a means for demonstrating openness, trustworthiness, and commitment to the community.

The Web is a crucial part of issue discussion (Web Watcher). Shell UK began to put information on its Web site to keep its publics and audiences informed of the policy development progress, technical information about the Brent Spar, and government review of various proposals. Greenpeace engaged in a Web site battle. Greenpeace did not argue with the technical analysis as much as it criticized the use of the ocean as a toxic-waste dumping ground. Most objective observers thought Greenpeace hyperbolized the issue, but its morality stance forced Shell UK to change its strategy for disposing of the oil collection buoy (Heath, 1998).

Coombs (1998) quite accurately pointed out that the Web has become a valuable communication resource for activists. Activists can post their issue positions. These can be searched by interested readers. Instead of spending money to reach interested publics, audiences, and followers, these people come to the Web site. Such Web sites give a global reach for the dissemination of information, evaluation, and policy messages. They can be updated instantly.

Companies and governmental agencies sometimes even link with specific Web sites to demonstrate their openness and responsiveness. Such Web sites allow for issue monitoring and analysis. Frequently asked questions (FAQs) signal what the discussants believe are the crucial issues. Discussion rooms gather the comments by critics, making these readily available for issue monitors and analysts.

Interactive vehicles have strong potentiality for fostering discussion rather than division. Such vehicles empower the participants. They allow stakeholders to ask questions, express concerns, and obtain desired information. Forums can be created that prevent opposing issue advocates from dominating the discussion of issues. For instance, instead of creating a forum with an "open mike," organizations have recognized the advantages of hosting an open house. Tables are made available so that concerned citizens can meet with experts and issue advocates. They can talk and obtain information, rather than listen to endless and often unproductive presentations by opposing sides who take turns at the "open mikes."

Issue communicators have learned that steady, continual, and open communication does more good than one-shot issue advertising. That does not mean that issue advertising is not a valuable tool, but it needs to be part of a larger set of issue communication vehicles. For instance, companies recognize the virtue of using multiple vehicles, including the Internet and employee publications, to equip employees with information, evaluations, and policy positions they can use to support the company point of view.

Collective decision making and strategic negotiation are crucial parts of the efforts to resolve issues. Some activists do not like to participate in such forums, for exactly the same reason that some companies, industries, and governmental agencies do not. Such recalcitrant players like to control the information, persuasive arguments, and policy statements. That communication style leads to division rather than reconciliation.

This section has reviewed communication response options, including strategies for developing issue position papers and for selecting and using communication vehicles. The last part of this chapter provides a brief review of how public relations practitioners can evaluate the success of their issues management program.

▶ Evaluating Issues Management Programs

The primary sign of a successful issues management program is that it keeps issues from becoming crises. Some issues can be killed because they lack merit. They cannot sustain themselves because they lack the information and evaluation to justify change.

Some issues, however, seem unlikely to end. Certain industries are likely to work on issues related to environmental quality for the foreseeable future. Environmentalists, for instance, work to hold industries and governmental agencies to ever-higher standards. Animal rights groups, such as PETA, will oppose the killing of animals until that practice stops. For such issues, evaluation focuses less on the outcome than on the process. It is not a matter of ending the issue, but keeping it from derailing the organization's mission.

Research is a valuable means for measuring success. Inherent in the process of issue monitoring is the use of research to measure support for various issue positions. Key publics' and audiences' opinions are important. If their tendency is to agree with the organization's issue position, that is good news. If they differ from the organization, it needs to make strategic changes.

As well as surveying the opinions of audiences and publics on the issue, companies, industries, and governmental agencies can use surveys to determine whether they are considered to be trusted, credible participants in the issue discussions.

Content analysis of media and community forum comments can indicate whether an issue is ending, dying, or continuing. Similar monitoring efforts can be devoted to seeing whether the power structures of society, such as legislative bodies, are continuing to discuss and take action on issues. Evaluative research can examine whether prestigious figures are taking stances that legitimize the issue or key issue positions.

Evaluation can focus on the content of issues. Are the informative and persuasive messages proposed by the organization being accepted or rejected by the issue discussants? Is the controversy ending or escalating? Is the relationship becoming harmonious or contentious?

Conclusion

Issues management is not only a process but also a way of thinking and responding. It was developed in a highly defensive reaction to critics of corporate policies who loudly voiced their discontent in the 1960s and 1970s. Since then, issues management has become a defining approach to responding to societal change and criticism.

The wise practitioner knows that he or she cannot truly manage issues if "manage" is thought of as being synonymous with "control the outcome." But as important voices in society, organizations of all kinds have become the speakers who shape issues. They frame the issues. They provide information, persuade, create relationships, collaboratively work with others to make decisions, and cocreate meaning.

In this way, issues management can help public relations practitioners to work for a more fully functional society. The society is one where voices of many kinds work together to solve problems and build mutually beneficial relationships.

Professional Reflection

The Brilliant Evolution of Issue Management

**Anthony Jaques
Senior Practitioner in
Issue Management
Author of *Don't
Just Stand There***

As a quirk of time and fate, I am one of those public affairs practitioners who began working in the field of issue management—initially in a government role and later in a corporate environment—when the discipline was still in its early days and when I was unaware that such a discipline existed.

Like many of my contemporaries, what we did seemed like a logical extension and application of basic but sound public affairs practices. And it is no coincidence that this concept of issue management—the application of proven practices within a formalized framework—has been one of the strengths of issue management as it has developed since the early days.

Despite almost three decades as a recognized business and academic discipline, the great strength of issue management remains its fundamentally simple principles— to identify and define issues early enough to facilitate proactive intervention; to set objectives to enable the achievement of goals designed to work toward positive planned outcomes; to apply the proven tools of public affairs in assigning and achieving tactics designed to deliver these outcomes; and to put processes in place to measure and communicate progress.

When I was first exposed to issue management as a formal discipline, I soon became dismayed that these brilliant fundamentals risked being overshadowed by an excessive emphasis on process and analysis which threatened the beautiful simplicity which underlies the discipline. Indeed some of the thinking within issue management was verging on the classic "paralysis by analysis."

As one commentator remarked in the early 1980s, "Corporations spend more time trying to label issues than they devote to managing issues."

It is undeniable that effective issue management demands robust processes to identify issues early, to analyze those issues and to assign them properly considered priorities.

But in my experience it is equally undeniable that identification, analysis and prioritization are of no tangible value when they do not lead to action. Issue management is an active verb which demands action to work toward real, bottom-line outcomes.

From the early 1990s onward there seems to have been a swing toward a more action-oriented focus. Part of this has been the realization among professional issue management practitioners that issue management processes must be robust enough to survive in an increasingly aggressive "show me" management environment where every function is evaluated on its contribution to the corporate bottom line.

I would like to think that I contributed in some small way to this trend by the development of my own four-step issue management action plan which was published in the book *Don't Just Stand There: The Do-It Plan for Effective Issue Management.* My "Do-It Plan" published in 2000 was a deliberate counter to the excessive complexity of multi-stage work process models which owed more to overdependence on computer-based systems than to intrinsically sound strategic planning.

It is therefore perhaps ironic that the other key element in the renewed action focus of evolving issue management is itself made possible only by computers—namely the democratization of issue management fueled by growth of the Internet.

Issue management was largely developed by and for corporations and their consultants, and they continue to exercise a powerful role in the promotion and shaping of the tool. But it is growing into a much wider discipline which has been embraced by activists, NGOs (nongovernmental organizations) and community groups, particularly through empowerment by the Internet.

While many of the activists and NGOs may not use the syntax and vocabulary of formal issue management, there is no doubt that they are helping extend the boundaries of what is possible.

Indeed some commentators such as the Canadian Ross Irvine now argue that activists and NGOs are pioneering new applications of

communication theory to issue management and that, in some respects, they are in fact showing the way to the corporate rivals.

This has caused consternation in some sectors, especially among some old-school practitioners and conservative think tanks who appear to regard the intrusion by activists and NGOs as a challenge and a risk. In my view this arises at least in part through confusing the activists' sometimes unwelcome messages and content with recognition of their innovation and creativity.

Corporations and governments—typically the target of activists and NGOs—need to develop a proper modus vivendi to accommodate this democratization of issue management.

However, for all the innovation and crossover into other public affairs activities, there remains a very real need to maintain and continue evolving the formal discipline.

In that respect I was privileged to lead an international project for the Issue Management Council to develop a tool to help organizations benchmark their own progress and achievement in implementing the issue management discipline itself. It quickly became evident that it is not possible to identify a "best model" which would apply across all organizations and circumstances. But it also became clear that there is a good amount of common ground on what an effective issue management system should deliver, and on which characteristics are demonstrated by excellent models.

The result was to crystallize such characteristics into defined indicators of Best Practice, which were published in 2004 in the newsletter and on the Web site of the

Professional Reflection

Issue Management Council (www.issuemanagement.org).

Looking forward it seems clear that the academic and theoretical basis of issue management will continue to be developed and sustained by the corporate sector and organizations such as the Issue Management Council. But it is also clear that the democratization of the discipline will continue apace and the professional practitioners must be more willing to learn and adapt.

Issue management is a brilliant tool which has the power to transform organizational culture and values, to motivate and mobilize citizens and to help make lasting change

to government and society. But to do this it must continue to balance academic and intellectual rigor with street-smart implementation.

Over a long period of writing about, teaching and practicing issue management I have remained firmly committed to an early realization—the two greatest obstacles to effective issue management are (1) failure to set a clear objective and (2) inability or unwillingness to take action. No matter how issue management evolves in the future, I am convinced that these should continue as our guide.

SOURCE: Reprinted with permission from Anthony Jaques.

FURTHER EXPLORATION

10

Ethical Quandary: Building Issues Ethics on Moral Principles

Explain at least three ethical reasons that you would use when advising a client or your nonprofit organization's executive management that wants to take a stand on an issue that has the potential of maturing into a change in legislation or regulation. You know or fear several facts, which could have explosive consequences regarding your current and future tax status as a nonprofit organization: (1) The client/organization is engaged in fund-raising activities that cost a great deal and yield very little income; (2) executives in the organization spend lavish amounts of money on their salaries, trips, consultants, and office space and furnishings; and (3) executives routinely and falsely claim the organization serves the needs of hundreds of hungry and homeless people and that they lobby for increased governmental funding to help these people.

An issue has arisen because of an investigative report by one reporter. Other reporters are also trying to do stories on the organization. One of the concerns expressed by these reporters is that many nonprofits may be engaged in similar kinds of activities. Management wants to challenge claims made by the one reporter that the nonprofit has falsely alleged that it needs donations and contributors to its fund-raising because the number of members of the community who need social services has increased. You believe this claim to be untrue but cannot get a straight answer from the executives. The organization has asked you to file an annual report that shows that only modest amounts have been spent on overhead: executive salaries, trips, consultants, and offices.

Ethical decisions can be based on high moral principle—doing what is right—and on pragmatics—what works is good. Would you build your case on these principles?

What three points would you make to guide the selection of public relations responses to the rhetorical problem? How are these three points connected to the strategic responses you would advise making to solve the rhetorical problem? Can you draw on Chapter 9 to help you address the ethics of this case? Must you be sure the organization is "good" before you can communicate effectively on its behalf?

Summary Questions

1. Define the term *issue* and discuss the difference between issues of fact, value (evaluation), and policy.

2. Explain how changes in public policy can serve as threats and opportunities. Why does issue management work to reduce the costs borne by an organization?

3. Explain the legitimacy gap and indicate its implications for changes in operations and communication as an organization seeks to reduce the gap. Why do activists try to increase the gap?

4. What does issue management have to do with narratives (especially those by reporters and activists), influencing choices, and aligning interests?

5. How can issue management help managements to position their organizations and set objectives?

6. Define corporate responsibility. Why is it important to issue management?

7. What are the steps and strategies issues managers use to monitor issues? Where do issues originate? Why is scanning like radar? How are issues identified and analyzed? How are issues monitored? How can issue monitoring help an organization to know how to set its issue priorities? Why is a matrix desired for the structure of an issue-monitoring and analysis team?

8. What does it mean when people say they need to "frame" an issue? What communication options are unique to issue communication? What is the nature of a rhetorical problem for issue management? Why is collaborative decision making such a vital part of issue communication? What should go into an issue position paper?

9. List six tools, including the Internet, that you might use in issue communication. How can they serve the purpose of effective efforts to reach targeted audiences?

10. How do you evaluate the success of issue management?

Exercises

1. Select an organization, and identify three issues that pose opportunities or threats. How should the organization position its strategic business plan to avoid collisions over these issues? Are you looking at issues related to a company, industry, governmental agency, or nonprofit? How can the issues affect the future of the organization?

2. Think of an issue as a narrative. It is likely to be presented in the media so that there are good and bad characters. Discuss an issue that is important to you. What are the plot, theme, and scripts that characterize this issue?

3. Why should issues managers try to align the interests of their clients and those of the persons or organizations who are pressing an issue? Think of an issue that is important to you. What are the interests that can be aligned? Can you explain the conflict or controversy over the issue in terms of misaligned interests?

4. Think of an issue that is important to you. How does it pose threats or offer opportunities to two or more businesses, industries, nonprofits, or governmental agencies?

5. Reexamine the discussion of a legitimacy gap. Explain why a legitimacy gap occurs. Taking an issue that is important to you, use the concept of the legitimacy gap to explain why an issue exists. Identify whether this is an issue of fact, value, or policy—or more than one.

6. Revisit the challenges in the issues-monitoring section above. Select an organization. Prepare a short report for "management." In the report, indicate three issues you have found through scanning. Identify the issues by type of motivator (safety, equality, environmental quality, or fairness) and by type of issue (fact, evaluation, or policy). Analyze the issue to determine three message points that are central to the issue. Identify the organization (or industry sector or nonprofit category) and its publics. Indicate what the publics believe the problem to be and why they are cognitively involved with the problem. Predict the factors that will keep the issue alive or cause it to decline. Identify sources of information where you can track this issue.

Recommended Readings

Berger, B. K. (2001). Private issues and public policy: Locating the corporate agenda in agenda-setting theory. *Journal of Public Relations Research, 13*, 91–123.

Brown, J. K. (1979). *The business of issues: Coping with the company's environments.* New York: Conference Board.

Chase, W. H. (1984). *Issue management: Origins of the future.* Stamford, CT: Issue Action.

Crable, R. E., & Vibbert, S. L. (1985). Managing issues and influencing public policy. *Public Relations Review, 11*(2), 3–16.

Dennis, L. B. (Ed.). (1996). *Practical public affairs in an era of change: A communications guide for business, government, and college.* Lanham, MD: University Press of America and Public Relations Society of America.

Nelson, R. A. (1996). Activist groups and the new technologies: Influencing the public affairs agenda. In L. B Dennis (Ed.), *Practical public affairs in an era of change: A communications guide for business, government, and college* (pp. 413–422). Lanham, MD: University Press of America and Public Relations Society of America.

Tucker, K., & Trumpfheller, B. (1993). Building an issue management system. *Public Relations Journal, 49*(11), 36–37.

Selecting Media, Technologies, and Communication Tools

11

"Favorite University": Using Many Tools to Build Academic Relationships

P revious chapters have introduced their specific topics by featuring a carefully selected, actual vignette. This chapter takes a different tactic. To feature the discussion of media types and tools that practitioners use, this chapter asks you to consider one of the most available examples: your college or university. These organizations strive to create, maintain, and restore strategic relationships. Think of "Favorite University," a fictional college or university that utilizes many media types as it works with its stakeholders.

Start by considering the print media that campuses utilize. Campus newspapers offer the university many communication opportunities. Student reporters feature campus activities, including sports and arts. They announce important events and procedures, such as class and enrollment schedules. In this reporting, professional communicators provide much of the information that is ultimately relayed by the reporters to student readers. Campuses use newsletters to communicate with employees, as well as memos. These newsletters feature faculty, student, and staff accomplishments. They report changes in policy and present views of senior university administrators. Newsletters, as well as the campus newspaper, offer space to announce student and campus arts and entertainment events. Colleges use annual reports to describe the challenges they are facing as well as the strategies and accomplishments that shape the future of the academic and research programs. Departments and

programs publish materials that inform readers of activities, policies, accomplishments, and challenges. For instance, many academic programs and departments publish booklets and pamphlets that tell what they offer and what is unique about them. Athletic programs, as well as the arts, give details about sports, theater, and music.

Campuses use newsletters and various reports to communicate externally. Much of this information is targeted at alumni, donors, community leaders, and legislators (especially if the college or university receives state funding). Universities as well as individual academic programs circulate recruiting materials to prospective students and their parents. They send prospective employers information about academic and research programs and student accomplishments. Brochures are designed to support fund-raising activities. Sports information

Reaching Alumni Through Print

SOURCE: Reprinted with permission from Western State College, Crested Butte Printing & Publishing, and artist Dale Russell Smith.

directors utilize media relationships to draw attention to the athletic program to feature athletic accomplishments and to attract fans, alumni, and donors.

Electronic tools are used along with print. Campus radio and television stations, as well as those in the community, provide outlets of campus news. Campus radio and television stations work to attract donors as well as support fund-raising initiatives for other programs. Although today, they are being replaced by other media, videos are prepared to target key audiences, prospective students and their parents, athletes and professional coaches, and contributors to the arts, for example. Campuses are quickly moving to use the Internet as a key communication tool. They make their library facilities available for student, faculty, and public use. They feature faculty, programs, and research accomplishments. Web sites service students by helping them to know academic and social calendars. Campuses often place their catalogues and student handbooks online. This valuable information allows students to explore academic programs, shop for classes, and have policy and procedures information readily available. Such sites often have special rooms for alumni. Students can use Web sites to enroll in classes. Faculty use them to communicate with students.

To communicate about themselves, campuses compose their histories, develop feature stories, issue media releases, and provide faculty and administration as spokespersons for the campus and on topics relevant to the faculty's scholarly interests. Campuses provide lecture series. They invite featured speakers. They engage in forums with other organizations in the community.

Universities use multiple channels to reach diverse markets, audiences, and publics. They work to increase awareness, to tell (inform) about themselves and to attract and persuade students, donors, and supporters. Campuses use many vehicles to listen to their constituents, including meetings, interviews, and surveys. Sometimes campuses engage in collaborative decision making needed to build long-term, mutually beneficial relationships. They publicize and promote their academic, research, athletic, arts, and service programs. Many public relations tools serve the purpose of generating financial support for academic, research, athletic, and artistic programs. Tools are used to attract employers that seek their next generation of talented graduates.

Events are vital tools used by campuses, especially sports, homecoming, and graduation. Commencement attracts parents, relatives, and friends to campus and portrays it in a favorable, even joyous light. This event focuses substantial attention on student accomplishments to demonstrate the quality of students and the academic programs that prepare them for their careers. Arts and entertainment use events, such as announcements of art exhibits and featured musical and theater achievements and productions.

This chapter explains how communication is scheduled to coincide with key events and to be sustained over time. Campuses realize that they need to communicate all of the time, but do so in carefully developed cycles and patterns. News on athletic events and accomplishments becomes more or less frequent depending on the schedule and success of the teams. For instance, if a team is doing well, the amount of information supplied on the student athletes is likely to increase around tournament times. Outstanding players receive special attention. The end of the semester as well as the beginning are key communication times, receiving more attention. Campuses often engage in highly publicized fund-raising. During these periods, the amount and varied types of communication increase. Statements describing the financial needs of the campus increase as budgetary discussion in legislatures goes into full swing. Thus, communication is sustained throughout the year but is likely to increase in volume and type when specific markets, audiences, and publics (MAPs) need to be reached. Vehicles are designed to work in coordination. For instance, as a budgetary request is made to the state legislature, related information might be supplied to alumni, community leaders, and students/parents to inform them of the needs of the campus and to persuade them to lend their support in legislative sessions. Today and in the foreseeable future, the Web will play a vital role in communication. As a Web Watcher, compare your campus Web use with that of other colleges or universities. How well does each achieve its communication objectives?

Strategic Selection of Communication Channels

Today's public relations professionals select from an assortment of communication channels and tools. Over the years, unique mixes of media and other communication tools have been utilized. In this regard, don't forget how architecture and other tools have served the needs of communicators as they have dealt with reputation, relationships, issues, risks, crisis, publicity, and promotion.

Traditional channels include newspapers, television, magazines, and radio, as well as speeches and meetings. In recent years, public relations professionals have added new public relations tools to their arsenal: fax transmissions, satellite feeds, Internet, Web sites, multimedia presentations, and CD-ROMs to build mutually beneficial relationships. Practitioners have many tools to select from in their efforts to build specific kinds of relationships.

In planning to communicate with a target MAP, practitioners assess the quality of each relationship to determine what needs to be done or said to strengthen, build, or repair it. Once a practitioner decides to communicate with the key MAP, media planning identifies the best and most cost-effective means to interact with it. As practitioners formulate a media plan, they ask how much exposure each medium generates with various targets. How often should a message be repeated to promote and publicize a product or service? Where should messages be positioned within a medium? Sometimes it is better to have a story in the business section than on the front page. How should they be designed to take advantage of the unique characteristics of each medium? Should ads be placed, or should efforts be made to obtain free media attention? Which media and communication tools do the most to foster the desired relationships?

Selection of channels and tools varies by relationship and public relations function. For publicity, the goal of any public relations professionals must be to use tools that maximize the reach and frequency with which a target MAP is exposed to the client organization's messages, while managing costs. For collaborative decision making, meetings and chat rooms on the Web might be two tools that increase the interaction needed to resolve conflict.

For these reasons, pause for a moment to reconsider the strategic planning logic developed in previous chapters. Recall Chapter 4 discussed research and Chapter 5 explained strategic planning. Those chapters set the foundation for action (Chapter 6) and evaluation (Chapter 7). Skilled practitioners couple strategically useful ideas with the logics of ethics and legal considerations, theory, strategic issues management, and publicity/promotion (which will be discussed in Chapter 12). All of that material comes together when the practitioner is ready to communicate. One of the central realities of today's public relations is the need to know a lot and think strategically before starting to communicate. By the time you are thinking seriously about media, you will have engaged in situational assessment to determine what rhetorical problems need to be solved. That solution may involve one or many message development options. Those message development options may require strategic consideration of the content of the message to be used and the tools that will be employed in its use. Now you are ready to seek to use a medium. (In the case of crisis, that choice might be made by others.)

That strategic planning and response logic is summarized in Figure 11.1. A quick review of that figure can assist your recall of the strategic options that culminate in the choices featured in this chapter. After you identify your objectives, consider the situation, identify the rhetorical problem, determine the best response to that problem, and strategically form messages to address that problem, what is left? You have to decide which communication channels and tools can and must be used to respond to the needs and concerns of the MAP you are addressing.

The selection of a communication channel is a strategic decision. Sometimes practitioners have no choice. If they receive a media inquiry, they respond to that inquiry, often questions raised privately or publicly by a reporter. At other times, practitioners create a plan that is to be implemented. Channels may be unidirectional or interactive.

After a target MAP has been identified, the savvy practitioner selects the most cost-effective channels of communication for the greatest impact. Selecting channels may entail a media mix strategy that will ensure repeat exposure and saturation. The selection of communication channels and the media mix strategy should always be based on accomplishing organizational objectives. Such selection may be made in concert and coordination with marketing and advertising specialists. It may result in integrated communication whereby each of these disciplines tailors messages to their MAPs. To be a successful practitioner, you need a working knowledge of spoken, written, visual, and multiple media channels.

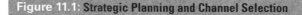

Figure 11.1: Strategic Planning and Channel Selection

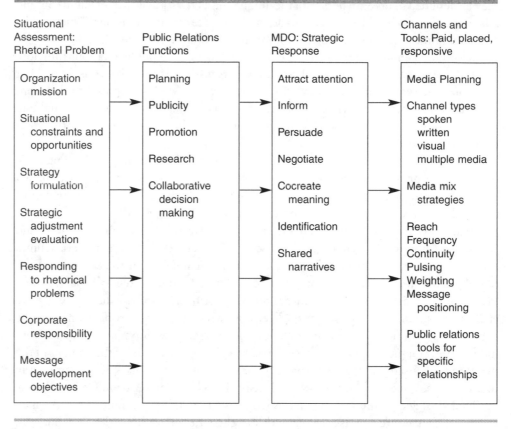

To help you understand the elements of selecting and using channels and tools, we remind you of the importance of strategic planning, move to a discussion of media mix strategies, and conclude with specific public relations tools for each relationship.

As we discussed in Chapter 5, you need a strategic public relations plan that can help the organization accomplish its strategic business plan. To implement the public relations plan, you will be asked to select message development objectives (MDOs), design messages, and place them in the channels as well as use public relation tools that have the greatest impact. This plan can be designed to accomplish specific objectives, such as execute a publicity campaign. It can prepare for contingencies, such as crises.

Any selection of tools and channels can be sharpened by realizing that some are routine and others are situational. If you are engaged in publicity and promotion, you are likely to work with media relationships to see that your organization receives news coverage on a routine, regular schedule. For instance, you might work for weekly, monthly, quarterly, annual, or special occasion coverage. This schedule is typical of retail sales, travel, and entertainment. You want monthly or seasonal coverage of products featured for purchase. For nonprofits, you may strive for quarterly reports in local media to keep donors and users of the nonprofit abreast of its programs and financial needs.

In addition to routine choices, you have situational choices. For instance, if your organization encounters a crisis, you might use tools such as press conferences involving senior management. You would not do that to feature the seasonal sales of gardening tools or seasonal fashion changes, for instance.

If you are working for a nonprofit, your annual report and your three major fundraiser events of the year might be routine. If a pending legislative change threatens the mission of the organization, you are likely to select channels and tools sensitive to this situation.

In addition to these choices, you have to decide what is your territory, what is the territory of advertising, and where you might connect with and support one another. You might want to revisit the discussion of marketing, advertising, public relations, and integrated communication in Chapter 1. Publicity strategies might support advertising and be part of the organization's integrated communication effort. You might have advertising support your public policy issue campaign. You might create an integrated communication campaign in which you partner with advertising.

This discussion becomes clearer by considering four sets of media circumstances under which you are likely to be asked to select the channels through which to communicate with the key MAPs. These choices are paid, placed, responsive, and interactive.

▶Paid

A *paid* channel requires that you buy time or space. Advertising departments purchase time on television or radio. Newspapers, magazines, radio stations, and television stations sell space or time. Advertising relies on this means to ensure that its messages reach the desired MAP when and where those messages can do the most good. If they did not buy the time or space, those messages might not be aired or printed.

Paid advertising is usually not the responsibility of public relations practitioners. They may participate in this communication decision in their support for an organization's integrated communication effort. They also need to know the advertising schedule and media placement so they can work to augment the reach of those messages through traditional public relations tools.

Some public relations tools are "paid." If you put up a Web site, it is a "paid" channel. If you publish an employee newsletter, you have to "pay" for publication costs: the cost of paper, ink, and distribution. You might use an event, which costs money, in coordination with a media advertising blitz to attract attention to the opening of a new store or a shopping center. You have to pay for the costs of the event, but you don't buy the time or space from a media outlet.

▶Placed

One unique talent of a public relations professional is his or her ability to get reporters, editors, and news directors to print or air a story about an organization, product, service, or community relations project, or even a need felt by some group that is being helped by a nonprofit organization. This use of the media is referred to as *placed*. In the jargon of public relations, you place a story by using your media relationships to persuade the reporter or editor that the story needs to be told in a particular way.

Placement of stories requires astute understanding of the journalistic needs of reporters. Each day, reporters, editors, and news directors have X amount of space or time to fill with news and features. They look for stories. They want to feature news-worthy events in their community, such as improvements in a school district or upcoming nonprofit activities. A company may engage in an interesting community relations endeavor, such as having employee volunteers plant trees, engage in a fund-raising fun run, or fix up the homes of the elderly. Each is a good story. The messages create a favorable positive image and reputation for community commitment.

This behind-the-scenes activity is one of the strategic strengths of effective public relations. The messages reach people through a second party—reporters, editors, and news directors—and may include third-party favorable comment. For instance, an elderly person may thank the organization for the improvements. Those messages seem untainted and credible. Even if they get their story told, they cannot control what is said, where and when it is said. So, placed stories are more credible, but the sponsor will have to settle for the story being told in other people's words.

▶Responsive

A third category of communication can be called *responsive*. This means that a reporter, editor, or news director has decided to report on some activities in a community. An activist group or outraged employees demand a response from an organization. For instance, the story may center on low test scores for local school district students, problems of local residents (such as the cost of medicine for the elderly), or pollution caused by industrial processes.

Rather than looking at this situation as a threat, you might see it as an opportunity. Think realistically. The story is going to be told even if you prefer that it not be. If you are representing the school district, you can explain why the scores are low and what is being done to improve them—or that a bond election is needed to raise money to enhance the quality of education. If you are representing a nonprofit that deals with the elderly, you can use this opportunity to request financial and community support to help them deal with their problems. If your client is a manufacturer, you can take this opportunity to demonstrate how the industry continues to abate its pollution. Instead of fearing this opportunity to communicate, seize it. You have a forum. You can get your story out—at no cost to your client. To do so, you need to be responsive.

▶Interactive

One of the most powerful changes in media availability for public relations is the innovation of the Internet and Web. As you recall, we feature Web Watchers throughout the book to familiarize and remind you of the innovative ways in which the Internet is used for public relations. One of its features is *interaction*.

Interaction is also possible through spoken channels, such as a conversation with a reporter or a public hearing—a vital tool for government relations. Practitioners may create committees where local citizens come together to discuss the performance of the company. In such interactive, give-and-take sessions, people can learn from one another. They can voice concerns, raise questions, respond, and listen to one another. Practitioners may engage in open-house sessions in which key publics are invited to visit facilities and learn about the organization. Such meetings are important for transparency. These can lead to collaborative decision making, a topic discussed in detail in Chapter 13.

The Internet and Web offer excellent opportunities for interactive public relations. Customers can ask questions about products, seek advice on how to get the most value from a product, and voice complaints. One does not have to look far to find home pages that allow for dialogue on issues. Companies now invite chat. Two or more organizations can actually engage in a "town meeting" on the Internet. An interested public can watch this dialogue simply by using links or storing favorites in their Web address books. One cost-effective element of this dialogue is that it is available to interested publics on a 24/7 basis. Whereas companies and other organizations used to spend large amounts of money pushing information outward through the media on a "to whom it concerns" basis, they now can store the information so that interested users can find it and compare issue positions.

Based on our discussion of paid, placed, responsive, and interactive media utilization, let's draw two conclusions before we continue. One is that placed and responsive discussion of products, services, image, and public policy issues is typically thought to be more cost-effective than is the paid discussion of these matters. With advertising costs on the rise, organizations look for cheaper means to get their messages across to key MAPs. Public relations can assist in that regard.

The second conclusion is that placed and perhaps even responsive uses of the media have more credibility than paid communication. Paid communication is widely believed by MAPs to be suspect and lack credibility. Articles and news reports seem more objective because the facts have been evaluated and filtered by reporters, editors, and news directors. Home pages may seem to lack credibility of advertising, but some experts think that they are more credible because people know that a company can be easily criticized for putting out false and misleading statements. Web critics can call attention to and debate positions. So, sponsors are more careful in what they say and how they say it. This is part of the strategic benefit of public relations practitioners who know that communication can help or harm relationships.

The next section examines specific types of channels. That discussion offers insights into the strengths and weaknesses of the various channels as ways of linking organizations to their MAPs.

Channels: Linking Organizations and MAPs

Public relations professionals select from an assortment of channels. MAPs may choose the channels through which they want to exert influence or seek information and opinion. Emerging and changing technology make more channels available to the practitioner and its MAPs. One interesting trend is that MAPs are increasingly likely to seek information on demand and exert influence, a desire satisfied by the Internet.

For these reasons, practitioners need to understand the nature of the various channels. To create a cost-effective plan, professionals identify, use, and respond to several categories of channels: spoken, print, visual, and multiple channels, especially new technologies and events.

▶Spoken Channels

Spoken channels range from face-to-face interpersonal interaction and oral presentations to the voices of spokespersons that might be transmitted by radio, video, television, or Web site. Traditional approaches about public relations practice tend to feature written communication, such as press releases, newsletters, and reports. What people may fail to appreciate is the vast amount of spoken interaction that occurs in public relations practice. A conversation between two or more persons is often the most effective form of communication. This may be particularly important for media relations, lobbying, and fund-raising. Even in this era of television, the tradition of U.S. presidents giving radio addresses is alive and well. Thousands of miles were logged during the 2004 presidential race in the United States by the presidential and vice-presidential candidates speaking to live, local audiences. This creates a bit more intimacy in politics in a vast nation with a large population.

Speakers Bureau

Speakers bureaus bring MAPs and organizational speakers together. Practitioners write speeches for executives. They work with other members of the organization to prepare messages and develop effective delivery skills.

Speakers bureaus are widely used to provide information to audiences such as community groups, nonprofit organizations, professional societies, neighborhood clubs, and groups of concerned citizens. This communication channel increases an organization's visible presence in the community and fosters personalized interaction between the organization and its MAPs.

Public relations practitioners tout the expertise of key members of the organization and seek speaking engagements for them. For example, colleges or universities maintain speakers bureaus. Professors are featured to interested audiences and groups based on their expertise. In this manner, each college or university provides a service to the community by making its experts available. This tactic can increase community relationships that help in fund-raising and attract students.

Press (Media) Conferences

Media relations is vital to the practice of public relations. A press conference lends an opportunity for two-way communication,

Media Relations in Action

SOURCE: Copyright © EPA/Shawn Thew/Landov.

dialogue between an organization's spokespersons and members of the media. Organizations stage press conferences to feature newsworthy information. They also schedule them in response to a crisis.

Press conferences can be spontaneous or regularly scheduled. The spontaneous press conference arises out of an unplanned or unscheduled news event. For example, your university may schedule a news conference to announce that a professor received a prestigious award or that an athlete achieved stellar performance. Representatives of the university and the professor or the athletic director meet the press and answer questions about the award. The regularly scheduled press conference is usually referred to as a *briefing*. Many times, public officials will have regularly scheduled press conferences, even when there is nothing special to report. The regularly scheduled press conferences help keep reporters up-to-date on developing stories or the general status of the organization.

Backgrounders, Press Parties, and Media Tours

Backgrounders often are conducted over lunch. They give the opportunity for a spokesperson to share in-depth information with a reporter, member of government, or key donor, for instance.

Press parties often entail a reception that features some person who can be available for reporter inquiries on a more personal basis. For instance, a museum or art gallery might have a press party with the artist (or a major scholar on the art) as featured guest. Parties allow organizational officials and members of the media to become acquainted and to open channels of communication. It is standard practice for a host to make a presentation toward the end of the event, and usually press packets are presented, either upon arrival or departure. Media reporters, in this case art critics, may be more receptive to the organization after the informal chat. Media participants view the occasion as an opportunity to develop potential contacts and news sources.

Press tours provide an opportunity for members of the media to become more familiar with a specific aspect or project of an organization. There are three types: the press junket, the familiarization trip, and the editor's tour. The *press junket* refers to trips in which the press are invited to tour several facilities or cities or company plants over a short period of time. The press might be given the opportunity to tour a new manufacturing plant that is about to start operation. The press might accompany a nonprofit spokesperson to a relief center for flood victims. The press might visit an old-growth forest to see its rich ecology.

A *familiarization trip* is usually provided by members of the travel and entertainment industry, such as convention and visitors bureaus. The goal is that once media representatives see firsthand what a location is like, they will write favorable articles. The *editor's tour* targets key editors at specific media. In this example, editors are afforded informal time to meet and have their questions answered. The event may be a background briefing or an explanation of one of the organization's positions. The goal is to develop relationships and news sources in the event of future interaction. Such trips are also used when members of a community are invited to open houses by companies and reporters are encouraged to visit key crucial sites, for instance, the environmental responsibility programs used to prove companies'

Tree Planting Draws the Media

SOURCE: Copyright © REUTERS/Jagadeesh NV/Landov.

corporate responsibility. For instance, if a company sponsors a tree-planting program, reporters often are invited to attend—and even to help.

Ethical questions can arise with this sort of public relations activity. Sometimes media and public relations professionals feel that press tours are potentially unethical. When are free travel and free gifts appropriate and inappropriate? Both media and public relations professionals have attempted to answer this question. As a professional, you have several options: First, do not violate the Public Relations Society of America (PRSA) Code of Ethics, which expressly forbids lavish gifts and free trips that are unrelated to a news story. Second, be sensitive to policies and procedures of the various media. Ask ahead of time so that there is no misperception of inappropriateness in the arrangement. Review the discussion of this topic in Chapter 9.

Collaborative Decision Making

Meetings, hearings, and negotiations occur in an oral channel and are typically face-to-face, although now they can occur on the Web. Concerned citizens may meet with company representatives. Outraged activists may engage in negotiations with company and government officials. You may host town meetings at which persons can speak to an audience from an open microphone. You might arrange a large hall so that concerned individuals can go from table to table to meet key individuals who represent various interests in a controversy, listen to them, voice concerns, and pick up information. Chapter 13 offers extensive detail to expand your understanding of this communication option.

Personal Interviews

Personal interviews offer a private, formal or informal, one-on-one opportunity for questions and answers between reporters and a featured spokesperson—someone other than the public relations person. Key reporters, for instance, a major reporter of a national business magazine, might be given an exclusive interview with a corporate chief executive officer (CEO).

The communication skill of the featured person is critical to the success of an interview. The organization's representative must be skilled at handling the questions. When answering a question, the representative will want to present his or her message points.

Print interviews differ from those with radio or television reporters. In print interviews, information is filtered by the media writer. In radio and television interviews, listeners hear the person's voice—sound bites—and make inferences about the person's character and credibility. In television interviews, viewers have an opportunity to both see and hear the person being interviewed. This can have tremendous impact on how the messenger and the message are received.

As you prepare yourself or others for an interview, realize four primary considerations: First, know the subject matter and message points you want to make. Second, make your message points in brief and concise statements. Responses should be kept to 30 seconds or less, with minimal detail or example. Third, relax. Speaking with a microphone in your face or with a huge camera pointed at you is not an everyday occurrence. Being confident and composed is a vital part of the organization's persona. Fourth, keep in mind that you are the message. Think about how you want to be perceived, and enact that persona.

Analyst Meetings

In investor relations, companies go on tour to discuss their earnings, actual and projected, with analysts who use such opportunities to gain insights into the organization. These meetings can assist analysts in getting to know the corporate executives. At those events, executives and investor relations specialists can understand the concerns and expectations of persons who analyze the financial performance of their company and the industry in which it competes.

Oral Presentations

Officials of organizations often speak to audiences about topics relevant to the relationship between the organization and the MAP. Senior officials speak at annual shareholder meetings or the annual gala of a charitable organization. They meet with employees, followers, or donors, as the case might be. The president of a university, for instance, might meet with large alumni groups during the year to personalize the relationship between them and the college.

Radio

Radio features oral communication. Speed, flexibility, and mobility characterize radio as a medium. Messages can be placed on air almost instantly. The messages can be obtained through face-to-face interviews, a press conference, or even a telephone interview.

Radio reaches people through three general formats: news, talk, and entertainment. In primary entertainment format programming, newscasts can be local or national and are usually on the half hour. Many communities have a talk radio station that devotes major time segments to news, commentary, policy issue discussion, community bulletins, call-in talk shows, editorials, and public service announcements. The president of a college can use a talk show to discuss academic and athletic achievements of the institution but also to emphasize the need to raise funding so the campus can provide more computers to students struggling to master the "information age."

Practitioners encourage the host and producer of talk radio shows to invite a key spokesperson for your organization to be a featured guest. The person can reach key segments of your MAPs. Comments directly from the spokesperson seem candid and unfiltered. Comments that are made live by a spokesperson seem more authentic and credible because they are spontaneous.

Spoken communication channels are powerful because they are personal. They are costly in many instances. Imagine how much 1 hour of company time costs for the CEO to meet with a key MAP. Calculate this figure by dividing 2,080, the typical number of paid work hours in a year, into the executive's salary—let's say, $1 million. Now you know what the cost is for having the "boss" speak in public. You are cheaper, but less credible. Face-to-face has impact. Talk radio has some of that same feel but reaches a larger audience.

For these reasons, oral channels play a vital role in the media plan. The goal is to achieve the biggest bang for the buck.

▶Print Channels

Print media and other written channels play a central role in the practice of public relations. The strategic practitioner will plan to use a mix of print channels (also mixed with other channels) that best place an organizational message before each target MAP.

Newspapers

Media relationships are vital to the practice of public relations. Reporters constantly need news stories. Each day, they have to fill a specified amount of space or time with interesting stories to attract and keep readers. Reporters define themselves as watch-dogs of the public interest, using investigative reporting to inform their readers. Skilled public relations professionals who have strong media relationships can assist reporters in developing interesting and vital stories—to the mutual benefit of both parties.

Newspapers help maintain a sense of community. Note that the name of the city, town, or community is often featured in the name of the newspaper—even in *USA Today*. Newspapers allow for extended coverage of an issue or topic of interest. Do you know that the amount of news—in terms of sheer copy—on the evening or nightly news (30-minute segment less advertising time) equals the news text on the front page of a newspaper? Newspapers tend to reach better-educated and more issue-oriented people than do television and radio. In large cities, community newspapers are also very popular. They can cover topics that are not of interest to the general reader, but are for the local reader.

If you think about the section structure of a newspaper, you can imagine the array of stories you might pitch to reporters and editors to run that address products, services, topics, issues, and activities relevant to your client's mission. You might get front-page headlines for some major activity. For instance, if you are doing public relations for an environmental group, you could draw front-page attention to some company's or governmental agency's failure to meet environmental standards. If your client is a business, you could make major announcements on the front page, at least the front page of the business section. You might sponsor a nonprofit fund-raiser and get coverage in the special events or social (lifestyle) section. The list goes on and tantalizes the imagination of skilled practitioners. At a university, you could get coverage for athletics in the sports section and for the arts (theater, arts, and music) in the lifestyle or arts and entertainment section.

Of special note is the number of community-based newspapers. These media outlets cover a smaller geographic area and serve a defined community. They provide an opportunity for the professional practitioner to target specific areas or people with a message.

Usually, readers of the community-based newspaper are active in their community and like to be informed on matters that affect the community. Opinion leaders such as these are vital to a public relations effort.

Magazines

Magazines, as a specialty channel, offer several advantages to the public relations professional. First, magazine subscribers constitute a specialty MAP that is active and interested in the topic of the magazine. Because they are active users of information, subscribers tend to keep the magazine for longer periods of time; magazines have a longer shelf life than some other channels—especially electronic ones such as radio and television. Magazines are passed along (also called "secondary circulation") to friends and family, thereby extending exposure. Thus, if the concern is to reach a specialty audience or to guarantee long-term exposure to an organizational message, magazines are the channel of choice.

Second, specialty magazines offer prestige to a paid advertisement or placed story. Practitioners compete to get their clients and key executives featured in news magazines. They work hard to get technical specialists and other top thinkers featured in magazines that specialize in business-to-business communication or feature special issues such as environmental discussions.

Third, magazines offer practitioners the opportunity to place photos that are relevant to some aspect of their stories. Newspapers rarely publish photographs, whereas magazines tend to thrive on them. (Nevertheless, don't forget the possibility of getting photographs included with your story in a newspaper.)

Magazines pose problems of frequency and timeliness of publication. Most magazines are published on set dates throughout the year. Deadlines are set well in advance for copy and content and are thus not very flexible. What magazines lack in terms of frequency and timeliness, they make up for in sheer impact.

Direct Mail

Over the years, direct mail has become a highly specialized channel of communication. Professionals in advertising, marketing, public relations, and politics have become skilled in the design and use of direct mail. Researchers have examined the combination of paper, color, and messages to determine the most effective design and best practices of direct mail.

As a channel, direct mail has certain advantages. It can narrowly target a segment of a MAP. Many companies specialize in up-to-date addresses and phone numbers of people grouped by MAP segmentation variables. The parameters of the target group, however, must be clearly defined for direct mail to be effective.

Direct mail messages can be tailored for the target MAP. Most professionals use direct mail when they want to reach a target MAP with a "personalized message." Personalized messages usually reflect the values, beliefs, or opinions of the target group in a sensitive manner. Personalized messages can be attack mail pieces that seek to discredit, for example, a political candidate or a company that offends an activist group's ethical standards. Because mail is opened in the privacy and convenience of one's home, there is little competition for the attention of the recipient. By the same token, most direct mail is never opened or read.

Finally, direct mail has many restrictions due to postal house regulations. Size, shape, stamp, or bulk mail certification location all affect the cost and timeliness of mailing. Another problem relates to the maintenance of mail lists. As people change jobs, relocate, or buy homes, many do not complete a change of address with the post office. Direct mail firms have a difficult time keeping up with the changes. Good firms continually update and verify people on their lists.

Activists and other nonprofits may be able to use direct mail more successfully than can businesses. The same can be true of governmental agencies. People assume they are "being sold" something if it comes from a business. They are angered when they are tricked into believing that such is not the case until they open the envelope. But a nonprofit, even during solicitation, is seeking money or other support for a community interest, rather than a narrow business interest.

Direct E-Mail

The Internet allows sources to provide information in exactly the same way that the postal service does. Instead of sending direct mail through the postal service, it can be sent to targeted readers. On the upside, people can be targeted because of interest or allowed to sign up (or opt out) to be on e-mailing lists. The downside is "spam." People are truly annoyed to have to pay in real cost and time to deal with spam. It's hard to imagine that much gain is achieved by persons who send mass e-mails to persons they hope are interested. It's sort of like shooting into a flock of birds, hoping to hit one. Also, however, people often pass notes and bulletins to friends through e-mail networks.

Media Releases

Media releases are also called *press releases*. As the number of papers has declined, practitioners have tended to call them "media releases," realizing they go to all media, not just the press. The media release is the staple for notifying reporters, editors, and news directors of key events and information. They can be used to take positions on issues, to publicize or promote an event, or to draw attention to the reputation of the organization as well as its products and services. Releases can reply to news stories that have been written about the client organization. We mention many instances of press releases throughout the book and direct your attention to them at sponsoring organizations' Web sites. Many organizations post their media releases on their home pages at their Web sites.

See Box 11.1 for a PETA (People for the Ethical Treatment of Animals) news release. They speak out in defense of animals on many issues. They use a variety of events announced through press releases to call attention to their protest activities and point to actions against animals that they think are particularly offensive. The PETA media release included here is dated 1996. As a Web Watcher, go to PETA's home page and look around. You will find lots of "media" materials combined at the site. Also, you will find an extensive list of media releases. Compare what was said in 1996 to what is being said today.

BOX 11.1 ATTRACTING MEDIA ATTENTION THROUGH SENSATIONALISM

WE'D RATHER GO NAKED THAN WEAR FUR

For Immediate Release: December 27, 1996

Contact: Bruce Friedrich 555-555-0000 (pager), or 555-555-5555, ext. 555

Sioux Falls, S.D.—Wearing nothing but Santa hats and holding a banner reading, "We'd Rather Go Naked Than Wear Fur," members of People for the Ethical Treatment of Animals (PETA) and Animal Rights Advocates of South Dakota will expose holiday shoppers to their message:

Date	Time	Place
Monday, December 30	12 noon	Eiler's Furs, 2524 W. 41st St.

PETA members will brave the elements to keep fur sales cold during the holiday shopping season. The strippers hope that by showing some of their skin, they will save animals' skins.

Fur sales have fallen 50 percent over the last 10 years. According to a 1995 Associated Press poll, the majority of Americans surveyed believe killing animals for fur is always wrong.

PETA has made headlines worldwide marching "au naturel" for animals in Anchorage, Alaska; Paris; Milan, Italy; Tokyo; New York; Hong Kong; Chicago; and Moscow.

This fall in New York, Marcus Schenkenberg and Joel West joined a dozen other Boss models who disrobed for a "Turn Your Back on Fur" protest in Times Square. Boss Models has signed an agreement with PETA to be the first fur-free modeling agency. Other "naked" fur foes have included Christy Turlington, Cindy Crawford, and Kim Basinger.

People for the Ethical Treatment of Animals
XXX Front Street, Norfolk, VA 23510
555-555-PETA

SOURCE: The PETA press release was downloaded from their Web site (Web Watcher): http://www.peta.org

An organization can send media releases to the media on its strategic list by using regular mail, e-mail, fax, or news services. One of the roles of practitioners (and interns) is to constantly update media lists so the names, phone numbers, addresses, fax numbers, and e-mail addresses are current. E-mail is a highly efficient means for sending media releases, because you can have the list of receivers set up in the computer address book and send all of them virtually at the same time. They also arrive in the offices of reporters, editors, and news directors in an electronic form that makes them easy to move into the news agency computers and prepare for print or electronic news copy. Faxes can also be sent via mass distribution. Public relations agencies and organizations set fax machines with names and numbers of the reporters. They put the fax in the machine, select the strategic distribution, and let the machine do the rest. With one touch of the button, the press release is sent to newsrooms in the community, and even across the country and around the globe. Some organizations create newsrooms at their Web sites and allow reporters entry by issuing passwords. In this way, reporters can have access to lots of news information about the organization. They can get more by visiting the home page.

Media releases can also be in the form of video news releases. They allow television stations to have video to play in support of the news report made by reporters. You can also send audiotapes to radio stations. Many home pages are constructed so that reporters can download video clips available there.

Releases can also be distributed through services. Businesses charge to disseminate press releases to specific media outlets. These outlets are either specified by the practitioner or the practitioner selects press wire companies that specialize in certain media outlets. You can stay abreast of news wire services by looking at ads in professional publications, such as *PR Tactics, The Strategist,* or *Communication World.* Associated Press, MediaLink, and Reuters are among the leaders in this industry.

Newsletters, Brochures, and Handbooks

These print channels keep certain targeted groups informed, such as employees or members of a nonprofit organization. These channels are widely and routinely used by government agencies. If you look around a college campus, you will find a wide array of these public relations tools.

These informational pieces are used as collateral with other strategic communication efforts. They can be cost-effective or cost-prohibitive, depending on the detail and choices made in the design and quality. They have the advantage of containing lots of information that readers can select to read, based on their particular interests. They can be passed on to other interested readers. Also, they often provide highlights and tidbits of information in a chatty, easy-to-read style. Many topics are covered to appeal to a wide or narrow MAP, as the case might be. A campus might have an orientation handbook to help new students navigate the pitfalls of the campus—a special problem, for instance, for students who are on campuses larger than their hometowns.

Modern computer technology has made this class of written channels more convenient to use. Software programs provide templates for the user to fill in information. Desktop publishing with laser printing can reduce the costs and increase the quality of these communication channels. Such materials can be pressed in print and placed online as well.

Using print channels as public relations tools offers a wide array of opportunities to define and enact the persona of the organization. For instance, campus materials could feature the mascot and the school colors. This approach gives life and voice to the interesting members of the academic community, combining text and pictures to tell the story.

Company, Nonprofit, and Agency Periodicals

Company magazines serve to inform employees and retirees from the company. They provide information on current events, key dates, and people. They build and maintain organizational pride as well as promote good relations with MAPs. Companies realize that their employees are some of their best ambassadors. For that reason, they want to keep them up-to-date on products, financial developments, and public policy issues. If the company needs for persons to write to members of Congress on key issues, well-informed and highly motivated employees are one of the best "activist" groups on which to call.

Similar kinds of publications are used by nonprofit groups. Outstanding examples can be found in the toolboxes of national and international environmental groups. The Audubon Society publishes *Audubon* magazine. It is a slick publication, containing beautiful photographs of nature, as well as examples of the misuse of the environment. Such publications announce key environmental dates and legislative discussions, and contain legislative alerts. As key legislation is pending, magazines of this sort, which typically contain feature stories, encourage readers to write letters to Congress. Similar publications are published by the National Wildlife Federation and the Wilderness Society, to name only a few. This tool is not limited to environmental groups, but they demonstrate powerful examples of how print along with photography can inform and persuade key audiences and publics.

Governmental agencies publish magazines to inform their key constituencies. An interesting example is *Initiatives,* which is published by the Waste Policy Institute for the U.S. Department of Energy Office of Science and Technology in the Office of Environmental Management. The magazine contains discussions of technologies that are used to remediate nuclear waste materials. It features technical problems and success stories. It explains how, through community involvement, citizens help select and monitor the use of technologies to assist in cleaning up nuclear sites in the locales.

Periodic Reports

Most organizations provide some annual review of their performance. Over the years, periodic reports have become very specialized. They are used to promote organizational performance, highlight leadership, and maintain relationships with investors. Performance may include a financial summary. These summaries are used by businesses, nonprofits, and government agencies. They state how much money was raised through the organization's activities, how the money was utilized for its objectives, and how effective it was in the management of these resources.

Publicly traded companies must publish what is called a "10K." Those reports give full financial disclosure, as prescribed by the Securities and Exchange Commission, of the financial status of the company. Once those documents are prepared, companies typically create a glossy version. Those financial documents routinely contain three primary sections. One is the letter to the shareholders. The letter provides an opportunity for the chief officers to address strategic topics that help interested readers to understand the current and future financial status of the company. Corporate annuals also include details on major departments, divisions, product lines, operations, and personnel. They also contain the "Notes to the Financial Statement" section. It features a key summary of the data included in the 10K.

Companies produce "human" side annual reports. Some feature their philanthropic and community relations activities. Some companies that suffer careful environmental scrutiny produce annual reports that feature their environmental improvements. Phillips Petroleum Company and Baxter International were among the first companies to publish such a document, just two of a wide array of companies that use this vehicle to reach and build bridges with key stakeholders and stakeseekers. Originally, these HSE (health, safety, and environmental) reports were published like a magazine or a newsletter. Today, they are more likely to be published online. As a Web Watcher, go to companies, especially those that engage in activities needing environmental sensitivity, to see whether they report their program and progress; timber companies, mining companies, and pharmaceutical companies are likely candidates. Also, you might look at oil companies and chemical-manufacturing companies. Earlier in the book, we pointed to ChevronTexaco as one of the leaders in such reporting.

Nonprofit agencies enhance their fund-raising efforts by producing an annual report to tell their donors, supporters, and service users about their annual strategic plans and accomplishments. For instance, the YMCA of Houston routinely presents its financial statement so people can be assured that their money reaches those deserving of the organization's activities. It features the number of persons who take advantage of programs, such as the thousands of children who learn to swim safely as part of its summer swim program. It focuses on key employees and volunteers. This publication contains lots of pictures of volunteers, donors, and the persons who benefit from the activities and services provided by the nonprofit.

Environmental groups publish annual reports that contain financial statements to demonstrate their wise stewardship of members' and donors' dollars. They provide details on their strategic plans, key issues, and accomplishments.

Governmental agencies also provide annual reports. The list is endless. If you look, and not all that hard, you are likely to find annual reports by civic associations, municipal governments, and county governments, as well as state and federal agencies. Individual politicians publish their reports. These tools tell citizens about vital services that are available to them and demonstrate the wise stewardship of tax dollars to help citizens' lives to be better.

Advertorials

Advertorials are paid advertisements in magazines and newspapers. Most present the sponsor's point of view on a public policy issue or other topic, such as the reputation of a controversial company or industry. The *New York Times* reserves a page for op-ed ads.

Publishers require that the name of the sponsor be clearly identified with the ad so that it is not confused with an editorial written by the editorial staff of the paper or magazine. Mobil Oil Company (now part of ExxonMobil) was a leader in the development and use of such advertisements starting in 1970, when it began to use such ads to defend itself, its industry, and large industry from activist and media attack. See the "Case Problem" in Box 11.2.

BOX 11.2 CASE PROBLEM: MOBIL OIL COMPANY REDEFINES ITS MEDIA RELATIONSHIPS

An example of media relationship building began when Mobil Oil Company executives were shocked on December 29, 1973, to read a story about oil tankers that appeared on the front page of the *New York Times.* The story confirmed public rumors that oil companies were holding tankers in New York's lower harbor to force the price of oil to rise. A great deal of suspicion surrounded the oil industry's business activities in the 1970s. The price of gasoline went up dramatically. Its availability declined, so that filling stations rationed gasoline. Working for an accurate story, New York newspapers asked the Coast Guard whether tankers were being held back to slow the importation of oil. The Coast Guard said that was not being done. Nevertheless, a story was written, printed, and repeated in other media. Even if untrue, this information as reported could hurt the reputation of the company—and the industry.

These news reports could damage the public trust a company or industry needs to do business properly. Mobil responded in a confrontational way (Schmertz, 1986). It described how the queuing of ships in the harbor was routine, a safe way to proceed in an orderly fashion to maximize safety results. Using that queuing procedure, oil tankers could navigate so they were less likely to collide with other ships. Safety procedures were being employed. Ships were not being delayed or held back to drive prices up. This confrontation with the media continued. Mobil decided to use op-eds to reach the public. It undertook an issue advertising campaign to blast unfair reporting practices and condemn the practice of reporters who hide behind the First Amendment rather than practice journalism in an ethical manner.

What would you do? Indicate the media and communication tools you would use to reach targeted MAPs with the messages relating information about the practices of the oil industry.

Collateral

Print channels involve words. Images are also important. Many interesting and powerful tools have been used by public relations practitioners over the years. Refrigerator magnets are an excellent tool for keeping your message before your MAP. They feature product or brand names. They can be used to remind people of safety messages. Those messages can include emergency numbers and measures.

Children love to color. Organizations provide coloring materials that have educational, informational value. For instance, the Natural Resources Conservation Service (NRCS) of the U.S. Department of Agriculture provides educational material that children can use at home or in the classroom to learn about nature and conservation measures. Coloring sheets are quite popular for this purpose. Children learn about animals, plants, water, soil, and ecosystems as they color these sheets. As a side benefit, these sheets end up on the kitchen table as the children explain to adults what they have learned. They have a shelf life once they are put up on the refrigerator (held in place with an NRCS magnet) or family bulletin board.

Calendars are another print vehicle. They can feature the activities of an activist group. They might advise the family on environmental activities that could be performed each month of the year. The color pictures can reinforce people's appreciation for the beauty of nature.

▶Visual Channels

Visual channels differ from written or spoken channels in that they appeal to the eye. People are exposed to a large amount of visual stimuli as a means of communication. Images are designed to convey certain ideals or values unique to a particular target group. For instance, an oil company, such as Chevron, might use images of environmental responsibility to shape its reputation. Chevron used these images in its "People Do" campaign. Activists often use images, such as atrocities, to draw attention to some issue, such as environmental irresponsibility. Images of mutilated turtles are featured by Ridley turtle advocates at their home page (Web Watcher: See the Web page for HEART). Smoking industrial stacks have become the sign of industrial pollution.

Television

Television is the dominant form of visual communication, although it may be challenged by the Internet. Television combines sight, sound, and motion to tell a story, attract attention, or convince an audience. It has high message impact and reach. Much of the product and service messaging on television is created through advertising professionals, but public relations experts develop newsworthy stories and events to attract reporters' attention. Television talk show and news feature segments offer public relations opportunities, as well as pose threats. Even the casual observer notes the number of times during a week when favorable or unfavorable attention is focused on a product, service, issue, or organization.

Organizations turn to cable television as a means to publicize or promote their products and services, as well as to discuss key issues. Cable (including satellite) industry growth has further segmented the television-viewing audience. Cable companies specialize in programming for certain viewers, thus allowing practitioners to be highly selective in their targeting of messages. In some areas, cable television can target geo-demographically and psychographically, allowing for even greater targeting precision. This is called *narrow casting*.

Cable costs less than mainstream television. Due to the variety of programming, organizations can pick combinations of time segments to better position their message when their target group is viewing.

Motion Pictures

Movie viewers are a captive audience that may be attracted to discussions of controversial topics. Over the years, industrial corruption, pollution, and worker safety have been recurring themes. Topics depicted in film create threats for practitioners. Activist practitioners may actually seek to position their themes in such films. Products that are used by movie characters can become more popular. Thus, practitioners may pitch their products and even offer money to defray the production costs of the movie if the director will have the star use the product. Do you think that it is coincidence when a popular star drives a particular automobile or drinks a specific brand of soft drink in a key moment in the film?

This medium has at times been controversial. Popular culture created by films and books can shape the opinions of key publics on controversial subjects. Popular views, for instance, of nuclear energy and radiation have been the grist for films, television shows, and literature. This technology is safely used in many industrial and medical settings that tend not to have dramatic visual content potential. The vile possibility is often more commercial than the safe reality.

Outdoor Displays

As you drive down the busier streets in your city, take a moment to reflect on the large number of outdoor displays. Hundreds of displays in all shapes, sizes, and colors compete for your attention. Creative displays catch your attention and remind you of the characteristics of a product or service when you go to make a purchase. Billboards are even used to raise and discuss issues. They are especially good to announce special events.

Outdoor displays can be high-reach and high-frequency communication tools. Displays can be targeted to geographic areas. They create or reinforce awareness and recognition of a product or service. They can be relatively inexpensive depending on the location and the potential exposure to people. They are best used in combination with other media, as opposed to a stand-alone communication strategy.

Videos

Videos can feature aspects of an organization, such as the technological achievements of employees. They allow employees to hear and see one another, as well as the executives. Environmental groups have used videos to discuss the problems of endangered species and animal population recovery. They can demonstrate the atrocities of elephants slaughtered for ivory or gorillas massacred for their hands and heads. They show the success of people working together to save species, including before-and-after footage of environmental damage and remediation. They allow for dramatic presentation unique to television but are accessible to anyone who has a VCR. Video clips are becoming a standard part of Web presentations.

▶Multiple Media: New Technologies and Events

Each year, professional practitioners generate new forms of communication based on advancements in technology. Computer-assisted communication has opened the Internet and Web as especially potent communication tools. These also pose threats because they can suffer from cybersabotage. Rumors and false information can circle the globe in minutes, as friends and relatives pass information to one another by using their e-mail address forwarding systems.

Internet

The Internet has changed the way organizations interact with key constituents. It offers fast, effective interactive communication with minimal interference, especially by reporters who tend to alter information before passing it along in their news reports and opinion statements. Communication can be public, as in chat rooms, or private, between individuals. People utilize the Internet in the comfort of their homes or offices, at a time that they designate. Look up the Web site of almost any company, and you can find everything from annual reports to advertisements to individual biographies to dialogue buttons to leave a message. Just for fun, visit the Web site of the White House, and leave the president, the vice president, or the first lady a message.

The Internet poses many problems. A lot of misinformation and disinformation exists on the Internet. This information, such as scary comments about products, can be sent by friends to friends who simply forward messages to preset networks. Rumors travel fast on the Internet.

Practitioners can use the Internet for research, such as focus groups and customer surveys, publicity, promotion, or to stay up-to-date on current events. They can invite and respond to reporter inquiries. They can access databases. They can invite the comments of students, customers, donors, critics, or other interested MAPs. Web sites add a new dimension to the Internet. Companies provide Web site access to products, service, or people.

Web sites can become identifiable by "sound marks." That means that each time a person accesses your organization's Web site, they can be greeted by a characteristic trademark sound. You can have video clips of your key spokespersons. You can have a virtual-reality meeting. You can let the browser view a meeting or watch an event, such as environmental activities to remediate a wetland. You can have clips of elderly people thanking your employees for painting their houses.

The Web site allows for links to related sites. It offers users the opportunity to obtain information on demand. These users can obtain layers of information. For instance, you might explain a technological innovation in terms that can be understood by a layperson, while you provide another Web page for the technically sophisticated user to get far more detail.

Web sites can be printed. Thus, users become a source of text that they print and distribute at will.

Webs allow for sound clips. If you are interested in increasing environmental activism, you might have the sounds of different birds. You can make such sites more interactive and appealing to children, for instance, by inviting them to match sounds to species.

The Web allows for a virtual reality. You can install a camera in the boardroom of your activist organization and allow users to hear the annual discussion of activist priorities. You can place a camera at a construction site and allow employees to see the progress. You can have cameras at various global locations in your multinational corporation and have people in those countries tell about themselves and their customs.

CD-ROMs

CDs can be used for a variety of purposes, including storing information, retrieving information, and sending personalized communication. Some companies have turned to the CD-ROM format instead of or in addition to their traditional printed annual report. Using computer graphics and interactive technology, organizations can demonstrate the nature of their business and provide information directly to key constituents.

1-800 Phone Numbers

By dialing a toll-free telephone number, customers can receive information from businesses—as well as voice complaints. Donors can pledge money. Activist followers can voice support to their activist organization. Citizens can request information from a government agency. Companies that sell turkeys know that not everyone knows how to prepare one as guests are scheduled to arrive for some seasonal holiday. By providing assistance to the cook, the company can have a happy, satisfied customer. Recall that the best predictor of a future purchase is a person's satisfaction with a product or service. Wise automobile manufacturers want angry or concerned customers to have easy access to customer service, instead of firing off angry letters to consumer editors or congressional representatives. Organizations that manufacture harmful, even deadly, products have felt the obligation to place a 1-800 number on the container (and now alongside the Web site address) to give the user access to expert advice in the safe and wise use of the product.

Multimedia

This is one of the underutilized new technologies. These can be created as stand-alone computer applications or set up on a Web site. This use of the technology allows for many media—sight, text, and sound—to come together. A major university in Australia used multimedia to help teachers understand cultural diversity. They could read about it (text). They could hear video clips of children who had experienced its positive side as well as the negative side of mistreatment. The user could navigate through various pages to locate curriculum. It could contain lists of contacts and success stories. The rich experiences of meeting persons, listening to students, and attending conferences could be had from browsing a computer.

Events

Events are a staple tool of public relations. They are an older form of multimedia. For instance, a trade show is an event. Your company might have a booth. Persons who visit your booth can talk to your representatives. They can pick up pamphlets and brochures. They can watch a video.

Events can be galas where affluent donors gather. They can also be community walks where neighborhood coalitions unite against drug dealers. Charities use events to raise funds. Supporters may pay—willingly contribute—to attend the event, and the "money goes to charity." These events attract reporters and photographers. The day after the event, the lifestyle section is likely to carry a story and show pictures. You are wise to create photo opportunities and to have materials available for the press. Have the same materials available at your Web site so the busy reporter can download your story and translate it into his or her story of the event.

This section has featured types of channels and many of the public relations tools that exemplify each. We can use this information to further refine our thinking about

	Figure 11.2: Selecting Channels and Tools to Link With Stakeholders						
				Channels and Tools			
	Print	*Radio*	*Television*	*Web Site*	*Event*	*Collaborative Decision Making*	*Face-to-Face*
Stakeholder 1							
Stakeholder 2							
Stakeholder 3							
Stakeholder 4							

NOTE: This planning chart allows the user the option of specifying the specific channels and tools that are to be used to communicate with each specific stakeholder.

our media plan. As is demonstrated in Figure 11.2, you can think of each stakeholder group by row and each public relations tool by column. In this way, you can imagine and plan for using the best tools to reach and interact with each of the stakeholder groups.

Media Planning

A media plan considers cost-effectiveness, return on investment (ROI), which we discussed in Chapter 5. Organizations want the "biggest bang for the buck." Unless they are responding to others, they can engage in selecting the best fit between the medium and advantage to the relationship. Where is the best point of engagement between the organization and its target MAP?

A media plan reflects strategic choices whereby a mix of planned, placed, and responsive channels are used to increase the likelihood that each targeted MAP will receive the message required to accomplish the desired objective. The simple equation is that a larger budget can buy more time and space and commit more public relations resources to creating and pitching stories to the media. A larger budget can fund more events or bigger, more splashy (attention-gaining) events.

Figure 11.3 depicts a typical format for a media/channel schedule. The different media are listed as rows, with time periods depicted as columns across the top. Reach and frequency can be reported for each week, then cumulatively for the month. Costs involved for each medium are also reported, with subtotals for each medium and an overall total.

A plan might call for placing a story for a business-to-business client on a monthly, quarterly, or annual basis. That story might also be pitched to television and newspapers (especially for a business section or a business newspaper). It might also be pitched to a general magazine as well as a trade publication. So, the plan can indicate frequency of pitch—the target of getting news out in these venues. The plan can specify exact names of publications. It might also specify the type of placement desired. For instance, a business-to-business client might want several articles per year featuring its product

Figure 11.3: Media/Channel Schedule

Days:	Period 1 1234567	Period 2 1234567	Period 3 1234567	Period 4 1234567
Medium:				
Magazines	xxxxxxx		xxxxxxx	
Specialty	x	x	x	x
Cost				
Medium:				
Newspaper	xxxx	xxx	xx	x
Cost				
Medium:				
Television	x	xxx	xx	xxx
Cost				
Total Cost				
Reach/Frequency per Period				

and to be featured in stories on competing products. It might want to publish a letter to the editor on a technical topic and to get a favorable review for its innovation. Part of the pitch can be tied to events. An event might be created by the company. A trade show is an event where products and services are displayed in a competitive, holistic arena.

Information about the costs associated with commercial time is compiled by Standard Rate and Data Services (SRDS). SRDS compiles and publishes the cost of individual newspapers, magazines, radio, and television stations. This information is sold to subscribers, such as advertising and public relations firms.

Professionals use SRDS in their media plans to calculate the cost per thousand (abbreviated CPM, with M representing "mil" or thousands). CPM is the cost to deliver one unit of commercial time or space to 1,000 audience members. CPM is used for comparative purposes within a medium. Rate structures differ across mediums; therefore, CPM is not a good indicator of different mediums.

The basic formula is that CPM is equal to cost per unit of time or space multiplied by 1,000 and then divided by the medium's reach. CPM must be calculated for each medium in the media plan. An average cost can be determined for the entire media plan by adding the CPM and dividing by the number of mediums.

As professionals wrestle with the trade-offs of reach, frequency, and continuity and begin to compare various media plans based on gross rating points (GRPs), they consider how much exposure can be generated by uncontrolled media, which we have defined as placed. Uncontrolled media should be a component of any media plan because it adds value to the overall media effort and demonstrates the usefulness of professional public relations practice.

After careful consideration and strategic thinking, you should be ready to propose the elements for a cost-effective media plan that achieves organizational objectives with maximum effective reach and frequency. Using any combination of GRPs, CPM, and uncontrolled media, your media plan should address management concerns for cost-effectiveness. Your plan should identify primary and secondary media as the appropriate channels for the communication effort. Is that all there is to strategic planning for selecting media and communication channels? Are there any considerations for mixing various media to accomplish organizational objectives? If you answered yes or "There should be," then you are on track with your strategic thinking.

Media Mix Strategies

Commercial space and time are expensive for any organization to purchase. For this reason, marketing budgets have expanded beyond advertising costs to seek the assistance of public relations to increase reach at a lower cost. How does one balance budget limitations and strategic planning for media and communication channels? Over the years, advertising, marketing, and public relations professionals have developed strategies to mix media in a communication effort. The term *media mix* refers to the simultaneous use of different mass media. Mass media include newspapers, magazines, radio, television, direct mail, or any communication channel that is mass mediated. One of the newest additions to this list is the Internet.

A media plan should consider the kinds of tools that can best be used, or are required, to reach and interact with the target MAP. For instance, a plan might feature print options that include a news story, a feature story, a major book that addresses key issues, and a series of stories in an employee, donor, or member newsletter. This brief illustration is intended to remind you that you have many public relations tools options for each medium.

Strategic media mix ensures that members of a target MAP will be exposed to a message at some point in time during a 4-week media plan. A media mix, when properly planned, can enhance the potential for exposure and reduce the amount of media purchased—thereby achieving cost-effectiveness. Seven media mix strategies can aid your selection of media and communication channels: reach, frequency, continuity, pulsing, flighting, weighting, and message positioning.

▶Reach

One major goal of strategic communication is to reach a specific MAP with one or more messages. *Reach* is defined as the number of people or percentage of a particular target MAP reached at least once in a media purchase or by a placed story—or one to which you respond. Some professionals refer to "cumulative reach" to account for the number or percentage of a target audience over the life of the media buy or placement.

Reach recognizes that some individuals enter or exit a MAP at different times or dates and that some individuals will never be exposed to a message. For example, you might watch the 10:00 evening television news on some days and not others. Some weeks may go by where you may be working and do not watch the news at all. In this instance, you would be in and out of reach and some weeks be completely unreachable.

Groups of 1,000 each	Week 1	Week 2	Week 3	Week 4
Figure 11.4: Example of Reach in a Population of 10 Individuals				
1	e	re	re	ne
2	e	re	re	ne
3	e	re	re	ne
4	ne	ne	ne	ne
5	ne	ne	ne	ne
6	e	ne	ne	re
7	e	ne	re	ne
8	e	re	ne	ne
9	ne	ne	e	ne
10	ne	ne	e	ne

NOTE: "e" indicates exposure, "re" a repeat exposure, and "ne" no exposure.

Figure 11.4 illustrates the concept of reach. For the illustration, imagine that a target of 10,000 customers were exposed to a message over a 4-week period of time. Some individuals were repeatedly exposed, while some were not exposed until the later weeks. For example, individuals in Groups 1, 2, 3, and 7 were exposed to the message in Week 1 and in subsequent weeks. Individuals in Groups 9 and 10 were exposed to the message only once in Week 3. Individuals in Groups 4 and 5 were not exposed to the message. In this illustration, cumulative reach is 80% (8 out of 10 were exposed to a message).

Consideration of television as a communication medium leads to useful concepts such as rating, households using television, and audience share. *Rating* refers to a percentage of all households that actually tune in to a particular program. For example, a rating of 25 means that 25% of all households are watching that program. Households using television (HUT) accounts for only those households using television at the time research is conducted, not all television households. HUT is utilized to calculate share. The concept of *audience share* expresses a television program's actual viewership in relation to all households operating a television at the time of research.

▶Frequency

Frequency is the number of times a message is repeated. Individuals may be exposed to a message once, twice, or three or many more times during the cycle of a media buy. As with reach, individuals move in and out of an audience at different dates and times, thus reducing the frequency with which they would be exposed to a message. The minimum period of time to calculate frequency is 4 weeks.

The major concern with frequency is that message content tends to be learned slowly over time. This realization is important.

Repetition builds individuals' recall or retention of the message, with the hope they will increase product purchase or service usage. Professionals are constantly challenged to decide how many times a message should be repeated. The minimum number of exposures that will maximize the likelihood of a product purchase is called the *minimum effective frequency* (MEF). As you can tell, some organizations keep their messages in constant view. To demonstrate this point, consider three products whose names you encounter each day. If you think for a moment, you will realize that three is a mere fraction of the number of products that come to mind.

Reach is essentially a measure of the number of people who will receive your message in a given period of time. Strategic communication is designed to reach MAPs. As you think of publicity and promotion, you recognize that marketers try to reach you as often as possible, frequently, all of the time, and so on.

▶Continuity

As a media mix strategy, *continuity* ensures that a message will continually appear before a target MAP. Continuity, as a media mix strategy, while ideal, tends to be very expensive to present the message on a continual basis, one exposure after another. While you will have maximum control over the medium, costs accumulate quickly with each exposure.

The concept of continuity alludes to the distribution of exposures over successive media purchases, placements, and responses. Whereas reach accounts for numbers of individuals exposed to a message and frequency accounts for frequency of message exposure by individuals, continuity is concerned with exposures or frequencies over time. Most likely an organization will make several media purchases and placements over time for a single product to reach its target market. Continuity is a concern for consistency in the reach and frequency over time.

Continuity can occur because you encounter the same message—such as a brand name and its association with one or two attributes—repeatedly. For instance, you are likely to see and hear the words "Coke" and "Pepsi" frequently throughout a day, week, or month. You may encounter the words in advertisements, on the packaging, at places where it is sold, and when it sponsors events. The latter publicity and promotion effort adds value to the advertising campaign.

Thus, continuity is the same message repeatedly encountered or a variation on the message. Each variation adds depth or breadth to the message. "Coke/Pepsi refreshes." "Coke/Pepsi tastes good." "Coke/Pepsi adds to your lifestyle." The name is repeated— continuity. Themes are repeated that define the name—continuity.

You have to consider the issue of saturation. Continuity results from repeated paid or placed stories, but after a while, audiences may pay less attention because they feel saturated with your messages. Your messages no longer contain information that is fresh and valuable to the target. Thus, if you have nothing new to say, waiting a while to continue your discussion can be a strategic option. You may also force yourself to look harder for a new, novel, and interesting angle with which to combat the saturation factor.

All of this is different if you are working in a major or a minor market. A major market is characterized by many media. A large city is typically a major market. In contrast, a minor market is one with a limited number of media outlets. A big player, such as a major employer in a small town, can achieve continuity but suffer saturation. The local audience may tire of stories—too many messages—that add little to what it wants to know about the company, nonprofit, or governmental agency.

▶Pulsing

A *pulsing* strategy employs a continual low level of advertising or story placement with higher bursts of messages at specific times. For example, a college or university may communicate continually but use pulses such as an annual alumni drive or fund drives for the library or the public radio station. The campus might feature the extraordinary achievement of a student or a faculty member. A nonprofit group may pulse using some issue. For instance, a major public policy issue, such as an unfavorable change in environmental laws, may be the impetus for a fund-raising drive by an environmental group.

When using a pulsing strategy, the minimum number of message exposures should be the continual portion of the strategy. Steady and predictable presentation of information sustains the flow between the organization and its MAPs. That steady flow becomes the foundation for the pulses that create extra punch at strategic times.

▶Flighting

Flighting is a media mix strategy that employs a medium, discontinues its use, employs the medium, discontinues its use, and so on. Think of flighting as a start-and-stop strategy. Most organizations cannot afford to purchase continual media space or time. The alternative is to be in and out of the market in bursts that are compatible with product characteristics.

Flighting is a popular media-scheduling strategy, particularly with organizations with limited funds. A nonprofit group cannot afford to communicate continually, so it may opt to communicate during major events or at specific seasons. Businesses use flighting to feature their quarterly earnings reports, for instance, as they build relationships with their investors. To avoid saturation, a company or a school district, for example, may use flighting in strategic ways to capture MAPs with new, vital, self-interested, and novel information.

▶Weighting

Professionals are faced with a problem of increasing message exposure to a certain demographic segment or geographic area, or other profile of its MAPs. In such cases, *weighting* is the proper media mix strategy.

Weighting can reflect consumption, media use patterns, or psychodemographic or geodemographic patterns. Weighting by consumption allows an organization to have message exposure mirror peaks and valleys in consumption. A good example is a candy products organization. As consumption increases around Halloween and Easter, the organization would increase communication; it would decrease communication in the slower-consumption months. To balance its message delivery load, a company might, for instance, weight its commercial messages to feature those peaks and valleys of consumer activity. During market lows, for instance, when consumption is lower, the organization might take that opportunity to spend more time communicating with its employees. News stories could feature the success of its marketing efforts and pay credit to the hard work of employees to meet customer demand. Weighted in this way, the staff of the public relations department stays busy throughout the year by weighting which audiences it communicates with at specific times during the year.

Weighting by media use patterns allows an organization to increase messages when media usage is high and, conversely, to decrease communication when media usage is low. For example, a college or university publicizes its arts and humanities in the lifestyle sections of the newspapers and in similar features on television and radio. Likewise, they tout their athletic achievements on talk shows devoted to sports.

Weighting by geographic patterns allows an organization to increase communication activity in certain geographic areas over others. For example, beef jerky may be purchased more by individuals living in western states, rather than individuals living in eastern states. In this case, an organization would concentrate its communication activities in western states and maintain the lowest effective frequency rate in eastern states.

▶Message Positioning

Organizations strategically position their messages where a target set of individuals is most likely to encounter them. As we discussed in Chapter 5, MAPs will pay attention to a message when they are self-interested—involved—in that message. When MAPs are cognitively involved or self-interested, they are likely to pay attention to messages. They are likely to read, listen to, or teleview entire messages or longer messages.

Public relations practitioners can increase the level of cognitive involvement of their MAPs. This can be done by connecting a message to the self-interest of the target and communicating at those times when self-interest is high. For instance, summer months are the best time for health organizations to communicate about the cosmetic and health consequences of extreme exposure to sunlight. Reporters looking for stories may be interested in those that relate to specific times of the year. Human interest stories at Christmas feature the plight of children who have little prospect of receiving presents. These human interest stories can be promoted by charitable organizations that seek donations to help make the holiday more cheery for families in special need. Colleges and universities often feature the tradition and heritage of programs, such as art, music, and theater, as they publicize and promote each new production, concert, or exhibit.

These strategic best practices guide the development of the media plan. The plan is a means by which strategic communicators seek to communicate key messages at times when the impact is likely to be greatest.

Conclusion

Media practices and characteristics play a big role in the professional practice of public relations. Some people have featured media relations as the end-all of public relations. This is not the case. It is much more than getting news and publicity. Media are tools.

Like the tools in a workman's toolbox, each has its unique application. A kitchen holds an amazing array of tools to prepare various meals, and in different ways. Such variety is part of the arsenal of the public relations practitioner. Planning, selecting, and utilizing media define the work of many practitioners, but not the entire profession.

Relationship development assumes communication. One of the important challenges facing public relations practitioners is to be stewards of information. The excellent practitioner wants to be the first and best source of information on all matters relevant to clients or employers. Media are a means for giving and getting information. Although at times, the process is best thought of as monologue, over time, a real dialogue emerges. Many voices compete for space, time, and credibility. The best voices are responsive and interactive. They build, maintain, and restore relationships for mutual benefit.

Ethical Quandary: Buying Lunch or a Story?

FURTHER
EXPLORATION

11

As you are beginning to pitch a story to a reporter, you arrange for a backgrounder. You invite him to lunch and say that you will pay. As you are about to leave for lunch, your boss (or client, as the case might be) calls, and you indicate you are going to lunch with the reporter. The boss (or client) says, "Tell the reporter that we do a lot of advertising in his newspaper (or on the radio or television station). Let him know that we expect a lot of placed coverage and expect it to be positive. Stress the advertising dollars we spend. Also, offer him samples of some of our products so that he can see how good they are." Using your own judgment and professional codes, identify the ethical issues that arise from this situation. How do you handle this quandary?

Summary Questions

1. Explain the difference between paid, placed, and responsive media. Locate an example of each.
2. Adopt an organization, and locate its communication tools. Categorize them by channel. Identify the stakeholder each is designed to communicate with.
3. Define the following concepts: Reach, frequency, continuity, pulsing, flighting, weighting, and message positioning. Imagine that you are planning the annual public relations activities for a college or university. Demonstrate that you understand each of the terms by indicating how it would be incorporated into your planning.
4. Develop a media plan for the creation, maintenance, and repair of a strategic relationship. Identify the public relations tools you would use on behalf of a specific client.
5. Extend the plan developed in item 4 above. Indicate how each of the tools could be used for achieving reach, frequency, continuity, pulsing, flighting, weighting, and message positioning.
6. Visit a Web site. Explain why it is multimedia. Find one that includes text (print), sound, video, and interactive exchange.

Exercises

1. A national jewelry company specializes in the manufacture and sale of college graduation rings. If this company were to ask your public relations class for strategic advice in publicizing and promoting its graduation rings at your campus, what would you recommend? How would you personalize the message to students at your campus? Design and plan a promotional campaign. Be sure to make suggestions for reach, frequency, and the media mix. Obtain the advertising rates from your school newspaper and develop a budget for a your proposed campaign. Is your plan cost-effective? How many rings must you sell to justify the cost of the campaign?

2. Select an organization, and chronicle its public relations efforts over the duration of several days or weeks. What tools does it use? How does it stage its press releases (and the media attention it receives) to keep its stories fresh?

3. Locate a sample of several types of public relations tools for various kinds of relationships. Identify these by typology—the kind of tool. Write a short planning essay that demonstrates your insights into the purpose that each tool serves and why it is a useful or required part of a media plan.

4. Identify an event that is occurring. Look at the stages in the communication about the event and how the organization prepares MAPs for it. See which tools the organization uses at the time of the event. Watch for the use of communication tools to draw the story together after the event. What message emerges from the story of the event?

5. Watch television news (including sports and entertainment venues), listen to radio, and read a newspaper for 1 month to identify the organizations that place their stories. Identify why those organizations appear to be successful in having their stories appear.

6. Explore the integration of media tools. Select a "client" organization and identify all of the media tools that it is currently using. Don't forget to look at its Web site. Do you find the same messages placed in different tools?

7. Monitor the tools that are used by a college or university. Identify the primary MAPs that are targeted with each one of the tools. Identify how these fit together into a package designed to achieve the mission of the institution.

8. Identify public relations tools that achieve the following media-planning objectives: paid, placed, responsive, reach, frequency, continuity, pulsing, flighting, weighting, and message positioning. Locate examples of each of the following channels: spoken, print, visual, new technologies, and events.

Recommended Readings

Fuhrman, C. J. (1989). *Publicity stunt! Great staged events that made the news*. San Francisco: Chronicle Books.

Hallahan, K. (1994). Public relations and circumvention of the press. *Public Relations Quarterly, 39*(2), 17–19.

Hallahan, K. (2000). Strategic media planning: Toward an integrated public relations media model. In R. L. Heath (Ed.), *Handbook of public relations* (pp. 461–470). Thousand Oaks, CA: Sage.

Heath, R. L. (2005). *Encyclopedia of public relations*. Thousand Oaks, CA: Sage. (The encyclopedia is loaded with details on media, media planning, media tools, and media techniques.)

Hunt, T., & Grunig, J. E. (1994). *Public relations techniques*. Fort Worth, TX: Harcourt Brace.

Johnson, M. A. (1997). Public relations and technology: Practitioner perspectives. *Journal of Public Relations Research, 9*, 213–236.

O'Keefe, S. (1997). *Publicity on the Internet*. New York: Wiley.

Schmertz, H. (1986). *Good-bye to the low profile: The art of creative confrontation*. Boston: Little, Brown.

Schultz, D. F., & Glynn, C. J. (1989). Selecting channels for institutional public relations. *Public Relations Review, 15*(4), 24–36.

Thorson, E., & Moore, J. (1996). *Integrated communication: Synergy of persuasive voices*. Mahwah, NJ: Lawrence Erlbaum.

Wilson, L. J. (1995). *Strategic program planning for effective public relations campaigns*. Dubuque, IA: Kendall/Hunt.

12

Publicity, Promotion, and Writing

Publicizing and Promoting *Harry Potter*

Harry Potter and the Goblet of Fire, the fourth book in the *Harry Potter* series of children's books, appeared at booksellers on July 8, 2000. Sales of this book enjoyed increased visibility through a marketing communication effort that relied primarily on publicity and promotion and very little on advertising. This publicity and promotion campaign was a spectacular example of return on investment. The campaign cost very little and generated enormous amounts of awareness and motivation. It tapped existing attitudes. Prior to the appearance of the fourth book, publicity and promotion about the *Harry Potter* series had largely been word of mouth, sporadically fed by publicity statements that stressed the popularity of the books and dedicated efforts of the author, J. K. Rowling, who wrote the books for the amusement of her daughter and her daughter's friends. A single, unemployed mother, she wrote the first book while staying warm in coffee shops in Edinburgh, Scotland. The first book launched with lots of speculation about its success. By the fourth book's publication, the author had become an icon, and the books were widely and enthusiastically read.

News about the first three books spread largely through conversations as children and their parents told one another about Harry's adventures. Children asked their parents to buy the books for them. They saved their allowances. They shared the books with friends. Parents read the adventures to children who were too young to read but who nevertheless

Building Anticipation for *Harry Potter*

SOURCE: Copyright © Landov.

enjoyed the fantasy and adventure. Many children would read the stories for themselves later. Much of the publicity focused on the phenomenal success of the books and their ability to encourage children to curl up with books, instead of merely relying on television and computer games for their adventures.

Word of mouth had played the dominant role in creating awareness, informing readers and parents about the first three books, persuading them to buy and read the books, and cocreating the meaning that wove a rich fabric of fun and fantasy about Harry's adventures. Many children reported having read each of the first three volumes more than once. Delighted parents secretly or openly enjoyed how the stories fueled their imagination. Long before the fourth book went on sale, it was destined to join the other three books on the fiction best-seller list.

Publicity and promotion are narrative public relations functions. They create and sustain a story that is deemed newsworthy by reporters and other members of society. Publicity creates or responds to a story. Promotion keeps the story alive. Promotion often requires that a single theme be established as the story line. Then, details are added to enrich and sustain the story development.

Promotion used suspense—an element in the series. It featured an anticipation narrative leading to the day when bookstores could sell the book. By agreement, they could not sell before midnight on the day the book was to become available. The campaign captured the drama of the children who love the suspense associated with the adventures of this young student of wizardry. The publicity led to promotion, which launched a story told by reporters, who helped children and their parents learn about the book's launch date and described the steps needed for the child to get a copy as soon as possible. Reporters told of children reserving copies and standing in lines, and warned of children being disappointed at not finding a copy they could purchase. These promotional stories were spiced with quotations by delighted children who had read the first three books. They yearned to have the new book in hand and reveled in the continuing adventures of this boy and his friends, with whom they had identified. Delighted parents, satisfied book store personnel, and media reporters focused on one message point: All were delighted by the lively interest the series had inspired in children to read; that was a mutually beneficial relationship for all involved in the integrated communication campaign, which relied heavily on publicity and promotion.

By the time the fourth book in the series was available to be purchased, the publicity and promotion had established several message points:

- The date and time the new book would be available—not one minute before July 8, 2000.
- The number of books in the first printing (3.8 million for sale in the United States—this was an industry record for the number of books published for a first printing), the number of pages (734), the weight of the book (2.7 pounds), and the price of the book ($25.95).
- The title of the new book: *Harry Potter and the Goblet of Fire.*
- The continuity of the characters, plots, specialized vocabulary, and themes established in the series. This promotion narrative indicated that one of the established characters close to Harry dies and Harry discovers girls at age 14.
- The continuing success of the author of the series, J. K. (Joanne Kathleen) Rowling.
- The financial success of the book (along with movie rights and merchandising).
- The impact the book had on children's interest in reading.

340

The book went on sale at 12:01 a.m., July 8, 2000, even though some copies had been sold earlier in the week, in violation of the vendors' agreement with the publisher. Imagine parents staying up and standing in line (by themselves or with their children) to get the book. July 8 was a Saturday. The children could rest and read all day, as well as all of Sunday, to see whether the new book was as enjoyable as they hoped. (Note: You don't want a publicity event where the children cause family trouble by being up late on a weeknight. Also note that the release occurred during the summer, when reading would not interfere with school assignments.) Some parents even used this occasion as the basis for birthday parties. *Harry Potter* became the theme of sleepovers, and each child received his or her own copy.

The story of Harry's education centers on his adventures, and those of his friends, as a student of witchcraft at Hogwarts School of Witchcraft and Mystery. After a blighted early childhood as an orphaned member of a relative's home (his parents were killed by an evil wizard named Voldemort), Harry blossomed as a student of witchcraft, excelling at sports and some classwork. He enjoyed many life-threatening adventures, made more dangerous by the fact that some teachers were in conspiracy with the evil wizard. He was raised as a Muggle (non-witch) until his soon-to-become friend Hagrid arrived to take Harry to school, where he could learn the craft of his parents, who were strong, brave, gifted, and good wizards.

The publicity and promotion narrative featured many levels, each for different markets and audiences. Part of the publicity was planned and executed by the publishing company and the companies that owned merchandising rights. One of the key message-positioning techniques was to use narrative suspense. The title was a guarded secret until a bit more than a week before release. Booksellers had to sign an affidavit promising secrecy about the title and plot; they could not sell the book earlier than 12:01, July 8. Some publicity speculated about what its title might be. The *Wall Street Journal* reported that it might be named *Harry Potter and the Doomspell Tournament*, but wisely observed that it would sell very well even if it were titled *Harry Potter and the Brown Paper Bag*. Advanced information—likely to have been included in a media kit circulated to all major and minor media outlets—contained pictures of Harry and data about the cost and physical appearance of the book, but not the plot or title.

Unlike the usual publicity efforts for a potential best seller, no reviews were allowed prior to initial sales. Publicity to promote books usually begins with practitioners sending review copies to reviewers. Those reviews are solicited and even courted. The good ones are featured in the publicity materials. The bad ones are ignored or discredited. Thus, for most book releases, publicity efforts are devoted to getting "buzz" started through reviews. The narrative logic of these publicity efforts is simply that if critics like the book, so will readers. Believing that reviewers would spoil the fun of the mystery for the children, the release of *Harry Potter* the fourth was cloaked in secrecy so that children (and parents) could experience the adventure through their own minds, unbiased by a jumble of narrative and character facts gleaned from reviews.

Individual bookstores planned special event publicity. The *Wall Street Journal* reported, for example, that the Enchanted Forest children's bookshop in Dallas would feature broom decorating. Harry and the other young wizards rode brooms. Days after he first arrived at Hogwarts, he had mastered his specially selected broom (Nimbus 2000) and became adept at using it to play quidditch, a soccer-like game played on broomsticks. The Enchanted Forest bookstore would also have wand making, a hat that talks, live owls (as a means for sending messages between wizards), and a magic show. Treats would be served: Bertie Bott's Every Flavor Beans, chocolate frogs, and sloat sandwiches. These treats would be catered by the Leaky Cauldron. Similar bookstore events were held at other stores around the United States.

Publicity was not only used to drum up advance sales of the fourth book but also focused on selling a wide range of collateral merchandise. At a merchandising show, Warner Brothers (which bought the merchandising rights along with the movie rights for the *Harry Potter* series) featured a 3,000-square-foot mock-up of Hogwarts School.

Hundreds of people waited in line at the event. Each could receive some promotional freebies. This included Bertie Bott's Every Flavor Beans (Mystical Morsels) or chocolate frogs. These favorite treats are enjoyed by Harry and friends. In the story, however, everyone has to worry about the flavor of the next bean because they truly could be wretched. They are all of the flavors of the world, some of which are truly unpleasant. This and other promotional efforts were planned, with the goal of grossing $1 billion in sales.

Publicity accounts as well as the actual results of this publicity ran in newspapers across the nation and appeared on air. The *Wall Street Journal* featured the *Harry Potter* promotion in its marketplace section on June 16, 2000. All of these accounts resulted from the skilled efforts of practitioners who wanted to keep the conversations and comments about the *Harry Potter* books alive and vibrant. National Public Radio ran a feature on June 30, 2000. That account included actual audio comments by children who anticipated the book and expressed appreciation that the plot had been secret so each could experience the book in her or his own fashion. They had learned from the publicity announcement that "someone close to Harry dies" in this volume. They speculated, in true mystery narrative, who that person might be. Online, they could express who that person might be and which favorite characters they wanted to return in subsequent books.

Prior to the official release of the book, some copies were inadvertently (or intentionally) sold. The offending vendors said the sales were inadvertent. One of the vendors was an international chain that could and did receive publicity for selling the book. Its name was mentioned in news stories about the sales.

Harry Potter publicity appeared on the Web. These Web sites appealed to children. They displayed pictures of Harry, discussion chambers, vocabulary, quizzes, and interviews with the author, J. K. Rowling. One site gave children the opportunity to vote for characters they wanted to see return in subsequent volumes. Scholastic Books had a site, as did Warner Brothers, which was used for a casting call of British children who wanted to be in the movie scheduled for release in 2001. News stories were a prominent part of the Web sites. Lots of details appeared about the book, including comments by children who read the "early sales" of *Harry Potter* 4. Details emphasized the sales and highlighted the fantasy.

The Web sites dealt with the controversy that surrounded efforts to ban the books, especially in schools. Some parents were disturbed by the books' favorable image of witchcraft and at the fact that Harry and others took drugs (potions).

Over time, this publicity and promotion campaign increased the reach, as more and more people learned of the book's release and heard about the events surrounding that release. Media outlets communicated frequently about it, therefore achieving the publicity and promotion goals of increased frequency. Frequency of reports increased as the release date approached and shortly after the release. The book was positioned as a positive experience for children and their parents. Media mix occurred as print, radio, events, the Web, and television were used to communicate with interested persons.

Harry's face appeared on the corner of the cover of *Newsweek* the week before the book's release. That issue with the magazine contained an exclusive interview with the author, who was recently awarded the Order of the British Empire. Harry appeared on the cover of the next issue of *Newsweek.* Magazine cover publicity is one of the coveted plums of effective public relations.

Local libraries took this opportunity to generate publicity for themselves. They reported the preparations they had made to purchase copies of the book and expedite placing it into circulation. They had ordered extra copies to meet the demand and created waiting lists so children could wait for their turn to read the book.

This publicity and promotion campaign is an excellent example of cocreated meaning. The meaning that was used for the publicity and promotion grew from the characters, plot, and story type—mystery—that had been established in the first three books; Hogwarts School; Bertie

Bott's Every Flavor Beans (Mystical Morsels); chocolate frogs; and wands, brooms, and talking hats. Children would understand these terms from reading the books, and so would their parents. This was cocreated meaning. The meaning of the book and events developed, as symbolic convergence theory suggests, because children and parents shared their experiences with the books. As they read the stories, they shared experiences with children and parents around the world. As they dreamed of the fourth book, they shared that experience. As they read and lived the adventures in their minds, they shared an experience.

On the day after the release, newspapers carried stories of the excitement of bookstores that had created events to amuse children and their parents while they waited for the book to go on sale. News accounts reported interviews of

delighted children. Pictures featured the children carrying their copies of the book. Photos captured the costumes of store personnel who had dressed especially for the promotion. These news stories featured the dominant theme that reading is fun and that *Harry Potter* gave children reasons to read.

The publicity and promotion fostered and utilized this shared experience of anticipation and gratification. The desired outcome was a mutually beneficial relationship that led to subsequent marketing opportunities. These opportunities, however, depended on how well the book and merchandising satisfied the expectation of its demanding customers, who made strategic entertainment choices. The book had to be good or the disappointment would be devastating to the sales of that book and subsequent books in the series.

A s a budding public relations professional, imagine the mix of materials that would be included in a media kit for promoting *Harry Potter*. Also think about the writing style and information that would be appropriate for press releases to the business publications that discussed the market successes of these books. This was likely to have huge financial implications, especially for publicly owned companies. (Note: Adjacent to this story was the concern that Amazon.com would not make a profit on its sale of *Harry Potter* books because it would have to spend extra for first-day delivery—to compete with the brick-and-mortar bookstores such as the Enchanted Forest, which could not only deliver copies requested in advance by parents and children but could also add to the buzz by having a festive *Harry Potter* atmosphere, which likely would lead to sales of other bookstore items.)

So, one audience is the media reporters, which segment into feature, entertainment, and business. Each needs different information. Then, you have three apparent markets: children, parents or other relatives, and libraries. No one wants to be left out. Each wants to have the first printing. Would you need to have read the first three books to do publicity on this project? Would you want to have read the fourth book before you began promoting it?

If we think only of the communication tactics and events leading up to the first-day sales, we can miss the important promotional role that public relations performs. Let's imagine that you are charged with the responsibility of promoting the sales of the books for 3 months after the initial day's sales. What would you do? Would you have children give their testimonials? Is that ethical? Would you have parents give testimonials? What meaning are you trying to cocreate? What narrative are you playing out? What identifications are you attempting to develop?

Today's public relations focuses attention on the relationships between organizations and their markets, audiences, and publics (MAPs). An organization becomes meaningful to MAPs by what it does and says. Public relations helps it "do and say" in a strategic fashion that leads to satisfying relationships.

Market relationships help organizations to compete for the resources granted by customers, donors, followers, members, students, alumni, and legislators who fund government agencies. This discussion zeros in on two of the primary functions of public relations: publicity and promotion. It explores the aspects of the practices whereby practitioners work to influence the choices of MAPs.

Publicity and promotion add to the marketing voice of the organization. Communication managers have several primary methods they can use in their efforts to communicate with MAPs. They can use advertising—pay for their messages to appear in the media. They can add public relations to their advertising program—attract reporters' attention to newsworthy stories of which the organization is a part. If professionals carefully integrate the two communication functions, they achieve an integrated communication program.

This chapter explains how publicity and promotion are an integral part of each organization's strategic planning and implementation efforts to achieve its mission and vision. This chapter describes the processes of publicity and promotion, as well as featuring the tactics basic to these communication functions. The chapter concludes with a section that addresses the writing skills that are needed for a successful publicity and promotion campaign. Typically, publicity and promotion require strategic thinking in planning the steps in a campaign. Ultimately, the ability to succeed at publicity and promotion depends on the practitioner's planning and communication skills. These allow the practitioner to tell a story that is clear, coherent, compelling, and convincing. Effective writing is the heart and soul of the execution of publicity and promotion.

This chapter explains the concept of message points and demonstrates how they can be used to help an organization be successful in its efforts to gain attention, inform, and persuade. A message point is a fact or opinion that the sponsoring organization wants MAPs to receive, think about, remember, and recall when it is relevant to the decision a person is making.

Giving Voice to the Organization

Today's public relations practitioner gives voice to organizations. As a strategic response to the mission and situational analysis, this voice attracts attention, informs, persuades, cocreates meaning, and makes decisions with publics in a collaborative mode. Voice advances the interests of the organization through publicity and promotion. These public relations functions give vitality to the organization's efforts to generate revenue. Practitioners perform these functions regardless of whether the organization is a business, nonprofit, or government agency. Each organization needs income. Publicity and promotion are used to attract donors, followers, citizens, legislative supporters, and customers, as the case might be.

Recognizing the role of publicity and promotion in the practice adds depth to your appreciation of the nature of the practice. Much of the discussion of public relations points to the strategic role it plays before, after, and during a crisis. Those dramatic and high-tension moments often move public relations to the front page or top-of-the-hour news coverage. They shine the spotlight on the practitioner who, among others, becomes "the spokesperson for the organization." Such dramatic moments give the profession its glamour and even lead to some of the disrepute that surrounds the practice. These dramatic moments can give budding practitioners a false sense of what public relations people do. They may fight fires, especially during a crisis, but they spend far more time attracting positive attention to the organization. They create methods by which communication can be used strategically to foster positive relationships between the employer and its supporters—MAPs.

This process requires the ability to listen, a major public relations function. Strategic public relations, based on the logic of solving rhetorical problems, listens to its MAPs by performing situational analysis. Listening gives a foundation for knowing what to say and thinking strategically of the best ways to frame and present appealing messages:

1. Knowing the challenge required to achieve the mission and vision in this particular situation.

2. Knowing what needs to be said and done to meet the challenge.

3. Knowing how to develop and frame the message to meet the challenge.

4. Knowing how to write the message.

5. Knowing how to deliver the message so that it reaches its target.

This fifth step in this strategic public relations process, strategically using channels and public relations tools, is featured in Chapter 11. The first two steps were developed in Chapters 4 and 5 and expanded in Chapter 6. Now, we need to fill in the center of this challenge. To start that discussion, the next section explains how publicity and promotion are strategic functions used to build mutually beneficial relationships.

▶Publicity and Promotion as Strategic Functions

Planning becomes more strategic when it is framed in terms of the total effort of the organization to create and implement its business plan. The public relations plan is designed and implemented to support the organization's strategic business plan. These are framed in terms of management by objectives:

- Mission and vision statements
- Situational assessment
- Strategy formulation
- Strategic adjustment and relationship development
- Evaluating the strategic plan

Chapter 3 gave insights into the strategic process of knowing which relationships you must build, maintain, or repair. Then, you were challenged to select public relations strategies to accomplish those objectives. This line of thinking has three components: (1) Understand the dynamics of each relationship, (2) think in terms of message development objectives (MDOs) needed for each relationship, and (3) select appropriate public relations tools to create mutually beneficial relationships. To define MDOs, we advise that you consider the following:

- Gain attention.
- Provide useful information (informing) desired by each specific market, audience, or public.
- Persuade and be persuaded through dialogue within appropriate and ethical limits.
- Engage in collaborative decision making.
- Cocreate meaning through narratives, identification, and symbolic convergence.

A logic guides strategic planning to address MDOs. It begins by listening—conducting research or being attentive to MAPs. It entails observing the messages and deciding which stakeholders agree and disagree with the message positions that are relevant to the organization's interests. This analysis focuses on the stake held by the stakeholders and considers the conditions under which the stakeholder will grant or withhold the stake. When the organization and the stakeholder agree, the relationship is positive, and when they disagree, it can be negative. Positive relationships lead to stake giving; negative relationships result in stake withholding.

Practitioners conduct various amounts and types of research in preparation for publicity and promotion campaigns. Research sheds light on which narratives exist in a situation and lets practitioners know which story they need to tell to attract attention, share information, persuade an audience, and cocreate meaning. Research reveals the information and motives MAPs have and what they further need to know to act in ways that foster mutually beneficial relationships with your client organization.

Practitioners are wise to understand as much as possible about what they know and how aware they are of your organization or its products and services. You should investigate how much information they have, whether it is correct, and whether they are predisposed to act favorably on the information and the relationship they have with your organization, as well as with its product and services.

Chapter 8 featured theoretical foundations that give you insight into how people become attentive, how they acquire and interpret information, and how they are convinced and motivated to act in various ways. Chapter 5 outlined McGuire's 12 steps of opinion formation and behavior as part of the discussion of objectives. These stages are useful focal points for conducting situational analysis. As you think about how and why to communicate with the targets of your message, you need to consider where each is in terms of the stage in this model. Some need to be exposed to the message. Thus, publicity and promotion seek to attract the person's attention. Others need reasons to understand your organization, as well as its products and services, so they have reason to like them. The story needs to be repeated so that it sticks in the mind of markets and audiences. They need examples to help them think the behavior will benefit them and so they can consolidate their opinions and behaviors in a way that is favorable to your organization. Thus, you should consider the following elements as useful for publicity and promotion:

- Being exposed to a message
- Attending to a message
- Liking or becoming interested in a message
- Comprehending the message
- Acquiring the skills to use the information and evaluation contained in the message
- Yielding to the message
- Storing the message content in memory
- Recalling the message content from memory
- Deciding on the basis of the information retrieved
- Behaving in a manner that is based on the information
- Reinforcing behavior that leads to positive outcomes
- Consolidating behaviors that are positive so that they become routine and repeated

As you think about publicity and promotion, you are wise to imagine where in the 12 steps of opinion formation and behavior your MAPs are. You might need to attract attention through publicity for a new product. You might use promotion to give people the information and incentive to acquire skills for interpreting your message. You might increase the chances that a market or audience can recall the name of your product at the time they choose one product as opposed to another. And your promotion might focus on reinforcing behaviors so that people's opinions and behaviors consolidate. A happy repeat customer is the foundation of a successful operation. It also assumes that the person has been able to form a mutually beneficial relationship with your organization.

This line of analysis and the strategic responses that follow result from efforts organizations make to respond to choices. The choices that MAPs make pose challenges to those who practice today's public relations.

Conceptualized as part of the organization's planning and implementation efforts, publicity and promotion are strategic functions designed to accomplish specific outcomes that serve the interest of the organization by building mutually beneficial relationships with its MAPs. To contribute to the success of organizations, they give voice to those organizations. They tell the story of the organization, as well as about its products, services, personnel, and relationships. The next section offers a narrative rationale for strategic publicity and promotion.

▶ Publicity and Promotion as Strategic Narratives

Publicity consists of the strategic processes of creating and responding to a story. Promotion requires that a series of strategic tactical functions be performed over time to keep the story alive. To create and sustain a story, practitioners give some information at various stages in the evolution of the story. Practitioners may formulate different story lines or plots, all of which merge into one story.

Human beings like stories. They think in terms of stories. They describe what occurs in their lives by bringing details to life as stories. They watch movies and sitcoms, as well as sporting events. These have plot, drama, theme, characters, situation, and scripts. Humans tell stories about their daily activities. When students make excuses for missing their assignments, they craft stories—whether they are true or not.

Reporters are in the narrative business. News consists of narratives. Reporters engage in research to understand a story. They write the story so that they can tell it accurately and fully—and in a manner that attracts listeners, readers, and viewers.

Today's public relations practitioner realizes that communication can be used to tell a story. Publicity is the public relations function that creates a story or responds to evolving stories. Promotion keeps that story alive for a longer period of time. In these ways, public relations attracts attention, informs, persuades, and cocreates meaning.

To promote and publicize requires that practitioners be able to help organizations create and tell stories. These stories need to appeal to MAPs. They need to appeal to reporters.

Reporters are trained storytellers. Part of their education centers on what makes a story newsworthy. They develop techniques that make them more interesting and appealing storytellers. They are drilled to conduct research by asking simple questions that are basic to narratives: who, what, when, where, how, and why? Who are the persons in the story? What are their characters and motives, and the other human elements of the story? What happened? What events led to, occurred during, and followed the key moments of the story? When did this occur? How did it happen? Why did it happen?

As you pitch a story to a reporter, remember he or she was trained to think in these narrative terms. So, as you design your press release, conduct the press conference, or pitch the story, think in narrative terms that feature who, what, when, where, how, and why. This line of discussion will be expanded later in the chapter when we discuss writing techniques, but for the moment, this overview suffices to introduce you to the elements of story from the reporter's point of view.

You might take a rhetorical narrative approach to the development of publicity and promotion. To bring this analysis to life, we illustrate it with the elements of the

Harry Potter publicity and promotion campaign. Consider the following elements of a narrative:

- *Narrator(s):* Who tells the story? In what context? For what reason(s)? What personae are presented in the story?

    The *Harry Potter* story is narrated by the publisher, which wants to reveal details about the release of the book in ways that tantalize the reader. Reporters become narrators by reporting on the book, the success of the series, the popularity of the characters, and the details of how bookstores create events that capture the essence of mystery and witchcraft.

- *Auditors:* To whom is the story told? In what context? For what reason(s)? How do the auditors interpret the story?

    The primary auditors of the story are customers—people who want the book—and those who are interested in children reading. One set of auditors includes the investment community, who like successful business stories. Children are not only narrators, sharing the fun they have with the *Harry Potter* mysteries, but are also auditors.

- *Plot:* What plot and theme are central to the story? Do different narrators tell the same story but with different plots or themes? Do the characters enact the same story in the same way? Does the story lead to a mutually satisfactory resolution and the development of a mutually beneficial relationship?

    The *Harry Potter* plot has two themes. One is the continuation of the story that began in the first volume. The second is the way in which the publisher and the book vendors worked together to create a wonderful marketing experience for children. The test of the quality of the book depends on its appeal to the children. Do the children find it as fascinating as they had hoped? Are they pleased?

- *Moral:* What is the moral of the story? Do people use the same story to make different points? Are the morals compatible or incompatible?

    The moral of the *Harry Potter* book is that good wins over evil. The moral of the promotion is that good books attract and interest young readers.

- *Characters:* Who are the characters of the story? How are they featured? What archetypal characters emerge? What motives drive the choices of the characters?

    The *Harry Potter* story features four sets of characters. One is made up of persons who create and narrate the story, the publisher, and the public relations and marketing personnel. The second consists of persons who help enact the drama of the release, primarily the bookstore owners, and thousands of other persons who maintained the secrecy of the plot. The third is the children and their parents, who hope the book would be enjoyable. The fourth is the commentators who share their insights. Some were narrators who told the story of the release. Others commented on how *Harry Potter* stories had given children incentives to read.

- *Location of the story (internal to the organization or external):* Where does the story transpire?

    One location was the bookstores, the events they would hold, and the fun they would create. Here, the drama of getting the book was played out. A second location was that imaginary land of Hogwarts School. Children who are caught up in the story are likely to see it in terms of the narrative of *Harry Potter*.

- *Relationship:* What relationship is enacted by the actors? What metaphor describes this relationship? Is the relationship mutually beneficial?

    Some may see this marketing effort as exploiting children, just another way to use hype to market a book. Another analysis might take a different tack. Do the children and their parents enjoy the drama of the promotion? Does it add to the enjoyment of the book? Does it feature reading and give children more incentive to read? Do the children and their parents think the experience was mutually beneficial? Did they get their money's worth?

If this narrative works to further the relationship children and their parents have with the publishing company and the author of the series, then they have cocreated meaning. The essence of this narrative publicity and promotion campaign is its ability to build on the meaning that has been cocreated by the first three books in the series. The next section reminds you that communication and positioning are strategically used to increase the likelihood that MAPs will make choices that favor your organization and build mutually beneficial relationships with it.

▶ Publicity and Promotion as Strategies for Influencing Choices

Public relations tries to influence the choices people make. It responds to those choices, perhaps reinforcing some choices and suggesting alternatives. An automobile dealership seeks to reinforce the decisions of customers who bought from it. It seeks to change the choice made by customers who purchased from a competitor. Publicity and promotion are vital public relations functions that organizations use to interact with people who are making various choices: to gain awareness, to become informed, to be persuaded, and to cocreate meaning.

Some of those choices deal with purchase preferences. They also relate to the decisions people make as they decide which nonprofits to support with their time, contributions, donations, and memberships. People choose to buy or not buy and to buy one product instead of another. People choose to give or not to give and may give to some charities or belong to some nonprofits but not others.

These choices call for public relations that operates in a wrangle of competing voices, each of which seeks to influence other persons. Whether businesses or nonprofits, competitors seek the attention of the same customers, donors, and contributors. They compete for purchases, loyalty, charitable donations, and contributions. They work to create, maintain, and repair relationships.

Public relations responds to the choices people make. During a crisis, for instance, some people choose to believe that a company or other type of organization is "guilty as charged." Others choose to take the side of the organization. In this sense, crises entail publicity, perhaps unjust and undeserved publicity. The organization may decide either to communicate until the storm of crisis subsides or to take advantage of this time to increase its publicity. In the latter sense, savvy practitioners recognize that when they receive lemons, it may be wise to decide to make lemonade.

This book assumes that people are more willing to do business with organizations with which they have good and mutually beneficial relationships (Ledingham & Bruning, 1998). To build effective relationships, the organization must align its interests with those of its MAPs.

Publicity and promotion offer public relations functions that help build relationships because organizations become known as sources of information, persuasive influence, and shared meaning with their MAPs. They help people make choices that are mutually beneficial, which can entail developing aligned interests.

▶Publicity and Promotion as Strategies for Aligning Interests

Practitioners recognize the limitations of communicating with MAPs in terms of their clients' interests instead of the interests of those persons they are trying to reach. Since the chapter on theory, we have emphasized the importance of aligning interests and communicating with persons who are involved in the topic or are motivated to be involved with the topic advanced by the practitioners. Sometimes practitioners respond to the needs and interests of audiences to obtain information, become aware, be persuaded, and cocreate meaning.

Public relations message objective development fosters an alignment of interests between an organization and those persons whose goodwill it needs to achieve its mission. Interests align where people understand one another, agree with one another, and are satisfied by the benefits they receive from the relationship. Understanding, agreement, and satisfaction constitute shared zones of meaning. A zone is a shared point of view on some topic, issue, or choice.

One objective of public relations is to work to cocreate meaning that supports the mutual interests of the organization and its key stakeholders. This can entail changing some zones and demonstrating how others align with one another. Zones align because of shared facts, evaluations, or conclusions. They can align through shared identifications and when the values used by the company are those used by MAPs. For instance, physicians and parents want to promote children's health for compatible but different reasons. Their interest in children's health is an aligned zone.

Customers want a good product at a fair price. Publicity and promotion need to let them know about products, where they are sold, and why they are a fair price for the value received.

As always, we need to keep in mind the parallels for public relations between nonprofits, businesses, and government organizations. Donors and members are the customers of the nonprofit. They want a good product—the service of the organization to achieve some beneficial end. Thus, the community symphony is a nonprofit. The goal is to use publicity and promotion to increase attendance and patronage of the symphony. To do so, the interests of the symphony and music lovers must align. They share a zone of meaning regarding the enrichment music brings to people's lives.

Publicity and promotion focus on this zone supplying information, persuasion, and motivation so that the symphony sustains itself financially and the public enjoys classical and classic pop music. That is an aligned interest that is mutually beneficial. Publicity and promotion sustain the relationship by listening to the public and communicating about the symphony.

One strategic MDO choice is deciding which message points are central to the solution of each rhetorical problem. A message point is a basic unit of thought (information, attitude, belief) that needs to be understood, evaluated, and accepted under the circumstances. For instance, if you were promoting the grand opening of a new store, you might quickly think of the message points that need to be established with the key market:

- The name of the store
- Location of the store
- Store hours
- Date of the opening
- Special attractions, such as sales or entertainers
- Featured products or services

If a celebrity or musical group is going to be part of the grand opening, that information becomes a message point. Perhaps the opening is going to be associated with a charitable fund-raiser. That information becomes a message point. In this way, the practitioner has in mind the rhetorical problem (notifying people of the opening and motivating them to visit the store) and the substance of the message that needs to be set into play to solve the rhetorical problem. This would be the message of a promotion.

In that sense, the message is all of the information and persuasive appeal, the cocreated meaning, that you want each customer to recall and act on when the day of the grand opening arrives. This meaning defines how the interests have aligned. The nonprofit needs money to accomplish its charitable goals, and its contributors believe that those goals solve problems and serve the interests of society. That means their interests align.

With these principles in mind, the next section develops the logic of publicity. Publicity uses stories in placed media and responsive media (perhaps in conjunction with paid media) to attract attention, inform, and persuade as the foundation for motivating markets and audiences. The section features steps for accomplishing a publicity plan: setting objectives, using research, developing message points, creating and implementing the tactical plan, and evaluating the success of the plan.

Publicity in Action

Publicity generates news. It features information about a business, nonprofit, or government agency. The news often focuses on the activities of the organization, such as a grand opening, or on a product or service.

The art and science of publicity come together when reporters and editors get information from a practitioner and use the information in a news report because they believe that it is newsworthy. Each day, reporters create stories based on information supplied by practitioners. This media relationship benefits the organization, which has its story told, as well as the reporter, who is looking for newsworthy information.

Either directly, through a presentation of information to the press, or indirectly, by creating a newsworthy event that reporters cover, the practitioner works to get his or her client's story told. It becomes available to the targeted MAP through the media and subsequent conversations that the news story creates. Whereas publicity is a one-news-story project, promotion occurs over time through a series of publicity efforts. Thus, publicity becomes the heart of the publicity and promotion duo.

▶ Publicity and Objectives

What do you want to accomplish with your publicity efforts? It is not enough to answer that you want "some publicity." That's a weak answer. As noted in Chapter 5, objectives need to be more specific and focus on information, attitude, and/or behavior. Generating publicity itself is a process, not an outcome. Publicity provides message points that targeted MAPs can use as they make strategic choices: which products to buy, where to buy them, when they are on sale, where to work, where to invest. The information provided in publicity supports relationships because it helps people to make informed and wise decisions. Those decisions, in turn, can benefit your client. Your client, with your professional assistance, demonstrates that it is committed to serving its market, employees, community, and investors.

So publicity planning begins by setting objectives that serve the business and public relations plans. If we think about the publicity and promotion leading up to the new *Harry Potter* book release, the objective was to generate sizable first-day sales for the book, a behavior objective. The business logic was to create buzz surrounding the book and sell lots of copies.

▶ Research and Publicity: Listening to Markets, Audiences, and Publics

Research is the foundation for strategic and public relations planning. As you develop your publicity plan, you might recommend the use of a survey, for example, to determine whether people in a community know about your nonprofit if you are helping a client to open a new office there. If they are aware of it, what do they know about it—its mission, the persons it serves, the problems it solves, its financial needs, and the success it has had (information)? Your survey might address the extent to which the audience believes it is a worthy nonprofit, deserving their donations and voluntary support (attitude). The final step is to research the motivation your target market and audience feel toward contributing to and supporting the nonprofit (behavior).

You might conduct other sorts of research as well. For instance, if the publicity event entails live entertainment, what kind of music is most appealing to your target audience? What sort of food is most appetizing? Do you need activities to entertain children so that their parents will not be distracted during the event? Do you build the event around the children, as was the case for the *Harry Potter* book, and have activities that appeal also to the parents? To answer these kinds of research, you would not conduct a survey, but might interview key people. Research helps you to understand the audience's awareness, information, persuasion, and shared meaning. This situational assessment allows you to plan the publicity to respond to the audience and to build stronger relationships.

▶Developing Message Points

Message points are the key ideas that you want the targeted MAP to remember when they need the information to make decisions. If your client is a nonprofit that is launching its fund drive, what are the message points that you want the MAP to receive, remember, and act on?

- The name of the organization
- The starting date of a fund drive
- The need for money
- The good the money does
- The human element of charity
- The social problems that are solved through the charity
- Where, when, and how money can be contributed
- Telephone numbers and Web addresses where additional information can be obtained
- Time, place, and nature of the event kicking off the campaign
- The reputation of the organization

These message points are incorporated into a variety of specific MDOs that are delivered through the tactical plan in order to achieve the plan's objective(s). To illustrate the strategic use of publicity, recall the vignette that opened Chapter 6. It featured a marketing communication campaign designed to establish specific message points about Nabisco's Chips Ahoy! cookies. That tactic nearly backfired, requiring a public relations response to a disconcerted group of schoolchildren to repair a potentially damaged relationship. The response illustrates how MDOs are used to pursue information, attitude, and behavior objectives.

Recall the story, that a teacher used real-life problems to help children learn to count. She wanted to make counting important to the children, to show them that counting helped them to gain information they could use. This teaching technique created a rhetorical problem for Nabisco. Nabisco advertised that each 18-ounce bag of Chips Ahoy! contained at least 1,000 chocolate chips. The teacher challenged the children to count the chips in several bags. They did. The totals they counted ranged from 340 to 680—far below the advertised claim. The children were shocked. They wondered whether there is truth in advertising.

Children in those classes sent nearly 100 angry letters to Nabisco expressing concern and outrage about the false advertising claims. That is the rhetorical problem.

What is the solution? A company spokesperson visited with the teacher; she learned that the children had counted only the chips they could see in each cookie. To demonstrate the number of chips in each bag of cookies, she placed a bag of cookies in a colander and soaked them until only the chips remained. She asked the students to count the number of chips again. The total number was 1,181 (Blackburn, 1997). This was an excellent example of customer relationship building by using publicity. It rests on the creation of a platform of fact the children could use to understand the quality of the product—as well as the reputation of the company.

The goal of this publicity effort was to prove several informative message points. It sought to demonstrate the company's commitment to customer relationships. In this way, the company and the children cocreated meaning and aligned interests. Nabisco had informational objectives to pursue. The following informative message points emerged during the publicity effort:

- Each bag of Chips Ahoy! contains at least 1,000 chocolate chips.
- Nabisco is willing to prove its advertising claims through public scrutiny.
- Nabisco responds to customer inquiries.
- Nabisco makes responsible marketing communication claims that can be trusted by its customers.

Situational analysis asks key questions: What attitudes are at play? Are they likely to lead to the wisest, most mutually satisfying outcomes? Do attitudes need to be changed? Can they be changed? Which can be reinforced? What changes need to be made by the client organization in light of prevailing opinions? MDOs are a strategic persuasion response to the rhetorical problem. Create a box, put the name "Nabisco" in it, and see what attributes you can imagine the children and their parents would associate with the company as a result of this publicity event. Note also that this publicity event could be the basis for advertising that would appeal to children and parents, and that advertising would make the point regarding the number of chips in each bag.

To this end, would the following be desirable terms for defining Nabisco?

- Nabisco is an honest company.
- Nabisco is an open company.
- Nabisco respects children as customers.
- Nabisco supports public education practices.
- Nabisco tells the truth.
- Nabisco makes a good product.

You can use this logic to think about any organization's reputation. Its reputation is the attitude people have about the organization.

Ultimately, Nabisco wants markets to keep buying the cookies (a behavior). The situational analysis led Nabisco to conclude that the children had used the wrong research method to calculate the number of chips in a bag of cookies. One publicity strategy would be to send a letter to the children. A more dynamic method would be to work with the children so that they cocreate meaning. Then, based on that outcome, messages could be released that could be reported to other customers. These publicity messages would not only increase the reach of the information about the number of chips but also demonstrate the corporate responsibility of Nabisco and show that it is an honest company worthy of continued patronage. Public relations messages are targeted to solve problems by addressing issues. Each issue can call for a different message or a different combination of messages. In the case of Nabisco, the company used a corrected version of the test methods used by the children. Nabisco crafted a message that showed it was honest and cared about its customers; it worked with the children and did not attack them. The information provided by Nabisco helped customers to maintain a positive attitude toward Nabisco and continue buying the cookies. Publicity, as part of the public relations plan, supported the business plan.

Once message points have been selected, the publicity effort requires the creation and implementation of a tactical plan. The plan is the means by which people receive messages and engage in communication with the organization.

▶Creating and Implementing the Tactical Plan

The tactical plan constitutes the steps and strategies that are used to get the messages to the intended MAP. Effective publicity requires a sound understanding of how the media operate, how reporters develop stories, what constitutes a story, how media outlets prefer to receive information, how important deadlines are, and which deadlines reporters and their outlets impose. Practitioners rely on media relationships as they implement their publicity plans. Publicity can take many forms.

News and Press Releases

Media releases such as news or press releases alert media reporters, editors, and news directors to key stories. They are a staple of publicity because they are the conventional vehicle by which public relations people send information to reporters. Today, these can be sent through e-mail. Reporters can be notified that one or more press releases are available at the client's Web site.

News releases are typically one- or two-page statements crafted to appeal to the news interests and needs of reporters. They may also include a video news release. These are short tapes that include footage and sound that can be used on television.

The objective of a news release is to attract attention to the story and convince the reporter the information contained in the release is newsworthy. News releases need to be brief and to the point. They can alert the reporter to additional sources of information, including the practitioner and the Web site. They contain all of the key message points. They need to be written in AP style, the style of the news industry. Sentences should be short and crisp. The same standard applies to paragraphs. The document must be double-spaced. It needs to grab the reporter's attention in the first two lines. It should not build up to the key point. It builds from the key point that is designed to "hook" the reporter's and reader's or viewer's interest. Box 12.1 provides a summary of how to write a news release, along with a sample release.

(Text continues on page 362)

BOX 12.1 WRITING A MEDIA RELEASE

The media or news release, sometimes called a "press release," is one of the first documents public relations practitioners learn to write. It is an informational document designed to entice a journalist into writing a story. The idea is that the journalist reads the news release, is interested in the information, and writes a story based on the news release and/or additional information he or she collects for the story. Understanding the format and content requirements for a news release will improve the odds of your material making it through the clutter and into the news media.

Format and Content

A news release is highly stylized. Two sample news releases are used to illustrate the style. The sample news releases follow a generic format, a common set of rules used to construct a news release. Keep in mind that organizations might have a preferred "house" style that is different from the one presented in this chapter. When you start a job or internship, check to see what the preferred style is for news releases. There are nine basic elements to the format of a news release. Each of these nine elements is identified in the "Elm Industry" news release:

1. Organizational ID [A]: the name, address, telephone number, and other contact information of the source should appear at the top of the first page. This can be done with organizational letterhead or by having specialized release letterhead. While typically found at the top, the letterhead may actually place the contact information at the bottom of the page.

2. Contact [B]: This is the person or persons the journalist should contact if he or she has any questions or needs additional information. Provide a complete list of contact information, including telephone numbers, fax number, and e-mail address. You may actually provide more than one potential contact person and his or her contact information.

3. Release Date [C]: Most releases will be for "immediate release." Recently, some releases include no release date unless you are asking for an embargo for a later time. For embargos, include the date only when absolutely necessary and do not include the time of day unless it is important. Embargos are suggestions, and there is nothing to prevent the journalist from using the information ahead of time.

4. Headlines [D]: Determine whether the media outlet wants headlines. If a headline is included, it is usually placed in capital letters and/or underlined. If one is not included, leave one or two inches so a headline can be inserted later. Public relations writers are split on the topic of headlines in news releases. Some say it is very important to catch someone's attention, while others feel it is a waste of time.

5. Dateline [E]: This is the start of the body of the news release. It contains the origin (city and state) and date (month and year). Remember to follow AP style for state and month abbreviations.

6. Lead Paragraph [F]: This covers the who, what, when, where, why, and how for the news release. The lead must be both informative and compelling to the reader. Why read the rest of the news release if the lead is pointless and/or dull? This lead paragraph is two to three sentences long, so your writing ability must meet the challenge of presenting the central information in a way that is both concise and interesting. It is important that you feature the news values in the lead paragraph. From the start of your release, the journalist should know what news values your message embodies. For local media outlets, it is critical to place the local news value in the lead paragraph.

7. Body [G]: The body of the news release is your message. Keep the body short, one page when possible, but never more than two pages. We knew a journalist who loved to show people an eight-page news release as an example of how bad public relations people can be at their jobs. The body of a good media release follows an inverted pyramid style. The inverted pyramid means you place the most important information first and the least important information last. As you go down the body of the news release, each paragraph is less important than the one before it. If there is space, the last paragraph can be a boilerplate. A boilerplate is a two- or three-sentence description of your organization.

8. Traditional End Marks [H]: It is common to mark the end of a release with "-30-," "ENDS," or "XXX." These are simply conventions that let the reader know the release is over.

9. Slugline [I]: When you need a second page, a slugline is placed at the top of the second page. The slugline is a short, key word (one word) identification of the news release's subject and the page number. The page number will read "2/2," meaning two of two pages. On the first page, instead of a traditional end mark, you place "-more-" at the bottom of the page. This lets the reader know he or she should look for another page. The slugline and "more" are very helpful if the two pages of the news release are separated. The samples include a one-page and a two-page news release.

In addition to these nine elements, a news release should be double-spaced, left-justified margin only, on 8.5"-by-11" paper, and have margins of 1" to 1.5". These format "rules" are designed to help the journalist reading the news release. Wide margins, double-spacing, and inverted pyramid allow a journalist to edit on the news release itself and to quickly identify the important information in a release. The organizational identification tells the journalist the source of the message, while the contact information provides a resource for gathering additional information. Journalists are unlikely to create a story if they have no means for collecting additional information for it. The dateline helps to clarify the timeliness and local nature of the news release. The other elements simply guide the reader through the message. Violating these generic rules will not make your news release stand out in a good way. You will be perceived as amateurish or poorly skilled if your release deviates from these generic rules. Following the format for a news release is the first check a journalist uses in determining whether to read it or to recycle it.

ONE-PAGE NEWS RELEASE

Elm Industry, LLC [A]

25 Sane Parkway

Niles, Ohio 44446

330-652-7777

Contact [B]

Janet McNabb

Phone: 330-652-7521

Fax: 330-652-3920

E-mail: jmcnabb@elmin.com

http://elmin.com

FOR IMMEDIATE RELEASE [C]

SIMS NAMED HR PROFESSIONAL OF THE YEAR [D]

Columbus, Ohio—May 1, 2004 [E]—Kyle Sims, human resources director at Elm Industry, LLC in Niles, has been named "Ohio's Human Resource Professional of the Year." Each year, the Ohio Association of Human Resource Professionals (OAHRP) honors one of its 450 members with this honor. The announcement was made at an afternoon award ceremony in Columbus, Ohio, that honored human resource professionals from around the state. [F]

Kyle has worked at Elm Industry for 15 years. She has served the last 10 as director of human resources. "Ms. Sims is known for her dedication to employee concerns," said Elm Industry President Drew Carey. "She represents the good qualities held by all of our fine employees."

A committee composed of three officers from OAHRP and two members elected by the memberships select the professional of the year. The committee reviews approximately 30 applications per year for the award. These applications include letters from various people who work with the professional. The committee looks for professionals who exemplify the best the human resources can be. [G]

-30- [H]

TWO-PAGE NEWS RELEASE
Elm Industry, LLC [A]
25 Sane Parkway
Niles, Ohio 44446
330-652-7777

Contact [B]
Janet McNabb
Phone: 330-652-7521
Fax: 330-652-3920
E-mail: jmcnabb@elmin.com
http://elmin.com

FOR IMMEDIATE RELEASE [C]
SIMS NAMED HR PROFESSIONAL OF THE YEAR [D]

Columbus, Ohio—May 1, 2004 [E]—Kyle Sims, human resources director at Elm Industry, LLC in Niles, has been named "Ohio's Human Resource Professional of the Year." Each year the Ohio Association of Human Resource Professionals (OAHRP) honors one of its 450 members with this honor. The announcement was made at an afternoon award ceremony in Columbus, Ohio that honored human resource professionals from around the state. [F]

Kyle has worked at Elm Industry for 15 years. She has served the last 10 as director of human resources. "Ms. Sims is known for her dedication to employee concerns," said Elm Industry President Drew Carey. "She represents the good qualities held by all of our fine employees."

A committee composed of three officers from OAHRP and two members elected by the memberships select the professional of the year. The committee reviews approximately 30 applications per year for the award. These applications include letters from various people who work with the professional. The committee looks for professionals who exemplify the best the human resources can be. [G]

-more- [I]
Sims Award 2/2 [I]

Kyle is a 1980 graduate of Niles McKinley High School and a 1984 graduate of Kent State University with a degree in management. In 1988 she earned her MBA from the University of Akron. She is an accomplished golfer and volunteer for the American Red Cross.

Elm Industry manufactures propane tanks and related accessories. Elm Industry has 105 employees.

-30- [H]

Media Kits

Media kits may be included with the media release or made available on request. The kit contains collateral material that is relevant to the story. Some of this collateral material might include fact sheets. It might include objects and other items, including pictures, that reporters could use to gain additional information as well as incorporate into their news story. Media kits can contain CD-ROMs, which allow for reporters to receive a huge amount of information in a convenient medium. CD-ROMs also can provide pictures, sound, television footage, voices and other actuals, and graphics. They are interactive. This is especially important when reporters can gain insights by, for instance, operating some system.

The media kit for the *Harry Potter* promotion could include the names and images of the covers of the first three books. It should include a summary of the plot of each book, as well as the names of key characters and some of the parts of the books that children find entertaining, such as chocolate frogs, broomsticks, talking hats, and wands. These may be standard parts of a wizard book, but they are uniquely treated in the *Harry Potter* series. A good kit adds depth and detail to support points made in the media release. The kit should include material that adds interest to the story and can be used as part of the news story. For instance, graphics and pictures might be a vital part of the *Harry Potter* release. You might include a chocolate frog.

Media Lists

Media lists consist of the names of reporters who are targeted for each publicity story. Lists are used to pitch the story. To pitch a story, practitioners call reporters to alert them to the forthcoming media release or to call after the release to see whether additional information can be provided to strengthen the reporters' stories. Reporters cover different stories. The *Harry Potter* story might be pitched to the entertainment or children's reporters. It might also be pitched to publishing-trade magazine reporters, those who cover the publishing industry. The pitch might be to business reporters. The key for developing media lists is to segment the lists by types of reporters who are most likely to be interested in the story. A good media list is accurate and up-to-date. It is well-defined so that the pitch is made to reporters in terms of what they would see as the story value.

Media Calls

Media calls occur as practitioners pitch and follow up on the media releases they issue. Calls can be made through the Internet but typically transpire over the telephone. They give reporters an opportunity to listen to practitioners to learn the story value and to become more interested and excited about the story value in the media release. A good media call is short and to the point. It focuses on the news value of the story. It answers questions. If questions are raised that can't be answered at the moment, the practitioner must get the information to the reporter as quickly as possible. Otherwise, this media relationship becomes strained.

Press Conferences

Press conferences allow reporters to meet with key members of an organization. They begin with a statement, which could be the essence of the media release. This statement is followed by a question-and-answer session whereby reporters can ask questions and gain additional information and clarification. Although backgrounders usually occur in a one-on-one setting, press conferences allow for additional background information to be supplied by practitioners to help reporters get a richer sense of the story, its context, and key details.

Press conferences can be done in person or via videoconferences. Organizations may stage a videoconference by having representatives communicate with reporters from a room that is equipped with video cameras. Reporters can observe the representatives and hear them. Videoconferences are interactive. They allow reporters to ask questions. Sometimes a center will be created for the reporters where the spokespersons for the organization can see and hear them as well. Videoconferences can bring people together in interactive communication, while eliminating travel costs. This can be especially important for a global press conference, which is called on relatively short notice.

Events

Events play a prominent part in publicity because they generate stories. They make major newsworthy announcements. Events are a staple of publicity as well as of promotion. They attract media attention and foster identification among key MAPs. Publicity can be achieved through the general media and those controlled by the organization, such as pamphlets, flyers, brochures, and newsletters. Speeches are a staple of publicity. They feature the ideas of an executive of the organization and are a staple of the speakers' bureau.

Public Service Announcements (PSAs)

Publicity can include the use of public service announcements (PSAs). These are prepared ads (often pro bono) used by nonprofits to convey information, image elements, and persuasive messages. They are run by television and radio stations for free, as part of their commitment to community service, a licensing requirement.

Talk Show Appearances and Special Interviews

One of the keys to publicity is the ability to increase the media visibility of key spokespersons. Many opportunities exist, including talk show appearances, special exclusive interviews, and presentations at key forums. Cable outlets as well as radio constantly search for interesting interviewees. Organizational spokespersons need to be knowledgeable, comfortable in communicating in those forums, and knowledgeable of the media interview protocols. For instance, hours of preparation may be required for a 5-minute interview on television. However short that time appears to be, it gives an executive the opportunity to reach a key and large audience with a placed or responsive message.

Web Sites

Press releases can invite reporters to Web sites. Organizations can use e-mail messages to alert reporters to important new information that is available at a Web site, including those that are not sponsored by the organization engaging in publicity. For instance, a nonprofit might publicize the magnitude of the challenge it is addressing by suggesting that reporters visit a government agency Web site that presents data on the magnitude of a problem, such as abandoned children.

As is the case with CD-ROMs, the Web site is interactive. It can provide text, sound, voice actuals, interview comments in text or sound, video clips, and interactive operations or processes.

Strategic Partnerships

Businesses, governmental agencies, and nonprofits have learned the publicity value that can be created through strategic partnerships. A strategic partnership blends the interest of a company and a nonprofit group, for instance. Let's say that a company seeks to diversify its workforce and requires students who have traditionally not studied or excelled in science to increase those skills. The company might partner with a community group that seeks underserved students and mentors them in science and mathematics. Its personnel may give employee service hours to help instruct classes in these topics.

Events have some of the same publicity potential as strategic partnerships. For instance, a company can publicize its social responsibility by holding an event at which it gives a check to a charity. The charity can publicize its activities by creating an event in which it honors a company that gave money that is helping to solve social problems. Government agencies have become skilled at creating partnerships with companies and nonprofits. The agencies can then count on their partners using their communication vehicles to communicate with key MAPs to announce the achievements that have resulted from the partnerships.

Publicity requires knowing the key message points that need to be put across to meet the needs and interests of each MAP. In a press release, a PSA, a speech, or other public relations vehicle, the message content is typically limited in terms of the number of message points than can be conveyed. They may be limited to 5 to 10, depending on the length of the statement. The key is not to say a lot in one of these messages, but to say it in ways that gain the most impact. A series of statements over time may be a promotion.

Publicity requires strong working relationships with reporters, editors, and news directors. Experienced practitioners know that if they want to pitch a story successfully to reporters, they build up credits by being an accurate, reliable, available, responsive, and open source of information. Media relationships are not a one-shot event; they are groomed, sustained, and repaired over time.

To close this section on publicity, we list several guidelines that are important when working with the media. These guidelines apply to personal contact with reporters but are also vital to the design and operation of Web sites that have become a vital part of media relationships. They have become a source of information reporters can use in addition to personal contacts with organizational spokespersons. They are valued sources of information reporters can peruse and download as backgrounders and to serve as quotations. They are a repository of press releases that serve as a history of various stories that might interest reporters:

- Monitor the work of key reporters so that you know what they think is a newsworthy story.
- Learn to pitch a story to reporters in terms of a strong and interesting news angle.
- In media contacts, establish rapport by listening to reporters to hear their opinions of this and other stories.
- Be sure the reporter receives a full set of details, including the names (with proper spelling) and titles of the relevant persons. If the material is technical, provide backgrounders that help the reporter to understand all of the details that can increase the chances he or she will see this as a story. Also supply details and explanations so the reporter has every opportunity to tell the story completely and accurately.
- Include pictures (and you might make them available through special files at your Web site). Be sure that you have attached a clearly handwritten or typed caption for pictures that includes names, places, and other key information the reporter needs if the picture is printed or aired. Similar guidelines are important for the release of video clips and audio actuals.
- Be available to answer follow-up questions that may arise as the reporter develops the story.
- Connect each new story with previous ones. You are wise to think of the activities of your organization as constituting a narrative. Each newsworthy event or activity is merely an episode in the ongoing narrative of your organization. The development of a new product is, for instance, another episode in the company's narrative of innovation. Another family helped through the community services of your nonprofit is another episode in the saga of your charity. Another successful conservation erosion abatement project is another newsworthy moment in the history of your governmental agency. Think in narratives.
- Have positions and message points developed before you pitch a story or start a news conference. Know the story that you want to tell. Have the details, including a news "hook," that give life and interest to your story.
- When appropriate, give reporters access to members of your organization or the persons served by it. Bring more voices into a story but work to give the story coherence, theme, and focus.
- If questions are asked that you cannot answer, promise you will get the details to the reporter in a timely fashion—that means so he or she can meet his or her deadlines. Keep that promise, or suffer a damaged relationship because you let the reporter down in the performance of his or her job.
- Be sure that the reporter gets the story he or she wants. Know the facts and interpretations that you want to push into the story.
- Don't press the reporter to tell your story. Don't ask when the story will run or how big it will be. Don't threaten the reporter with statements such as "You take my time but don't run my stories." Realize that each story is another

opportunity to build, maintain, or destroy the relationship you and the reporter need with one another. Negotiate, build, maintain, repair, and sustain the relationship to be sure it is mutually beneficial.

- Create events that are meaningful, not what has been termed *pseudo-events*. Reporters can tell the difference. They avoid pseudo-events because they don't want to be duped into providing free time and space to a story that benefits only the sponsor. Thus, if you want to demonstrate your community commitment, sponsor an event with a nonprofit partner whose goodwill adds luster to the sponsor's reputation. If you are a nonprofit, select events that make a point. Some activist organizations walk a fine line between merely creating an event and having a function event that contributes something to society. An event such as using fashion models to protest killing animals for fur is just an event, while an environmental group that sponsors a "clean-river day" that includes getting the community involved in removing trash from the river is actually contributing to the community. The mounds of trash and debris, including old tires, becomes a media event and photo opportunity for top-of-the-hour and front-page news.

- Develop an event so that it makes a point relevant to the story you are developing. Notify the media of the event. The media may help to attract the attention of your market and audiences to the event. You may also invite targeted groups of people by several means, including direct mail invitations, Web sites, and newsletters. Prepare the event carefully so that it runs smoothly; otherwise, the poor preparation and execution are likely to become the news story. Make sure that you greet the reporters and help them to develop their story, including giving them opportunities for photographs and television footage. Provide a press kit that contains information and materials relevant to the event. Give the reporters workspace and special parking so they have easy access to the event. Introduce them to featured persons who can provide interviews about the event. Supply them with follow-up material, including measures of the success of the event, such as the number of people who attended. For instance, if your event entails competition for children, you would want to be sure the reporters know the names and ages of the children and the awards that each won. The narrative of the event is in the telling of the story by what happens, when it happens, where it happens, why it happens, who made it happen, and how it happens.

Guidelines and suggestions such as these feature the narrative aspect of publicity. Publicity entails creating and successfully pitching a story to receive placed news about your organization. It requires responses to evolving news stories that affect your organization.

Once you have a story started through publicity, you may want to sustain it and build it over time. Whereas publicity is one story episode, promotion entails creatively putting together many episodes, each of which is a reportable story. In that way, practitioners work to achieve media visibility over a period of time for the purposes of promotion of their organization or its products or services. They want to increase favorable media attention through placed and responsive media coverage.

WEB WATCHER: PR NEWSWIRE

"PR Newswire" is an electronic distribution service for news releases and other publicity materials and a monitoring service to track media coverage generated by publicity. Its Web site is http://www.prwire.com/. The PR Newswire is over 50 years old but saw the value of the Internet to publicity and became a leader in the Internet-based distribution and monitoring of publicity materials. While at the Web site, answer the following questions. How do you go about submitting a news release to PR Newswire? What is an access report, and why would a public relations department find one useful?

Promotion: Building a Message Over Time

Publicity creates a story. Promotion expands or sustains that story, by adding detail and developing new plot or theme lines. The sale of the fourth book in the *Harry Potter* series was an excellent opportunity for a promotion. It was a story that could sustain itself over several days, even weeks. Lots of people and events occurred during that time. Some of the attention reporters gave to the new book grew out of their human interest reporting, but it required that information be made available to reporters (placed stories) and answers be given to their inquiries (responsive), such as the title of the book and events that would be held by bookstores. The promotion also included exclusive interviews with the author of the book.

Promotion requires a story that can be sustained over several days, weeks, months, or years. A promotion campaign to open a new major-league baseball stadium might require months. The approval of the stadium would be one element of the story. Construction is another element. As the date for opening the stadium arrives, many stories need to be told, including how people will find parking and the sorts of food venues that will be featured. A sports story focuses on how well individual players will do because of the configuration of the field. Some parks favor pitchers, whereas others give advantage to home run hitters. Fan and player interviews abound on opening day.

▶Sustaining a Narrative

Promotion requires a story told in segments over time. Details need to be given strategically over time. Each new moment of the larger story needs to be designed to attract reporters' attention and convince them that parts of the larger story deserve to be told. Even companies that have been in business for decades promote their images through their longevity. Companies like to feature milestones such as turning 100 years old. Nonprofits like to feature the numbers of people they have served over the decades. These narrative details are the grist of promotion.

Situational analysis asks key questions. What series of statements can and should be made to provide and highlight details that are situationally relevant to the needs and interests of MAPs? Recall the discussion of Nabisco's publicity problem that surrounded students who were engaged in testing whether each bag of Chips Ahoy! contained as many chocolate chips as Nabisco claimed. We can think of the story of the Nabisco spokesperson meeting with the children, who used the correct method to count the chips and thereby proved that Nabisco was honest and truthful in its advertising. If we think of that story as one event, it is publicity. If we see that story as part of the ongoing efforts Nabisco makes to promote its products, then we see that publicity effort as part of a sustained promotion campaign.

As part of an ongoing series of statements, the message provided by Nabisco management focused on its commitment to its customers through sustained efforts to provide them with accurate information about its product: Keep demonstrating the quality of the company's products and the accuracy of its advertising claims. Demonstrations of the product, cookies, in class made the children (and through them the product purchasers) aware of the product and the company that markets them.

Promotions are a sustained means to attract attention, supply vital information, and persuade MAPs to use a particular set of evaluations. A promotion conveys a few message points at a time. Recall the discussion in Chapter 2 of the promotional activities used by Edward Bernays on behalf of Lucky Strike cigarettes. His campaign was designed so that each stage provided some key bits of information to the targeted market. Promotions center on events. Often these events are staged in a series, such as a product promotion tour, an investor relations road show, or a fund-raising event such as that for "Jerry's Kids" for muscular dystrophy each Labor Day. Organizations spend time and money creating an amazing array of promotional activities, such as product launches, store openings, and image or reputation building by demonstrating the organization's commitment to key interests.

Promotions sustain narratives over time. Each statement of a promotion should add one or more message points that collectively build into a coherent message.

Promotions provide the same message through many communication vehicles, each of which is designed to reach some MAP based on their geodemographic or psychodemographic profile. Different media attract different markets and audiences. As a part of the story is told through one medium, it reaches a segment of the targeted market or audience.

One principle of integrated communication is that if a consumer encounters repeated messages in many situations, the total impact can be greater than a repeated message in the same medium. Consistency in the presentation of message points, message themes, organizational image, logo, and name of the organization add to its brand equity. *Brand equity* requires that markets and audiences receive messages that feature the essence of the organization. The name of the organization and its logo are vital to differentiating and presenting the essence of the organization, along with its products and services.

A quick example adds depth to the explanation of brand equity. John Deere, which manufactures farm and residential lawn equipment, is one of the most recognizable logos in the United States. The company enjoys extraordinary brand equity as establishing the standard of excellence for its product lines. Most persons who "buy green" recognize they pay for the color as well as the quality—evidence of brand equity. One of Deere's competitors takes advantage of that positioning by indicating that its riding mower is equal to or superior to the one by Deere in quality features but costs $800 less. That company uses the question in its advertising: "Is the color green worth $800?" In 2000, Deere made strategic changes in its logo. This company, established in 1837, has changed its logo only eight times in nearly 170 years. The last previous change came in 1968, when the company also adopted the slogan, or tag line, "Nothing runs like a Deere." The yellow and green colors stay the same, but the logo of jumping deer and name changed in 2000. The deer was redesigned to give it an even more dynamic appearance, suggesting that it really does run fast and giving the impression that the company is determined and capable of being dynamic. The size of the lettering of the company name that accompanies the deer was increased to be even bolder.

▶ Promotion and Organizational Persona

Personae are vital to the narratives organizations tell. Narratives are stories that feature characters. An organization's persona is like a character in a play, novel, or film. It needs to be clearly defined and presented in a manner that is convincing and fosters a mutually beneficial relationship with stakeholders and stakeseekers. The *persona* or *character* enacted by an organization results from the residue of what key MAPs know of its actions and statements.

Through public relations and advertising, an organization features its character in the context of the larger narrative, such as community service through charity. A college or university is an excellent example a of a persona. Each college or university wants to differentiate itself so that it exhibits a particular persona. It might be a tier-one research institution. It might specialize in agriculture. It might be a small, elite liberal arts college. It might have an excellent sports program.

The personae of organizations are demonstrated by what they do and say. Part of the rhetorical problem facing public relations professionals is knowing the narratives that align with the interests of their stakeholders and stakeseekers. Promotion seeks to tell an organization's story to targeted, selected groups of people so they and the organization can create, repair, and sustain a mutually beneficial relationship.

Research and situational analysis need to examine the narratives that are important to each of the targeted groups. People think in terms of narratives. Situational analysis figures out the narrative that needs to be enacted to achieve the mission of the organization given the situation in which it finds itself.

Narratives must exhibit fidelity. That means that the facts presented and portrayed by the organization must be verifiable and fit with the facts known—accepted—by MAPs. Narratives must meet the standard of probability. That means that they must be coherent and not internally inconsistent (Fisher, 1987).

Graphics and other visual presentations are vital to conveying the narrative messages and personae of organizations. Public relations messages predominantly consist of words, but they are also presented in conjunction with pictures and in graphics. The organization's logo on the stationery used for the press release is a good example of how graphics are featured in promotion. Events give an opportunity for the name and logo of the organization to be featured. Web pages are a striking example of the use of pictures and graphics to make some important point—and to present an organization's persona. Graphics often present facts relevant to the information being presented and rhetorical argument being made. Graphics can dramatize issues, feature a product's attributes, and feature the traits the organization wants to use to define its persona.

Graphics may be thematic and constitute evidence presented in support of public relations claims. One striking example is the environmental images of nature utilized in Chevron's "People Do" campaign. This campaign features pictures of natural settings and events to highlight the company's commitment to operate in environmentally responsible ways. Print advertisements typically use graphic presentations and drawings to augment the images portrayed on television. Graphics and pictures can be powerful demonstrations of the facts, conclusions, and evaluations presented in public relations messages.

▶ Promotion and Brand Equity

A persona is the residue of the encounters MAPs have with the organization. Personae can be inferred from ad message content, communication tactics, kinds of issues addressed, and the relationship the source states, implies, assumes, or seeks with key publics.

A persona can affect how key publics react to the organization's public policy stance, and its public policy stance helps establish its persona. For instance, Mobil Oil Company (now ExxonMobil) developed a bold advocacy persona as it attacked critics of the oil industry, especially those who alleged that an oil embargo existed without being able to prove that conclusion. As Mobil became more aggressive in its stance, it asserted that it was defending the public against irresponsible reporters who avoided facts, or created them, and then hid behind the First Amendment (Schmertz, 1986). A persona can also affect and be affected by perceptions of its products, services, fund-raising activities, and impact on the community. A persona influences how well the organization is received in the marketplace and public policy arena. For example, as the local hospital needs to replenish its blood supply, it appeals to donors and creates campaigns that build and call on established relationships. Some of those relationships exist with companies and other nonprofits that call on employees and members to participate in the drive. The hospital speaks for the needs of the community. The companies and nonprofits speak about their commitment to the community and the alignment of their interests with it. MAPs react to an organization's persona based on their identification with it. Thus, they identify with Mobil as being an aggressive advocate for free enterprise that is not intimidated by the press, and the hospital and other organizations foster identifications with the health of the community.

Companies, in particular, strive to achieve brand equity as a means for increasing market advantage and market share—or their share of a market. We can even think in terms of "mind share." Brand equity is the marketplace advantage they gain because of the identity they establish with their customers and other stakeholders.

Savvy communication personnel plan to communicate with targeted audiences in ways that feature the positive attributes of their organizations. They develop message points and use carefully designed and strategically placed logos to define and differentiate themselves from their competition. The logo should feature the brand essence of the company, its products, its employees, and its customer relationships.

All of these actions and statements can add value to the organization because it dominates or enjoys a larger share of the top-of-the-mind thoughts about itself, or its products or services. Brand equity predicts the likelihood the organization will receive preferential thoughts and treatment by the organization's constituents.

Brand equity is the positioning value of the name and identity of the organization as measured by the perceptions of its key audiences. This means that organizations with strong brand equity enjoy a visibility and reputation that differentiates them positively in comparison to their competitors. Watches are an example. Some watches are positioned and their brand equity is managed so that they are leaders in the lower-cost, multiple-function "plastic electronic watch" segment of the market. In contrast, other watch companies seek the brand equity that they are the top end of the market and are worn only by "persons of distinction." Equity comes when people believe that the organization, or its products or services, adds value to their life. This value is partly symbolic and partly actual. It demonstrates market differentiation that influences purchase preferences, including wants, even if they cannot be fulfilled. Some expensive cars, such as Porsche and Ferrari, have brand equity because people want them, even though they cannot afford them.

Brand equity is the unique, differentiated essence (character) of an organization or its products or services. Essence is that carefully defined and refined kernel of meaning that uniquely distinguishes one organization from another, especially through marketing communication that also ties the organization, product, or service to the identity of the person who uses or prefers the product, service, or organization. Texans respond emotionally and intellectually to the brand of pickup they drive. It may become part of their personal legacy that is also linked to the legacy of the product in Texas. They have pickups that are "Texas Tough." The essence of the product is its unique kind of toughness that is itself unique, because Texas Tough is tougher than any other kind of toughness.

Brand equity can be developed through integrated communication, including promotion. Brand equity expresses the essence of the organization. Its essence might be expressed in terms of its communication style, such as "objective advocate," "policy innovator," "informed source," "tough debater," "outraged activist," "children's advocate," "environmental protectionist," "product innovator," and "friendly advisor."

CHALLENGE BOX

Think of organizations that you believe exhibit or achieve each of the personae mentioned, and consider the personae you believe are presented by organizations with which you are familiar.

An organization's persona is revealed through its communication strategies, which it may develop through advertising and promotion. For instance, an "informed source" persona was used by the U.S Council for Energy Awareness (USCEA) in its "Energy

Updates." USCEA was a public information organization that was created to influence key publics' understanding and appreciation of the use of nuclear energy to generate electricity—nuclear generation. It presented small bits of information in each "Energy Update," which it ran in a series for several years in leading newspapers, such as the *Wall Street Journal*. It participated in public policy debates and governmental hearings on the safety and economic impact of nuclear fuel to generate electricity.

Nonprofit activist groups have rhetorically redefined the personae of government and private sector organizations. Activists try to reframe the power bases of society. They strive to "publictize" the private sector into their view of the public interest; that is, they believe that industry should adapt to the opinion of the public. Environmental groups often employ this tactic. They challenge private owners of land to act responsibly so that their use of the land does not harm wildlife that "belongs to the public." This dialectic of public and private interests is the heart and soul of public relations (Heath, 1993; Pearson, 1989).

Advocates of public policy issue positions exhibit personae that are vital to the campaign they are waging. The same can be said for the marketing and fund-raising efforts of organizations. Governmental agencies work to define and portray personae aligned with their missions and interests of key MAPs. For instance, the FBI and the Justice Department seek different personae than do welfare agency departments such as the Department of Education and the Department of Housing and Urban Development (HUD). The Department of Commerce differs from the Department of Defense.

Similar tailoring exists for activist group personae and brand equity. Some activist groups—Greenpeace, for example—seek to position themselves as (portray a persona of being) extreme, active, and radical demanders of policy change. In contrast, the Audubon Society is more staid, and the World Wildlife Fund positions itself to support research and fund species preservation.

Universities strive for unique personae based on their academic programs, admission and graduation standards, athletic programs, campus mascots, students, alumni, and faculty. Fund-raising organizations tailor their missions and demonstrate their personae as a vital part of their efforts to generate and apply funds in ways that foster and sustain long-term relationships between donors and benefactors of those funds.

In Chapter 6 we referred to four key concepts that can be used in strategic positioning. Here those concepts are applied to specific organizations:

- *Differentiation:* Public relations can help to differentiate one organization from its competitors. This requires using messages to demonstrate that its products, services, issue positions, operations, mission, and marketing strategies (including fund-raising) make it unique—different from other organizations. For instance, the World Wildlife Fund features itself as a nonprofit that uses research and collaborative decision making to preserve species. It quietly uses publicity and promotion to feature its program accomplishments. Greenpeace, in contrast, differentiates itself as an organization that uses outrage and confrontation to publicize environmental issues and promote activism.
- *Associations:* Public relations can use messages that demonstrate to the client organization that it is associated with positive characteristics that align with

the interests of the MAPs. For instance, publicity and promotion associated the release of the fourth *Harry Potter* book with adventure and intrigue.

- *Identity:* Public relations can make statements that define the organization, such as proving that it is a bold advocate, technical expert, wise advisor, defender of the environment, or protector of abused women. Mobil sought to demonstrate that it was a bold advocate for free enterprise and fairness in journalistic reporting as it defended oil companies against allegations that they were engaging in an embargo to raise gasoline prices. The USCEA was a technical expert commenting on the safety, environmental benefits, and national security that can be accomplished by using nuclear energy to generate electricity. Women's shelters create the identity that they protect women and children against physical and mental abuse.

- *Goodwill:* Public relations builds relationships by using messages to demonstrate how organizations operate with goodwill and commitment to customers, neighbors, employees, alumni, followers, and donors. Marketing communication statements feature product/service quality at prices that are fair. Relationships can indicate to employees and neighbors how committed the organization is to benefiting the community. These statements can be made on behalf of companies, nonprofits, and governmental agencies. Governmental agencies, for instance, like to feature how the citizens' tax dollars are being used wisely for the community.

People identify with organizations that align with their interests and share their zones of meaning. Through dialogue, employees and management build a persona that can establish mutually satisfying relationships with one another and with their customers, and align interests. Employees identify with the organization where they work. Managements identify with employees. Products are featured by using messages that customers can use to identify with the organization. We often call this *brand loyalty*. Customers may disidentify with a product or organization when they see the purchase of the product or the support of the organization as conflicting with their identities. Students identify with their school or university. They proudly wear T-shirts and sweatshirts as well as display bumper stickers that express their academic affiliation. They identify with one another through their shared identity. They chant this identity at sporting events. They identify with other students from that school or university. Persons with commitment to environmental protection identify with environmental groups and disidentify with organizations that they believe harm the environment. Viewed this way, identification is cocreated meaning, shared zones of meaning (even campus rivalries), and aligned interests.

Identification can predict product purchase and other favorable granting of financial stakes, such as donating to a charity or enrolling in a college. It may be a vital part of the reason why students choose one college over another. It seems to be key to alumni association membership and sustained contributions to alma maters. If people identify with animals and other parts of the environment, are they likely to join and support environmental movements? If they identify with the targeted group of a nonprofit, such as cancer victims, are they likely to support its efforts? For that reason, we can understand why people support the American Cancer Society. The list of identifications is endless.

Based on the rhetorical problems facing their organizations, public relations professionals use MDOs to create identifications through cocreated meaning. Promotion is a public relations function that over time not only adds to the meaning it shares with others but also demonstrates how the organization shares the meaning of its markets and audiences. Promotion may demonstrate how the organization adheres to the attitudes preferred by the MAP. Identification can emerge through collaborative decision making whereby organizations and key publics work together to solve problems. Promotion can be used to demonstrate this working relationship. It tells the story, over time, of the successful operations of the organization in cooperation and harmony with its MAPs.

▶ Promotion Through Multiple Public Relations Tools

Because promotion transpires over a longer period of time than does publicity, it requires the use of a wider array of public relations tools. The tools of publicity are those needed to get one news story. Promotion requires a sustained series of stories, and tools are a way to get those stories to the targeted markets and audiences. Also, because the story is sustained for a longer period of time, promotion can use many tools to reach different markets and audiences.

To create, maintain, restore, and enhance market relationships, practitioners can select from a long list of tools:

Using Events for Promotion

SOURCE: Copyright © Graham Barclay/Bloomberg News/Landov.

- Press releases and media kits
- Product (service) releases and stories
- Feature releases and stories
- Customer applications, testimonials of satisfied customers
- "How-to" releases and events
- Expert columns (real estate, cooking, automobiles)
- Events
- Road shows, media tours, trade shows, product shows
- Videos, books, booklets, catalogs, pamphlets, and Web sites
- Briefings and backgrounders
- Samples and coupons

Harry Potter gives us an excellent example. In 2005, the sixth book in the series, *Harry Potter and the Half-Blood Prince*, was released. The promotion was exactly the same as it was in 2000. The same theme, agreement, excitement, testimonials, and positive comments created another page in this narrative. Network and local television and print coverage featured this ongoing adventure. Children were interviewed who had read the previous five books "dozens of times." The author, J. K. Rowling, was interviewed. Reporters even commented on the fun they and their children had with this fantasy. Again, the theme of excited children enjoying reading was central to the entire narrative. The Web again played a vital role in the promotion of the legendary adventure that has been translated into many languages, sold around the world, and used as the basis of hit movies.

Promotion is used to build stronger relationships with employees. Several tools are worth considering as an organization communicates with its employees to build mutually beneficial relationships:

- Employee newsletters
- Community relations through employee involvement in the community's goodwill projects
- Annual events, such as health fairs and company outings
  - Annual reports
  - Financial
  - Community relations
  - Environmental relations
  - Membership relations
  - Constituent relations

- Web sites and the organization's Intranet
  - Discussion rooms
  - Issue forums
  - Links to other discussants
  - Organizational policy and progress announcements

- Speakers bureaus
- Conference presentations
- Workshops and seminars
- Support for professional and trade associations

Tools can be adapted to the rhetorical challenges of promotion. Promotion needs a variety of tools to sustain the flow of information, persuasion, cocreated meaning, and identification. Publicity and promotion share some tools but differ in their use. Promotion requires the repeated us of the same tool or a mix of tools to sustain a story and to reach the targeted MAPs.

▶ Promotion as Proactivity

Today's public relations stresses the importance of being proactive rather than reactive. To understand these choices requires a bit of discussion. Over the years, many strategic public relations responses have been tried. One is the standard "No comment." That statement is perhaps the loudest one an organization—through its spokesperson—can make. It always conveys a negative tone. It hints that the spokesperson is aware of facts and evaluative judgments on issues that would be condemned if made public. The statement signifies an unwillingness to answer questions and be open to stakeholders.

It indicates that the organization prefers a closed rather than open communication style. It asks the MAP to "trust" it. The relationship tends to be one-sided.

"No comment" can suggest that the organization has not figured out what is happening, or has happened, and therefore is not well managed. Those two words often speak loudly to convince audiences that the allegations made about the organization are true. This weakens the organization's position to respond later and commits the organization to a reactive rather than proactive stance.

Reactivity occurs when an organization is caught off-guard by an issue that emerges before it is aware of the issue and can respond to it. Given this rhetorical problem, practitioners and scholars have expended a lot of thought to figure out the best ways to identify, analyze, and monitor issues in preparation for responding to them.

The argument against being reactive is that either the organization is faced with accepting a defensive position (clearly "No comment" is defensive) or getting to the table after the meal is well under way. That means that other parties—issue advocates, media reporters, activist groups, and disgruntled customers, for instance—have had time to define the issue, build support for their view of it, and take the moral high road. That stance can leave an indefensible position for the organization under attack.

Massive product recalls that result only after a product has received sustained media bashing exemplify this problem. Firestone tires have several times been associated with design or manufacturing flaws that had resulted in substantial injury and death. Such was the case for the "Firestone 500," which occurred in 1978 and required a recall of 14.5 million Firestone radial tires. Similar problems occurred in 2000 with a series of tires that were mounted on Ford Explorers. Many lawsuits against the company brought this issue to light, based on 46 deaths and at least 300 blowout incidents. This caused a public relations—market relationship—problem not only for Firestone (a division of Bridgestone) but also for Ford. This story erupted into top-of-the-hour and front-page news in August 2000. Television reporters went to Firestone stores to interview managers and customers. They reported frustrated customers and long waits for inspections to detect tire flaws. Recall procedures were announced as well as the specific series of tires involved and the manufacturing facility where they were produced. The total recall was 6.5 million tires. Critics had bashed the company and its products before a substantial marketplace response occurred. Family members of persons killed in car accidents made network and local news, as did persons who where severely injured during the blowouts. The *Wall Street Journal* (August 10, 2000) reported that awareness of this problem began to occur in the early 1990s as lawsuits were filed for sudden and violent tire failure.

Bridgestone/Firestone admitted that it did not have a database that would have alerted it to the mounting complaints, even though complaints had been voiced to the National Highway and Transportation Safety Administration, which relayed those complaints to Bridgestone/Firestone. Company engineers had carefully studied the tires and concluded that they were safe. Examining the slowness of Bridgestone/Firestone to respond to this market relationship fiasco, the *Wall Street Journal* ran three stories on August 10, 2000, including a front-page story under the headline "How the Tire Problem Turned into a Crisis for Firestone and Ford."

Third parties addressed the issue. In an August 14, 2000, editorial in the *Wall Street Journal*, Brock Yates sought to give a less hysterical tone to the problem. Drawing on his credibility as editor-at-large for *Car and Driver* magazine, he acknowledged that a batch of tires manufactured at one plant was likely to be at fault. He noted Ford's recommendation that a lower tire pressure be used to give the tires a smoother ride, despite Firestone's advice that a higher pressure would reduce tire friction and heat buildup. He pointed to the media, liability attorneys, and activist groups such as Public Citizen and Strategic Safety as fanning the flames of hysteria.

Ford defended its reputation by advertising safety information about the tires. It identified the vehicle models that used these tires. It advised owners on how to inspect their tires and where to look to see whether the tires had been manufactured in the plant where the defects had occurred. It supplied 1-800 numbers and a special e-mail address for its customers to use to get information about the tires. It made itself accessible to its customers.

Sage practitioners offer this advice: "Be proactive; get out in front of a rhetorical problem, an emerging issue, as soon as possible." Identify, analyze, and monitor issues to respond to them in the earliest stage possible. That advice encourages organizations to avoid being put into a defensive position. Johnson & Johnson's response to the Tylenol problem continues to be one of the best examples of a proactive and open response by a company. Deaths resulted in Chicago because people took Tylenol capsules that were laced with cyanide. The company executives used a national teleconference to meet the media. They made a product recall. They issued statements indicating that the tampering occurred after sales to the stores. They changed to using caplets instead of capsules and began using tamper-proof packaging.

That advice assumes, perhaps incorrectly, that if the organization beats its critics to the punch, it can "win" the issue and avoid having to change some policy or activity that offends them. That kind of proactivity can't work. If the opposition is angry and tenacious, it will press the issue to see the problem corrected and its solution implemented.

Proactivity means getting involved with a rhetorical problem by working for a mutually beneficial solution before the interested parties expend unnecessary time and money—human and monetary resources—as well as exhaust their goodwill to solve a problem. Proactivity might entail making positive changes to reduce the criticism of the key MAP. Proactivity may be achieved by getting information into the public dialogue while the issue is fresh and points of view are being accepted, evaluated, and digested.

Proactivity demonstrates a strong desire to act in the best interest of the community to foster and maintain mutually beneficial relationships. Proactivity empowers the critics and gives them less incentive to be hostile toward your client. Proactivity increases the likelihood that all stakeholders will listen to, respect, and regard the points of view advocated by one another. Early action can reduce the likelihood that polarization leads to destructive communication styles.

Proactivity entails getting at the front end of the rhetorical problem as quickly as possible. Texaco faced an intense situation when tape recordings surfaced that, at least in the minds of some, had top executives using racial epithets. Texaco needed to decide how it would respond. The recording was not of high quality and was obtained by stealth, perhaps with the intention of embarrassing others on the management team. Experts in the analysis of sound disagreed as to what words were actually said. Thus, as a strategy, Texaco could have debated the accuracy of the tapes in public—and perhaps ended up winning the case by demonstrating that the *New York Times* reporters and editors had misheard the tapes, which were not as damaging as alleged. At times, public debate or aggressive advocacy can be proactive. But in the case of Texaco, it was likely to bog down in semantics, giving the appearance that the company was defensive about its employment policy. So, the chief executive officer went on the offensive. He sought to ensure that the company achieved the desired level of corporate responsibility. The company communicated its commitment to change and to continue to announce its achievements to become more diverse. It wanted to be a good organization communicating well. Proactivity allows organizations the opportunity to get their information out—to increase the chance that they can say what they want—through the media, as well as through other channels.

Proactivity, then, may be more a matter of communication philosophy than it is a matter of timing. It demonstrates a commitment to several principles:

- Be community oriented.
- Seek to put the best available information into play.
- Carefully analyze the information that is in play, and invite analysis of the information.
- Express evaluations, listen to others' evaluations, and invite evaluations—genuine dialogue.
- Seek outcomes that feature "win-win" alternatives.
- Be open, candid, and honest.
- Listen, give regard, and respond in ways that demonstrate a commitment not merely to defending a position but also to fostering dialogue that can lead all interested parties to achieve a mutually satisfying, beneficial outcome.
- Seek to establish mutually beneficial relationships.

As we close this section, recall that we defined publicity and promotion as creating and responding to news media attention and coverage. Publicity and promotion seek to create and sustain a narrative to create attention, inform, persuade, and cocreate meaning. Sometimes, the narrative comes to the organization. The organization can respond reactively or proactively. The best practices of public relations stress the advantages to be gained by proactive response.

As we near the end of this chapter, consider this case study: *Who Wants to Be a Millionaire?* How would you answer that question if you had the opportunity to publicize and promote a new television program?

Realize that successful television programs are rare. Many fail to materialize or even be aired. Others struggle to achieve an adequate market or viewing audience. The challenge of producing a television program is to formulate a unique concept and have it mature into a successful program that attracts a large and loyal audience. Once that is accomplished, the advertising time achieves high value. Then, the program is a financial success.

We tend to ignore or not observe the role of advertising and public relations in the integrated marketing communication effort used to launch a new television program. "Buzz" is created through ads about the "fall lineup" or "new replacement programming." The real incentive for much of this "buzz," however, is likely to result from public relations. The communication plan for a new program launch calls for publicity and promotion. It entails getting trade reporters, entertainment reporters, and media commentators to talk about a new program that is about to be launched. These people need information about the program so that they can understand the entertainment principle of the program. If the program is a sitcom, the publicity is likely to focus on cast, situation, and plot. What about the publicity for an evening game show? That might be a different challenge.

Television viewers are a market—and an audience. Current viewers of a show or channel are a market. Viewers who can be attracted to a show or channel are an audience. Television executives seek to keep current viewers and attract new ones to fight the battle of ratings. The higher the ratings, the more they can charge for advertising and the more revenue they generate.

Launching a new television show can be risky. It has no market, only audiences to be attracted. Such was the case for *Who Wants to Be a Millionaire?* the ABC blockbuster originally hosted by Regis Philbin. Within days of airing, the show had become so popular that the phrase "So, is that your final answer?" had become part of the conversations of viewers across the United States.

Public relations helped to attract that audience and form a market. The launch occurred in the standard manner. Philbin and Michael Davies, the show's executive producer, held a press conference at the Television Critics Association semiannual event. From this media launch, they worked to attract other reporters, particularly television writers and critics. This requires having a good story and mutually beneficial relationships with reporters. Reporters want stories. Organizations want their stories reported.

The publicity and promotional efforts featured several aspects of the show. One was the phone-in process by which contestants qualified. This increased the national appeal of the program. Viewers could see contestants from small and large towns in every state of the nation. These were ordinary people wanting to become extraordinary. Public relations persons featured this Everyman appeal, even if they did have to battle the criticism that most of the contestants were young white males.

The objective of the publicity and promotional effort was to make the program appealing. It was designed to get people to talk about the show. The combination of news reports and interpersonal conversation attracted huge audiences and shaped them into a loyal market. For more details, read Alison Stateman (2000), "The Money Pit: How PR Helped Make 'Millionaire' a TV Blockbuster."

Conclusion

People often think public relations is just publicity and promotion. While public relations is much broader, publicity and promotion remain important tools for practitioners. The key is to be strategic, not random, in the use of publicity. A skilled

Gaining Publicity for a Historic Accomplishment

Terry Benczik
The Port Authority
of New York and
New Jersey

On the surface, it didn't seem like anything that reporters in a tough media market like New York City would think newsworthy. But this is a story where the best parts are subterranean. The Holland Tunnel was about to be designated a National Historic Landmark by the federal government, and my job as a Supervising Public Information Officer at the Port Authority of New York and New Jersey was to work with the Tunnels, Bridges and Terminals Department in putting together a press event and then getting the media to come. At first, I didn't have much hope.

But I had a sentimental reason beyond just wanting to do a good job. When I was a little girl, my family would drive to New York City from New Jersey on special occasions, and inevitably, as we reached the exact marker that delineated the New Jersey/New York border, my father would say, "Do you know how many people actually died building this tunnel just so people like us could drive through here?"

The 1.6 mile Holland Tunnel structure was the world's first long underwater vehicular tunnel, a marvel of the age when President Calvin Coolidge opened it in November of 1927. This facility defined the technology and has been the prototype for virtually all underwater tunnels built in the world.

Today, it is still one of the busiest anywhere.

In modern times, many have come to take the tunnel for granted. Realizing the general public knew very little about how the tunnel was built or even how it got its name helped us to plan our strategy. If we could just make history come alive and explain the invention, precision and innovation involved, perhaps there was a chance to get someone to cover this.

The story of the Holland Tunnel is a story of hope, tragedy and triumph. During a brutal winter in the early 1900s the Hudson River froze for an entire week and no ferries could get to Manhattan. There was a brief food shortage. After that, it was decided that a tunnel would be constructed between Manhattan Island and New Jersey. Clifford Milburn Holland, a brilliant young engineer, was given the impossible task of overseeing the design and construction of this mammoth enterprise. There was a "can-do" spirit in the air. One thousand workers called sandhogs labored in shifts around the clock working in pressurized caissons under the river to dig the tunnel through the riverbed. During seven years of construction, 13 sandhogs lost their lives. Holland, a 36-year-old father of four, endured impossible hours to accomplish the miracle the public was expecting from him. But Holland had a weak heart. He died the day before workers tunneling through from each side would meet in the middle. Milton Freeman, the engineer who succeeded him, died five months later of pneumonia. It remained for Ole Singstad, the ventilation engineer, to finish the job. The day the tunnel opened, the public had great expectations. People from all over came to the tunnel to "walk under water" to and from the island of Manhattan. It was a glorious celebration. The next day the tunnel opened to traffic and people just kept driving back and forth for the fun of it.

So how could reporters and members of the public born many decades later understand the context? How could a historic designation be relevant or interesting today? I began by writing a six-page history of the Holland Tunnel, chronicling the lives of the heroic men who built the structure. Next, I put together a series of "fun facts" about the Holland Tunnel versus the Lincoln Tunnel, listing everything from the amount of vehicles that have passed through since their opening to the number of tiles on the wall.

The next step was working on the event. Those planning the ceremony had discovered the address of Clifford Holland's only surviving daughter, Benita Holland Low. Ole Singstad's grandchildren were also invited. And the advance publicity for the event brought forth an 85-year-old woman named Anne Tracy, who as a girl of 17, went to the opening ceremony with her mother and joined thousands to walk through the tunnel on its first day. About a week before the designation, I started making phone calls, targeting reporters who write interesting features. I faxed the history to whoever would read it. I made sure traffic reporters had the "fun facts" to pepper through their broadcasts and had enough information about the event to "talk up." Many were surprised to learn the tunnel had a namesake.

There was a wealth of historic photos. I sent some out in advance. Though they were black-and-white stills, the pictures of workers covered in grime and perspiration breaking through rock were entirely moving.

The day of the event, major New York and New Jersey newspapers, television stations and radio stations all came, as did wire services and syndicates. Benita Holland Low reminisced about how her father would take her to visit the tunnel on Sunday, his day off. She remembered how the tunnel then smelled of mud and water and how special it was to be with her father. Ole Singstad's granddaughter said that Singstad joked often about having "brought traffic to Manhattan." And many reporters gravitated to Anne Tracy to hear her recapture the excitement of opening day.

That evening and the next day, there was press coverage everywhere we looked. Reporters talked about the tunnel as something that meant more than just asphalt and tiles. The best part was opening the *New York Times* the next day and seeing a photograph of Benita Holland Low holding a plaque honoring her father's accomplishment. Holland Low was just 8 when her father passed. The event was a way of helping today's tunnel users understand Clifford Holland's genius and sacrifice . . . and the sacrifice of the 14 others who honorably paved a well-traveled road with the most they had to offer: their lives. Their accomplishment is something my father never forgot.

I learned from this event that with patience and education people are willing and able to recognize the accomplishments of the past. And that sometimes the past can help you to see an everyday part of your life . . . such as a tunnel, in a whole new way.

SOURCE: Reprinted with permission from Terry Benczik.

public relations practitioner creates publicity and promotion in order to achieve public relations and business objectives, not simply to create attention. We also returned to the concept of message development objectives (MDOs) and showed how they can be used to pursue information, attitude, and behavior objectives. The idea was to illustrate how writing strategies used in publicity and promotion are used strategically to address rhetorical problems.

FURTHER
EXPLORATION
12

Ethical Quandary: Facts or Fiction?

You have been approached to create publicity and promotion for a small company that features the use of exercise, special diet, and herbal pills to reduce weight. The company has, among other investors, a national celebrity who is known for constantly working to reduce weight. You are told that this celebrity will make a series of statements indicating that she is losing weight based on this company's plan. One of the message points that you are expected to promote is this: "Our special diet products contain reduced fat." Another message point is as follows: "Our herbal pills increase the body's ability to use fat." Review the Public Relations Society of America (PRSA) and other professional association guidelines from Chapter 9. Review the guidelines for product claims established by the Federal Trade Commission and the Food and Drug Administration.

What three ethical issues do you need to resolve before you agree to take this company as a client (or to undertake this publicity and promotion campaign as an employee)? As you think about these ethical problems, also consider the guidelines for clear and readable communication. How would the standards of cocreated knowledge and shared evaluations affect your decisions about the ethics of this case?

Summary Questions

1. Define and differentiate publicity and promotion. Explain how publicity and promotion are part of the strategic business planning steps. What are publicity and promotion used to achieve?

2. Explain how publicity and promotion influence choices. Describe how publicity and promotion connect to message development objectives (MDOs).

3. Discuss how publicity and promotion can be used at some or all of McGuire's 12 steps of opinion formation and behavior.

4. Explain how publicity and promotion influence choices, are strategic narratives, and help organizations to align their interests to those of markets and audiences.

5. Taking a strategic approach to publicity, explain why it begins by setting objectives and includes conducting research (situational assessment), entails developing messages and message points, and creates and implements a tactical plan. In your answer, define message points.

6. Select four of the vehicles for implementing the publicity tactical plan. Define each of those vehicles. Describe the strategies for using each effectively to gain publicity.

7. List the elements of a news story that constitute reporters' education and their approach to a story. Indicate how those elements of a story are a narrative. Explain how publicity and promotion create and sustain stories.

8. Indicate the guidelines that are required for effective publicity aimed at increasing reporters' interest in the story and for developing and publicizing events.

9. Promotion requires telling a story that lasts. Two elements are important to promotion. One is the persona of the organization and its products and services. A second is its brand equity. Explain the connection between publicity, organizational persona, and brand equity. In your answer, include the concepts of differentiation, association, identity, and goodwill.

10. What are the challenges and advantages of taking a proactive approach to promotion?

11. List at least six guidelines for developing public relations documents effectively.

12. Demonstrate how key answers to MDOs can increase your ability to tailor messages to your targeted markets and audiences.

Exercises

1. Dissect a news story from radio, television, the Web, or a newspaper. Identify the reporter's answers to the following narrative elements: Who, what, when, where, how, and why. Now think in terms of the narrative characters. Who are they, and what about their nature and character make this an interesting story? What are the scripts that sustain the story? What is the theme of the story and its plot? Who tells the story? What is the relationship between the narrator and those to whom the story is told? Why is this story told? Why is it told in this fashion? What is the location of the story? How are relationships a part of this story? What are the theme, plot, and moral of the story?

2. Locate and analyze press releases on an organization's Web site. Identify what you believe is the news value and the news hook for each release. Identify the organization's persona, the relationship it is building with a target MAP, and the plot, theme, scripts, contexts, and characters of the narrative.

3. Conduct a case study of a publicity or promotional campaign. Identify and discuss the way that it was designed to accomplish one or more message development objectives (MDOs).

4. Locate and analyze some public relations materials used in a publicity or promotion effort. Review the criteria of effective writing discussed in this chapter. Analyze the extent to which the materials conform to those standards.

5. Select a person or organization for which you develop a publicity or promotion campaign. Identify the objectives that the campaign should achieve. Connect those to the business objectives of the individual or organization. Conduct situational analysis. Develop tactical options. As part of the tactical options, select the message points that need to be established. Indicate the market or audience for which the message points are intended. Define the campaign in terms of the 12 steps in the McGuire model and in terms of MDOs. Write a media release that you would issue to launch the campaign. Identify three reporters or media outlets you would issue the release to. Explain how you would pitch the release by featuring its news value and news "hook." Indicate three elements of the story that you might use for promotion. How would you evaluate the success of this publicity or promotion campaign?

6. Identify three goals you set for yourself to increase your mastery of grammar, spelling, and punctuation.

Recommended Readings

Aaker, D. A. (1996). *Building strong brands.* New York: Free Press.

Beard, C. K. (1998). Web site worthiness: How some organizations reap rewards. *Public Relations Tactics, 5*(11), 28–29.

Bible, G. (1996). The world's most valuable brands: Blind faith. *Financial World, 165*(10), 50–65.

Brown, K. (1997). How the best writers do it. *Quill, 85*(5), 11–14.

Cain, D. (1997). Do the right thing: Designing contests for kids. *Promo, 10*(4), 110.

Center, A. H., & Jackson, P. (1995). *Public relations practices: Managerial case studies & problems* (5th ed.). Upper Saddle River, NJ: Prentice Hall.

Coombs, W. T. (2005). Lucky Strike Green campaign. In R. L. Heath (Ed.), *Encyclopedia of public relations* (pp. 495–498). Thousand Oaks, CA: Sage.

Durham, D. (1997). How to get the biggest bang out of your next spokesperson campaign. *Public Relations Quarterly, 42*(1), 38–41.

Goldstein, N. (Ed.). (1998). *The Associated Press stylebook and libel manual* (fully updated and revised edition). Reading, MA: Perseus Books.

Harris, T. L. (1998). *Value-added public relations: The secret weapon of integrated marketing.* Lincolnwood, IL: NTC/Contemporary Publishing Group.

Hearit, K. M. (2005). Battle of the currents. In R. L. Heath (Ed.), *Encyclopedia of public relations* (pp. 68–70). Thousand Oaks, CA: Sage.

Heath, R. L. (1994). *Management of corporate communication: From interpersonal contacts to external affairs.* Hillsdale, NJ: Lawrence Erlbaum.

Heath, R. L. (2005). Promotion. In R. L. Heath (Ed.), *Encyclopedia of public relations* (pp. 650–652). Thousand Oaks, CA: Sage.

Hines, B. (1998). Unleashing the power of branding. *Public Relations Strategist, 4*(2), 24–26.

Howard, C. M. (1997). Marketing communications: Teamwork and sophisticated sequencing will maximize results. *Public Relations Quarterly, 42*(4), 23–25.

Lubove, S. (1998). Get smart: A reporter's take on good PR practices. Public *Relations Tactics, 5*(10), 20–21.

Lyon, L. (2005). Publicity. In R. L. Heath (Ed.), *Encyclopedia of public relations* (pp. 714–716). Thousand Oaks, CA: Sage.

Maynard, R. (1996). The lighter side of promotions. *Nation's Business, 84*(7), 48.

Newsom, D., & Carrell, B. (2001). *Public relations writing: Form and style* (6th ed.). Belmont, CA: Wadsworth.

Newsom, D., Turk, J. V. S., & Kruckeberg, D. (2000). *This is PR: The realities of public relations* (7th ed.). Belmont, CA: Wadsworth.

Papinchak, K. M. (2005). P. T. Barnum. In R. L. Heath (Ed.), *Encyclopedia of public relations* (pp. 94–97). Thousand Oaks, CA: Sage.

Ries, A., & Ries, L. (1998). The power of publicity. *Public Relations Strategist, 4*(4), 18–20.

Seitel, F. P. (2004). *The practice of public relations* (9th ed.). Upper Saddle River, NJ: Prentice Hall.

Spethmann, B. (1998). Happy birthday to us. *Promo, 11*(5), 36–39.

Stateman, A. (1999). Hello, Dalai! Publicizing the Dalai Lama and the Tibetan cause. *Public Relations Tactics, 6*(8), 1, 16.

Stateman, A. (2000). The money pit: How PR helped make "Millionaire" a TV blockbuster. *Public Relations Tactics, 7*(1), 9, 29.

Treadwell, D., & Treadwell, J. B. (2005). *Public relations writing: Principles in practice* (2nd ed.). Thousand Oaks, CA: Sage.

Tucker, K., Derelian, D., & Rouner, D. (1997). *Public relations writing: An issue-driven behavioral approach* (3rd ed.). Upper Saddle River, NJ: Prentice Hall.

Wilson, L. J. (2000). *Strategic program planning for effective public relations campaign* (3rd ed.). Dubuque, IA: Kendall/Hunt.

13 Collaborative Decision Making

When Interests Collide

Imagine you work for ChemBurn, a company that specializes in building and operating industrial incinerators. Your facilities burn industrial chemical waste, which includes many toxic chemicals. ChemBurn has an excellent safety record. It is the safest organization in the industry and has never had a major incident. Still, people do not like the idea of living near a facility that burns toxic chemicals. Residents voice concerns not only about accidents, such as sudden releases of high amounts of hazardous chemicals (safety motivator), but also about the air quality, such as continual exposure (health motivator) to chemical or environmental toxins. People worry that even small amounts of toxic pollution could harm their children. Based on research, you and the technical members of the company have reviewed, you know that ChemBurn meets or exceeds all Environmental Protection Agency (EPA) requirements for air quality. In general, research as well as your experience leads you to conclude that people would prefer not to have one of your facilities in their community. Even as they make that decision, you also know the local residents understand that your company provides jobs, pays local taxes, and serves as a customer for local businesses.

ChemBurn has purchased land in northeastern Ohio. The location is the site of a former steel mill operation that closed in the late 1970s. There is a need for an industrial incinerator facility in the area. Currently, industries must ship their burnable toxic chemicals to Kentucky.

Analysis indicates the facility would be highly profitable. ChemBurn would have a large customer base and have a competitive edge in cost for these customers. The new facility would boost stock prices and increase ChemBurn's profit margin. However, you know from past experience that getting state and federal licensing approval to build an incinerator facility is never easy. Your plant needs to obtain licenses ensuring safe operations. These require that public hearings be held. You know that public hearings can be a constructive forum to hear, listen to, and address concerned citizens' doubts and fears. You also know that hearings allow for endless public harangues by a few vocal activists. Some make sound sense. Others do not. Some merely use these forums for political expediency.

As a thoughtful and strategic public relations practitioner, you begin by analyzing your markets, audiences, and publics (MAPs). Your target MAPs include local residents, politicians, environmental groups, and the news media. All four types of stakeholders—and stakeseekers—can play an important role in ChemBurn's plans. Politicians will ultimately make the decisions to issue the permits necessary to operate the facility, but they will be influenced by public outcry. Local residents must live near the facility. They can pressure politicians to deny the permits. Environmental groups can organize opposition. Working with local residents, they can form a powerful alliance against the proposed facility. The news media will be a major source of information and opinions (evaluations) about the proposed facility and have been used by past opponents to generate negative feelings against ChemBurn and to build political pressure.

The situation is ripe for conflict and will require collaborative decision making. History suggests that people will oppose the facility. You can hear the conflict storm building, imagine the angry crowds at public hearings, and anticipate the headlines as the media bash your efforts to achieve a sound business decision and solve a community problem. Collaborative decision making is a way to make the conflict productive and to produce a mutually beneficial outcome. As noted in Chapter 3, collaborative decision making is a message development objective that allows all parties to contribute and to have a voice in decision making. ChemBurn will want to include residents, environmental groups, and politicians in the decision-making process. The news media can help by reporting all the events to other interested MAPs. By being open to the media, everyone can understand the decision-making process. Let us consider two possible options, cooperation or competition with MAPs.

The cooperation option could begin by holding interactive community meetings. At the meetings, representatives from ChemBurn can explain what the facility is, the air standards, and the safety features. Community members and environmental groups can express concerns and ask questions of the ChemBurn representatives. The community meetings would be repeated each time a major step is taken in licensing, planning, and

construction of the project. Community members and environmental groups can appoint members to a planning team. That way, stakeholders are kept informed of and have a voice in the project. The goal is to have the community and environmental groups become comfortable with and willing to support the final proposal. News media reporters and editors can report all the activities of the planning team and the community meetings. Once the planning team approves the proposal for developing the location, politicians will be asked to vote on it. The politicians should be willing to support a plan that is being endorsed by local residents and environmental groups. Winning that support is one of your responsibilities.

All of that planning and collaboration is one option. Another option, the competitive option, could involve engaging the enemy in battle. ChemBurn can focus its messages on job creation and ignore community safety and environmental concerns. Politicians and some residents can be lured to the siren's call of more jobs, tax revenues, and spending in the local economy. ChemBurn defines the issue their way, as an economic concern, and looks to win over some local support and the politicians. Which option will produce the quickest results? Which option will be cheaper to implement? Which option is most likely to succeed? Which option is mostly likely to produce a long-term, mutually beneficial relationship between ChemBurn and its various MAPs? Which option is the more ethical? These questions are frequently asked of today's public relations practitioners.

P ublic relations is committed to community building. The best evidence of that commitment is the use of collaborative decision making to build relationships. Public relations is a monologue if managements and senior practitioners believe they can create policy positions on controversial positions and sell them to their MAPs. Dialogue brings parties together to resolve differences and solve some problem that could harm their relationships.

Today's public relations has willingly embraced this philosophy of the practice because it is ethical and effective. It demonstrates the rhetorical principles of public relations: the good organization communicating effectively. This chapter discusses in detail the principles and best practices of effective collaborative decision making.

Collaborative Decision Making as a Strategic Function for Giving Voice to an Organization

Public relations can help organizations to take strategic actions needed to avoid or resolve conflict. Conflict is a major rhetorical problem that practitioners are expected to solve. Let's open this section with an adage: If MAPs think a problem exists, then a problem exists. This principle reminds strategic planners to realize that they must address and solve problems, not merely deny or avoid them.

When a conflict occurs, some organizations turn immediately to the legal department for advice and action. That can be a problem, because lawyers are trained to defend their client's interest—perhaps at the expense of other interests. Traditional public relations was often practiced in a similar spirit. In contrast, today's public relations finds virtue in using collaborative decision making to solve conflict.

Conflict can result from deeply held interests and evaluations that support mutually exclusive choices. Conflict is not mere disagreement. It is a clash over differences about which people feel strongly—are cognitively involved. They are willing to punish, impose penalties on, those who block their efforts to resolve the conflict.

Planning for Collaborative Decision Making

To understand the role of conflict, think about your own reaction to organizations that violate your expectations. If a store treats you rudely, do you want revenge? If advertising claims about a product are misleading, do you want revenge? If a company operates in ways that you think harm your health or safety, do you want revenge? If a company or other organization damages the environment, do you want revenge? MAPs have plenty of incentive to challenge organizations. For this reason, rhetorical problems arise!

Conflict can be resolved by several methods. Contemporary literature, as well as best practices of today's public relations, suggests that competition can be an unconstructive, even destructive, approach to resolving conflict. Whereas most experts advocate a "win-win" spirit as being constructive to resolving conflict, competition very often fosters—and indeed is so defined as—a "win-lose" approach to conflict. One party wins, but at the expense of the other parties that are interested in the outcome. Court cases typically result in a win-lose outcome.

Conflict can be resolved by negotiation, a form of compromise. It assumes that through give-and-take, parties can work out their differences. Through dialogue, they trade concessions for what they truly want from the decision. Negotiation is a means for working through the available choices so that all parties compromise.

Collaborative decision making, according to Conrad (1985), is a process during which the interested parties believe "that they should actively and assertively seek a mutually acceptable solution" and are "willing to spend large amounts of time and energy to reach such an outcome" (p. 243). Collaborative decision making requires that interested parties work together to create an outcome that best satisfies each other's needs and interests. Collaboration is joint problem solving. It can lead to a solution for a shared problem in a manner that satisfies the needs and interests of all parties.

Collaborative decision making fits the process of strategic planning that we have featured in other chapters:

- *Mission and vision statements:* What the organization wants to accomplish will be supported by some and opposed by others. Collaborative decision making can help the organization position itself so that it reduces friction and maximizes support. Positioning requires effective communication with the key stakeholders.
- *Situational assessment:* The opinions of key publics shape the environment in which the organization operates. Collaborative decision making requires that public relations practitioners carefully monitor the environment for conflicts that can affect the destiny of the organization. The assessment looks for key stakeholders and listens to their opinions.
- *Strategy formulation:* Strategies of collaborative decision making can be divided into two broad categories. It requires a good organization that is committed to effective communication. To be a good organization, it must be committed to build relationships that reduce conflict and acknowledge the concerns of stakeholders. The second strategy is to build dialogue with other interested parties to examine ideas, information, and issues, looking for best solutions to problems.
- *Strategic adjustment and relationship development:* As issues change, strategies need to be adapted to them to reflect these changes. Public relations practitioners need to adapt to the dynamics of conflict so that they work to align interests and resolve the issue.
- *Evaluating the strategic plan:* As always, practitioners need to be able to assess the extent to which their strategic choices and the implementation of their communication efforts have been successful. If harmony increases and conflict decreases, the conflict has been wisely managed. If conflict and friction continue and even increase, then new strategic options are needed.

Effective strategic planning leads to narratives that feature the organization as being committed to the interests of its stakeholders. Successful organizations will receive favorable news coverage and support of their stakeholders.

▶ Collaborative Decision Making as Strategic Narratives

Strategic narrative was a key theme in the chapters on publicity, promotion, and issues management. That theme supplies the rationale for collaborative decision making as well. Today's public relations centers on the development and enactment of narratives. No better narrative demonstrates an organization's commitment to its stakeholders than the ongoing drama of its concerted efforts to work with them to achieve mutually beneficial relationships.

Empowerment results when individuals, groups, and organizations look back to admire their accomplishments. Success is the basis for empowerment. Empowerment results when people, organizations, and media reports focus on successful problem solving. One of the startling trends in community relationship building, as will be demonstrated throughout this chapter, is organizations' commitment to work with the community to solve problems.

As was demonstrated in the opening vignette, ChemBurn was willing to demonstrate its commitment to the community to work in concert to listen and respond, to solve problems. In this way, the narrative that occurred in the community focused on harmony rather than conflict. Media reports capture these positive efforts. News stories feature the drama of a community with aligned interests working for relationships that empower them.

▶ Collaborative Decision Making as Strategy for Influencing Choices

Choices can divide an organization from its stakeholders. If the stakeholders believe the organization is limiting their choices, they are likely to oppose the organization. Conflict results. Relationships can be damaged.

Customers can believe that companies limit the ability to buy safe products. Employees challenge companies' efforts to limit wages and working conditions. Environmentalists oppose the efforts of businesses and government to set the levels of environmental damage.

Choices of this kind can be made through collaborative decision making. They can entail battles that result in damage to reputations and relationships.

Today's practitioners recognize the virtue of involving stakeholders in key decisions. They know they can diffuse conflict if they allow affected publics and audiences to help make choices that affect their interests.

As was demonstrated in the opening vignette, citizens do not want ChemBurn to make choices that could affect their health, their safety, and the quality of the environment without listening to and considering community concerns. ChemBurn is wise to aggressively seek and heed public advice on its operations. Collaborative decision making is a proactive response to potentially damaging conflict.

▶Collaborative Decision Making as Strategy for Aligning Interests

When organizations engage in collaborative decision making, it proves their sincere commitment to align their interests with those of their MAPs. Conflict tends to occur when MAPs worry that organizations' interests collide with their (the MAPs') interests. Markets believe that product quality and safety drop when companies want to maximize profits. Employees conclude that companies pay lower wages to make higher profits. Citizens worry that their health and safety are harmed in the name of profits. When companies stop and make key decisions with citizens, it demonstrates that their interests align.

ChemBurn was willing to demonstrate its desire to operate profitably and protect citizens' health and safety. When a company or other organization opens itself to public scrutiny, it shows its commitment and goodwill. It demonstrates that it cares about the persons who could be affected by its policies and operations. Collaborative decision making requires working with others to make decisions. It entails listening to the concerns of MAPs. To solve problems requires aligning interests by solving problems so that one interest does not suffer at the expense of another.

For these reasons, collaborative decision making is a valuable means for giving voice to the organization. Today's public relations practitioners know that relationship building takes time, money, and effort.

Collaborative Decision Making: A Valued and Needed Public Relations Function

Collaborative decision making is not quick. It is not cheap, and it is not easy. It takes time to discuss and resolve differences while making a decision. Over the last several years, however, collaborative decision making has become a valued and needed public relations function. At one stage of the practice, media relations was probably the defining function of the practice. Today, in sharp contrast, many organizations have recognized that public relations can play an instrumental role in resolving conflict between them and their key stakeholders. Collaborative decision making is a vital function for discovering and achieving mutually beneficial relationships.

Consider a situation in which you and three friends are going out to dinner. It may be quicker if you pick the restaurant than trying to reach a decision that satisfies the four of you. If you do this, does it guarantee that everyone will be satisfied? In fact, even with collaborative decision making, not everyone will be fully satisfied, but at least all feelings and preferences would be considered as the decision was made.

Likewise, it costs money to make changes to business plans and policies to satisfy critics who call for new government regulations. Each organization must spend money to comply with the new regulations. It is not easy to resolve conflicts and reach a mutually agreed-upon decision. Conflict can escalate and turn negative, or people may simply try to avoid it. Either way, the conflict does not become productive—does not lead to resolution that benefits both parties. Collaborative decision making is not always possible or desirable. Key publics may have no desire to be part of the decision-making process or may not be able to add anything to the process, or time may be too short for collaborative decision making.

This section has provided the background information necessary to develop a collaborative-decision-making approach to your practice of public relations and helped you know when it is appropriate. It is an important strategy for cocreating meaning.

Collaborative decision making is given prominence in today's public relations. It is one of five message design objectives and is considered valuable enough to warrant its own chapter. So you should ask, "Why is collaborative decision making so valuable?" and "Does public relations really need to use collaborative decision making?" This next section will address these questions.

▶ The Value of Collaborative Decision Making

The fields of organizational psychology and organizational communication have studied the effects of collaborative decision making for years, under the guise of *participation decision making* (PDM). PDM gives employees a voice in decisions that affect their work life. PDM gives employees a feeling of control over the workplace (Witt, Andrews, & Kacmar, 2000). The feeling of control results in numerous benefits: greater job satisfaction, increased productivity, increased understanding of the organization, more positive attitudes toward management, and greater fulfillment of higher-order needs (Miller, 1999). Moreover, the employees feel better about the decisions and are more willing to support them (Witt et al., 2000). We believe similar benefits occur when PDM is applied to public relations—when organizations use collaborative decision making.

PDM facilitates the empowerment of employees. Empowerment has become a buzzword in organizations that often loses its meaning. True empowerment occurs when people feel they can and have accomplished tasks in an organization: They are no longer powerless to effect change. They gain control over what is done in the organization and the conditions under which it is done.

Employee relationship building offers many examples of the positive impact of collaborative decision making. Employees' feeling of being empowered results from their awareness that collective efforts have made a positive difference. Table 13.1 lists some of the broad topic areas over which employees might have control. However,

Table 13.1: Areas of Employee Control

1. Identification of problems in the workplace
2. Development of alternatives for solving workplace problems
3. Evaluation of alternatives for solving workplace problems
4. Selection of alternatives to use for solving workplace problems
5. Implementation of the alternatives and follow-up evaluation of the alternatives

not all employees are willing to take the greater responsibility for their own work that accompanies empowerment (Eisenberg & Goodall, 1997). PDM is a process, a way for workers to have a say in decisions. PDM is actually a feeling gained when employees have a voice and are involved in making decisions (Barge, 1994). Each area represents an increase in responsibility for the employee and implies greater control over the decision.

Organizations and MAPs can work together on a number of different types of decisions. Community groups might be involved in decisions regarding the location of a facility or access roads, the type of volunteer work a company's employees engage in, or what social issues an organization should address. Customers and activists might be involved in decisions about the type of products a company produces, the nature of a company's advertising, the suppliers a company uses in third-world countries, the disclosure of the exact location of overseas suppliers, and the creation of codes of conduct for suppliers. Stockholders might be involved in decisions about where a company invests its money and where a company locates its own overseas facilities. These are but a few of the wide range of opportunities for collaborative decision making.

The central argument for collaborative decision making is that it builds mutually beneficial relationships. If stakeholders are involved in decision making, they should be more satisfied with their relationship to the organization, view the organization more positively, feel better about the decision, and be more willing to support the decision. Table 13.2 draws a parallel between the organizational and public relations benefits of PDM. Our logic is consistent with James Grunig's (1992) call for two-way symmetrical public relations. Dialogue, two-way communication between organizations and stakeholders, is central to the two-way symmetrical model of public relations. Collaborative decision making is one form of two-way communication and a perfect forum for a dialogue.

Collaborative decision making adds value because it can reduce costs. Class action lawsuits have come to require enormous settlements, in the billions. They offer huge financial rewards to attorneys. They give customers, employees, citizens, and other offended

Table 13.2: Public Relations Benefits of Participation Decision Making (PDM)	
Benefits in Organizational Literature	*Benefits for Public Relations*
1. Increased job satisfaction	Increased satisfaction with MAP-organization relationship
2. Increased understanding of the organization	Improved alignment of goals
3. Increased positive feelings toward management	Increased positive feelings toward the organization
4. Increased willingness to support the decision	Increased willingness to support the decision
5. Feel better about decisions	Feel better about decisions
6. Increased productivity	Improve organization's ability to operate in its environment

parties the feeling of revenge. People use them to punish organizations: businesses, government agencies, and nonprofits.

Research by Murphy and Dee (1992) underscored the reality that negotiation and compromise are not easily achieved. Examining the relationship between companies and polarized activist groups, they discovered that each side in a policy battle espouses an ideological position that may differ from its behavior. For instance, one side might espouse a particular environmental position, but act in ways that do not correspond to that ideology. Company and activist ideological positions may be quite similar in principle, but each side may opt for different solutions to the shared problem. Neither group wants to embrace that similarity as the basis for negotiating solutions. The differences between activist groups and the targets of that activism seem to reach a point at which issues become personalized and compromise is a matter of losing face. This is not a pretty prospect for resolving public policy differences.

To continue what we discussed in Chapter 10, Shell UK used collaborative decision making to reduce the cost of disposing of the Brent Spar oil buoy. Its strategic business plan called for a decision that disposed of the buoy in the manner that was most environmentally responsible and cost-effective. Despite its best-laid and well-executed plans, Greenpeace derailed Shell's planning efforts. Nevertheless, Shell UK received substantial applause for using collaborative decision making. If it was at fault, the error was in not anticipating the potential for Greenpeace intervention. Whether Greenpeace would have participated in collaborative decision making is questionable. Activists use conflict to raise the cost of business activities. That cost pressures companies into decision making that can privilege a narrow agenda of activist groups.

In additional financial costs, social costs are also important. Organizations can strain their relationships with their MAPs. They damage their goodwill. They harm their brand equity and reputation. Good relationships with stakeholders increase organizations' ability to accomplish their goals.

The value of collaborative decision making results from reduced business costs, increased ability to generate revenue, and better rapport with MAPs. Research indicates that communities are more willing to support chemical-manufacturing companies that pose safety, health, and environmental quality problems if the companies communicate effectively with the communities. Companies increase their acceptance by demonstrating that they care for the air and water quality in the community and are working to ensure the health and safety of the citizens if a chemical release occurs (Heath & Palenchar, 2000).

Scene of the Conflict: Brent Spar

SOURCE: Reprinted with permission from Greenpeace.

▶ The Need for Collaborative Decision Making

One of the compelling needs for collaborative decision making results from the incentive on the part of businesses, government, and nonprofits to achieve aligned interests. Thirty to 40 years ago, the standard model was for industry to impose its will on the public, assuming that the public would be motivated to align its interests with companies' interests. That model has changed—dramatically. Starting with the activist 1960s, the equation began to reverse. Activists sought out industry and government to align their interests with those of the activists.

Do stakeholders really want to be involved in collaborative decision making? As with PDM in organizations, stakeholders must be willing to take the responsibility for their involvement in decision making. The 20th century witnessed a rise in stakeholder activism. A wide array of stakeholders became willing to contact an organization to voice their concerns. Those stakeholders are quite able to attract media attention and thereby to make their concerns public. Stockholders are filing more resolutions to change corporate policies and governance. Customers complain or condemn an organization publicly, and social activists expose and confront corporate misconduct (Coombs, 1998, 1999). Stakeholders want and expect more dialogue, honest and open interaction with organizations to solve mutual problems. Stakeholders believe communication should be two-way between themselves and an orgnization. This new stakeholder activism results from often narrowly self-interested organizational practices. Organizations have encouraged communication from stakeholders because such communication is critical to maintaining an effective organization—stakeholder relationships—one premised on mutual benefit (Grunig & Grunig, 1992; Heath, 1994, 1997).

Technology facilitates stakeholder communication with the organization as well. E-mail, discussion groups, and chat forums all promote two-way, interactive communication. E-mail provides an easy way for stakeholders to send messages to an organization. But the authors of those e-mails expect a meaningful and useful response. A discussion group, sometimes called a "newsgroup," is an electronic bulletin board devoted to one topic. People post messages, and other people reply in private or post a reply to the entire newsgroup.

Organizations have learned to promote and facilitate such conversation rather than ignore or seek to stifle it. Shell Oil is an example of an organization that sponsors discussion groups on its Web site to encourage stakeholder discussions and expressions of opinions. Shell Oil maintains various discussion groups on its Web site. A chat forum is a "real-time" discussion that includes members of an organization and MAPs. Organizations have learned that they can listen to their critics and concerned publics as well as respond to them. Many retailers, such as "Martha Stewart Living," sponsor chat forums for MAPs as a way to generate Web traffic and revenues.

But what does this all really mean for public relations? An organization should give the stakeholders what they want. Stakeholders increasingly want to interact with and influence organizations. Furthermore, technology is facilitating that interaction. Collaborative decision making should become a part of that communication mix because of the benefits it can generate. If stakeholders want to participate in decisions, an organization should try to facilitate collaborative decision making. Technology makes it even easier, as geographic location is no longer required for a meeting. People from around the world could be part of a collaborative-decision-making team that meets in cyberspace. The technology for such meetings exists and is relatively cheap. Organizations seem to have stakeholders willing to be involved in decisions and the technology for making such groups easier to form and to operate. It is logical that organizations will increase the use of collaborative decision making.

One of the compelling needs for collaborative decision making comes from the value that results from an honest effort to solve problems and resolve conflicts. Public relations entails relationship building. These relationships should lead to mutual benefits. Dialogue is essential to this outcome.

Collaborative Decision Making in Action

A mutually beneficial relationship implies that all parties participate in its creation and maintenance. That participation should include decision making. Today's public relations professionals have become increasingly aware that they are wise to counsel employers and clients on strategies that build these relationships. One of the strategies begins with the realization of the pitfalls that result from efforts to impose unilateral decisions on stakeholders. Unilateral decisions result when one party in the relationship makes the decisions that affect the other members of the relationship but does not reflect their input.

Today's practitioners suggest that organizations and stakeholders collaborate on important decisions. The organization and the stakeholders should contribute and have a voice when all are affected by the decision. The organization and stakeholder must decide on a course of action both can accept. This often means working through conflict—differences in how to solve the problem. All parties are more likely to benefit when each has its perspective heard and integrated into the decision.

For public relations, collaborative decision making involves three essential factors: (1) small groups/teams, (2) decision making, and (3) conflict. Small groups or teams are created to make the collaborative decision. Representatives from the organization and the stakeholders meet as a group to make the decision. The decision making for collaborative-decision-making groups involves solving a problem. The organization and stakeholders are making a decision about how to resolve a problem. In the opening vignette, ChemBurn and its stakeholders are trying to decide the best way to build and to operate the facility—solve the problem about the organization's operation. Conflict occurs when people or groups are interdependent and have conflicting goals or values (Putnam & Poole, 1987).

Collaborative decision making acknowledges that organizations and MAPs are by definition interdependent. They engage in collaborative decision making to resolve conflicting goals or values. ChemBurn and its stakeholders had different goals for the new incinerator. ChemBurn was interested in profit, while the community was concerned about safety. By understanding the three essential factors involved in collaborative decision making, we should be able to implement collaborative decision making more effectively. To make collaborative decision making work, people must be able to handle conflict in a productive fashion.

▶ Conflict

It is only natural that a group will have conflict or that people will perceive incompatible goals or values. Conflict can be very useful to a group. Vigilance is based on conflict; people will argue for and against positions. The key is cooperation, the willingness to maximize the gains for all parties involved in the conflict (Daniels, Spiker, & Papa, 1997). If people are willing to cooperate, conflict becomes productive. When people become overly competitive, viewing the situation as "win-lose," it becomes destructive. People vary in terms of being competitive or cooperative (Baron, 1983). To build mutually beneficial relationships, people must draw out their cooperative side for the good of the group.

Although people will react differently to conflict, they will have a typical way of handling disputes. Kilman and Thomas (1975) developed a popular set of five conflict management styles:

1. *Avoidance:* Choose not to address the conflict.

2. *Accommodating:* Give in to the demands of the other party and smooth feelings more than resolve differences of opinion.

3. *Competition:* Try to force the other party to accept your demands.

4. *Compromise:* Split the difference; both parties win some and lose some.

5. *Collaborative:* Work together to find a solution that benefits both parties. Collaborative approaches to conflict help the key parties to align their interests as a major step toward achieving mutually beneficial solutions and building relationships that reflect those shared interests.

Group members should learn to recognize these conflict management styles and be encouraged to use the collaborative style. Even the compromise style can have positive results, but the other three are problematic in a collaborative-decision-making situation (Daniels et al., 1997). Conflict is part of the decision-making process and a reason for engaging in collaborative decision making, a point we will address later in the chapter.

The strategies used to resolve conflict affect whether it is productive or destructive. Bargaining, or negotiation, is one strategy for dealing with conflict. Putnam and Poole (1987) defined it as follows: "Bargaining constitutes a unique form of conflict management in that participants negotiate mutually shared rules and then cooperate within these rules to gain a competitive advantage over their opponent" (p. 563).

Bargaining is formal. It does have rules that the participants create and follow; it involves representatives or groups; parties involved in the conflict will select representatives who represent the entire group; and it is often used to resolve intergroup or interorganizational conflict (the conflict can be between groups or between organizations) (Miller, 1999).

ChemBurn serves as an illustration. The conflict could be between ChemBurn, a community group, and an environmental group (interorganizational conflict). Each of the three organizations selects representatives for the collaborative-decision-making team. The team sets rules for the discussion and presentation of the problem and proposals. Under these circumstances, the collaborative-decision-making team would be using negotiation and bargaining.

Bargaining can be subdivided into two strategies, distributive and integrative. *Distributive bargaining* occurs when a party tries to maximize its gains while minimizing its loses. Communication is often deceptive, and sides will try to withhold information to create a bargaining advantage. *Integrative bargaining* occurs when parties work to maximize the gains for both sides (cooperation). Communication is open, and information is shared (Miller, 1999). A collaborative group that uses bargaining will reinforce the need for and use of integrative bargaining strategies. Leaders and members of a group must remember to maximize cooperation during conflict. Cooperation is the only way to make the conflict productive.

Throughout this book, we have focused on mutually beneficial relationships as the centerpiece of public relations. Conflict can pose a threat to mutually beneficial relationships when MAPs perceive the organization's policies as nonbeneficial. Stakeholders might escalate conflict as a way to force a change in organizational policies. In the fall of 1990, NBC and CBS announced plans to scramble satellite transmission of professional football games. The National Football League (NFL) would have prevented the free transmission of games to sports bars. Two sports bar owner coalitions formed and threatened a boycott of the Miller Brewing Company and other prominent sponsors of NFL broadcasts. Miller arranged for meetings between the leaders of the coalitions and the networks. The coalition explained the value of showing out-of-market games in their sports bars. The networks dropped the scrambling plan a few days after the meetings, citing technical problems with scrambling. Miller admits that it became involved in the situation only because of the threatened boycott. Miller did not want a significant share of its customers angry in the highly competitive beer market.

Collaborative decision making is one way to prevent or to resolve conflict between an organization and any of its MAPs. Of course, it is a radical measure to make a MAP part of the organization's decision-making process. Collaborative decision making shares power and information with stakeholders. Not all organizations will be comfortable with such sharing.

To be a wise and effective public relations counselor, you may need to be able to build a case that convinces management of the virtues of the collaborative-decision-making process. You may need to help executives to appreciate the benefits of collaborative decision making in conflict resolution.

To maintain a mutually beneficial relationship, an organization must identify and resolve conflicts with MAPs. An effective resolution is one in which a MAP sees the outcome as beneficial to itself. James Grunig recommended early detection and resolution of conflict in his model of strategic management of public relations (Grunig & Repper, 1992). Chapter 3 emphasized the importance of finding an early solution to problems in the organization-MAP relationship. The sooner the conflict or potential conflict is identified, the less effect it will have on the relationship, and the less damaging the aftermath will be. The key functions of public relations require practitioners and other executives to listen to their critics and to respond proactively to those concerns.

Conflict with MAPs is bound to occur. With so many MAPs, an organization cannot help but develop incompatibilities. Collaborative decision making is one way to resolve incompatibilities. Organizational members might anticipate conflict at the latent, perceived, or felt stages of conflict. Or conflict may not be noticed until the manifest stage. Whatever the stage, MAPs may be brought into the decision-making process. Ideally, the conflict is identified at an early stage. MAPs can voice their concerns and help to shape the decision, thereby increasing the likelihood of MAPs accepting the decision. Collaborative decision making is used to involve MAPs in the relationship. There is a chance to cooperate and align interests through collaborative decision making.

For example, an environmental group called "Earth Island" and the Bumble Bee Tuna company had a conflict over tuna fishing. Earth Island wanted an end to drift net tuna fishing (which also caught up dolphins), while Bumble Bee wanted to honor existing contracts. By changing the existing contracts to incorporate dolphin-friendly fishing practices, Bumble Bee and Earth Island were able to align interests. The alignment was made possible by a series of meetings for collaborative decision making: Both parties had to agree on what constituted an acceptable decision.

Collaborative decision making builds mutually beneficial relationships by ensuring two-way communication and being proactive. The communicative give-and-take involved in the decision-making process is a form of dialogue. The earlier discussion of small-group decision making reveals the dialogue format. The organization is being proactive; it is considering the MAPs when making a decision. By being part of the process, a MAP can ensure that its perspective is heard and shape the final decision. Again, the ideal is to find a mutually beneficial solution early in the conflict.

▶ Relational Decision Making

Not every decision that affects the organization-MAP relationship will be collaborative. Moreover, there is more than one form of collaborative decision making. Table 13.3 identifies and defines a range of decision-making options for relationship-related decisions. A proactive decision is made by the organization alone (unilateral). However, the organization is proactive by considering how the decision will affect MAPs and how they will react to it. The needs of the MAPs are factored into the decision-making process. Informed decisions solicit varying degrees of input from the MAPs before the organization makes the decision. Informed-decision 1 (I1) asks MAPs for comments about the decision. Informed-decision 2 (I2) has MAPs participate in a discussion about the decision.

In each case, the organization retains the authority to make the decision, while the MAPs act in an advisory capacity. Participative decisions are joint ventures where the organization and its MAPs each have a say in the decision. The power to make the decision is shared (bilateral). No decision is made until the parties can agree. Mandated decisions are made by the MAPs. Organizations are not the only ones who make decisions that affect the organization-MAP relationship. A MAP may boycott

Table 13.3: Relationship Decision Options		
Proactive	(PO)	Organization makes a decision but considers how it will affect markets, audiences, and publics (MAPs) and how MAPs will react to it.
Informed	(I1)	Organization solicits feedback from MAPs but makes the final decision.
	(I2)	Organization involves MAPs in a discussion about the decision but makes the final decision.
Participative	(PA)	Organization and MAPs are equal partners in making the decision.
Mandated	(M1)	MAPs receive limited input from the organization but make the decision.
	(M2)	MAPs involve the organization in a discussion about the decision but make the final decision.

an organization, donate money, or endorse an organization's actions. Organizations can try to influence mandated decisions in one of two ways. Mandated-decision 1 (M1) has the organization offer its position or provide some input. Mandated-decision 2 (M2) allows the organization to be part of a discussion, while the MAP retains the right to make the final decision.

All but the proactive decision involves some degree of collaboration. I1 and M1 are the least collaborative. In each, one participant has limited input. I2 and M2 become a little more collaborative. One party joins the discussion but has no decision-making power. In the participative decision, the parties each have power over the final decision. Table 13.3 elaborates on these decision-making options.

This analysis gives us reason to reemphasize the elements of relationship building that are vital to today's public relations. These connections are presented in Box 13.1.

BOX 13.1 RELATIONSHIP BUILDING THROUGH COLLABORATIVE DECISION MAKING

- *Openness:* fosters two-way communication that involves listening/sharing valuable information and is open, responsive, respectful, candid, and honest. Collaborative decision making requires openness. Each party must express its opinions and listen to the opinions of the other parties. Without a free and fair exchange of ideas and concerns, collaborative decision making will fail.

- *Trustworthiness:* builds trust by being reliable, nonexploitative, and dependable. Trust is strained by conflict. To move along the steps in collaborative decision making, each party must not only come to trust the other, but must act in ways that foster trust. Trust is built through demonstrating a cooperative commitment to positive change.

- *Cooperation:* cooperates to make decisions by engaging in collaborative decision making that ensures that the needs/wants of the organization and its stakeholders are met. Collaborative decision making is a constructive approach to decision making because it creates a cooperative atmosphere. Each party must cooperate to identify, analyze, propose solutions, evaluate solutions, and implement solutions that build a long-term relationship.

- *Alignment:* aligns interests, rewards, and goals with those of its stakeholders. Conflict presumes that some interests are in conflict. Careful analysis, however, is likely to reveal interests that are in common. Collaborative decision making works best when the parties look for and find the alignment between their interests, instead of featuring their differences. One party to the decision making is likely to frustrate the process if it believes that its interest is not appreciated by the others. Each side needs to work to achieve positive alignment.

- *Compatibility of views/opinions:* fosters mutual understanding and agreement and cocreates meaning. Conflict results from incompatible views/opinions. However, it cannot be resolved unless the parties share certain views and opinions as a foundation. Collaborative decision making is a process that helps parties to discover and implement their compatible views/opinions.

- *Commitment:* supports the community by being involved in it, investing in it, and displaying commitment to it. An organization can say that it is committed to its stakeholders' interests. To engage in collaborative decision making demonstrates this commitment.

Guidelines for Decision Choices

Stakeholder theory realistically notes that an organization cannot please all of the stakeholders all of the time. The reason is that different stakeholders can make conflicting demands on an organization. Similarly, a decision that helps one organization-MAP relationship may hurt another. Nor does an organization have the time and resources to make all decisions collaboratively.

Vroom and Yetton (1963) have proposed several decision-making steps that are vital to constructive conflict resolution. These are featured in Box 13.2. These decision-making styles were originally developed to assist corporate managers to build better relationships with their employees. That context is still relevant to the challenges facing today's public relations practitioners, who share the responsibilities for creating mutually beneficial employee-and-follower relationships. These styles become even more relevant when we substitute the phrase "organization through its management team, including public relations," for *manager.*

BOX 13.2 FIVE DECISION-MAKING STYLES

Autocratic 1: Manager makes the decision himself or herself (organization through its management team, including public relations, makes the decision by itself, with its interests primarily and even exclusively in mind).

Autocratic 2: Manager collects needed information from followers, then makes the decision (organization through its management team, including public relations, collects needed information from its stakeholders, then makes the decision).

Consultative 1: Manager discusses the problems with followers individually, then makes the decision (organization through its management team, including public relations, discusses the problems with stakeholders individually, then makes the decision).

Consultative 2: Manager discusses the problem in a group with followers, then makes a decision (organization through its management team, including public relations, discusses the problems in a group with stakeholders, then makes a decision).

Consensus Seeker: Manager shares problem with followers, and they collectively make a decision (organization through its management team, including public relations, discusses the problems with stakeholders, and they collectively make a decision).

Seven questions help guide executives' decision making as they work proactively to decide when collaborative decision making is a valued option.

1. Does the problem possess a quality requirement?

2. Do you have sufficient information to make a high-quality decision?

3. Is the problem structured?

4. Is acceptance of the decision by followers (stakeholders) important for effective management?

5. If you were to make the decision yourself, will it be accepted by followers (stakeholders)?

6. Do followers (stakeholders) share the organization's goals?

7. Will followers (stakeholders) be in conflict over how the problem should be solved?

For a detailed discussion of the model, see *Leadership and Decision Making,* by V. H. Vroom and P. W. Yetton (1963).

As is demonstrated in the boxed feature, organizations need a set of guidelines to help them choose when to engage in collaborative decision making. Figure 13.1

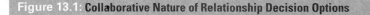

Figure 13.1: **Collaborative Nature of Relationship Decision Options**

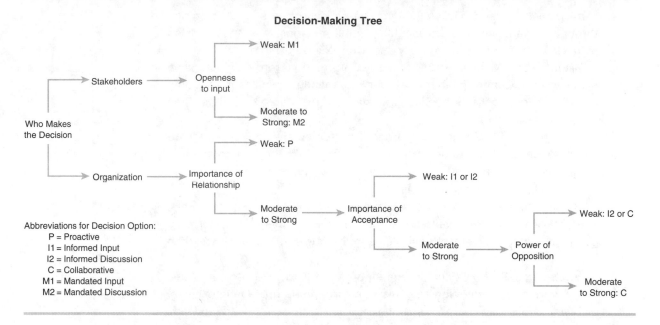

Decision-Making Tree

presents a decision tree for making such decisions relevant to collaborative decision making. The decision tree is patterned after Vroom and Yetton's contingency theory of leadership.

The contingency theory of leadership is a model that prescribes what type of decision making an organization should use in a given situation. The model offers five types of decision making, which are defined in Box 13.2. A manager answers seven questions, which are also listed in the box. The questions form a "decision tree." Based on the answers to the questions, the manager is given a range of decision-making options to use in the given situation.

The decision tree begins by asking, "Who makes the decision?" If stakeholders make the final decision, the only option would be mandated decisions. The choice between M1 and M2 depends on how open the MAP is to organizational input. The next question concerns "importance to the relationship." Not all decisions have a significant effect on relationships. Most decisions made by either an organization or a MAP are routine and impact the other very little. When a decision does not affect the relationship, a proactive decision is good enough. The third question concerns "importance of acceptance." Does the organization need the stakeholder to accept the decision? Collaboration should increase acceptance of a decision. If acceptance is not very important, I1 or I2 are acceptable. The decision still impacts the relationship, so you want the MAPs to have some input into the decision.

The final question concerns "threat of the opposition." If MAPs dislike the decision, they can actively oppose rather than accept it. Your task is to determine which

MAPs are affected by a decision, how the decision will be received by each MAP, and the relative threat of each MAP. Not all organization-MAP relationships are important all of the time. The importance of a MAP depends on the situation and the threat posed by the MAP. During a recall, customers are a top priority, while the community is very important during plans to get rezoning for an expansion. The organization will focus on MAPs relevant to the situation. An organization must consider clusters of relationships with MAPs and not look at each relationship in isolation (Rowley, 1997). MAPs often have goals and values that conflict with one another. Box 13.3 illustrates conflicts among MAPs. Conflicting demands means that not all MAPs will be happy with every decision. You should anticipate how key MAPs will react to a possible decision. Your focus will be on those who might have a negative reaction. Organizations do need to rank order MAPs in terms of importance to determine which MAPs they must please. One measure of importance is the threat a MAP would present if it were upset by a decision.

BOX 13.3 CASE STUDY: DAYTON-HUDSON: THE COST OF BUILDING RELATIONSHIPS

In the summer of 1990, Dayton-Hudson, a retail chain that includes Dayton's and Target, decided to end 22 years of contributions to the local chapter of Planned Parenthood. This meant a loss of $18,000 for the chapter. Dayton-Hudson said it wanted to avoid the abortion issue. The money had always been used for educational programs, never to fund abortion clinics. The local chapter of Planned Parenthood was part of a consortium of state groups dedicated to women's issues. The consortium contained 170 organizations and a membership of over 200,000 women. Within a week, the consortium had organized and publicized protests against Dayton-Hudson, including a rally that urged people to return the "Christmas Bear" stuffed-animal promotion offered by Dayton's. Thousands attended a rally outside a Dayton's store in suburban Minneapolis. Members of the consortium began returning cut-up credit cards to Dayton-Hudson as well. Dayton-Hudson also witnessed a run on returns, with customers citing the funding as the reason for the return. Within a few weeks, Dayton-Hudson restored the grant. The grant restoration triggered protests, a letter-writing campaign, and boycotts from right-to-life groups. Dayton-Hudson did not respond to the new protests and left the grant intact. Ann Barelew, vice president of corporate public relations, observed, "We couldn't possibly win" (Snyder, 1991, p. 17).

The threat presented by a MAP can be assessed using three criteria: (1) power, (2) legitimacy, and (3) willingness to act. A MAP has power when it can make an organization do something it would not do otherwise. For example, as mentioned, the activist group "Earth Island" made Bumble Bee Tuna change the nature of its contract with Thai fishers to protect dolphins from being caught in tuna nets. A MAP has power when it can disrupt an organization's operations. A strike by employees, new government safety regulations, and stockholder resolutions are examples of possible disruptions. MAPs can enhance power through coalitions and ability to act. Coalitions reflect the power of numbers. The more MAPs that unite, the more powerful they become. For instance, if customers and stockholders unite, an organization is faced with a powerful coalition. Ability to act means the MAPs have the resources (e.g., money) and skills to take action against an organization (Coombs, 1998; Mitchell, Agle, & Wood, 1997).

The National Resources Defense Council (NRDC) used a well-financed and professionally done campaign to have Alar, a chemical agent used to improve apple ripening, removed from the market. The NRDC had enough funding to hire a public relations agency. The agency coordinated a massive publicity effort to promote the dangers of Alar. The publicity included using celebrity spokespersons, such as actress Meryl Streep. In one month, public awareness of Alar's threat went from 0% to 95% (Center & Jackson, 1995). The NRDC used money and professional communication skills to make people aware that Alar was a potential cancer threat to children.

Sometimes an organization has legitimacy when it is perceived as desirable or appropriate. MAPs are more of a threat when their concerns—objections to a decision—are perceived as legitimate by other MAPs. An organization looks bad when it is seen as ignoring legitimate concerns. For this reason, McDonald's suffered when it overlooked legitimate demands by customers to reduce the heat of its coffee in the 1990s. The end result was an embarrassing lawsuit victory by an elderly customer. Willingness is the MAPs' desire to confront the organization about the concern. The salience of an issue results from the importance of the concern to MAPs and/or deadline for taking action. Wal-Mart planned to build a new store in a small town in South Carolina. Residents and businesses united to prevent the intrusion of "Sprawl-Mart" into their "village" atmosphere. The decision to build in the local area had high salience, and a zoning commission meeting date added a time dimension to the willingness to take action on the issue. The high willingness led to many acts of confrontation with Wal-Mart. You should assess all three of the threat criteria when evaluating MAPs. Of the three criteria, power is the most important one. Never ignore a powerful MAP. Legitimacy and willingness add to power to increase the threat posed by a MAP (Coombs, 1998; Mitchell et al., 1997).

MAPs that threaten the organization must be included in the decision-making process. If they oppose the decision, it could hinder the organization's ability to operate. If the MAPs are relevant and a threat, a decision should be collaborative. If the stakeholder is relevant but a minor threat, informed discussion, or collaborative should be used. There is still a need to involve powerless stakeholders. First, it is a sign of respect for the relationship, and second, you can never be sure when a powerless MAP may find the resources to become powerful. For instance, two customers do not seem very powerful. Ford Motor Company felt the same way. However, a Web site created by two angry Ford owners led to one of the largest recalls in the automotive industry. Debra and Edward Goldgehn created the "Flaming Ford" Web site after their 1985 Ford Ranger burned to a black blob in their driveway. They argued the problem was a faulty ignition switch that Ford should be replacing. Their Web site posted evidence of the problem and listed the makes and years of Ford vehicles with the problem. Ford had resisted a recall for years and had undergone three federal investigations on the subject. According to many media accounts, the Flaming Ford Web site attracted enough national attention to push Ford into a recall. In April of 1996, Ford recalled over 8.7 million vehicles at a cost of between $200 and $300 million (Coombs, 1998).

The decision tree offers basic guidance on when to involve MAPs in collaborative decision making. Two other factors will affect the decision to engage in collaborative decision making:

1. *Information factor:* You will involve MAPs that can have an informed discussion of the decision. Moreover, you want to involve MAPs when they have important information pertaining to the decision that the organization lacks.

2. *Time factor:* You will select the decision style that fits your time frame. An immediate decision does not fit well with a participative style, because it is too time-consuming. We must be pragmatic when making decisions: Understand when constraints require us to take less-than-ideal actions.

The previous sections have explained the strategic rationale for collaborative decision making as a means for creating positive narratives and aligning interests. Discussion has explored the nature of conflict and the need as well as the value of effective conflict resolution. Analysis has examined the nature of small-group decision making and the processes of collectively identifying, solving, and resolving problems. This discussion has justified the use of collaborative decision making as a vital public relations function. Practitioners are expected not only to be expert in their ability to counsel management when collaborative decision making is wise but also to know how to engage in true decision making. In this way, these practitioners can help to reduce conflict and demonstrate the organization's ability and willingness to solve mutual problems. Citizens' advisory boards or panels are an example of tools that can be used in collaborative decision making.

WEB WATCHER: COLLABORATIVE EFFORTS TO IMPROVE AIR TRAVEL SAFETY

The federal government is trying to harness the power of collaborative decision making to improve the safety of air travel. A variety of government and private organizations are sharing information and working together on this initiative. The Web address is http://www.metronaviation.com/cdm/what scdm.html. While at the Web site, answer the following questions. Who are some of the groups involved in the project? What are these groups doing that qualifies as collaborative decision making? How will the project result in mutually beneficial relationships for the groups involved?

Selecting Collaborative-Decision-Making Tools

Collaborative decision making builds relationships and solves problems in concert. It grows out of the organization's desire to achieve its mission and vision. It becomes an important rhetorical strategy once situational assessment reveals that critics are building a power base of conflict that can frustrate this goal.

By identifying and analyzing zones of meaning, practitioners locate agreement and disagreement. Agreement rarely makes the news. Disagreement constitutes a rhetorical problem, a challenge to harmony. Disagreement can lead publics to become activists and increases the potential for media inquiry. Media reporters feast on disagreement.

Conflict has bottom-line consequences. Disagreement can affect markets. Consumers and manufacturers can disagree regarding the quality or price of products. Disagreement can harm fund-raising efforts on the part of nonprofit organizations. Potential donors may disagree that a sufficient need exists for them to contribute their money. Followers may disagree with one activist group, environmental, for instance, and agree with the agenda of another. Which are they likely to support with their money?

Conflict can affect employee relationships. It may harm follower or alumni relationships. For these reasons, practitioners should scan for damaged relationships as part of their situational analysis.

Government officials can employ the principles of public relations to create zones of meaning that foster harmony among citizens. Sometimes that is easier said than accomplished. A community is a mix of interests. Sometimes they are compatible. At other times, they conflict. One case of conflict focuses on the question, "But would you kill Bambi?" Across the nation, deer populations cause about $1 billion in property damage each year. Deer populations have increased because their food is ample and predators such as mountain lions and wolves are insufficient in numbers to balance nature. Deer are beautiful, cute, and docile. They can be a nuisance by destroying gardens and landscaping. Should cities and other governmental agencies allow supervised hunts? What other measures should be employed to control the deer population and reduce their damage? *What would you recommend?*

Situational analysis of this issue reveals a highly polarized society. People are either for the deer or for their control, by whatever means will work. Both publics recognize a problem, experience high levels of cognitive involvement, and therefore become active. Compromise is often difficult. Collaborative decision making may work, but it requires commitment to succeed in joint problem solving. As the process moves forward, each side is likely to fear that the process works only for one side or the other—the ostensible "winner." Zones are at odds: animal protection versus property rights. The conflict continues because the zones are at odds, not aligned. Government executives and public information officers are challenged to find the acceptable solution and create harmony—mutually beneficial relations.

What strategic message objectives and communication processes can solve this problem? The message points need to feature information and persuasion, which subdivide into attitude formation and behavior. Thus, to understand the issue of deer populations, information needs to be gathered and analyzed. Attitudes need to emerge that favor a solution based on aligned interests. The sides need to work together cooperatively to solve the problem and see that the solution is implemented.

To understand the impact of "wild" deer on the local environment, including residents' property, requires knowing something about the total financial impact, the number and kinds of deer involved, and the means for deer population management. Through dialogue, message points of fact and evaluation are weighed, leading to the formation of a policy. Collaborative decision making helps determine what the key message points are, which facts and evaluations are best because they withstand public scrutiny, and which policy solves the collectively experienced problem.

BOX 13.4 STEPS IN COLLABORATIVE DECISION MAKING

- Identify the goals of the engaged parties. Find out what each wants in terms of a preferred solution. Learn the reasons (facts and evaluations) why each party believes in its goals.
- Discover the common ground in the goals of the engaged parties. Find where the greatest amount of agreement is. See where the interests align.
- Uncover the points of disagreement.
- Analyze points of disagreement to determine which ones can be corrected or abandoned as being less important, incorrect, or unproductive.
- Disclose impediments to resolving the differences and solving the joint problem. Impediments can be lack of information, conflicting attitudes and evaluations, and systemic processes such as feelings of disempowerment, lack of trust, lack of control, disproportionate distribution of costs and rewards, and traditions ("We've always done things that way").
- Seek to eliminate impediments.
- Disclose positive incentives and thinking processes that support achieving a mutually satisfying outcome.
- Build on positive incentives and systems to find remedies to disincentives and dysfunctional elements of the system.
- Propose and analyze solutions to discover which ones maximize the wins and minimize the losses of the interested parties.
- Narrow and select solutions that seem most satisfying.
- Agree on solutions to be tested to determine whether they solve the problem in ways that maximize wins and minimize losses for the interested parties.
- Test the solutions.
- Evaluate, reevaluate, retest, and refine until a workable and satisfying solution is achieved.

We can cast this line of thinking into a "concurrence model," which uses a series of questions to determine the similarity/dissimilarity and agreement/disagreement that exists between the organization and each relevant stakeholder/stakeseeker in the specific rhetorical problem. When conflict is high, we have competing and unaligned zones of meaning.

- What do you want the group to know?
- What do they know?
- What do you want them to believe?
- What do they believe?
- How do you want them to evaluate the circumstances of the situation?
- How do they evaluate the circumstances of the situation?
- What criteria do they use?
- What criteria do you want them to use?
- What conclusions do want them to draw?
- What conclusions do they want to draw?
- Where is there difference?
- Where is there agreement?
- How significant is the agreement?
- How substantial is the disagreement?
- Which differences can be reduced or eliminated?
- Is the relationship strengthening or deteriorating because of differences?

Keep in mind that concurrence can be looked at from the point of view of each MAP as well. For instance, what do you believe, and what do they want you to believe? If we put this analysis into the context of a rhetorical problem, we can think of it this way: Differences that are strongly held are likely to be threats; they can lead to conflict. Opportunities arise out of agreement and unmet challenges.

The case of deer population control is a conflict that ultimately stops on the desk of government officials, who not only have to achieve a mutually satisfying solution, but often assist the members of the community in their efforts to implement the solution. After examining the deer population problem, government officials who are expected to help community members solve this problem were offered this advice:

- Involve key publics from the outset.
- Communicate constantly, employing additional channels so that the media do not control the message.
- Recruit and nurture allies.
- Bring in impartial experts to help obtain facts and generate creative solutions.
- Educate the media to the full story.
- Demonstrate the problem so that interested parties see the big picture.
- Respect differences and avoid public debate, in preference of collaborative decision making.

These principles can guide practitioners' rhetorical choices in using collaborative decision making for relationship building. The process needs to be open, candid, honest, fact based, and evaluative to reach the best solutions to shared problems. It requires a constructive communication style:

1. Listen to and appreciate others' points of view.

2. Demonstrate respect for the rights, concerns, arguments, information, convictions, and solutions of the opposing parties.

3. Be open and responsive.

4. Build trust through shared control and empowerment.

5. Align interests (attitudes and beliefs).

6. Negotiate and engage in collaborative decision making to reach a solution that maximizes the wins for the interested party and advances the good of the community.

7. Achieve dynamic change and adaptation for a growing relationship.

Viewed this way, collaborative decision making is not only a methodology. It is also a philosophy that is fundamental to today's rhetorical approach to public relations.

Citizens Advisory Committees: Working Together

Over the years, wise executives and savvy public relations practitioners have learned many lessons the hard way. The same can be said for government officials who have created and implemented policies and then battled citizens over those policies. The lesson learned is simple: Involve community members from the start if they are going to be or are affected by a problem and its solution.

Industry and governmental public relations practitioners and other managers have steadily increased the opportunities for community members to be involved in crucial decisions. This responsive attitude has often resulted from a realization that an angry public will not be denied. It also follows mandates from the U.S. government that people will receive information when manufacturing and other processes can affect their health, safety, and environmental quality.

The experiences and innovations by the chemical-manufacturing industry serve as an example for this discussion. This industry has been under fire for at least two decades and has learned many lessons worth sharing. Responding to governmental mandates and recognizing that it needs to be a better citizen, the chemical-manufacturing industry, starting in the mid-1980s, set out not only to reduce emissions but also to improve its relationships with its employees and neighbors. The efforts of this industry help to demonstrate the virtues of involving people in community-industry decisions. Part of the innovation led to the use of citizens advisory committees and panels and, ultimately, a public-facing Web site with individual company performance data.

In 1985, the Canadian chemical-manufacturing industry began what it calls its "Responsible Care® Program." The program was then adopted in the United States in 1988, through the American Chemistry Council (ACC), formerly the Chemical Manufacturers Association, and it is now present in 52 countries, globally. Through Responsible Care®, the chemical-manufacturing industry committed itself to be a better steward of the environment in terms of water and air quality. It obligated itself to communicate better with the persons who live and work near its facilities. Responsible Care® companies sign documents committing themselves to higher environmental, health, safety, and security performance. They take pride in using this program to guide improved performance and to eliminate the "bad apple" syndrome, the company that brings criticism onto an industry because it will not behave more responsibly.

Responsible Care®

Improving Performance, Sharing Results

Responsible Care®
Good Chemistry at Work

Responsible Care® is the U.S. chemical industry's award-winning initiative to improve performance that has resulted in emissions reductions of 70 percent and a worker safety record that is four times better than manufacturing as a whole.

Participation in the Responsible Care initiative is mandatory for members of the American Chemistry Council. Widely recognized as one of the largest and most successful performance initiatives advanced by any industry, Responsible Care helps America's leading chemical makers go above and beyond government requirements and share their progress with the public.

Responsible Care®
Good Chemistry at Work

- Emissions reductions of 70 percent.

- A worker safety record that is four times better than manufacturing as a whole.

- Implementing a comprehensive security code that has become a model for U.S. industries.

- And talking candidly about all of these important issues with more than 300 community advisory panels across the nation.

- These are just some of the ways Responsible Care® is making a difference.

- A difference we can measure.

Delivering Measurable Results

For more than fifteen years, the American Chemistry Council's Responsible Care® initiative has led the way to a cleaner environment, safer facilities and a more secure nation. We know this because Responsible Care companies routinely measure and track their performance. The Responsible Care initiative establishes a comprehensive series of standardized performance measurements through which individual companies and the industry track and publicly report their results on an annual basis.

Sharing Progress and Activities

Through www.ResponsibleCare-US.com, the public can track industry's progress in emissions reductions, worker safety, product stewardship, security, economics, and more. Responsible Care companies also candidly share their performance results and discuss other important issues with approximately 300 community advisory panels across the country.

Providing Assurance Through Independent Review

To drive improved performance, a key component of Responsible Care's modern management system is mandatory certification by independent, accredited auditing firms. These firms audit headquarters and chemical facilities to assure that every Responsible Care company has in place a rigorous framework to achieve and verify results.

Extending Responsible Care

The Responsible Care Partnership Program extends the Responsible Care ethic beyond America's chemical product makers to their customers, shippers and others engaged in the business of chemistry. Through the Responsible Care Partnership Program, approximately 100 companies are working together to raise the performance of chemical distribution and use nationwide.

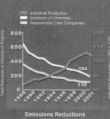

Emissions Reductions
Based on TRI Data and IP Index for business of chemistry

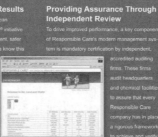

Trends in Occupational Injury and Illness Incidence Rates

Manufacturing 7.2
Business of Chemistry 3.3
Responsible Care Companies 1.8

A Cleaner Environment

Since 1988, Responsible Care companies and the business of chemistry have reduced emissions 70 percent while increasing production 25 percent.

A Safer Workplace

The incidence of worker illness and injury among Responsible Care companies has declined 51 percent since 1990. Members of the American Chemistry Council have illness and injury rates one-half that of the business of chemistry as a whole and one-fourth that of all of manufacturing.

A More Secure Nation

Security has always been a top priority for America's chemical makers, but soon after the terrorist attacks of September 11, 2001, Responsible Care® companies took the lead in securing our facilities: a critical part of the nation's infrastructure. Without waiting for government direction, these companies quickly adopted the Responsible Care Security Code, an aggressive plan to further enhance security of our facilities, our communities and our products.

Under the Security Code - which addresses site, cyber and transportation security - companies are required to conduct comprehensive security vulnerability assessments, implement security enhancements and obtain independent verification of those enhancements. Implementing the Security Code under a strict timeline is mandatory for members of the American Chemistry Council and Responsible Care Partners.

Responsible Care companies invested more than $800 million in 2003 alone to enhance security at their facilities. The Security Code been praised by the highest levels of government and has been recognized in law and regulation by the United States Coast Guard, the City of Baltimore and the State of Maryland.

To learn more about Responsible Care visit: www.ResponsibleCare-US.com

Building Relationships Through Responsible Care®

SOURCE: © 2004, American Chemistry Council.

In 2004, the American Chemistry Council (ACC) decided to go one step further in its efforts to improve stakeholder outreach. In May 2004, it launched a first-of-its-kind, public-facing Web site that shares individual member company data with the public. The Web site, http://www.responsiblecare-us.com, remains, to date, the only such industry Web site. Data are updated annually, and new metrics are being evaluated on an ongoing basis.

One of the first collaborative initiatives was the formation of Local Emergency Planning Committees (LEPCs). These were mandated by the EPA, which believes that people have a right to know about chemicals manufactured, transported, and stored in their communities. LEPCs are composed of industry emergency response experts, chemical company executives, local government officials (elected officials and emergency response experts, such as the fire chief), concerned citizens, and media reporters. LEPCs have been more successful in creating workable emergency response plans than they have been in building communication bridges with area residents. Through LEPC discussion, experts are better prepared for such emergencies. Through community outreach efforts, citizens have become informed of the protective measures they should take under those circumstances. Warning systems using radios, telephones, and sirens have been put into place. Area residents have been informed about these warning systems. They have been told what to do in the event of an emergency (Heath & Abel, 1996; Heath & Palenchar, 2000).

All of that planning and communication is well and good, but it has not totally met the industry, local government, and community resident needs. Long and tedious technical discussions of emergency response systems, equipment, and protocols do not interest most area citizens for long. They have other issues they want to discuss, such as levels of emissions of harmful substances. To solve this rhetorical problem, industry groups (such as the East Harris County Manufacturers [EHCMA] near Houston, Texas) and chemical-manufacturing companies and refineries have created an alternative communication vehicle. These are called *citizens advisory committees* (CACs) or *community advisory panels* (CAPs).

These committees use professional facilitators to conduct their business. They are funded by the industry but are designed to be operated by interested community members. They bring together area residents, technical experts who can explain chemical hazards, plant managers who can explain manufacturing processes, and members of local government (elected and professional). They are designed to foster dialogue, lead to collaborative decision making, and build trust through open and constructive cooperation.

Building and operating effective CACs requires an understanding of and willingness to embrace community members' comments and to operate in an open fashion with a commitment to reduce the actual and perceived impact of the industry on the health, safety, and environmental quality of the community. A CAC should offer a neutral meeting place where interested parties can come together, share ideas and concerns, and solve problems of mutual interest. Several best practice guidelines are essential for creating and operating an effective CAC:

- Be proactive by taking the initiative to create CACs and support their operation when conflicts occur or appear to be imminent.
- Have a facilitator who is impartial. This person may be a community leader. Industry or the government may have to hire a professional facilitator. In any event, the key publics should be involved in selecting and reviewing the performance of this person.
- Empower the facilitator to run the meetings in a fair and open manner.
- Create and adhere to agendas and operating principles.
- Use public media to notify community members about the CAC, its agenda, its meeting places and times, each meeting's agenda, its members, and its conclusions and recommendations. Keep the community aware of the CAC. Be sure that the community knows what it is and what it does.
- Ensure a fair and balanced membership. The interests of all parties need to be met for the CAC to be a successful means for collaborative decision making.
- Meet frequently and regularly. Meeting frequency may depend on the sorts of issues and conflicts that need attention. The public needs to influence the frequency of such meetings.
- Ensure input. Allow participation. Maintain patience as people seek to understand and express their sentiments about technical issues.
- Notify the community of the success and problems that result from the work of the CAC.
- Implement solutions that are recommended by the CAC.

Citizens advisory committees serve many purposes. They can help to identify and solve problems. They are an excellent means for monitoring issues. They give participants the opportunity to share and receive information, form attitudes, and adopt behaviors. They are a means for cocreating meaning by building shared narratives and fostering identification—valuable message development options.

Conclusion

This chapter has featured the advantages and techniques of collaborative decision making. We have discussed why organizations would consider it as an option, three essential factors related to collaborative decision making, and how to assess when best to employ it. We have spent a lot of time addressing conflict because it drives the need for collaborative decision making. Conflict can be positive if handled in a cooperative manner. We have identified factors that shape whether or not conflict becomes positive or negative. We want you to understand conflict and to be able to establish situations where it can be used constructively. Our focus has been on conflict and collaborative decision making as it relates to the organization-MAP relationship. We have stressed the roles that effective crisis response and risk communication can play in building relationships. Collaborative decision making is a vital public-relationship-building function.

Let's end the chapter by returning to the ChemBurn vignette, which opened the chapter as an illustration of conflict's positive and negative potential. ChemBurn is well-advised to use collaborative decision making in its efforts to build a chemical incinerator. The decision is important to ChemBurn's relationships with various MAPs. ChemBurn needs MAPs to accept the decision. Refusal to accept the decision could cause delays or prevent construction of a facility altogether. The MAPs in this case are a threat. By forming a coalition, the MAPs could convince the local politicians to deny permits or slow down construction with protests and litigation. The MAPs have power; concerns over safety are legitimate; and the MAPs are willing to act. The vignette's idea of a planning group, the cooperative option, is a form of participative decision making, the most collaborative of the decision-making styles. While not easy or quick, working together will ensure that a resolution is mutually beneficial and not harmful to relationships with the organization. The competitive option will harm relations and promote a negative aftermath to the conflict. When the stakes are high, an organization is well-advised to utilize collaborative decision making.

Ethical Quandary: Sharing as Collaborative Decision Making

FURTHER EXPLORATION

13

You are one of your organization's representatives on a collaborative-decision-making team. Your organization is the regional airport authority that needs to expand the runways to accommodate the growth of your airport. Because the noise will affect local residents, three neighbor associations are represented on the team, along with the airlines currently using the airport and the local chamber of commerce. The airlines' ability to offer more routes is affected by the decision. The chamber of commerce has a stake in the development because expansion could increase business revenues. The initial sound survey is out, and it shows the noise level from various types of planes in the surrounding area. The sound survey is very favorable for the least-expensive configuration for runway expansion. However, you know that the airport authority is finalizing plans to bring in a new air carrier. The plans hinge on approval of the expansion, because the new carrier needs longer runways for its jets. That carrier uses a type of jet that is not covered in the sound survey and will be louder than any existing planes used at the airport.

Do you share this information with the planning team? If you do, a new sound survey would have to be conducted, and the results could favor a more expensive runway configuration. There is also a greater potential for delay, which could cause the authority to lose the potential new contract. Your airport authority is in heavy competition with another regional airport just 40 miles away. It is possible the new carrier could switch to your competitor. What is the downside if you do not disclose the information? What is your final choice, and why?

Summary Questions

1. Explain how collaborative decision making is a strategic public relations function. How does it identify and solve problems and resolve conflict? How does collaborative decision making create narratives and align interests?

2. What is the value of collaborative decision making? Explain why it is needed as a tool the organization can use to achieve its strategic plan.

3. Collaborative decision making involves three factors. What are these factors? Define a small group. What is democratic leadership? Why is democratic leadership vital for collaborative decision making? What should members of a small group do to ensure that it functions effectively?

4. Identify and explain the five steps of the reflective decision-making process.

5. List the five conflict management styles. Which is best for collaborative decision making?

6. Demonstrate that you understand the connection between the factors of relationship building and collaborative decision making.

7. Explain each of the steps in the collaborative decision-making process. Using those steps and other best practices and communication styles, list and explain the tactics needed for effective collaborative decision making.

8. What is a citizens advisory committee? Why were these developed? How can they be used strategically as a collaborative-decision-making tool?

Exercises

1. Attend a meeting of a city council or similar decision-making body. Does this body engage in collaborative decision making? Why do you draw that conclusion? What strategies and communication styles could be used to make the organization more effective in its collaborative decision making? Does it seem to prefer monologue to dialogue? How good are its relationships with its constituencies?

2. As you participate in small-group decision making, use your knowledge of collaborative decision making to see why the group operates as it does. Do the members meet the responsibilities of being involved in a small group? Do the groups use vigilant decision making and the reflective-thinking method?

3. Find an instance of an organization that is or has been engaged in conflict. From the statements it made, determine which of the conflict management styles it used. Was this style appropriate to solving its public relations rhetorical problem?

4. Conduct a case study of an organization that has been embroiled in conflict. Assume that the organization is your employer or client. Critique the organization's strategic approach to conflict resolution. Focus your analysis on the extent to which it used appropriate conflict resolution strategies and the best communication style. Was the organization able to demonstrate that it could comply with the requirements of building and sustaining mutually beneficial relationships?

5. Identify an organization that is or was confronted with the crisis. Did the organization seem prepared to follow the guidelines and best practices of crisis preparation and response?

6. Locate an organization that is engaged in risk communication. Is the organization one that creates the risk—or is offended by it? Identify the risk issues, the information, evaluations, and behaviors that seem to be at the heart of the conflict. Does the organization meet the guidelines and best practices of effective risk communication? Take the organization on as an imaginary client. Develop a plan that should be used to reduce conflict, engage in collaborative decision making, and build a mutually beneficial relationship with the key constituencies.

7. Select a company (or industry), governmental organization, or nonprofit (including activist groups). Write a plan for the organization to use to reduce conflict. Include in your plan the situational analysis that supports your conclusions. Provide advice that is justified by the key points discussed in this chapter that you recommend to management. Give the details for a communication plan that includes the use of collaborative decision making groups as well as messages that are communicated to key stakeholders. Explain how this plan can create, repair, build, and maintain relationships with specific markets, audiences, and publics (MAPs).

Recommended Readings

Christen, C. T. (2004). Predicting willingness to negotiate: The effects of perceived power and trustworthiness in a model of strategic public relations. *Journal of Public Relations Research, 16,* 243–267.

Plowman, K. D., Briggs, W. C., & Huang, Y. H. (2001). Public relations and conflict resolution. In R. L. Heath (Ed.), *Handbook of public relations* (pp. 301–310). Thousand Oaks, CA: Sage.

Smith, M. F., & Ferguson, D. P. (2001). Activism. In R. L. Heath (Ed.), *Handbook of public relations* (pp. 291–300). Thousand Oaks, CA: Sage.

14

Building a Career

Personal Planning for a Public Relations Career

Let's imagine the following scenario, which happens each day and every year across the country in programs that teach public relations. Two public relations students, Linda and Carol, attend the same school and earn the same grades in their courses. Both have taken many communication and other academic courses. They have completed courses titled "Public Relations Principles" and "Public Relations Writing." Now they are about to start their junior year. They both plan to enroll in advanced courses in public relations, such as public relations campaigns, public relations research, and case studies.

Planning Is No Accident

SOURCE: Courtesy of the PRSSA University of Houston Chapter 2005.

At this point, their preparation begins to go in different paths. Planning for a public relations career is more than simply completing course work. Public relations is a competitive field. Choices made early in college can affect employment opportunities and long-term career satisfaction. Students need to set personal goals early in their careers.

Linda has carefully considered three key points: (1) her minor, (2) an internship, and (3) her portfolio. Linda is minoring in consumer behavior in order to learn more about segmenting and understanding markets, audiences, and publics (MAPs). She has an internship planned for this summer to apply what she has learned in the classroom. She also has collected samples of her public relations work and will use her internship and membership in PRSSA (Public Relations Student Society of America) to develop more materials for her portfolio. Linda held the office of public relations director for the PRSSA chapter in her sophomore year and was elected chapter vice president in the spring. She is scheduled to attend the PRSSA national conference during the fall. She regularly serves as an aide to the local PRSA (Public Relations Society of America) chapter at its monthly meetings. She helps members locate their nametags; in doing so, she gets to know their names. They know her and recognize her interest in the profession. She sits beside and visits with different professionals each month during the lunch meetings.

Carol has not thought much about these points. She picked sociology for a major because it was easy. She has no plans for an internship, nor has she kept a file of her public relations work. She says she is too busy to join PRSSA. She doesn't help the PRSA chapter.

Ask yourself, who is more likely to get a job if the two apply for the same position? Will one have an advantage? Why so? Which path are you taking in your career preparation?

How will you answer the question that may be posed by your parents, acquaintances, or children? So you are in public relations—what do you do? Why did you pick that profession? You need some definitive statements to help you respond to people who make comments once they know you are in public relations. As you pursue that practice, you will learn the many perceptions people have of what public relations people do. Some—perhaps many— of these perceptions are not all that flattering. A professional knows how and when to explain and defend his or her profession.

The purpose of this chapter is to guide your career preparation in public relations. The success of your career in large part depends on your professional preparation and continued career development. The sooner you think about and set goals for your public relations career, the better your preparation will be.

This chapter is about preparing for a career in public relations, not just getting a job. A career means you will be spending your work life in the profession and want to advance in your profession. Getting a job means doing the minimum to get an entry-level job. Think seriously—do you want a job or a career?

Job or Career?

What do public relations professionals do? They perform specialized roles and functions. We have explored these roles in general detail in previous chapters. The functions of public relations are to publicize, promote, listen/research, engage in collaborative decision making, and perform strategic planning. They achieve these functions by performing message development objectives (MDOs): create awareness, inform, persuade, negotiate, and cocreate meaning. These functions and MDOs are vital to the definition of the professional practice.

▶ Managerial Roles and Technical Functions

The profession is roughly divided into levels of practice. Many of the previous chapters in this text have featured the sorts of activities that are typical of what managers do and what technicians do. Now we take the time to discuss this in a concentrated manner. Your insights into the practice help you study and prepare to enter the profession. One way to focus your attention on this preparation is to imagine the sorts of questions that an interviewer will ask as you seek to demonstrate that you are qualified to serve as an intern, to become an entry-level employee, or to move upward in status, authority, and responsibility. We want to help you think about what you want to be "when you grow up." What do you want to be doing in 10 years? When parents, other relatives, and acquaintances ask, "What do public relations persons do?" or "What will you do in public relations?" we want you to have a sound set of answers.

In 1993, the PRSA Foundation published a report that you can use to gain additional insight into what public relations practitioners do. The report was titled *Public Relations Professional Career Guide*. It examined the functions and tactics performed by today's public relations practitioner. The report gave us additional insight into the differences in activities between entry-level technicians, supervisors, managers, directors, and executives. The core responsibility and skill required at all levels was effective writing.

The report gave a lot of detail about the sorts of daily, weekly, and annual activities that are performed by each of the five professional levels. Most studies make less dramatic differentiations, limited to technician and managerial. That sort of reduction may oversimplify the roles and functions, but it is more manageable, for instance, in a textbook discussion such as this. Let's grasp the differences between the levels with this generalization.

Technicians primarily engage in writing, research, and the development of the means by which the messages will be delivered. For instance, a technician might be responsible for researching stories and gathering information about a corporation's performance as a first step to create the employee newsletter. This person may write news stories for this newsletter and lay out the newsletter in a form that makes it ready for printing. The person may work with a printing company to publish the newsletter. The person might see that the newsletter is circulated to all employees. Today's practitioner may put this newsletter on the company Intranet. It might go on the Intranet and not be printed on paper.

Supervisors are likely to do some of these technical functions, but the primary responsibility of supervisors is to assign work to technicians, guide the work performance, support the technicians' efforts, and oversee and coordinate the work of several technicians. Both the technicians and the supervisors may work with agency and contract personnel who perform similar functions.

Managers and executives are much more engaged in strategic planning than they are in the execution of the plans. This planning occurs at both the executive management levels and the public relations department levels. For instance, instead of researching and writing stories for the newsletters, executives and managers set policy guidelines for content and purpose of the newsletter. They convince management that it adds value to the organization.

With these broad generalizations in mind, we can focus even more on the skills that differentiate these levels of practitioners. The PRSA Foundation report zeroed in on four kinds of skills. It reported the importance of the skills for the performance of each of the practitioner levels, as follows:

- *Technical and craft skills:* These are very important for technicians but decrease in importance for each higher level. They are quite low in importance, for instance, to executives and managers.
- *Interpersonal skills:* These are of medium importance or higher for all levels, but they are especially important to the managers and executives who have to counsel executives and sell business to clients—including the executives of the organization.
- *Conceptual and problem-solving skills:* The report indicated that these are of medium importance to all levels. Today's public relations practitioner, however, is likely to be more successful if his or her conceptual and problem-solving skills are high. They are less vital to persons who perform routine tasks but are very important to persons who lead the profession and engage in strategic responses to rhetorical problems. Many senior practitioners describe themselves as "problem solvers." So, conceptual problem-solving skills are vital for those who work at this level.
- *Consulting and teaching skills:* The report indicated that these were of low importance to all levels. Nevertheless, mentoring and development are vital parts of professional experiences. Supervisors and managers spend a lot of their time developing the skills of the persons who work below them. Executives coordinate and counsel.

PRSA has not been the only group to explore the profession to better understand what practitioners do and what they bring to the organizational table. Glen M. Broom (Broom, 1982; Broom & Dozier, 1986; Broom & Smith, 1979) and various research associates have defined the public relations practice by distinguishing a variety of roles. This research features four roles that can be used to differentiate the activities that practitioners routinely perform: expert prescriber, communication facilitator, problem-solving process facilitator, and communication technician.

Think about each of these to help yourself conceptualize the sorts of roles and functions that persons perform in professional public relations capacities. The *expert prescriber* is a senior counselor, one who draws on years of practice to advise management what actions and messages need to be used to solve the rhetorical problems confronting them at the moment and over the long term. This sort of person could be an organizational insider, but is often a consultant. Some consultants who have achieved this level of practice might be senior members of public relations firms. They might work as a "one-person" operation. They might be on retainers to large organizations, and/or they could be on call to provide highly specialized expertise. Some of these persons have developed such a professional reputation that they can charge hundreds of dollars per hour and thousands of dollars per day for their professional services. These persons truly have "been there and done that."

The *communication facilitator* is a senior boundary spanner, one who performs communication roles and functions to increase the quality and quantity of information flow from the organization to MAPs. Perhaps of even more importance, this person helps the MAPs to get their information, opinions, attitudes, and beliefs set on the decision table before senior management. This person is expected to facilitate two-way symmetrical communication between the organization and its stakeseekers/stakeholders.

The third category of public relations practitioners discovered by Broom and his associates is called *problem-solving process facilitator*. What functions do persons in this category perform? This combination of roles and functions can best be understood by comparing it to the expert prescriber. Whereas the organization asks for and follows the advice of the expert prescriber, the problem-solving process facilitator works with the executives of the organization to define the rhetorical problem and consider several solutions. The solutions are weighed and compared. Out of that problem-solving process—facilitated by this professional—a decision is made and implemented.

The fourth category of public relations professional is the *communication technician*. This person might be relatively new to the field and is employed because of his or her strong communication skills. Or the person might be a more senior person who executes the development and use of the standard public relations tools. This person might spend most of his or her time writing: employee newsletters, press releases, news stories, feature articles, speeches, and the like. The person might do editing and layout. The person could as well do the video scripts and production for the department or the agency. Most of this person's day is devoted to the practice of the sorts of communication skills that are featured in strong public relations, journalism, speech communication, and radio or television programs. We often call these *basic skills*. They are the foundation of the profession.

Persons who are entering the field do so for the most part by performing the role of communication technician. Thousands of persons employed in public relations engage in this practice as part of all of their jobs. Some individuals never do the other roles. They enjoy being highly skilled communication technicians. As glamorous as the other roles are at times, no public relations department or agency can exist without employing or contracting excellent communication technicians.

Technicians may be involved in the strategic design and execution of public relations tools, but they are rarely involved in larger issues of public relations strategic planning. They rarely become involved with the strategic business planning of organizations. They do very little situational analysis. They rarely analyze rhetorical problems, but may participate in the design and execution of messages created and developed in response to such analysis.

Elsewhere in this chapter, we discuss salaries, but let us pause to suggest here that expert prescribers earn the highest salaries or consulting fees. The order of the other roles in terms of size of consulting fee or salary is as follows: problem-solving facilitators, communication facilitators, and communication technicians (Broom & Dozier, 1986).

So, we have reviewed the four-part taxonomy of public relations professional practice. How else can we help you imagine the sorts of career options that lie before you? One way to do that is to indicate that instead of the four-part model, we can limit the role-function typology to two categories: public relations manager and public relations technician. One is primarily responsible for counseling, situational analysis, rhetorical problem recognition, strategic planning (business and public relations), and strategic execution of business and public relations plans. The other is a communication technician. The technician is largely expected and assigned to implement the strategic plans created by the managers.

This first section of the chapter has helped to focus your attention on the nature of a profession and the sorts of functions and tactical skills that are important to it. The next section explores careers by examining the occupational outlook, qualities of successful practitioners, and ways to hone those skills.

"I Want to Practice Public Relations"

This section opens with a statement that people may express boldly, proudly, or tentatively. Let's think about our imaginary students in the opening vignette, Carol and Linda, who are learning to be practitioners. At some point in their lives, they have to say to themselves, their professors, their friends, and their acquaintances, "I want to practice public relations." An issue of ethics is central to making that decision and is likely to be implied or stated in the responses others make to it. But even more important, if Carol or Linda made this statement to members of their families, we can imagine family members asking three questions: Are there public relations jobs? What qualities are needed to succeed in public relations? How can you acquire the knowledge and skills necessary to succeed?

▶Occupational Outlook

As a future or current public relations practitioner, you must want to know about the employment outlook in your chosen field. The news is mixed. The good news is the job growth rate. The U.S. government projects job growth for entry-level positions to be much faster than average (increase 36% or more) through 2006. Job growth for manager positions is projected to be faster than the average (increase 21% to 35%) through 2006.

The bad news is the amount of competition for those jobs. Public relations has become a popular major in colleges and universities for many reasons, one of which is the number of jobs. That good news masks the challenge that the more people there are competing for jobs, the more well prepared each successful candidate must be.

The U.S. government rates competition for both entry-level and manager-level public relations jobs to be keen; there will be fewer job openings than job seekers. Opportunities will continue to exist, but you must act strategically to place yourself in a position to secure one of these jobs. Yes, thinking strategically begins even before your job does. In the opening vignette, Linda was being strategic; she was thinking about and working hard to develop skills and build her portfolio, while Carol was not. You must learn what qualities employers are seeking in a job candidate and how you can acquire, demonstrate, and refine those qualities. The process will not be easy, but hard work will be rewarded.

Your next question might be, "How much can I expect to earn?" That is not an easy question because it depends on the type of organization you work for, your experience, and your responsibilities. Below are figures and job titles used by PRSA:

Title	Salary
Entry level	$18,000 to $22,000
Account executive	up to $35,000
Public relations director	$35,000 to $40,000 in small to medium organizations $40,000 to $60,000 in a large organization
Public relations executives	$75,000 to $150,000

Your skills can increase your salary. Investor relations specialists make about 30% more than the average salary. Practitioners who work in environmental and risk communication are paid better than most of their counterparts. Practitioners who are mastering the Web are not only more employable but are also receiving higher-level starting salaries. Those with technology skills command higher pay as well.

▶ Qualities of a Successful Practitioner

A public relations career begins with an entry-level job and progresses to a managerial position. An entry-level position is a technician role. The practitioner creates materials such as news releases, brochures, newsletters, and media lists. The technician is told what to create and is uninvolved in the planning and decision-making process. For instance, the technician is told to create a membership newsletter for a nonprofit organization, but he or she does not decide that a newsletter is needed or how it fits into the organization's strategic plan. In contrast, managers are defined by decision making and planning. Managers decide what should be done and why it should be done. A manager would decide that a newsletter was necessary to help achieve some facet of the organization's strategic plan. Managers also often counsel their clients and executive counterparts on ways to position the organization so that it can achieve and maintain mutually beneficial relationships.

Different qualities are needed for the technician and manager roles. A technician starts with basic skills, such as writing, but must acquire planning-related skills to advance to management. Today's practitioners must be able to engage in strategic planning to respond ethically and effectively to rhetorical problems.

Too often, students and entry-level practitioners think only of the first job/technician role. As a result, there has been a shortage of applicants for public relations manager jobs for over a decade. Practitioners must think beyond the technician role if they want to have successful careers that include movement into a management position.

One of your immediate educational objectives should be to learn which qualities your prospective employers want in their candidates. Many public relations books contain lists of such qualities. Below is a list of the personal traits and intellectual qualities identified by PRSA:

- Analytic thinking
- Ability to work well under pressure
- Imagination and creativity
- Communication skills
- Self-confidence
- Diplomacy
- Organization and planning skills

Two high-tech skills are noted as well: Internet research skills and the ability to utilize a wide range of software. A similar list is provided by the Commission on Public Relations Education (1999).

The Commission on Public Relations Education believes the following knowledge should be acquired by students who are preparing for a career in public relations (see also the comments by John Paluszek, 2000, "Public Relations Students: Today Good, Tomorrow Better"):

- Communication and persuasion concepts and strategies
- Communication and public relations theories
- Relationships and relationship building
- Societal trends
- Ethical issues
- Legal requirements and issues
- Marketing and finance
- Public relations history
- Uses of research and forecasting
- Multicultural and global issues
- Organizational change and development
- Management concepts and theories

In addition to this knowledge, the Commission on Public Relations Education recommends the following skills:

- Research methods and analysis
- Management of information
- Mastery of language in written and oral communication
- Problem solving and negotiation
- Management of communication
- Strategic planning
- Issues management
- Audience segmentation

You may note that some of the traditional assumptions about the role of public relations as media relations seem less central to the knowledge and skills in this list.

In addition to who you are, you need to think about what you know and learn. Practitioners look for entry-level people who bring leadership skills as well as demonstrate knowledge of business practices and economics. Even if you are intending to work in nonprofits, you need to understand business principles and best practices.

You should be current on the events in your community, profession, state, and nation. Senior practitioners believe that entry-level practitioners need to read at least two newspapers each day. You should read one news magazine each week. You should consume radio and television news. You need to be aware of all of the sections of the news, including business and financial news.

You should read interesting books and novels. You should watch television programs other than network sitcoms. You need to understand the world, the way it works, how people act, and the broader issues typically explored in the humanities and social sciences. You should develop the habit of reading at least two newspapers every day. Senior practitioners are "news junkies."

A refined and detailed list of qualities was created from a massive research effort launched in the late 1990s. A 12-page survey was completed by 108 practitioners and 150 public relations educators from across the country. One section asked respondents to evaluate what students should be able to do on the job—qualities of a good hire. Separate answers were given for entry-level (technician) and advanced-level (managerial) positions. Respondents were given options ranging from 1 "not desired" to 7 "highly desired." We will consider the top qualities from each list.

►Entry Level (Technician)

The entry-level qualities were reduced to 10 items, with each item rated at 6.27 or higher by practitioners. The qualities include skills, what people should be able to do; knowledge, what people should know; and personal attributes, how people should act. These are featured in Table 14.1.

Table 14.1: Entry-Level Skills, Knowledge, and Personal Attributes

Trait	Mean	Skill, Knowledge, Attribute
1. Is self-starter	6.63	Personal attribute
2. Can write media releases	6.57	Skill
3. Is organized	6.54	Personal attribute
4. Possesses interpersonal skills	6.53	Skill
5. Can think critically and solve problems	6.49	Skill
6. Is flexible	6.44	Personal attribute
7. Can use word processing/e-mail	6.37	Skill
8. Knows current events	6.36	Knowledge
9. Takes criticism	6.30	Personal attribute
10. Has basic knowledge of mass media	6.27	Knowledge

The entry-level skills are fundamental to public relations. They reflect what technicians do in their jobs. Writing news releases and word processing are necessary for the entry-level practitioner. Critical thinking and interpersonal skills are valuable in any workplace. The personal attributes are common as well: self-starter, organized, flexible, and takes criticism. When learning to write for an editor (your manager), taking criticism is a must. Entry-level practitioners use the criticism to improve their writing and to adjust to the style of the manager. Basic knowledge of the mass media fits with the media relations tasks that frequently fall to entry-level personnel. Students should recognize the importance of knowledge/interest in current events. Too often, college students insulate themselves from current events; they focus on campus and local events. It is important to avoid this insulation if you are to become more marketable. All it takes is an effort to watch and/or read the national and world news. A former student of one author who is now an entry-level practitioner set up his computer so that each morning when he turned on his machine, it would display news related to the industry in which he worked.

▶Advanced Level

The PRSA Foundation report that we discussed above suggested that a hierarchy of skills and activities distinguish the entry-level person from those at more advanced levels. Some practitioners are quite satisfied to remain at lower levels, if that means they write more and engage in planning and counseling less. Agencies and other organizations are wise to have a stable of competent writers who can perform that vital function.

In addition to the entry-level skills, however, agencies and other organizations need people to do more advanced-level activities. For instance, an agency can't survive if its account executives can't work effectively with clients. The agency will sink if it does not have senior practitioners who are adept at acquiring new business and keeping old clients happy.

Whether in an agency or other organization, one or more practitioners need advanced-level skills. The study reported in the entry-level section above also examined advanced-level personal skills, knowledge, and attributes. The advanced-level list is composed of eight items. Each item was rated a 6.00 or higher by practitioners. The results are presented in Table 14.2

Table 14.2: Advanced-Level Skills, Knowledge, and Personal Attributes

Trait	Mean	Skill, Knowledge, Attribute
1. Works well in team effort	6.51	Personal attribute/skill
2. Handles media professionally	6.47	Skill
3. Demonstrates critical listening	6.37	Skill
4. Has field experience in PR	6.23	Knowledge
5. Knows crisis management	6.12	Knowledge
6. Has research skills	6.06	Skill
7. Knows issues management	6.05	Knowledge
8. Knows PR's management team role	6.03	Knowledge

The advanced-level qualities reflect the managerial role's emphasis on planning and decision making. Notice that research appears as an important skill, along with "handling the media" and "critical listening." The only personal attribute is "works well in a team," an attribute that is also a skill, as people can learn how to improve their group communication skills. Once more, the small-group nature of public relations work is apparent. Knowledge shifts to a higher level of planning and decision making with crisis management, issues management, and public relations' management team role. Finally, as one would expect, field experience in public relations is required for advanced-level positions. The entry-level qualities are a base that practitioners must build on to progress from the first job to a career. We now turn our attention to how you can acquire, demonstrate, and refine these highly desired qualities.

Acquiring, Demonstrating, and Refining Qualities, Knowledge, and Skills

At the beginning of this book, we had you imagine what you would do if your new boss asked you to prepare a press release soon after you had started your first job. Do you think that this book and other discussions have come closer to preparing you for that assignment? No one book or course can cover the entire range of knowledge and skills you will need in your career. You need to use your undergraduate education as a series of building blocks. You need to choose wisely and strategically to build the foundations for that career. Then, you may need to use graduate education and continuing and professional development to hone your knowledge and skills.

Chapter 2 discussed the need for public relations to become a profession. Part of becoming a profession is standardized education/training. Although public relations education/training is not standardized, it is obvious that you should be acquiring and refining expected qualities from your public relations education that you can demonstrate to employers. Education/training, like a career, should be ongoing. The undergraduate degree is the starting point. Your undergraduate degree provides the entry-level qualities and creates a base for advanced-level qualities. A graduate degree is recommended for refining the advanced-level qualities. Continuing education is a way to refine qualities by updating them or adding new ones. Finally, accreditation is a way to show your commitment to the profession as well as demonstrate your desirable qualities. In this section, we will examine undergraduate education, graduate education, continuing education, and accreditation as ways to acquire, demonstrate, and refine desired qualities.

▶ Undergraduate Education: "A Port of Entry"

In 1999, the Commission on Public Relations Education produced a report titled "A Port of Entry." This report outlined academic preparations for students who seek to become practitioners. Viewing colleges and universities as ports of entry, the commission wanted to suggest curricular guidelines. "The Commission's goals were to determine the knowledge and skills needed by practitioners in a technological, multicultural and global society, and then to recommend learning outcomes—what students should know and be able to do—for undergraduate, graduate and continuing education" (Commission on Public Relations Education, 1999, p. 3).

With competition for public relations jobs being strong, a degree in public relations is an advantage. Too many schools claim to teach public relations. However, they offer only a few courses that are not integrated into an actual sequence. The most recent Commission on Public Relations Education, a project sponsored by PRSA with membership from all major professional and academic communication associations, recognized this problem.

The commission recommended at least five clearly identifiable public relations courses as the minimum for a major. The five can include the following: Introduction to/Principles of Public Relations; Public Relations Writing and Production; Public Relations Research, Measurement, and Performance Evaluation; Public Relations Case Studies/Strategy Implementation; and Supervised Work Experience in Public Relations/Internships. The commission cautioned, "Programs that offer minors should make it clear that a minor in public relations is not sufficient to prepare a student for the professional practice of public relations" (Commission on Public Relations Education, 1999, p. 23). As you read this book, we hope you are in a program that offers a true major. Employers should recognize the value of a true major over a minor only.

You should plan your curriculum so that it adds up to a well-defined and supported undergraduate education. In your sophomore year, you would set out your curriculum plan as well as your support plan. You should identify your career goals. Be realistic. Think in terms of short- and long-term goals. Assess your skills. Be willing to take classes that give you knowledge and strengthen your skills. Allow the classes to have a positive impact on you. Learn something that is useful, particularly in ways that support your personal plan. One way to prepare your plan is to look at the lists of courses we mention here, as well as the skills, knowledge, and personal attributes that are featured. Ask yourself where you can acquire these, both in courses and through extramural activities.

An important outcome from your undergraduate education is a portfolio. Your portfolio is an organized collection of your public relations work. It is the embodiment of your résumé and demonstrates your skills. For instance, your résumé may say you know Web design. Your portfolio would include at least one sample of a Web site you designed—a demonstration of your ability to apply a skill. Typical materials in your portfolio would include writing samples (news releases, brochures, magazines, newsletters, etc.), PowerPoint slides and disk, sample Web site and disk, surveys, data analysis and summary, audio and/or visual public service announcements, and short public relations documents, such as a crisis management plan or a position paper on an issue. The key is to keep all of the public relations materials you create for classes and outside the classroom. Select the best pieces for inclusion in your portfolio. Remember to make any suggested revisions to materials completed in class. The instructor is providing feedback for a reason; taking criticism is a desired outcome. Organize the materials logically. Your organization depends on the material you have to work from. Ask instructors and public relations professionals for advice on your portfolio. Box 14.1 provides more details about how to construct a student's portfolio.

BOX 14.1 YOUR PORTFOLIO

Throughout this chapter, we have noted the need for a portfolio and briefly described one. In this box, we provide more detail on what the portfolio is and how to prepare one. A portfolio is simply a collection of your work samples. These samples demonstrate your skills and abilities. The portfolio works with the résumé. The portfolio brings to life the skills and abilities you list on your résumé.

You begin preparing your portfolio by identifying the skills you want to emphasize. Clearly identify those skills and locate any materials you have created that demonstrate the skills. Portfolio pieces should be your best work. Make sure the copy is clean and includes any suggested revisions. Portfolio pieces may include PowerPoint presentations, brochures, newsletters, news releases, awards, in-house magazines, budgets or planning documents, or problem analysis reports. The pieces depend on what you have done and what skills you would like to feature in the portfolio. It is possible to modify your portfolio to match the job. You may add and remove pieces depending on the specifics of the job. For instance, a media relations position would feature news releases and media contact lists, while an employee relations position would feature newsletters and in-house publications. Limit your portfolio to around 10 items when you show it to a prospective employer.

The next step is to organize the portfolio pieces. You might arrange them chronologically or by level of complexity. There is no set format for organization. What you want to remember is *easy access* and *short explanations.* Make it easy for someone to take a piece out of the portfolio for closer inspection. Use plastic holders that allow a document to be easily removed. Employers don't like it when pieces are difficult to access. Prepare a short explanation for each item and place it near the item. The explanation clarifies the skills demonstrated in the piece. Finally, practice your presentation of the portfolio. You want to be able to talk through the portfolio smoothly and expertly. It always helps to have others critique your presentation so you can improve it. Be sure to mention in your cover letters that you have a portfolio and will bring it to the interview. Advanced warning allows the potential employer to consider the portfolio review as part of the time needed for the interview.

Most curricula feature some combination of five courses that feature public relations principles, writing, campaigns, cases, and practicum. The five classes are just the basics. Additional courses that would be useful include Ethics, Visual and Interactive Communication, Public Relations Management, Issues Management, Crisis Management, Public Relations Internship, Marketing Communication, and International Public Relations. Your school may not offer courses using these exact titles. If that is the case, look for courses that offer the desired content areas. You may even have to take classes from departments other than the one offering the public relations major. The important thing is to learn the desired content.

The classroom is only part of the undergraduate educational experience. The internship counts as a class but is also a bridge to outside-the-classroom experiences. Outside experiences can provide insight into what public relations people actually do on the job (what public relations work is like), provide connections to the professional community, give you a chance to apply your skills and knowledge, and provide an opportunity to develop portfolio pieces. Internships can help you to see whether the career is right for you. One author had a student who switched from radio broadcasting to public relations after her radio internship. She found radio was not what she wanted to do. Her public relations internship went much better, and she was very happy with the career switch. The 1999 Commission on Public Relations Education noted the value of outside experiences: "It is imperative that public relations students have the opportunity to apply skills and principles they learn to the professional arena" (p. 22). You can find valuable suggestions in Table 14.3, "Beyond the Classroom," which lists common extramurual, outside-of-class experiences and what they can offer students.

The outside-of-classroom activities you engage in depend in large part on you. Instructors may bring in guest lecturers, set up public relations career days, or coordinate a community service/learning project as part of a class. However, students can initiate and bring to life any of the beyond-the-classroom items. Clearly, some are easier than others. The most difficult is establishing a student professional organization such as PRSSA. There are strict rules and guidelines for the process. The easiest is to subscribe to a public relations listserv. You are limited only by time constraints and your own ambitions. Do not be afraid to become an active participant in your own public relations training. Remember, the competition for jobs is keen, and better training improves your odds of moving to the top of an applicant list.

In addition to all of the attention you give to your major, select your minor carefully. Experience suggests that too many students consider the minor an afterthought

Table 14.3: Beyond the Classroom

Activities	Outcomes
Professional organizations (e.g., PRSSA)	Portfolio materials, application, connections
Student-run PR agencies	Portfolio materials, application
Student competitions (e.g., Bateman)	Portfolio materials, application
Work on student media	Portfolio materials, application
Community service/learning projects	Portfolio materials, application
Shadow days	PR work, connections
Guest speakers	PR work, connections
PR career days on campus	PR work, connections
Mentoring match-ups	PR work, connections
Subscribing to PR listservs	PR work, connections
Internship*	Portfolio materials, application, connections, and PR work

*May count as course credit

or look for something that is easy or fun. Poor reasons to pick a minor include hearing it is "easy" or "it takes the fewest hours to earn." You should select a minor for one of two reasons. First, the minor will help in the area of public relations you have selected for a specialty. Second, the minor provides skills that would be useful in general to a public relations specialist.

As the later part of this chapter will discuss, there are many specialty areas within public relations. Let us consider a few to see the value of the minor specialty fit. Parks, recreation, and tourism is an excellent minor for specialists in travel and tourism public relations. Some colleges offer programs in hotel and restaurant management. Finance is essential if you hope to be involved in investor relations. Political science is beneficial to an issues management specialist in government relations. International trade and/or foreign language would be critical to an international public relations specialist. Human resources is excellent for a specialist in internal (employee) public relations. If you know early on in your college career that you want to be a public relations specialist, work to match the minor to the specialty. As the "Context" section will detail, minors are critical to some public relations specialties and helpful to all. A business minor is an excellent option. It prepares you to talk with executives in business and understand how they operate. It is vital to anyone who aspires to work at the corporate levels or in a major agency.

Many skills would benefit any public relations practitioner. A list of these knowledge and skills courses would include marketing, journalism, graphics, applied computer science, statistics/research methods, consumer behavior, and foreign language skills. Marketing and consumer behavior provide greater insights into MAPs. Journalism and graphics help to refine writing and design skills. Statistics/research methods improve your research and analysis skills. Applied computer science provides skill in applications, including Internet and Intranet. Foreign language skills are useful in a business environment that is increasingly global. Knowing a language could be the difference between going overseas for an assignment or staying home.

Bottom line, minors are a serious consideration. The sooner you know whether you want to specialize in an area of public relations, the easier it will be to select a minor. The safe option is to select from the list of general skills. But do think about the decision carefully. Look through your college's course catalogue to see what minors are available and the requirements for each. There really are no "wrong" minors. Some courses you may take just for personal interest. One author had a friend who minored in Eastern philosophy with a major in pre-med. He is now a physician who knows a lot about Buddhism and Zen. However, a minor can be an advantage in your career. Just be sure to make an informed choice about your minor. Be strategic, and consider how it fits into what you think you want to do with your life.

One of the last considerations on most students' minds is education after finishing the undergraduate degree. The following sections all deal with that subject. As noted throughout this book, the practice of public relations changes over time. Societal trends, changes in business, and new technologies all transform the practice. Some form of additional education is necessary to remain current. For example, today many practitioners are learning new Internet-based skills. Prior to the Internet, many practitioners needed to learn more about research. Research is a skill in greater demand, and many early public relations programs did not prepare students to execute research, so they had to learn it later. Moreover, promotion may require you to seek additional education. Still other people simply love to learn new things. Whatever your motivation, a master's degree, continuing education, and accreditation are all possible options for your future.

▶Graduate Education: The Master's Degree

The 1999 Commission on Public Relations Education described a master's degree in public relations as "preparation for public relations management leadership, career development, and to make contributions to society and the profession" (1999, p. 24). The master's degree is dedicated to the advanced-level qualities identified earlier in the chapter and prepares practitioners to become public relations managers. The emphasis is on theory and research. Practitioners learn theory and research so that they can apply it to solving problems and taking advantage of opportunities faced by their organizations. The master's degree is a form of career advancement.

▶Continuing Education

Continuing education is another name for lifelong learning. It is a way for practitioners to add new or refresh old skills and knowledge. Both entry-level and advanced practitioners benefit from the process. Two types of continuing education may be in your future: certification programs and workshops and seminars. The two differ in terms of formality and time commitment. The certification program is the most formal and requires the greatest time commitment.

▶Certification Programs

Certification programs are abbreviated degree programs. Participants must complete a set number of hours that cover specific topics. Most colleges require that participants have an undergraduate degree and enroll as a graduate student. However, the requirements are not as stringent as for a master's degree program. Fewer total hours and classes are required. The participant might take a mix of college courses, workshops, and seminars as ways to complete the required number of hours. Still, the certification program is structured, and participants must meet and fulfill all the requirements. Depending on time constraints and professional goals, a certification program might be a person's best option for career development.

▶Workshops and Seminars

Workshops and seminars provide an alternative to classes. These are usually one- or two-day intensive sessions on a topic such as crisis management, budgeting, or Web site utilization. Most are offered from private vendors rather than colleges. Both PRSA and IABC (International Association of Business Communicators) offer a number of workshops and seminars each year on both the national and chapter levels. PRSA

Summer 2000 Seminars ranged in cost from $25 to $625 dollars and included the following topics: Crisis Communications Planning; Public Relations: Research, Measurement, and Evaluation; Strategic Public Relations Planning; Media Relations: Building Relationships to Deliver Your Message; Public Relations Programming: A Comprehensive Approach; Building and Evaluating an Employee Communications Program; and Leadership and Management of the Public Relations Function. Depending on the vendor, the price can be rather steep. However, the cost is a business expense that your employer may pick up, or you can write off on your taxes. Check the vendor carefully to be sure the topic is what you need/want and that the quality is high. Workshops and seminars are a quick way to stay current or to sharpen skills and knowledge. Again, depending on time issues and professional development goals, workshops and seminars may be a person's best option for career development.

▶ Professional Meetings

Organizations such as the PRSA and IABC hold monthly and annual meetings in which senior practitioners, academics, and other specialists share their knowledge and promote what they believe to be best practices.

Many professional organizations also have special interest groups that meet to share insights and provide networking and bonding experiences. Special interest groups might be created for all of the key specialty areas of public relations, such as issues management or tourism.

Professional associations and meetings may also feature unique aspects of the profession. For investor relations practitioners, the National Investor Relations Institute offers networking and career development support. The same is true for practitioners who specialize in public affairs, education, and many other parts of the profession.

PRSA and IABC professionals provide liaison with PRSSA and student IABC chapters. This is a valuable mentoring opportunity that can help students to become more familiar with the profession. One of the valuable connections gives students the opportunity to have their résumés and portfolios reviewed by professionals.

▶ Accreditation

As we noted at the beginning of the chapter, members enter organizations through a process we called *assimilation*. It consists of anticipatory socialization, encounter, and metamorphosis. Undergraduate education and all that goes with it are largely supportive of the socialization process and to some extent the encounter phase. The new member of the profession learns what it requires, and prepares to enter the profession. In the final phase, the member of the profession matures to the point that he or she becomes committed to mastering the knowledge and skills of the profession. The person is proud to be a member of the profession. He or she knows that it adds value to society as well as to the employer or client organizations.

As this maturation process continues, we find professional practitioners becoming teachers and mentors. They earn accreditation as a badge of having accomplished a major level of achievement. They serve their local and national professional organizations. They are officers of these organizations. They become honored fellows. Toward this maturation, one of the key steps is becoming accredited.

Accreditation can be used in conjunction with the other three forms of career development. Accreditation means you have passed a series of examinations offered by a professional organization. Upon successfully completing accreditation, a person earns the right to place the marks of accreditation next to his or her name. Both PRSA and IABC offer accreditation. PRSA grants the initials APR (Accredited in Public Relations) while IABC uses the initials ABC (Accredited Business Communicator). It is a sign of professional achievement and a statement of commitment to the public relations profession. Accreditation is another step toward professionalization. Accreditation is designed to show a high level of competencies. While it does not carry the same weight as a lawyer passing the bar, it does show detailed knowledge of the field.

What does it require to become Accredited in Public Relations, or APR? To take the APR examination, a practitioner needs 5 years of experience in full-time practice of public relations or teaching public relations. The examination has written and oral sections. The written section is a daylong examination that is divided into two sections. The morning session covers testing of general knowledge of public relations. The afternoon session is devoted to a case study. The practitioner chooses one of several case studies and then writes a public relations plan to address the case.

The topics covered in the examination include the following: the evolution of the public relations practice, socioeconomic and political factors that affect the field, the theoretical bases of public relations, public relations management and roles, campaign and program planning, research, communications and public opinion theory, strategy planning, news media relations, special events, crisis management, evaluation of public relations, public relations law, and the Universal Code of Professional Standards for the Practice of Public Relations.

The accreditation examinations provide evidence you have mastered your craft. It is another way to demonstrate your knowledge and skills. While you might learn new skills or polish existing skills and knowledge when preparing for the examinations, their purpose is to indicate achievement and not learning. The undergraduate degree provides the base of the knowledge you need to become a practitioner, with an emphasis on entry-level qualities. A master's degree provides the qualities for advanced-level qualities. Certificate programs, workshops, and seminars are ways to refine old qualities and learn new ones. Education can facilitate your career development throughout the entire span of your work life. Think of education as a tool for improving your practice of public relations. The competition for the good public relations job is fierce, and with the proper preparation, you can be in a strong position to win that competition.

Contexts of Public Relations Practice: Many Types of Relationships

Public relations is a very broad field. A number of specialty areas of public relations are based on the context in which public relations is practiced. Chapter 3 made that point when it addressed several of the key types of relationships that are central to the practice of public relations. We also featured key public relations functions in chapters on research, publicity, promotion, issues management, and collaborative decision making. In this section, we review five major context areas, identify key aspects of the specialty, and recommend preparation designed for the specialty.

Many different ways can be used to differentiate and organize the various contexts of public relations. One is by types of stakeholders and their unique relationship needs: media relations, community relations, investor relations, customer relations, employee relations, alumni relations, and member relations. Another is by industry or topic: association, food and beverage, health, travel and tourism, environment, and technology. Another is by basic type of public relations: nonprofit, corporate, and agency. As background, you may want to return to the salary list above that reports recent data on the pay of public relations practitioners. While covering all the contexts is beyond the scope of this chapter, we have selected five contexts that present special preparation and career issues.

▶ Travel and Tourism

The travel industry is a broad area, with strong growth and potential for public relations work. The travel industry includes four areas: (1) transportation, (2) lodging, (3) amusement and recreation, and (4) visitor and convention bureaus. Transportation features the airline industry and cruise ships. Lodging, such as hotels and motels, provide people places to stay. These run the range from extravagant five-star hotels to a Motel 6. Amusement and recreation include parks and entertainment centers. Disney World is the premier amusement park, but there are many others around the world. Smaller recreation centers such as "Game Works" provide high-tech arcade amusement, while there are many outdoor parks, ski resorts, beaches, and so on for those who enjoy the outdoors. Visitor and convention bureaus try to attract tourists and convention goers to specific cities or regions.

Travel and tourism are key drivers in the global economy (Sallot, 2005). In 1998, nearly 7.6 million jobs in the United States were directly related to the travel industry. During the 1990s, the travel industry grew 27.7%. The industry is expected to grow another 21% by the year 2006. The jobs are not all low-paying anymore, either. Practitioners should not overlook this growing industry as a potential job option.

THE FLORIDA KEYS

Most people know the Florida Keys and Key West as a great getaway. One of the most unique places on earth. Calm. Serene. Laid back. Just the right setting to recharge your batteries and rejuvenate your spirits.

But a getaway to the Florida Keys and Key West is much more than peace and quiet. And not just because of the legendary fishing and the world's most spectacular dive sites.

The Keys mean history. Art. Theater. Museums. Shopping. Fine dining. Entertainment. And much more. All told, 120 miles of perfect balance between natural beauty and extra-ordinary excitement. Between relaxation and activities. Between the quaint and the classic.

And you'll find our accommodations just as diverse as our pleasures. From some of the best camping spots in the country to luxurious hotels. From charming bed-and-breakfasts to rustic, family-owned lodgings. In other words, we've got something for everyone.

In the next few pages you'll get to know what your Florida Keys vacation can and will be like. What you'd expect. And what will surprise you. Our fame and our secrets. We figured we owed it to you.

After all, we wouldn't want you to get here and wish you had booked just a few more days.

Use these color codes to go directly to the information or accommodations for a specific district.

▮ KEY LARGO	▮ MARATHON
▮ ISLAMORADA	▮ THE LOWER KEYS
	▮ KEY WEST

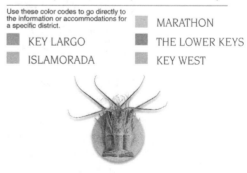

Could You Convince People to Vacation Here?

SOURCE: Courtesy of the Monroe County Tourist Development Center.

Travel and tourism are often oversimplified. It is said all you have to do is to attract customers, get them to your business, and make sure they have a good time. Ideally, you want repeat customers and positive word of mouth. You would like people coming back to your resort each year and telling their friends how great a place it is for a vacation. Public relations can help to attract and to keep customers and/or visitors. The five functions of public relations can be helpful in getting out positive information. For instance, a resort might conduct research to determine the demographics of its visitors. A plan is crafted to increase awareness and a favorable impression of the resort. Promotion and publicity are executed in the media, heavily used by the target demographic. The relationship is maintained through follow-up messages to past guests about changes and specials. An example is how a resort in Las Vegas, such as the Mirage, sends information to former guests via e-mail. There is a clear need for crisis management in travel and tourism. While not routine, airplanes do crash or go off runways, cruise ships have fires or breakdowns, hotels have fires or food poisoning, people are injured or killed on rides, and geographic areas experience violence against tourists.

Travel and tourism are active on the Internet. One of the primary uses of the Internet is to research and book travel. Online travel revenues exceeded $3 billion in 1998 and are projected to increase. Hence, it is logical to have a strong Internet presence if your organization is in the travel industry. All 50 U.S. state tourism offices have Web sites. Across the four areas, travel and tourism professionals agree there is a need to be online. Here are some guidelines for travel and tourism online: First, you must decide what information you wish to disseminate to MAPs and arrange it on an easy-to-navigate Web site. Place information a customer would want to know, and make it interactive. A hotel, for example, would want to post room rates for its various seasons and occupancy, a description of services, pictures of rooms and other areas or the hotel, sample menu items from the restaurant, and an online reservation system—the information a potential guest would like to know. Second, make sure you publicize the Web address in your other promotional materials. Third, it is a good idea to monitor and place your comments on travel listservs and bulletin boards. To maintain your ethics, always identify your employer.

Most sites allow people to book airline flights, cruises, rental cars, and hotels. Some even allow you to book a tee time on major golf courses and to make rail reservations. Expedia has a currency converter and posttravel advisories for the U.S. State Department. Travelnow even has message boards where people exchange travel information and a traveler review area where people review vacation spots. These travel sites are a good way to stay current on the field. You learn about what your competition is doing (e.g., specials they are running) and how your organization is portrayed on the sites. If you are not in the industry, the sites can be very helpful if you are planning a business or pleasure trip.

A practitioner should select a minor in some area related to travel and tourism. Search your university's course offerings carefully, because few offer a major in travel and tourism. Classes might be offered in geography, parks and recreation, hotel and restaurant management, or physical education. Check out your local convention and visitors bureau or amusement parks for potential internships. A minor and a relevant internship are your best bet for getting a job in the travel and tourism area.

▶ Nonprofit Organizations

Nonprofits can be the most personally rewarding contexts in which to practice public relations. Anyone who has a strong interest in some societal problem can find a corresponding nonprofit organization that has been created to solve that problem. Students have mixed impressions of nonprofits. Some don't realize that major nonprofits have substantial budgets and often have dozens of employees and volunteers working in public relations. They often provide the richest internship experience because they have lots of public relations needs and challenge personnel to know a lot and do a lot. Agencies and corporations, by contrast, may offer narrower experiences during an internship.

Nonprofits offer unique opportunities. Some of them are old, well established, highly respected, and well-endowed. Some nonprofits are new and tailored to address the problems of society that did not exist many years ago. Taken as a spectrum, they have missions and visions that focus on solving a huge array of human, societal, and environmental problems.

Nonprofits offer wonderful career development opportunities. Students find internships in nonprofits to be especially useful in giving them a wide array of skills.

Nonprofit public relations is the lowest-paying specialty area. These organizations devote greater resources to helping clients than to lining employees' pockets. Still, many people are attracted to nonprofit work because of their missions. They work for organizations that have social consciences consistent with their own. Research suggests people are happiest when they work in an organization that shares their values. Many practitioners find nonprofit work very rewarding. Nonprofit covers a wide array of organizations, including those that deal with human services, culture, environment, health, religion, education, relief, and foundations. Human services try to improve people's lives in some way. YMCAs, the Salvation Army, American Red Cross, and Girl Scouts of the USA are all human service nonprofit organizations. Cultural organizations include those that deal with the arts, museums, zoos, and aquariums. The Smithsonian Institute, Metropolitan Opera, Museum of Modern Art, and American Museum of Natural History are all cultural nonprofit organizations. Environmental groups look to protect our natural resources. The World Wildlife Fund and Nature Conservancy are environmental nonprofit organizations. Health organizations try to promote wellness and to treat diseases. Shriners Hospitals for Children, the American Cancer Society, Inc., and the American Heart Association are all health-oriented nonprofit organizations.

Religious organizations are organized around any faith and center on weekly worship meetings. However, religious organizations provide a wide array of community services, such as soup kitchens and homeless shelters. Examples include any of the churches you see in your town and organizations such as the Salvation Army. Education refers to schools and includes K–12, universities, and colleges. If you are reading this book, the odds are you are currently a client of an educational institution. Look around the campus to see how many different public relations activities are enacted by your school. Any school you have attended during your lifetime will be an example of an educational organization. Relief organizations are private versions of governmental welfare agencies designed to help people in need. Relief organizations include CARE USA, Habitat for Humanity International, and World Vision Federal Way. Foundations are organizations

Positive Contributions of Nonprofits

SOURCE: File Photo/Habitat for Humanity International.

that invest a large sum of money (their capital) and use the interest from the capital. Foundations use the interest by giving grants to people or groups who apply for money. Some well-known foundations include the Ford Foundation and the Bill & Melinda Gates Foundation, a new and well-funded foundation that supports efforts to help people through better health and learning.

Nonprofits share a need for fund-raising and volunteers. Nonprofits have limited budgets, which may come all or in part from donations; hence the need for fund-raising. Securing funding may be essential to continued operation or for expanding services. While people are generous, there is only so much money donated each year, and nonprofits do compete with one another. Table 14.4 provides a list of the categories and percentage of donated money they receive. According to Kathleen Kelly (1991), an expert in fund-raising and public relations, fund-raising can benefit greatly from public relations. The five MDOs can be used to help raise money and keep donors giving on a regular basis. A supplement to fund-raising is merchandising. Cultural organizations have been successful at merchandising as a way to generate funds. Sales from museum stores, such as the Detroit Institute of Art or San Diego Zoo merchandise, are another source of funding. Public relations can help to promote the existence and use of such stores.

Fund-raising and spending must be monitored carefully in nonprofit organizations. Abuses in spending can hurt future efforts to solicit funds. The United Way stands as a shining example of improper spending. In 1992, William Aramony, the president of United Way, was forced to resign. In addition to his $400,000-a-year salary, people were upset by the public disclosure of plush offices, limousines, private jets, country club memberships, gambling junkets to Las Vegas, and a massive expensive account,

Table 14.4: Contributions	
Type of Nonprofit	*Percentage of Annual Giving in the U.S.*
Religion	43.0%
Education	14.4%
Health	9.4%
Human services	9.1%
Foundations	7.9%
Culture	5.8%
Relief	5.8%
Environment	3.1%

all paid for with United Way contributions. A bad year for the United Way was 1992, when giving dropped because people saw the agency as wasteful. The National Charities Information Board recommends that a charity should try to spend at least 60¢ for each dollar contributed on its charitable purpose. The rest of the money can go toward overhead costs. As Kelly noted, fund-raising is done as a means to an end. Fund-raising allows the organization to accomplish its objectives, such as curing a disease or feeding the hungry. Nonprofits should create and make public an annual report that details giving to and spending by the charity. If you are contacted to give money to a charity, you should ask for such information if you are not familiar with the charity. Public relations can help to create and to disseminate vital information about giving and spending.

Most nonprofits rely on the hours donated by volunteers in order to operate. Volunteers work with scouts, sell tickets and operate coatrooms, deliver meals, or help with secretarial work. The nonprofit must attract and keep volunteers—recruitment and retention. Research can identify potential volunteers and why they want to volunteer. Nonprofits must learn the demographics for potential volunteers and their motivations for volunteering (the "why"). A plan can be constructed to use publicity and promotion to recruit volunteers and a system developed to make sure volunteers receive the intrinsic rewards they desire. Volunteers and the organization need a mutually beneficial relationship, and public relations can help them to achieve it. For instance, one motivation for volunteering is career development. Volunteer activities are an excellent way to gain public relations experience and to build one's portfolio. You may be motivated to volunteer in order to develop some job skill. Your experience would be negative if that opportunity, such as developing publicity materials, did not materialize.

Because of their smaller budgets, nonprofits often are less technologically sophisticated than their corporate cousins. However, nonprofits are increasingly using the Internet. All of the major U.S. charities have Web sites. Cultural nonprofits often have extensive sites that are very educational, as well as outlets for selling merchandise, soliciting donations, and attracting volunteers. What college or university does not have a Web site? Even K–12 schools and local churches are establishing sites. Technology has reached even the most "remote" regions of the public relations practice.

Preparation for nonprofit should emphasize being a generalist. With small staffs, the nonprofit practitioner must be able to perform all public relations activities. You will be writing newsletters, planning special occasions, and handling media inquiries, to name but a few. Some extra courses in desktop publishing would help, since you probably will not have a graphics staff at your disposal. Nonprofit work is when sociology is a viable minor. Many sociology departments offer courses that examine the function and structure of different types of nonprofits, such as health and religion. Check to see whether your sociology department offers courses related to nonprofit organizations.

▶ Public Relations Agencies

Agency work is different from the other contexts. Agencies are independent of a client organization. They work for clients and are not part of the organization's structure. Agency work is like being a lawyer at a law firm rather than an in-house counsel. Agency work demands some special skills and raises unique ethical questions.

WEB WATCHER: MONSTER.COM

As a Web Watcher, visit Monster.com, which has become a major force in helping people find employment. Part of the site provides free advice to people looking for jobs. The section is called "Career Advice," and the address is http://content.monster.com/. Visit the site, select the "Interviewing Tips," and answer the following questions: What are the main headings for the categories of interviewing tips? Look through the tips, and find one that you think is useful.

Working at an agency means soliciting and keeping clients. Soliciting clients requires proposal writing and presentational skills. Clients look for the best agency to represent them. This means you must write and present a proposal—explain why you are the best choice to represent them. Many senior practitioners lament the lack of spoken presentation skills among new practitioners. The skill is very valuable in an agency. You need to keep the client happy once you land the account. You are basically relationship building with the client. You must ensure that the relationship remains mutually beneficial if you are to retain the client. You practice public relations for and with the client.

In an agency, you are frequently assigned to a client. But what if you have a philosophical difference with the client? Hill & Knowlton had a string of high-profile, controversial clients in the 1990s. They represented the Catholic Bishops' anti-abortion campaign and the People's Republic of China after Tiananmen Square. Could you work effectively on an anti-abortion campaign if you were pro-choice or promote the People's Republic of China if you held strong beliefs about protecting human rights? The answer for many people is "no." That is why many, but not all, agencies allow employees to remove themselves from a client if they have a philosophical disagreement. You just need to establish that the difference is significant for you. One example of the policy is to have employees detail their personal values and beliefs. If a client is in conflict with a stated value or belief, the employee can exempt himself or herself from that account. For example, you indicate a strong desire to protect the oceans from pollution. You would not be assigned to a client that was one of the leading polluters of the oceans. Agencies want people who are totally committed to a client, including what the client stands for. Before accepting a position at an agency, you should find out what its policies are regarding client assignments.

Hill & Knowlton raises the larger issue of representing controversial and unethical clients. Some agencies maintain that public relations is like law and that everyone has a right to representation. As long as the client does not ask the agency to engage in unethical behavior, the client should be represented. Some consider this to be a financial argument: You represent anyone who can pay and requests ethical actions. In the United States, you do have the right to legal representation. No such rule exists for public relations. Find out whether your potential employer has guidelines for accepting and rejecting clients. Even if you do not work on the account, you may not want to work with an agency that serves unsavory clients. Agency work adds a few wrinkles to ethical concerns.

Agency work is increasingly high-tech, regularly using the Internet and e-mail. Agencies have found they must keep up with technology and equipment if they are to stay competitive. Some public relations firms even specialize in Internet and Intranet design and applications.

So how should you prepare if you plan to go into agency work? We have two recommendations: First, take at least one course in presentational skills. This might be an advanced public speaking course or a media use course. Be sure it includes an opportunity to use PowerPoint or some other presentational software. PowerPoint is not needed for every presentation, but is considered part of an effective corporate speaker's arsenal. Second, take courses that expose you to Internet usage and design. This may mean taking a course or two in applied computer science. This does not mean you become an expert in Web page design. But you should understand the basics and be able to have a meaningful conversation with the true Web designers. Internet skills are necessary for agency work.

▶ Investor Relations

Investor relations (IR) is one of the most specialized and highest-paying specialties in public relations. The high pay is a direct result of the need for special training. Your job involves attracting and keeping investors. As noted in Chapter 9, the Securities and Exchange Commission (SEC) closely monitors and regulates information from a company that can affect its stock price. That is the context for investor relations: financial information. At minimum, an IR practitioner will need a major in business and perhaps an MBA. The stakes are high and the information complicated. The IR specialist must know financial terminology and SEC regulations, and understand the stock market thoroughly. The IR specialist releases and tracks financial information, monitors the creation of all necessary financial documents for the SEC, and aids in the preparation of the annual meeting.

News releases are more complicated in IR than in any other specialty of public relations. IR specialists must meet SEC guidelines, and failure to do so can result in fines. The SEC wants to ensure that potential investors are not misled and that prices are not artificially moved. Online investing has made information tracking more difficult. Information, correct or incorrect, about a company can affect its stock price. The explosion of online trading includes a massive amount of investment information being posted on the Web. One source of information is that provided by the company's Web site. The IR specialist should oversee the financial sections of the company's Web site, which are usually substantial. Visit the Web sites of a *Fortune 500* company and see how much financial information is available. The Web site is an important investment tool these days. Online investors scour the Internet, searching for additional information to help them "make money." Not all of the information is accurate. While individual investors are cautioned to evaluate online investment information, the IR specialist must work to protect the company from misinformed online information that will hurt stock prices (Cherry, 2002; Mahoney & Wessendorf, 1996).

The IR specialist must monitor the primary sources of information used by online investors. The online sources for investors can be divided into two groups: Web brokers and investor boards. Web brokers are simply brokers in cyberspace. The brokers, for a fee, aid in researching stocks and making trades. As an IR specialist, you would want to make sure a broker's posted research for your company is accurate. Major Web brokers include Charles Schwab, Datek, and American Express. Investor boards are bulletin boards or chat rooms where anyone can post information about a company. Most postings are anonymous, and many are wrong, but they can move the market. Popular investor boards include AOL Message Boards, Clearstation, Company Sleuth, Iexchange.com, Raging Bull, Silicon Investor, and Yahoo! Finance. The IR challenge is to monitor these boards for inaccurate postings about your company. Company Sleuth can be a big help. This site lets you search a company's name, and it will find all the postings on the major investment boards and send you an e-mail when new postings appear.

So you have found some inaccurate postings. What do you do next? You have at least two options. First, you can post the correct information at the site. Be sure to clearly identify yourself as an investment specialist for the company. Hopefully, your message will be more credible than an anonymous posting of inaccurate information. Second, you can file a lawsuit against the anonymous poster if the information is a serious problem. By filing a "John Doe" lawsuit, you can silence misinformation and find out who has posted the information. The Ethical Quandary for this chapter provides the details and downside about the lawsuit option.

Your understanding of financial terminology comes into play when creating financial documents. Moreover, you must know what each document is, how it is to be prepared, and the deadline for its preparation. Any mistake can result in fines from the SEC. For example, a "10-K" is filed annually with the SEC by March 31. It is a detailed financial document with strict guidelines for what it must contain. It is an informational document. An annual report is more of a promotional document but covers information similar to the 10-K. The annual report must be filed 90 days after the end of the reporting year (Downes & Goodman, 2002).

IR requires special knowledge as well as mastery of a specialized language. Here are some terms unique to that aspect of the practice.

Prospectus	A document issued when a company goes public. It tells the story of the company, its management, and its competitors. It tries to generate interest in the stock.
Going Public	A company sells securities to the public in order to raise capital. The company must register the stocks and securities with the SEC.
Proxy Statement	Arrives with the annual report and tells stockholders when and where the annual meeting will be. It also presents information about board elections and policy changes to be considered at the annual meeting.
Publicly Traded	A company's stock is publicly traded when anyone can buy it on an open market, such as the New York Stock Exchange or the NASDAQ.
Divestiture	A company sells off an unwanted business or asset.

| Form 10-Q | A quarterly report required of all publicly held companies. |
| Acquisition | One company buys another company. |

The annual meeting is required by law. It is an important part of corporate governance—how an organization is operated. Each year, stockholders must meet to take care of company governance. Technically, the stockholders own and run the company. In reality, the stockholders select a board of directors. The board selects the chief executive officer (CEO), who then runs the company. Each year, members of the board of directors are selected and resolutions voted on at the annual meeting. Resolutions can come from management or from stockholders. Stockholder resolutions are often socially oriented, addressing environmental or human rights issues. Some sample stockholder resolutions from the year 2000 include not using genetically engineered foods, noting on labels that a product uses a genetically engineered ingredient, establishing a ratio between CEO compensation and lowest-paid worker, and freezing executive compensation during periods of downsizing. The annual meeting can be drab or exciting; it depends on the company. Ben & Jerry's and Southwest Airlines are known for their fun and exciting meetings.

Corporate governance brings up a problem that can plague the IR person. The past decade has seen a number of reports about highly overpaid CEOs. These men and women get huge salaries and bonuses, even when the company performs badly. An example would be Linda Wachner, CEO of Warnaco, an apparel maker. Wachner's base salary was $2.7 million (second highest at the time in the U.S.), and Wachner's annual bonus was $6 million. During her tenure as CEO, Warnaco lost money and stock value. The board was heavily criticized for overpayment and for not trying to correct the problem. Boards come under fire from stockholders for these enormous salaries because the boards approved the deals. Some boards have been sued by stockholders, while other companies have seen stockholders revolt by voting in new boards and selecting new CEOs. This is a rare move, but it does happen. The IR specialist will be in the middle. Part of his or her job is to justify large salaries and address stakeholder complaints. All relationships have problems, and the IR specialist must try to keep the stockholder-organization relationship mutually beneficial.

▶ Integrated Marketing Communication

Chapter 1 discussed the concept of integrated marketing communication (IMC), the cooperative relationship between marketing, public relations, and advertising. In this section, we focus in more detail on that vital public relations context.

A formal definition of IMC is "a strategic business process used to plan, develop, execute and evaluate coordinated and measurable persuasive brand communication programs over time with consumers, customers, prospects and other targeted, relevant external and internal audiences" (McGoon, 1998, p. 15). IMC is a way to integrate various communication functions into one planning system—an organization coordinates its messages in order to create "one sight" and "one sound." While IMC sounds simplistic, there is a need for such coordination. We shall review the variety of communication functions, the basics of integration, and the benefits from IMC.

MAPs have a variety of contact points with organizations. Here are but a few: products, stationery, packaging, advertisements, publicity, salespeople, customer relations people, marketing materials, annual reports, employee publications, and a building's exterior. All of the contact points provide an opportunity for communicating with a MAP. But what qualifies some of these contact points as communication? The Duncan Message Typology helps to explain how the contact points are communication. Duncan's Message Typology divides the contact points into four types of messages: planned, inferred, maintenance, and unplanned. *Planned messages* are deliberate and are the typical communication options, such as advertising, public relations, and sales promotion. *Inferred messages* are the impressions people have of an organization. Everything a company says or does can help to form an impression. *Maintenance messages* are how a company and its employees interact with customers. *Unplanned messages* include investigative reports, product recalls, industrial accidents, attacks/protests from activist groups, and employee gossip. Many of the unplanned messages would fall under crisis management (Moriarty, 1994).

So what does a list of contact points mean? Well, the point is that an organization has a large number of contact points with MAPs and that different units in an organization are responsible for the contact points. For instance, contact points for the same MAP may come from advertising, purchasing, human relations, investor relations, customer service, or public relations. If the units do not coordinate their efforts, there is a strong chance that inconsistencies could occur. Integration is a way to promote consistency. Integration begins by auditing all organizational contact points. You must discover how the organization reaches its various MAPs. You then coordinate contact points for the same or overlapping MAPs. *Overlap* means some people are part of more than one MAP. For example, employees can be customers and investors too. Next, cross-functional teams are created: People from the various areas meet as a team to discuss their actions and how they can be coordinated. Finally, a shared performance measure is created and used. This will allow for comparison of performance between different units. This is just a rough outline of an IMC program. You would want to consult books on the subject for a more detailed understanding of IMC.

Organizations have known for a long time that consistent messages are better than inconsistent ones. Inconsistent messages create confusion and erode an organization's credibility. IMC believes that coordinated messages create a synergy that you would not get from isolated messages—the integrated messages have a greater impact on MAPs. Moreover, IMC promotes efficiency and effectiveness. Coordination eliminates conflicting messages and redundancy, thereby making the organization more efficient. The coordination would include planning and budgeting. Imagine that three units communicate with the same MAP. The IMC team decides which unit is best suited for the specific task. That unit receives the bulk of the budget for the task and leads the effort, resulting in savings in cost and effort. A consistent message should increase the effectiveness of the message. The organization becomes more effective because of the synergy from the consistent messages (Gonring, 1994; Moriarty, 1994).

From Student Leader to Young Professional

Gail Liebl, APR
Senior Counselor
Morgan & Myers, Inc.
Minneapolis, Minnesota

NOTE: This entry was written in 1998. At that time, Gail was working hard to make the transition from student to practitioner. She listed these accomplishments:

Minnesota PRSA Associate Member

Minnesota PRSA Student Relations Committee Co-Chair

PRSSA Immediate Past President

My Public Relations Discovery

As a college freshman, I vividly recall seeing a brochure that said, "Public Relations Student Society of America (PRSSA): Everything you need to know about public relations." My thoughts were, "people . . . relating to people . . . I can do that!" Previously, I knew that I would pursue a career in mass communications, but until that moment, I had never heard of public relations. Coming from a small town of 1,100 people in northern Minnesota, it wasn't a word that was brought up between discussions on field work and when to feed the livestock.

Five years later in 1997, as I gaze at my business card that says, "Gail Liebl, Public Relations Associate, Morgan & Myers/The Thoms Group," I never dreamed I'd make it this far.

Ready to Open Doors—PRSSA Was My Key

I began my pursuit of a public relations career at a very early age. As an 18-year-old college freshman, I attended a PRSSA meeting the first week of my college career. By spring quarter, I was elected PR Director for the Moorhead State University's PRSSA chapter. As a sophomore, I was selected to be the delegate for the PRSSA National Assembly in New Orleans. This was my first exposure to PRSSA at the national level, and from that moment on, I knew that I wanted to one day be national president of PRSSA.

I returned to my chapter after the assembly and was elected chapter president. The following year I was elected to the national committee as Midwest District Director, in which I oversaw activities for 18 chapters in a five-state area. Finally, as a senior, I put it all on the line and ran for national president. It was an interesting match of candidates—a Fashion Institute of Technology student from New York and me, "the farm kid from Minnesota." Luckily, I came out on top and began to reconstruct a new national organization. That year, the assembly decided to abolish district lines and construct a national committee with a president, vice president and eight vice presidents in charge of specific areas of interest.

Never Pass Up Professional Development Activities—The Sky Is the Limit

Serving as PRSSA National President was perhaps the greatest learning experience of my life, and the best preparation I could've ever asked for to prepare me for my first job. PRSSA taught me the joys and difficulties of leading a team toward a specific goal and the gratitude of helping my fellow peers.

It is because of PRSSA that I have many interesting days in the world of public relations. Coincidentally, my supervisor was my PRSSA professional advisor. It was a fluke of luck where I was at the right place at the right time—but was also prepared.

As I had mentioned, I came from a small town in northern Minnesota where opportunities are limited. Just driving into Minneapolis was enough to get my heart racing. I dreamed of living in the "big city" and living the life of a public relations executive. Much of my dream has become a reality, but I've quickly learned the glamour isn't what I expected.

My First Public Relations Job

The first full-time job that I accepted was in February 1997 with Morgan & Myers/The Thoms Group, a medium-sized public relations agency in Minneapolis. Morgan & Myers specializes in food and agricultural public relations, but the largest account was 3M Company.

Within the first couple of weeks, I quickly learned about the "glamorous" job of clip reports in which I cut clips out of newspapers for hours. My first client was 3M Office Ergonomics. I didn't even know the true definition of "ergonomics" when I joined the team. After I finished the clip report, I had the opportunity to meet our 3M client. I must admit, I was a bit intimidated at our first meeting. Here I was, a fresh-out-of-college grad that would soon be offering public relations counsel to clients twice my age.

Wake-Up Call to the PR Profession

I had many shaky days at first trying to learn the ropes of agency life. It seemed so ironic that I spent the past five years of my life planning for a job in an agency—I completed five internships prior to graduation, fulfilled all course requirements for my concentration in public relations and climbed the PRSSA ladder as high as it would take me—yet, I felt like I knew absolutely nothing! I remember how confused I was, trying so hard to remember not only how to write AP style, but to fill out

a purchase order, bill to the correct job code, enter my time weekly, code my activities in 15-minute increments, fax this, FedEx that, budget for a newsletter, add in mark-up, develop editorial outlines, etc.

My goal is not to scare college graduates entering the field, I just want them to know that if you want to succeed in the fast-paced world of public relations, your schedule is no longer your own. I try to fully utilize my Franklin Planner, but your tasks change quickly throughout the day. I can attempt to focus on a client project for a couple of hours, but if another client calls with an emergency, you must be flexible and react.

The only thing I truly miss about college life is ownership over my own schedule. Perhaps the greatest challenge I've needed to overcome was knowing that my work isn't done until all deadlines have been met. It was so different in college. I was up at 6:00 a.m. for morning track practice, at class from 8:00 to noon, worked for three hours, back to track practice, and then to the library for studying. Yes, it was a monotonous schedule, but it was mine and I controlled it.

Every Day Is an Adventure

Now, as a working professional, I've learned to be more flexible with my time. Don't get me wrong; working in public relations is very demanding, but also very rewarding. Every day is a new day filled with adventures. I never know when new projects will pop up, or when I'll need to call the media with important press information. It has taught me the true meaning of being a flexible individual, which is one of the key elements to succeeding in this business.

I'd love to tell you about a normal day in the life of a first year professional, but without a schedule or a routine, every day has the promise of new surprises. I am blessed with diverse accounts, so I can honestly say that I have never been bored. My clients range from the Toro Company to 3M Office Ergonomics, 3M Industrial Tape and Specialties Division and 3M Integrated Solutions. My activities can vary from preparing an editorial calendar and writing newsletter copy for Toro, to writing a press release on 3M's new adhesive labels, to coordinating a media kit for office ergonomics, to my favorite project, being the sole account person handling the largest collateral piece ever done out of our agency. This project, which consumed my time for 5 months, included coordinating all activities with 3M marketers, the designer, printer and the 3M clients. It was a big step for me to sell public relations activities that reached six figures to men old enough to be my parents.

Another key piece of advice is to never let age stand in your way when you enter this field. I am 23 years old, and have recently completed projects for 3M that will be distributed globally. Remember, it is your talent and capabilities that count. If you can demonstrate your abilities to your client, you can quickly overcome age barriers and build a reputation on your accomplishments rather than on your generation label.

The Facts About Your First Job in PR

With only a year of experience, the amount of knowledge I've gained by working in a public relations agency is priceless. Many students may take the fast route to bigger money after graduation, but I would like to challenge PR graduates to pursue jobs in the profession as hard as they can. No, the pay isn't wonderful, but I am prepared to pay my dues because I know it will pay off in the future. I can't think of any other profession that allows such diversity. As I mentioned, every day is a new

adventure—and I don't think many people can say that about their current jobs. Many walk into their companies at 8 a.m. do what they've been doing for years, and leave at 5 p.m. In the world of public relations, your day can be filled with stimulating brainstorming sessions, a challenging pitch to the media, the opportunity to interview someone new and the chance to say you've made an impression on someone's life through your story or information.

Public Relations. Demanding? Yes. Rewarding? Yes. Stressful? Yes. Boring? Never.

If you are ready to challenge yourself to the fast-paced lifestyle, you too can reap the rewards. If you are just starting your career, get involved in your PRSSA chapter and become a leader. Without my experiences in PRSSA, I would've been shocked by the public relations world. However, due to the diversity of experiences I had gained, I felt confident and prepared to not only meet but also greet the challenges of client relations and deadlines. I've learned the earlier you start, the easier it gets.

I consider myself lucky to be a public relations professional. I owe much to the public relations professionals that guided me along the way. Jon Riffel and Betsy Plank, the founders of PRSSA, have become a second set of "grandparents" to me. They helped me see that it didn't matter where you came from— what mattered was your desire to succeed. They are shining examples of the public relations professional I hope to be.

I hope you will feel the excitement and desire to succeed in public relations, and I look forward to seeing you in the profession.

SOURCE: Reprinted with permission from Gail Liebl.

So what does IMC mean for public relations practitioner preparation? There are two key points for your preparation: First, you may need to work closely with other communication units, such as advertising and marketing. Therefore, you should be familiar with their language and functions. We discussed the overlap of functions among the "big three" in Chapter 1. You may want to learn more by taking a course in marketing and/or advertising. Another option is to do some exploring on your own. Visit the Web sites for the American Marketing Association (and the American Advertising Federation), http://www.aaf.org. Read through the Web sites, and get a feel for the terminology they use and the types of functions they seem to perform. A good place to start is with mission statements and declarations of principles. The more you know about marketing and advertising, the easier it will be to work on cross-functional teams with people from those areas. Second, get practice working on teams. Students seem to find group work either very rewarding or painful. People in organizations feel the same way. Volunteer to work on teams in organizations you belong to; the practice will help. Another option is to take a course in small-group communication or team building to learn more about how teams should work. You could use an elective course in your plan of study to build team skills. Too often, employers place people in teams but never train them in how teams should work. Team skills are something you should try to refine before you reach the workplace.

Conclusion

A successful public relations career does not happen by accident. Public relations jobs will continue to be available, but you will have to demonstrate you are better than your competition. To enhance your chances, you must be strategic about career development: You must set your goals and work toward them. It begins by selecting a university or college that has a true public relations major. One indicator is whether or not the school has a PRSSA chapter.

PRSSA chapters are granted only if a school meets the requirements for public relations courses. Your education does not stop in the classroom. Find ways to learn beyond the classroom, through involvement in student organizations, internships, and career shadowing. Carefully choose your minor and elective courses. Choose those that best prepare you for the general public relations practice or the specific area of public relations you wish to pursue. The next step is to develop your portfolio. This means keeping samples of what you create in class and outside of class. Your portfolio will be more well-rounded if you engage in outside-of-class activities. Finally, consider your options for career development.

Accreditation and seminars are excellent ways to show your dedication to the field and/or to develop new skills. Weigh the benefits of a master's degree or certificate program. Consider how each might improve your career opportunities. Public relations learning extends well beyond your undergraduate degree if you hope to stay current in the practice and to develop as a professional. We hope this chapter stimulates your thinking about your career, inspires you to set personal goals, and provides guidance on how you can achieve those goals.

Ethical Quandary: Presenting Your Case

Imagine for a moment that you have read an advertisement for an entry-level public relations practitioner in a nonprofit that really appeals to you. The nonprofit provides shelters for families that are suffering financial problems and have been living on the street. You have heard that the professional practitioner is very talented and a wonderful mentor. You recall your professors telling classes that nonprofits help build professional skills quickly because they have lots of communication needs and therefore thrust new hires into projects that they might not experience in a major company until they had been there for 3 to 5 years. You really want this job.

Here are the key qualifications that result in this ethical quandary: The job calls for a degree with a specialty in public relations. It requires a 3.0 grade point average, a demonstrated record of community involvement, and knowledge of Excel, PowerPoint, and any of several graphics programs. You know you will be expected to show your portfolio. The prospective boss has been a past president of the local PRSA chapter.

Knowing these facts, you sit down to redraft your résumé. You have a 2.89 grade point average. You have done a lot of work with your church, but most of it has been with the youth athletic program there. You know Excel reasonably well, but don't know PowerPoint or a graphics program. You have some stuff for your portfolio. You have writing samples that were provided in some of your classes, but they were not your writing. You can download lots of stuff from the Web and present it as your work. No one can monitor the entire Web. You always said you were going to join PRSSA, but never did. You attended two meetings in your senior year. You helped with a bake sale because one of your friends worked at it that day.

List the ethical choices you have to make. Prepare the key parts of your résumé. What do you include in your portfolio, and what do you say on the résumé? You have 7 days before the interview. Can you add to your résumé in that length of time and still tell the truth?

Ten years from now, what would you tell a person in your position that you did?

Summary Questions

1. What must the field of public relations have to actually be a profession?

2. What do the stages of anticipatory socialization, encounter, and metamorphosis have to do with your career planning?

3. What skills, knowledge, and personal attributes should you have to be a successful practitioner?

4. What are the four role-functions of public relations that have been studied by Glen Broom?

5. What are the differences in knowledge and activities of entry-level technicians, supervisors, and managers/executives in public relations?

6. How good is the occupational outlook for practitioners over the coming decade? Are the opportunities for managers better than for entry-level practitioners? What salary ranges seem reasonable in today's market?

7. What is a portfolio? Why is it important to your career aspirations? What should a portfolio contain?

8. Name five courses that you should have to be a public relations student, according to PRSA and others. What courses might you expect to take as a graduate student? How can you continue your education after college? What knowledge and skills are listed by the Commission on Public Relations Education?

9. What is accreditation? What are the titles that accredited practitioners earn? What are you supposed to have accomplished, and what do you need to know to become accredited?

10. What are some of the contexts in which you could work as a practitioner? How is each different? What are the professional development requirements that are unique to each?

Exercises

1. Write a five- to six-page essay that defends public relations as a profession. In the essay, address the following points: (1) specialized skills and knowledge of the profession; (2) the body of public relations literature; (3) the beneficial role public relations plays in society (see previous chapters, especially Chapter 1); (4) the identity of a practitioner (we suggest you avoid "spin master," "flack," and "PR guy"); (5) a code of ethics; and (6) learnable practices and standards of accreditation.

2. Interview a professional practitioner. Write a short biography of this person. Address at least the following points: Why did the person enter the profession? How did the person become educated into the profession? What has the person's career path been? Is the person involved in supporting the profession? If so, how so? What are this person's career aspirations? How will this person achieve those goals? What is the best advice this person can give to a budding practitioner such as you? What is the biggest warning that you should heed?

3. Prepare a strategic plan of your academic preparation to be a practitioner. Have it reviewed by a teacher and a practitioner. What did you learn from the review? What changes do you plan to make? How well does your list of knowledge and skills compare with that recommended by the Commission on Public Relations Education?

4. Practitioners want entry-level technicians to be interested in and knowledgeable of current events. Answer the following questions: What was the front-page story in your local paper today? What was the lead story in any of the past 5 days of the *Wall Street Journal*? What was the cover story of the latest of any national news magazine? Where did the Dow Jones and NASDAQ close yesterday? Name

the president or prime minister of three countries other than your own. Name two national nonprofit organizations. Who are your federal representatives? Name a book on the fiction and nonfiction best-seller list. Name a television talk show.

5. Select a public relations context. Develop a short paper in which you describe the role practitioners perform in that context. Include an explanation of the knowledge, professional skills, and personal attributes that increase a practitioner's success in that context. Perform a Web search to help document your case. Try to locate a practitioner through the Web whom you can quote on some aspect of your paper.

Recommended Readings

Burns, R. L. (1999). Looking back at 30 months of self-employment. *Public Relations Tactics*, 6(3), 20.

Commission on Public Relations Education. (1999, October). *A port of entry: Public relations education for the 21st century.* New York: Public Relations Society of American.

Coombs, W. T., & Rybacki, K. (1999). Public relations education: Where is pedagogy? *Public Relations Review, 25*, 55–64.

Drake, J. W. (1999). Speaking out of school: Collaboration in the field sparks innovation in the classroom. *Public Relations Tactics*, 6(9), 28–29.

Gaschen, D. J. (1999). PR students should learn to do the math. *Public Relations Tactics*, 6(9), 37.

Neff, B. D., Walker, G., Smith, M. F., & Creedon, P. J. (1999). Outcomes desired by practitioners and academics. *Public Relations Review, 25*, 29.

Paluszek, J. L. (2000). Public relations students: Today good, tomorrow better. *Public Relations Strategist, 5*(4), 27–28.

Rybacki, D., & Lattimore, D. (1999). Assessment of undergraduate and graduate programs. *Public Relations Review, 25*, 65–76.

Sharpe, M. L. (1999). A Sharpe perspective on PR education. *Public Relations Tactics*, 6(2), 30.

Stacks, D. W., Botan, C., & Turk, J. V. (1999). Perceptions of public relations education. *Public Relations Review, 25*, 9–10.

Toth, E. L. (1999). Models for instruction and curriculum. *Public Relations Review, 25*, 45–54.

15

The Future of Public Relations

Globalism and Cyberspace

Global Blunders Cost Money

The Mexican government was searching for a company to handle its telecommunications. The two finalists were a U.S. firm and a French firm. The U.S. firm pitched its proposal first. The proposal reflected the cultural values and preferences of the United States. The U.S. firm emphasized its superior technology in a fast-paced, high-energy, and tightly organized presentation. The representatives of the U.S. company left Mexico City the night of the presentation. The U.S. firm's communication style reflected a focus on business. The nature of the presentation and the firm's use of time indicate time was defined as precious and to be used for work. The content of the presentation focused solely on business concerns such as technology.

The French firm stayed for a 2-week visit to get to know their Mexican counterparts. Their presentation was loosely connected and emphasized their history in Mexico and past contract with the Mexican government in the 1930s. The French firm's communication focused on interpersonal relationships. The schedule of this company allowed ample time for personnel and government officials to get to know one another. The content of its presentation reflected past relationships. The French firm won the contract. Its view of culture was more consistent with Mexican culture than was the view of the U.S. firm (Trompenaars & Hampden-Turner, 1998). Culture does matter in communication. At its heart, the practice of public relations entails many communication and positioning functions that should be sensitive to cultural preferences. Culture should be a central concern of international public relations.

Experts agree globalism and cyberspace are two of the dominant forces that will shape public relations in the 21st century (e.g., Greer & Moreland, 2003; Sriramesh & Vercic, 2003). Why? The answer is simple. All business is now global, and most businesses utilize the Internet in some fashion. Through evolving technology and the growth of international business, every business competes globally. Each day, more companies become global, with operations in more than one country. The *Handbook of Public Relations* devotes an entire section to the globalization of public relations. Heath (2001) observed that "the future of public relations cannot escape the global influence" (p. 626). Another section of the *Handbook* is dedicated to public relations and cyberspace. This chapter frames the future of public relations in terms of these two important and related trends.

Public Relations
in a Shrinking World

Global business operations take many forms. One is the giant multinational that has operations in many countries: manufacturing, distributions, research and development, and marketing. These giants sometimes have the power to topple governments and shape the economic futures of nations. These organizations must balance and respond to challenges that result, for instance, from operations that are affected by many cultures. Such giants are challenged to communicate within and across cultures and in a variety of languages. Multinationals often construct public relations teams composed of people from different countries and cultures. Team leaders need to understand cultural differences and how to integrate various cultures into a functional team (Wakefield, 2001).

Globalization, especially with the advantages of the Internet, has reshaped the way many small businesses can operate and has created challenges for large multinational organizations. Once, small businesses simply lacked the advertising and public relations budgets to reach markets around the world. The Internet, with its many search engine capabilities and specialized discussion groups and Weblogs, has brought these small companies and interested customers together. Search engines, discussion groups, and Weblogs create the "awareness" that cannot be accomplished with limited advertising dollars. Faxes, the Internet, and the Web bring people closer together by speeding things up and making communication easier.

Larry Foster (1999), then vice president of public relations for Johnson & Johnson, observed,

> There are . . . some dark and disturbing clouds on the horizon. The darkest is the tendency of many large multinational companies to make international public relations management the victim of benign neglect.
>
> As a result of this neglect, the international public relations/public affairs function has not developed in large corporations as it should. (p. 3)

Governments, nonprofits, activists, and nongovernmental organizations (NGOs) also operate in ways that are increasingly global and utilize public relations. The Red Cross, Greenpeace, and Amnesty International are but a few of the global NGOs. A primary reason that governments and NGOs enter the global arena is a concern with international business and technology. Governments try to protect and expand their share of international business, while NGOs often protest over unfair or destructive business practices.

Many examples illustrate that point. South American countries have fought tariffs in Australia for beef imports. Amnesty International has protested human rights violations in Nigeria. The Internet and the Web make public relations and global protests much easier and cheaper to accomplish. Zapatista rebels in Mexico, an NGO, used the Internet to update people about their struggles. Similarly, Greenpeace used the Internet to describe its occupation of the Brent Spar oil buoy. Greenpeace listed its complaints about the way in which Shell UK intended to use the ocean as a "cesspool" to dispose of the retired oil buoy. Because of the Internet and Web, international organizations find it easier and quicker to monitor and to inform their followers, audiences, and publics about problems in different areas of the world. Just ask the management at Nike how quickly a local issue can become a global one (Coombs, 1998; Heath, 1998).

We start our journey through international public relations by defining terms. We must specify what international public relations is before we can understand its practice. We must also understand and appreciate culture and its impact on communication and public relations. From there, we can consider several ethical challenges specific to practice globally. A discussion of the Internet follows the examination of globalism.

Red Cross: An NGO in Action
SOURCE: Copyright © REUTERS/Russell Boyce/Landov.

Coming to Terms With a Global Presence

You will hear a variety of terms used to describe the globalism of public relations: *international public relations, transnational public relations, multicultural public relations*, and *intercultural public relations*. This section explains these terms, shows how we use the term *international public relations*, and highlights the essential factors involved in international public relations.

Both international and transnational public relations denote challenges faced by practitioners who work for organizations that operate in two or more countries. For instance, BMW launched a driver safety campaign in the United States from its headquarters in Germany. The message went from Germany to the U.S market, audience, and driver-safety-conscious public. Multicultural and intercultural public relations denote that professionally prepared messages go between two different cultures. The BMW safety campaign was between two different cultures as well as between two countries. Messages can be between cultures (multicultural) in a single country. Canada is both English and French, Belgium has German and French cultures, and Switzerland contains French, Italian, and German cultures.

WEB WATCHER: INTERNATIONAL PUBLIC RELATIONS ASSOCIATION

As a way to get some feel for international public relations, use this Web Watcher. The International Public Relations Association (IPRA) is a global collection of public relations practitioners. Visit its Web site at http://www.ipra.org/index.htm. Find the discussion of its history that explains how IPRA developed. Next, look at the members of its council. While at the Web site, answer the following questions: How many different countries are represented? Are certain continents represented more than others? Find another public relations association based outside of the United States and find out its stated purpose.

We use *international public relations* to refer to both of these options—the messages and other relationship development strategies are between different global cultures and countries. International public relations is simply public relations practiced between countries and cultures; although a country such as the United States has many cultures, the significance of culture is even more dramatic when it is defined by unique countries. The same five public relations functions occur, and the same five message design objectives are used. Although cultures differ, professional practices perform publicity, promotion, research, collaborative decision making, and strategic planning. Practitioners attract attention, inform, persuade, negotiate, and cocreate meaning. Although these practitioner functions and message development objectives (MDOs) are universal, how they are performed is highly sensitive to cultural differences. Culture shapes how practitioners utilize the functions and MDOs. An effective way to initiate the discussion of international public relations is to examine culture.

Culture is a core component of international public relations. International business demands that organizations interact with markets, audiences, and publics (MAPs), some of which the company has never dealt with before. Interactions bring culture to the forefront. When Kentucky Fried Chicken moved into India, the executives of the company had never dealt with the MAPs in India before. The culture in India made these MAPs unique and new for the strategic thinking and planning by Kentucky Fried Chicken. The challenge of globalism for public relations is to learn how to communicate with these new MAPs and to develop mutually beneficial relationships with them. Being fluent in a language is helpful, but not enough. An international practitioner must be fluent in a culture. Culture shapes communication and how relationships are developed.

So what is culture? There are as many definitions of *culture* as there are of public relations. Geert Hofstede (1984), a well-known and respected researcher of culture, defined it as "the collective programming of the mind which distinguishes members of one human group from another" (p. 21). In his system, cultures are built on values; values create the collective programming. Collective programming means that people share patterns of thinking, feeling, acting, and reacting. People in the same culture will see and react to events in a similar fashion. People from different cultures can see and react to the same event in very different ways.

These differences in collective programming make intercultural communication challenging. Recall the French and U.S. telecommunications firms featured in the opening vignette for this chapter. Each viewed the business presentation situation differently. The U.S. firm focused on its business practices, while the French emphasized the relational/personal aspect of how it conducts business for a client. The French businesspeople were successful because the collective programming and cultural assumptions they made were more consistent with the programming of the Mexican officials. That firm knew and could respond to the relationship expectations of their potential business partners.

It seems odd that something so central to our thoughts, feelings, and actions can be nearly or completely invisible to us. But culture is nearly invisible to the people living in it. All of our major institutions—family, education, and government—help to teach us about our culture. Culture is taught and passed from one generation to the next. We do not stop to think about the values we are learning and how they help us to form a collective programming. Only when we experience other cultures do we begin to see the differences and thereby understand the values of our own culture.

A member of the U.S. telecommunications company may have realized the following after losing the contract: "They made the decision based on social concerns, not just the business concerns, the way we do in the United States." Trying to understand cultural differences and their effect on business has spawned an entire industry, which prepares businesspeople for dealing with different cultures. Preparing for another culture assumes we have comparison points for cultures: ways to measure and to understand them and the people who live in them. Before we get to comparison points that highlight the profound differences between cultures, however, it is instructive to review the debate between globalization and localization in international public relations.

▶ Transnational, Multinational, International: What's in a Name?

As public relations becomes more international, practitioners debate whether the practice should be governed by globalization or localization. This discussion focuses on whether some or all of the practices of public relations are universal across boundaries and cultures. As a future practitioner, you should be aware of this debate. We consider three points relevant to this discussion.

First, the globalization approach is based on the idea of the "global village"—that the world is becoming more and more alike. Moreover, people assume business is business anywhere in the world. Hence, public relations can be practiced in the same way in every culture. A large multinational corporation with branches in 20 countries need create only one public relations program at its home office and use it in all 20 countries. Botan (1992) called this practice "transnational public relations" and deemed it an ethnocentric approach to public relations. Persons who think that way assume their way of practicing public relations is the best and perhaps only way. That view of globalization assumes only one standard of what public relations is and how it should be practiced everywhere in the world. It is ethnocentric because it does not take into account unique aspects of public relations in each country or region. Globalization can create errors because it ignores the impact of culture on public relations actions.

As Taylor (2001) observed, in some countries, relationship building may not be the core function of public relations. Some activities that U.S.-based firms may not define as public relations can be considered public relations in other countries. In Latin America, for example, public relations has a very political function (Simoes, 1992). We need to consider the presuppositions we have about public relations when we are involved in international public relations. More specifically, we need to be flexible in understanding what public relations is and is not in various countries (Taylor, 2001).

In contrast to globalization, localization, sometimes called *internationalization,* calls for tailoring practices to fit the culture. Our large multinational corporation would hire local public relations practitioners in each culture to develop public relations plans for that country. Localization can create problems when the multinational wishes to create a unified public relations action in all 20 countries. You would have 20 public relations units operating independently. Coordination and consistency suffer under localization.

A third line of thought tries to merge the best ideas from globalization and localization. This approach has been called the *generic principles* approach. The generic principles approach claims that certain public relations practices are common around the world and may need only slight adaptation to fit any specific culture. Adaptation would include how to apply the public relations plan within a specific culture and how to modify the objectives, if need be, to match the culture. Culture becomes an important variable in the public relations process affecting research, planning, implementation, and evaluation—the basic process of public relations. Local public relations personnel are hired to advise the multinational on how best to adapt its public relations actions. As we will discuss later, hiring local talent is a key to successful international public relations (Wakefield, 2001). But how do we understand cultures in order to successfully adapt public relations activities?

▶ Global Challenges: The Routine and Unique

To appreciate the challenges of international public relations, we need to understand what practices are routine across country boundaries and cultures. We also should identify the unique challenges of global public relations.

Addressing this issue, Wakefield (2001) noted, "Some form of media relations occurs almost everywhere, as do advertising, promotionals, communication with targeted

Pepsi: Global Brand Management

SOURCE: Copyright © REUTERS/Claro Cortes IV/Landov.

publics, issues and crisis management, and a growing amount of community relations" (p. 641). By this point in your study of public relations, these elements of the practice should seem familiar. For instance, because of the close connection between government ministers or bureaucrats and business practices, government relationships are a vital part of international public relations. In some countries, the practice is heavily devoted to building relationships with government officials.

Creating brand and organizational identity and equity is a challenge. As companies and nonprofits go abroad, they bring a lot of cultural baggage that reflects their home countries. For instance, the United States has exported fast food around the world. Today, one of the universals of travel is the ability to recognize McDonald's golden arches and Coca-Cola at every stop. As products and companies go abroad, they collide with local businesses. They change marketing patterns. At first, they lack market and audience awareness. They may arouse publics' outrage, whereas they are taken for granted in other countries.

Communication practices are different across borders and cultures. The content of messages needs to be tailored to the assumptions, values, and narratives of each target MAP. The style might be different. In the opening vignette, we contrasted the aggressive U.S. style versus the interpersonal style of the French. Politeness and careful interpersonal rituals are often part of the interaction styles of countries outside of the United States. Without fully appreciating the fact, U.S. organizations and practitioners can be viewed as arrogant and ignorant simply because of the U.S. public relations and corporate communication style (Taylor, 2001).

Practices can be quite different. Some countries assume that media relationships require a business relationship. This can include placing ads in the newspapers or on the radio or television if you want to publicize or promote your story. It can entail a bribe. Employee relationships in the United States may rely heavily on a company newsletter and the annual picnic. In other countries, religious events may be part of employee relationships. In some countries, companies celebrate employees' birthdays. Activists have learned that when they show up asking local people to cease poaching and destroying forests, they are asking for a dramatic change of lifestyle that includes traditional ways of feeding a family.

Comparing Cultures

To understand culture, we must find ways to assess and to compare cultures. Only then can we begin to appreciate the differences and similarities between them. There are two very popular and accepted comparison points for intercultural public relations: Hall's (1981) idea of contexting and Hofstede's (1984) four cultural dimensions. This section will explain each and relate them to public relations and relationship building. Keep in mind that international public relations operates on two levels: internal communication and external communication. The internal level involves the interaction between employees in an organization and between practitioners from different cultures. When working with local practitioners, intercultural communication occurs between practitioners from the home office and the local practitioners with whom they work. The external level involves the messages sent from the organization to external MAPs.

▶ Hall's View of Culture as Context

In *Beyond Culture*, Edward Hall (1981) developed the idea of *context* in communication. Context explains how we attach meaning to a message. People draw on two sources when trying to understand what something means: transmitted information and stored information. Transmitted information is what is said in a statement, the words, pictures, graphics, and such. Stored information refers to shared experiences and represents what is not said. Stored information is much like an inside joke between friends. You say "saltshaker" and your friends laugh. They laugh because they have stored information; they know the story behind the words. Stored information comes from knowing one another—having shared experiences. Stored information represents part of the context for the message.

Organizations using communication, internally and externally, may fail to be successful in building relationships if they are not aware of and able to tailor messages and communication style to the contexts of their MAPs. This observation further demonstrations the skills needed for international public relations and the fact that practitioners need to communicate with people from their points of view, not that of the organization.

Explaining his theory, Hall distinguished between high- and low-context cultures. A *high-context culture* derives meaning from the stored information and relies little on the transmitted information. People in the culture share knowledge and experience. They can anticipate what others will say. What is not said is understood. Meanings are implicit. Relationships are extremely important in the high-context cultures. Through relationships, people come to share the experiences that help them to create the meaning for their messages in high-context countries. Small talk is a valuable part of business communication in a high-context culture. In contrast, a *low-context culture* derives meaning from the transmitted information and relies little on the stored information. People use verbal messages to communicate meaning because they cannot rely on the context for meaning.

Context leads to differences in how and what people communicate. Communication in high-context cultures is indirect rather than direct, demonstrates low reliance on words, views silence as a virtue, views promises as being as good as written contracts, and heavily emphasizes the social aspect of business as very important (small talk about family and personal concerns are valued in business). Communication in low-context cultures is direct, relies heavily on words, sees silence as problematic, prefers a written contract to promises, and focuses on business (small talk is unimportant to business). Table 15.1 summarizes the key communication differences between high- and low-context cultures.

Figure 15.1 presents the context level for a number of major countries. It is easy to see that communication problems can occur between high- and low-context cultures. Not only can meanings be difficult to exchange, but people can be offended by another's normal communication practices. A Norwegian in China might be direct, demand a written contract, and ignore small talk. All of these actions would offend his or her Chinese counterpart. One must be sensitive and adapt to differences in context.

Table 15.1: Key Communicative Differences in Context

High Context	Low Context
– Directness is rude; indirectness smoothes over interpersonal problems	– Directness is valued
– Greater emphasis on close interpersonal relationships	– Focus on business side
– Weak emphasis on written word	– Strong emphasis on written word
– Personal promises are binding	– Personal promises are not binding
– Low reliance on words	– High reliance on words
– Silence is respected	– Silence creates anxiety
– High uncertainty avoidance	– Low uncertainty avoidance
– High face-saving	– Low face-saving

Figure 15.1: Examples of Context by Country

Countries by Context

High

    Japan

    Arabic countries

    Latin American countries

    Italy

    England

    France

    U.S. and Canada

    Scandinavian countries

    Germany

    Switzerland (German-speaking part)

Low

Public relations practitioners must adapt their messages to fit the relevant context. This adaptation often requires research but also demonstrates one of the keys to international public relations. People who are raised in or have become familiar with contexts will communicate more effectively than people who lack that cocreated meaning. Messages, either internal or external, cannot be direct in a high-context culture. Compliance-gaining provides a useful example. *Compliance-gaining* is a form of statement designed to get a person to do something. There are a number of different compliance-gaining strategies a person might use.

Table 15.2 lists and defines some common compliance-gaining strategies. You might need to use compliance-gaining on both the internal and external levels. Convincing someone to accept a proposal (internal) or change unhealthy behaviors (external) are examples of compliance-gaining. Based on your understanding of context, which compliance-gaining strategies would be best for a low-context culture, and which would be best for a high-context culture?

A discussion of context is incomplete without addressing face. *Face* is the image a person wants to project in public, his or her public persona. High-context cultures place a strong emphasis on face and helping people to save face, or protect and maintain their public image. This explains why high-context cultures prefer indirectness. Direct criticism or refusal (saying no) would threaten another person's face and therefore should be avoided. Low-context cultures do not have such strong concern about face.

Imagine you are at an idea-generating session for a public relations project. Your manager suggests a theme for the message. You think the idea is bad and will be ineffective. Context dictates how you will communicate that message to your manager. In the United States, you would be direct and explain why the idea would not work. How

Table 15.2: Compliance-Gaining Strategies Defined

Compliance-gaining strategies are messages used to get a person or people to do something. Public relations people use compliance-gaining strategies in persuasive efforts.
Partial List of Compliance-Gaining Strategies (Marwell & Schmitt, 1967)

1. Promise: People are given rewards if they comply.
2. Threat: People are given punishment if they fail to comply.
3. Liking: Be friendly and helpful so people are in the right frame of mind to comply.
4. Pregiving: Reward people before you make the request so that they feel obligated to comply.
5. Aversive stimuli: Punish people until they comply.
6. Debt: People are reminded of past favors done for them.
7. Moral appeal: People are immoral if they do not comply.
8. Self-feeling (positive): People will feel better about themselves if they comply.
9. Self-feeling (negative): People will feel worse about themselves if they fail to comply.
10. Esteem (positive): People you respect will think better of you if you comply.
11. Esteem (negative): People you respect will think less of you if you do not comply.
12. Altruism: I need your help, so do it for me.
13. Altercasting (positive): A person with good qualities would comply.
14. Altercasting (negative): A person with bad qualities would not comply.

would you communicate that same message in a high-context culture? Review Table 15.1 and identify other possible context errors that could occur when engaging in either internal or external communication between high-context and low-context cultures.

Face can be a factor in the development of relationships. If an organization communicates with people in a manner that threatens their face, relationships are likely to deteriorate. Two domestic cases illustrate how this can happen within a country. First, employees who worked for Exxon lost face as the company was battered over its oil spill from the tanker Exxon Valdez. Employees were confronted with statements such as "that oil spill company you work for." Persons who shop at the Gap could have felt that their face was threatened when they learned that members of the family who manage the company owned old-growth timber in California. Gap has a persona that appeals to youth who like natural products and a natural look. Clear-cutting old-growth forests threatened that face.

▶ Hofstede's Dimensions of Culture

In *Culture's Consequences*, Geert Hofstede (1984) studied workers in a variety of different countries. From those data, he derived four dimensions of culture, which are commonly called "Hofstede's Dimensions." The four dimensions are (1) uncertainty avoidance, (2) masculinity-femininity, (3) individualism-collectivism, and (4) power distance. These dimensions represent values that are central to a culture. Since practitioners base strategies and tactics on values, Hofstede's Dimensions are extremely valuable to international public relations.

Uncertainty avoidance is a culture's comfort level with the unknown or ambiguity. Low-uncertainty-avoidance cultures accept and are comfortable with the unknown. They tolerate ambiguity. High-uncertainty-avoidance cultures dislike the unknown and prefer the comfort of certainty. Low-uncertainty-avoidance cultures are less resistant to change, are more willing to take risks, have a greater potential to engage in protest, are more accepting of foreigners, can accept broad guidelines, and will break rules for pragmatic reasons. High-uncertainty-avoidance cultures demonstrate a greater resistance to change, are less likely to take risks, have a low potential for protesting, are suspicious of foreigners, prefer specific instructions, and will rarely break rules. High-uncertainty-avoidance cultures include Greece, Portugal, and Belgium. Low-uncertainty-avoidance countries include Singapore, Denmark, and Sweden.

High-uncertainty-avoidance countries will follow processes that have rules and favor ideas that have limited risk. Your internal and external messages must stress stability and risk avoidance. Moreover, activism will be low. You cannot expect stakeholders to challenge an organization over a problem. That does not mean the problems do not exist or are not important. It simply means that you as a practitioner must work harder to find and to address the problems. Conversely, a low-uncertainty-avoidance culture will favor messages that promote change and can involve risk. Stakeholders will be comfortable bringing forth problems for you to resolve, making your job a little easier in one respect.

The *masculinity-femininity dimension* relates to a culture's enactment of gender roles. The dimension operates on two levels, expected gender roles and cultural traits. For expected gender roles, a masculine culture communicates strong recommendations for male and female roles in society. Feminine cultures are more open to genders engaging in any role they choose (e.g., women being physicians and men being nurses). On a second level, masculinity-femininity refers to values related to work and family. Masculine cultures see work life as central to one's life, have a strong need for achievement, are less benevolent, are money/object oriented and independent, and favor economic growth over environmental concerns. Feminine cultures view work life as less central, have a low need for achievement, show greater benevolence, are people oriented and interdependent, and favor the environment over economic growth. Some strong masculine cultures include Japan, Australia, and Venezuela, while some strong feminine cultures include Sweden, Norway, and the Netherlands.

The masculine-feminine dimension has serious ramifications for corporate social responsibility. Masculine cultures will downplay the value and importance of being socially responsible, while feminine cultures will deem it essential. You will need all of your persuasive skills to convince a business in a masculine country that it must demonstrate corporate social responsibility in a feminine culture. Japanese companies, for example, have been very resistant to the idea of corporate social responsibility in the low-uncertainty-avoidance culture, creating conflict in many U.S. locations where they operate. For the Japanese, social responsibility ends with providing jobs and tax revenues. U.S. communities have come to expect more. A company is expected to become part of the social fabric of the community. Because corporate social responsibility is often linked to public relations, it is a public relations concern. On the internal level, different cultures expect different commitments to work and family. Men in masculine cultures are often upset by what they consider to be the lack of work commitment from their female counterparts. Male workers stay late to finish projects. Female workers leave at 5:00 to spend time with their families. You will need to recognize and adapt to different work and family priorities.

The *individualism-collectivism dimension* describes the relationship between an individual and the collective/group. Individualistic countries are inner directed and favor the individual over the group. In contrast, the collectivistic cultures are outer directed and favor the group over the individual. The individualistic culture emphasizes the personal life, the "I" consciousness, individual initiative, independence, and directness. The collectivistic culture emphasizes the work life and the "We" consciousness, discourages individual initiative, and values interdependence, indirectness, and a concern for face. There is a strong parallel between context and the individualism-collectivism dimension. High-context cultures tend to emphasize collectivism, while low-context cultures emphasize individualism. Strong individualistic cultures include the United States, Australia, and Great Britain. Strong collectivistic cultures include Colombia, South Korea, and Taiwan.

On the internal level, decision making can be very different. Collectivistic cultures favor consensus: All must agree. People work together and try to promote harmony. Disagreement over a decision poses a threat to harmony. There is also a clear value distinction that is relevant to public relations messages. An appeal to the family or good of the group works in a collectivistic culture, while an appeal to "self" works best in an individualistic culture. Consider a message designed to get people to take high blood pressure medicine. A collectivistic campaign would stress taking the medicine for your family. If you were to die because you did not take your medicine, your family would suffer. An individualistic campaign would stress taking the medicine to save your own life and future. Always search for the values that undergird a dimension. These values will be very useful when constructing public relations messages.

The *power distance dimension* refers to how willing people are to accept the unequal distribution of power. In a high-power-distance culture, people accept the unequal distribution of power, such as status differences (e.g., nobles and commoners). People in a low-power-distance country will not accept and are uncomfortable with large power or status differences. In low-power-distance cultures, inequities are bad, people should be interdependent, all should have equal rights, and all people should be treated similarly regardless of power. In high-power-distance cultures, inequities are expected, a few people should be independent and the rest dependent (conformity is important), the powerful are entitled to privileges, and powerful people should be treated better than the rest. High-power-distance countries include the Philippines, Mexico, and Venezuela. Lower-power-distance cultures include Austria, Israel, and Denmark.

Decision making is affected by power distance. An authority appeal will work much better in a high-power-distance than a low-power-distance culture. Decision making is not collaborative in high-power-distance countries; it is a sign of weakness and to be avoided. In fact, you would get little, if any, response from workers in a high-power-distance country if you asked them for input on a decision. Low-power-distance cultures expect collaborative decisions and would be upset by an authoritarian approach common in high-power-distance cultures.

Hofstede has added a fifth dimension in more recent works: Confucian dynamism. *Confucian dynamism* refers to certain ethics found in Confucian teachings. A culture strong in Confucian dynamism will emphasize thrift and perseverance, while a culture weak in this dimension will emphasize immediate gain and reward. A clash could arise when trying to determine when results should be seen from a public relations effort. A country with a strong Confucian perspective would accept a long time to yield results, while a country with a weak Confucian perspective would expect to see quick yields (Taylor, 2005).

As a case study, consider how culture affects business practices: doing business in India.

In 1990, India was emerging as an excellent location for foreign direct investment (FDI). The ruling Congress Party began eliminating old laws that prevented or restricted FDI. The policies reversed decades of India being xenophobic and preventing foreign investments. Enron, a U.S. energy company, was one of many U.S. companies to invest in India. (You may recall that since this event, Enron had to file for bankruptcy and eventually suffered huge changes as a company because the senior executives failed to abide by Securities and Exchange Commission [SEC] requirements for a publicly traded company.)

While it was a robust company, Enron was often engaged in international business ventures. In India, Enron's contract included an agreement to a build a liquefied-natural-gas-based power plant in the state of Maharahtra. Enron was actually the lead company in a consortium that held the contract. In June of 1995, the Shir Sena Party, a conservative opposition party to the Congress Party, won local elections in Maharahtra. The new state government canceled the Enron contract because the leaders felt the energy costs would be too high, bribes were used to win the agreement, and the plant was an environmental hazard.

During this same time period, U.S. business publications and Internet sites began warning against FDI in India. Stories claimed there was an antiforeign backlash in India and that American companies were no longer welcome. Enron, along with other companies such as PepsiCo, decided to stay. In October of 1995, the new state government began negotiating a new contract with Enron. In January of 1996, Enron signed a new agreement. The plant would now cost $1.8 billion instead of $2.8 billion and charge 22% less for the power. Why would Enron stay and sign yet another contract?

Enron officials realized the canceled contract was political, not a business maneuver. A strong locally sensitive government relations program would have uncovered that fact. The Shir Sena and its coalition partner the Bharatiya Party had used antiforeign themes in the local elections. The antiforeign theme is an old Indian political strategy, in part motivated by the anticolonial spirit that resulted as countries have reestablished their political and economic independence. However, Shir Sena also realized the value of FDI such as the Enron facility. The "new contract" allowed the Shir Sena Party to live up to its campaign talk and show it could negotiate a better deal than the Congress

Party. The case reflects a growing need for relationships with local government as part of the international public relations mix of an organization working in India. Understanding and working with local governments had become a critical factor in the success of foreign companies in India. Enron understood and played along with the local political game. The contract changed, but Enron remained a key player in a developing market.

Cultural differences do manifest themselves in public relations practices. Japanese practitioners emphasize new technologies as communication tools. They were among the first to embrace video newsletters, live satellite broadcasts for internal communication, and video news releases. A Japanese practitioner would even use a narrative comic book *(manga)* to reach an adult public. In the United States, a narrative comic book would be reserved for children (Cooper-Chen & Kaneshige, 1996). In France, advertorials (bylined articles) would be inappropriate, but they are used in the United States. Preparation for a press conference in India will emphasize the food, snacks, and beverages to be served, because it is more of a social function than a news function (Sriramesh, 1996). China has slowly realized that a public relations practitioner is more than a receptionist who entertains guests (Chen, 1996).

We often assume that European countries are united and homogeneous. That is a dangerous assumption. Public relations planning will vary greatly in Europe. In Italy and Spain, plans are a low priority and are rough outlines, while in Germany and France, the plans are important and detailed. Employee newsletters in Italy have an informal feel and would include personal information. In the United Kingdom, the employee newsletter reflects a formal view of top-down communication that centers on hard facts (Mole, 1991).

Culture can influence how practitioners approach problems. For public information campaigns, there are three basic strategies for getting people to change their behaviors: educate, engineer, and enforce. *Educate* means you tell people what they should do, they appreciate the information, and they change their behaviors on their own. For instance, you tell people their odds of surviving a car crash are greater if they wear a seatbelt. People think living is a good idea, and they are motivated to wear their seatbelts. *Engineer* means you structure the environment so that people must change their behaviors. The old automatic seatbelts were a form of engineering. *Enforce* means you create laws or rules that make people change behaviors. It is common in the United States to be given a ticket if you are not wearing a seatbelt, so people wear seatbelts to avoid the fine. Based on context and Hofstede's dimensions, create cultural profiles that would be very appropriate and very inappropriate for the three forms of behavior change. Use only the factors you feel are relevant to each type of behavior change. That means you may not use every dimension or even context for each profile.

Let us revisit the opening vignette to see how Hall's and Hofstede's ideas can explain the Mexican contract bidding. Mexican culture is fairly high in context, collectivisitic, masculine, and high power distance. The high-context and collectivistic factors help to explain the social emphasis in Mexican business. Both cultural factors emphasize knowing people before doing business with them. The United States and France share a moderately low context and strong individualism, although France is closer to Mexico on both factors. The French seemed better able to adapt to the social aspects of Mexican business. Perhaps the French firm had more experience in international business and more fully appreciated the need to adapt its practices and styles to those of its potential client.

Public Relations Functions and Communication Styles

Culture is a very broad concept and can be manifest in anything people create, say, or do. The insights of Hall and Hofstede offer glimpses into the perils of international public relations. Beyond their work, however, additional insights can be gained. Today's public relations practitioners are aware of the cultural influences that include decision making, language, gestures, business etiquette, media systems, government practices, and religious/belief systems. Each of these manifestations of culture creates unique challenges for the international practitioner.

▶ Decision Making

People will base decisions on fact, faith, or feelings. Cultures vary in terms of which factor they emphasize when making a decision. *Fact-based decisions* are comfortable for Westerners. People use facts, data, or objective information to make decisions. A decision might be based on how people responded to a survey. *Faith decisions* are based on a set of beliefs that can be religious or political. Iran has based its government and decision making on the Koran, while China uses the teachings of the Communist Party even as it becomes a global economic powerhouse. A decision would be based on whether or not an action was consistent with religious beliefs (Morrison, Conaway, & Borden, 1995).

Feeling decisions are based on personal relationships. Is the person a friend, or do you feel comfortable with the person? Many collectivistic cultures, such as Thailand, use feeling-based decisions. A decision would be based on whether or not you feel a positive connection to the other people involved in the decision. Both the internal and external levels must be sensitive to people's bases for decisions. Using data to convince people to change behaviors or support a policy is ineffective if the cultures rely on faith or feeling for their decision making. Going back to our opening vignette, the Mexican culture is more feeling based. The French presentation was more oriented toward feelings. In contrast, the U.S. presentation was unsuccessful because it relied totally on facts and ignored the importance of interpersonal relationships.

▶ Language

There is no global language, so international practitioners must deal in multiple languages, which may have subtle or profoundly different regional vocabularies and meanings. An international practitioner should be fluent in at least one other language if he or she plans to practice overseas. It is ethnocentric to assume people in another country will adapt to your language. The 1999 Report of the Commission on Public

Relations Education recommended a foreign language because of the coming globalism of public relations.

Speaking a language is not the same as knowing a language. We must be aware of linguistic equivalence; a translation is an equivalent but not an exact reproduction of meaning. Language is complicated, and errors in translation are common. For instance, Kentucky Fried Chicken ran an advertisement in China that included the line "Eat your fingers off." General Motors Chevrolet Division failed to recognize how the name of one of its automobile models would be interpreted in Latin America. The model, called "Nova," was very popular in the United States. Nova can be understood in Spanish to mean "No go," not the brand equity an automotive company wants to achieve (Ricks, 1999).

Great care must be taken when translating. Any international business should carefully screen translators. Once again, hiring local talent can be beneficial because a local practitioner will have greater language skills than someone who has just learned the language. Take all precautions to be precise with business translations.

▶ Gestures

An American waves a hand showing five fingers, and a Nigerian is insulted by the gesture. Americans may casually sit back so the soles of their shoes are exposed to others in the room. Arabs find this offensive. Like language, gestures are not the same everywhere. Take time to learn about the gestures in a target culture. Find out what they consider acceptable and unacceptable and which of your common gestures would be inappropriate in the new culture. As in the law, ignorance is no excuse for cultural faux pas. Use your research skills to prevent mistakes created by using the wrong gestures. Gestures apply to internal-level interactions and the visual aspect of external messages.

If you have business contacts with Japanese clients, you might accept a business card and quickly put it aside—put it in your wallet and sit on the wallet. That is often the custom in the United States. We try to be unobtrusive during the exchange of business cards. The Japanese spend time studying cards they have received. They bow their heads in respect to the card, which they hold in both hands. Then, they acknowledge the person whose card they studied with a respectful nod and pleasant smile. For a Japanese businessperson, it is quite insulting to have someone pay passing interest in a business card, which he or she then sits on (Morrison et al., 1995).

▶ Business Etiquette

Imagine you are at a business dinner. How should people be seated? How should people be addressed? Should there be toasts, and who should give them? Many Eastern cultures seat according to age, as a sign of respect. Some cultures use very formal address, including titles and surnames, while others are informal and use given names. Certain cultures expect toasts and have an established format for how they should be given, while others do not toast at dinner. Other questions you may face include the following: Does a meeting/appointment begin on time, or are people expected to be late? Do you need a letter of introduction to set up a meeting? Who should be included in a meeting? Business interactions are full of opportunities to inadvertently offend people (Morrison et al., 1995).

Be a good researcher and learn the business etiquette of the culture you plan to enter. For instance, in Thailand, you should be on time, use formal titles in greetings, arrange for a letter of introduction from an intermediary, and never touch anyone on the head. While shallow, books on "How to Conduct Business in 'X' Culture" are a starting point. Such books help you to avoid mistakes your host would expect anyone to know, such as forms of address. While these books are not academic and detailed, they will teach you the basics you need to prevent mistakes and insults. Business etiquette skills are indispensable on the business level.

▶Media Systems

Not all media systems are just like the one in your home culture. You will want to learn who controls the media systems and what type of content they use. Control and access to the media vary. Some media may be owned and operated by the government, political parties, or private businesses. In Japan, access to the media is controlled through clubs, while in Greece, it is important to be friends with a journalist if you want a story placed. Content varies as well. Some newspapers may specialize in political news, while others focus on business.

Any sharp media relations person will review editorial processes and content preferences before pitching an idea to a media outlet. Moreover, countries vary in terms of which media are the most used and most credible or even whether media relations is useful at all. Again, local knowledge is invaluable to successful practice in international media relations (Zaharna, 2001).

U.S. practitioners, for instance, are aware that reporters in their own country have a code of ethics that prohibits receiving even the smallest gift from a practitioner. When these same practitioners go abroad, they may have to learn about and know how to deal with bribes. One prominent southwestern practitioner told the story of meeting with a reporter to give a backgrounder about a client in Mexico. After the discussion, which was quite cordial, the journalist said bluntly, "Reporters in my country do not make very much, so we like to receive money from companies to help us meet our bills and care for our families." The practitioner said, "I am unfamiliar with such practices. How much does it cost to help me get you to cover my story?" The reporter replied, "How important is the story to you?" This scenario could happen in many other countries around the globe.

External-level activities must take the media systems into account. First, you must learn whether media relations is important in the country. It could be that government relations are much more important than media relations. Second, you must learn which media are the most important, which are the most credible and/or most widely used. Third, you must understand how to go about placing information in the media. Will a simple press release do? Will you need to become close friends with media representatives in order to place a story? Will you need to pay to have a story placed? Will you need to spend money on advertising to also have a story placed? Do not assume media relations operates just like at home, because that can lead to some very unpleasant and failed situations.

▶Government Practices

In Chapter 9, you learned about some of the U.S. laws and regulations that affect public relations. Be sure to review the political system in a country as it relates to public relations. Which laws and regulations protect and/or restrict the practice of public relations? For instance, grassroots lobbying might be inappropriate or illegal in a country (Zaharna, 2001).

Know the laws and regulations relevant to public relations. Local knowledge could save you time and fines by helping you to navigate the legal waters surrounding public relations in a country. If nothing else, you must learn the value of government relations and the nature of the process. The value indicates how much time to devote to government relations, and the nature allows you to understand how to use the process.

▶Religious/Belief Systems

Some countries base decisions on religious/belief systems. Understanding the main religious/belief systems in a country provides additional insights into the values of a country. Moreover, different religions have different holy days and religious holidays. You should plan business activities so that they do not conflict with religious days. In the United States, the focus has traditionally been on the Judeo-Christian religions. The Middle East has a strong influence from Islam. India has a strong Hindu following, while Buddhism is found in various countries throughout the Far East. Not all belief systems are considered religions. *Feng shui,* from the Far East, is an excellent example of a belief system that is relevant to business. Feng shui considers how physical surroundings affect *chi,* the inner force that flows through every living thing. The idea of "the Force" in the Star Wars movies is loosely based on chi. A good chi leads to success in life, including business and family. A good chi is balanced and strong. The layout of a building or room affects the movement of energy and thus the chi of people in that building or room. For instance, a hallway that simply ends can create negative chi because there is no flow of energy. A fountain with running water placed at the end of such a hallway would correct the problem by creating movement or energy. Feng shui is gaining popularity in Western business for office designs (Kennedy, 1998).

But how does feng shui affect business? Donald Trump tells the story of Eastern businessmen who refused to rent office space from him in New York City because the building was not certified by a feng shui master. Trump had never heard of feng shui— but wanted to rent the space. He called in a feng shui master, who inspected the property. The building was certified after a few changes were made, and the space was leased to the Eastern businessmen. As most architects and interior designers will tell you, the principles of feng shui are sound. The principles maximize airflow and sunlight, both of which benefit people. You may find local practitioners do not want to meet in your offices because they have poor chi. If your client is in a joint venture with a company steeped in an Eastern culture, you may need to have office space designed and approved by the principles of feng shui. It would be prudent to understand the basics of feng shui if you plan to practice public relations in the Far East.

One example of a religious belief system is Buddhism, which is based on four noble truths and five precepts:

Noble Truths

1. Life is suffering *(dukka)*.

2. Desire *(tanha)* is the cause of suffering.

3. Removing desire is the cure for suffering.

4. Following the Eightfold Path removes desire.

Five Precepts

1. Do not kill.

2. Do not steal.

3. Do not lie.

4. Do not be unchaste.

5. Do not take drugs or drink intoxicants.

Even though these truths may be phrased in words familiar to you, don't assume that they mean for others what they do for you.

Thus, skilled practitioners are students of the world, its people, and their beliefs. A skilled practitioner will review past research in order to discover information that could be useful for his or her current situation. It follows that international practitioners should review research in the field for possible insights. However, the practice of international public relations has exploded, while the research on the subject lagged behind. A quick journey through the international public relations research will illustrate the limited knowledge it has to offer practitioners.

This section has demonstrated some subtle and profound cultural differences. The section is designed not only to help you understand and appreciate cultural differences but also to serve as a warning: Don't take culture for granted as you practice public relations internationally.

Roles and Public Relations Models

Roles and public relations models were among the first variables studied in international public relations research. Taylor (2001) identified the application of the public relations models and the comparison roles (as a form of contextualized research) as two of the major research paths in international public relations. Roles research examines whether practitioners in a country are primarily technicians or managers. Technicians create public relations materials, while managers have responsibility for planning and decision making. *Public relations models* refers to the four models of public relations developed by James Grunig and Todd Hunt (1984): press agentry, public information, two-way asymmetrical, and two-way symmetrical.

Current thinking places the four models on two continua. The craft continuum is based on one-way communication: from practitioners to MAPs. The press agentry model suggests getting attention any way possible, with no regard for the truth. The public information model recommends disseminating accurate information to MAPs. The professional continuum is based on two-way communication: Practitioners and MAPs exchange messages. The two-way asymmetrical model relies on persuasion, while the two-way symmetrical model uses conflict management. Research promotes two-way symmetrical as the best way to practice public relations. A variety of studies have examined the public relations models used in various countries (e.g., Holtzhausen, Petersen, & Tindall, 2003). Although these models are popular, not all public relations researchers are comfortable with how they portray the practice.

When applied to countries with a relatively short history of public relations, the role and models research finds that (a) practitioners are mostly technicians, (b) practitioners use craft models, and (c) practitioners aspire to use professional models. The reasons for these findings are limited training in public relations and lack of management support for public relations (Coombs, Holladay, Hasenauer, & Signitzer, 1994; Ekachai & Komolsevin, 1996; Jamais, Navarro, & Tuazon, 1996).

Research sheds light on the basic structure of the practice and offers some insight into public relations development. However, research directed at understanding how international public relations works, or should work, is limited. It may also miss some of the crucial dimensions of international practice. For instance, the definition of public relations we use may be too narrow and ignore how some cultures use public relations. A substantial part of public relations in countries around the world entails working with government officials. That fact is true for businesses, nonprofit organizations, and governmental agencies.

One benefit of the models research was the discovery of two new models, the personal influence model and the cultural interpreter model. The *personal influence model* is a quid pro quo system: The public relations practitioner does a favor for a stakeholder, and the stakeholder does a favor for the practitioner. Media relations is the most common target in the personal influence model, but government and activist stakeholders can be targets as well. Japan, India, Greece, and South Korea were all found to practice a form of the personal influence model (Sriramesh, 1992, 1996).

The *cultural interpreter model* uses the expertise of local practitioners. Managers will consult with the local practitioner on public relations concerns. This is consistent with the recommendation in international business to hire local talent.

Oddly, we know little about culture's effect on public relations (Sriramesh & Vercic, 2003; Taylor, 2004). This is unfortunate because culture, through communication, should have a significant influence on public relations. As Sriramesh, Kim, and Takasaki (1999) noted, there is "the need to link culture with public relations so that we can understand the native's point of view when we observe and practice public relations globally" (p. 289). Sriramesh is one of the few researchers to connect international public relations with culture. He used power distance to explain the current state of Indian public relations and collectivism to understand Japanese media relations. India is a high-power-distance country. Public relations personnel tend to be younger and at lower levels in the organization, so they must follow the dictates of senior managers. The power distance is compounded by the fact that most managers are from wealthier, more elite families. As a result, Indian practitioners are mostly technicians with small offices and no air-conditioning (Sriramesh, 1996).

Japanese practitioners place a strong emphasis on media relations. *Nomunication* and press clubs are essential to Japanese media relations. *Nomu* means drink, and Japanese practitioners combine it with communication to describe media relations. Media relations involves socializing with media representatives over drinks. Press clubs offer a setting for nomunication. Press clubs, which are physical spaces set aside for reporters to meet and collect information, evolved from social clubs. The setting promotes the simultaneous distribution of information and prevents "scoops." This system reflects a collectivistic culture. People get to know one another personally, even in business, and information is shared with the group (Sriramesh et al., 1999). More research needs to apply culture as an explanatory device for international public relations practices. Such research will yield insights into how to effectively practice international public relations.

Cultures of Markets, Audiences, and Publics

If you recall the discussion in Chapter 3, you will appreciate the discussion in this section even more. That chapter offered insights in the ways that you could analyze the opinions and behaviors of MAPs. The chapter advised you to always look at an organization's image, its products and services, its relationships, and the like from the perspectives of the people with whom it is working to build mutually beneficial relationships. This section adds detail to that discussion by featuring the role culture plays in the process of relationship development.

You may ask, "How does understanding public relations in 'X' country help me to practice international public relations?" The answer is twofold. First, research tells you how public relations works in a particular country. If you are engaged with that country, you will have some insights into how public relations works there. You will better understand the practice before you become a part of it. Second, if we understand culture's effect on communication, we can use the information to construct more effective external- and internal-level messages. Culture becomes another factor we consider when analyzing the MAPs, including the local practitioners who will be advising your public relations efforts in their countries. We are better prepared for international public relations when we have an understanding of the culture we are about to engage.

But what does it mean to be "prepared"? Let us return to the five functions of public relations and the five MDOs to explain preparation. The five functions and MDOs are generic principles; they can be found in the practice of public relations anywhere around the globe. However, what constitutes a specific use of one of the functions and how important each is will change from culture to culture. For instance, publicity is quite different in the United States, Japan, and Greece. In the United States, it is common to send press releases; in Japan, access to a press club is essential; while in Greece, paying for placement is accepted.

We can expect the similar variations for the other four public relations functions. Planning should be different in high- and low-uncertainty-avoidance cultures. The high-avoidance cultures will plan every detail carefully, while the low will have more general plans of action. The functions will reflect different emphases as well. Promotion might be the dominant function in one culture, while relationship building is more important in another. Preparation means you have some idea of how each function works and its relative value in a culture.

Negotiation and collaborative decision making are likely to be different in various countries around the world and across cultures. In one country, a battle over corporate policy or product safety might be waged in the media. The activists make their case, and the company responds. The dialogue continues. In other countries, this sort of conflict might be adjudicated by a government official. Any effort on the part of either the activists or the company might be their undoing. The bureaucrat does not want discussion before the decision, nor after it. His or her word is final!

Similar strategic preparation is needed to tailor MDOs to cultural differences. We must understand how to use each MDO effectively—how to operationalize it in a specific culture. Let's consider attention as an example. What is attention-getting in the culture? Attention can be related to specific colors, design layout, and message appeals. But what colors, layout, and message appeals work best in that culture? If you do not know the answer, you should know enough to ask someone the question. The same concerns exist for information, persuasion, collaborative decision making, and cocreation of meaning.

Collaborative decision making and cocreation of meaning may be especially problematic. As noted earlier, high-power-distance and high-uncertainty-avoidance cultures do not care for activism. Hence, MAPs are unlikely to actively or even passively become involved in collaborative decision making. The idea of collaboration will be new to them and may make certain MAPs uncomfortable. You will have to devise original ideas for how to make collaborative decision making work in cultures in which it does not fit well. Cocreation of meaning centers on shared interpretations of the events. Different cultures can have different meanings for the same event.

Risk, for instance, can be positive or negative depending on one's culture. While cocreating meaning across cultures is not impossible, it is much more difficult than when the organization and MAPs are from the same or similar cultures. Realize that cocreating meaning will take greater effort in the international arena. By "preparation," we mean that you understand the need and are ready to adapt the functions and MDOs to different cultures.

Ethics and International Public Relations Practice

International public relations is a hotbed for ethical issues. Cultures and values clash, often involving what is right or wrong, proper or improper conduct. For instance, what do you do when bribery is common in a country but your ethics—and your profession's code of ethics—preclude its use? Bribery is a serious matter in public relations because it can affect the practice. Kruckeberg and Tsetura (2003) did a global assessment of bribery in the newspapers industry. They created an index that evaluated 66 countries on the degree to which cash can be used to get news coverage. Bribery was most common in China, Saudi Arabia, Vietnam, Bangladesh, and Pakistan. Finland was the country least likely to trade news for cash (Kruckeberg & Tsetura, 2003). Practitioners face an ethical dilemma when cash is expected to get publicity.

The ethical discussions for international public relations mirror the localization/globalization debate to a degree. If you recall, in the United States, practitioners do not violate the Public Relations Society of America (PRSA) code if they give something of modest value to reporters. By their code, reporters are prohibited from receiving favors of monetary value. International practitioners may be confronted with ethical quandaries that the U.S. code does not adequately address. That quandary can be compounded when international practitioners suggest the use of bribes to get coverage in the United States. In this section, we shall review this debate and then present an integrated option based on codes of conduct used in the garment industry.

The terms *relativism* versus *universalism* are quite relevant in matters of culture. What is relative in one culture may be considered to be universal in others. History abounds in examples where clashes of various magnitudes occurred between people of different cultures simply because some thought certain values to be relative, while others approached the values as universal.

Thousands of laws relate to business that vary from country to country. Furthermore, moral tastes differ from country to country as well. The problem for an international business is how to decide what is ethical in all of its locations. International ethics can be divided into two schools of thought, relativism and universalism. Relativism argues for the acceptance of local differences. "When in Rome, do as the Romans do." Universalism argues for one unified ethical code that is applied everywhere in the world. Some claim relativism demonstrates respect for cultures while universalism is a form of ethnocentrism. Others believe relativism is an excuse to not strengthen ethical codes while universalism is the only fair system.

Dean Kruckeberg, a public relations educator and scholar, has written extensively on the need for a universal code of ethics in international business. Kruckeberg (1996) suggested that we view organizations as moral agents; an organization has freedom of choice and can make reasoned choices. Therefore, organizations have an obligation to follow an ethical code. A universal code should be built around a respect for human rights that seeks to protect people from degradation and physical harm. His view is that such a code can still be adapted to tolerate moral tastes but must stay true to the commitment for human rights.

Identifying and agreeing on what constitutes human rights may be easier said than done. Just because something is difficult does not mean we should not do it. International organizations need to develop codes of conduct, and public relations practitioners should provide their input. Because of their responsibility to MAPs, practitioners should have a strong sense of ethical conduct.

The garment industry is an excellent example of the need for and development of codes of conduct. The 1990s were filled with reports of various garment makers, including Nike and the Gap, using sweatshops, forced labor, child labor, or mistreatment of workers such as beatings. To be accurate, vendors hired by the garment makers were responsible for most of the abuses. Thus, many garment makers drafted Standards of Vendor Engagement, codes of conduct vendors must meet in order to do business with the company. Dayton-Hudson Corporation's Standard of Vendor Engagement includes the following:

1. Safe and Healthy Workplace: Workplaces must be safe, healthy, and in compliance with all local laws.

2. Forced or Compulsory Labor: No vendor will be used who employs forced or compulsory labor, including labor used as political coercion or as a punishment for expressing peaceful political views.

3. Disciplinary Practices: No vendor will use corporal punishment or other forms of mental or physical coercion, such as denial of bathroom breaks.

4. Nondiscrimination: Workers should be selected according to their abilities to perform the job and not based on personal characteristics or beliefs. Vendors must not discriminate in their job selection.

5. Working Hours and Overtime: Vendors must not have employees work more than 60 hours per week on a regular basis except for overtime that is compensated fairly and in compliance with local laws. This means employees cannot be forced to work overtime.

6. Fair Wages: Vendors must provide wages and benefits that allow a respectable living and are appropriate in light of national practices and pay.

7. Child Labor: Vendors may not use child labor, anyone under the age of 14, regardless of the country's laws.

The garment industry provides proof that organizations can draft codes of conduct that can be applied to all operations around the globe. This does not mean that drafting and enforcing the codes is easy. An organization must constantly monitor its vendors. If an organization does not catch a "bad" vendor, you can be assured some part of the human rights advocacy network will. An international organization must take the time to develop a viable code of ethics. Public relations should be a part of the process, since it will fall to the public relations people to explain charges of misconduct.

Recall the topic featured in the vignette at the beginning of Chapter 9. It featured a continuing battle surrounding Nike's business practices. Workplace ethics is a controversial issue that has haunted many multinational companies. International human rights groups watch closely and use severe power resources to battle against worker exploitation.

Below are 18 items from the Human Rights United Nations Declaration. Human rights has been advanced as one basis for a universal code of ethics for international public relations. However, some of the items may infringe on a government's laws, and a country might see such items as a threat to their sovereignty. In fact, the items could be said to have a Western bias. In a group with classmates, review the items, and identify those items you feel would be difficult to apply everywhere in the world. Your discussion will give you an idea of how difficult it is to agree on universal principles.

1. Right to life, liberty, and security.

2. No slavery.

3. Freedom from torture or from cruel, inhumane, or degrading punishment.

4. All people are protected by the law.

5. Right to a tribunal for acts violating fundamental rights.

6. No arbitrary arrest, detention, or exile.

7. Right to a tribunal to judge criminal charges.

8. Presumed innocent until proven guilty.

9. Right to protection against arbitrary interference with privacy or family.

10. Freedom of movement and residence within a state.

11. Right to leave and to return to your own country.

12. Right to seek asylum from another country.

13. Right to marry and have families.

14. Right to own property.

15. Right to freedom of thought, conscience, and religion.

16. Freedom to express opinions.

17. Right of peaceful assembly.

18. Right to take part in government.

Final Advice to Future International Public Relations Practitioners

Reading this chapter does not prepare you to be a practitioner on the international scene. Our objective is to make you aware of the myriad concerns you must address on an international level and to guide your preparation for such a career. We end with four pieces of advice for those wanting to practice international public relations.

1. *Language skills.* If you want to work in a country other than your own, you must learn the language. You cannot expect people in another country to adapt to your language; you must adapt to theirs. Business is conducted in the language of the host country. Get as many language skills as possible in school, including

conversational skills and business applications, if your school offers them. Living and working in a language is different from translating passages from a book. Work on your application of the language.

2. *Culture skills.* Learn as much as you can about the culture you are about to enter. This includes the points outlined in this chapter and the history of a country. As with any job, show an employer you have done your homework—you have learned not only about their organization but also about their culture. Studying abroad is a useful tool for learning about culture. It is not enough to read about culture; you learn it much better by living in one for an extended period of time. This also provides an opportunity to work on language skills. A bonus is to get an internship as part of the study abroad experience. You will be able to directly sample the culture at work through the internship and have an impressive item on your résumé.

3. *Current events.* The world is at your fingertips in the news media. Pay attention to the world by following current events. Knowledge of current events is valued highly in public relations but becomes even more important at the international level. You must be well-informed if you are to know what is happening and how it might affect your organization on a local and international level. Start immersing yourself in current events now. This will build a wider base of knowledge than starting after you graduate. Public relations people deal in information, and current events are an important part of that information.

4. *Translation.* Be very careful when you have documents translated. Be sure to hire translators who are familiar with your type of organization and who have strong references. It is also a good idea to "back translate." Let's say you need to translate a document from German to Russian. Have one translator make the translation from German to Russian. Then have a second translator make the translation from Russian back to German. Compare the original and translated German versions to see whether the meaning is the same. International businesspeople value accurate translation, so make sure you do your best to get accurate translations for your messages.

This advice follows the suggestions offered by Wakefield (2001):

A team leader should be well versed in international issues and events, skilled in cultural integration, and knowledgeable about public relations strategizing. Local officers should be experienced in local public relations and also able to make valuable contributions to the overall strategies of a global public relations unit. (p. 646)

Adding her voice to those calling for attention to the challenges of international public relations, Taylor (2001) called for "increased education, cultural sensitivity, and increased professionalism" (p. 637). This section of the chapter has offered you direction, but only you can know whether you can meet this challenge. The challenge of globalism is here to stay.

As this section of the chapter has demonstrated, international public relations is a rapidly developing, exciting, and challenging specialty of public relations. The new MAPs that come with new countries create challenges. Practitioners must try to understand these new MAPs if they are to form lasting relationships with them. Culture is the key to understanding and adapting to new MAPs The basic functions of public relations remain, but what this constitutes and how those functions and MDOs are applied will change. You must learn which MAPs are the most important to you, which channels provide the best access to reach them, and which values appeal to them, to name but a few of the challenges. It is critical to tap local talent to aid in your learning process. Think of local practitioners as a key source of information to include in your cultural research efforts.

International public relations does not always involve living and working in another country. Foreign agents will want to engage in some form of public relations in your home country. You become the local expert who is part of a larger international public relations effort. While not as exciting as traveling or living in another country, it is a form of international public relations. As with any other public relations specialty, preparation is the key to success. You will need some language skills and experience with other cultures. This means you should have at least a language minor and study abroad.

You also should take courses that expose you to the basics of international business and begin to follow international current events. If you want to become an international worker, you must become a citizen of the world. Even if you do not plan to become an international practitioner, you should become familiar with the basics of international public relations. Remember, the globe is shrinking. You will have more and more difficulty in avoiding the trend. Technology unites the world and means all business is global to some degree. Better to be prepared when you encounter the new MAPs than to be caught short and try to play catch-up.

Technology and Public Relations Practice

You have probably noticed that the Internet gets mentioned frequently in this book, because it is essential to today's public relations. Our discussion of the practice in this chapter and Chapter 12 featured a number of Internet applications and addresses. As noted in Chapter 2, technology does affect the practice of public relations. The Internet and related Intranet are the current technologies of note, so they are the focus of this section. The Internet is a computer-assisted network that allows people to communicate with one another as well as with various kinds of organizations. The Intranet is a similar computer-assisted network that operates only within an organization.

Throughout the book, we have used Web Watchers to foster your interest in using the Internet as a continuing source of information. Practitioners are learning that it must be monitored like all other channels. In fact, it requires special skills because of its vast size and the ability of any person to put messages there for anyone to find and consider. As much as it offers alternative channels of communication, it is also the source of cybersabotage. The role of the Internet is one of the defining differences between what might be called "old" and "new" public relations. Public relations in the century prior to the creation of the Internet relied heavily on skilled practitioners gaining access through news reports to readers, listeners, or viewers. As such, communication often took a shotgun approach. Shoot enough pellets into the air, and some will strike the target. Today's public relations presents the Web home page as a target that any interested user of information can find through a search, link, or direct access. It is available, as we have come to say, 24/7.

The practitioner literature is filled with stories about the need to be Internet savvy and the growing use of Intranets for internal communication (e.g., Callison, 2003; Hachigian & Hallahan, 2003; Kent, Taylor, & White, 2003). In this section, we explore the ramifications of technology on public relations practice, with an emphasis on the Internet. We begin by reviewing some of the current applications of technology. From there, we examine writing for the Internet. We conclude with a note of caution about new technologies.

▶ Applications

You are hard-pressed to find a content area of public relations that does not use the Internet. IR specialists post a wealth of information on corporate Web sites. Nonprofits disseminate information, solicit donations, and recruit volunteers online. Government offices provide contact information to constituents. Schools post information of use to students, parents, and alumni. Intranets are used by many organizations to facilitate the flow of information between units. It is much quicker to download a document from the organization's Intranet site than to call or e-mail another person in the organization and request the same information. More important, the new technologies can be used as part of the five functions of public relations.

Publicity can be generated through the Internet. Organizations can send press releases via e-mail. Also, a Web site can attract publicity. The "Flaming Ford" Web site mentioned in Chapter 13 is an example of one that drew media attention. Another example is the Web site Metabolife constructed in anticipation of a negative story being run on ABC's *20/20*. Metabolife, leading seller of the controversial weight-loss supplement ephedra, placed its own, unedited footage of ABC's interview with its leader, Michael Ellis. The site urged people to watch the entire interview before watching the edited piece on ABC. The implication is that the media distorts information through editorial decisions. The Internet can be used as part of promotional efforts. Web sites can carry the same messages being delivered in other media. Promotional efforts often mention the Web site address. At the Web site, people can get additional and more detailed information. "Thetruth.com" campaign against tobacco companies illustrates a Web site as part of a promotion. Each television advertisement carries the Web site address. People can go to "thetruth.com" and learn more about the anti-tobacco claims made in the television spots. Metabolife also ran a series of radio spots that urged people to visit the Web and view the raw footage before ABC aired its piece.

The Intranet becomes a tool for planning. People can exchange information and work on schedules in cyberspace. People can even hold planning sessions via the computer. Research becomes faster. As previously noted, the Intranet speeds up the collection of information inside of an organization. Externally, the Internet provides access to government association databases, comments by MAPs in discussion groups, Weblogs, track actions being planned by the government (pending bills and regulatory decisions), breaking news, and Web sites that attack your organization. Relationship building is facilitated, as MAPs have an easy way to interact with the organization. Web sites provide information MAPs may want, while e-mail and discussion groups make it easier to exchange messages with people in the organization. Chapter 13 discussed the highly interactive Web site used by Shell. Relationships become stronger through the type of interaction made possible by the Internet.

So what does it mean that the Internet and related technologies are found in different content areas of public relations and are used in the five functions? Our point is that the Internet and Intranet are here to stay: They are now part of the media mix a public relations practitioner has at his or her disposal. You should learn the basics about the Internet just as you should learn the basics of any other media you might use on the job. The next section gives an overview of what a practitioner might want to know about the Internet.

▶ Writing for the Internet

Our discussion of Internet writing concentrates on online press releases and Web sites, the two most common Internet applications a practitioner will use. Each medium has its own demands, which shape writing for that medium. Ochman (2000), a specialist in Internet writing, contends that the typical press release format does not work for the e-mail/Internet variation. Internet press releases are frequently delivered via e-mail, so the e-mail format creates restrictions. The e-mail has two demands: (1) short attention spans and (2) computer screens. The e-mail message flow for people increases almost daily. People have very little time to devote to e-mail messages, so they must be short. People typically read e-mails on their computer screens. Again, this requires short messages.

A traditional press release is around 350 words, with as many as 100 words in the lead paragraph. For releases sent by distribution services such as Business Wire or PR Wire, e-mail press releases are recommended to have a total of 200 words and 40 or less words in the lead paragraph. The e-mail press release should have only five paragraphs, with each being two or three sentences in length. The information can be presented with bullet points and use 6 words or less to describe what the organization does. The bottom of the release can be used for additional information. The contact name, phone numbers, e-mail address, and URL for the home page can be above the headline or at the bottom of the release. The e-mail press release gets people interested, while the Web site delivers the detailed information.

Another option for the e-mail press release is for the practitioner to send the release directly to a reporter. For a direct e-mail press release, keep it to three paragraphs, and treat it as a pitch letter or memo. Just remember online press releases are e-mails that people read on their computer screens. They should be able to read all the critical information (the three or five key paragraphs) without scrolling down the screen (Kent & Taylor, 2003; Ochman, 2000). This is the same logic that recommends a traditional press release to be one page.

Public relations practitioners also get involved in developing Web sites. A set of five standard criteria have evolved for evaluating Web sites:

1. *Accurate:* The information at the site is correct.

2. *Expert:* The people providing the content are experts on the topic.

3. *Objective:* The information is not biased and avoids exaggerated claims.

4. *Current:* The information is up-to-date.

5. *Comprehensive:* There is extensive information provided at the site.

If you are involved with a Web site, you should make sure it meets the five criteria (Witmer, 2000).

A Web site has two basic parts, content and technology. The *content* is what appears on the site. As a practitioner, you should always be responsible for the content part. Content is a reflection of the objectives of the Web site and the MAPs you hope will access the Web site. The Web site is used strategically to achieve specific objectives. *Technology* is the programming that makes the site run—places the text and graphics on the site.

The practitioner's relationship to technology can vary. First, you could be the expert. Your job is to design and to build the site. You must know the program or programs used to create what people will see at the site. This requires Internet expertise and at least a minor in applied computer science. Second, you could be the advisor. You work with a technical expert to design the Web site. You should know the basic rules of Web page design (layout, not the programs) so that you can have informed discussions with the technical people. Third, you could be a content provider. You should know the vocabulary of the new technologies. You must know such terms as *home page, hot link, Intranet,* and *hypertext.* This does not mean you must know the code necessary for writing Web pages; most programs will write without code these days. But you must know what the technical people are talking about. You should focus on knowing the content of the page, such as what objectives are to be reached, what MAPs will use the site, and what information needs to be on the site.

Diane Witmer (2000), a leading expert in public relations and the Internet, discussed a number of issues related to Web design in her book *Spinning the Web: A Handbook for Public Relations on the Internet.* Based on her book and other sources, we offer five Web site design concerns that a public relations practitioner should understand:

1. *Know why you are creating the site.* It is amazing to ask a roomful of practitioners how many are on the Internet. Then ask how many know why their organizations are on the Internet. The number drops dramatically from question 1 to question 2. You must know the objectives to be achieved by the Web site and the target MAPs for the Web site. Like any other medium, a Web site is effective only if it is used properly. Just being on the Internet is a weak reason for having a Web site. Your Web site, like other messages, must be targeted and help the organization to realize its strategic plan.

2. *Maximize the interactivity of the Web site*. The unique characteristic of a Web site as a medium is its ability to be interactive. Give Web surfers what they want and expect: interactivity.

3. *Organizations must be ready to respond to questions and comments*. Members of the organization will need to respond to e-mail messages and discussion group postings placed on a Web site. In the late 1990s, Sears was slow to use the interactive elements on its Web site because its people were not ready to respond to incoming messages.

4. *Make the site easy to navigate*. A Web site should be easy to move around in and have useful navigation aids. Avoid dead ends—a page should have buttons returning people to the home page or the beginning of the area they are exploring. Do not have people go three or four links deep into your Web site and provide no easy way to return. Provide a site map, an outline of the links at your Web site. It is very helpful to sketch a site map and all links between files before constructing the Web site. Planning will improve the logic of the design and thus improve navigation.

5. *Keep the design elements simple*. You give some people Web software, and they go wild. You have flaming logos, rotating planets for bullets, and more frames than an art museum. Clean and simple is better than outrageous. Do not overuse graphics or frames. Both slow a page's loading time, and frames can hinder navigation. Monthly, new software appears that allows Web designers to do new things to their sites. Remember, just because you can do it does not mean you should do it. The Web site should be designed for the intended user, not just the design team. Consider how the target MAPs will approach and use the Web site. They may not have the team's technological savvy or advanced computer systems. Simple designs will allow people to navigate and to load your Web site in a reasonable amount of time. If your page is slow in loading, the compressed time on the Internet may lead people to move on to some other site. People are on the Internet because they want things in seconds.

▶ Caveat 1: One of Many

The excitement over the "Net" must be tempered. While expanding rapidly, the Internet is only one of many media tools or channels available to public relations practitioners. Do not be blinded by technology and the "hype" of a technology. There is a danger that new practitioners believe the Internet is the source of all information and the answer to all questions. That may be a very dangerous belief. While vast, the Internet does not contain all the information you might need and will provide a lot of "bad" information as well. All practitioners must be careful consumers of Internet information and still know other techniques for gathering information besides keystrokes. Nor is the Internet always THE media for reaching people. Ask yourself, "Does my target MAP use the Internet, and do they believe information they find on the Internet?" You still must carefully evaluate each communication medium.

Let us consider an example that illustrates the Internet as part of the media mix. In 2000, Seton Hall University, in New Jersey, had a devastating fire in a dormitory that killed three students and injured 62 others. The Seton Hall Web site provided basic information, such as where parents could contact their children. Would parents

Bertil Flodin
Partner, Gullers Grupp
Stockholm, Sweden

International Public Relations From a European Perspective

1. Do Europeans share the same perceptions of public relations?

2. Does the infrastructure allow us to practice public relations in the same manner all over Europe?

3. Are the relationships to governments and journalists the same all over Europe?

4. Is the international approach performed only by companies?

It seems necessary to be international today. Business is global, politics is global, relationships are global, and modern information technology makes it easier than ever to communicate.

But "international" does not necessarily mean interaction between people geographically wide apart. Even within the borders of Europe, the implications are evident.

Let me raise four questions from a Swedish perspective, just to give you an idea of what it means to be a practitioner working with international public relations within Europe:

To answer the first question, let us look at the results of a research study of 25 European countries, where I was a member of the research group. The study searched for the common ground of public relations in Europe. The findings indicate that there are several different perceptions of the concept of public relations within Europe.

Some of the respondents argued that public relations is about managing relations, while others said it is about managing communications. Some wanted to include market communications as a part of public relations practice, while others absolutely refused to do so. The study revealed that although we do have much in common in the way we perceive public relations, we also have strikingly different interpretations.

of students in that dormitory want information only from a Web site? What about displaced students? How should they be kept abreast of developments? A Web site is fine for those not personally involved in the fire, such as media representatives, students not in the affected dormitory, and the parents of unaffected students. Those affected by the fire needed a much more personal channel, such as direct contact by phone for parents and in person for students. Technology is seductive. The Internet is quick and trendy to use. This means it can be easily misused as well.

Continuing with the second question, we can state that the infrastructure in Europe differs considerably. There is, for example, a vast difference in household penetration of personal computers and Internet connections within Europe, making a common media strategy impossible. This is especially obvious if we compare Eastern and Western Europe, the former lagging behind so far. We also have numerous examples of big companies overlooking the importance of history and local culture when trying to enter the European market.

The answer to the third question is a clear No. When the European Union institutions send information to the Swedish government, they often expect it to be secret. To their surprise, they learn that Sweden's Right to Information Act makes almost all governmental documents open to the public as soon as they are received. Obviously a public relations practitioner needs to be aware of the different traditions and legislative protocols that exist within different European countries.

Also, working habits differ considerably among journalists from different European countries. This becomes evident every time there is a national disaster serious enough to attract international interest. Journalists' demand for openness, transparency, access to decision makers and respect for the integrity of the individual vary tremendously from country to country.

The last of the four questions is of course rhetorical. Activists, consumer organizations and strong environmental movements, to name a few, have demonstrated what it means to work internationally. Through a variety of meeting places in Cyberspace, decentralized structures and very efficient systems of distributing information, these organizations have demonstrated the power and possibilities of working internationally.

It is imperative to be international today. But as I have tried to show with my examples from Europe, one needs to be aware of and adapt to the cultural, political, religious and historical variations that exist all over the world. Genuine dialogue and careful environmental scanning are prerequisites for successful international public relations.

SOURCE: Reprinted with permission from Bertil Flodin.

▶ Caveat 2: Hidden Ethical Concerns

Your organization has a Web site that MAPs visit. Polls show many Web site visitors have no idea how easy it is for people to track their movement on the Internet. Tracking visitors on Web sites raises a number of questions with ethical implications. Should your organization track visitors? What type of information should they collect about visitors? Should the organization sell the information to others? Should you notify

people that they are being tracked when they arrive at your Web site? Should you give visitors the option of deactivating your tracking software? Or maybe you require people to register to use the site; they can use the site free of charge if they fill out an informational survey. Who will have access to that information? As a practitioner who must place the public interest first, a warning about tracking, an option for deactivating the tracking, and an option to preclude the sale of collected information would seem appropriate and ethical. The new technologies associated with the Internet have great potential for surveillance and for abuse. Your involvement with the Web site should extend to policy concerns about tracking. Management and the design team should consider the ethical ramifications of their tracking decisions. As a practitioner, part of your responsibility is to represent the public interest in Web use discussion, such as tracking.

As we near the end of this discussion, consider the following case problem. If you've been on the Internet, you know there is a lot of garbage out there. People feel free to say and to comment on anything, including organizations. So what does your company do if someone or a group of people is posting nasty messages about your company? Maybe they are posting negative comments on an investment board or have created a Web site critical of your company. One option is to sue. Let us consider an investing example.

A group of people post negative investment information about PharmCo on "Raging Bull," a popular investment board. The information wrongly states the organization will fail to meet Food and Drug Administration (FDA) standards on two promising drugs. Do you simply post a response from the investor relations department, or do you sue to silence your critics? Using charges such as defamation, you could sue the posters. This is called a "John Doe lawsuit." You then ask a judge for a subpoena to force Raging Bull to release the Internet addresses of the posters. The subpoena is given to Raging Bull, and they are most likely to comply. Within a few weeks, you have the Internet address and can track down the people posters— get the John Doe's real identity. While a quick solution, lawsuits have downsides. First, your company looks like a bully. A large company goes after some average people posting messages. Second, the John Doe lawsuits "chill" discussion—make people less likely to post messages openly. As a practitioner, chilly discussion is in opposition to the ideas of building mutually beneficial relationships. A chill prevents even factual criticism from being aired. You want stakeholders to air criticism because it gives you an opportunity to resolve the problem and keep a relationship intact or improve it.

Reserve the lawsuits for the most serious problems. If trade secrets are being posted or employees are violating their contracts, that is a time for a lawsuit. Another is if a rash of inaccurate postings is being used to manipulate your stock prices, either up or down. Such manipulation is a crime, and the SEC may become involved. Reserve lawsuits for real crimes in cyberspace, not for a few people venting their anger against your client.

What guidelines would you recommend for your organization when it came to using John Doe lawsuits? How might you deal with a Web site that criticizes your organization over products, practices, or policies? How would you distinguish between legitimate criticism/complaints, parody, and unfair attacks?

Conclusion

This chapter has focused on two points that are central to public relations' future: (1) international public relations and (2) the Internet and related technologies. International public relations is a rapidly growing context area of public relations. Practitioners increasingly will need to appreciate how culture affects relationship development between organizations and MAPs from different cultures and countries. Culture is becoming a basic knowledge set for practitioners. We used the term "Internet" to represent a collection of related technologies, including Web sites, e-mail, Weblogs, and discussion groups. The Internet has great potential for facilitating dialogue between organizations and MAPs and requires new skills that are becoming essential for practitioners. Chapter 15 has been a continuation of Chapter 14. International public relations is a context area of public relations that warrants detailed attention. The Internet is a "new" communication channel that must be integrated into a practitioner's toolbox. Both topics suggest additional or specialized preparation required of tomorrow's public relations practitioners.

Ethical Quandary: Clashing Cultures: Justice in Singapore

FURTHER EXPLORATION

15

In 1994, an 18-year-old American pled guilty to vandalism in Singapore. He and a Singaporean youth had spray-painted graffiti on a number of cars over a 10-day period. By law, Michael Fay was sentenced to 4 months in jail, a $3,500 fine, and six strokes of the cane. This touched off a debate between elements in the United States and Singapore.

The *New York Times* led the anticaning campaign with editorials. They said caning was a violation of human rights and too brutal. It was called "medieval torture." The editorials asked people to flood the Singapore embassy with phone calls (the number was printed in the paper) and listed the names of the heads of various U.S. companies doing business in Singapore. People were asked to write to these companies and demand that these companies pressure the Singapore government to drop the caning.

No companies did pressure the government. Three companies said it was not related to business and was a judicial matter they should not be involved in.

The Singapore government responded harshly. They felt Americans wanted a double standard and were refusing to respect the rights of other countries. Singapore felt it was a matter of sovereignty and nationalism. They also labeled the attempts to generate economic pressure as economic aggression. In the end, Fay received two strokes of the cane. The caning did draw blood.

Do you believe U.S. companies should have pressured Singapore to not cane Fay? Why or why not?

There are no wrong or right answers. Your job is to justify your decision—explain your answer thoroughly. The paper should be about a page (three to five paragraphs in length). Be sure to explain your reasoning in detail.

Summary Questions

1. Why is international public relations becoming more important each day?
2. What is the difference between *international* and *transnational?*
3. What is culture, and why does it matter to international public relations?
4. What are some of the differences between high- and low-context cultures?
5. What is power distance? Uncertainty avoidance?
6. How do feminine and masculine cultures differ?
7. How do individualistic and collectivistic cultures differ?
8. How is culture manifested in decision making, and how can that affect international public relations?
9. What are some aspects of business etiquette, and why does it matter to international public relations?
10. What unique, ethical problem does bribery present to international public relations?
11. How do new technologies fit with the five functions of public relations?
12. What unique demands does the Internet place on writing?
13. What are the six Web design concerns?
14. What are some hidden ethical concerns with using the Internet?

Exercises

1. Conduct some basic research on a foreign country. At the very least, identify the following: major language spoken, literacy rate, major media outlets, and form of government. How might this information be of use if you were assigned to coordinate public relations efforts in that country?
2. Many countries have their own public relations organizations. Find one of these organizations on the Internet. Locate its definition of *public relations* and compare it with the definition used in this book. Locate its statement/code of ethics and compare it with the statement of the Public Relations Society of America. What insights in practicing public relations in that country might be gained through its definition of public relations and code of ethics?

Recommended Readings

Coombs, W. T. (1998). The Internet as potential equalizer: New leverage for confronting social irresponsibility. *Public Relations Review, 24,* 289–304.

Heath, R. L. (1998). New communication technologies: An issues management point of view. *Public Relations Review, 24,* 273–288.

Heath, R. L. (2001). Globalization—the frontier of multinationalism and cultural diversity. In R. L. Heath (Ed.), *Handbook of public relations* (pp. 625–628). Thousand Oaks, CA: Sage.

Sriramesh, K., & Vercic, D. (2003). *The global public relations handbook: Theory, research, and practice.* Mahwah, NJ: Lawrence Erlbaum.

Taylor, M. (2001). International public relations: Opportunities and challenges for the 21st century. In R. L. Heath (Ed.), *Handbook of public relations* (pp. 629–638). Thousand Oaks, CA: Sage.

Taylor, M. (2004). Exploring public relations in Croatia through relational communication and media richness theories. *Public Relations Review, 30,* 145–160.

Taylor, M. (2005). Intercultural communication theory. In R. L. Heath (Ed.), *Encyclopedia of public relations* (pp. 428–430). Thousand Oaks, CA: Sage.

Trompenaars, F., & Hampden-Turner, C. (1998). *Riding the waves of culture: Understanding diversity in global business.* New York: McGraw-Hill.

Wakefield, R. I. (2001). Effective public relations in the multinational organization. In R. L. Heath (Ed.), *Handbook of public relations* (pp. 639–648). Thousand Oaks, CA: Sage.

Witmer, D. F. (2000). *Spinning the Web: A handbook for public relations on the Internet.* Reading, MA: Longman.

References

Chapter 1:
Strategic Relationship Building

Aristotle. (1952). Rhetoric (Trans. by W. R. Roberts). In R. M Hutchins (Ed. in chief), *Great books* (Vol. 2, pp. 593–675). Chicago: Encyclopaedia Britannica.

Bryant, D. C. (1953). Rhetoric: Its function and its scope. *Quarterly Journals of Speech, 39,* 401–424.

Burke, K. (1969). *A rhetoric of motives.* Berkeley: University of California Press.

Isocrates. (1929a). *Against the sophists* (Trans. by G. Norlin). *Isocrates* (Vol. 2, pp. 160–177). Cambridge, MA: Harvard University Press.

Isocrates. (1929b). Antidosis (Trans. by G. Norlin). *Isocrates* (Vol. 2, pp. 182–365). Cambridge, MA: Harvard University Press.

Lentz, C. S. (1996). The fairness in broadcasting doctrine and the Constitution: Forced one-stop shopping in the "marketplace of ideas." *University of Illinois Law Review, 271,* 1–39.

Mead, G. H. (1934). *Mind, self, and society.* Chicago: University of Chicago Press.

Public Relations Society of America. (2003). *Public relations tactics: The blue book.* New York: Author.

Quintilian, M. F. (1951). *The institutio oratoria of Marcus Fabius Quintilianus* (Trans. by C. E. Little). Nashville, TN: George Peabody College for Teachers.

Wallace, K. R. (1963). The substance of rhetoric: Good reasons. *Quarterly Journal of Speech, 49,* 239–249.

Weaver, R. M. (1953). *The ethics of rhetoric.* Chicago: Henry Regnery.

Weaver, R. M. (1970). *Language is sermonic* (R. L. Johannesen, R. Strickland, & R. T. Eubanks, Eds.). Baton Rouge: Louisiana State University Press.

Woodrum, R. L. (1995). How to please the CEO and keep your job. *Public Relations Strategist, 1*(3), 7–12.

Chapter 2:
History of Public Relationships

Bernays, E. L. (1928). *Propaganda.* New York: Liveright.

Chase, W. H. (1982, December 1). Issue management conference—a special report. *Corporate Public Issues and Their Management, 7,* 1–2.

Cutlip, S. M. (1994). *The unseen power: Public relations. A history.* Hillsdale, NJ: Lawrence Erlbaum.

Cutlip, S. M. (1995). *Public relations history: From the 17th to the 20th century. The antecedents.* Hillsdale, NJ: Lawrence Erlbaum.

Ewen, S. (1996). *PR! A social history of spin.* New York: Basic Books.

Ewing, R. P. (1987). *Managing the new bottom line: Issues management for senior executives.* Homewood, IL: Dow Jones-Irwin.

Garbett, T. (1981). *Corporate advertising: The what, the why, and the how.* New York: McGraw-Hill.

Griswold, G. (1967). How AT&T's public relations policies developed. *Public Relations Quarterly, 12,* 13.

Heath, R. L. (1997). *Strategic issues management: Organizations and public policy challenges.* Thousand Oaks, CA: Sage.

Heath, R. L. (2005). *Encyclopedia of public relations.* Thousand Oaks, CA: Sage.

Hiebert, R. E. (1966). *Courtier to the court: The story of Ivy Lee and the development of public relations.* Ames: Iowa State University Press.

International Association of Business Communicators. (2005). Retrieved July 7, 2005, from http://www.iabc.com/

Lee, I. L. (1907). Indirect service of railroads. *Moody's Magazine, 2,* 580–584.

Lubbers, C. A. (1996). George Creel and the four-minute men: A milestone in public relations history. In A. F. Alkhafaji (Ed.), *Business research yearbook* (pp. 719–723). Lanham, MD: University Press of America.

Olasky, M. N. (1987). *Corporate public relations: A new historical experience.* Hillsdale, NJ: Lawrence Erlbaum.

Public Relations Society of America. (2005). Retrieved July 7, 2005, from http://www.prsa.org

Raucher, A. R. (1968). *Public relations and business: 1900–1929.* Baltimore: Johns Hopkins University Press.

Renfro, W. L. (1982). Managing the issues of the 1980s. *The Futurist, 16*(8), 61–66.

Schultze, Q. J. (1981). Advertising and public utilities: 1900–1917. *Journal of Advertising, 10*(4), 41–44, 48.

Starr, C. (1969). Social benefit versus technological risk. *Science, 165,* 1232–1238.

Stauber, J. C., & Rampton, S. (1995). *Toxic sludge is good for you: Lies, damn lies, and the public relations industry.* Monroe, ME: Common Courage.

Tye, L. (1998). *The father of spin: Edward L. Bernays & the birth of public relations.* New York: Crown.

Chapter 3: Managing Mutually Beneficial Relationships

Betz, E. K. (1996). *Nonprofit public relations: Building mutually beneficial relationships with corporations.* Unpublished master's thesis, University of Houston, Texas.

Broom, G. M., Casey, S., & Ritchey, J. (1997). Toward a concept and theory of organization-public relationships. *Journal of Public Relations Research, 9,* 83–98.

Burke, K. (1969). *A rhetoric of motives.* Berkeley: University of California Press.

Ewell, E. (1996). Strategically reaching the gay market. *Public Relations Strategist, 2*(4), 30–35.

Fisher, W. R. (1987). *Human communication as narration: Toward a philosophy of reason, value, and action.* Columbia: University of South Carolina Press.

Heath, R. L. (1994). *Management of corporate communication: From interpersonal contacts to external affairs.* Hillsdale, NJ: Lawrence Erlbaum.

Hill, J. W. (1958). *Corporate public relations: Arm of modern management.* New York: Harper & Brothers.

Ledingham, J. A. (2005). Relationship management theory. In R. L. Heath (Ed.), *Encyclopedia of public relations* (pp. 740–743). Thousand Oaks, CA: Sage.

Ledingham, J. A., & Bruning, S. D. (1998). Relationship management in public relations: Dimensions of an organization-public relationship. *Public Relations Review, 24,* 55–66.

Ledingham, J. A., & Bruning, S. D. (2000). *Public relations as relationship management: A relational approach to public relations.* Mahwah, NJ: Lawrence Erlbaum.

Quesinberry, A. A. (2005). Identification. In R. L. Heath (Ed.), *Encyclopedia of public relations* (pp. 403–405). Thousand Oaks, CA: Sage.

Chapter 4:
The Value of Research

Coombs, W. T., & Holladay, S. J. (2002). Helping crisis managers protect reputational assets: Initial tests of the situational crisis communication theory. *Management Communication Quarterly, 16,* 165–186.

Hill, J. W. (1958). *Corporate public relations: Arm of management.* New York: Harper & Brothers.

Holladay, S. J. (2005). Sampling. In R. L. Heath (Ed.), *Encyclopedia of public relations* (pp. 763–764). Thousand Oaks, CA: Sage.

Honesty and ethical standards. (1983, July). *Gallup Report,* No. 214, p. 19.

Honesty and ethical standards. (1993, July). *Gallup Report,* No. 334, pp. 37–39.

Kelly, O. (1982, September 6). Corporate crime: The untold story. *U.S. News & World Report, 93,* pp. 25–29.

Kinnick, K. N. (2005). Communication audit and auditing. In R. L. Heath (Ed.), *Encyclopedia of public relations* (pp. 158–161). Thousand Oaks, CA: Sage.

Lenskold, J. D. (2003). *Marketing ROI: The path to campaign, customer, and corporate profit.* Columbus, OH: McGraw-Hill.

Lerbinger, O. (1997, Winter). Corporate use of research in public relations. *Public Relations Review, 3,* 11–19.

McDonald, M., & Dunbar, I. (2004). *Market segmentation: How to do it, how to profit from it*. New York: Butterworth-Heinemann.

Nurses remain at top of honesty and ethics poll. (2000, November). *Gallup Poll Monthly*, No. 422, pp. 45–48.

Stacks, D. W. (2002). *Primer of public relations research*. New York: Guilford Press.

Stewart, T. D. (2002). *Principles of research in communication*. Boston: Allyn & Bacon.

Chapter 5:
Elements of Planning

Ajzen, I., & Fishbein, M. (1980). *Understanding attitudes and predicting social behavior*. Englewood Cliffs, NJ: Prentice Hall.

Coombs, W. T. (2005). Objectives. In R. L. Heath (Ed.), *Encyclopedia of public relations* (pp. 583–584). Thousand Oaks, CA: Sage.

Davidson, J. (2000). *Project management: 10 minute guide*. Indianapolis, IN: Macmillian USA.

Hallahan, K. (2005). Communication management. In R. L. Heath (Ed.), *Encyclopedia of public relations* (pp. 161–164). Thousand Oaks, CA: Sage.

Heath, R. L. (1994). *Management of corporate communication: From interpersonal contacts to external affairs*. Hillsdale, NJ: Lawrence Erlbaum.

Hunger, J. D., & Wheelen, T. L. (1993). *Strategic management* (4th ed.). Reading, MA: Addison-Wesley.

Martin, P., & Tate, K. (1997). *Project management memory jogger*. Salem, NH: Goal/QPC.

McGuire, W. J. (1989). Theoretical foundations of campaigns. In R. E. Rice & C. K. Atkin (Eds.), *Public communication campaigns* (2nd ed., pp. 43–65). Newbury Park, CA: Sage.

Petty, R. E., & Cacioppo, J. T. (1986). *Communication and persuasion: Central and peripheral routes to attitude change*. New York: Springer-Verlag.

Stacks, D. W. (2005). Benchmarking. In R. L. Heath (Ed.), *Encyclopedia of public relations* (pp. 74–76). Thousand Oaks, CA: Sage.

Turney, M. (2004). *Take ten steps for a strategic public relations plan*. Retrieved July 10, 2004, from http://www.nku.edu/~turney/prclass/readings/plan2.html

Chapter 6:
Taking Action

Ad Council. (2004). *Mission*. Retrieved June 25, 2005, from http://www.adcouncil.org/campaigns/

Blackburn, T. (1997). Nabisco comes through when the chips are down. *Public Relations Tactics, 4*(3), 4.

Sledzik, W. E. (1997). Killing Bambi: The deer population explosion challenges public officials and PR pros. *Public Relations Tactics, 4*(3), 1, 13, 25.

Chapter 7:
Evaluation of Public Relations Efforts

Grunig, J. E. (1983). Basic research provides knowledge that makes evaluation possible. *Public Relations Quarterly, 28*(3), 28–32.

Ledingham, J. A. (2005). Relationship management theory. In R. L. Heath (Ed.), *Encyclopedia of public relations* (pp. 740–745). Thousand Oaks, CA: Sage.

Chapter 8:
Public Relations Theory in Practice

Albrecht, T. L. (1988). Communication and personal control in empowering organizations. In J. A. Anderson (Ed.), *Communication yearbook 11* (pp. 380–390). Newbury Park, CA: Sage.

Anderson, R. V., & Ross, V. (2002). *Questions of communication: A practical introduction to theory* (3rd ed.). New York: Bedford/St. Martin's.

Benoit, W. L. (1995). *Accounts, excuses, and apologies: A theory of image restoration.* Albany: State University of New York Press.

Benson, J. A. (1988). Crisis revisited: An analysis of the strategies used by Tylenol in the second tampering episode. *Central States Speech Journal, 38,* 49–66.

Bowen, S. A. (2005). Excellence theory. In R. L. Heath (Ed.), *Encyclopedia of public relations* (pp. 306–308). Thousand Oaks, CA: Sage.

Cameron, G. T., Cropp, F., & Reber, B. H. (2001). Getting past platitudes: Factors limiting accommodation in public relations. *Journal of Communication Management, 5,* 242–261.

Coombs, W. T. (1995). Choosing the right words: The development of guidelines for the selection of the "appropriate" crisis response strategies. *Management Communication Quarterly, 8,* 447–476.

Coombs, W. T. (2004). Impact of past crises on current crisis communication: Insights from situational crisis communication theory. *Journal of Business Communication, 41,* 1–25.

Coombs, W. T., & Holladay, S. J. (1996). Communication and attributions in a crisis: An experimental study of crisis communication. *Journal of Public Relations Research, 8,* 279–295.

Coombs, W. T., & Holladay, S. J. (2001). An extended examination of the crisis situation: A fusion of the relational management and symbolic approaches. *Journal of Public Relations Research, 13,* 321–340.

Coombs, W. T., & Holladay, S. J. (2002). Helping crisis managers protect reputational assets: Initial tests of the situational crisis communication theory. *Management Communication Quarterly, 16,* 165–186.

Coombs, W. T., & Schmidt, L. (2000). An empirical analysis of image restoration: Texaco's racism crisis. *Journal of Public Relations Research, 12*(2), 163–178.

Davies, G., Chun, R., da Silva, R. V., & Roper, S. (2003). *Corporate reputation and competitiveness.* London: Routledge.

Davies, J. C., Covello, V. T., & Allen, F. W. (Eds.). (1987). *Risk communication.* Washington, DC: Conservation Foundation.

Driskill, L. P., & Goldstein, J. R. (1986). Uncertainty: Theory and practice in organizational communication. *Journal of Business Communication, 23*(3), 41–57.

Fombrun, C. J., & Van Riel, C. B. M. (2003). *Fame & fortune: How successful companies build winning reputations.* New York: Prentice Hall.

Fuchs-Burnett, T. (2002, May/July). Mass public corporate apology. *Dispute Resolution Journal, 57,* 26–32.

Grunig, J. E. (Ed.). (1992). *Excellence in public relations and communication management.* Hillsdale, NJ: Lawrence Erlbaum.

Grunig, L. A., Grunig, J. E., & Dozier, D. M. (2002). *Excellent public relations and effective organizations: A study of communication management in three countries.* Mahwah, NJ: Lawrence Erlbaum.

Hearit, K. M. (1994, Summer). Apologies and public relations crises at Chrysler, Toshiba, and Volvo. *Public Relations Review, 20,* 113–125.

Heath, R. L. (Ed.). (2005). *Encyclopedia of public relations.* Thousand Oaks, CA: Sage.

Heath, R. L., & Abel, D. D. (1996a). Proactive response to citizen risk concerns: Increasing citizens' knowledge of emergency response practices. *Journal of Public Relations Research, 8,* 151–171.

Heath, R. L., & Abel, D. D. (1996b). Types of knowledge as predictors of company support: The role of information in risk communication. *Journal of Public Relations Research, 8,* 35–55.

Heath, R. L., & Douglas, W. (1991). Effects of involvement on reactions to sources of messages and message clusters. *Public relations research annual* (Vol. 3, pp. 179–194). Hillsdale, NJ: Lawrence Erlbaum.

Heath, R. L., & Gay, C. D. (1995). Working with experts in the risk communication infrastructure: Another challenge for public relations practitioners. *Public Relations Review, 21,* 211–224.

Heath, R. L., & Gay, C. D. (1997). Risk communication: Involvement, uncertainty, and control's effect on information scanning and monitoring by expert stakeholders in SARA Title III. *Management Communication Quarterly, 10,* 342–372.

Heath, R. L., Liao, S., & Douglas, W. (1995). Effects of perceived economic harms and benefits on issue involvement, information use, and action: A study in risk communication. *Journal of Public Relations Research, 7,* 89–109.

Heath, R. L., & Palenchar, M. J. (2000). Community relations and risk communication: A longitudinal study of the impact of emergency response messages. *Journal of Public Relations Research, 12,* 131–161.

Heath, R. L., Seshadri, S., & Lee, J. (1998). Risk communication: A two-community analysis of proximity, dread, trust, involvement, uncertainty, openness, knowledge, and support/opposition to chemical companies. *Journal of Public Relations Research, 10,* 25–56.

Ihlen, O. (2002). Defending the Mercedes A-class: Combining and changing crisis-response strategies. *Journal of Public Relations Research, 14,* 185–206.

Krimsky, S., & Golding, D. (1992). Reflections. In S. Krimsky & D. Golding (Eds.), *Social theories of risk* (pp. 355–363). Westport, CT: Praeger.

Ledingham, J. A. (2003). Explicating relationship management as a general theory of public relations. *Journal of Public Relations Research, 15,* 181–198.

Ledingham, J. A. (2005). Relationship management theory. In R. L. Heath (Ed.), *Encyclopedia of public relations* (pp. 740–743). Thousand Oaks, CA: Sage.

Lerbinger, O. (1997). *The crisis manager: Facing risk and responsibility.* Mahwah, NJ: Lawrence Erlbaum.

Nathan, K., Heath, R. L., & Douglas, W. (1992). Tolerance for potential environmental health risks: The influence of knowledge, benefits, control, involvement, and uncertainty. *Journal of Public Relations Research, 4,* 235–258.

Neuliep, J. W. (1996). *Human communication theory: Applications & case studies.* Boston: Allyn & Bacon.

Palenchar, M. J., & Heath, R. L. (2002). Another part of the risk communication model: Analysis of communication processes and message content. *Journal of Public Relations Research, 13,* 127–158.

Petty, R. E., & Cacioppo, J. T. (1986). *Communication and persuasion: Central and peripheral routes to attitude change.* New York: Springer-Verlag.

Shin, J. H. (2005). Contingency theory. In R. L. Heath (Ed.), *Encyclopedia of public relations* (pp. 191–193). Thousand Oaks, CA: Sage.

Sturges, D. L. (1994). Communicating through crisis: A strategy for organizational survival. *Management Communication Quarterly, 7,* 297–316.

Chapter 9:
Ethical and Legal Restraints on Public Relations Practice

Bivins, T. H. (1992). A systems model for ethical decision making in public relations. *Public Relations Review, 18,* 365–383.

Burke, K. (1966). *A grammar of motives.* Berkeley: University of California Press.

Fitzpatrick, K. R. (1996a). Public relations and the law: A survey of practitioners. *Public Relations Review, 22,* 1–6.

Fitzpatrick, K. R. (1996b). The role of public relations in the institutionalization of ethics. *Public Relations Review, 21,* 21–33.

Fukuyama, F. (1995). *Trust: The social virtues and creation of prosperity.* New York: Free Press.

Hanson, K. O. (1996). Ethics and public affairs: An uneasy relationship. In L. B. Dennis (Ed.), *Practical public affairs in an era of change: A communications guide for business, government, and college* (pp. 423–434). Lanham, MD: Public Relations Society of America and University Press of America.

Heath, R. L., & Ryan, M. (1989). Public relations' role in defining corporate social responsibility. *Journal of Mass Media Ethics, 4,* 21–38.

Jackall, R. (1995). Practical moral reasoning in public relations. *The Strategist, 1*(2), 14–18.

Kruckeberg, D. (1997). Testing your public relations E.Q. *The Strategist, 3*(1), 31–35.

Lazarus, D. (2004, May 5). *Union, SBC talks resume.* Retrieved July 7, 2005, from http://sfgate.com/cgi-bin/article.cgi?file=/chronicle/archive/2004/05/05/BUG8V6FKBR1.DTL

Leeper, R. V. (2005). Copyright. In R. L. Heath (Ed.), *Encyclopedia of public relations* (pp. 201–202). Thousand Oaks, CA: Sage.

Seib, P., & Fitzpatrick, K. (1995). *Public relations ethics.* Forth Worth, TX: Harcourt Brace.

Stateman, A. (1997). Making a splash with the swimsuit issue. *Public Relations Tactics, 4*(5), 4.

Trademark law. (2004). Retrieved June 15, 2005, from http://www.law.cornell/edu/topics/trademark.html

What is copyright protection? (2004). Retrieved July 7, 2005, from http:/www.whatis copyright.org

Chapter 10:
Monitoring and Managing Issues

Chase, W. H. (1984). *Issue management: Origins of the future.* Stamford, CT: Issue Actions.

Coombs, W. T. (1998). The Internet as a potential equalizer: New leverage for confronting social irresponsibility. *Public Relations Review, 24,* 289–303.

Davis, G. F., & Thompson, T. A. (1994). A social movement perspective on corporate control. *Administrative Science Quarterly, 39,* 141–173.

Ewing, R. P. (1987). *Managing the new bottom line: Issues management for senior executives.* Homewood, IL: Dow Jones-Irwin.

Hainsworth, B., & Meng, M. (1988). How corporations define issue management. *Public Relations Review, 14,* 18–30.

Hearit, K. M. (1996). The use of counter-attack in apologetic public relations crises: The case of General Motors vs. Dateline NBC. *Public Relations Review, 22,* 233–248.

Heath, R. L. (1997). *Strategic issues management: Organizations and public policy challenges.* Thousand Oaks, CA: Sage.

Heath, R. L. (1998). New communication technologies: An issues management point of view. *Public Relations Review, 24,* 273–288.

Johnson, J. (1983). Issues management—what are the issues? An introduction to issues management. *Business Quarterly, 48*(3), 22–31.

Renfro, W. L. (1993). *Issues management in strategic planning.* Westport, CT: Quorum Books.

Sethi, S. P. (1977). *Advocacy advertising and large corporations: Social conflict, big business image, the news media, and public policy.* Lexington, MA: D. C. Heath.

Tucker, K., Broom, G., & Caywood, C. (1993). Managing issues acts as bridge to strategic planning. *Public Relations Journal, 49*(11), 38–40.

Chapter 11:
Selecting Media, Technologies, and Communication Tools

Schmertz, H. (1986). *Good-bye to the low profile: The art of creative confrontation.* Boston: Little, Brown.

Chapter 12:
Publicity, Promotion, and Writing

Blackburn, T. (1997). Nabisco comes through when the chips are down. *Public Relations Tactics,* 4(3), 4.

Fisher, W. R. (1987). *Human communication as narration: Toward a philosophy of reasons, value, and action.* Columbia: University of South Carolina Press.

Heath, R. L. (1993). A rhetorical approach to zones of meaning and organizational prerogatives. *Public Relation Review, 19,* 141–155.

Ledingham, J. A., & Bruning, S. D. (1998). Relationship management in public relations: Dimensions of an organization-public relationship. *Public Relations Review, 24,* 55–65.

Pearson, R. (1989). Business ethics as communication ethics: Public relations practice and the idea of dialogue. In C. H. Botan & V. T. Hazelton Jr. (Eds.), *Public relations theory* (pp. 111–131). Hillsdale, NJ: Lawrence Erlbaum.

Schmertz, H. (1986). *Good-bye to the low profile: The art of creative confrontation.* Boston: Little, Brown.

Stateman, A. (2000). The money pit: How PR helped make "Millionaire" a TV blockbuster. *Public Relations Tactics,* 7(1), 9, 29.

Chapter 13:
Collaborative Decision Making

Barge, J. K. (1994). *Leadership: Communication skills for organizations and groups.* New York: St. Martin's Press.

Baron, R. A. (1983). *Behavior in organizations: Understanding and managing the human side of work.* Boston: Ally & Bacon.

Center, A. H., & Jackson, P. (1995). *Public relations practices: Managerial case studies & problems* (5th ed.). Englewood Cliffs, NJ: Prentice Hall.

Conrad, C. (1985). *Strategic organizational communication: Cultures, situations, and adaptation.* New York: Holt.

Coombs, W. T. (1998). The Internet as potential equalizer: New leverage for confronting social irresponsibility. *Public Relations Review,* 24(3), 289–303.

Coombs, W. T. (1999). *Ongoing crisis communication: Planning, managing, and responding.* Thousand Oaks, CA: Sage.

Daniels, T. D., Spiker, B. K., & Papa, M. J. (1997). *Perspectives on organizational communication* (4th ed.). Dubuque, IA: Brown & Benchmark.

Eisenberg, E. M., & Goodall, H. L., Jr. (1997). *Organizational communication: Balancing creativity and constraint* (2nd ed.). New York: St. Martin's Press.

Grunig, J. E. (1992). Communication, public relations, and effective organizations: An overview to the book. In J. E. Grunig (Ed.), *Excellence in public relations and communication management* (pp. 1–28). Hillsdale, NJ: Lawrence Erlbaum.

Grunig, J. E., & Grunig, L. A. (1992). Models of public relations and communications. In J. E. Grunig (Ed.), *Excellence in public relations and communication management* (pp. 285–326). Hillsdale, NJ: Lawrence Erlbaum.

Grunig, J. E., & Repper, F. C. (1992). Strategic management, publics, and issues. In J. E. Grunig (Ed.), *Excellence in public relations and communication management* (pp. 117–157). Hillsdale, NJ: Lawrence Erlbaum.

Heath, R. L. (1994). *Management of corporate communication: From interpersonal contacts to external affairs.* Hillsdale, NJ: Lawrence Erlbaum.

Heath, R. L. (1997). *Strategic issues management: Organizations and public policy challenges.* Thousand Oaks, CA: Sage.

Heath, R. L., & Abel, D. D. (1996). Proactive response to citizen risk concerns: Increasing citizens' knowledge of emergency response practices. *Journal of Public Relations Research, 8,* 151–171.

Heath, R. L., & Palenchar, M. (2000). Community relations and risk communication: Longitudinal study of the impact of emergency response messages. *Journal of Public Relations Research, 12,* 131–162.

Kilman, R., & Thomas, K. (1975). Interpersonal conflict handling behavior as a reflection of Jungian personality dimensions. *Psychological Reports, 37,* 971–980.

Miller, K. (1999). *Organizational communication: Approaches and processes* (2nd ed.). Cincinnati, OH: Wadsworth.

Mitchell, R. K., Agle, B. R., & Wood, D. J. (1997). Toward a theory of stakeholder identification and salience: Defining the principles of who and what really counts. *Academy of Management Review, 22,* 853–886.

Murphy, P., & Dee, J. (1992). Reconciling the preferences of environmental activists and corporate policymakers. *Journal of Public Relations Research, 8,* 1–34.

Putnam, L. L., & Poole, M. S. (1987). Conflict and negotiation. In F. Jablin, L. L. Putnam, K. Roberts, & L. W. Porter (Eds.), *Handbook of organizational communication* (pp. 549–599). Beverly Hills, CA: Sage.

Rowley, T. J. (1997). Moving beyond dyadic ties: A network theory of stakeholder influence. *Academy of Management Review, 22*(4), 887–910.

Snyder, A. (1991, April 8). Do boycotts work? *Adweek's Marketing Review,* pp. 16–18.

Vroom, V. H., & Yetton, P. W. (1963). *Leadership and decision making.* Pittsburgh, PA: University of Pittsburgh Press.

Witt, L. A., Andrews, M. C., & Kacmar, K. M. (2000). The role of participative decision-making in the organizational politics-job satisfaction relationship. *Human Relations, 53,* 341–357.

Chapter 14:
Building a Career

Broom, G. M. (1982). A comparison of sex roles in public relations. *Public Relations Review, 3,* 110–119.

Broom, G. M., & Dozier, D. M. (1986). Advancement for public relations role models. *Public Relations Review, 12,* 37–56.

Broom, G. M., & Smith, G. D. (1979). Testing the practitioner's impact on clients. *Public Relations Review, 5,* 45–49.

Cherry, S. R. (2002, November). Corporate boards failing investors. *Insight,* pp. 24–25.

Commission on Public Relations Education. (1999, October). *A port of entry: Public relations education for the 21st century.* New York: Public Relations Society of American.

Downes, J., & Goodman, J. E. (2002). *Dictionary of finance and investment terms.* Hauppauge, NY: Barron's Educational Series.

Gonring, M. P. (1994). Putting integrated marketing communications to work today. *Public Relations Quarterly, 39*(3), 45.

Kelly, K. S. (1991). *Fund-raising and public relations: A critical analysis.* Hillsdale, NJ: Lawrence Erlbaum.

Mahoney, W. F., & Wessendorf, C. K. (1996). How to get investors online. *Financial Executive, 12*(1), 41–43.

McGoon, C. (1998). Cutting-edge companies use integrated marketing communication. *Communication World, 16*(1), 15.

Moriarty, S. E. (1994). PR and IMC: The benefits of integration. *Public Relations Quarterly, 39*(3), 38–45.

Paluszek, J. L. (2000). Public relations students: Today good, tomorrow better. *Public Relations Strategist, 5*(4), 27–28.

Sallot, L. M. (2005). Travel and tourism public relations. In R. L. Heath (Ed.), *Encyclopedia of public relations* (pp. 861–863). Thousand Oaks, CA: Sage.

Chapter 15:
The Future of Public Relations

Botan, C. H. (1992). International public relations: Critique and reformation. *Public Relations Review, 18,* 149–159.

Callison, C. (2003). Media relations and the Internet: How *Fortune 500* company Web sites assist journalists in news gathering. *Public Relations Review, 29,* 29–41.

Chen, N. (1996). Public relations in China: The introduction and development of an occupational field. In H. M. Culbertson & H. Chen (Eds.), *International public relations: A comparative analysis* (pp. 121–153). Mahwah, NJ: Lawrence Erlbaum.

Coombs, W. T. (1998). The Internet as potential equalizer: New leverage for confronting social irresponsibility. *Public Relations Review, 24,* 289–304.

Coombs, W. T., Holladay, S., Hasenauer, G., & Signitzer, B. (1994). A comparative analysis of international public relations: Identification of similarities and differences between professionalization in Austria, Norway, and the United States. *Journal of Public Relations Research, 6,* 23–39.

Cooper-Chen, A., & Kaneshige, M. (1996). Public relations practice in Japan: Beginning again for the first time. In H. M. Culbertson & H. Chen (Eds.), *International public relations: A comparative analysis* (pp. 223–238). Mahwah, NJ: Lawrence Erlbaum.

Ekachai, D., & Komolsevin, R. (1996). Public relations in Thailand: Its functions and practitioners' roles. In H. M. Culbertson & H. Chen (Eds.), *International public relations: A comparative analysis* (pp. 155–170). Mahwah, NJ: Lawrence Erlbaum.

Foster, L. G. (1999). *Building global bridges: 1998 Atlas Award lecture on international public relations* (International Section monograph). New York: Public Relations Society of America.

Greer, C. F., & Moreland, K. D. (2003). United Airlines' and American Airlines' online crisis communication following the September 11 terrorists attacks. *Public Relations Review, 29,* 427–441.

Grunig, J. E., & Hunt, T. (1984). *Managing public relations.* New York: Holt, Reinhart & Winston.

Hachigian, D., & Hallahan, K. (2003). Perceptions of public relations Web sites by computer industry journalists. *Public Relations Review, 29,* 43–62.

Hall, E. T. (1981). *Beyond culture.* Garden City, NY: Doubleday.

Heath, R. L. (1998). New communication technologies: An issues management point of view. *Public Relations Review, 24,* 273–288.

Heath, R. L. (2001). Globalization—the frontier of multinationalism and cultural diversity. In R. L. Heath (Ed.), *Handbook of public relations* (pp. 625–628). Thousand Oaks, CA: Sage.

Hofstede, G. (1984). *Culture's consequences: International differences in work-related values.* Beverly Hills, CA: Sage.

Holtzhausen, D. R., Petersen, B. K., & Tindall, N. T. J. (2003). Exploding the myth of the symmetrical/asymmetrical models in the new South Africa. *Journal of Public Relations Research, 15,* 305–341.

Jamais, K. H., Navarro, M. J., & Tuazon, R. R. (1996). Public relations in the Philippines. In H. M. Culbertson & H. Chen (Eds.), *International public relations: A comparative analysis* (pp. 191–206). Mahwah, NJ: Lawrence Erlbaum.

Kennedy, D. D. (1998). *Feng shui: Tips for a better life.* Toronto, Canada: Storey Books.

Kent, M. L., & Taylor, M. (2003, Spring). Maximizing media relations: A Web site checklist. *Public Relations Quarterly, 47,* 14–18.

Kent, M. L., Taylor, M., & White, W. J. (2003). The relationship between Web site design and organizational responsiveness of stakeholders. *Public Relations Review, 29,* 63–77.

Kruckeberg, D. (1996). A global perspective on public relations ethics. In H. M. Culbertson & H. Chen (Eds.), *International public relations: A comparative analysis* (pp. 81–92). Mahwah, NJ: Lawrence Erlbaum.

Kruckeberg, D., & Tsetura, K. (2003). *A composite index by country of variables related to the likelihood of existence of "cash for news coverage."* Gainesville, FL: Institute for Public Relations.

Marwell, G., & Schmitt, D. R. (1967). Dimensions of compliance-gaining behavior: An empirical analysis. *Sociometry, 30,* 350–364.

Mole, J. (1991). *When in Rome . . . A business guide to cultures & customs in 12 European nations.* New York: AMACOM.

Morrison, T., Conaway, W. A., & Borden, G. A. (1995). *Kiss, bow, or shake hands: How to do business in sixty countries.* Holbrook, MA: Bob Adams.

Ochman, B. L. (2000). Communicating online. Retrieved July 10, 2004, from http://www.whatsnextonline.com/realitypr.html

Ricks, D. A. (1999). *Blunders in international business.* Malden, MA: Blackwell.

Simoes, R. P. (1992). Public relations as a political function: A Latin American view. *Public Relations Review, 18,* 189–200.

Sriramesh, K. (1992). Societal culture and public relations: Ethnographic evidence from India. *Public Relations Review, 18,* 201–211.

Sriramesh, K. (1996). Power distance and public relations: An ethnographic study of Southern Indian organizations. In H. M. Culbertson & H. Chen (Eds.), *International public relations: A comparative analysis* (pp. 171–190). Mahwah, NJ: Lawrence Erlbaum.

Sriramesh, K., Kim, Y., & Takasaki, M. (1999). Public relations in three Asian cultures: An analysis. *Journal of Public Relations Research, 11,* 271–292.

Sriramesh, K., & Vercic, D. (2003). *The global public relations handbook: Theory, research, and practice.* Mahwah, NJ: Lawrence Erlbaum.

Taylor, M. (2001). International public relations: Opportunities and challenges for the 21st century. In R. L. Heath (Ed.), *Handbook of public relations* (pp. 629–638). Thousand Oaks, CA: Sage.

Taylor, M. (2004). Exploring public relations in Croatia through relational communication and media richness theories. *Public Relations Review, 30,* 145–160.

Taylor, M. (2005). Intercultural communication theory. In R. L. Heath (Ed.), *Encyclopedia of public relations* (pp. 428–430). Thousand Oaks, CA: Sage.

Trompenaars, F., & Hampden-Turner, C. (1998). *Riding the waves of culture: Understanding diversity in global business.* New York: McGraw-Hill.

Wakefield, R. I. (2001). Effective public relations in the multinational organization. In R. L. Heath (Ed.), *Handbook of public relations* (pp. 639–648). Thousand Oaks, CA: Sage.

Witmer, D. F. (2000). *Spinning the Web: A handbook for public relations on the Internet.* Reading, MA: Longman.

Zaharna, R. S. (2001). "In-awareness" approach to international public relations. *Public Relations Review, 27,* 135–148.

Index